"She's done it again! Like her seminal first book, *Understanding Payments - A Whistle Stop Tour into What You Thought You Knew*, Neira Jones' *Beyond Payments* provides a comprehensive manual on the complicated and often mysterious domain of decentralised payments. Neira takes us on a wild ride through the ins and outs of this ever-evolving world and she does so in a fun, thoughtful and imminently approachable manner. For fans of her first book, you'll be happy to know that Neira's delightful characters John and Suzie make a return, as do her tremendously helpful figures and tables!"

Tiffany Anzai Hill, *Director & Senior Commercial Counsel, APAC & MEA, Nium*

"The world of payments is changing and changing fast. Can you keep up? Some are asking what's happening and others what's happened. Neira and I, and some others, ask: what's happening next? This book gives you some clues to the answers. Read it and learn."

Chris Skinner, *CEO, TheFinanser.com*

"I came away enlightened, informed and intrigued. Enlightened, because the clouds lifted from a previously misunderstood topic. Informed, because I can now understand the origins of these new models, technologies and mechanisms and appreciate where they fit in. And intrigued, because despite the authoritative explanations, I believe we still don't know for sure where these innovations will take us – but I have a much better idea than most."

Tony Craddock, *Director General, The Payments Association*

"It's payments Jim but not as we know it !". Having nailed the world of bank and card payments in her last book, Neira has done it again in *Beyond Payments* – taking the fast evolving and ever more complex world of digital payments and decentralised finance, and again breaking it down into the fundamentals of how things work, who makes things work and why. She assesses and summarises the challenges involved, illustrating the flow and providing real life examples, and always in her very readable, fun style. Like many of us Neira has a passion for 'payments' and her genuine interest and enthusiasm shines through. If Understanding Payments was a must read for anyone wanting to understand our current payments world, then Beyond Payments is an essential for anyone wanting to understand the future world of payments."

Jeremy Nicholds, *Managing Director, Judo*

"Neira Jones has done it again. Her first book on payments laid out the fundamentals and the complexity of payments. In *Beyond Payments* she elucidates how blockchain technology and digital and virtual assets might change the way we and those institutions that make money – central banks – understand representations of monetary value and payments. A must read if you want to understand evolving field of blockchain technology, who runs it, and how assets can be exchanged and traded using this technology."

Stanley Skoglund, *Partner, Minerva Partnership Consultancy*

"*Beyond Payments* is a must-read for anyone involved in the payments industry. As a brilliant continuation of *Understanding Payments*, Neira masterfully simplifies a complex and evolving field, making it both engaging and highly accessible. This book is essential for professionals looking to deepen their knowledge and stay ahead in the rapidly changing world of payments."

Mike Chambers, *Northey Point*

"Well, what I can say this is the book to educate, demystify and get excited about the new way of transacting. If you have ever wanted to know more about the world beyond payments, you will not be disappointed. Neira's expertise shines through, with thorough research whilst ensuring it stays relevant and easy to follow. Well done my dear, can't wait for the next book too!"

Claire Pearson, *Head of Technical Operations, Fnality International*

"Neira has done it again. Having thought that Neira had written the bible of payments with her first book, beyond payments will answer every question that a professional will require from anything relating to payments and the emerging markets that surround this. This book demystifies the many complex aspects of the payments industry enabling a less technical audience to get deeper into subjects they have avoided in the past or for specialists to be able to pick the book up and get to the chapters that they are interested in. As an executive that struggles to keep up with the pace of innovation and change in financial services and payments in general, beyond payments is the perfect reference book that I will regularly turn to to equip me with the knowledge to have an opinion with the background required across multiple subjects."

Andy McDonald, *CEO Cloudapps, Business Coach' Formerly at ACI worldwide, Retail Decisions, Moneybox, NCR*

"I will always advocate that Bitcoin and Bitcoin alone is the only option for digital payments, however, Neira has done a masterful job of unpacking the complex and opaque landscape of digital assets and gives the reader a framework and mental model within which they can navigate the ever growing ecosystem."

David Parkinson, *CEO, Musqet*

"In *Beyond Payments* Neira Jones provides readers with a comprehensive guide to the fast-moving world of decentralised payment ecosystems. She provides a detailed and up to date review of blockchain fundamentals, smart contracts, cryptocurrencies, value tokens and central bank digital currencies amongst other topics, with examples of the various types that have been developed and implemented globally. Helpfully, the book includes clear explanations on how they differ, their applicability and implications. This book helps readers decipher often confusing jargon, debunk myths and delivers practical advice in an easy-to-read style backed up by original hand drawn illustrations. It covers next generation payment concepts in more depth than was possible in her initial book *Understanding Payments*. A wide range of people will benefit from reading *Beyond Payments* including those with a direct responsibility for payments and others with an interest in learning about the latest digital payment technologies. I have learnt much by reading this book, endorse it, and encourage others to make the time to read it thoroughly."

Mark McMurtrie, *Director, Payments Consultancy Ltd and Ambassador, The Payments Association*

"Neira Jones' *Beyond Payments* is an insightful and compelling continuation of her previous work, *Understanding Payments*, providing readers with a comprehensive view of the rapidly evolving payment landscape. The book adeptly navigates the complexities of both centralized and decentralized payment systems, making it accessible to a broad audience, from industry professionals to curious newcomers.

She employs clear language and engaging illustrations to demystify intricate concepts such as blockchain technology, digital currencies, and the implications of decentralized finance (DeFi) and also addresses regulatory challenges and the need for a cohesive understanding among various stakeholders in the payment ecosystem. Neira reinforces the notion that knowledge is key to navigating this complex industry and highlights the implications for businesses and consumers alike, making this an essential read for anyone navigating the future of digital finance. It is structured to facilitate learning, with chapters that can be read independently, allowing readers to focus on specific topics of interest. Overall, *Beyond Payments* is well researched featuring practical insights and real-world applications and serves as a valuable resource for anyone looking to grasp the future of financial transactions."

Janusz Diemko, *CEO Xelopay, Angel Investor Mentor, Industry Enthusiast and Consultant*

". . . *Beyond Payments* - from centralised to decentralised and everything in between . . . the title says it all! Compelling and compulsive reading, a truly invaluable resource and comprehensive reference work for anybody involved or passing through the ever evolving payments landscapes. Insightful and challenging, this is a 'must have' addition to your libraries."

Ken Lipton, *Chairman, Paycross*

"Neira has written another 'must read' reference book. She explains with unique clarity the fundamentals of various decentralised payment ecosystems from blockchain to smart contracts and dApps, from layer 2 to DeFi, from cryptocurrencies to CBDCs, explaining implications and opportunities. She provides also a simple framework for comparisons, which helps understanding the specific concepts/cases, a powerful methodology ready for broader application. With her continuous research and efforts, Neira makes important and complex concepts understandable to the community of professionals who are interested in developing the payment ecosystem (and not only) leveraging new technologies and infrastructure. If you haven't yet, get a copy."

Flavia Alzetta, *CEO, NED, Advisor*

"I had the pleasure of reviewing Neira's previous book, *Understanding Payments*. I was blown away by the context and detail of the subject matter. Having just reviewed Neira's new book *Beyond Payments* again, I was impressed by how Neira crafted the subject in a manner that is both simple to digest and a compelling read simultaneously. There is no doubt that Neira's depth of experience in this field is outstanding, along with her unique ability to articulate to the reader in such terms that even inexperienced folks could digest the goodness of this book. Both payments experts and regulators can reference this outstanding piece of work along with Neira's previous book *Understanding Payments* as 'Payments Industry Encyclopaedias'."

Soteris Vasili, *Chairman Vasili Advisory*

"Neira's latest book has certainly helped me to understand better the new frontiers. Highly recommended for those who (like me) have come from the more traditional card and account-to-account payments world (explored brilliantly in Neira's first book), and who want to understand better the fast developing worlds of blockchain, CBDCs, etc. Her evident grasp of the detail combined with her very accessible communication style bring clarity to what can be a somewhat opaque set of topics!"

Jim Wadsworth, *GM, innovator & thought leader in open banking & payments*

"I was honored when Neira asked me to review her second book, *Beyond Payments*, and was not disappointed with the read. Although the contents of *Beyond Payments* is still targeted for the largely uninitiated payments enthusiast, it, by necessity, gets more into the technology weeds, particularly when covering the broad and complex subjects of crypto currencies and blockchain. As was true with her first writing endeavor, *Understanding Payments*, her new offering helps the reader understand those and other challenging topics using easy-to-understand language mixed with a bit of humor and lots of examples. I was particularly impressed by the deep research that was required on Neira's part and the obvious efforts she made to provide the latest statistics, data, and news. *Beyond Payments* will, undoubtedly, become required reading for executives considering forays into digital payments of all types."

Gary Yamamura, *President, Edept LLC*

"Neira's latest book, *Beyond Payments* is a tour de force in the world of decentralised payment systems. Filled with helpful diagrams and detailed descriptions, this book is, at the same time both a primer and a deep-dive into what is still a relatively poorly understood area. Even though I have been advising companies engaged in decentralised finance for over a decade this is a book that I am going to keep near at hand so that I can reach into its capacious contents whenever I have a doubt."

Rahul Matthan, *Partner, Trilegal*

"Another great achievement in explaining a complex matter and very useful addition to an otherwise undocumented subject matter."

Alison Donnelly, *Director, fscom*

"In the complicated, continually evolving, and controversial world of cryptocurrencies, blockchain, DLTs, stable coins, and CBDCs, you could spend a lifetime trying to understand it. Neira has done an incredible job providing a well-balanced view with summaries, detailed explanations and fantastic diagrams. I've worked in this area for 15 years and thought I had a pretty good grip on it, I was captivated as I reviewed the book. I highly recommend this book for anyone working in financial services and Fintech, whether you're designing the next web 3 platform or just trying to understand what it's all about."

John Davies, *CTO, Incept5*

"I found Neira's first book invaluable, and I can't wait to get stuck into book 2 – it will no doubt be a crucial resource for me and my team. Neira's knowledge and ability to make concepts and details accessible and understandable is a such a benefit to us all in the industry – thank you again for taking the time to create this important body of work."

Paul Horlock, *Chief Payments Officer, Retail and Business Banking (RBB), Santander*

"Neira's comprehensive approach to payments present and future is a field guide for those joining our industry and a terrific reference for those of us who have been here a while."

Dave Birch, *Author, advisor and commentator on digital financial services*

"*Beyond Payments* builds on its predecessor, *Understanding Payments*, offering readers invaluable perspectives into the rapidly evolving payments landscape. Drawing on her extensive experience and expertise, Neira has crafted a detailed guide that is essential reading for all payment practitioners. Both providers and buyers in the industry will find *Beyond Payments* to be an easily digestible user guide for navigating the future world of payments."

Stuart Campbell, *Head of Payments at TLT LLP*

BEYOND PAYMENTS

This is a book about payments, and how they are evolving, from centralised to decentralised and everything in between, and the new opportunities they present.

In the world of payments, we are experiencing an inexorable move towards decentralisation, standardisation, and automation. New business models have emerged, existing ones have evolved, and some have disappeared, whilst regulation struggles to keep pace. As the puzzle becomes more complex, each player not only needs to understand where they fit in, but how they can remain relevant in a fast-evolving and extremely competitive industry. This book takes the reader through the fundamentals of the various decentralised payment ecosystems. From blockchain to smart contracts and DeFi, jargon is debunked, and myths are busted. For each concept, a simple framework is used, enabling comparison: mechanics, economics, risks, and the future outlook. It gives the reader a unique classification framework of virtual assets and explains the regulatory landscape. Drawing on real-life examples, the book weaves together the underpinning principles, legislation, and key stakeholders.

As a follow-up to *Understanding Payments*, it is a must-have reference book for the evolution of payments. It provides practical applications, offers insights into the key disciplines, and equips anyone in the payments industry with an understanding of the key issues and opportunities.

Neira Jones has more than 25 years' experience in financial services and technology, and advises and coaches organisations of all sizes on payments, fintech, RegTech, cybercrime, information security, fraud, and regulations. She also provides payment security expert witness services and is a Panel Member for the UK Payment Systems Regulator.

BEYOND PAYMENTS

From Centralised to Decentralised and Everything In Between

Neira Jones

Routledge
Taylor & Francis Group
LONDON AND NEW YORK

Designed cover image: marchmeena29 / iStock / Getty Images Plus

First published 2025
by Routledge
4 Park Square, Milton Park, Abingdon, Oxon OX14 4RN

and by Routledge
605 Third Avenue, New York, NY 10158

Routledge is an imprint of the Taylor & Francis Group, an informa business

British Library Cataloguing-in-Publication Data
A catalogue record for this book is available from the British Library

ISBN: 978-1-032-76997-4 (hbk)
ISBN: 978-1-032-75865-7 (pbk)
ISBN: 978-1-003-48076-1 (ebk)

DOI: 10.4324/9781003480761

Typeset in Joanna
by codeMantra

For Product Safety Concerns and Information please contact our EU representative:
GPSR@taylorandfrancis.com
Taylor & Francis Verlag GmbH, Kaufingerstraße 24, 80331 München, Germany.

CONTENTS

INTRODUCTION

Payments are pervasive

For my first book, Understanding Payments, I set out to democratise payments knowledge. Rather than providing a textbook, my objective was to offer a reference in plain and accessible language, with plenty of illustrations and much debunking of myths. I finished writing it in August 2023, and from the feedback I have received so far, I think I may have achieved that objective. I am at once relieved and delighted.

For those who read my first book, you will know that it came with an underlying warning: payments are pervasive, and they evolve rapidly, and what may be true today might not necessarily be true in the future. This means that a few years after publication, whilst the fundamental mechanics of traditional payment systems may largely remain the same (in principle at least), that book will need a serious update, and I look forward to that. The main reasons for the update will be changes in behaviours (including geo-political and socio-economic factors), technology, and regulations.

DOI: 10.4324/9781003480761-1

Already, and for the last couple of decades, we have experienced an inexorable move towards decentralisation, standardisation, and automation. This has taken many forms, from cloud technologies to open standards, Everything-as-a-Service, not forgetting the many forms of artificial intelligence. New business models emerged, existing ones evolved, some disappeared, criminals and malicious actors continued to innovate, and regulations continued to struggle to keep pace (as they are hampered by long regulatory cycles).

Decentralisation, through Distributed Ledger Technology (DLT), and blockchain in particular, has been attracting attention for a while, especially in the world of payments. Google searches on the words "blockchain and payments" and "distributed ledger technology and payments" return 39.5 million and 11.1 million results respectively at the time of writing. Evidently, "blockchain" and "distributed ledger technology", are relevant to payments. But these terms are confusing to most people, and abundant media reporting of crypto investment scams, whilst rightfully raising general risk awareness, don't really contribute much to well-rounded and informed education. Unless you're an institutional investor or a savvy crypto enthusiast, confusion still reigns.

In my first book, I briefly introduced the world of blockchain technology and virtual assets when describing the spectrum of centralised payment infrastructures and how payments touch every aspect of our lives. In this book, we continue our tour of this fascinating world by further exploring the universe of decentralised payments. Today, as both centralised and decentralised payment ecosystems continue to evolve in parallel, and increasingly intermingle, we still don't really need to understand payments, we just want to send money, buy things, or use services. At some point, a payment will take place, but this is only secondary to the primary goal, and therefore, as consumers, we object to jumping through seemingly unnecessary hurdles… And we want reassurance that our money is safe with those to whom it has been entrusted. When we tap our mobile phone on a card reader to buy our morning coffee, we don't need to know that data could have travelled from our favourite coffee shop, through multiple entities and networks in the value chain to reach our account provider, and eventually come all the way back to inform us that our payment was approved, before we can walk out with our coffee. We may even get loyalty points if we're a regular customer, and if we paid with a crypto card, we may have accumulated reward points in the form of crypto tokens. Whichever way we pay, we have more options than we've ever had before.

Payments continue to evolve and converge fast

A couple of decades ago – at least in the UK, one of the most advanced markets – we wouldn't have dreamt of payments being so convenient, instantaneous, and ubiquitous. We thought nothing of bank payments taking three days or more to process. We still had cheque books, and much cash in our wallets. Today, we may still have a cheque book somewhere, just in case, probably a few years old, and we may carry some cash to pay the window cleaner. But increasingly, even the window cleaner may carry one of those purpose-built devices enabling them to take card payments, or even just use their own phone. Payments have evolved to fulfil a consumer need driven by technology, especially smartphones.

Everyone knows PayPal. They started allowing UK customers to buy and sell cryptocurrency in 2021, bringing this into mass consciousness. Due to new UK regulations on the promotion of crypto assets[1] that came into force in October 2023, PayPal announced that they would stop offering this service until at least early 2024,[2] allowing themselves time to comply with the new rules. At the time of writing, the service had still not resumed in the UK,[3] but in June 2024, PayPal, not missing an opportunity to participate without having to carry the new regulatory burden, partnered with MoonPay (a service allowing users to buy and sell cryptocurrencies) to allow MoonPay customers to use PayPal as a method to buy and sell crypto currencies in the UK and Europe.[4] In March 2023, Shopify, the popular ecommerce platform for small to medium-sized businesses, launched a suite of blockchain commerce tools to enable merchants to mint and list NFTs (Non-Fungible Tokens) through the Shopify NFT minting app without having to use a dedicated platform such as Opensea or Rarible.[5] Twitter (now X) has always had ambitions of becoming a payments company, and Elon Musk has made it his mission to turn X into a "super app" for financial services as well as a social media platform, or even into a bank.[6] In 2022, WorldPay started offering merchants direct settlement in the USDC stablecoin.[7] In April 2023, X deployed a feature in partnership with eToro, a social trading platform, to let users trade stocks, financial assets, and cryptocurrencies. In the same month, Ralph Lauren opened a Web 3-centric store allowing customers to purchase items with cryptocurrency and launched an NFT for special perks.[8] In May 2024, Visa made what is probably the announcement of the decade,[9] in a bid to become a "network of networks", combining payment rails (cards, account-to-account, identity, and much more). Of course, not to be outdone, Mastercard also made a major announcement in May 2024 with the launch of their "Crypto Credential" solution enabling blockchain transactions between Latin America and Europe.[10]

Looking back a couple of decades, we wouldn't have dreamt of payments being so multi-layered.

Payments are becoming more complex

Nearly 70 years from the launch of the first modern credit card (BankAmericard), and nearly 20 years from the launch of the first 24 h/day, 365 days/year (near) real-time payments scheme (the UK Faster Payments System), the world of payments has evolved at a relentless pace. In my first book, "Understanding Payments", I covered the fundamentals of payments infrastructures, and these infrastructures are evolving. Centralised and decentralised payment ecosystems are converging, and regulatory complexity continues to increase. At the same time, businesses strive to make consumer payments ever more convenient.

Let's pause for a second and consider how much innovation and technological advancements were deployed in just the past five years. Imagine the investments made in payments infrastructures and processes over that period. Consider how Big Tech players, such as Apple, Google, and Facebook, inserted themselves in traditionally closed payments ecosystems, forcing incumbent players to interact with them due to consumer demand. Spare a thought for regulators and standards bodies trying to keep pace with the evolution of centralised payments, and the recent struggle of having to add decentralised payments into the mix. And no one actually agrees on what that mix is, or how it should be defined or governed: is it centralised or decentralised? Is a crypto asset a security, or considered property, or just a medium of exchange?

In April 2023, I was so staggered to see Robert F. Kennedy Junior, a US 2024 presidential candidate, get it so wrong by describing FedNow, a newly launched real-time payment system, as a Central Bank Digital Currency (CBDC), that I must reproduce his post in Figure 0.1.

← Post Reply

Robert F. Kennedy Jr
@RobertKennedyJr

The Fed just announced it will introduce its "FedNow" Central Bank Digital Currency (CBDC) in July. CBDCs grease the slippery slope to financial slavery and political tyranny.

While cash transactions are anonymous, a #CBDC will allow the government to surveil all our private financial affairs. The central bank will have the power to enforce dollar limits on our transactions restricting where you can send money, where you can spend it, and when money expires.

A CBDC tied to digital ID and social credit score will allow the government to freeze your assets or limit your spending to approved vendors if you fail to comply with arbitrary diktats, i.e. vaccine mandates.

The Fed will initially limit its CBDC to interbank transactions but we should not be blind to the obvious danger that this is the first step in banning and seizing bitcoin as the Treasury did with gold 90 years ago today in 1933.

Watch as governments, which never let a good crisis go to waste, use Covid-19 and the banking crisis to usher in a new wave of CBDCs as a safe haven from germ-laden paper currencies or as protection against bank runs.

https://www.cnbc.com/2023/03/15/long-awaited-fed-digital-payment-system-to-launch-in-july.html

5:55 PM · Apr 5, 2023 · **8.6M** Views

Figure 0.1 Fudge and confusion.

That a senior official can display such a lack of knowledge and remain unchecked is frightening. I am hoping that those who read my first book know better.

In any instance, RFK Jr can be forgiven for his lack of knowledge (if not for the dissemination thereof, but unfortunately, he continues to be very active on social media on this topic. After all, he is not a payments professional. But in this fast-evolving, complex and multi-faceted industry, can we really say that technology suppliers, payments services providers, retailers, regulators, and standards bodies, amongst others, understand all the nuances of the evolution and revolution that are happening in parallel in the payments world? Do we agree on the definition of a digital asset? Can we describe what DeFi is? How do crypto wallets work? Why are CBDCs such a much-researched, controversial, and sometimes emotional topic worldwide? Do we even understand what a distributed ledger is and where it can be used? Or what implications the metaverse has on payments?

As the puzzle becomes more complex, ecosystems players not only need to understand where they fit in, but they also must remain relevant in a fast-evolving and extremely competitive industry. Market pressures have forced a blurring of boundaries between all infrastructures. Ongoing market consolidation and growing innovation have only added to the confusion. Stakeholders continue to struggle with this constant change as they try to understand the relevance of other parts of the various ecosystems and take advantage of the opportunities available to them. Getting this knowledge is not only desirable but necessary, and sourcing the relevant knowledge is still tough.

If you perform a Google search on "blockchain payments books", you get in excess of 100 million results, most of which only cover blockchain technology, or specific aspects of cryptocurrencies, or specific use cases. Most of these are academic books, and this seems to be confirmed by a recent bibliometric analysis on "blockchain-based payment systems"[11] which identified 1,511 publications, 0.5% of which were books, 5.8% book chapters, and only 6.7% under the "Business, Management" category. But don't get me wrong, this is not a book about blockchain, or distributed ledger technology, or virtual assets, or the metaverse – many authors have done this very well already – although I will cover the fundamentals. This is a book about payments, and how they are evolving, from centralised to decentralised and everything in between, and the new opportunities they present.

Why I wrote this book

The payments industry continues to be fascinating, why make a book about it boring? This is not a textbook, it is written in plain English in a style accessible to all, and my cartoons featuring John and Suzie make a reappearance.

This book will appeal to those wanting to continue their journey from "Understanding Payments" at the fundamental level to incorporate those evolutionary, and sometimes revolutionary, elements that go beyond traditional payments. Whilst those new to the industry may find it hard to follow without an understanding of fundamentals (e.g. authorisation, clearing, settlement, which are covered in "Understanding Payments"), some chapters (e.g. Chapter 1, *Blockchain fundamentals*, or Chapter 5, *Digital and virtual assets*) can be read independently, and the book's glossary and references are extensive and there to help.

This book is primarily for the ducks, and will help them remain calm on the surface, whilst maximising the value of the paddling underneath (yes, the duck makes a reappearance too, and for those just looking for a succinct summary, jump to that icon). Private sector corporations, regulators, law firms, retailers, investors, professional services firms, security advisors, educators, and other curious minds, should find it a useful tool. From traditional financial services institutions jumping on the decentralisation bandwagon, to innovators and new entrants creating new business models and capitalising on modern technologies, to regulators trying to cope with it all and maintain some sort of integrity, whilst fostering innovation in increasingly complex ecosystems that facilitate the exchange of value in ways never thought of before.

This book will take readers through the fundamentals of the various decentralised payment ecosystems: from blockchain to smart contracts and dApps, from layer 2 to DeFi, from cryptocurrencies to CBDCs, jargon will be debunked, myths will be busted, and facts will be presented. It will also explain the potential interactions with centralised infrastructures, their implications, and how parallels can be drawn. For each concept, simple frameworks will be used, enabling comparison: mechanics, economics, metrics, risks, and future outlook. In the absence of consistent regulations (which will be highlighted where present), it will provide readers with unique categorisation frameworks (e.g. virtual assets, consensus protocols). It will also present practical applications, real-life examples, and offer insights into the key disciplines involved, giving readers an understanding of the key issues, risks, governance challenges, and opportunities. It may not answer all the questions – after all, this industry is vast and fast-moving – but it will equip readers with the knowledge to ask the right questions and know where to find the answers.

Finally, this book is not about blockchain, or DeFi, or crypto (although it covers all these and more), it is about payments in a brave new world. Halfway through writing this book, which was originally much bigger than what you will read here, I realised that I needed to split it into two parts: in "Beyond Payments", we will cover the decentralised infrastructures, the virtual assets that run on them, and the markets where they can be traded; in "Payments Unbound", the next book, we will cover in more detail the challenges and opportunities that decentralised markets present.

I hope this will continue to democratise payments knowledge and become a practical reference, at least for a little while.

Neira Jones
August 2024

Figure 0.2 Let's go! © Neira Jones 2024.

Notes

1 "PS23/6: Financial Promotion Rules for Cryptoassets" Financial Conduct Authority website. Available at: https://www.fca.org.uk/publications/policy-statements/ps23–6-financial-promotion-rules-cryptoassets (Accessed 3 July 2024).

2 "PayPal to Halt UK Crypto Sales Until 2024" 16 August 2023. Available at: https://www.reuters.com/technology/paypal-halt-uk-crypto-sales-until-2024-2023-08–16/ (Accessed 16 October 2023).

3 "What Can I Do with Crypto on Paypal" Paypal Help Centre. Available at: https://www.paypal.com/uk/cshelp/article/what-can-i-do-with-crypto-on-paypal-help893 (Accessed 3 July 2024).
4 "MoonPay and PayPal Crypto Purchasing Integration Expands to Include UK and EU Customers" *The Block*, 12 June 2024. Available at: https://www.theblock.co/post/299617/moonpay-and-paypal-crypto-purchasing-integration-expands-to-include-uk-and-eu-customers (Accessed 3 July 2024).
5 "Shopify Launches Blockchain Commerce Tools for Merchants" 5 March 2023. Available at: https://medium.com/@observer1/shopify-launches-blockchain-commerce-tools-for-merchants-6d51663fa36a (Accessed 16 October 2023).
6 "Elon Musk Wants X to Replace Users' Bank Accounts within a Year" 27 October 2023. https://www.finextra.com/newsarticle/43200/elon-musk-wants-x-to-replace-users-bank-accounts-within-a-year (Accessed 31 October 2023).
7 "Worldpay to Offer Merchants Direct Settlement in USDC" April 2022. https://www.finextra.com/newsarticle/40022/worldpay-to-offer-merchants-direct-settlement-in-usdc (Accessed 31 October 2023).
8 "Ralph Lauren Opens Crypto-friendly Store in Miami's Design District" 4 April 2023. Available at: https://ww.fashionnetwork.com/news/Ralph-lauren-opens-crypto-friendly-store-in-miami-s-design-district,1503510.html (Accessed 16 October 2023).
9 "Visa Reinvents the Card, Unveils New Products for Digital Age" Visa website. Available at: https://usa.visa.com/about-visa/newsroom/press-releases.releaseId.20686.html (Accessed 29 May 2024).
10 "Mastercard Issues New Crypto Announcement: Key Details Revealed" *U Today*, 29 May 2024. Available at: https://u.today/mastercard-issues-new-crypto-announcement-key-details-revealed (Accessed 29 May 2024).
11 "Blockchain-based Payment Systems: A Bibliometric & Network Analysis" 2022 https://arxiv.org/ftp/arxiv/papers/2212/2212.03790.pdf (Accessed 16 October 2023).

1

BLOCKCHAIN FUNDAMENTALS

Introduction (a different corner)

This is a long chapter and designed to be modular. I aim to introduce all things fundamental about blockchains, and sometimes, this means going into the details (not everyone is interested in that). For those only wanting to understand the basics, the duck is always there to remind you of the key takeaways. Also, sometimes, I have to introduce a term or a concept that is covered in detail in other chapters, but this will be signposted, and glossary entries will be highlighted in bold.

Traditional payment ecosystems recap

In my first book, "Understanding Payments – A Whistle-Stop Tour Into What You Thought You Knew",[1] I covered the fundamentals of the various centralised payments ecosystems, and I offered a quick glimpse into the decentralised world. In this book, we'll continue our journey into the fascinating world of payments, but because I aim to provide readers with a standalone reference

DOI: 10.4324/9781003480761-2

point, this introductory section will give a summary of the main differences between traditional and emerging payment ecosystems, so that we're all on the same page. Please feel free to skip this section if you know enough.

Most readers will be familiar with standard payment terminology, at least when related to card rails and bank rails, and the following terms should already be familiar:

- **Acquirer, card scheme, issuer**
- **Payment scheme, payment service provider (PSP), third party PSP (TPP)**
- **Authorisation, clearing**
- **Settlement, settlement agent**

For a quick refresher on terms, please look at the glossary (entries appear in bold in the text).

For completeness purposes, I will briefly recap transaction authorisation, clearing, and settlement here. Since these processes work similarly on card and bank rails, I will use the card rails (**four-party model**) for illustrative purposes (as the processes are more complex than on the bank rails, and if you're familiar with one, it's easy to understand the other) (Figures 1.1–1.3 illustrate this).

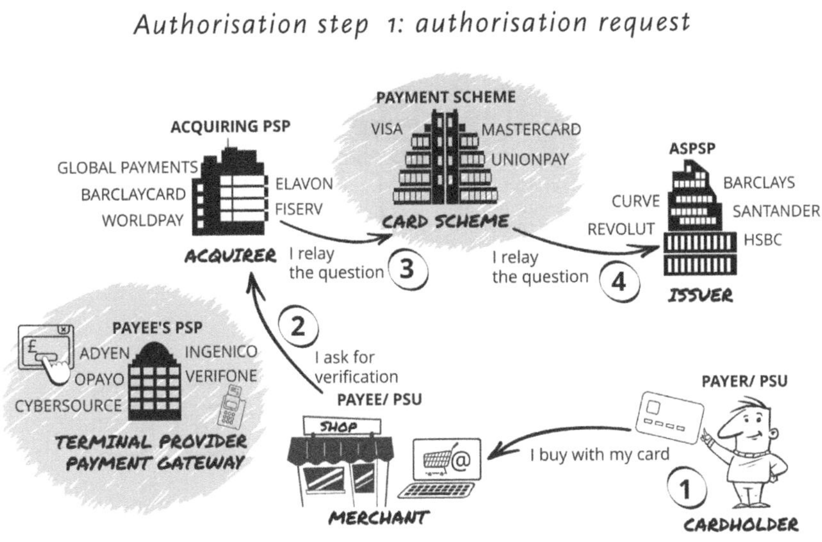

Figure 1.1 Authorisation request. © 2024 Neira Jones.

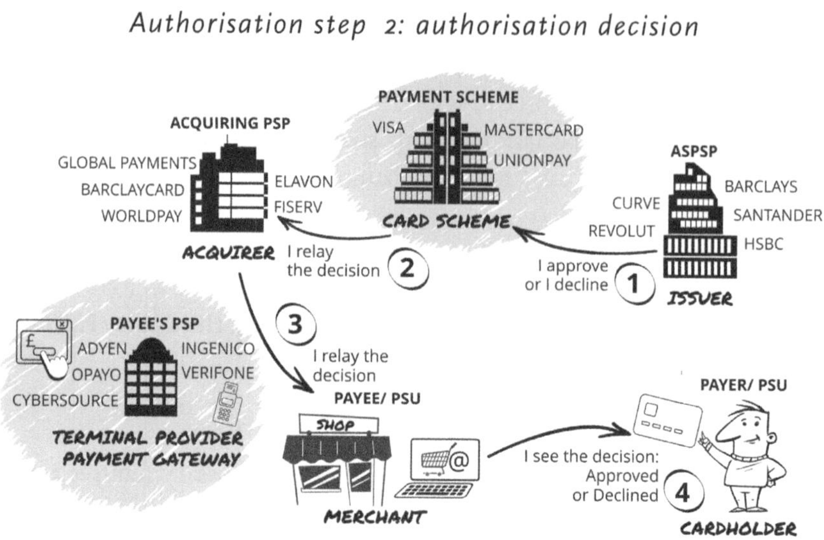

Figure 1.2 Authorisation decision. © 2024 Neira Jones.

On the card rails, once the issuer has authorised the transaction, the clearing process will allow for all transactions to be reconciled, a process orchestrated by the **card scheme** (aka the **payment scheme**).

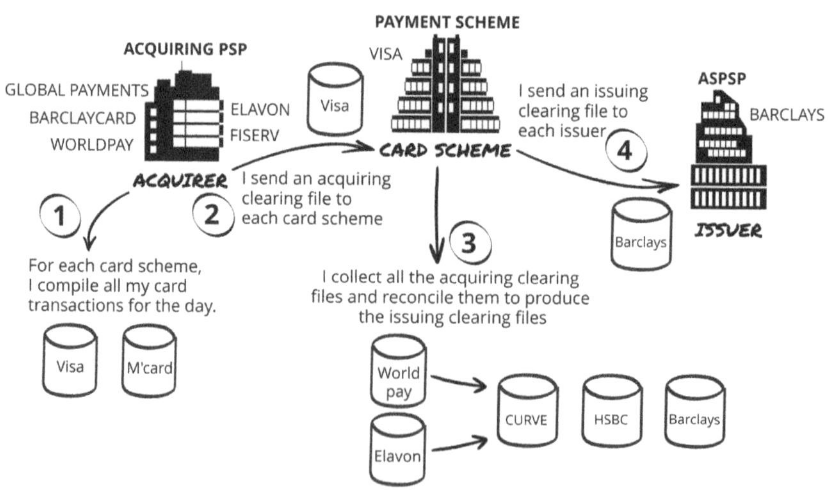

Figure 1.3 Clearing. © 2024 Neira Jones.

Clearing

The clearing process occurs between centralised trusted entities: the acquirer, the card scheme, and the issuer. These entities perform functions on behalf of the whole network, essentially providing a centralised trust framework.

Since clearing is only a transaction information reconciliation process, no funds movement occurs. The finality of the transaction is ensured by the settlement process, and on the card rails, this has two steps (Figures 1.4 and 1.5 illustrate this).

Interbank settlement

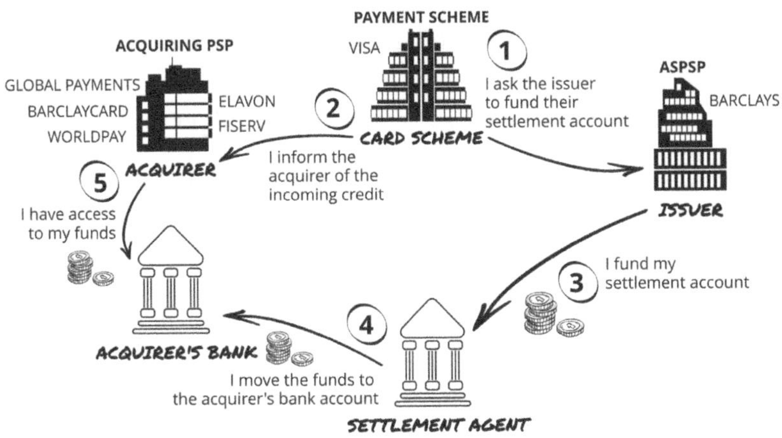

Figure 1.4 Interbank settlement. © 2024 Neira Jones.

At this stage, funds have moved between issuers and acquirers, and this process is facilitated by the settlement agent (e.g. a bank), another centralised trusted entity that provides a function on behalf of the whole network.

Merchant settlement

At this final stage, the merchant receives their funds, and the acquirer controls this process as the trusted entity.

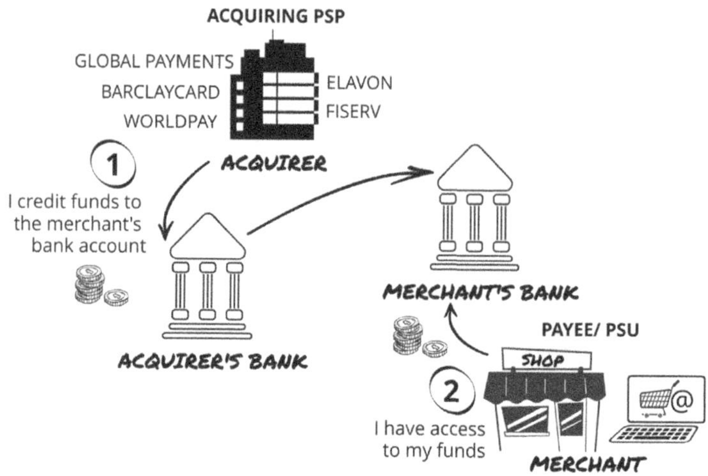

Figure 1.5 Merchant settlement. © 2024 Neira Jones.

Centralised vs. distributed ledgers

Traditional card and bank rails both use centralised mechanisms where trusted entities perform essential functions to maintain the integrity of the network:

- The payment scheme clears the money on behalf of the network.
- On the **card rails**, settlement is performed by banks chosen by the card schemes.
- On the **bank rails**, settlement is usually performed by a **central bank**.
- The movement of funds is orchestrated by a trusted central entity acting on behalf of the network.

The technology is centralised too, usually through standard databases and file systems. Traditional **centralised ledgers** took a long time to develop, and banks and financial services institutions largely provided the infrastructure. Of course, traditional financial services institutions, especially banks, are plagued with legacy systems,[2] despite digital transformation efforts over the past couple of decades.[3] Indeed, despite some moves to modern technology infrastructures, such as cloud computing, modern programming languages,[4] and modern messaging standards such as ISO 20022, a substantial share of the world's financial services systems still run on **COBOL**, and skills are scarce[5] (note from the author: showing my age here, I could have a go and help in an emergency! 😉). Of course, we have seen a surge of neo-banks and other PSPs showing the way to true digital transformation and customer interactivity, leading incumbents to try and emulate them, with variable success. Our world is slowly moving towards more interactivity, and embracing **Web 2.0**, although **Web 1.0** still rules for incumbents.

Unsurprisingly, decentralised infrastructures, especially **distributed ledgers**, have been attracting much attention, both from new and existing players. Since 2021, 18 South Korean banks have deployed Bank ID, a blockchain-based decentralised identity solution operated by the Korea Financial Telecommunications and Clearings Institute (KFTC), enabling customers to access their accounts seamlessly across the member banks without having to log in separately to each bank, and the number of participating banks is rising.[6] JP Morgan started seriously exploring blockchain for payments in 2020,[7] and in November 2023, they launched programmable payments on their Onyx blockchain platform.[8] They even launched payments in space[9]! In November 2023, JPM reported handling $1 billion in daily transactions using their digital token JPM Coin[10] (Note from the author: granted, that figure is dwarfed by the $10 trillion handled by JPM daily).

What am I trying to tell you? The world is changing, and new technologies and infrastructures can't be ignored. Anyone with a passing interest in payments will know that we're inexorably moving towards cashless payments, more digital interactions, more collaboration between fintech and incumbents, more real-time interactions, more cross-border payments, more **multi-rail** interactions, more seamless **B2B** payments, more e-commerce, not forgetting changing behaviours and relentless technology advancements, which in turn lead to new business models. And with all this, regulators are playing catch-up.

Undeniably, payments are evolving fast. Consumers have driven the adoption of **peer-to-peer networking**, as evidenced by the pervasiveness of social networks, and the popularity of **peer-to-peer payment** apps, such as Cash App, Revolut, Venmo, or Wise (although these don't qualify as true "peer-to-peer" as their underlying infrastructure is still centralised, but more on that later, or in my first book "Understanding Payments"...).

With centralised ledgers, the integrity of traditional payment rails is ensured via centralised mechanisms, and this means that one entity (or set of entities) is responsible for ensuring the integrity of the whole network. The idea of eliminating the need for a central authority (or intermediary) to preserve the integrity of the network (e.g. authentication, processing, settlement) led to the development of **Distributed Ledger Technology (DLT)**.

Distributed ledger technology (DLT)

DLT is based on peer-to-peer networking, where peers communicate without the need for a centralised entity to act as an intermediary. Many confuse DLT and **blockchain**, using the terms interchangeably. Blockchain is one example of DLT, but not the only one, although blockchain is undeniably the most popular implementation. Think of DLT as facial tissue, and of blockchain as Kleenex™.

> **BOX 1.1 EXAMPLES OF DLT OTHER THAN BLOCKCHAIN**
>
> Whilst blockchain is the most popular implementation of DLT, there are others:
>
> **Hashgraph**[11]: an architecture claiming to be more scalable than blockchains by having a validation mechanism (consensus) based on virtual voting where participants continuously communicate, sharing information about the transactions they receive. An example of implementation is Hedera.[12]
>
> **Holochain**[13]: a new development claiming to be more scalable than blockchains because, unlike blockchains, it doesn't require all participating nodes to store and validate all of the data (as this creates a large amount of overhead and doesn't scale easily). The architecture is "agent-centric" rather than "data-centric", meaning that a Holochain application creates an encrypted peer-to-peer network between users directly with a concept of mutual accountability. Holochain positions itself as a **Web3.0** platform.
>
> **Directed Acyclic Graph (DAG)**[14]: a mathematical construct offering a conceptual representation of the ordering of a series of activities represented by circles, some of which are connected by lines representing the flow from one activity to another. Examples of implementations are NANO,[15] Obyte,[16] and IOTA.[17]
>
> **Tempo (Radix)**: the Radix DLT[18] uses a data structure called Tempo, where nodes rely upon the passage of logical time to validate transactions. Radix positions itself as a Web 3.0 platform.

With DLT, traditional centralised functions become distributed. Processes like authorisation, clearing, and settlement are shared across the network. For the remainder of this chapter, I will mostly cover blockchain infrastructures given that they are the most common implementation of DLT.

Professionals should remember the following:

- Blockchain is a type of DLT.
- The equivalent of the authorisation, clearing, and settlement processes is performed on the blockchain.
- The rules and governance of the ecosystem are also maintained by and enacted on the blockchain.
- The blockchain ecosystem ensures the movement of funds and there is no need for intermediaries.

Let's dig a little deeper.

What is a blockchain? (democracy)

How did blockchains come about?

First mentioned in 1991 by cryptographers Stuart Haber and W. Scott Stornetta in their paper "How to time-stamp a digital document",[19] the concept of a blockchain is not new. However, it didn't gain popularity until 2008 when the mysterious Satoshi Nakamoto wrote the Bitcoin **white paper**[20] (see Chapter 2, Box 2.9), and blockchains suddenly entered the world of payments, with the utopian promise of a self-governing democratic ecosystem. Launched in 2009, the bitcoin blockchain is the oldest and its original **cryptocurrency**, Bitcoin Core (BTC), still runs on the original bitcoin blockchain and remains the most popular cryptocurrency today. Blockchain technology made it possible to record bitcoin transactions without the need for central authorities to establish trust in a trustless environment or govern a monetary system. The bitcoin blockchain was followed by Ethereum's in 2015. Many other blockchains launched since (Figure 1.6 illustrates this).

A blockchain is a form of DLT where time-stamped "blocks" of data are stringed together in a "chain" on an "append-only" basis, following the age-old accounting principle of the general ledger where the history of transactions is immutable. These blocks of data are intermittently validated (through consensus) by users of the network (nodes) before they are

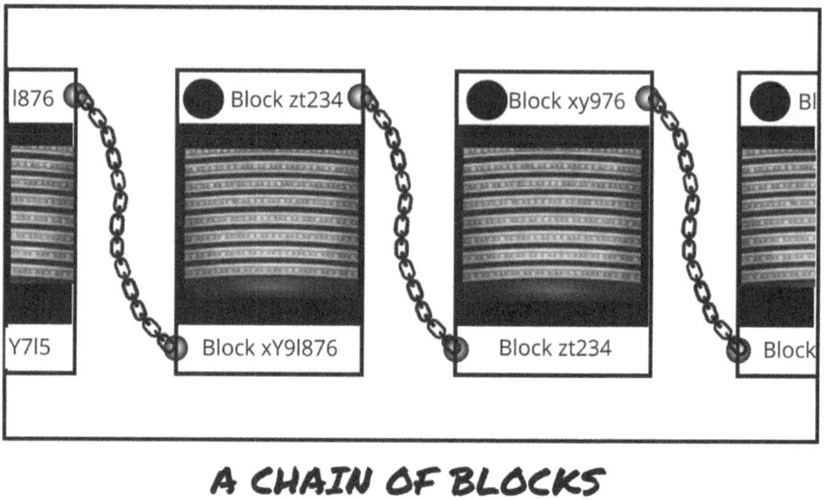

Figure 1.6 A blockchain: blocks chained to blocks. © 2024 Neira Jones.

permanently recorded on the blockchain (the ledger). Blockchain data will represent transactions (e.g. payments). Put simply, a DLT is a kind of distributed relational database with specific properties.

Of course, blockchains have to start somewhere, and there must be a first block added to the blockchain. As such, it's a special block that contains no reference to a previous one, since it is the first block. This block is called the genesis block.

BOX 1.2 THE GENESIS BLOCK

The **genesis block**, also known as "block 0", is the first block added to a blockchain after which every subsequent block is added. It's essentially the ancestor to which every other block can trace its lineage since every block contains a reference to the block preceding it.

The genesis block marks the launch of a blockchain and defines the format of all subsequent blocks. It's created differently from all subsequent blocks, and, in most blockchains, it will be hardcoded directly into the software, potentially including some initial coin/token supply (initial **coinbase transactions**).

Unlike regular blocks, the genesis block has no previous block to reference. In **Proof of Work (PoW)** blockchains, the genesis block may be pre-mined by the blockchain creator or a trusted group of individuals. In **Proof of Stake (PoS)** blockchains, the genesis block might be "seeded" by **validators** typically involving distributing the initial stake to the chosen validators.

The genesis block data is usually publicly available for inspection.

(PoW and PoS blockchain implementations are explained later on in this chapter, and definitions are in the glossary, but we don't need to understand the details right now).

What are the properties of a blockchain?

Figure 1.7 shows the generally accepted fundamental properties of a blockchain.

Figure 1.7 The four properties of a blockchain. © 2024 Neira Jones.

Immutability

Data recorded on a blockchain can't be changed or altered. It follows the general ledger principle where transactions are added sequentially (i.e. append-only) to record a new state. A blockchain ledger gives a permanent and unalterable history of transactions (semper eadem 😉). The data on the blockchain will remain there forever (well, as long as nodes are connected to it). Each block containing transactions (the data) on the ledger has a unique hash (see Figure 1.8 and Box 1.3) and contains the hash of the previous block (see Figure 1.6), and this is what gives **immutability** to blockchains. Immutability is important in environments that require auditability.

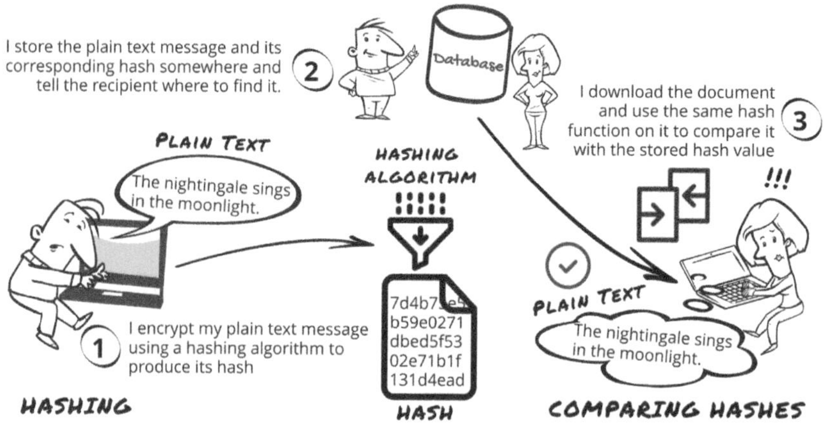

Figure 1.8 Hashing. © 2024 Neira Jones.

In Figure 1.8, if the stored document had been tampered with after John had uploaded it, when Suzie downloaded it and applied the hash function, the new output (hash) would have differed from the stored hash value, indicating that the document had been modified.

BOX 1.3 WHAT IS A HASH?

A **hash** is a mathematical function that converts an input of arbitrary length into an encrypted output of fixed length. This means that regardless of the original size of data used as input, the output is a unique string of characters that will always have the same size.

Hashing is used to secure stored data (data at rest), thus ensuring the integrity and authenticity of data stored on a blockchain. Hashed data can be checked against the original content to determine that the contents haven't been modified whilst in storage. Hashed data is different from encrypted data inasmuch as there is no decryption key (it is a one-way function) and it can't be decrypted.

Popular hashing algorithms include **MD-5** (one of the earliest, now considered unsafe), **RIPEMD-160** (RACE Integrity Primitives Evaluation Message Digest, also an established one, still considered secure), the **SHA** family (Secure Hash Algorithm, current version is SHA-3), and **Whirlpool**, but there are others.[21]

Hashes are commonly used to store passwords instead of storing plain text. This is helpful at the authentication stage where a user enters their password. The same hashing function would be used, and the resulting hash would be compared to the one that is stored. If the two match, you know the authentication was successful, and there was no need of storing the user's plain text password.

Security

Hashing is one aspect of security for blockchain infrastructures, and it ensures immutability.

In addition, **blockchain transactions are encrypted** between the sender and the recipient (see Figure 1.9) using **public key cryptography**, also known as asymmetric cryptography (see Box 1.4).

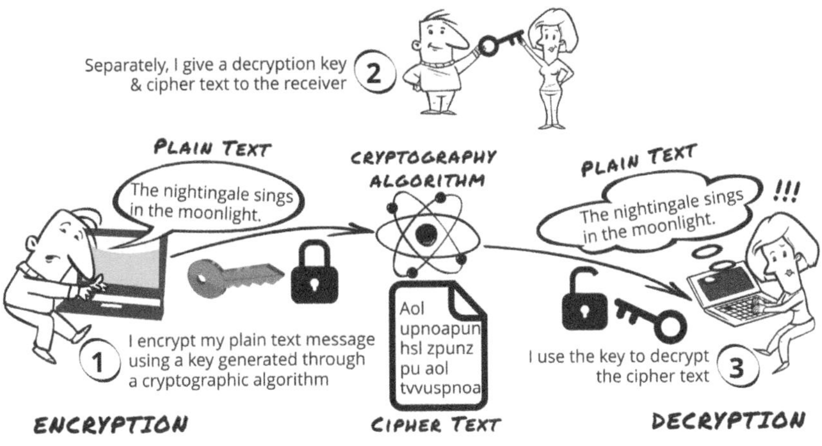

Figure 1.9 Encryption and decryption. © 2024 Neira Jones.

BOX 1.4 WHAT IS PUBLIC KEY CRYPTOGRAPHY?

Public key cryptography is an encryption method that uses two mathematically related, but not identical, keys – a **public key** and a **private key** – where each key performs a unique function. Public key cryptography is considered more secure and easier to manage than **symmetric cryptography** but is slower.

This method, used by blockchain networks and anywhere digital signatures are desirable, is also known as "asymmetric cryptography", "public key encryption", and "asymmetric encryption".

Well-known public key cryptography algorithms include Rivest-Shamir-Adleman (RSA), Elliptic Curve Digital Signature Algorithm (ECDSA), Digital Signature Algorithm (DSA), and Diffie-Hellman Key Agreement Protocol.

A bit of cryptographic history. Cryptographic techniques were made famous by the codebreakers at Bletchley Park[22] during World War II. Cryptographers, including the famous Alan Turing,[23] worked tirelessly to crack encrypted messages sent by the Germans using Enigma[24] machines. These machines scrambled messages using complex algorithms, turning them into seemingly nonsensical unbreakable code (**ciphertext**). But the Bletchley Park team had a secret weapon: their understanding of codebreaking techniques, using a process similar to hashing, where a fixed-length code (the scrambled message) is generated from the original message. By analysing patterns in these codes and using their knowledge of German communication habits, they were able to reverse-engineer how the Enigma machine worked and decipher the messages. Public key cryptography is similar: imagine two spies wanting to exchange secret messages without anyone eavesdropping. One spy broadcasts a complex padlock anyone can see (public key), but only the other spy has the unique key (private key) to unlock it. Messages secured with this public key can only be opened by the intended recipient, ensuring secure communication even on an open channel.

Transparency

Some participating nodes will store an entire copy of the ledger, meaning there isn't a single source of truth, and **everyone sees the same data**.

Of course, not all participants on the blockchain (i.e. nodes) get to fulfil all the required functions to maintain it (see *Who can do what?*).

Anonymity

I chuckle at that one, but I will say this: as long as no link between a **crypto wallet** address (see Chapter 6, *Transacting in a decentralised world*) and a real-world identity (e.g. card number, government ID, email address) can be established, the transaction on the blockchain will remain anonymous. To understand blockchains' anonymity and **privacy** features, we first need to understand how transactions are validated and added to the ledger (see *How are transactions validated? Reaching consensus*), and anonymity will be covered in the later section *Are blockchains private and anonymous?*

What are the characteristics of a blockchain?

If you compare them to traditional centralised networks, blockchains have three main characteristics: decentralisation, distributed trust, and peer-to-peer interactions (removing intermediaries) and Figure 1.10 illustrates this.

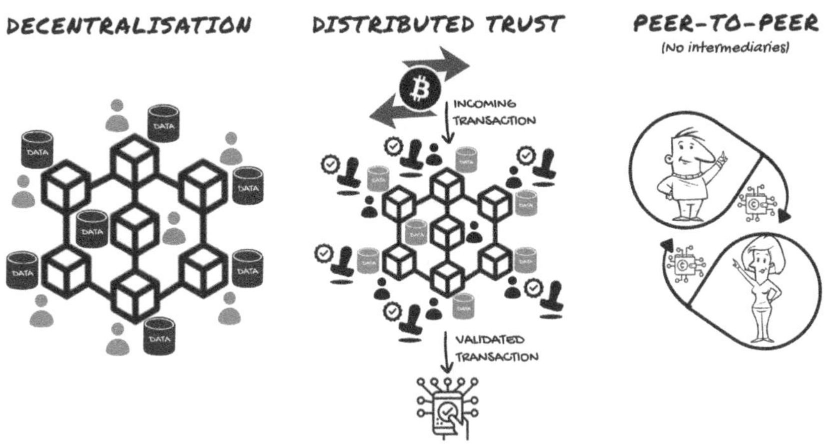

Figure 1.10 The three characteristics of a blockchain. © 2024 Neira Jones.

Decentralisation

Blockchains store and manage data by spreading responsibilities across multiple participants who can all see a copy of the same data using a distributed ledger. The network and hardware resources are owned and shared by the blockchain network members, and this means that no single entity owns either the data or the infrastructure.

Distributed trust

Blockchains minimise the trust required from any single participant in the network. The way data and transactions are validated is distributed across multiple participants in the ecosystem through a trust framework that incentivises ecosystem actors to cooperate with the rules defined by the blockchain; this means that transactions may be conducted on a blockchain without the transacting participants having to know or trust each other.

The blockchain **consensus protocol** is the main mechanism to achieve this, and it's a kind of economic game (see *How are transactions validated and settled?*). Not all blockchain network users will participate in the distributed trust framework, and blockchains will have the equivalent of participation models on centralised systems (e.g. **directly connected settling participant**, **indirect participant**, **principal**). However, these models don't generally rely on centralised entities for "membership" or "participation" (although this is not strictly true in all cases, see *Permissioned blockchains*).

The blockchain network participants engaged in the operation of the trust framework may be called **nodes** or **validators**, and the way they perform their tasks will depend on the type of blockchain used.

Peer-to-peer

The blockchain network performs functions on a **peer-to-peer** basis where participants interact directly with each other. Participants who transact on the network (e.g. trade cryptocurrency) will interact on a true peer-to-peer basis, with no need for trusted intermediaries (e.g. payment scheme, settlement agent) to provide the trust framework.

It's also worth noting that popular payment services commonly dubbed as "peer-to-peer", such as Venmo or Zelle, are not true "peer-to-peer" since they rely on centralised trusted intermediaries (e.g. payment schemes, banks).

Blockchain types (never trust a stranger)

Blockchain networks fundamentally differ from traditional payment networks, but they offer ecosystem actors various participation and access models similar to those seen in traditional centralised systems. To illustrate this difference, Figure 1.11 shows the various access models for participants on the bank rails: **directly connected settling participant**, **directly connected non-settling participant**, and **indirect participant**.

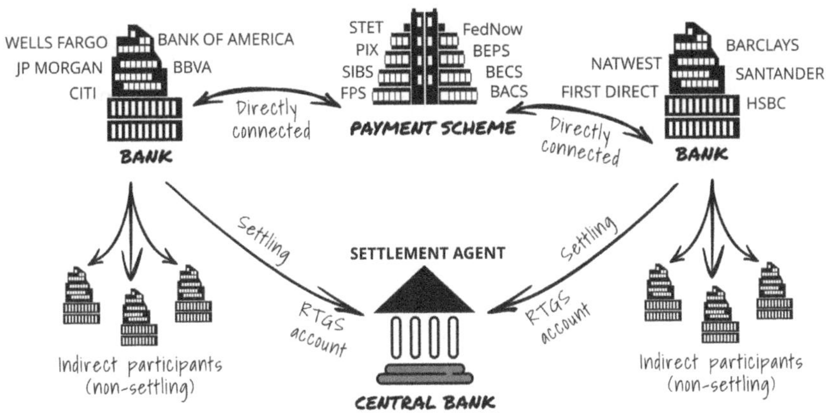

Figure 1.11 Participation models on the bank rails. © 2024 Neira Jones.

Figure 1.11 shows the participants who act as trusted entities to perform functions that ensure the integrity of the bank rails (i.e. payment schemes, banks); this is covered in detail in my first book, "Understanding Payments". These traditional centralised systems are heavily regulated and operate according to the applicable scheme rules, regulations, and standards, within the monetary policy set by the government.

The blockchain protocol

Blockchain networks will set their own rules, and the set of rules is known as the **blockchain protocol**, where, amongst other elements, the participation models will be specified (think of it as the rough equivalent of the "card scheme operating rules").

BOX 1.5 WHAT IS A BLOCKCHAIN PROTOCOL?

The **blockchain protocol** is the set of rules governing the operation of a blockchain network. Its core components include:

- **The consensus protocol**: the heart of a blockchain protocol, this defines how transactions will be validated and settled on the network.
- **The block structure**: this specifies the format of the data stored within each block.
- **The cryptography protocol(s)**: as cryptography is an intrinsic part of blockchains, the blockchain protocol defines which cryptography algorithms will be used and for what purpose.
- **The network protocol(s)**: this defines how blockchain nodes will communicate with each other and ensures reliable and secure data transmission as well as data synchronisation across the distributed network. Protocols common in traditional centralised infrastructures may be used (e.g. TCP/IP, UDP, HTTPS), but blockchain-specific protocols are not uncommon.

In addition, and depending on implementation, some blockchain protocols allow for the deployment of **smart contracts** (see *Quickly defining smart contracts and dApps*), incentive mechanisms, and governance models for decision-making regarding network upgrades, rule changes, resource allocation, etc.

Blockchains have two broad participation models: permissionless and permissioned, and Figure 1.12 illustrates their positioning, with some real-life examples seen in financial services.

Figure 1.12 gives examples of popular blockchains and where they fit in, showing Bitcoin, Ethereum, and Solana as **permissionless blockchains**, and Ripple as a **permissioned blockchain**, with Hyperledger Fabric, Quorum, and R3 Corda as established platforms for permissioned blockchain development and enterprise use-cases (rather than true blockchains themselves) (see Chapter 2, *Building blockchains and applications*).

Permissionless blockchains

With this model, any user can join the network and become a validating node if they have sufficient resources. The technology infrastructure

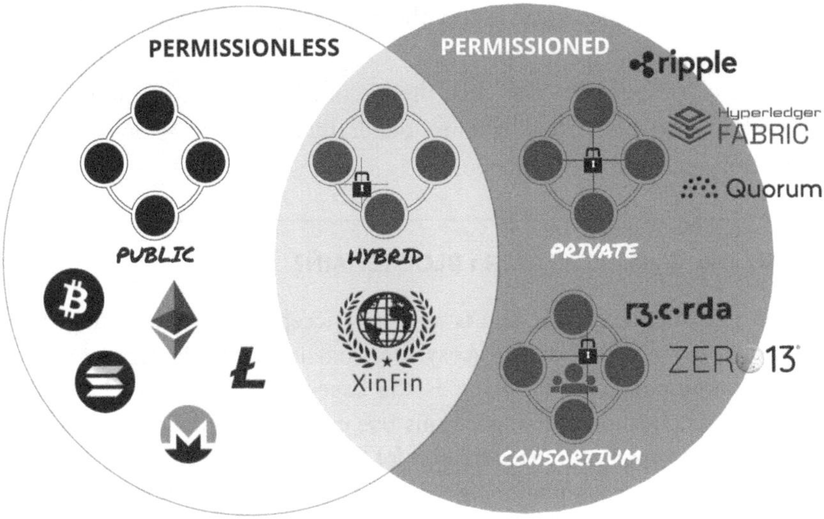

Figure 1.12 Permissionless, permissioned, and hybrid blockchains. © 2024 Neira Jones.

is **open source**, and this is the most decentralised of blockchain models, embodied through an open network where participants are unknown. Permissionless blockchains, whilst they offer a degree of anonymity (see *Are blockchains private and anonymous?*), enable everyone to see all transactions as these are recorded on a public ledger, which makes them unsuitable (at the basic level) where transaction privacy is a requirement.

Permissionless blockchains, also known as public or trustless blockchains, are the oldest established networks, and the Bitcoin and **Ethereum** blockchains are examples. These blockchains are completely independent of any single organisation, which means that even if the founding organisation ceases to exist, the blockchain will continue running as long as nodes are still connected.

They are primarily used for digital asset trading (e.g. **cryptocurrency**), **crowdfunding** and donations, and applications that require a high level of **decentralisation**, such as distributed file storage. They can also be used where immutable records with an auditable chain of custody are required, such as electronic notarisation or public property ownership records.

There is much jargon in the blockchain world, but unlike in payments, where we (more or less) agree on definitions, it's a bit more difficult to agree on definitions and classification in the blockchain world. Throughout this book, I will try to give you the most popular definitions, and the variations of which I am aware.

So here goes: blockchains, like the Bitcoin blockchain or the Ethereum blockchain, are main infrastructures generally referred to as Layer 1 (sometimes abbreviated L1) blockchains.

BOX 1.6 WHAT IS A LAYER 1 BLOCKCHAIN?

The term **Layer 1 blockchain** is generally accepted as representing the base layer in a blockchain ecosystem that is **permissionless** and for **general-purpose** use. It serves as the base infrastructure for building various applications serving various use cases. Some definitions might encompass **open source** technology for the underlying code and consensus protocol, whilst others might specify the use of an **established consensus protocol** such as Proof of Work (PoW) or Proof of Stake (PoS). The Bitcoin, Ethereum, and **Solana** blockchains are Layer 1 blockchains by that definition.

It is important to note that other interpretations exist: Hyperledger Fabric is often defined as a Layer 1 blockchain although it is a framework used to develop permissioned blockchains (see Chapter 2, *Building blockchains and applications*), not a blockchain itself (but permissioned blockchains developed using Hyperledger Fabric could be classified as Layer 1); Ripple is also sometimes defined as a Layer 1 blockchain, although it is **permissioned**, with a **proprietary consensus protocol**, and designed for a **specific purpose** (i.e. **cross-border** payments). I'll let you make up your own mind.

In any instance, if we take the broad definition of a "base layer" blockchain, I think the industry agrees on the terms "**mainchain**", "**mainnet**", and "**parent blockchain**", regardless of whether they are classified as "Layer 1" or not.

Permissioned blockchains

By contrast to permissionless blockchains, permissioned blockchains are closed networks in which only a select number of parties interact and participate in the trust framework. Think of them as the rough equivalent of **closed loop** networks in centralised infrastructures.

They are only partially decentralised as all participants are known (e.g. these will be verified through KYC as on centralised systems).

This model restricts access and rights to certain nodes. The technology is not as distributed as in permissionless blockchains, which enables more flexibility in customisation as the decision-making process is confined to a select number of known participants, enabling diverse configurations and incremental decentralisation as required.

Also, because they are generally smaller than permissionless blockchains and fewer participants are involved in transaction validation, they can process transactions faster than public blockchains. A permissioned blockchain enables the transacting parties to be known only to each other and to keep transactions secret from other participants; this is useful where transaction privacy must be preserved, such as in trade finance and money market applications.

Purists often claim that permissioned blockchains are not "true blockchains" because they compromise some of the fundamental properties and characteristics of blockchains (e.g. decentralisation, anonymity, distributed trust, transparency). Some even call them BLINO[25] (Blockchain In Name Only) and I sympathise 😉.

Permissioned blockchains are primarily used in financial services (e.g. asset ownership, trade finance) but they have also enabled new use cases such as supply chain monitoring and tracking, healthcare, goods authentication, claims settlement, and identity verification. I let you decide whether such implementations will stay the course (many haven't). Furthermore, not all blockchain applications are decentralised (see Chapter 2, *Blockchain application types*).

Permissioned blockchains, with their immutable (unchangeable) and auditable (verifiable) ledgers, could be useful for payment processes where trust and a clear record of events are crucial. For example, in **arbitration**, the immutable record on a permissioned blockchain can serve as a tamper-proof source of evidence for dispute resolution. Authorised participants, likely including arbitrators, can access and verify this record, streamlining the process, reducing the risk of manipulation, and offering a new model for trusted third parties. This model leverages cryptographic security and DLT for enhanced transparency and efficiency.

Hybrid blockchains

As the name suggests, hybrid blockchains incorporate features from both permissionless and permissioned blockchains. Depending on the deployment and requirements of the founders, they may have a combination of:

- both public and private ledgers,
- both public and private nodes.

There are several use cases for hybrid blockchains, including:

- Global trade and finance, and banking, where operational efficiency is desired,
- Government, enabling required control whilst allowing general access for use cases such as aid, voting, public identity services, healthcare records, research, etc.
- Supply chains, where tracking, monitoring and authenticity proofing are desirable,
- IoT, where device access can be through a private blockchain for security purposes, and some network features can be made public depending on information-sharing requirements,
- Enterprise services, where blockchain properties may be beneficial.

Comparing blockchain models

Blockchain applications are numerous, and when considering their use, **professionals should compare their properties, characteristics, pros, and cons depending on the planned application.**

Table 1.1 compares the properties of various architectures.

You will realise from Table 1.1 that the fundamental properties of blockchains (see *What are the properties of a blockchain?*) are not always totally observable in all blockchain models.

Professionals should remember:

- **Immutability and security** are sacrificed in favour of other properties in private, consortium, and hybrid blockchains.

Table 1.1 Comparing properties of databases and blockchain models. © 2024 Neira Jones

Properties	**Standard Database**	**Public Blockchain**	**Private Blockchain**	**Consortium Blockchain**	**Hybrid Blockchain**
Immutability	As immutable as the owners make it	Yes	Partial		
Security	As secure as the owners make it	High	Security levels depend on the design		
Transparency	Only accessible to those granted access by the owners	High: transaction data visible to anyone, open source	Low: access is restricted to authorised participants	Transparency levels depend on the design	
Anonymity	Not anonymous as systems rely on centralised authorisation and authentication	Users may remain anonymous if no correlation can be established with real-world identities	Low anonymity as access is restricted to authorised participants who are known to each other		Anonymity levels depend on the design
Example use cases	An online banking application, a digital payment wallet (e.g. PayPal, Apple Pay)	A crypto wallet (e.g. Coinbase)	Blockchain applications involving regulated products or services (e.g. securities, trade settlement)		Land and property registry (i.e. private for records management, public for viewing)

- **Transparency** is sacrificed in private blockchains, and transparency levels depend on the design of consortium and hybrid blockchains.
- **Anonymity** levels depend on the blockchain implementations, and even public blockchains can't claim total anonymity.

Table 1.2 compares the characteristics of the various architectures, including standard centralised databases.

It becomes apparent from Table 1.2 that all fundamental characteristics of blockchains (see *What are the characteristics of a blockchain?*) are not necessarily present in all blockchain models.

Professionals should remember:

Whilst public blockchains exhibit all the fundamental characteristics of blockchains, private, consortium, and hybrid blockchains sacrifice decentralisation, distributed trust, and peer-to-peer interactions in favour of other factors (e.g. control, performance, privacy).

Table 1.3 gives the pros and cons of the various architectures and details the factors influencing design.

Do you need a blockchain?

I won't bore you by giving you a decision-making flowchart as to whether your project needs a database or a blockchain because technology evolves all the time and what might have been true a few years ago may no longer be true today.

In addition, the real-life examples I gave in the previous tables, whilst correct at the time of writing, may change rapidly as blockchains may evolve from one model to another, or even disappear altogether. For example, We.Trade, an IBM-backed consortium blockchain founded in 2018 with several European member banks, shut down in June 2022 after running out of cash.[26]

In any instance, I give a few references for decision flowcharts[27,28,29] at the end of this chapter so you can decide. I won't indulge in producing another one.

Table 1.2 Comparing characteristics of databases and blockchain models. © 2024 Neira Jones

<table>
<tr><th>Characteristics</th><th>Standard Database</th><th>Public Blockchain</th><th>Private Blockchain</th><th>Consortium Blockchain</th><th>Hybrid Blockchain</th></tr>
<tr><td>Decentralisation</td><td>Low</td><td>High</td><td>Low</td><td>Medium</td><td>Decentralisation levels depend on design</td></tr>
<tr><td>Distributed trust</td><td>No</td><td>Yes</td><td colspan="2">Only to selected participants</td><td>Trust distribution levels depend on design</td></tr>
<tr><td>Peer-to-peer (no intermediaries)</td><td>Peer-to-peer interaction levels depend on design (e.g. client-server)</td><td>High</td><td>Low</td><td colspan="2">Peer-to-peer interaction levels depend on design</td></tr>
<tr><td>Examples</td><td>A traditional banking or payment application</td><td>Bitcoin blockchain, Ethereum blockchain</td><td>Ripple, implementations of Quorum and Hyperledger Fabric</td><td>ZERO13, implementations of R3 Corda</td><td>Xinfin</td></tr>
</table>

Table 1.3 Pros and cons of databases and blockchain models. © 2024 Neira Jones

	Standard Database	**Public Blockchain**	**Private Blockchain**	**Consortium Blockchain**	**Hybrid Blockchain**
Independence from censorship	No	Yes	No	No	Partial
Performance	Fast, but depends on design	Slow, but depends on design	Fast		
Scalability	Yes	No[a]	Yes		
Security	Can be compromised	Yes	Can be compromised		
Governance	The owner can change the rules at any time	All participating nodes must approve (or not deny) changes	The owner can change the rules at any time	A designated set of participants can change the rules at any time	Hybrid, depending on role and function
Trust	Centralised	Decentralised	Semi-centralised		
Participants	Identified and trusted	Anonymous, anyone	Identified and trusted		Hybrid, depending on role and function
Access	Only authorised	Public	Only authorised		
Data integrity	Read, write, update, delete	Read, write	Read, write, update, delete as per blockchain protocol		Hybrid
Privacy of transactions	It depends	No	Yes		
Technology	Client-server centralised	DLT			
Use cases	Various	Cryptocurrency Document validation	Asset ownership Supply chain	Banking Research Supply chain	Healthcare records Land registry

[a] *Note:* without scaling solutions (see *Are blockchain scalable?*).

Professionals should remember that blockchains are not a panacea to all systems development woes. You may consider their use if:

- The problem can't be resolved faster and cheaper with existing technologies.
- The participants in the transactional system can't be individually trusted.
- A centralised entity (or set of entities), who may perform functions on behalf of the whole network, can't be trusted by all participants.
- Absolute immutability of transaction history is required.
- It is difficult to decide who should be in control of the data.
- You are working with digital assets.
- Your software developers are not bound and controlled by a common interest.

Of course, if you still can't decide, you can look at what's involved in building blockchains and applications in Chapter 2 for more details.

Now that we understand the various types of blockchain infrastructures, their properties, and characteristics, let's examine how transactions are performed.

How are transactions validated and settled? (the eyes of truth)

In the previous sections, I briefly introduced the concepts of validation and consensus as mechanisms to preserve blockchain networks' integrity and security. There's a bit more to it.

What is a consensus protocol?

The **consensus protocol** is probably the most well-known aspect of a blockchain. It is the set of rules defining how a distributed network of nodes ensures the blockchain ledger's security and integrity and how transactions will be added to it. Think of it as a democratic voting system where everyone participates in the decision-making process without needing trusted intermediaries or central authorities.

The most well-known consensus protocols are Proof of Work (**PoW)** and Proof of Stake (**PoS)**.

Proof of Work (PoW)

PoW is a blockchain consensus protocol by which validating nodes, the **miners**, compete to solve a cryptographic puzzle. Whomever solves the puzzle first gets to add their block to the chain. The process of adding new blocks in PoW blockchains is called mining.

A **miner** is a node in a PoW blockchain network that participates in the transaction validation process.

A miner listens to the network and gathers valid transactions to fit in a block. Miners ensure the integrity and security of the blockchain network by completing tasks including verifying and processing transactions, ensuring consensus, and preventing fraud (e.g. **double-spending**, see Box 1.8).

As miners do this all at the same time for all transactions, which blocks get added to the chain is determined by the PoW consensus protocol.

Mining is the process by which a new block will be added to a PoW blockchain and where miners compete to solve a complex mathematical problem.

The first miner to solve the problem gets to broadcast their block to the network and if consensus amongst participants is reached that the block is valid, the new block is added to the chain, creating an immutable record.

This resource-intensive process is the reason why PoW blockchains are often criticised for their energy consumption.

Mining is a bit like trying to solve a Rubik's cube whilst running a marathon.

Proof of Stake (PoS)

PoS is a blockchain consensus protocol by which validating nodes, the **validators**, stake their own funds, a process referred to as **staking**. A **coin** or **token** is picked randomly from all staked funds. The owner of the "winning" coin gets to add their block to the blockchain. The process of adding new blocks in PoS blockchains is called **staking**.

A **validator** is a node in a PoS blockchain network that participates in the transaction validation process.

Unlike in PoW blockchains which involve solving complex mathematical puzzles, validators are only required to stake (i.e. lock up) their funds to participate in the process, and the winning validator is selected according to the PoS consensus protocol.

Once a validator is selected, they gain the right to create a new block including validating incoming transactions to include within. This new block is then broadcast to the network and if consensus on block validity is reached, the new block is added to the chain.

Staking is the process by which a validator will be selected to gain the right to create a new block for a proposed addition to the blockchain ledger.

The PoS consensus protocol will select the winning validator according to factors including the amount of their stake, the duration held, and the validator reputation.

Staking consumes far less energy than mining and has a lower barrier to entry for prospective participants as they only need to have enough coins/tokens to stake.

Byzantine fault tolerance

As a rule of thumb, PoW and PoS are the predominant consensus protocols for permissionless blockchains, whereas permissioned blockchains tend to use **Byzantine fault tolerance (BFT)**, hybrid, or proprietary consensus protocols.

This is because permissionless blockchains implement trust frameworks designed to address (usually large) distributed networks of unknown and untrusted participants. By contrast, permissioned blockchains must implement trust frameworks for comparatively smaller distributed networks of participants known to each other, a model with its own challenges.

The Byzantine's General Problem

As explained in Tables 1.1 and 1.2, whilst public blockchains exhibit all the fundamental characteristics of blockchains, permissioned and hybrid blockchains may sacrifice decentralisation, distributed trust, and peer-to-peer interactions in favour of other factors (e.g. control, performance, privacy), and this would be reflected in their chosen consensus protocol. This is because permissioned (and hybrid) blockchains may be adversely affected by Byzantine faults, whilst designed to be more performant (fast finality or settlement) than their permissioned counterparts.

The **Byzantine General's Problem** is conceptual in distributed systems where components may fail and insufficient information on whether a component has failed makes decision-making difficult.

The allegory stems from an example where a group of generals, each commanding a portion of an army, must coordinate an attack or retreat on a city. However, some generals may be traitors and provide false or conflicting information to other generals, making coordinating the attack or retreat difficult.

The challenge is for the loyal generals to reach a consensus, despite the presence of traitors and potentially unreliable communication mechanisms, to ensure that they either all attack or all retreat to avoid defeat.

In blockchains, the problem describes the challenge of achieving consensus among nodes in the presence of unreliable or malicious actors. This is particularly relevant to permissioned blockchains, where participants are known and (hopefully!) trusted entities who may abuse their influence through Byzantine faults.

Byzantine faults include **Sybil attacks, DDoS attacks, Eclipse attacks, packet tampering, time synchronisation attacks**, double-spending, **collusion**, etc. The consensus protocol must therefore be resilient to malicious or compromised nodes who may send conflicting information, become unresponsive, or deliberately attempt to disrupt the network's operation.

There are various mitigating features that a blockchain protocol may implement to resist Byzantine faults, including imposing thresholds on the number of nodes required to validate, node reputation systems, redundant communication channels, message replication, audits, network monitoring and intrusion detection, and cryptography.

BFT characteristics

Consequently, **Byzantine fault tolerance (BFT)**, or variations/hybrids of it, is a popular consensus protocol used in permissioned blockchains. Aside from the standard processes explained in earlier sections (e.g. validation, block formation, compliance), BFT adds several steps to ensure resilience to malicious nodes and the consensus steps are explained below:

- **Communication**: nodes interact with each other to decide on the ordering and validity of transactions.
- **Quorum**: to reach consensus, a threshold of correct nodes (the quorum) must agree on the validity of transactions. This is usually two-thirds of the nodes, but individual blockchain protocols may vary this proportion depending on other factors (e.g. network size, security, desired level of fault tolerance).
- **Voting**: nodes independently validate transactions and communicate with other nodes to vote on proposed transactions or blocks.
- **Consensus**: If the number of votes agreeing on the validity and ordering of transactions reaches a "super majority" (at least two-thirds of the quorum), consensus is achieved, and transactions are finalised (i.e. settled).

Unlike PoW or PoS which have a specific mechanism for achieving consensus (i.e. mining, staking), consensus protocols based on BFT rely on voting, quorum systems, and messaging within a (smaller) network of known entities. These are designed to ensure that the blockchain can still achieve consensus and maintain its integrity and security even in the presence of Byzantine faults.

Recap on consensus protocols

Aside from PoW, PoS, and BFT, there are many other blockchain consensus protocols, some of which may be variants of any of these, some may be proprietary to specific blockchains (or DLTs), and some may be hybrids.

Table 1.4 gives more details on the consensus protocols of which I am aware, with real-life examples at the time of writing.

Whilst the examples in Table 1.4 are current at the time of writing, blockchain design evolves rapidly, and it is advised to check up-to-date documentation.

Table 1.4 A detailed view of consensus protocols. © 2024 Neira Jones

Proof of Work (PoW)	**Proof of Stake (PoS)**	**Byzantine Fault Tolerance (BFT)**	**Hybrid Protocols and Others**
Hashcash Example: original PoW	**Pure Proof of Stake (PPoS)** Examples: Algorand, Avalanche	**Practical Byzantine Fault Tolerance (PBFT)** Examples: Hyperledger Sawtooth, Quorum	**Proof of Elapsed Time (PoET)** Examples: Hyperledger Sawtooth, IOTA Streams, Symbiosis
Proof of Work (PoW) Examples: Bitcoin, Litecoin	**Casper** Example: Ethereum 2.0	**Federated Byzantine Agreement (FBA)** Example: Stellar	**Proof of Reputation (PoR)** Examples: GoChain, U2U Chain, Lition, Ontology, Daostack (ran out of money)
Ethhash Example: Ethereum 1.0	**Nominated Proof of Stake (NPoS)** Example: Polkadot	**Delegated Byzantine Fault Tolerance (dBFT)** Example: NEO	**Proof of Commitment (PoC+)** Example: Signum
CryptoNight Example: 1st version of Monero	**Delegated Proof of Stake (DPoS)** Examples: EOS, Tron, Lisk, Ark, Gnosis	**Ripple Protocol Consensus Algorithm (RPCA)** Ripple proprietary	**Directed Acyclic Graph (DAG) based** Example: IOTA (Tangle), Nano (Block Lattice)
Equihash Example: Zcash	**Bonded Proof of Stake (BPoS)** Example: Cosmos	**HoneyBadgerBFT** Example: Hedera Hashgraph	**Expected Consensus (EC)** Example: Filecoin

Proof of Work (PoW)	Proof of Stake (PoS)	Byzantine Fault Tolerance (BFT)	Hybrid Protocols and Others
RandomX Example: 2nd version of Monero	**Liquid Proof of Stake (LPoS)** Example: Tezos	**Tendermint** Example: Cosmos, Binance Chain, Crypto.com Chain	**Proof of Burn (PoB)** Example: Slimcoin
Cuckoo Cycle Example: Grin	**Ouroboros** Example: Cardano		**Proof of Authority (PoA)** Examples: Ethereum (in some private or test networks using the Clique consensus algorithm), VeChainThor
Proof of Space (PoSpace), also called Proof of Capacity (PoC) Examples: Chia, Storj DCS, Arweave, Siacoin, Turtlecoin	**Proof of Deposit (PoD)** No current example		**Raft** Examples: Hyperledger Fabric
			Proof of Formulation (PoF) Example: Fleta (although, this blockchain seems to have disappeared[30])

Figure 1.13 shows the more common consensus protocols available at the time of writing and their applicability to blockchain types.

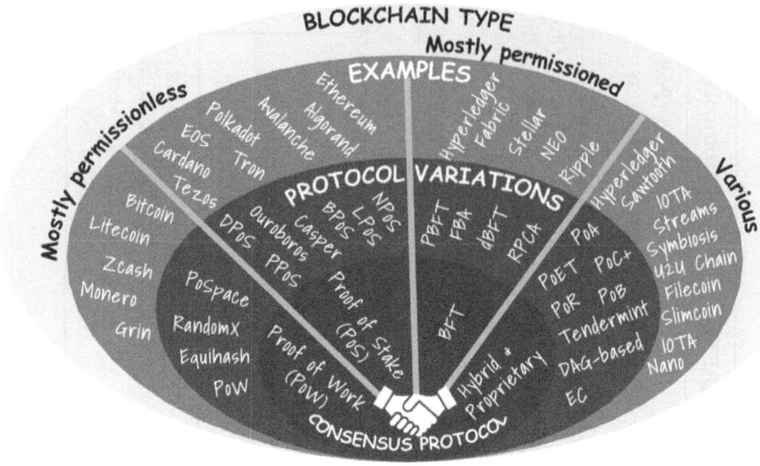

Figure 1.13 Consensus protocols. © 2024 Neira Jones.

Of course, the world of blockchains (and other DLTs) is very dynamic, and this picture will change over time.

Professionals should remember the following:

- **Blockchain consensus protocols vary across implementations**, and it is important to check up-to-date official documentation to understand the operation of a particular blockchain.
- PoW, PoS, and BFT are the more commonly used consensus protocols, but hybrid and proprietary protocols also exist.
- As a broad generalisation, **PoW and PoS are mostly used by permissionless blockchains**, although some prominent permissionless blockchains also use hybrid protocols.
- **Permissioned blockchains mostly used variants of BFT** and hybrid or proprietary protocols.

Validation vs. consensus

My first book covered authorisation, clearing, and settlement for centralised payment ecosystems. It may be surprising to some that these processes (the basic three steps) still exist for blockchain infrastructures; they are just performed differently due to their distributed nature.

For blockchains, "validation" and "consensus" are different concepts. The validation process ensures that transactions are "valid" (e.g. not malicious, no double-spending, etc.), whereas the consensus process determines the order in which validated transactions will be added to the blockchain ledger (remember, a blockchain is an immutable sequential ledger). As such, "validation" comes before "consensus".

Each time a transaction is conducted on a blockchain, it is broadcast to the nodes participating in the validation process.

At the validation stage, no new transaction is added to the ledger, making this step equivalent to authorisation and clearing on centralised networks (see Figures 1.1–1.3).

For transactions to be added to the ledger, the network must agree, and this is achieved through a consensus protocol which is the set of rules by which participating network nodes reach an agreement. The process by which a validating node gets selected to propose a new block for addition to the blockchain is called **mining** (PoW) or **staking** (PoS).

Once consensus is reached, a new block (i.e. a batch of valid transactions) is added to the blockchain and is henceforth immutable, making this step equivalent to the settlement process in centralised systems (see Figures 1.4 and 1.5).

The end-to-end process is illustrated in Figure 1.14.

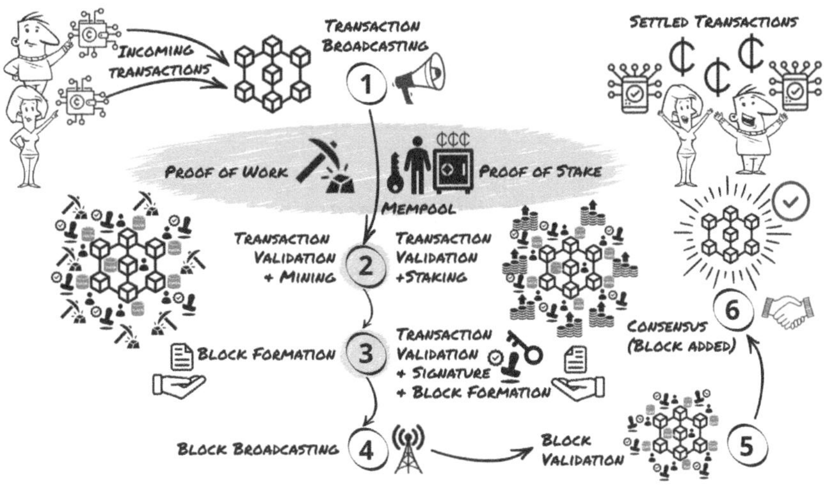

Figure 1.14 How consensus is reached for PoW and PoS blockchains. © 2024 Neira Jones.

After block broadcasting, the network must agree that the valid block will be recorded on the ledger, which is achieved through consensus.

Quickly defining smart contracts and dApps

This is a "fork" from the flow of this chapter (😉 inside joke, but you'll have to read Chapter 3, *An introduction to blockchain forks*) to understand it, or look up the term in the glossary, or for a quick peek, Chapter 3, Box 3.2).

Since I will use the terms "smart contract" and "dApps" a few times in the remainder of this chapter, you probably don't want to wait until you read Chapter 2, *Building blockchains and applications* to understand these in detail, so here are simple definitions that'll do the job for now:

A **smart contract** is simply code stored on a blockchain that automatically executes when its pre-defined conditions are met. Based on the "If, Then" principle, they are typically used to automate the execution of an agreement between participants in a trustless environment, without the need for intermediaries.

A **dApp** (**d**ecentralised **App**lication) is a software application built on DLT, such as a blockchain, consisting of a smart contract at the backend and a front-end user interface. The user interface is just like any app and is usually built using traditional web technology. Since smart contracts are typically public on the blockchain, anyone can inspect the code and transactions associated with the dApp.

Now, let's get on with the blockchain transactional process.

Submitting transactions

In the world of blockchains, there is a cost associated with getting transactions processed and this is generally referred to as the transaction fee.

As a user initiates a transaction through their preferred interface (e.g. **crypto wallet**, **dApp**, see Chapter 2, *dApps* and Chapter 6, *Transacting in a decentralised world*), they will specify several data elements as part of the transaction input, including the amount, the **transaction fee** they are willing to pay, the recipient's **public key**, and a **digital signature** (proof of ownership), as shown in Step 1, Figure 1.14. These data elements are used by validating nodes to verify the validity of the transaction and prioritise it for inclusion in a block.

Transaction fee

Blockchains rely on transaction fees to incentivise miners or validators to process transactions and ensure network stability. These fees vary depending on the blockchain type (e.g. PoW, PoS) and network congestion, but blockchains may implement a minimum fee requirement – often called a base fee – which users must pay:

- **Proof of Work (PoW)**: users pay a base fee and can optionally offer a higher fee to speed up transactions during congestion.
- **Proof of Stake (PoS)**: Ethereum uses a system where users pay a price for the computational effort required by their transaction. The network adjusts the base fee based on congestion.

How fees are calculated will be explained in detail in Chapter 3, but for now, that's all we need to know.

Digital signature

Aside from transaction fees, a user needs to submit a proof of ownership of the assets traded in the transaction. You already know that blockchain transactions are secured by public key cryptography (See *What are the properties of a blockchain?*). Therefore, a user will need to create a digital signature to prove they own the assets being transferred, using the following steps:

- **Hashing the transaction**: the user's wallet first creates a hash of the transaction details (e.g. sender, recipient, amount), as shown in Figure 1.8.
- **Creating the digital signature**: next, the user's **private key** is used to cryptographically sign the hash generated in the first step, thus creating a digital seal.
- **Public key verification**: the recipient will then use the sender's **public key**, which is freely available for anyone to see to verify the validity of the signature (see Figure 1.9 and Box 1.4). This verification confirms

that the transaction originated from the owner of the corresponding private key and hasn't been tampered with during transmission.

The digital signature will be used as part of the transaction validation process.

Figure 1.15 compares public/private key authentication and standard authentication.

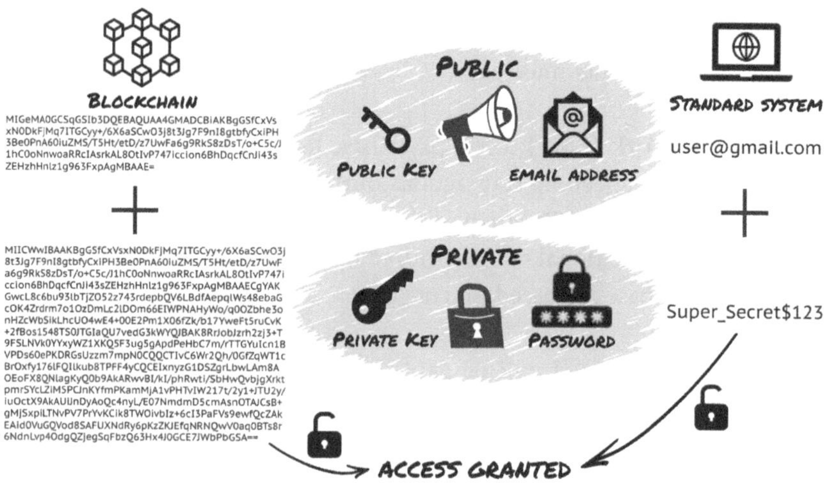

Figure 1.15 Public/private key authentication vs. standard authentication. © 2024 Neira Jones.

Of course, email (or user ID) and password combinations are not known for being particularly secure on their own, which is why, in practice and in traditional systems, we supplement them with additional factors and overlay services (e.g. **biometrics**, **3D Secure**).

Professionals should remember the following:

Digital signatures are fundamental to transaction validation, and characteristics of public and private keys include:

- A public key allows a user to receive blockchain transactions.
- A user needs the private key to "unlock" a transaction and prove that they own the underlying asset (e.g. cryptocurrency) received in the transaction. The private key proves that the holder of the key owns the asset.

- A public key can be shared freely (just like an email address), and anyone can send transactions to it (i.e. the receiving address).
- Public and private keys are generated together, and a single private key can only have one associated public key, and this combination is known as a "key pair".
- The mathematical relationship between the private and public keys is designed to be one-way, making it computationally infeasible to derive the private key from the public key.
- If users lose their private keys, they lose access to their assets (and there are many horror stories![31]). It is therefore important for users to ensure that their private keys are safe.

The user's preferred blockchain interface (e.g. a crypto wallet) will ensure that transactions are in the correct format and that these transactions are then broadcast to the blockchain network for processing.

Validating transactions

The first step of transaction processing is transaction validation, where validating nodes listen to the network for incoming transactions in order to validate them. The equivalent of this stage on centralised networks would be the transaction authorisation process. However, unlike centralised networks where trusted authorities would authorise transactions (e.g. issuer, bank), blockchains rely on a distributed network of trust where validating nodes perform this function.

Validating nodes may all validate incoming transactions, and these pending transactions are stored in a staging area (see *The mempool*), as they wait to be finalised.

BOX 1.7 WHAT BLOCKCHAIN NODES PARTICIPATE IN THE VALIDATION PROCESS?

On a blockchain network, there may be different types of nodes, and, depending on the implementation, these include full nodes, masternodes, light nodes, miners, and validators (see *Who can do what?*).

Only specific types of nodes can participate in transaction validation and these validating nodes may be referred to as validators (PoS) or miners (PoW), whilst other nodes (i.e. full nodes) ensure the security and integrity of the ledger and validate blocks (i.e. a batch of transactions, see Figure 1.6) before they can be included in the ledger.

Both miners and validators may perform block validation if they are also full nodes, but the specifics depend on the blockchain implementation (see Table 1.8).

In steps 2 and 3 in Figure 1.14, it becomes apparent that PoW blockchains consume more resources (extensive computational work required for mining) than PoS blockchains (selection done through staking). When Ethereum moved its consensus protocol from PoW to PoS in September 2022 (aka "The Merge"), a report published by the Cambridge Centre for Alternative Finance in December 2023 claimed a reduction in energy consumption by approximately 99.99%.[32]

In any instance, validating nodes must have enough resources (e.g. computing power, stake) to participate in this distributed trust framework and this is why blockchains reward validating nodes for their efforts through incentives (see *Incentives and penalties*).

The mempool

Transactions submitted by users will be stored in a staging area called the **mempool**. Think of it as a temporary storage facility where the transactions are "pending".

Each full node (see Table 1.8) maintains its own mempool which contains the transactions received by the node but not yet included in a block (i.e. not validated). Full nodes will then communicate with each other to share information about their respective mempools to ensure that all nodes have a similar understanding of pending transactions. Therefore, no central authority manages a single unified ledger; rather, the mempool is a dynamic environment where transactions are added and removed based on network activity and miner/validator behaviour.

Miners/validators will select pending transactions from the full node's mempool to include them in their block according to how they prioritise transaction processing.

Transactions in the mempool (sometimes referred to as the "transaction pool") are called "unspent" because they have not yet been added to the blockchain (i.e. they are pending, aka not settled) (see Figure 1.14 and Table 1.5).

As a parallel with centralised systems, the transaction in a mempool is partly "authorised" and partly "cleared". Note from the author: Sorry! This is the best generalisation I can give you, as it really depends on the blockchain implementation, but one thing is for sure: the transaction in the mempool is "pending", and it could remain in that state for a very long time if validating nodes don't prioritise it for processing.

The steps taken to ensure that transactions are valid will depend on the blockchain protocol, but the core principles are similar across blockchain implementations. These may include transaction fee evaluation, security and integrity of transactions, formatting, fraud prevention (e.g. double-spending), chronology assurance, and compliance.

Transaction fee evaluation

Validating nodes will verify that the transaction includes a fee that meets the minimum network requirement (the base fee), which helps ensure network stability. Transaction fees are an incentive for validating nodes, as processing transactions requires them to spend a certain amount of computing power (i.e. mining) or other resources (e.g. stake). For faster processing by validating nodes, users submitting transactions may elect to pay more than the minimum fee requirement set by the blockchain, whilst transactions with lower fees may have to wait longer. Additionally, a transaction can fail if it demands more resources than specified. However, when prioritising transactions, validating nodes may also be influenced by network conditions, block size, and specific protocol rules, and they can adopt strategies to maximise revenue (please see Chapter 4, *Validating nodes and transaction fees*) for more detail).

Now that validating nodes have evaluated the transaction fee, it's time to get on with the other validation steps.

Digital signature verification

The validating node will verify that the private key is associated with the legitimate sending address (public key) and that the digital signature hasn't been tampered with. This ensures that the transaction was indeed initiated by the private key's owner (see Figures 1.9 and 1.15). This is the authentication of the sender.

Transaction format validation

This will involve verifying that the transactions follow the prescribed format, syntax, and structure for the blockchain used and that all the fields are present, as prescribed by the blockchain protocol. This is a bit like using standard messaging like **ISO 8583**, **ISO 20022**, or **SWIFT**, to draw a parallel with centralised payment systems.

Validating nodes may use the transaction size as one way to prioritise which transactions they will process as they take up less space in the blocks they are building, enabling them to fit more transactions in a block.

Double-spending prevention

BOX 1.8 WHAT IS DOUBLE-SPENDING?

Double-spending refers to the attempted spending of the same funds twice, which creates a discrepancy between the actual amount of funds available and how it is recorded on a ledger.

Double-spending is extremely improbable in centralised payment systems because they have mature processes, established regulations, robust security, and trusted intermediaries overseeing all transactions, from payment instruction to settlement.

Double-spending is an issue for blockchain infrastructures as these don't rely on trusted intermediaries and operate a distributed trust model where participating nodes ensure the system's integrity. To prevent double-spending, blockchains use various mechanisms including the consensus protocol, the validation of transactions by nodes before they are added to the blockchain ledger, and transaction timestamping.

When validating nodes try to prevent double-spending, they aim to ensure that funds are available for the transaction. One of the fraud prevention mechanisms is to ensure that the inputs (unspent transaction amounts) used in a transaction have not been spent in any previous transaction.

The **Unspent Transaction Output (UTXO)** model, commonly used in PoW blockchains (e.g. Bitcoin and Bitcoin-based blockchains) and some PoS blockchains (e.g. Cardano, Zilliqa, Tezos), enables the blockchain to keep a consistent and unbroken chain of ownership through the tracking of UTXOs where every transaction can be traced back to its origin through the series of unspent outputs. The UTXO model is generally preferred by blockchain projects that focus on privacy.

Other blockchains (e.g. Ethereum, Solana, Avalanche, Polygon) may use account-based models where the account balance is checked rather than individual unspent amounts. Blockchain projects more focused on scalability and performance may prefer this model.

Chronology

A blockchain is an immutable sequential ledger of transactions (see *What are the properties of a blockchain?*), so timing is important. Blockchains may use different mechanisms to achieve chronologic integrity, and as you may have guessed, this involves mathematical and cryptographic techniques.

For example, transactions may have a **nonce** field (depending on the blockchain implementation), an identifier unique to each transaction sent from a specific address, used to verify sequential order to prevent replay attacks.

Another time consistency verification mechanism is timestamp verification, where validating nodes ensure that the timestamp is within the allowed range to ensure that the chronological order of transactions on the blockchain ledger remains consistent.

BOX 1.9 WHAT IS A NONCE AND HOW IS IT USED?

In mathematical terms, a **nonce** – contraction for "number used once" – is a number, often a positive integer, used only once for a specific purpose. It is commonly used in computer science and cryptography, particularly in hashing and cryptographic protocols.

In some blockchain implementations, a nonce may be included in individual transactions by the user's crypto wallet (or other facility used to interact with the blockchain). The user's wallet keeps track of the nonce associated with their address (public key) and ensures each transaction has a unique and sequentially increasing nonce. By having users include a nonce, blockchain networks ensure that transactions are processed in the correct order and prevent replay attacks.

A nonce may also be used for a different purpose in PoW blockchains where it is a field in the block header (see *Block formation*). Here, validating nodes (miners) must find a value for the nonce that, when combined with the other block header data, produces a hash (see Figure 1.8) that meets certain criteria (specified by the blockchain consensus protocol). Miners adjust the nonce repeatedly (this is resource-intensive) until a valid hash is found (i.e. below the difficulty target, see Table 1.5), signifying that they have successfully mined a block.

A **replay attack** is a network attack where an attacker intercepts and maliciously retransmits data that was validly communicated between two parties.

In cryptocurrency or financial transactions, a replay attack involves the unauthorised and fraudulent re-broadcasting of a valid transaction for illicit gain.

In traditional centralised financial systems, replay attacks are unlikely to succeed as these systems usually have robust security and fraud prevention measures, such as authentication, transaction verification, security standards, stringent regulations, and of course, centralised control.

In decentralised systems, such as blockchain networks, replay attacks can be particularly problematic because of the distributed nature of the trust framework. This is why these systems implement measures such as timestamps, usage of nonces, digital signatures, message authentication, etc.

Compliance

Transactions must adhere to the consensus rules defined by the blockchain protocol (see Chapter 3, *Blockchain operations and governance*). This includes rules related to block size, block interval, and other protocol-specific parameters. Each blockchain protocol must be examined separately to understand this in more detail.

Regardless of the mechanisms to get to a valid block of transactions, creating a block is commonly known as "block formation", and this must happen before the block can be added to the ledger.

Block formation

Block formation will broadly be a similar process on all blockchain implementations and describes how a block will be formatted. Specific details are included in the block template as dictated by the blockchain protocol. It involves the following steps:

- **Collection of valid transactions** to include in the candidate block as users broadcast transactions.
- **Creation of an additional transaction**, which will be the first transaction in the block, and specifies the rewards that the block creator will get. It may include newly minted coins/tokens and transaction fees. This transaction is referred to as the **coinbase transaction** for PoW, and in PoS, it may be called a staking reward transaction, validator reward transaction, or block reward transaction, although the term coinbase transaction may also be used.
- **Creation of a block header** which is a data construct used to ensure the integrity of a block. As such, the block header will typically include a version number (referring to the validation rules used), the hash of the previous block, a **Merkle root** (see Box 1.10) for all transactions including the coinbase transaction, a timestamp, the digital signature of the block creator, and additional fields specific to the protocol.
- **Creation of the block hash**: this represents the hash of the entire block and serves as a unique identifier for the block (which will be included as a reference in the next block).

Table 1.5 shows the data constituents of the block header for both PoW and PoS implementations.

Please note that in Table 1.5, the various data elements listed neither represent an exhaustive list of all possible data elements in a block header

Table 1.5 Comparing PoW and PoS block headers. © 2024 Neira Jones

Steps	**Proof of Work**	**Proof of Stake**
Version number	The version of the block template or protocol being used	
Hash of previous block	A reference to the hash of the previous block in the blockchain, creating the chain of blocks	
Merkle root	The **Merkle root** of all transactions included in the block (including the coinbase transaction or equivalent)	
Timestamp	The time at which the block was created	
Digital signature	Digital signature of the miner who mined the winning block	Digital signature of the validator who was selected to create the block
Protocol-specific data	**Difficulty target**: this represents the mining difficulty level set by the blockchain protocol that miners have to achieve when mining the block (i.e. find a hash that is below the difficulty target) **Bits**: a compact representation of the difficulty target. Used by the blockchain protocol to adapt to changes in the network's hashing power, ensuring that the block interval remains within the desired range **Nonce**: a random unique number that miners have to adjust when trying to find a valid hash (i.e. below the difficulty target) **Block size limit**: the maximum allowable block size, which is particularly relevant in PoW blockchains with dynamic block size limits **Chain ID**: some PoW blockchains may include a version number for the blockchain itself	**Validator set**: contains the validators' public keys to authenticate their inclusion in the set as this proves their authorisation to participate in the consensus process **Nonce**: this is different from PoW. Here the nonce may be included in the block header to ensure that a specific block proposal is unique, and validators check it to prevent replay attacks **Digital signatures** of validators in the validator set who confirm the block's validity **Staking information**: such as the amount of cryptocurrency staked by the validator set, and the duration of the staking commitment **Validator status**: to indicate whether validators in the validator set are actively participating or on standby **Validator voting power**: in some PoS implementations, validators may have varying degrees of influence depending on their staked cryptocurrency. This weight factor may be included in the block header **Validator rotation**: in some PoS implementations, data relating to the rotation schedule or criteria for selecting validators

nor will these elements always be present in all blockchain implementations. For more specific details, looking at each blockchain's technical documentation is advisable.

The Merkle root is an important cryptographic concept and security mechanism used to validate transactions in a block, and for this, the concept of a Merkle tree must be understood.

BOX 1.10 WHAT IS A MERKLE TREE?

A **Merkle tree** is a mathematical construct used in blockchain infrastructures commonly used to ensure block integrity in various blockchain implementations.

This data structure summarises the transactions within a block by hashing each transaction individually, and then the individual hashes are hashed again in pairs, repeating the process until a single hash is obtained representing all the transactions. This final hash is the **Merkle root** and is included in the block header.

When other validating nodes receive the proposed block, they verify its integrity by recalculating the Merkle root using the received transactions, and then checking whether it matches the Merkle root included in the block header. This is an efficient way of validating block integrity without re-validating each transaction within the block.

From transaction broadcasting to block formation and broadcasting

Now that a validating node has created a valid block, it must be proposed to the network in order to eventually reach consensus that the block is valid. Table 1.6 compares transaction validation and block formation stages for PoW and PoS blockchains.

After block formation, we can draw a parallel with centralised systems and say that all transactions in the block have been "authorised and cleared".

Table 1.6 Comparing PoW and PoS transaction validation to block broadcasting. © 2024 Neira Jones

Steps	**Proof of work**	**Proof of stake**
Transaction broadcasting	Users initiate transactions through their interface (e.g. crypto wallet, dApp), including details such as transaction amount, fee they are willing to pay, recipient's public key, nonce (see Box 1.9), digital signature, etc. The specific data elements depend on the blockchain implementation	
Validating node selection	**No selection** Any validating node may choose to validate incoming transaction	**Staking** Validating nodes lock up an amount of the native blockchain coin/token as collateral (the stake)
Pending transactions	Validating nodes validate incoming transactions and include them in their mempool	Validating nodes validate incoming transactions and include them in their mempool. In some PoS implementations, transaction validation and block formation are simultaneous, in some others, transaction validation happens before block formation
Block formation	Validating nodes select a set of transactions from their mempool to include in a new block For each block, a block header will be created, including a reference to the previous block's hash, a timestamp, a Merkle root (see Box 1.10) of the selected transactions, and nonce **Mining** Miners compete to find a nonce that, when combined with the block header, results in a hash that meets a certain criteria	A validating node is automatically selected according to the protocol using several factors (e.g. amount staked, length of time the stake has been held, previous participation, network reputation, commitment, etc.) The selected validator selects transactions from the mempool and then creates a new block (or proposes their already formed block), including a timestamp, the hash of the previous block, the Merkle root, and their signature
Block broadcasting	The first miner to find the valid hash has the right to broadcast their block to the network	The selected validator has the right to broadcast their block to the network

Reaching consensus

Comparing Proof of Work and Proof of Stake

Whilst the consensus rules will differ at the detailed level depending on the blockchain consensus protocol (e.g. PoW, PoS), the various steps to reach consensus are broadly common to all protocols as illustrated in Figure 1.14.

Validating nodes participate in an economic game determined by the consensus protocol (Steps 2 and 3 of Figure 1.14), and the winning node gets to broadcast the valid block to the rest of the network (Step 4, Figure 1.14) for its proposed inclusion in the blockchain ledger.

This step involves yet more validation steps: validating nodes will validate both the proposed block and the transactions within (Step 5, Figure 1.14). If consensus is reached regarding the block's validity, the block gets added to the chain (the ledger), as shown in Step 6, Figure 1.14.

At that point, the transaction is recorded on the ledger, and users are notified of their successful transactions. This is the rough equivalent of the settlement process on centralised networks and what ultimately gives blockchains their immutability.

Table 1.7 summarises this for PoW and PoS protocols.

Validating nodes may get rewards once the block is added to the blockchain ledger.

Of course, each blockchain will have its own consensus protocol and rules, and, to understand this in more detail, these must be examined separately.[33,34]

Rewards and incentives

You're probably wondering how validating nodes get rewarded or incentivised. Whilst this will be covered in detail in Chapter 3, I must now introduce the concept of a token or coin, which are the lifeblood of Layer 1 blockchains.

Whilst most permissionless Layer 1 blockchains use coins to reward and incentivise participants, there are alternatives, including reputation systems where participants are rewarded with reputation scores based on their contribution to the network, eliminating the need for a coin altogether (e.g. Stellar blockchain).

Table 1.7 Comparing PoW and PoS: reaching consensus. © 2024 Neira Jones

Steps	**Proof of Work**	**Proof of Stake**
Block validation	Other validating nodes will verify the validity of the proposed block by independently hashing the block header with the provided nonce and verifying the Merkle root to confirm the validity of transactions within the block	Other validating nodes verify the validity of the block by checking the proposer's signature, the Merkle root, and ensuring that they have the required stake to participate in block creation
Consensus	If the proposed block is deemed valid, nodes incorporate it in their local copy of the blockchain and spent transactions are removed from the mempool Some blockchains require that a transaction be validated by at least 51% of validating nodes, but others may set a higher threshold for approval	If the proposed block is deemed valid, other nodes accept it and consensus is often reached using mechanisms that involve a certain percentage of the total stake, rather than node count In some PoS blockchains, this stage may also involve voting amongst a subset of validators to finalise the block (delegated Proof of Stake)
Block finalisation	The block is added to the blockchain (settlement)	

Permissioned blockchains may feature coins, but these are not essential to their operations as their focus is on streamlining transactions and data sharing within a closed network of trusted participants (e.g. XRP for Ripple).

BOX 1.11 WHAT IS A COIN OR TOKEN?

In most cases, the terms **coin** and **token** are used interchangeably. For the purist, this is not technically correct as a coin is native to the blockchain on which it lives, is created when the blockchain itself is created (e.g. BTC for Bitcoin, ETH for Ethereum), and can't be transferred to another blockchain without conversion.

A token is not native to the blockchain on which it exists but leverages its infrastructure and may be used for a variety of applications, making the often-used "native token" a misnomer, as only a coin is "native". But that's a moot point (see Chapter 5, *Digital and virtual assets*) and it's usually easy, depending on context and application, to determine whether you're talking about a coin or a token.

A coin is a digital asset that resides and functions on a particular Layer 1 blockchain. It serves various purposes, including:

- **Incentivising participation**: in permissionless blockchains, it is used to reward miners or validators who maintain the security and integrity of the blockchain. The Bitcoin and Ethereum blockchains are prime examples (see Chapter 4, *Incentives and penalties*).
- **Facilitating transactions**: a coin acts as the primary medium of exchange within the blockchain network, enabling users to pay transaction fees (see Chapter 4, Under the hood: *transaction fees*). In some cases, they may also be used as a store of value.
- **Governance**: in some blockchains, coins can be used for voting on network upgrades and proposals, granting coin holders a say in the blockchain's future. This is not, however, the primary purpose of a coin, and governance will be covered extensively in Chapter 4, *Token utility*.

In addition, some blockchains may have a pre-defined maximum supply of coins and some coins may be programmable making additional functionality beyond transactions possible, such as accessing specific services (see Chapter 4, *Tokenomics*).

Finally, tokens can eventually become coins when a project develops its own blockchain and migrates its tokens to the new blockchain as a coin. Successful migrations include Binance Coin (BNB), Tron (TRX), and Zilliqa (ZIL), which all previously existed as tokens on the Ethereum blockchain.

When can a transaction be considered final?

You would be forgiven for thinking that the transaction is considered "final and irreversible" once the block containing it is added to the blockchain at the block finalisation stage, seemingly completing **blockchain settlement**. This is not, strictly speaking, the case. When the block containing the transaction is added to the blockchain, that transaction is considered "recorded", and for it to be considered truly "final and irreversible", multiple blocks need to be added to the blockchain after the block containing that transaction.

This is a security measure, not a technical one, used to mitigate the effects of blockchain reorganisations (see Chapter 3, *Blockchain operations and governance*) and combat fraud (i.e. make it more difficult for malicious actors to reverse transactions). Think of it as a rough equivalent of managing **settlement risk** on traditional financial settlement infrastructures.

The number of blocks that must be added to the blockchain after the block containing the recorded transaction has been added depends on the blockchain and its approach to security, and this number, expressed in minutes, is usually called the **confirmation depth**, and sometimes "confirmation number". For example, low-value time-insensitive transactions may only require two to six blocks to be added before the transaction is considered final, whilst ten or more new blocks may be required for high-value or time-sensitive transactions.

Therefore, the **confirmation time** is calculated from the time a transaction is recorded (i.e. its containing block has been added to the blockchain) to the point when the required number of new blocks have been successfully added (i.e. the confirmation depth) and is dependent on the average block creation time.

Consequently, **block finality** (aka blockchain settlement) is achieved only after confirmation time. This is a dynamic metric, and blockchain explorers usually track it. On some blockchains, confirmation times can be several hours or even days[35]…

Users will be notified of the status of their transaction, and the way this is done will depend on the interface used. For example, a wallet may show a transaction as "pending" or "unconfirmed" when initiated, and this may change to "successful" or "completed" after confirmation time. For public blockchains, users can use blockchain explorers to search for their transaction ID (see *Blockchain information services*).

Validating nodes may receive economic rewards as a result of their contribution to the community (see Chapter 3, *Incentives and penalties*).

Who can do what? (working on it)

Full nodes, miners, and validators

Technically, a blockchain infrastructure consists of a network of connected nodes (i.e. computers). To draw a parallel with centralised payment ecosystems, these are the ecosystem actors (e.g. payment schemes, direct and indirect participants, settlement agents), and similarly to centralised payment ecosystems, blockchains also have different participation models and ecosystem actors.

In centralised payment ecosystems, taking the example of the card rails, a card scheme will provide the network infrastructure (e.g. **Visanet** for Visa), the operating rules (e.g. Visa operating regulations), the participation models (e.g. principal member, affiliate member), and the environment and processes that enable that ecosystem to operate and for participants to derive value. Similarly, blockchains will feature the blockchain infrastructure (e.g. the Ethereum blockchain) and the blockchain protocol (the Ethereum protocol) that will define how the network should operate.

Depending on the blockchain implementation, special types of nodes will participate to perform vital functions to ensure the integrity and security of the network, and terminology will vary. However, in general, there is the concept of a **full node** in both PoW and PoS implementations, and this "uber node" is essential to the operation, integrity, and security of the blockchain as it stores an entire copy of the blockchain ledger. Think of full nodes as the backbone of a blockchain network as decentralisation and security increase proportionally with the number of full nodes it possesses.

In addition, different types of nodes may perform other functions. For example, transaction validation is performed by **miners** in PoW blockchains and **validators** in PoS blockchains.

At a high level, the fundamental responsibilities of validating nodes and full nodes are shown in Table 1.8 (although it is advisable to look at the current documentation or technical specifications for each blockchain):

Table 1.8 Comparing PoW and PoS: types of nodes involved in validation. © 2024 Neira Jones

Activity	**Proof of Work**		**Proof of Stake**
	MINER	**FULL NODE**	**VALIDATOR**
Transaction validation	Yes	Yes (as they validate blocks)	Yes
Block formation	Yes (all miners)	No	Yes (only selected validator)
Data storage	Stores the block template and uses temporary storage during mining Long-term storage of mined blocks for auditing and historical analysis purposes (optional)	Stores an entire copy of the blockchain Maintains a mempool	Only the selected validator stores the block template (temporary storage) May store varying amounts of data depending on blockchain design, and therefore may store an entire copy of the blockchain
Block validation	No (unless they are also full nodes)	Yes	Yes (depending on implementation, it's more common in PoS blockchains for validators to be full nodes when compared to miners in PoW blockchains)

Table 1.8 proves that PoS blockchains are less resource-intensive than PoW blockchains.

There are however more node types than just full nodes, miners, and validators. Similarly to centralised payment systems, taking the card rails as an example, one single entity may perform several functions (e.g. an acquirer provides **acquiring** services, but may also provide merchants with a **payment**

gateway), such as when a full node is also a miner or a validator. The most common types of nodes and their connectivity are shown in Figure 1.16.

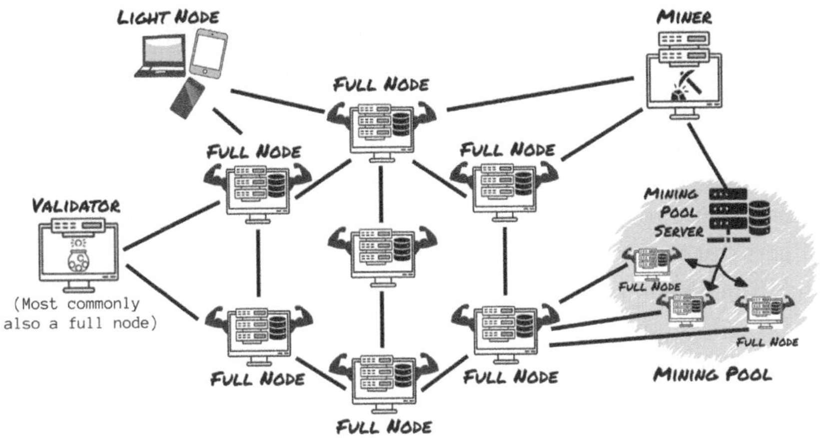

Figure 1.16 Common blockchain node types and connectivity. © 2024 Neira Jones.

As shown in Figure 1.16, full nodes are the backbone of a blockchain, and resource requirements will vary depending on the blockchain consensus protocol.

Note from the author: not all types of nodes are shown here, as this is only to illustrate interactions, also, as you know by now, a validator (PoS) and a miner (PoW) can't be part of the same blockchain infrastructure.

PoW mining resources and services

We've already ascertained that PoW mining is resource-intensive and requires a lot of computing power, which makes mining only accessible to those able to afford it.

A **mining rig** is a specialised computer designed to help PoW miners solve the complex cryptographic puzzles required by the protocol.

Whilst mining rigs have all the generic features of standard computers (e.g. CPU, RAM, motherboard, power supply, cooling system), they are so much more than that. They incorporate specialised chips such as

Application-Specific Integrated Circuits (ASICs) and Graphics Processing Units (GPUs). Beyond the hardware, they incorporate lightweight mining-specific operating systems (e.g. HiveOS, RaveOS) and specialised mining software to interact with specific PoW blockchains and maximise miner earning potential. Suppliers of mining rigs include Bitmain,[36] Canaan,[37] and MicroBT.[38]

Of course, what characterises a mining rig is its computing power and chip manufacturers compete in the supply of ASICs and GPUs, including Samsung Electronics, TSMC, Nvidia, AMD, and Bitmain (it's big business!). Miners can expect to spend between $500 and $2,000 for a basic model, and from $5,000 to $10,000 and beyond for cutting-edge hardware.

There are, however, two ways to lower this barrier to entry and miners have options beyond solo mining:

- **Mining pools**: where individual miners combine their computing resources, known as their **hashing power**, into one pool that competes as one entity to solve the cryptographic puzzle. Typically, a mining pool will have a mining pool server which enables miners to connect to the mining pool's full nodes which are themselves connected to other full nodes in the blockchain.

  The role of the mining pool is to communicate with the pool's full nodes for access to the latest blockchain data and transactions, to distribute transactions to participating miners, and to collect PoW cryptographic puzzle solutions from participating miners and submit them to the blockchain network for validation.

  Some mining pools may implement the Stratum[39] communication protocol (most common) between the pool server and miners to give miners more control over the transactions they receive, whilst GetWork is an older protocol less commonly used, and custom protocols may also be implemented.

  The more hashing power, the more chance the mining pool has to solve the puzzle faster and earn the block reward (see *Rewards and incentives*). Rewards are distributed amongst the pool members according to their hashing power contribution.

  Examples of BTC mining pools are Foundry USA,[40] Antpool,[41] F2Pool,[42] Braiins Pool[43], but there are also multi-currency operators such as Poolin,[44] ViaBTC,[45] and BTC.com.[46]

- **Mining-as-a-Service (MaaS)**: where service providers rent out their hashing power (including hardware and software) to individuals or businesses interested in earning mining rewards.

  The fees charged to users and cryptocurrencies supported will depend on the service provider. For example, they may require an initial deposit representing the hashing power to be rented or offer pay-as-you-go options. The individual or business can start mining normally without incurring an infrastructure outlay. Rewards are then paid out regularly after service fees are deducted.

  Also known as "cloud mining". Examples are Nicehash[47] and Kryptex.[48] Hashflare was a MaaS provider, but its founders were arrested in 2022 on fraud and **money laundering** charges.[49] Another player, Genesis Mining, stopped taking on new customers in 2020,[50] and HashOcean unexpectedly disappeared in 2016, the circumstances remaining obscure, and customers potentially lost significant sums of money[51] (although this is not easy to verify). Caveat emptor.

In addition, those with the resources to acquire expensive computing power have launched new businesses to create **mining farms**, which are dedicated facilities with specialised equipment (mining rigs) for mining cryptocurrencies in PoW networks. Unlike mining pools and MaaS providers, which are targeted at those with no or little access to resources, these primarily attract investors as they require a high initial investment and could potentially give high returns. Farms may also join mining pools to leverage collective power. Examples are Canaan, Bitmain, Riot Blockchain,[52] Hut 8 Mining,[53] Argo Blockchain,[54] Marathon Digital Holdings,[55] Iren (formerly Iris Energy),[56] and CleanSpark,[57] all of which are publicly listed companies, except Bitmain (privately owned, headquartered in China).

Many of the companies listed may serve several purposes. For example, Canaan operates a mining farm and sells mining rigs. The Argo Blockchain operates a mining farm but also provides some MaaS options. BTC.com operates a mining pool (Poolin) and runs a mining farm.

PoS staking resources and services

As shown in Figure 1.14 (steps 2 and 3), PoS blockchain consensus (staking) is far less resource-intensive than in PoW (mining), and therefore doesn't require specialised equipment. Validators use standard servers, virtual private servers, or cloud instances as provided by the likes of Amazon Web Services (AWS), Google Cloud, or Microsoft Azure. In some cases, particularly in smaller PoS networks, validators may use consumer hardware such as laptops or desktop computers.

As explained in *PoW mining resources and services*, miners in PoW blockchains may not always have the necessary resources to mine new blocks, and several avenues are available to them (e.g. mining pools, MaaS). Similarly, validators in PoS blockchains may, of course, have enough coins/tokens to be able to stake (solo staking), but other avenues are available to them:

- **Stake delegation**: this allows coin/token holders to delegate their stake (voting power and staking rights) to other validators or entities of their choice if they don't have the resources or expertise to run a validator node and still want to participate in the consensus protocol and earn staking rewards.

  Delegators retain control of their stake and can withdraw delegation at any time. Coin/token holders running validator nodes may also self-delegate to their own node to enhance their reputation and probability of being chosen.
- **Staking pool**: validators can join or create staking pools (a somewhat similar concept to mining pools in PoW) where the pool operator aggregates the delegated stakes to operate a validator node on behalf of the pool members.

  An alternative model is where staking pools function as intermediaries, allowing users to delegate their stakes to validators chosen by the pool operator as the pool doesn't operate a validator node.

  Regardless, staking pools share rewards proportionally to their member's contributions and typically charge fees deducted from the staking rewards.

  These pools can be small (targeted at individual investors or validators) or large-scale operations (targeted at institutional investors) and depending on size, may offer professional infrastructure management, security, risk management, optimisation services, and even portfolio management across multiple blockchains.

As they delegate their tokens to the pool, participants have limited control over their staked assets.

Examples include Staked.us,[58] Figment,[59] Blockdaemon,[60] and Rocket Pool.[61]

- **Staking-as-a-Service (StaaS)**: those unable to run a validator node may leverage the infrastructure and expertise of these providers by delegating their stake to them to increase their chance of earning staking rewards.

  StaaS providers may offer infrastructure, node management, and validator hosting. They typically charge a fee deducted from the staking rewards which are distributed amongst participants according to their contribution. Participants have more flexibility and control over their stake when compared to staking pools.

  Examples included Huobi Pool and OKEx, but these had shut down at the time of writing. Some exchanges also offered these services, such as the Kraken staking pool, but this shut down in February 2023, and as regulations became more stringent worldwide, other exchanges were forced to shut down staking operations in some jurisdictions.[62]
- **Cross-chain staking**: validators may participate in cross-chain staking protocols that enable them to stake their coins/tokens across multiple blockchains to maximise their stake and reduce their risk exposure to a single blockchain. Examples include Cosmos,[63] Polkadot,[64] Ankr.[65]

In addition, those with the resources may operate **staking farms**, which are large-scale staking operations and validators may delegate their stake to the farm's infrastructure in exchange for professional infrastructure management, security, risk management, optimisation services, and even portfolio management across multiple blockchains. Staking farms will charge a fee deducted from the staking rewards distributed amongst participants according to their contribution.

What are light nodes?

Light nodes, also referred to as "lightweight clients", "light clients", or SPV clients (Simplified Payment Verification, mostly in the context of

Bitcoin), are by definition more efficient than full nodes and can run on a wide range of devices, including smartphones and tablets, as they have comparatively modest CPU, memory, and storage requirements. However, they require a stable and sufficiently fast internet connection to participate in the network.

The exact configuration of a light node will, however, depend on the specific blockchain and usage, but they always prioritise low resource consumption to enable network participation for a wide range of devices.

A **light node** is a generic term for a computer (the node) running a piece of software (the client) specifically designed to interact with a blockchain efficiently and with minimal resource requirements as it only downloads some blockchain data (e.g. block headers, specific transaction information).

They are sometimes referred to as "stateless clients" because, unlike full nodes, they don't record the entire state of a blockchain.

As such, light nodes rely on full nodes for most functionality (see Figure 1.16).

Now that the resource requirements for PoW and PoS blockchains are understood, it becomes apparent that miners can't use light nodes for mining activities because of their intense computational work. However, in theory, PoS validators (most commonly also full nodes) could run a light node instead.

These lightweight clients might have additional functionalities and storage requirements that differ from standard user-focused light nodes. Although I can't find actual examples at the time of writing, some blockchains (e.g. Cosmos,[66,67] Tezos[68]) explored the concept, and it is advisable to look at recent developments to determine whether this type of implementation will catch on.

Typically, light nodes are used by external users who want to interact with a blockchain without storing the entire blockchain. For those wanting to delve further, I recommend the Nervos knowledge base resource entitled "The Ultimate Guide to Blockchain Light Clients".[69]

Light node usage in payments

There are many ways in which light nodes can be leveraged for payments, including:

- **Crypto wallet users**: by leveraging light nodes, users can view their balances and transaction history, and submit transactions. Some crypto wallets may include a built-in light node (typically non-custodial wallets, see Chapter 5, *Transacting in a decentralised world*), but others may use external light node service providers such as Infura,[70] Alchemy,[71] Blockdaemon,[72] Quicknode,[73] and many more.
- **Merchants accepting cryptocurrency payments directly**: merchants directly accepting cryptocurrency payments are, at the time of writing, still uncommon, as this requires technical expertise and resources. However, theoretically, if they want to focus on autonomy and data privacy, such merchants may run a light node to verify (without intermediaries) that transactions are valid, broadcast confirmed transactions to the blockchain network, and monitor the blockchain.
- **Merchants accepting cryptocurrency payments through a crypto payment processor**: this is a more common scenario and may appeal to a broad range of crypto-friendly merchants and those who want to enable access to a wide range of cryptocurrencies. Merchants will typically receive a settlement from the service provider in the cryptocurrency they were paid in, although some fiat conversion may be available, which exposes them to cryptocurrency volatility.

  These service providers, such as Coinbase Commerce[74] and BitPay,[75] may leverage light nodes within their infrastructure (although this is difficult to verify). As an example, Ralph Lauren partnered with BitPay in April 2023.[76] For those wanting to dig further, BitPay has an extensive directory of merchants[77] using their services to accept cryptocurrency payments.
- **Merchants accepting cryptocurrency payments through a mainstream payment processor**: this is a more common scenario and would appeal to merchants that prioritise faster settlement times, especially for cross-border transactions, and are keen to avoid cryptocurrency volatility. In this scenario, the payment processor would offer a broader range of payment processing solutions, including fiat currencies and

cryptocurrency (although the range of cryptocurrencies supported may be smaller than those offered by crypto payment processors).

The payment processor would convert cryptocurrency payments into stablecoins (e.g. **USDC**, see Chapter 5, *Digital and virtual assets*) and then settle the amount in fiat currency (although settlement in cryptocurrency may also be provided). Typically, the payment processor, such as Checkout.com[78] and WorldPay,[79] would partner with a crypto service provider, such as Fireblocks[80] (see Chapter 2, *A special kind of BaaS: payments*), who may leverage light nodes as part of their infrastructure to verify the validity of incoming transactions and track their confirmation status. In this context, think of Fireblocks as a **payment orchestration** facility across multiple blockchains for merchant cryptocurrency payments and settlement. In any instance, this is still an emerging phenomenon and will evolve over time.

At the time of writing, mainstream processors have limited stablecoin support, with USDC being the most commonly used stablecoin for settlement purposes.

- **Merchants accepting payments at the POS (Point of Sale)**: This is still a developing area, but some service providers exist and may leverage light nodes as part of their infrastructure for efficiency purposes (since we're talking about retail environments where transaction speed is important).

  These solutions usually are software-based facilities (e.g. shopping cart plugins, **SDKs**, APIs, POS tools) and may be suitable for merchants both virtual (e.g. the equivalent of a traditional **payment gateway**) and physical (e.g. the equivalent of a **softPOS**) wishing to accept payments in various cryptocurrencies or those focused on privacy. They however require the merchant to have some level of technical expertise as they would need to have a **crypto wallet** (see Chapter 6, *Transacting in a decentralised world*). Service providers include specialised crypto payment processors such as BitPay,[81] CoinPayments,[82] NOWPayments,[83] and ForumPay[84] (see Chapter 2, *Crypto payment processors*).

  In addition, traditional card payment terminal manufacturers may partner with crypto processors to offer merchants the ability to accept cryptocurrency payments, as was the case with Ingenico and Binance in 2023[85] and 2024[86] (where Binance may be leveraging light nodes as part of their infrastructure).

- **Crypto ATMs (Automated Teller Machines)**: crypto ATMs may leverage light nodes when users buy or sell cryptocurrencies to verify transactions on the relevant blockchain and retrieve balances for specific addresses, allowing users to see their available balance before initiating transactions.

  Of course, crypto ATMs may also choose to operate full nodes for specific blockchains (which would be a trade-off between security and efficiency).

  Crypto ATMs are increasingly under regulatory scrutiny, but some geographies are becoming more tolerant.

  Providers include Bitcoin Depot[87] (Canada, United States), Coinflip[88] (Australia, Canada, Puerto Rico, United States), Localcoin[89] (Canada, also allowing Interac e-Transfer®), Kurant[90] (Austria, Germany, Spain), värdex[91] (Switzerland), BitcoinMat[92] (Czech Republic, Greece, Slovakia), and BTM[93] (Mexico). At the time of writing, the manufacturing of crypto ATMs seems to be shared between General Bytes[94] and BitcoinATM.com[95] (incorporating Bitstop and Genesis Coin), although this is difficult to verify as market data is scarce.
- **Interbank settlement and merchant settlement**: Visa, a major card scheme, partnered with Circle[96] to enable acquirers to perform stablecoin settlement for credit and debit card transactions processed through Visanet.[97] This is transparent to the cardholder, but unlike in the standard settlement process (see Figures 1.4 and 1.5), Visa uses its own Circle account to perform interbank settlement in USDC, resulting in faster settlement and potentially lower costs (e.g. avoiding foreign exchange fees). At this point, acquirers have the option to settle with merchants in fiat currency in the usual way or in USDC, as WorldPay have done since 2022[98] and Checkout.com since 2023[99] – both WorldPay and checkout.com achieved this through partnership with Fireblocks.

  What has that got to do with light nodes? I hear you say. Well, Circle, as the issuer of the USDC stablecoin (see Chapter 4, *Stablecoins*), maintains its infrastructure and is likely to use light nodes to efficiently interact with the blockchain for monitoring reserve balances and activity, (as they have a specific focus on transparency and regular audits). However, this doesn't influence the settlement process between Visa, acquirers, and merchants.

For the eagle-eyed amongst you, you will have noticed that the examples I have given are mostly related to cryptocurrency usage. Blockchains have other potential applications, as we will examine throughout this book, but we'll just have to see how this develops.

What else can light nodes do?

As you might expect, light nodes have many more uses than payment-related activities.

Blockchain information services

These companies may leverage light nodes to efficiently gather data from the blockchain to provide information services for analysis and reporting purposes. To all my payment friends, think of these services as the rough equivalent of those offered by an **Account Information Service Provider**, or **AISP** (covered in my first book, "Understanding Payments – A whistle-stop tour into what you thought you knew"). They may serve different functions, as shown in Table 1.9.

Whilst blockchain explorers are simpler tools targeted at a broader audience, blockchain monitoring and analytics services mostly target business users, regulators, and law enforcement. They provide identification and traceability of transactions by classifying and investigating specific addresses, monitoring transactions, and analysing risk. They create risk models using data including the source and destination of funds, transaction amounts, and money flow history.

For all of you payment geeks and data scientists out there, examples of companies prominent in this space are Chainalysis, Ciphertrace (acquired by Mastercard in 2021[121]), and Coinfirm, and they are particularly helpful in fighting money laundering (in this context, blockchain analysis companies may be referred to as "blockchain forensics").[122] It is interesting to watch the traditional payment players as they get more involved in the blockchain space.

Other uses for light nodes

As this is still an evolving market, who knows what new services will emerge that will capitalise on the resource efficiency of light nodes, especially in our increasingly data-driven world? It is important to note that

Table 1.9 Main blockchain information services. © 2024 Neira Jones

	Blockchain Monitoring and Analytics Service Providers	**Blockchain Explorers**
Function	Sophisticated information services	The equivalent of a search engine
Scope	Usually support multiple blockchains, but some blockchain-specific services exist	Usually blockchain-specific but some services support multiple blockchains
Activity	Functionality will vary across services and may include: • Blockchain activity real-time monitoring • Alert systems triggered by user-specified criteria • Analytics, including transaction patterns, suspicious activity, risks related to addresses or transactions, trends, etc.	Functionality will vary across services and may include: • View block details • Search for specific transaction or wallet addresses • See blockchain current state (e.g. block information, transaction details, cryptocurrency supply)
Target audience	• Businesses involved in cryptocurrency trading, including crypto exchanges, wallets, payment firms, etc. • Law enforcement and regulators • Investors and traders	• Developers building applications on a blockchain • Users interested in specific transactions or blockchain activities • Anyone curious about a specific blockchain
Examples	• Chainalysis[100] • Ciphertrace[101] • Coinfirm[102] • Glassnode[103] • IntoTheBlock[104] • Nansen[105] • Dune[106] • coinglass[107] • coinmetrics[108] • The Block[109] • Delphi Digital[110] • Crystal Blockchain (Bitcoin-specific)	• Bitcoin: Blockchain.com,[111] mempool.space[112] • Ethereum: Etherscan,[113] Blockchair,[114] Blockchain.com • Tron: Tronscan[115] • Binance Smart Chain: BscScan[116] • Ripple: XRPscan[117] • Solana: Solscan[118] • Cardano: Cardano Explorer,[119] Cardanoscan[120]
Cost	Typically paid subscription model but may offer free service with basic functionality	Usually free or freemium model

light node implementations may vary depending on the application and the blockchain used, but at the time of writing, the following use cases exist:

- **dApp users**: those using decentralised applications (see Chapter 2, *dApps*) may leverage light nodes to interact with dApps without having to download the entire blockchain, essentially enabling those users with limited resources or bandwidth to interact efficiently with dApps on resource-constrained devices such as smartphones.

  This however means that there is reliance on trusted full nodes (see Figure 1.16) to provide valid data which may become compromised and provide unreliable information or expose the user to security risks.

  In addition, since light nodes can't independently verify all aspects of the blockchain state, users may be restricted in terms of functionality if the dApp requires full validation. Examples of dApps using light nodes include:

  - **non-custodial crypto wallets** such as Metamask[123] and Rainbow Wallet[124] (see Chapter 6, *Transacting in a decentralised world*).
  - **decentralised marketplaces**: an example of this is Opensea, a popular marketplace for trading NFTs (Non-Fungible Tokens, see Chapter 5, *Digital and virtual assets*). Opensea uses the Ethereum blockchain and external light node service provider Alchemy, allowing users to browse NFT listings and verify them on the blockchain without downloading the entire Ethereum history.
  - **prediction markets**: these services allow users to bet on the outcome of real-life events. An example is Prosper[125] (on Binance Smart Chain), which uses a light node infrastructure to allow users to view current predictions and historical outcomes without a full blockchain download.
  - **decentralised games**: in this context, light nodes can verify ownership of in-game assets and track game progress without requiring a full blockchain download. An example is Gods Unchained[126] (see Chapter 2, *GameFi: revolutionising gaming with DeFi*).
  - **decentralised file storage**: light nodes can be used to verify file availability and track data updates without a full blockchain download. An example is Arweave.[127]
- **Developers and researchers**: when building tools or researching, these users may leverage light nodes to interact with the blockchain

for testing or data collection. Potential research and development areas include:

- **scaling blockchain applications**: as blockchains grow, scalability becomes a challenge, and blockchain developers may see light nodes as a way to enable more participants in a network. For example, the Ethereum blockchain explored the use of light clients in November 2023.[128] See also *Are blockchains scalable?*
- **enhancing the security of IoT devices**: securing IoT devices is a complex matter, and researchers are exploring how light nodes can leverage blockchain security in that space.[129]
- **data sharing**: developers are exploring how light nodes can facilitate secure and decentralised data sharing. An example is the Filecoin[130] project, although they have different terminology for light nodes (look for "verification network", "proven retrieval", and where they say: "without requiring them to store the entire blockchain.").
- **decentralised identity**: researchers are exploring the use of light nodes in blockchain-based decentralised identity systems, such as in the Sovrin project.[131]

- **IoT devices**: low-powered by definition, these devices may leverage light nodes to interact with a blockchain efficiently. This is still a nascent field, and applications are scarce, but in theory, the following use cases can be considered:
  - **supply chain management**: imagine a network of IoT sensors attached to goods travelling through the supply chain. As these sensors can collect information (e.g. location, temperature, tampering), a blockchain could record this data transparently and permanently. By using light nodes, these sensors could interact with the blockchain without downloading the full ledger. An example is the VeChainThor project.[132]
  - **home automation**: smart homes are now part of our lives, and most are familiar with connected devices such as thermostats, door locks, and plugs. Traditionally a central hub might manage these devices, but a blockchain-based approach where smart home devices could act as light nodes could reduce the reliance on central servers. This idea is still under development.[133]

Other types of nodes

The blockchain space evolves rapidly, and as you may imagine, different constructs emerge, and other types of nodes get created to serve specific purposes on specific blockchain types. Of course, terminology will vary, but for completeness (as far as I can tell), I include some other node types you may encounter:

- **Authority nodes**: in permissioned blockchains (see Figure 1.12), which inherently rely on a pre-selected group of participants and a BFT (or variant thereof, such as PoA) consensus protocol (see Table 1.4), this is a type of trusted node responsible for granting access, maintaining network integrity, and in some cases validating transactions. These may be implemented as full nodes or limited functionality nodes dedicated to permission management.
- **Ordering service node**: in permissioned blockchains, this node ensures the transaction sequence and finality. Unlike public blockchains where miners compete to validate transactions and create blocks, permissioned blockchains rely on pre-selected, trusted nodes for ordering. The ordering service node receives transactions from various participants in the network, determines the order in which transactions are placed within a block (according to the chosen consensus mechanism, see Table 1.8), creates the block and distributes it to all participants. This ensures all participating nodes agree on the transaction sequence within a block. This is roughly equivalent to performing a centralised clearing function.
- **Consensus node**: this term may be used in permissioned blockchains and refers to validator nodes (a term which can also be used), as, unlike permissionless blockchains where access is open, permissioned blockchains restrict validation to a set of pre-defined trusted entities and the selection process for consensus nodes may vary depending on the chosen permissioned blockchain.
- **Masternode**: masternodes are full nodes with enhanced functionality most commonly found in PoS blockchains or those using hybrid protocols (see Table 1.4), and they usually have to stake a large amount of the blockchain's cryptocurrency to demonstrate commitment. Additional features may include instant transactions, private transactions, and

participation in governance voting. Examples of blockchains using masternodes include Dash,[134] Syscoin,[135] and Horizen (ZEN).[136]

- **Pruned full nodes**: a pruned full node is a way of implementing a full node with storage optimisation in mind and is not specific to any blockchain. Pruned full nodes are allowed to discard block bodies (i.e. the transactions) for old blocks (e.g. after a specific period of time, or when a storage limit is reached), whilst retaining the block headers.
- **Archival full nodes**: unlike pruned full nodes, these are the big boys as they store the entire blockchain and entire blocks (header and body). They perform all the tasks of a regular full node (see Table 1.8) and are the workhorses of a blockchain network as they provide a complete record of the blockchain ledger, but this comes at the cost of significant storage requirements. All blockchains require a certain number of archival nodes.
- **Super nodes**: very similar to masternodes, the only difference being that they don't usually facilitate private transactions. They are usually associated with newer PoS blockchains, such as Polkadot[137] and Cosmos.[138]
- **Lightning nodes**: this is a different type of node that doesn't operate on a mainchain (see Box 1.6). They are not full nodes or validators, but they are similar to light nodes since they don't hold an entire copy of the blockchain. However, their primary function is to facilitate fast, low-cost payments on a blockchain. For those familiar with traditional centralised payments, think of them as an overlay service that works with Layer 2 scaling solutions (see *Layer 2 scaling solutions*). Lightning nodes are only associated with the Lightning Network,[139] originally designed to address Bitcoin scalability issues, but also support other blockchains such as Litecoin.
- **Governance nodes**: this type of node is not present in all blockchains and is more common in PoS, permissioned or hybrid blockchains. They are designed to participate directly in on-chain governance processes, such as voting on proposals for protocol upgrades, fee structures, treasury fund allocation, or adjustments to blockchain parameters that may influence security or performance. These nodes may earn rewards for their participation in such activities.

You may come across the term **economic node**, which isn't very helpful as it is far too generic. It describes nodes that play a role in the blockchain's economic activities, such as participating in governance, voting, or deciding on protocol upgrades. They may not necessarily be involved in the creation or validation of new blocks, but they might.

Professionals should remember the following:

- A blockchain consensus protocol governs how transactions are settled on a blockchain (i.e. a block of transactions is added to the ledger). There are several types of consensus protocols, and even within one type of consensus (e.g. PoS), variations will exist depending on the blockchain.
- In PoW blockchains, all miners may validate transactions and participate in block formation (mining), which requires substantial computing resources.
- In PoS blockchains, all validators may participate in transaction validation but only the selected validator will perform block formation (through staking their funds), which is far less resource-intensive than in PoW blockchains.
- The data storage requirements and computing resources are much higher for miners (PoW) than for validators (PoS) as instead of mining (computational work), the latter stake coins/tokens to be selected to propose the next block.
- Only full nodes store an entire copy of the blockchain, maintain a mempool, and play an essential role in the operation and security of the blockchain.
- Validating nodes may be rewarded for their efforts. How rewards are given depends on the blockchain consensus protocol.

Are blockchains private and anonymous? (ain't nobody's business)

On privacy and anonymity

First of all, we have to be clear on terminology. Whether a blockchain preserves the **anonymity** of its participants depends on the blockchain, the participants, the process being performed, and the services being used.

We've already ascertained that blockchain transactions are secured by public key cryptography (see *Digital signature*), and therefore, users are identified by their cryptographic keys. If there isn't a way of linking the user's cryptographic keys with real-world identities, we can say that transactions performed by that user will remain private.

Of course, cryptographic keys can be linked to real-world identities, as is the case, for example, with (custodial) crypto exchanges (e.g. Binance, Coinbase) who will perform some due diligence on their customers as required by the laws of the jurisdiction in which they operate (see Chapter 6, *Transacting in a decentralised world*). This means that users' real-world identities will be known, regardless of which crypto asset they trade.

Table 1.1 highlights the difference in degrees of anonymity that may be offered depending on the infrastructure type, and Table 1.10 expands further by adding the **privacy** dimension.

Whilst anonymity can generally be achieved in public blockchains, these sacrifice privacy for transparency (the ledger is public). A more accurate term would be "pseudonymous" rather than anonymous. **Privacy and anonymity are not the same,**[140] although both are important, especially in payments.

Conversely, when looking at permissioned blockchains, we see that privacy is prioritised over anonymity, and this is particularly important in blockchains used in financial services where transaction privacy is crucial.

Having said that, some blockchains, such as Monero and Zcash, focus on privacy, and we'll examine these in a bit more detail next. It must be noted, however, that aside from blockchain infrastructures' privacy features, there are other ways to preserve anonymity and ensure privacy, and this is covered in more detail in Chapter 5, *Digital and virtual assets*, Chapter 6, *Transacting in a decentralised world*, and later in this chapter in *Are blockchains scalable – Layer 2 scaling solutions*.

Privacy-focused blockchains

Whilst public blockchains like Bitcoin offer transparency – as transactions are visible on the public ledger, thus revealing the sender, receiver, and transaction amount – they lack built-in features to preserve privacy, which, for some, may raise concerns about financial surveillance, or potential misuse of personal data.

Table 1.10 Anonymity and privacy in databases and blockchain models. © 2024 Neira Jones

Properties	Standard Database	Public Blockchain	Private Blockchain	Consortium Blockchain	Hybrid Blockchain
Anonymity	Not anonymous as systems rely on centralised authorisation and authentication	Users may remain anonymous if no correlation can be established with real-world identities	Low anonymity as access is restricted to authorised participants who are known to each other		Anonymity levels depend on the design
Privacy	As private as the owners make it	Low, as transparency is prioritised	Partial: participants are known to each other, but transaction details are only shared between them		Privacy levels depend on the design

This is why privacy-focused blockchains, such as Monero and Zcash, came about, as they aimed to offer unique characteristics to enhance user anonymity through the use of shielded transactions. Unlike the transaction flow covered in *How are transactions validated and secured?* shielded transactions obscure the sender, receiver, and transaction amount through a variety of core cryptographic techniques, allowing validators to verify transaction validity without revealing specific details. If you're not interested in the technicalities of these cryptographic techniques (e.g. zk-proof, ring signatures, confidential transactions, homomorphic encryption), just skip to *Are blockchains scalable?*

Zero-knowledge proof (ZKP, zk-proof)

A cryptographic tool allows a user to prove they possess specific information (e.g. sufficient funds for a transaction) without revealing the information itself to the validator, thus maintaining network integrity whilst protecting user privacy.

A commonly used type of ZKP is zk-SNARK (Succinct Non-interactive Argument of Knowledge), as implemented by Zcash.

Bulletproofs,[141] a relatively new variant of ZKP, is emerging as a more efficient mechanism allowing for faster verification speed and enhanced scalability, and several privacy-focused blockchains are exploring the concept, but no actual implementation existed at the time of writing.

Please note that ZKPs are not confined to privacy-focused blockchains, as this mechanism is often implemented in Layer 2 scaling solutions (see *Rollups*), as well as in some Central Bank Digital Currency (CBDC) implementations (see Chapter 7, *Central Bank Digital Currencies*).

Ring signatures

Another cryptographic technique (used alongside others) that allows a user's signature to be combined with the signatures of other users, creating a ring of possible senders (the anonymity set), making it computationally impossible to determine the actual sender of the transaction.

The number of ring signatures could be used as a metric representing the level of anonymity, as a larger set makes it more difficult to pinpoint the true source of a transaction. For example, Monero uses a minimum of 11 ring signatures, offering a robust level of anonymity.

Confidential transactions (CT)

A process by which the sender uses a cryptographic technique (commitment scheme) to create a unique, blinded value (commitment) that represents the transaction amount. This commitment hides the actual amount whilst still allowing verification of the transaction's validity on the blockchain network. Only the sender, possessing a special key, can reveal the actual amount.

In addition to hiding the amount, the sender also proves they have sufficient funds to cover the transaction. This is achieved through a mathematical concept called a "spending proof" which uses ZKPs. Validators can then verify the spending proof and confirm that the hidden amount doesn't exceed the sender's balance without knowing the actual amount.

In some implementations, CT can be more efficient than other privacy techniques such as ring signatures and potentially contributing to improved blockchain scalability. Examples of blockchains using CT at the time of writing are Elements,[142] Grin,[143] and Beam.[144]

Homomorphic encryption

A cryptographic technique that allows computations to be performed directly on encrypted data without decrypting it first, allowing parties to compute functions on private data without revealing the actual data, or to search for data without entirely decrypting it.

Depending on the implementation,[145] this can be resource-intensive and technically challenging but may provide enhanced transaction privacy and privacy-preserving **smart contracts** (see Chapter 2, *What is a smart contract?*). This is not yet mainstream technology, but several blockchains are exploring it.

Are blockchains scalable? (let it grow)

Decentralisation, as explained in *Blockchain characteristics*, is one of the fundamental characteristics of blockchains and refers to the meaningful distribution of computing power and control to a network of participants where no single entity is in control. This is obviously one of the major differences between (permissionless) blockchains and centralised payment ecosystems.

Security is achieved through the blockchain protocol's defences against malicious attacks, including validation, consensus, and other governance measures.

Scalability, the ability to process high transaction volumes and sustain growth as more users join the network, is essential for blockchain infrastructures if they aim to compete with centralised payment systems with high transaction throughputs.

Therefore, blockchains face the challenge of achieving the delicate balance between decentralisation, security, and scalability.

The CAP theorem

Without boring you with the technicalities, the CAP theorem (**c**onsistency, **a**vailability, and **p**artition tolerance) was first introduced by scientist Eric Brewer in 2000[146] and a formal mathematical proof was produced by Seth Gilbert and Nancy Lynch in 2002.[147] The CAP theorem describes the challenge faced by distributed systems[148] stating that they can deliver only two of the following three desired characteristics:

- **Consistency**: everyone sees the same data all the time, no matter where they connect.
- **Availability**: users will get a valid response from the network because all working nodes return a valid response for any request without exception or delay.
- **Partition tolerance**: the network will continue working even if the connection between two or more nodes is lost or delayed.

As an example, if a distributed system aims for consistency (everyone sees the same data all the time) and partition tolerance (resilience to network failures), availability (users can access the data when they need it) will have to be sacrificed (because ensuring distribution of both data and processing comes at the cost of performance).

Figure 1.17 illustrates this.

Distributed systems like blockchains, are faced with this challenge, and the CAP theorem was the origin of the blockchain trilemma which is described in Figure 1.18.

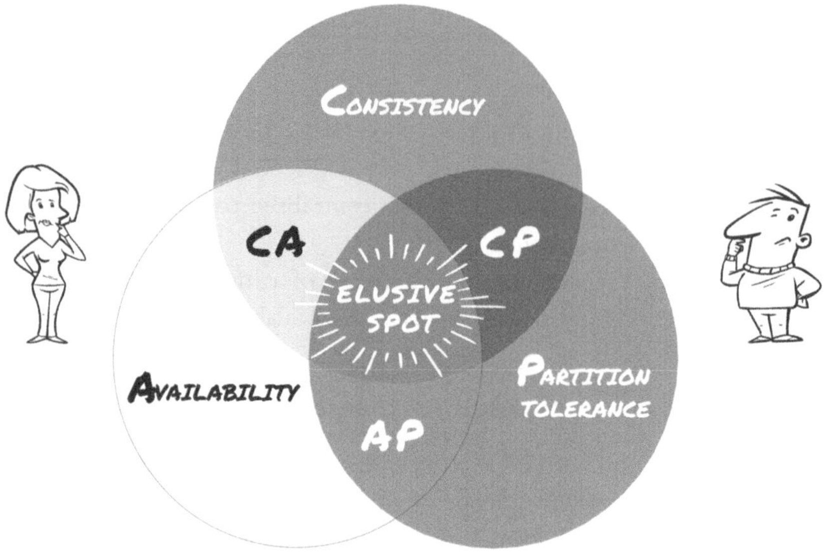

Figure 1.17 The CAP theorem. © 2024 Neira Jones.

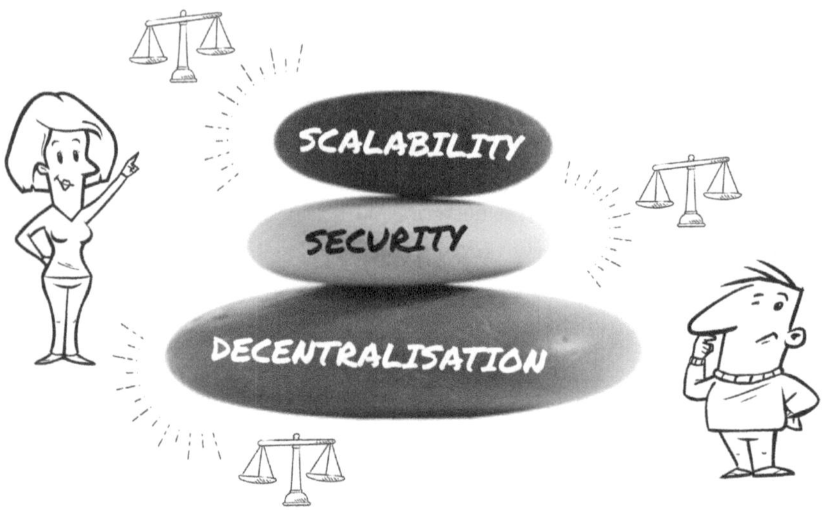

Figure 1.18 The blockchain trilemma. © 2024 Neira Jones.

The blockchain trilemma

Early blockchains, such as Bitcoin and the first version of Ethereum (pre-Merge), met the first two criteria (decentralisation and security), sacrificing the third one (scalability). As adoption grew and transaction volumes increased, these blockchains became limited by their own architecture (e.g. block size, number of validating nodes, consensus protocol), in turn, constraining transaction processing throughput, resulting in very slow transaction times. Consequently, users may pay higher fees to incentivise validating nodes to prioritise their transactions (see *Transaction fee evaluation*).

For example, the Bitcoin blockchain block size is 1 MB and a new block is added to the chain approximately every 10 minutes (**block interval**, see Chapter 4, Box 4.5). Whilst the average size of an Ethereum block is around 1–2 MB, it can dynamically go up to 12 MB, claiming a block interval of 12 to 20 seconds. Conversely, the Cardano block size is comparatively very small at about 0.1 MB, as they aim to create a block every 20 seconds (go and grab a cup of tea whilst you wait…). For those familiar with traditional settlement infrastructures, think of the block interval as the rough equivalent of the **settlement cycle**.

Similarly to the CAP theorem, the blockchain trilemma states that a blockchain system can't simultaneously achieve decentralisation, security, and scalability as each property places different demands on the network, and optimising one generally means sacrificing another.

For example, reducing the block interval or increasing the block size can improve scalability by allowing more transactions to be processed, but this can also compromise security by making the system more vulnerable to attacks. Similarly, increasing the number of nodes can improve decentralisation, but it can also reduce scalability by slowing down the consensus process.

If we take the example of Ripple, the focus on scalability and security dictates the sacrifice of decentralisation, as permissioned blockchains are prone to do.

Lastly, whilst security is foundational to blockchain architectures and would never be completely sacrificed, some blockchains may focus on decentralisation and scalability whilst achieving a "good enough" level of security. The relatively new Solana blockchain (born in 2020) is one example, as network outages and ongoing security discussions suggest[149] (I apologise to all Solana lovers out there, but this is the evidence at the time of writing…).

Figure 1.19 puts the blockchain trilemma in context.

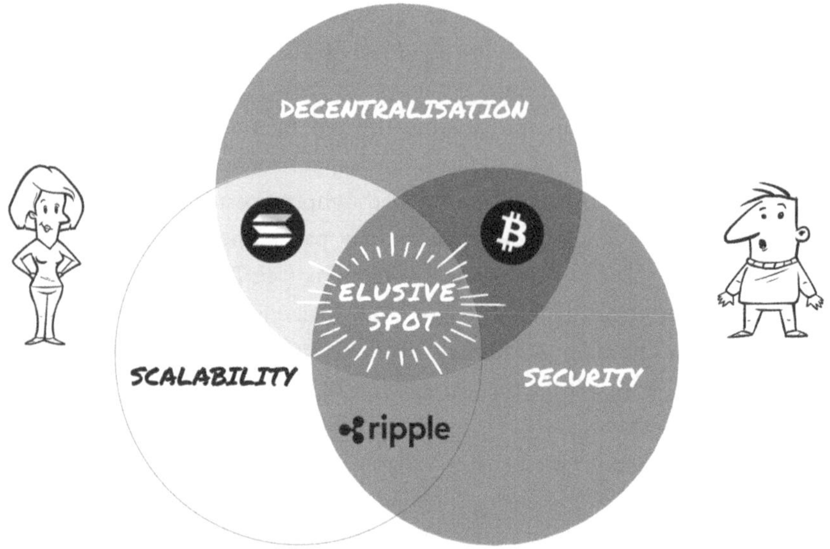

Figure 1.19 The blockchain trilemma in practice. © 2024 Neira Jones.

Understanding the blockchain trilemma is crucial when designing new blockchains, and developers must carefully balance the trade-offs. Research into blockchain scalability continues and new developments abound, which we will explore in the next sections.

In the meantime, as I always say, if you want to assess something, you must be able to measure it, which means having a set of agreed metrics, and I introduced some in the previous sections (e.g. transaction speed, block interval). Competing in the fast-moving consumer retail world where centralised payment infrastructures enable everyone to take transaction speeds for granted, blockchain networks still have some way to go. Figure 1.20 gives you a comparative scale between some dominant centralised payment infrastructures and popular blockchains. I've also added the dates when the various infrastructures were created to help assess the maturity and speed of technology evolution. A word of warning: whilst the figures in Figure 1.20 were current at the time of writing, they may look very different when you read this book. For an easy-to-read blockchain explorer dashboard presenting the performance of the most popular blockchains on one screen, try Chainspect.[150]

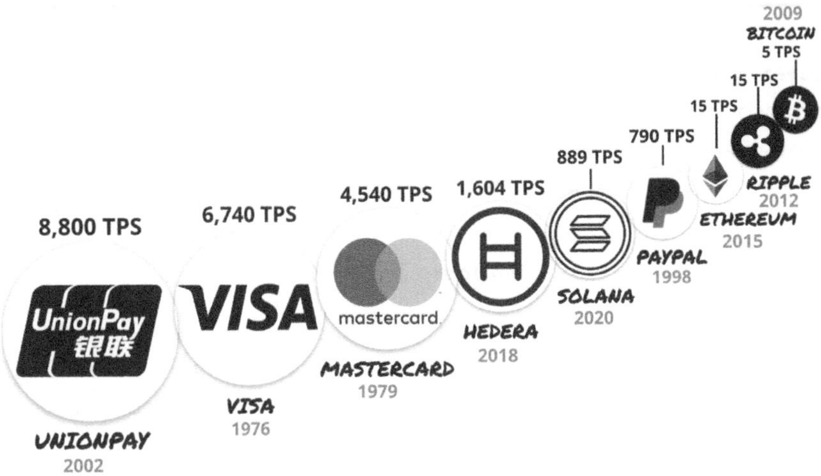

Figure 1.20 Transaction speeds: centralised payment networks vs. blockchains. © 2024 Neira Jones.

Surprised? Some may argue that Figure 1.20 doesn't relate to transaction speeds you may find through a Google search for the various infrastructures shown, and they are partly right. The transaction speeds given here refer to the actual volume of transactions per second (TPS), rather than theoretical TPS (what the infrastructure can theoretically sustain).

For example, VisaNet is theoretically capable of processing 65,000 TPS[151] and Solana is also theoretically capable of handling 65,000 TPS. The reality is of course different. When Ethereum migrated its infrastructure from PoW to PoS in September 2022 (The Merge), the expectation was that it would be able to reach 100,000 TPS, but at the time of writing, its maximum theoretical speed was 119 TPS, with an actual TPS of 15 (and a maximum recorded TPS of 62.34). Caveat emptor.

Going back to the question at hand, are blockchains scalable? Yes, they can be scalable, and this is achieved through **scaling solutions** which come in two types: Layer 1 scaling solutions (improvements to the main blockchain) and Layer 2 scaling solutions (third-party integrations that can be used in conjunction with a main blockchain to achieve scalability).

These scaling solutions target the "elusive spot" in Figure 1.19.

Layer 1 scaling solutions

Layer 1 scaling solutions augment the base layer of the blockchain protocol itself in order to improve scalability. Here, the protocol rules are changed directly to increase transaction capacity and speed whilst accommodating more users and more data, and this may include:

Changing block data

Involves changing the block in terms of size, structure, etc. For example, the Bitcoin Cash blockchain increased the block size from 1 MB to 32 MB. The Segwit fork of the Bitcoin blockchain changed how block data is organised, freeing up more space for transactions in a block without affecting network security (see Chapter 3, *Soft forks*). Zcash, a privacy-focused blockchain mentioned earlier, had a block structure similar to Bitcoin and subsequently introduced "joined shielded transactions" in a protocol upgrade allowing multiple shielded transactions to be combined in a single block entry, reducing overall data size, and improving scalability for shielded transactions.

Changing consensus protocol

A well-known example of this is Ethereum, which changed from PoW to PoS in September 2022 in an exercise dubbed "The Merge" (see Chapter 3, Box 3.4). Others include Solana (from Proof of History to a hybrid combination of BFT and PoS), Cardano (from Ouroboros PoS to an enhanced version of Ouroboros PoS), EOS (from DPoS to an enhanced version of DPoS), and NEO (from Delegated BFT to a hybrid combination of Practical BFT and Tendermint BFT). Please note that the transition to a new protocol takes time, and not all changes may guarantee an improvement in scalability, and changes may not always be accepted by the community (see Chapter 3, *Blockchain operations and governance*)...

Sharding

This concept involves breaking the state of an entire blockchain into distinct data sets called "shards", which are then processed in parallel, allowing for simultaneous work on numerous transactions. Think of it as a form of database partitioning. The MultiversX (formerly Elrond) blockchain is one example and is theoretically capable of processing over 100,000 TPS, however, the reality at the time of writing is 2.2 TPS when checking their own explorer[152]... Zilliqa, Near Protocol, Polygon, and Avalanche are other blockchains that use sharding, whilst Ethereum may have plans to implement it.

Transaction pruning

This involves removing transactions from a blockchain after a certain period of time determined by the protocol (meaning that most full nodes won't have to store an entire copy of the blockchain, thus increasing scalability). If a blockchain implements transaction pruning, most full nodes will be pruned full nodes, whilst several archival full nodes will still store an entire copy of the blockchain (see *Other types of nodes*). Bitcoin introduced this option in release 0.11.0,[153] and Zcash may also have introduced it.

Signature aggregation

This technique allows multiple transactions to be signed together with a single digital signature, reducing the transaction's size, and, therefore, the block size, thus improving scalability, especially where many small transactions are involved. Both Bitcoin and Ethereum may be exploring this option.

Final words on Layer 1 scaling solutions

Of course, technology will evolve, and I have no doubt that some clever people will find new ways to improve main blockchains at their core. And that's one thing that blockchains and traditional payment infrastructures have in common: they evolve fast. For example, Directed Acyclic Graph (DAG) sharding is a Layer 1 scaling solution proposal that combines elements of both DAGs and sharding. It proposes using a DAG structure within each shard of a sharded blockchain.[154] This is still theoretical, at the time of writing, and no implementations exist. Watch this space.

In this chapter, I concentrated on blockchain, the most commonly deployed DLT. However, for completeness purposes when addressing scalability, we must also mention the blockchain alternatives (see Box 1.1) such as Hashgraph, Holochain, DAG, and Tempo (Radix), which promise much in terms of scalability, and this is why I included Hedera (a hashgraph implementation) in Figure 1.20.

Also, for completeness purposes, I must mention a relatively new scalability research area for Layer 1 improvements: stateless blockchains.

You may have come across the term **stateless blockchain**, and the definition of alternative DLT infrastructures (e.g. hashgraph) may confuse as they share similarities with stateless blockchains since they don't store the entire transaction history, only the current state of the network.

Many will call Hedera (hashgraph) and IOTA (DAG) stateless blockchains, but these are not blockchains! You know me, I'm a stickler for correct terminology, and this space is confusing enough...

In any instance, stateless blockchains are a new concept, very much still at the research stage (at the time of writing). Essentially, a stateless blockchain is one that aims to improve scalability by only storing the current state of the network, effectively only remembering "who owns what right now" (as opposed to the whole history of all transactions).

Now that you understand blockchain consensus processes, it becomes clear that, in a stateless blockchain, verifying transactions without a complete history will be quite complex and can pose security challenges. This is why there are no known examples of stateless blockchains, although Ethereum is exploring the concept[155] whilst some claim that statelessness is impossible to achieve.[156] That's that cleared up, for now ...

Professionals should remember the following:

- Look at Layer 1 scaling solutions as the equivalent of a **major software upgrade** in traditional computer systems. Sometimes, the upgrade is backwards compatible with the previous version, sometimes it isn't. The same happens with blockchains, and given their decentralised nature, where everyone has to agree to a change, you can imagine that this may cause governance problems for blockchain implementations. More on that in Chapter 3.

- **Layer 1 scaling solutions require significant effort to implement**. For example, the transition of Ethereum from PoW to PoS was first proposed in 2016, then a new separate test chain (Beacon Chain) was conceptualised in 2016 and launched in 2020, testing and integration took place between Beacon Chain and Ethereum mainnet between 2021 and 2022, for the new Ethereum to go live in September 2022, making it a total of six years!
- **There is no guarantee that the expected improvements will actually happen**.
- The Layer 1 deployment techniques introduced so far (e.g. changing block data, changing consensus, sharding) don't represent an exhaustive list. Much research continues, and new developments will happen over time, introducing more techniques. It is always advisable to look at up-to-date documentation, white papers, etc.

Layer 2 scaling solutions

Layer 2 scaling solutions shift a portion of the transactional burden from a main blockchain to an adjacent infrastructure which then handles the brunt of the blockchain processing and only subsequently reports back to the main blockchain to finalise the results. Think of Layer 2 solutions as **overlay services** that sit on top of a Layer 1 blockchain.

On-chain and off-chain

Before going further, we must define what "processing" means. From the previous sections, you are now familiar with the transactional processes. But "processing" is not just about processing and validating transactions: it can mean record keeping, computation, data storage, dispute resolution, security, and much more.

The way processing will be conducted may happen **on-chain** (processing happens on a main – Layer 1 – blockchain) or **off-chain** (processing happens outside of a main blockchain, for example on a traditional transactional system or a Layer 2 blockchain-lite infrastructure).

In *How are transactions validated and settled?* we covered how the consensus protocol ensures the validity of transactions in Layer 1 blockchains. With Layer 2 solutions, since processing may be shifted to an adjacent infrastructure, proving the validity of a transaction is slightly different as they focus on faster transaction processing and scalability. Therefore, they are unlikely to use common Layer 1 consensus protocols such as PoW or PoS (although they may inherit some of the security features from the underlying Layer 1 blockchain, depending on what is processed on-chain or off-chain).

Of course, Layer 2 solutions have to communicate with their underlying Layer 1 blockchain, and this may be achieved through bridges.

BOX 1.12 WHAT IS A BRIDGE?

Think of a bridge as a gateway enabling a performance-focused Layer 2 solution to interact with their underlying high-security Layer 1 blockchain. There are two types of bridges, smart contract bridges (decentralised self-executing programmes, see Chapter 2, *What is a smart contract?*) and centralised bridges.

Smart contract bridges are the most commonly implemented and involve three generic steps: (1) secure the original asset on the Layer 1 blockchain, (2) issue a representation (i.e. a token) of the asset on the Layer 2 solution, a representation which is used to conduct faster transactions on the layer, and (3) return to Layer 1 to conclude the interaction, which involves destroying the Layer 2 representation of the original asset.

Smart contract bridges offer benefits including:

- **Decentralisation**: smart contract bridges promote decentralisation by removing the need for a trusted third party to operate the bridge.
- **Security**: smart contracts can be rigorously audited and configured to enforce specific rules for secure asset transfer. Their code is typically open source and auditable, allowing for transparency in their operation.
- **Transparency**: the open source nature of smart contract bridges allows for public scrutiny and helps ensure they function as intended.

Smart contract bridges may also pose challenges:

- **Complexity**: developing and maintaining secure smart contract bridges can be complex (see Chapter 2, *Building smart contracts*).

- **Vulnerability Risks**: smart contracts are susceptible to vulnerabilities if not properly designed and audited. A compromised bridge can lead to the theft of locked assets.
- **Limited Functionality**: smart contract bridges might have limitations regarding the types of assets they can support or the complexity of transactions they can handle.

Bridges can also be centralised (as may be implemented in side chains), in which case they would be operated by a trusted entity and may not involve smart contracts directly (although they may leverage smart contracts to lock and unlock assets on the Layer 1 blockchain). In this configuration, centralised bridges may be faster and easier to use, but the trusted entity operating the bridge introduces an element of centralisation and a potential single point of failure. In addition, centralised bridges may not offer the same level of transparency as smart contract bridges, as the underlying infrastructure might not be completely open source.

As research and development continue, in future, bridges may become interoperable and could allow asset movements across multiple blockchains.

Some of the solutions (e.g. rollups) use the concept of validity proofs and fraud proofs, or hybrid protocols (see Table 1.4) as part of their trust framework.

Validity proofs and fraud proofs

With the scalability and performance focus of Layer 2 solutions, some level of security still needs to be achieved (see *The Blockchain trilemma*). One mechanism is the **validity proof**, and this acts as an express-lane receipt, guaranteeing that a set of transactions is valid.

When transactions are processed on the Layer 2 infrastructure, validators on the Layer 2 network will create a cryptographic proof guaranteeing that all transactions in the set follow the rules.

This proof is then submitted to the Layer 1 blockchain which only has to verify the proof without the need of processing every transaction in the set. If the proof is valid, the Layer 1 blockchain accepts the transaction set for inclusion in the ledger.

As an additional security measure, Layer 2 solutions may use "fraud proofs", which encourages validators to act as watchdogs (and may be achieved through economic and non-economic incentives).

Fraud proofs are additional security measures used by Layer 2 solutions to encourage validators to ensure the integrity and security of the network.

If a Layer 2 validator suspects that a transaction is fraudulent, they may gather evidence (e.g. copies of transactions, data inconsistencies, senders, receivers) which is then transformed into a cryptographically verifiable proof (the fraud proof). The fraud proof is then submitted to the Layer 2 blockchain, thus raising the alarm.

Depending on the Layer 2 implementation, this fraud proof may also be escalated to the underlying Layer 1 blockchain. Depending on the ultimate designated authority (i.e. Layer 2 or Layer 1), the network will take corrective action after verifying the fraud proof, which if deemed valid, may result in potentially reversing the fraudulent transaction, alerting other network participants of the fraudulent activity, and penalising the malicious actor.

For those familiar with traditional financial systems, think of a fraud proof as a similar concept to a fraud investigation and **suspicious activity reporting (SAR)** as normally performed by fraud department staff in financial institutions, with added cryptography.

Fraud proofs are used in Layer 2 solutions to target fraudulent transactions, but fraud proofs may also be used on Layer 1 blockchains, in which case, they are mostly used to target specific validators acting maliciously (rather than transactions). This is because in Layer 1 blockchains, integrity and security are ensured by the consensus protocol (e.g. PoS,

PoW), and all processing is conducted on the main network (on-chain), which means that fraud proofs will be validated directly on the main network.

Ultimately, fraud proofs play an essential role in Layer 2 solutions but are less common on Layer 1 blockchains.

Now that we've sorted these few fundamental concepts out, let's have a look at the different types of Layer 2 solutions.

Plasma chains

These blockchain implementations introduce a hierarchy of blockchains, with a parent chain and child chains. The main blockchain acts as a secure foundation and sets the rules for the whole network, whereas the child chains handle transaction execution.

This means that all processing is conducted "on-chain", whether it is on the parent chain or child chains, bringing more security. Plasma chains[157] allow for the customisation of child chains to handle specific workloads (e.g. fungible or non-fungible tokens, see Chapter 5, *Digital and virtual assets*), and may use a different protocol from the mainchain to offer flexibility.

There are two types of plasma chains: plasma cash and plasma application, the former focuses on fungible coin/token transfers, whilst the latter can be used for more complex use cases (e.g. decentralised applications, see Chapter 2, *Blockchain application types*). Plasma chains are consequently quite complex to implement as managing interactions between main and child chains can be challenging, the reliance on fraud proofs may introduce additional complexity, and vulnerabilities on the child chain or the fraud proofs may potentially compromise the entire network (requiring a high level of security expertise for implementation).

A simpler variant of the plasma chain model is "nested blockchains", involving child chains which are closely coupled with the mainchain, usually implementing a modified version of the mainchain's protocol or one that is specifically designed to work with the main blockchain. Whilst transactions still happen on the child (nested) chain, the validation is achieved through the consensus specified by the underlying Layer 1 blockchain. This means that fraud proofs are not the primary focus, and therefore there is more reliance on the underlying Layer 1 blockchain when compared to plasma chains (which only use the Layer 1 blockchain for dispute resolution).

The OMG Network was a nested blockchain implementation on top of Ethereum, but it is no longer active, and another project inherited its community, whilst its OMG token was delisted by a number of exchanges.[158] Loopring started life as a plasma chain but transitioned to a rollup in 2021. Whilst the concept of plasma and nested blockchains has been explored by many, it hasn't gained much traction as other Layer 2 solutions have gained more favour (e.g. rollups).

Plasma and nested chains in a nutshell:

- Layer 1 blockchain (parent chain) verifies and records all transactions on the ledger.
- Child chains perform all computations.
- Child chains are not independent from their parent chain and rely on the Layer 1 consensus protocol.

Rollups

In theory, whilst rollups can be implemented as a Layer 2 solution on top of any Layer 1 blockchain, all current and working implementations are based on Ethereum (as far as I can tell). In principle, these are similar to plasma chains, since processing is offloaded from the Layer 1 to the adjacent chain (rollup chain), but with some important differences. Rollups communicate to their Layer 1 blockchain via a bridge (see Box 1.12) usually implemented through a smart contract (see Chapter 2, *What is a smart contract?*), and there are two types of rollups: **optimistic rollups (ORU)** and **zero-knowledge rollups (zk-rollups)**.

An ORU assumes that all transactions are valid by default (hence the optimism!), and therefore fraud proofs are a crucial element of their design (similar to plasma chains), and the mainchain verifies them and may potentially reverse an entire set of transactions if the fraud is proven. Examples of ORUs are Optimism[159] and Arbitrum.[160]

A zk-rollup includes a validity proof for every transaction in the batch, which is implemented through ZKPs (see *Zero-Knowledge Proofs (ZKP)*), in theory offering more security than ORU, which is why fraud proofs are not strictly necessary in this model. The reverse of the coin is that zk-rollups exhibit slower transaction processing than ORUs due to the complexity of zk-proofs, but zk-rollups may offer lower transaction fees and higher privacy.

Examples of zk-rollups are ImmutableX[161] (formerly Elrond), Loopring,[162] and zkSync.[163] Rollups are less complex to implement than plasma chains.

Rollups in a nutshell:

- Layer 1 blockchain records submitted batches of transactions from rollups on the ledger.
- Rollups perform all computations.
- Rollups are independent of their Layer 1 blockchain but submit batches of transactions (hence rollup) through a bridge usually implemented through a smart contract (ORU or zk-rollup) before submitting them to Layer 1 to verify the proofs and may reject batches instead of recording on the ledger.
- Rollups must continuously provide evidence (proofs) that that all rolled-up transactions are valid, and that the rollup is not compromised.

Side chains

Side chains are separate blockchains (although not fully-fledged ones) with their own consensus mechanism (e.g. PoS, PoA) that connect to a Layer 1 blockchain through a bridge (see Box 1.12), which is usually implemented through a smart contract.

Similarly to other Layer 2 solutions, side chains rely heavily on fraud proofs for security and dispute resolution, and they may also rely on validity proofs depending on the consensus mechanism used.

Polygon[164] operates an Ethereum side chain (Polygon POS) using PoS consensus, but they also offer a zk-rollup (zkEVM). Other examples of Ethereum side chains include Skale[165] and Ronin.[166] The RSK (Rootstock) BTC side chain uses a federated PoS consensus, and its bridge with the Bitcoin blockchain is implemented through a 1:1 **peg** between its native coin

(RBTC) and BTC, not through a smart contract. The Liquid Network[167] is a similar Bitcoin side chain, also using federated PoS and a 1:1 peg.

Side chains in a nutshell:

- Layer 1 blockchain records transactions from the side chain on the ledger.
- Side chains perform all computations and validate transactions as they have their own consensus protocol (often PoS).
- Side chains are independent of their Layer 1 and communicate with it through a bridge usually implemented through a smart contract (but a bridge can also be operated by a centralised trusted entity).
- The security of the side chain depends on the security of the bridge and the parties governing the bridge are responsible for attesting transaction validity and that the side chain is not compromised.

State channels

State channels are usually not blockchains but separate transactional infrastructures where participants can carry out multiple private transactions off-chain on a peer-to-peer basis, where only the first (open channel) and final (close channel) transactions are recorded on the underlying Layer 1 blockchain.

As such, they facilitate fast and cheap transactions without relying on the mainchain for every transaction. They rely on cryptographic signatures as validity proofs to demonstrate that a participant in the channel has the necessary funds to complete a transaction and that they haven't tampered with the current state of the channel balance. They may also use fraud proofs for dispute resolution.

They potentially attract privacy-focused users as the details of transactions within a channel remain off-chain. Examples of state channels include Lightning Network[168] (Layer 1 Bitcoin), Raiden Network[169] (Layer 1 Ethereum), and Celer[170] (multiple blockchains). At the time of writing, neither Raiden Network nor Celer had many applications built on them.

Those familiar with centralised settlement infrastructures will realise that this mechanism is somewhat similar to **deferred net settlement**.

State channels in a nutshell:

- Layer 1 blockchain records only the first (open channel, initial funding) and last transaction (close channel, settlement) from the state channel on the ledger.
- State channels are transactional channels where participants open and close channels through smart contracts on the Layer 1 blockchain on a peer-to-peer basis. A state channel performs multiple transactions between channel participants and maintains the channel balance without intervention from Layer 1.
- State channels have limited interaction with their Layer 1 (only the first and last transaction), but they may interact with the Layer 1 in case of dispute resolution (e.g. fraud proofs).
- The security of the state channel is achieved through digital signatures and cryptographic techniques (e.g. hash).

Validiums

A recent Layer 2 scaling development, specifically targeted at Ethereum,[171] validiums are not blockchains themselves and have no separate consensus protocol (they rely on the security of the mainchain). Rather similar to state channels, they operate an adjacent infrastructure dedicated to validium operations and data storage.

This means that, like rollups and state channels, transaction processing is performed outside the Layer 1 blockchain, but unlike rollups, detailed transaction data is stored on the validium (off-chain), and off-chain data accessibility and verifiability may be ensured through a group of stakeholders (e.g. independent nodes, storage providers) called the Data Availability Committee (DAC) or through a Data Availability Provider (DAP) which can be either centralised or decentralised.

Validiums leverage Merkle proofs to efficiently demonstrate the validity of a batch of transactions (see Box 1.10), and they may also implement fraud proofs or zk-proofs as additional security measures.

The Layer 1 blockchain only records the proofs on the ledger. As a new development in the blockchain space, there are few examples at the time of writing, but it seems that Starknet[172] has implemented a validium, and the Validium Network[173] and Arcana[174] both launched in 2024.

Validiums in a nutshell:

- Layer 1 blockchain only records the validity proofs of each batch of transactions submitted to it by the validium (not every transaction).
- Validiums perform all computations and validate transactions according to their own security mechanisms (e.g. sufficient funds, valid signatures, rule compliance, cryptographic techniques, zk-proofs).
- Detailed transaction data is stored off-chain (not on the Layer 1) and made available through a DAC or a DAP, which can be either centralised or decentralised.
- Validiums are independent of their Layer 1 and communicate with it through a bridge usually implemented through a smart contract (but a bridge can also be operated by a centralised trusted entity).
- Validiums have limited interaction with their Layer 1 (only state changes for each batch of transactions), but they may interact with the Layer 1 in case of dispute resolution (e.g. fraud proofs).
- Note from the author: I wonder what happens if a validium "dies", since transaction data is stored off-chain, and the Layer 1 only records proofs. Scary thought, which I'll let you ponder on.

Final words on Layer 2 scaling solutions

Well, I have no final words. This is a rapidly evolving space, and much research and development effort is being spent on blockchain scalability. Things will be tried, some will work, some won't, and it is therefore important to keep up-to-date with developments and official sites for up-to-date information. I'm pretty sure things will have changed when you read this book.[175]

Figure 1.21 gives you a quick reminder of the various Layer 2 scaling solutions and their main characteristics, with some examples of implementations and their launch dates.

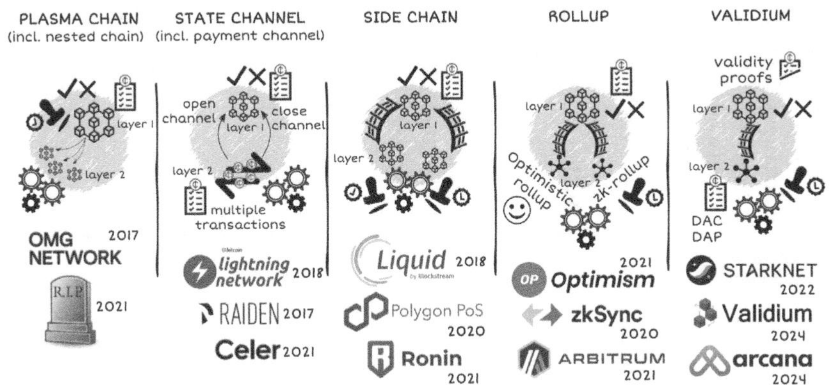

Figure 1.21 Layer 2 scaling solutions. © 2024 Neira Jones.

In any instance, Table 1.11 aims to give you examples of payment-related use cases for Layer 2 scaling solutions, you might recognise some of the names. I have omitted plasma chains as these seem to have been superseded by more modern alternatives, and validiums as they are too new. Please note that the services listed don't in any way constitute a recommendation or endorsement 😉...

Of course, I could have given many more use cases for Layer 2 scaling solutions, such as healthcare data management, identity, voting systems, and supply chain management. However, this is a "payments" book, so it's all you get for now...

Are all the real-life examples I've given successful? At least, most websites suggest that they are still operating at the time of writing. However, I had to remove some of the examples I originally gave by the time I finished writing this chapter because the pages returned the 404 error...

To determine success we must have a way of measuring it. This is not an easy task in blockchain infrastructures, as it means agreeing on metrics and critical success factors. How do you achieve this across disparate and distributed ecosystems, largely without regulations? I'll try to answer this in Chapter 4, *Tokenomics and metrics*.

Table 1.11 Examples of payments-related use cases for Layer 2 scaling solutions. © 2024 Neira Jones

Use Case	Rollups	Side Chains	State Channels
Payments, exchanges, wallets, cards, loyalty, swaps	**Exchanges**: Coinbase,[176] Binance,[177] crypto.com[178] on Optimism **Wallets**: Coinbase Wallet,[179] Metamask,[180] Brave Wallet[181] on Optimism. Argent[182] on Starknet **Payments**: Checkout[183] on ImmutableX **Swaps**: Uniswap,[184] Layerswap[185] on Optimism. Layerswap on Starknet. Hop[186] on Optimism and Arbitrum	**Exchanges**: Binance, crypto.com, bybit,[187] Coinbase, on Polygon POS **Wallets**: Huobi (iToken),[188] Metamask, all on Polygon POS. Ledger,[189] MEW[190] on Skale **Banking**: Nubank[191] on Polygon POS **Retail**: Flipkart[192] on Polygon POS **Loyalty**: Starbucks Odyssey,[193] Nike .Swoosh[194] on Polygon POS **Swaps**: Hop, Uniswap on Polygon POS	**Exchanges**: Kraken,[195] Coinbase, BitFinex,[196] all on Lightning Network **Payments**: zaprite,[197] Speed,[198] opennode,[199] Lightning Checkout,[200] all on Lightning Network **Wallets**: Cash App,[201] Trezor,[202] Ledger, Breez,[203] all on Lightning Network **Cards**: Moon,[204] Laser Eyes Cards[205] on Lightning Network **Swaps**: Boltz[206] on Lightning Network
Gaming	Mines of Dalarnia[207] on Optimism Metacube[208] on Starknet Gods Unchained[209] on ImmutableX Treasure[210] on Arbitrum	Axie Infinity,[211] Pixels[212] on Ronin Aavegotchi,[213] Decentraland[214] on Polygon POS	Zebedee,[215] Nakamoto Roulette,[216] LN Scratch,[217] Lightning Roulette[218] on Lightning Network
Marketplaces	Ventory Marketplace,[219] Pyramid[220] on Starknet OptiMarket[221] on Optimism OpenSea[222] on Arbitrum Rarible[223] on ImmutableX	OpenSea, Rarible, Draftkings[224] on Polygon POS Mavis Market[225] on Ronin	Lightning Bazaar,[226] The Bitcoin Shop.uk[227] on Lightning Network

Source: Various Layer 2 solutions websites.

Blockchain fundamentals – conclusion (where do we go from here?)

In this whistle-stop tour of blockchain fundamentals, we covered:

- A comparison between centralised and decentralised infrastructures
- The properties and characteristics of blockchains
- The various blockchain models
- The consensus protocols
- The blockchain participants
- The privacy and anonymity characteristics of blockchains
- The blockchain scaling solutions

I have tried to explain the jargon, lifting the veil on confusing matters, and drawing parallels with centralised systems. I have provided you with some classification and reference frameworks, but please don't take them as gospel. This industry is still nascent (in the greater context of settlement infrastructures), and some might disagree with the way I have presented things. At least, I hope I have equipped you with the tools to enable you to make up your mind. I have also given you my opinion on some aspects of the ecosystem, but feel free to disagree, as I always welcome a good debate!

If you read this book a few years from now, more innovation will have happened, features and applications will have emerged, innovative technologies will be used, and behaviours will have evolved. Some blockchain deployments may grow, others won't, some will disappear, and new ones will emerge. Advocates of blockchains will continue to advocate, detractors will continue to detract. Suffice to say, it won't be boring.

All the important terms introduced in this chapter can be found in the glossary and plenty of references are provided before you get to the next chapter.

I find blockchains technically interesting as they appeal to the nerd in me. They remind me of my coding days when C.J. Date's "An Introduction to Database Systems", Volumes 1[228] and 2[229] were my constant companions (I still have my first editions!). But as exciting as the technology might sound, we've only scratched the surface.

To continue on our journey of understanding blockchain ecosystems, we must understand how we build blockchains and the applications that run on them.

Let's go on the second leg of our trip.

Notes

1 Neira Jones. "Understanding Payments" ISBN 13 978-1032631349, 29 February 2024. Available at: https://www.routledge.com/Understanding-Payments-A-Whistle-Stop-Tour-into-What-You-Thought-You-Knew/Jones/p/book/9781032631349.

2 "Bank of England Slammed over Outdated IT and Culture" *Finextra*, 13 March 2019. Available at: https://www.finextra.com/newsarticle/33529/bank-of-england-slammed-over-outdated-it-and-culture (Accessed 11 January 2024).

3 "Bank of England Opens Settlement System to Blockchain" Pymnts.com, 26 June 2018. Available at: https://www.pymnts.com/news/b2b-payments/2018/bank-england-settlement-blockchain/ (Accessed 11 January 2024).

4 "Facilitating Firms' Use of Technology, Like the Cloud, to Increase Their Operational Resilience" Bank of England website. Available at: https://www.bankofengland.co.uk/research/future-finance/facilitate-firms-use-of-technology (Accessed 11 January 2024).

5 "The World Depends on 60-Year-Old Code No One Knows Anymore" pcmag.com, 1 December 2023. Available at: https://www.pcmag.com/articles/ibms-plan-to-update-cobol-with-watson (Accessed 11 January 2024).

6 "Welcome Savings Bank Implements Blockchain-based Bank ID for Enhanced Customer Convenience" *Medium*, 3 August 2023. Available at: https://medium.com/@coinness.gl/welcome-savings-bank-implements-blockchain-based-bank-id-for-enhanced-customer-convenience-f05a9e842b6b (Accessed 11 January 2024).

7 "JPMorgan Creates New Unit for Blockchain Projects, Says the Technology Is Close to Making Money" *CNBC*, 27 October 2020. Available at: https://www.cnbc.com/2020/10/27/jpmorgan-creates-new-unit-for-blockchain-projects-as-it-says-the-technology-is-close-to-making-money.html (Accessed 11 January 2024).

8 "JPM Coin Launches Programmable Payments" *Finextra*, 10 November 2023. Available at: https://www.finextra.com/newsarticle/43272/jpm-coin-launches-programmable-payments (Accessed 11 January 2024).

9 "Onyx by J.P. Morgan Launches Blockchain in Space" JP Morgan website, 2021. https://www.jpmorgan.com/technology/news/blockchain-in-space (Accessed 11 January 2024).

10 "JPMorgan: JPM Coin Handles $1 Billion in Daily Transactions" pymnts.com, 26 October 2023. Available at: https://www.pymnts.com/blockchain/2023/jpmorgan-jpm-coin-handles-1-billion-dollars-daily-transactions/ (Accessed 11 January 2024).

11 "Hashgraph Consensus: What It Is, How It Works" Investopedia, 13 August 2013. Available at: https://www.investopedia.com/terms/h/hashgraph-consensus-mechanism.asp (Accessed 12 January 2024).
12 Hedera website. Available at: https://hedera.com/ (Accessed 12 January 2024).
13 Holochain website. Available at: https://www.holochain.org/ (Accessed 12 January 2024).
14 Bitcoin Wiki, DAG. Available at: https://bitcoinwiki.org/wiki/dag (Accessed 12 January 2024).
15 NANO website. Available at: https://nano.org/en (Accessed 12 January 2024).
16 Obyte website. Available at: https://obyte.org/ (Accessed 12 January 2024).
17 IOTA website. Available at: https://www.iota.org/ (Accessed 12 January 2024).
18 RADIX website. Available at: https://www.radixdlt.com/ (Accessed 12 January 2024).
19 Stuart Haber and W. Scott Stornetta. "How to Time-stamp a Digital Document" January 1991. Available at: https://link.springer.com/article/10.1007/BF00196791 (Accessed 1 July 2023).
20 Satoshi Nakamoto. "Bitcoin: A Peer-to-Peer Electronic Cash System" Nakamoto Institute, 31 October 2008. Available at: https://nakamotoinstitute.org/bitcoin/ (Accessed 1 July 2023).
21 "Hashing Algorithm Overview: Types, Methodologies & Usage" Okta, 15 September 2023. Available at: https://www.okta.com/identity-101/hashing-algorithms/ (Accessed 15 January 2024).
22 "Who Were the Codebreakers?" Bletchley Park Website. Available at: https://bletchleypark.org.uk/our-story/who-were-the-codebreakers/ (Accessed 3 July 2024).
23 "Alan Turing FAQs" Bletchley Patk website. Available at: https://bletchleypark.org.uk/our-story/alan-turing-faqs/ (Accessed 3 July 2024).
24 "Enigma" Bletchley Park website. Available at: https://bletchleypark.org.uk/our-story/enigma/ (Accessed 3 July 2024).
25 Patrick McConnell. "BLINO (Blockchain in Name Only)" LinkedIn post, 1 August 2022. Available at: https://www.linkedin.com/pulse/blino-blockchain-name-only-patrick-mcconnell/ (Accessed 1 June 2024).
26 "we.trade Calls It Quits after Running Out of Cash" *Global Trade Review*, 6 June 2022. Available at: https://www.gtreview.com/news/fintech/we-trade-calls-it-quits-after-running-out-of-cash/ (Accessed 6 February 2024).
27 Sebastien Meunier. "When Do You Need Blockchain? Decision Models" *Medium*, 4 August 2016. Available at: https://medium.com/@sbmeunier/when-do-you-need-blockchain-decision-models-a5c40e7c9ba1 (Accessed 21 January 2024).

28 Mogen E. Peck. "Do You Need a Blockchain?" *IEEE Spectrum*, 29 September 2017. Available at: https://spectrum.ieee.org/do-you-need-a-blockchain (Accessed 21 January 2024).

29 "These 11 Questions Will Help You Decide If Blockchain Is Right for Your Business" World Economic Forum, 23 April 2018. Available at: https://www.weforum.org/agenda/2018/04/questions-blockchain-toolkit-right-for-business/ (Accessed 21 January 2024).

30 "Blockchain Mainnet Platform, Fleta's Roadmap Update and Website Renewal" 8 June 2021. Available at: https://medium.com/meverse/blockchain-mainnet-platform-fletas-roadmap-update-and-website-renewal-a6301542d3c7 (Accessed 8 February 2024).

31 "Paradise Lost: The 5 Biggest Bitcoin Private Key Horror Stories" *CoolWallet*, 17 May 2021. Available at: https://www.coolwallet.io/blog/bitcoin-lost-private-key-horror-stories/ (Accessed 3 February 2024).

32 "Ethereum's Climate Impact: A Contemporary and Historical Perspective" University of Cambridge, Judge Business School, 1 December 2023. Available at: https://www.jbs.cam.ac.uk/2023/ethereums-climate-impact-a-contemporary-and-historical-perspective/#paradigm-shift (Accessed 29 January 2024).

33 "Consensus Mechanisms" Ethereum website. Available at: https://ethereum.org/developers/docs/consensus-mechanisms (Accessed 29 January 2024).

34 "Running a Full Node" Bitcoin.org website. Available at: https://bitcoin.org/en/full-node#what-is-a-full-node (Accessed 29 January 2024).

35 "Average Confirmation Time for Bitcoin" Blockchain.com website. Available at: https://www.blockchain.com/explorer/charts/avg-confirmation-time (Accessed 7 April 2024).

36 Bitmain website. Available at: https://www.bitmain.com/ (Accessed 9 February 2024).

37 Canaan website. Available at: https://www.canaan.io/ (Accessed 9 February 2024).

38 MicroBT website. Available at: https://www.microbt.com/#/ (Accessed 26 May 2024).

39 Stratum website. Available at: https://stratumprotocol.org/ (Accessed 20 March 2024).

40 Foundry USA website. Available at: https://foundrydigital.com/mining-service/foundry-usa-pool/ (Accessed 8 April 2024).

41 Antpool website. Available at: https://www.antpool.com/ (Accessed 9 February 2024).

42 F2Pool website. Available at: https://www.f2pool.com/ (Accessed 9 February 2024).

43 Braiins Pool website. Available at: https://braiins.com/pool (Accessed 9 February 2024).
44 Poolin website. Available at: https://www.poolin.com/ (Accessed 9 February 2024).
45 ViaBTC website. Available at: https://www.viabtc.com/ (Accessed 9 February 2024).
46 BTC.com website. Available at: https://btc.com/ (Accessed 9 February 2024).
47 Nicehash website. Available at: https://www.nicehash.com/ (Accessed 9 February 2024).
48 Kryptex website. Available at: https://www.kryptex.com/en/ (Accessed 9 February 2024).
49 "Two Estonian Citizens Arrested in $575 Million Cryptocurrency Fraud and Money Laundering Scheme" Office of Public Affairs, 21 November 2022. Available at: https://www.justice.gov/opa/pr/two-estonian-citizens-arrested-575-million-cryptocurrency-fraud-and-money-laundering-scheme (Accessed 9 February 2024).
50 Genesis Mining website. Available at: https://genesis-mining.com/ (Accessed 9 February 2024).
51 "HashOcean Scam Victims Sign Petitions to FBI, Hackers to Reveal More Scams" *Cointelegraph*, 2 July 2016. Available at: https://cointelegraph.com/news/hashocean-scam-victims-sign-petitions-to-fbi-hackers-to-reveal-more-scams (Accessed 9 February 2024).
52 Riot Blockchain website. Available at: https://www.riotplatforms.com/ (Accessed 9 February 2024).
53 Hut 8 Mining website. Available at: https://hut8.com/ (Accessed 9 February 2024).
54 Argo Blockchain website. Available at: https://argoblockchain.com/ (Accessed 9 February 2024).
55 Marathon Digital Holdings website. Available at: https://www.mara.com/ (Accessed 9 February 2024).
56 Iris Energy website. Available at: https://irisenergy.co/ (Accessed 9 February 2024).
57 Cleanspark website. Available at: https://www.cleanspark.com/ (Accessed 9 February 2024).
58 Staked.us website. Available at: https://staked.us/ (Accessed 12 February 2024).
59 Figment website. Available at: https://figment.io/ (Accessed 12 February 2024).
60 Blockdeamon website. Available at: https://www.blockdaemon.com/ (Accessed 12 February 2024).

61 Rocket Pool website. Available at: https://rocketpool.net/ (Accessed 12 February 2024).
62 "Coinbase Suspends Staking Services in Four U.S. States" *CryptoDaily*, 15 July 2023. Available at: https://cryptodaily.co.uk/2023/07/coinbase-suspends-staking-services-in-four-us-states (Accessed 19 February 2024).
63 Cosmos website. Available at: https://cosmos.network/ (Accessed 12 February 2024).
64 Polkadot website. Available at: https://polkadot.network/features/cross-chain-communication/ (Accessed 12 February 2024).
65 Ankr website. Available at: https://www.ankr.com/staking-crypto/ (Accessed 12 February 2024).
66 "The Interchain Ecosystem" Interchain Developer Academy website. Available at: https://ida.interchain.io/academy/1-what-is-cosmos/2-cosmos-ecosystem.html (Accessed 24 March 2024).
67 "A Step-by-Step Guide to Join Cosmos Hub Testnet (gaia-13007)" *Medium*, 4 June 2020. Available at: https://medium.com/forbole/a-step-by-step-guide-to-join-cosmos-hub-testnet-e591a3d2cb41 (Accessed 25 March 2024).
68 "The Prevalidator" Tezos Agora Forum. Available at: https://tezos.gitlab.io/shell/prevalidation.html (Accessed 25 March 2024).
69 "The Ultimate Guide to Blockchain Light Clients" Nervos Knowledge Base, 2 October 2023. Available at: https://www.nervos.org/knowledge-base/ultimate_guide_to_light_clients (Accessed 26 March 2024).
70 Infura website. Available at: https://www.infura.io/ (Accessed 21 March 2024).
71 Alchemy website. Available at: https://www.alchemy.com/ (Accessed 21 March 2024).
72 Blockdaemon website. Available at: https://www.blockdaemon.com/ (Accessed 21 March 2024).
73 QuickNode website. Available at: https://www.quicknode.com/ (Accessed 21 March 2024).
74 Coinbase Commerce website. Available at: https:/www.coinbase.com/commerce (Accessed 23 March 2024).
75 Bitpay website. Available at: https://bitpay.com/business/ (Accessed 24 March 2023).
76 "Ralph Lauren Miami Store to Accept Crypto Payments" Coindesk, 4 April 2023. Available at: https://www.coindesk.com/web3/2023/04/04/ralph-lauren-miami-store-to-accept-crypto-payments/ (Accessed 23 March 2024).
77 Bitpay Merchant Directory. Available at: https://bitpay.com/directory/ (Accessed on 23 March 2024).
78 "Checkout.com Becomes the First PSP to Unlock Weekend Settlement for Merchants, Powered by Fireblocks' Crypto Payouts Debut" *Financial IT*,

7 June 2022. Available at: https://financialit.net/news/cryptocurrencies/checkoutcom-becomes-first-psp-unlock-weekend-settlement-merchants-powered (Accessed 24 March 2024).

79 Fireblocks Adds Worldpay as Network Partner for New Crypto Payments Engine" *Decrypt*, 24 October 2022. Available at: https://decrypt.co/112728/fireblocks-adds-worldpay-network-partner-new-crypto-payments-engine (Accessed 24 March 2024).

80 Fireblocks website. Available at: https://www.fireblocks.com/platforms/payments/ (Accessed 24 March 2024).

81 Bitpay website. Available at: https://bitpay.com/retail/ (Accessed 25 March 2024).

82 "Merchant Tools" CoinPayments website. Available at: https://www.coinpayments.net/merchant-tools (Accessed 25 March 2024).

83 NOWPayments website. Available at: https://nowpayments.io/pos (Accessed 25 March 2024).

84 ForumPay website. Available at: https://forumpay.com/payments (Accessed 25 March 2024).

85 Alex Rolfe. "Binance and Ingenico Begin Cryptocurrency Payments in France" *Payments Cards & Mobile*, 24 February 2023. Available at: https://www.paymentscardsandmobile.com/binance-and-ingenico-begin-cryptocurrency-payments-in-france/ (Accessed 25 March 2024).

86 "Ingenico, Binance and Nilos Join Forces to Facilitate Cryptocurrency Acceptance" Ingenico website, 21 March 2024. Available at: https://ingenico.com/en/newsroom/press-releases/ingenico-binance-and-nilos-join-forces-facilitate-cryptocurrency-acceptance (Accessed 25 March 2024).

87 Bitcoin Depot website. Available at: https://bitcoindepot.com/ (Accessed 25 March 2024).

88 Coinflip website. Available at: https://www.coinflip.tech/ (Accessed 25 March 2024).

89 Localcoin website. Available at: https://localcoinatm.com/ (Accessed 25 March 2024).

90 Kurant website. Available at: https://at.kurant.net (Accessed 25 March 2024).

91 värdex website. Available at: https://www.vaerdex.ch/ (Accessed 25 March 2024).

92 BitcoinMat website. Available at: https://bitcoinmat.org/Bitcoin_ATMs (Accessed 25 March 2024).

93 BTM website. Available at: https://www.btm.mx/ (Accessed 25 March 2024).

94 General Bytes website. Available at: https://www.generalbytes.com (Accessed 25 March 2024).

95 bitcoinATM.com website. Available at: https://bitcoinatm.com/ (Accessed 25 March 2024).
96 Circle website. Available at: https://www.circle.com (Accessed 24 March 2024).
97 "Visa Expands Stablecoin Settlement Capabilities to Merchant Acquirers" *Finextra*, 5 September 2023. Available at: https://www.finextra.com/newsarticle/42890/visa-expands-stablecoin-settlement-capabilities-to-merchant-acquirers (Accessed 24 March 2024).
98 "Worldpay from FIS Becomes First Global Merchant Acquirer to Offer Direct USDC Settlement, Driving Digital Currency Adoption to Businesses" FIS, 6 April 2022. Available at: https://www.fisglobal.com/about-us/media-room/press-release/2022/worldpay-from-fis-becomes-first-global-merchant-acquirer-to-offer-direct-usdc-settlement (Accessed 26 May 2024).
99 "Checkout.com Makes around-the-Clock Liquidity a Reality with Stablecoin Settlement" checkout.com, 15 March 2023. Available at: https://www.checkout.com/blog/checkout-com-makes-around-the-clock-liquidity-a-reality-with-stablecoin-settlement (Accessed 26 May 2024).
100 Chainalysis website. Available at: https://www.chainalysis.com/ (Accessed 26 March 2024).
101 Ciphertrace website. Available at: https://ciphertrace.com/ (Accessed 26 March 2024).
102 coinfirm website. Available at: https://www.coinfirm.com/ (Accessed 26 March 2024).
103 Glassnode website. Available at: https://glassnode.com/ (Accessed 26 March 2024).
104 IntoTheBlock website. Available at: https://app.intotheblock.com/ (Accessed 26 March 2024).
105 Nansen website. Available at: https://www.nansen.ai/ (Accessed 26 March 2024).
106 Dune website. Available at: https://dune.com (Accessed 26 March 2024).
107 coinglass website. Available at: https://www.coinglass.com/ (Accessed 26 March 2024).
108 Coinmetrics website. Available at: https://coinmetrics.io/ (Accessed 26 March 2024).
109 The Block website. Available at: https://www.theblock.co/ (Accessed 26 March 2024).
110 Delphi Digital website. Available at: https://delphidigital.io/ (Accessed 26 March 2024).
111 Blockchain.com website. Available at: https://www.blockchain.com/explorer (Accessed 26 March 2024).

112 mempool.space website. Available at: https://mempool.space/ (Accessed 26 March 2024).
113 Etherscan website. Available at: https://etherscan.io/ (Accessed 26 March 2024).
114 Blockchair website. Available at: https://blockchair.com/ethereum (Accessed 26 March 2024).
115 Tronscan website. Available at: https://tronscan.org (Accessed 26 March 2024).
116 BscScan website. Available at: https://bscscan.com/ (Accessed 26 March 2024).
117 XRPscan website. Available at: https://xrpscan.com/ (Accessed 26 March 2024).
118 Solscan website. Available at: https://solscan.io/ (Accessed 26 March 2024).
119 Cardano Explorer website. Available at: https://explorer.cardano.org/en (Accessed 26 March 2024).
120 Cardanoscan website. Available at: https://cardanoscan.io/ (Accessed 26 March 2024).
121 "Mastercard Acquires CipherTrace to Enhance Crypto Capabilities" Mastercard website, 9 September 2021. Available at: https://www.mastercard.com/news/press/2021/september/mastercard-acquires-ciphertrace-to-enhance-crypto-capabilities/ (Accessed 26 March 2024).
122 "Blockchain Forensics: How Authorities Track Crypto Transactions" crypto.news, 13 June 2023. Available at: https://crypto.news/learn/blockchain-forensics-how-authorities-track-crypto-transactions/ (Accessed 26 March 2024).
123 Metamask website. Available at: https://metamask.io/ (Accessed 26 March 2024).
124 Rainbow website. Available at: https://rainbow.me/en/ (Accessed 26 March 2024).
125 Prosper website. Available at: https://prosper.so/ (Accessed 9 August 2024).
126 Gods Unchained website. Available at: https://godsunchained.com/ (Accessed 27 March 2024).
127 Arweave website. Available at: https://www.arweave.org/ (Accessed 27 March 2024).
128 "Light Clients" Ethereum website, 23 November 2023. Available at: https://ethereum.org/en/developers/docs/nodes-and-clients/light-clients/ (Accessed 27 March 2024).
129 "Blockchain-Based Secure and Lightweight Authentication for Internet of Things" *IEEE Internet of Things Journal*, 9(5), 1 March 2022. Available

at: https://ieeexplore.ieee.org/document/9490334 (Accessed 27 March 2024).
130 Filecoin website. Available at: https://filecoin.io/ (Accessed 26 May 2024).
131 "Sovrin™: A Protocol and Token for Self-Sovereign Identity and Decentralized Trust" Sovrin Foundation, January 2018. Available at: https://sovrin.org/wp-content/uploads/Sovrin-Protocol-and-Token-White-Paper.pdf (Accessed 27 March 2024).
132 Ayush Mittal. "VeChain: Revolutionizing Supply Chain Management" *Medium*, 29 August 2023. Available at: https://medium.com/@sprayiton1122/vechain-revolutionizing-supply-chain-management-fc4eb16a94a4 (Accessed 27 March 2024).
133 Subhita Menon, Divya Anand, Kavita, Sahil Verma, Manider Kaur, N. Z. Jhanjhi, Rania M. Ghoniem, and Sayan Kumar Ray. "Blockchain and Machine Learning Inspired Secure Smart Home Communication Network" *MDPI*, 4 July 2023. Available at: https://www.mdpi.com/1424-8220/23/13/6132 (Accessed 27 March 2024).
134 Dash website. Available at: https://www.dash.org/ (Accessed 27 March 2024).
135 Syscoin website. Available at: https://syscoin.org/ (Accessed 27 March 2024).
136 Horizen website. Available at: https://www.horizen.io/ (Accessed 27 March 2024).
137 Polkadot website. Available at: https://polkadot.network/ (Accessed 27 March 2024).
138 Cosmos website. Available at: https://cosmos.network/ (Accessed 27 March 2024).
139 Lightning Network website. Available at: https://lightning.network/ (Accessed 27 March 2024).
140 "Privacy and Anonymity Are Not the Same, Yet Both Are Important" *Forbes*, 5 June 2024. Available at: https://www.forbes.com/sites/forbestechcouncil/2024/06/05/privacy-and-anonymity-are-not-the-same-yet-both-are-important/ (Accessed 5 June 2024).
141 "Bulletproofs in Crypto – An Introduction to a Non-interactive ZKP" Panther, 16 September 2022. Available at: https://blog.pantherprotocol.io/bulletproofs-in-crypto-an-introduction-to-a-non-interactive-zk-proof/ (Accessed 21 April 2024).
142 Elements website. Available at: https://elementsproject.org/ (Accessed 21 April 2024).
143 Grin website. Available at: https://grin.mw/ (Accessed 21 April 2024).
144 Beam website. Available at: https://beam.mw/ (Accessed 21 April 2024).

145 "Homomorphic Encryption" Chainlink, 21 December 2023. Available at: https://chain.link/education-hub/homomorphic-encryption (Accessed 21 April 2024).

146 Dr Eric A. Brewer. "Towards Robust Distributed Systems" PODC Keynote, 19 July 2000. Available at: https://people.eecs.berkeley.edu/~brewer/cs262b-2004/PODC-keynote.pdf (Accessed 13 June 2024).

147 "Brewer's Conjecture and the Feasibility of Consistent, Available, Partition-tolerant Web Services" *ACM SIGACT News*, 33(2). Available at: https://dl.acm.org/doi/10.1145/564585.564601 (Accessed 13 June 2024).

148 "What Is the CAP Theorem?" IBM website. Available at: https://www.ibm.com/topics/cap-theorem (Accessed 21 February 2024).

149 "Solana Confronts Another Security Hurdle Amid a History of Outages" *Blockworks*, 9 August 2024. Available at: https://blockworks.co/news/lightspeed-newsletter-solana-outage-patch (Accessed 30 August 2024).

150 Chainspect website. Available at: https://chainspect.app/dashboard (Accessed 10 May 2024).

151 "A Deep Dive on Solana, a High Performance Blockchain Network" Visa website, 31 August 2023. Available at: https://usa.visa.com/solutions/crypto/deep-dive-on-solana.html (Accessed 10 May 2024).

152 MultiversX explorer website. Available at: https://explorer.multiversx.com/ (Accessed 24 April 2024).

153 "Bitcoin Core 0.11.00" BitcoinCore website. Available at: https://bitcoin.org/bin/bitcoin-core-0.11.0/ (Accessed 10 May 2024).

154 "SharDAG: Scaling DAG-Based Blockchains via Adaptive Sharding" IEEE, 13–16 May 2024. Available at: https://ieeexplore.ieee.org/document/10597801 (Accessed 30 August 2024).

155 "Building a Stateless Ethereum Model" Consensys website, 20 October 2021. Available at: https://consensys.io/blog/building-a-stateless-ethereum-model (Accessed 10 May 2024).

156 "On the Impossibility of Stateless Blockchains" a16zcrypto website, 24 August 2023. Available at: https://a16zcrypto.com/posts/article/on-the-impossibility-of-stateless-blockchains/ (Accessed 10 May 2024).

157 "What Is Plasma and Why Is Vitalik Buterin into It All over Again?" *Blockworks*, 16 November 2023. Available at: https://blockworks.co/news/vitalik-buterin-plasma-hype (Accessed 13 May 2024).

158 "Serum (SRM) and OMG Network (OMG) Delisted from Major South Korean Exchanges" CoinUnited.io, 13 April 2023. Available at: https://coinunited.io/news/en/2023-04-13/crypto/cunews-serum-srm-and-omg-network-omg-delisted-from-major-south-korean-exchanges/ (Accessed 13 May 2024).

159 Optimism website. Available at: https://www.optimism.io/ (Accessed 13 May 2024).
160 "A Gentle Introduction to Arbitrum" Arbitrum website. Available at: https://docs.arbitrum.io/welcome/arbitrum-gentle-introduction (Accessed 13 May 2024).
161 "What Is ImmutableX?" Immutable website. Available at: https://www.immutable.com/blog/what-is-immutablex (Accessed 13 May 2024).
162 Loopring website. Available ate: https://loopring.org/#/ (Accessed 13 May 2024).
163 zkSync website. Available at: https://zksync.io/ (Accessed 13 May 2024).
164 Polygon website. Available at: https://polygon.technology/ (Accessed 13 May 2024).
165 Skale website. Available at: https://skale.space/ (Accessed 13 May 2024).
166 Ronin website. Available at: https://roninchain.com/ (Accessed 17 May 2024).
167 Liquid Network website. Available at: https://liquid.net/ (Accessed 13 May 2024).
168 Lightning network website. Available at: https://lightning.network/ (Accessed 17 May 2024).
169 Raiden website. Available at: https://raiden.network/ (Accessed 17 May 2024).
170 Celer website. Available at: https://celer.network/ (Accessed 17 May 2024).
171 "Validium" Ethereum website, 20 March 2024. Available at: https://ethereum.org/en/developers/docs/scaling/validium/ (Accessed 17 May 2024).
172 Starknet website. Available at: https://www.starknet.io/en/learn/what-is-starknet (Accessed 13 May 2024).
173 Validium Network website. Available at: https://www.validium.network/ (Accessed 27 May 2024).
174 "Behind the Scenes: Developing Arcana Network's Validium Infrastructure" 28 March 2024. Available at: https://arcana.network/blog/behind-the-scenes-developing-arcana-networks-validium-infrastructure (Accessed 27 May 2024).
175 "A Comprehensive Exploration on Blockchain Layer 2 Scaling Solutions" *Medium*, 28 October 2024. Available at: https://medium.com/coinmonks/blockchain-layer-2-scaling-solutions-d177d3bdeb00 (Accessed 28 November 2024).
176 Coinbase website. Available at: https://www.coinbase.com (Accessed 20 May 2024).
177 Binance website. Available at: https://www.binance.com/ (Accessed 20 May 2024).

178 Crypto.com website. Available at: https://crypto.com/ (Accessed 20 May 2024).
179 Coinbase Wallet website. Available at: https://www.coinbase.com/en-gb/wallet (Accessed 20 May 2024).
180 Metamask website. Available at: https://metamask.io/ (Accessed 20 May 2024).
181 Brave Wallet website. Available at: https://brave.com/wallet/ (Accessed 21 May 2024).
182 Argent website. Available at: https://www.argent.xyz/argent-x/ (Accessed 21 May 2024).
183 ImmutableX website, Checkout. Available at: https://www.immutable.com/products/checkout (Accessed 21 May 2024).
184 Uniswap website. Available at: https://app.uniswap.org/swap (Accessed 21 May 2024).
185 Layerswap website. Available at: https://www.layerswap.io/ (Accessed 21 May 2024).
186 Hop website. Available at: https://app.hop.exchange/ (Accessed 21 May 2024).
187 Bybit website. Available at: https://www.bybit.com/ (Accessed 20 May 2024).
188 Huobi wallet (iToken) website. Available at: https://www.itoken.com/ (Accessed 20 May 2024).
189 Ledger website. Available at: https://www.ledger.com/ (Accessed 23 May 2024).
190 MEW website. Available at: https://www.myetherwallet.com/ (Accessed 23 May 2024).
191 "Nubank Adds Two New Cryptocurrencies to the Nubank Crypto Experience" Nubank website, 20 December 2020. Available at: https://international.nubank.com.br/consumers/nubank-adds-two-new-cryptocurrencies-to-the-nubank-cripto-experience/ (Accessed 20 May 2024).
192 "Flipkart's Blockchain-based Firedrops Seeks More Use Cases" *The Economic Times*, 25 April 2024. Available at: https://economictimes.indiatimes.com/tech/technology/flipkarts-blockchain-based-firedrops-seeks-use-cases/articleshow/109572272.cms (Accessed 20 May 2024).
193 "Starbucks Taps Polygon for Its 'Starbucks® Odyssey' Web3 Experience" Polygon Labs, 12 September 2022. Available at: https://polygon.technology/blog/starbucks-taps-polygon-for-its-starbucks-r-odyssey-web3-experience-nbsp (Accessed 24 May 2024).
194 "Nike's Web3 Platform '.SWOOSH' Set to Launch On January 25" *Medium*, 24 January 2023. Available at: https://medium.com/@CryptoSavingExpert/nikes-web3-platform-swoosh-set-to-launch-on-january-25-15c77b6f1005 (Accessed 24 May 2024).

195 Kraken website. Available at: https://www.kraken.com/ (Accessed 20 May 2024).
196 Bitfinex website. Available at: https://www.bitfinex.com/ (Accessed 20 May 2024).
197 Zaprite website. Available at: https://zaprite.com/ (Accessed 20 May 2024).
198 Speed website. Available at: https://www.tryspeed.com/ (Accessed 20 May 2024).
199 Opennode website. Available at: https://opennode.com/ (Accessed 20 May 2024).
200 Lightning Checkout website. Available at: https://lightningcheckout.eu/en/ (Accessed 20 May 2024).
201 Cash App website. Available at: https://cash.app/ (Accessed 20 May 2024).
202 Trezor website. Available at: https://trezor.io/ (Accessed 20 May 2024).
203 Breez website. Available at: https://breez.technology/ (Accessed 20 May 2024).
204 Moon website. Available at: https://paywithmoon.com/ (Accessed 20 May 2024).
205 Laser Eyes Cards website. Available at: https://lasereyes.cards/ (Accessed 20 May 2024).
206 Boltz website: Available at: https://boltz.exchange/ (Accessed 20 May 2024).
207 Mines of Dalarnia website. Available at: https://www.minesofdalarnia.com/ (Accessed 21 May 2024).
208 Metacube website. Available at: https://metacube.games/ (Accessed 23 May 2024).
209 Gods Unchained website. Available at: https://godsunchained.com/ (Accessed 21 May 2024).
210 Treasure on Arbitrum. Available at: https://treasure.lol/ (Accessed 23 May 2024).
211 Axie Infinity website. Available at: https://axieinfinity.com/ (Accessed 23 May 2024).
212 Pixels website. Available at: https://play.pixels.xyz/ (Accessed 23 May 2024).
213 Aavegotchi website. Available at: https://www.aavegotchi.com/ (Accessed 20 May 2024).
214 Decentraland website. Available at: https://decentraland.org/ (Accessed 20 May 2024).
215 Zebedee website. Available at: https://zbd.gg/z/build-with-zbd (Accessed 20 May 2024).

216 Nakamoto Roulette website. Available at: https://nakamotoroulette.com/ (Accessed 20 May 2024).
217 LN scratch website. Available at: https://lnscratch.com/ (Accessed 20 May 2024).
218 Lightning Roulette website. Available at: https://lightning-roulette.com/ (Accessed 20 May 2024).
219 Ventory website. Available at: https://ventory.gg/ (Accessed 20 May 2024).
220 Pyramid website. Available at: https://pyramid.market/ (Accessed 23 May 2024).
221 OptiMarket website. Available at: https://optimarket.io/ (Accessed 23 May 2024).
222 OpenSea website. Available at: https://opensea.io/ (Accessed 23 May 2024).
223 Rarible website. Available at: https://rarible.com/ (Accessed 23 May 2024).
224 "Polygon and DraftKings Forms a Strategic Agreement" Polygon website, 18 October 2021. Available at: https://polygon.technology/blog/polygon-and-draftkings-forms-a-strategic-agreement (Accessed 20 May 2024).
225 Mavis Market website. Available at: https://marketplace.skymavis.com/ (Accessed 23 May 2024).
226 Lightning Bazaar website. Available at: https://lightningbazaar.com/ (Accessed 20 May 2024).
227 The Bitcoin Shop.uk website. Available at: https://thebitcoinshop.uk/ (Accessed 20 May 2024).
228 "An Introduction to Database Systems, Volume 1" C.J. Date, 1983, ISBN-13: 978-0321197849.
229 "An Introduction to Database Systems, Volume 2" C.J. Date, 1983, ISBN-13: 978-0201144741.

2

BUILDING BLOCKCHAINS AND APPLICATIONS

The ecosystem (C'mon everybody)

Introduction

This chapter is not as long as the previous one but is also designed to be modular as I aim to provide a foundational understanding of the technologies and services required to build blockchain networks, applications, and services.

Sometimes, this means going into the details (not everyone is interested in that). For those only wanting to understand the basics, the duck is always there to remind you of the key takeaways. For service provision, if you don't specifically want to dive into the weeds, jump to sections that start with "Choosing a…" as these summarise the main points.

In a few instances, I will introduce a term or a concept that is covered in detail in subsequent chapters, but this will be signposted with a quick definition, and glossary entries will be highlighted in bold.

DOI: 10.4324/9781003480761-3

What is a smart contract?

History and definition

Vitalik Buterin conceived Ethereum in 2013,[1] where he introduced the notion of smart contracts in his **white paper** "A Next-Generation Smart Contract and Decentralized Application Platform".[2] The Ethereum network went live in 2015 as a Proof of Work (PoW) blockchain, and as you already know, migrated to Proof of Stake (PoS) in September 2022 (aka "The Merge", see Chapter 3, Box 3.4). Vitalik's idea was to be able to record contracts in the form of a computer code, which would be activated automatically when certain conditions were met. This could potentially remove the need for trusted third parties to act as intermediaries (such as banks).

Since then, much hype and confusion have surrounded smart contracts. So much so that Vitalik himself, in a 2018 X (then Twitter) post I reproduce in Figure 2.1, regretted using the term in the first place. In my opinion, that's because there's nothing really "smart" about smart contracts 😉.

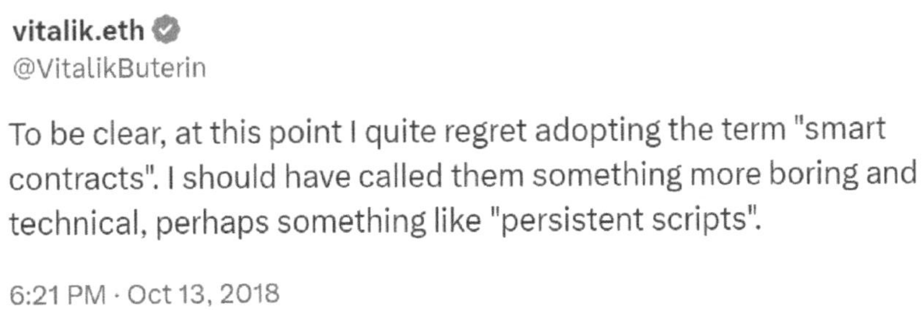

Figure 2.1 Vitalik Buterin on smart contracts.

BOX 2.1 WHAT IS A SMART CONTRACT?

A smart contract is digital code that offers a set of promises on predefined conditions agreed between the contracting parties and the main characteristics are:

- **They use blockchain technology to function**. In simple terms, this is the equivalent of what you would call an **overlay service**, such as

Request-to-Pay or **Variable Recurring Payment**, operating on top of centralised payment infrastructures.

- **The smart contract self-executes** when its conditions are met. It works on the "If, Then" principle, leaving no space for ambiguity.
- **Smart contracts can't interact with the real world**, but they usually will need real-world data to ensure that their conditions are met (e.g. asset prices, game results, etc.).
- Smart contracts form the backend of decentralised applications (see *dApps*).

The most popular blockchain for smart contracts is Ethereum, but there are others (e.g. Solana, Avalanche, Algorand, Cardano) as illustrated in Figure 2.2.

Foreseeing the potential of smart contracts, Vitalik Buterin envisioned a world where these contracts could power entirely new applications, independent of central control (decentralised applications or dApps).

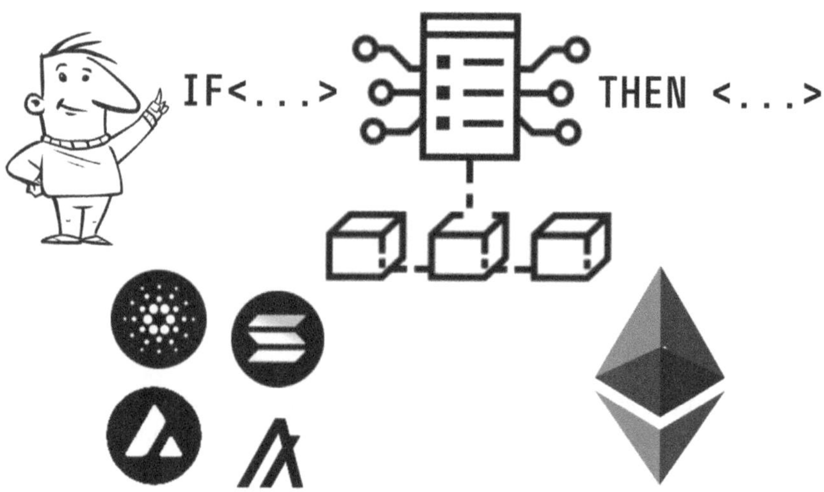

Figure 2.2 A smart contract. © 2024 Neira Jones.

Since we're going to use the term dApp quite often going forward, here's a simple definition:

BOX 2.2 WHAT IS A DAPP?

Decentralised applications (dApps) are blockchain-based distributed applications where the code and data are spread across multiple devices, eliminating a single point of control (or failure). Unlike traditional apps, dApps have a unique two-part structure:

- **Decentralised back-end**: at the heart of a dApp lies a smart contract, removing control from a central authority, and fostering trust and security in its operation. The smart contract encodes the dApp functionality. When a user interacts with the dApp, the smart contract code runs on all nodes, ensuring transparency and immutability.
- **Familiar end-user interface**: the user interface feels just like any other app, built using common web technologies for a seamless experience (see Table 2.3).

Smart contracts, usually publicly viewable on the blockchain, foster transparency and trust by allowing anyone to inspect the code and transactions associated with the dApp. Additionally, the underlying blockchain's consensus mechanism ensures agreement on the state of the dApp across the network and prevents manipulation by any individual node as the data associated with the dApp is stored on the public ledger, benefiting from the underlying blockchain's characteristics (e.g. immutability).

Several challenges stood in the way of Vitalik's vision of dApps: having a secure and accessible platform for dApps required solutions for standardisation, security, and decentralisation.

Ethereum virtual machine (EVM)

To address these challenges, Vitalik Buterin devised the **Ethereum Virtual Machine (EVM)**. This Ethereum-specific **Virtual Machine (VM)** provides a standardised environment for executing smart contracts. Think of it as a secure sandbox where code written in a familiar language can run on any EVM-compatible blockchain. In Chapter 1, I mention "Ethereum-compatible blockchains" (e.g. Avalanche as layer 1, and many layer 2 solutions such as Polygon, Arbitrum, and Optimism), you can now substitute that term for "EVM-compatible".

Having the EVM not only promotes **interoperability between blockchains** but also simplifies development. Additionally, the EVM enhances **security** by ensuring that smart contracts run in an isolated sandbox, preventing smart contract execution from directly modifying the blockchain state and thus mitigating the risk of vulnerabilities.

Finally, by **distributing smart contract execution** across a network of nodes, the EVM fosters decentralisation, a core principle of dApps. In essence, the EVM acts as the engine that powers the innovation of dApps within the Ethereum blockchain.

The Ethereum Virtual Machine **(EVM)** is an Ethereum-specific VM. By offering a familiar development environment, the EVM allows programmers to use existing tools and languages to create smart contracts, making blockchain development more accessible.

The EVM is probably the most well-known blockchain-specific VM, but smart contracts can be developed on non-EVM blockchains, including:

- **Solana VM (SVM)**: Solana, a performance-focused layer 1 blockchain, has its own VM. However, there are ongoing efforts to build an EVM on Solana, allowing developers to leverage existing tools and code.
- **Algorand Virtual Machine (AVM)**: Algorand, a layer 1 blockchain focusing on performance and low fees, uses its own VM, specifically designed for efficient and secure execution of smart contracts written in Teal, a low-level language.
- **Hyperledger Fabric VM**: This VM is designed for private and permissioned blockchains within the Hyperledger Fabric framework. It prioritises flexibility and modularity, allowing developers to customise the execution environment for specific use cases.

For completeness purposes, I should mention Cardano. Unlike Ethereum, EVM-compatible blockchains, and blockchains with their own VMs, Cardano isn't EVM-compatible, nor does it have a sandboxed VM environment. Cardano uses Plutus, its own smart contract language designed for formal verification of smart contracts. Smart contracts written in Plutus are compiled directly into machine code and executed on each Cardano node in the network. Formal verification of Plutus smart contracts can potentially enhance security compared to code execution in a VM, and this approach avoids the potential overhead of a separate VM layer, which could contribute to scalability. Drawbacks include the steep learning curve for Plutus and the limited interoperability with other platforms. This relatively new concept is sometimes referred to as "compile-to-chain" and Tezos is another example using this approach with their Michelson programming language.

Now that the concepts of smart contracts, blockchain-specific EVMs, and compile-to-chain examples have been introduced, let's look at an example.

A smart contract illustration

Let's imagine that John wants to buy Suzie's house. Suzie wants to sell her house for 2,000 ETH. John and Suzie don't know each other. They enter into a smart contract which contains the details of the transaction, and the steps are explained in Figure 2.3.

1. The **agreement is coded and stored** on the blockchain as Suzie sets the sale price and John agrees to buy at that price.
2. The **transactions are processed on the blockchain** (exchange of funds) as explained in Chapter 1, and **real-world obligations are fulfilled** (transfer house ownership).
3. Upon receipt of the funds from John, Suzie transfers the ownership of the house to John (in the real world). The **smart contract executes its conditions** by verifying that the funds have moved (on-chain), and that the ownership of Suzie's house has been transferred to John by using a service that allows the smart contract to interact with the real world. The **smart contract automatically finalises when all its conditions are met**.

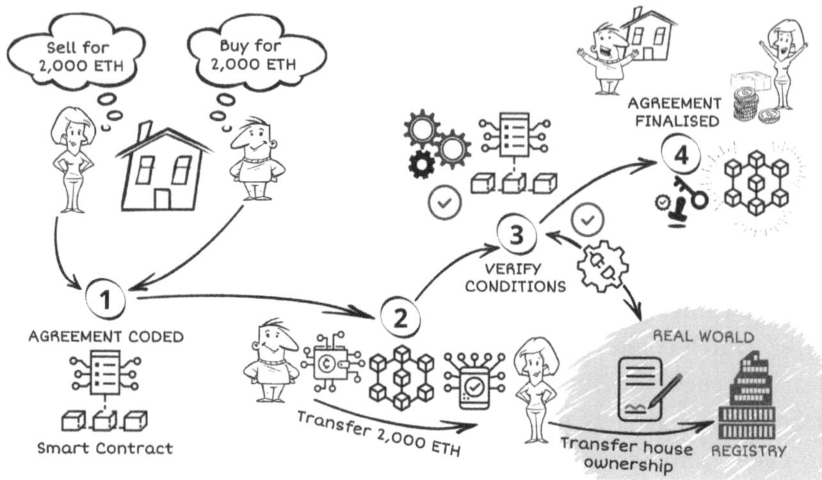

Figure 2.3 Buying a house through a smart contract. © 2024 Neira Jones.

4. All obligations have been discharged, Suzie has received the funds, John owns the house, and **the new state is recorded on the blockchain ledger**.

As we see from this example, John and Suzie didn't need to trust each other as the smart contract and blockchain infrastructure provided the trust framework. No intermediaries were involved.

In some geographies, smart contracts are recognised by law and may therefore be legally binding.

You may have noticed at step 3 that the smart contract needs an "intermediary" to interact with the real world, and this was also mentioned earlier in Box 2.1. In our example, the smart contract has to check whether ownership of the house has been transferred, which involves checking official records (e.g. land registry, recorder's office).

But blockchains, and therefore smart contracts, are isolated from the real world, essentially lacking the ability to fetch information from outside their own ecosystem. This is because, as you know by now, a blockchain is all about reaching consensus, so off-chain data couldn't be presented along with transaction data since other nodes would detect information coming from an "untrusted" source and reject it.

Therefore, the smart contract needs a data feed that is trusted by all nodes to provide off-chain, reliable, real-world, data.

Oracles

Oracles are third-party services that act as bridges, connecting blockchains to real-life (off-chain) data for smart contracts to use.

The types of data that a smart contract may want to query are numerous and include stock/asset prices, exchange rates, weather conditions, political events, games results, election results, geolocation and traceability information, static data (e.g. country codes), and much more. Unlike mythological oracles who communicate directly with god and can see the future, blockchain oracles can't see the future, they only retrieve information from the past (e.g. the official record of Suzie's house ownership changing to John).

Oracles perform their functions through APIs, proprietary corporate data feeds, and IoT feeds (e.g. sensors), and then relay the collected information to the smart contract as illustrated in Figure 2.4.

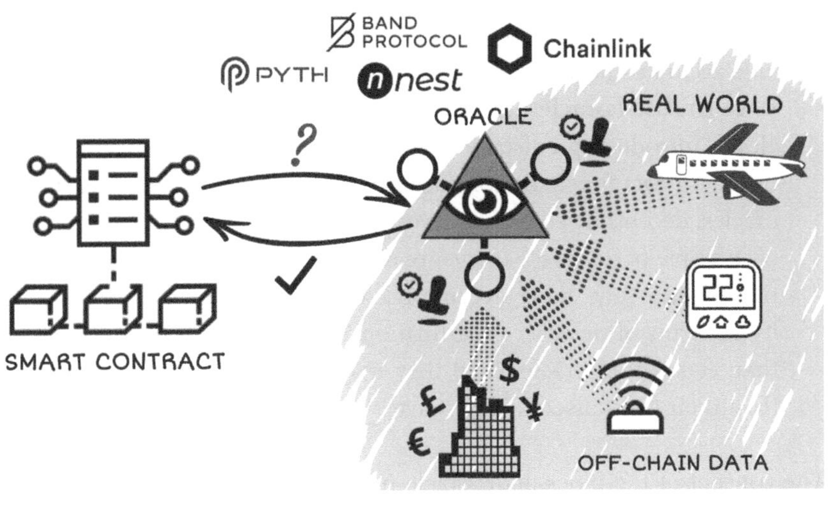

Figure 2.4 A blockchain oracle. © 2024 Neira Jones.

But how can an oracle be trusted? Here lies the blockchain oracle problem.

The core challenge of **the blockchain oracle problem** is securely connecting blockchains, inherently isolated environments, with real-world, off-chain data. This data is essential for smart contracts to function, but blockchains lack the ability to access it directly. Oracles act as bridges, fetching and translating external data, but ensuring its accuracy requires solutions that balance security with decentralisation. Security and trust issues arise when smart contracts depend on centralised oracles to provide off-chain information, potentially introducing vulnerabilities and single points of failure into otherwise decentralised systems. This problem underscores the need for robust, decentralised oracle solutions to maintain the integrity and security of blockchain applications that interact with external data. Solving this problem is crucial for unlocking the full potential of smart contracts.

There are two types of oracles:

- **Centralised oracles**: these rely on a single source for data controlled by the oracle provider, raising concerns about manipulation and single points of failure. They offer a straightforward, fast, and cost-effective solution for integrating basic off-chain data into smart contracts. The drawback is that users might not fully trust a single entity to provide accurate and unbiased data.
- **Decentralised oracles**: these address the limitations of centralised oracles by introducing a distributed network of nodes to gather and validate off-chain data for smart contracts. Unlike a single source in centralised oracles, decentralised oracles leverage the collective power and security of multiple participants to ensure data accuracy and prevent manipulation. Conversely, their decentralised nature can introduce complexity in terms of network coordination making them potentially slower than centralised oracles, and they may be more expensive to operate than their centralised counterparts.

The concept of the blockchain oracle problem directly relates to the challenges encapsulated by the blockchain trilemma (see Chapter 1, *The blockchain trilemma*):

- **Centralised oracles** offer security and scalability by relying on a single, trusted source. However, this approach sacrifices decentralisation, raising concerns about a single point of failure and potential manipulation.
- **Decentralised oracles** strive for decentralisation and security by distributing data validation across a network. However, achieving this can introduce complexity and potentially hinder scalability, leading to slower data retrieval compared to centralised solutions.

Therefore, oracles must implement solutions to address the trade-offs, and this is explained in Table 2.1.

Please note that the examples given in Table 2.1 will not necessarily exhibit all the mitigating features listed. In addition, I wasn't able to find references for centralised oracles, but a September 2023 Bank of International Settlements paper entitled "The oracle problem and the future of DeFi"[6] makes good reading.

If you want to understand why centralised oracles may present challenges, imagine a scenario where one is compromised, and a malicious actor manipulates the data feed for a particular asset. This would lead to unintended consequences or unfair outcomes for the applications relying on that data feed. For example, traders often use stop-loss orders to automatically sell assets if their price falls below a certain threshold. A compromised oracle could trigger these stop-loss orders prematurely, forcing traders to sell at a loss based on false data.

As ever with blockchain infrastructures, classification is difficult as, sometimes, you can't clearly categorise an oracle as either purely centralised or purely decentralised, including:

- **Centralised oracle with decentralised features**: whilst Chainlink[7] operates as a centralised oracle with a single entity managing the network (Chain Labs), it incorporates some decentralised aspects. These include a network of node operators who contribute to data security and reputation. Chainlink supports a vast array of data sources,

Table 2.1 Centralised and decentralised oracles: addressing the blockchain oracle problem. © 2024 Neira Jones

Mitigating the Oracle Blockchain Problem	**Centralised Oracles**	**Decentralised Oracles**
Scalability	Focus on specific and well-defined data sets to reduce the processing burden Implement mechanisms to cache frequently requested data or pre-aggregate data from multiple reliable sources	Leverage layer 2 scaling solutions Implement mechanisms to cache frequently requested data or pre-aggregate data from multiple reliable sources Develop specialised oracles for specific data types (financial data, weather data, etc.) to optimise data retrieval and validation processes for each use case
Security	Increase transparency by disclosing data sources and provide detailed information about the validation process Deploy Hardware Security Modules (HSMs) to store cryptographic keys and perform sensitive computations	Employ cryptographic techniques such as signature thresholds and multi-signature wallets to allow multiple nodes to collaboratively sign data without revealing their individual private keys Deploy incentivised dispute resolution mechanisms where nodes are rewarded for identifying and resolving data disputes Deploy decentralised key management systems to eliminate the risk of a single point of failure for cryptographic keys used by the oracle network
	Integrate with Trusted Execution Environments (TEE) which are secure and isolated off-chain environments (often called "secure enclaves") used for handling confidential data like financial information or trade secrets. Through multi-party computation (MPC) multiple nodes can collaboratively process sensitive data within a TEE without revealing their individual data points	

Mitigating the Oracle Blockchain Problem	**Centralised Oracles**	**Decentralised Oracles**
Decentralisation	Reputation systems: even within a centralised framework, the oracle provider can implement a reputation system for data sources where external entities providing data can earn a score based on historical accuracy	Blockchain interoperability to allow smart contracts to leverage data retrieved from another chain Applying formal verification techniques to the oracle code to mathematically prove the correctness and security properties of the system Leverage reputation systems where nodes with a proven track record of providing accurate data earn a higher score enabling users to prioritise data from highly rated nodes
Examples	Due to the very nature of centralised oracle deployments in any industry (e.g. confidentiality, competitive advantage), finding referenceable examples is difficult. Deployments may exist in a specific context or for internal enterprise-specific solutions, but these will be private	Band Protocol[3] is a cross-chain oracle that aggregates and connects APIs, price feeds, real-world event reports, and other data oracles to be used in all types of dApps and smart contracts Nest Oracle[4] was built specifically for the NEST cross-chain financial ecosystem. It retrieves data from various sources, including traditional financial APIs and public blockchains Pyth Network[5] is a price feed and market data oracle

including traditional financial APIs (e.g. market data), weather feeds, IoT sensor data, and real-world events. Financial services institutions such as SWIFT[8] and DTCC[9] have explored the use of Chainlink in capital markets.

- **Hybrid services**: Universal Market Access (UMA)[10] is an Ethereum-based protocol that functions as a hybrid oracle network, designed to facilitate DeFi contracts and crypto derivatives. It employs an "Optimistic Oracle" system, which assumes data is valid by default unless challenged within a specific time frame. If a dispute arises, it is resolved through a decentralised voting process involving UMA token holders, who are incentivised to ensure accurate data reporting. This hybrid approach combines the speed and efficiency of centralised data provision with the security and oversight of a decentralised community, allowing for quick data access whilst maintaining the integrity and trustworthiness essential for blockchain applications.

In any instance, blockchains and smart contracts can't directly access real-world data, and for this reason, they need oracles (at least at the time of writing). The future of oracles will hinge on specialisation, enhanced security, and interoperability. Imagine oracles optimised for specific data types, further secured by cutting-edge cryptography, and seamlessly retrieving information across blockchains. Artificial intelligence could revolutionise data analysis, identifying anomalies and even predicting trends. Whilst decentralisation remains a goal, hybrid solutions for optimal use cases may gain popularity. This evolution promises to not only empower smart contracts but also unlock entirely new blockchain applications reliant on secure, real-world data.

Where can smart contracts be used?

There are potentially several applications for smart contracts, including:

- Smart contracts for automation and efficiency:
    - Traditional financial processes often involve manual steps and paperwork, and these can leverage smart contracts for tasks such as **loan approvals** based on pre-defined criteria set within the code; **automatic release of funds** upon completion of specific

actions (e.g. property purchase); **streamlined trade finance processes** by automating document verification and payments upon fulfilment of conditions; **streamlined escrow processing** (amount, trust and authentication).
  - Traditional settlements can take several days due to manual processing and reconciliation, and smart contracts could: a**utomate settlements** by reducing manual intervention and leading to faster completion times; **potentially eliminate the need for intermediaries** in certain cases, further streamlining the process.
  - Traditional insurance processes can be resource-intensive and smart contracts could be used to streamline **insurance claims processing** and dispute resolution.
  - **Know Your Customer (KYC) streamlining**: smart contracts can be used to securely verify and store customer data, automating compliance checks and reducing onboarding friction.
- Smart contracts for enhanced traceability and record-keeping:
  - **Supply chain management**: smart contracts can be used to track the movement of goods throughout a supply chain, ensuring transparency and immutability of data. This can improve efficiency, reduce fraud, and enhance traceability.
  - **Ticketing and record-keeping**: smart contracts can be used to manage tickets for events or create permanent and verifiable records for important documents. This can eliminate fraud, streamline verification processes, and reduce the risk of loss or damage.
  - **Document provenance and authentication**: smart contracts can be used to track the origin and ownership history of important documents, reducing fraud and streamlining verification processes.
  - **Clinical trials**: smart contracts can be used to automate patient recruitment, data collection, and secure payments within a transparent and tamper-proof system.
  - **Gaming and collectibles**: smart contracts enable the management of in-game assets and create unique digital collectibles within blockchain games, enabling secure ownership and verifiable scarcity.
  - **Voting systems**: smart contracts would enable the creation of secure, transparent, and tamper-proof elections, potentially increasing voter participation and reducing fraud.

- **Internet of Things (IoT) integration**: smart contracts could be used to manage and automate interactions between connected devices, ensuring secure data exchange and potentially enabling new business models in the IoT space.
- **New business models**: smart contracts can enable entirely new business models that were not possible before due to limitations of traditional trust mechanisms. Some potential applications include:
  - **Decentralised marketplaces** where buyers and sellers can interact directly without intermediaries.
  - **Data monetisation**: smart contracts could enable individuals to control and sell their personal data securely to companies or researchers, creating a new data marketplace.
  - **Fractional ownership of assets**, allowing for greater accessibility and divisibility of ownership rights.
  - **Decentralised Finance (DeFi)**: new financial services are emerging, including peer-to-peer (P2P) lending, borrowing, decentralised insurance, and trading without relying on traditional intermediaries (DeFi is covered in detail later in this chapter).
  - **Decentralised Autonomous Organisations (DAOs)**: DAOs are essentially communities governed by smart contracts and could be used for various purposes like collective ownership or investment (this is covered in more detail in Chapter 3, *Blockchain operations and governance*).
  - **Self-sovereign identity management**, empowering individuals to control their data and securely share it with authorised parties (see Chapter 7, Box 7.3).

Here are two real-life examples I found interesting:

- **De Beers Group**: this diamond giant leveraged smart contracts to track diamond provenance in order to enhance transparency and help prevent the sale of conflict diamonds. The smart contract stores information about each diamond, including its origin, characteristics, and ownership history. Through smart contracts, De Beers encourages sightholders to use the Tracr[11] platform to register their ownership of diamonds purchased from them and update the diamond location, or ownership further down the supply chain. De Beers' Tracr blockchain keeps tabs on 1.5 million registered diamonds, and a recent 2023 partnership with Sarine[12] suggests that the project is doing well.

- **Livepeer**[13]: this decentralised streaming infrastructure leverages smart contracts to distribute revenue fairly to content creators. Viewers pay to access a live stream using cryptocurrency through a smart contract which distributes the revenue amongst content creators and node operators who contribute to the streaming infrastructure.

Of course, more possibilities will emerge as the technology evolves.

Blockchain application types

In the previous section, I mentioned dApps, but you may not be surprised to discover that not all blockchain applications are decentralised, similar to "not all blockchains are decentralised" (see *Chapter 1, Permissioned blockchains*).

Here, I try to classify the different types of blockchain applications, but I'm not the font of all knowledge. Some may disagree with my definitions and categorisations, which is fine in this nascent field, but at least they give you a framework that may help with understanding. Classification of applications in the blockchain space can be nuanced.

Centralised applications (CApps)

Centralised Application (CApp) is a broad term encompassing any application that interacts with a blockchain in some way and is **controlled by a single entity**. A CApp **primarily operates on blockchain technology** – leveraging one or more blockchains – but will have some elements built on traditional databases. A CApp may lack features like trustless transactions or native governance mechanisms and the level of centralised control can vary depending on the implementation. An example could be a loyalty programme managed by a company that uses blockchain to store points but has centralised control over how they are issued and redeemed.

Examples in financial services include:

- **Securitize**[14]: this platform provides an environment for the issuance and management of digital securities on a blockchain. Whilst the platform leverages blockchain technology across multiple blockchains for security and transparency, Securitize itself acts as a central authority, managing user access, compliance, and **asset tokenisation** processes. As you may imagine, Securitize is a regulated entity wherever it operates as securities are heavily regulated worldwide.
- **Compound**[15]: this platform allows users to lend and borrow cryptocurrencies in a peer-to-peer (P2P) manner. It offers features like earning interest on deposited crypto and borrowing assets at variable interest rates. Whilst the core functionalities rely on the Ethereum blockchain, Compound Labs maintains control over smart contract upgrades and protocol governance, although it allows for some community participation.

An example outside of financial services is Provenance,[16] a CApp built on the Hyperledger Fabric to track the origin and journey of goods throughout a supply chain. Whilst the core data (e.g. product information, location) resides on the blockchain for security and immutability, Provenance itself operates as a centralised application where user interaction primarily occurs through centralised servers managed by the Provenance Association, the single controlling entity.

In my first book, I introduced the "Regulations at the Edges Principle", I reproduce it here:

BOX 2.3 THE REGULATIONS AT THE EDGES PRINCIPLE

When something unregulated starts touching something regulated, regulations will soon affect the unregulated thing, until, in time, what is unregulated becomes regulated.

Neira Jones, August 2023

CApps will of course be affected by this principle, as it becomes obvious that using blockchain technology doesn't necessarily mean that regulatory compliance isn't a requirement.

Blockchain-enabled applications

Blockchain-enabled applications use blockchain technology for specific functionalities but might not be fully built on a blockchain. These applications may offer some level of decentralisation (e.g. data storage, traceability) and may have a permissioned access system. The level of centralised control can vary depending on the application and its use of blockchain technology. Permissioned blockchain deployments might offer more centralisation, whilst public blockchains can introduce a greater degree of decentralisation for specific functionalities. For instance, a supply chain management system could use blockchain technology to track the movement of goods whilst operating primarily on traditional databases.

Examples in financial services include:

- **TradeIX**[17]: this platform streamlines trade finance processes by using blockchain technology for secure document management and automating key steps. It integrates with existing trade finance systems, leveraging blockchain for specific functionalities but doesn't operate as a fully decentralised application.
- **Fnality International**[18]: this company provides a blockchain-enabled platform for the post-trade settlement of securities. They integrate with existing financial market infrastructure and use blockchain technology for automating processes and reducing settlement risks. Whilst Fnality offers some elements of decentralisation for specific functions, it remains a centralised platform overall and boasts 20 major institutions as shareholders: Banco Santander, BNY Mellon, Barclays, BNP Paribas, CIBC, Commerzbank, DTCC, Euroclear, Goldman Sachs, ING, KBC Group, Lloyds Banking Group, Mizuho Financial Group, MUFG Bank, Nasdaq, Nomura, Sumitomo Mitsui Banking Corporation, State Street Corporation, UBS, and Wisdom Tree. As an example, Fnality became the first **omnibus account** holder at the Bank of England.[19,20] The omnibus account allows a payment system operator to access the Bank's **RTGS** system in a new way where payment system's participants will be able to pool funds within a single account, allowing them

to utilise those funds to settle payment-related transactions across the payment system on a 24/7 basis.

An example outside of financial service is the IBM Food Trust,[21] an application that leverages blockchain technology to track foodborne illness outbreaks. Whilst it interacts with a blockchain for data storage and transparency, its core functionalities and data access are not fully decentralised, and it maintains a permissioned access system.

The examples given showcase how blockchain technology can be integrated into existing applications to enhance specific functionalities without requiring a fully decentralised or fully centralised structure. Suffice to say that these implementations, especially in financial services, will be subject to applicable regulations.

dApps

A dApp (decentralised application) is a software application built on a blockchain that achieves a significantly higher degree of decentralisation than a blockchain-enabled application. The dApp core functionality and data reside on the blockchain without a single point of control over the application or the data it stores.

It's also worth noting that "DApp", "dApp", and "Dapps" are all common abbreviations for decentralised applications, with "dApp" being the most widely recognised format.

A dApp consists of two main elements as illustrated in Figure 2.5:

- **a smart contract** at the back-end,
- **a front-end user interface**: just like any app, the user interface (UI) is usually built using traditional web technology (e.g. HTLM, CSS, Javascript, React, Vue.js) to enable user-friendly interaction with the smart contract back-end.

The level of decentralisation may vary depending on the blockchain (e.g. permissionless vs. permissioned) and the smart contract design (i.e. the level of control users have over the dApp).

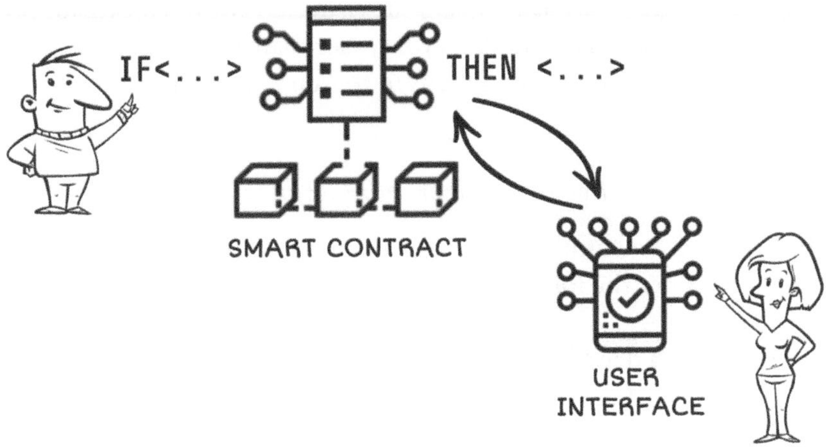

Figure 2.5 A dApp. © 2024 Neira Jones.

Whilst I will explain how to build dApps later in this chapter, I will only concentrate on the elements related to blockchain integration that may be unfamiliar for those used to traditional development (rather than detailing how to build a user interface). As for smart contracts, which form the back-end of the dApp, as these live on the blockchain, anyone participating in that network can inspect the code and transactions associated with it. This is an interesting concept and will be detailed later in *How to build a smart contract?* and *How to build a dApp?*

dApp implementations vary across industries:

- **Financial services**: borrowing, lending, and trading financial instruments without relying on traditional institutions.
- **Gaming**: managing in-game assets and creating P2P marketplaces.
- **Supply chain management**: transparent tracking of goods.

Popular dApps include Uniswap (on Ethereum blockchain) and PancakeSwap (on Binance Smart Chain), both leading decentralised crypto exchanges where users can swap cryptocurrencies with each other through transactions facilitated by smart contracts.

Because dApps essentially inherit the characteristics of blockchains (see Chapter 1, *Are blockchains scalable*), they may face challenges where transaction throughput is a requirement, such as in consumer payments.

Recap on blockchain application types

When considering using or building blockchain applications **professionals should consider the following:**

- **How much decentralisation?** Blockchain applications exist on a spectrum, from fully centralised (CApps) to fully decentralised (dApps). Professionals should consider the appropriate level of decentralisation based on factors like data privacy needs, regulatory compliance, and the desired level of trust.
- **CApp considerations**: CApps offer benefits like familiarity and existing infrastructure but come with central control and potential regulatory hurdles. Professionals building CApps should prioritise robust access controls and ensure compliance with relevant regulations.
- **Blockchain-enabled applications**: these applications leverage blockchain for specific functionalities, potentially improving efficiency or transparency. However, they may not offer full decentralisation. Professionals should carefully assess the degree of decentralisation achieved and potential reliance on centralised systems.
- **dApp considerations**: whilst dApps offer true decentralisation and increased trust, they can be more complex to develop and integrate. Scalability and user experience can also be challenges. Professionals building dApps should prioritise user-friendly interfaces and explore solutions for scalability.
- **Performance and scalability**: blockchain applications need to consider not just decentralisation and security but also performance and scalability. This means evaluating factors like transaction throughput, latency, and potential bottlenecks to ensure the application can handle user demand. These considerations are especially important for applications targeting high transaction volumes, such as consumer payments.
- **Regulatory landscape**: regulations are still evolving for blockchain applications. Professionals should stay up-to-date on relevant regulations and ensure their applications comply to avoid potential legal or operational roadblocks.

TradFi, CeFi, CeDeFi, and DeFi

If you're reading this book, you already understand traditional, centralised, financial services systems. In blockchain circles, **TradFi** is the term used to refer to these (which are extensively covered in my first book).

As blockchain technology became more interesting for specific use cases, the traditional financial services industry saw new ways of using blockchain characteristics and properties. This is exemplified in the previous section and is how the term "CeFi" was coined.

BOX 2.4 WHAT IS CeFI?

CeFi (Centralised Finance) is enabled by financial services CApps and/or blockchain-enabled applications where participants are financial services institutions who want to leverage the potential of blockchain technology to offer familiar financial services within a centralised framework. They can benefit from:

- **Centralised control**: whilst CeFi applications leverage blockchain technology, core functionality, such as user management, remains under the control of the institution using centralised systems.
- **Increased security**: the immutability of blockchain technology means that records are tamper-proof which can improve security for specific functionalities within CeFi applications, reducing fraud and errors.
- **Improved transparency**: a shared ledger between known participants on the blockchain allows for greater transparency in transactions and data, improving trust and auditability for CeFi institutions.
- **Streamlined processes**: blockchain technology can automate tasks like document verification or trade settlement steps, leading to faster processing times and reduced manual work within CeFi systems.
- **Compliance**: CeFi applications, such as custodial crypto exchanges, must comply with applicable regulations.

Whilst CeFi applications can leverage the security and transparency benefits of blockchain technology, their transaction throughput is often limited by the blockchain integration with traditional centralised infrastructure. This can hinder their ability to match the speed required for applications requiring high transaction volumes and fast transaction speeds such as consumer payments.

Given all this, you now won't be surprised to see that all the examples I gave earlier for CApps and blockchain-enabled applications in financial services are all in trade finance and settlement, with a notable absence of consumer payments use cases! (see also Table 2.2)

Because I aim to demystify jargon, let's pause for a minute before we move on to the next section and explain a few acronyms around this.

BOX 2.5 WHAT IS DeFI?

- **Decentralised finance (DeFi)** represents an alternative financial ecosystem built on blockchain technology. Unlike TradFi or CeFi, DeFi applications use dApps to facilitate P2P financial transactions and services without intermediaries. This fosters a more open and transparent financial system but also comes with inherent risks and limitations. Key characteristics include:
- **Decentralised control**: DeFi eliminates the need for central authorities and users maintain control over their assets through private keys or seed phrases, enabling self-custody and censorship resistance.
- **Security**: blockchain technology offers a high degree of security through cryptography and immutability. However, smart contract vulnerabilities and individual responsibility for asset security remain challenges.
- **Transparency**: transactions are recorded on a public, shared ledger, enabling anyone to view and verify them. This fosters trust and accountability within the DeFi ecosystem.
- **Streamlined processes**: smart contracts automate financial agreements and processes, potentially leading to faster transaction settlements and reduced operational costs compared to traditional financial systems.
- **Limited compliance**: DeFi operates largely outside the purview of traditional financial regulations. This can pose challenges for user protection and overall stability within the ecosystem.

Whilst DeFi offers a vision of a more open and accessible financial system, it's important to be aware of its limitations. Decentralisation can lead to complexity for users, potential security vulnerabilities in smart contracts, and a lack of regulatory oversight. DeFi is a rapidly evolving landscape, and navigating it requires a strong understanding of the associated risks and opportunities.

BOX 2.6 WHAT IS CeDeFI?

Centralised decentralised finance (CeDeFi) bridges the gap between CeFi and DeFi. Built by financial institutions as the core service providers, CeDeFi applications may leverage a blend of technologies: CApps, blockchain-enabled applications, and centralised systems. They offer functionalities typically associated with DeFi within a centralised framework, allowing for a familiar and more accessible user experience by combining DeFi functionalities with a familiar CeFi user experience. The key characteristics include:

- **Centralised control**: financial institutions maintain control over core functionalities like user management and account security, potentially enhancing user trust and streamlining onboarding processes.
- **Increased security**: the immutability of blockchain technology can potentially enhance security for specific functionalities within CeDeFi applications and the involvement of financial institutions and regulatory oversight could potentially enhance security compared to some DeFi protocols.
- **Transparency**: a shared ledger system can contribute to greater transparency within CeDeFi platforms, although the level of transparency may be impacted by centralised control compared to pure DeFi.
- **Streamlined processes**: blockchain technology can automate tasks, potentially leading to faster processing times within CeDeFi systems. An example could be automating smart contract execution for specific DeFi actions within the CeDeFi platform, reducing manual work and potentially expediting transactions.
- **Compliance**: CeDeFi applications operate within a regulated environment, ensuring compliance with applicable regulations and potentially fostering greater user protection and stability compared to DeFi. Specific functionalities offered by CeDeFi and regulations governing CeDeFi applications may vary depending on the jurisdiction.

CeDeFi applications leverage the security and transparency benefits of blockchain technology, but their performance is often limited by the blockchain integration with traditional centralised infrastructure. Whilst CeDeFi offers a blend of benefits from both CeFi and DeFi, it's important to note that it may not offer the same level of decentralisation, transparency, or user control over assets as pure DeFi platforms.

Table 2.2 TradFi, CeFi, CeDeFi, and DeFi: a comparison. © 2024 Neira Jones

Feature	**TradFi (traditional finance)**	**CeFi (centralised finance)**	**CeDeFi (centralised decentralised finance)**	**DeFi (decentralised finance)**
Control	Centralised	Centralised (financial institutions with blockchain integration)	Hybrid (centralised control for user management, potentially decentralised for specific functions)	Decentralised (no central authority, governed by code and community)
Technology	Traditional databases and infrastructure, traditional application development	Blockchain technology integrated with existing financial systems Traditional application development, CApps, blockchain-enabled applications	Hybrid Centralised infrastructure with blockchain for specific functionalities Traditional application development, CApps, blockchain-enabled applications	Primarily blockchain-based dApps
Regulation	Heavily regulated	Regulated	Emerging regulatory landscape	Largely unregulated
Transparency	Limited transparency	Improved transparency through blockchain for specific functions	Aims for transparency through a shared ledger but may involve some centralised control	Highly transparent (all transactions publicly viewable on a blockchain)

Feature	**TradFi (traditional finance)**	**CeFi (centralised finance)**	**CeDeFi (centralised decentralised finance)**	**DeFi (decentralised finance)**
Security	Relies on traditional security measures	Aims to leverage blockchain's immutability for enhanced security	Aims to combine centralised security measures with blockchain security features	Relies on smart contract security and network consensus
Accessibility	Generally accessible to most users	Accessible through established financial institutions	Accessibility may vary depending on platform	Accessible to anyone with an internet connection and a non-custodial crypto wallet
Innovation	Some innovation	Can offer some innovation through blockchain integration	Aims to combine traditional financial services with DeFi innovation	Highly innovative due to open-source development and experimentation
Complexity	Relatively simple and user-friendly	More complex than TradFi due to integration with blockchain	Can vary depending on the platform, potentially offering a mix of simple and complex features	Highly complex due to the decentralised nature and reliance on smart contracts
Examples	Banks, regulated payment institutions, investment firms, payment schemes	Custodial crypto exchanges offering fiat deposits or withdrawals, security token offerings on a blockchain	Platforms offering some DeFi features but with centralised control over user assets	Self-custodial wallets, decentralised exchanges (DEXs), trading, yield farming, peer-to-peer lending / borrowing protocols

Table 2.2 gives you a comparison between TradFi, CeFi, CeDeFi, and DeFi (we'll explore the latter in a bit more detail later).

Table 2.2 is yet another example of the Regulations at the Edges Principle (see Box 2.3) in action 😉.

More seriously, many will confuse TradFi and CeFi, and when you add CeDeFi and DeFi into the mix, the fog often thickens. I hope Table 2.2 cleared that up. I will not cover CeFi or CeDeFi in more detail as their characteristics are embodied in CApps and blockchain-enabled applications, which were covered earlier. But DeFi is worth a closer look.

Lifting the veil on DeFi

Box 2.5 gave you the standard definition of DeFi, and Table 2.2 positioned it against the other models. It may seem relatively simple (or not!), but there is still a lot of confusion around the term and where it applies. So here's an alternative definition:

> DeFi is a generic term for decentralised financial services with an open infrastructure operating on a permissionless basis using a blockchain settlement layer where users control their assets. Services may include investments, insurance, asset management, payments, lending, and trading.

To determine whether a financial service is DeFi, you must ask a few questions:

Of course, any service you might assess for its "DeFiness" may exhibit the characteristics shown in Figure 2.6 to varying degrees, but at least it's a good starting point.

To summarise, here are our four assessment questions:

1. **Is it a financial service or product involving a transfer of assets?** Typically, what you're looking for is for a transfer of value to take place. If no transfer of value takes place (e.g. decentralised oracle for financial services usage, decentralised storage service), the service wouldn't be classified as DeFi, even if used in financial services.

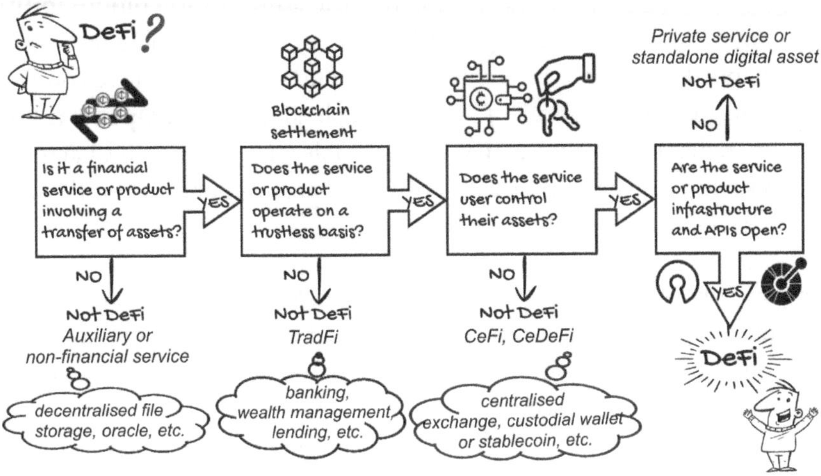

Figure 2.6 How will I know if it's really DeFi? © 2024 Neira Jones.

2. **Does the service or product operate on a trustless basis?** Whilst implementations may vary, DeFi products or services should operate on permissionless blockchains, which don't require trust in a counterparty or third-party intermediary, and their functionality is defined by smart contracts.
3. **Does the service user control their assets?** This means that the assets issued or managed by DeFi services can't be expropriated or altered by any party other than the account owner. The assets are however subject to the logic of the underlying smart contract code and the relevant DeFi protocols (which may affect the economic rights of account holders). For example, a custodial (centralised) exchange, where account holders are not in control of their keys, is not a DeFi service.
4. **Does the service operate on an open infrastructure?** This means that the underlying source code will be publicly available, which may take the form of an **Open-Source** infrastructure and Open APIs. This transparency fosters trust and empowers participants to create their own version or build derivative services on top of it. In addition, open APIs enable third-party developers to understand, extend, and verify the security of DeFi services. Open Source code and Open APIs allow for automated and permissionless access to DeFi services as well as **programmability** where DeFi instruments can be customised

and extended dynamically. This in turn brings us to **composability**, where these "financial Legos" (the programmable components) can be snapped together to create intricate products, from derivative contracts to insured loans. Think of it as the rough equivalent of **Open Banking** in TradFi. For example, a fiat-backed stablecoin (covered in Chapter 4), with its value pegged on a 1:1 basis to a fiat currency, can't be classified as DeFi, and hopefully, you know why 😉.

As you may imagine, DeFi is also characterised by its decentralised governance models, which is why regulators and policymakers get hot under the collar just thinking about it, but more on that in Chapter 3, *Decentralised Autonomous Organisation (DAO)*.

DeFi offers opportunities to earn rewards on cryptocurrency holdings. **Yield farming** is a strategy where users stake their crypto assets in DeFi protocols or platforms to generate returns. These returns can come in various forms, including protocol tokens native to a particular DeFi platform. By staking their assets, users help provide **liquidity** to the DeFi platform and earn rewards in the form of these tokens. In addition, some DeFi platforms offer interest on deposited assets, similar to a traditional savings account but with potentially higher yields. Yield farming can be a complex strategy and not for the faint-hearted. Users should be aware of the associated risks, such as **impermanent loss**, smart contract vulnerabilities, and high volatility.

Measuring the success of DeFi applications is complex, but one popular metric is **Total Value Locked (TVL)**, which represents the total value locked inside the DeFi platform. Think of it as the rough equivalent of total deposits for a bank, or assets under management for investment funds. A higher TVL will generally indicate a more established DeFi protocol, but it guarantees neither its safety nor its profitability. With this caveat in mind, yield farming potential can be explored using popular blockchain explorers such as coinmarketcap.com, or dedicated DeFi explorers such as defilama.com and dappradar.com, where TVL for the top platforms listed run in the billions of dollars. There are also some notable horror stories: yield farming platform Pancake Bunny (2021, $44 million loss),[22] Meerkat Finance exploit (2023, $31 million loss, leading to the collapse of the platform).[23]

Whilst yield farming may offer opportunities for those so-inclined, DeFi encompasses a broader range of services and instruments as the landscape continues to evolve. One noteworthy concept is the **flash loan**. Imagine borrowing a massive amount of crypto for a short period without any collateral. Flash loans enable this by leveraging smart contracts to execute a complex financial manoeuvre within a single transaction without any collateral (!). They are powerful tools for **arbitrage** opportunities in the hands of experienced users but carry significant risks due to their complexity, and potential exploitation if not executed flawlessly. There are a few horror stories: the DAO hack (2016 – $150 million loss),[24] Mango Market exploit (2022, over $100 million loss),[25] Deus Finance Exploit (2023, $6 million loss),[26] and Radiant Capital flash loan attack (January 2024, $4.5 million loss and October 2024, $51 million loss),[27] to name but a few.

GameFi: revolutionising gaming with DeFi

As DeFi attempts to disrupt traditional financial systems, its potential influence is reaching into the world of entertainment through a concept called **GameFi**. I include this here for completeness, although gaming is not strictly speaking "payments", but we can learn lessons, draw parallels, and payments companies may leverage opportunities.

GameFi represents the convergence of gaming and DeFi, creating a new wave of games where players can not only enjoy themselves but also earn cryptocurrencies or tokens by playing games. This fundamentally changes the traditional gaming model where players consume content without the potential to earn any financial rewards.

Play-to-Earn (P2E)

P2E games are the foundation of GameFi, rewarding players with coins or tokens for the time and effort they invest in playing. Players may earn rewards by completing quests and challenges within the game, engaging in competitive battles against other players, collecting and trading in-game assets, and owning and managing virtual assets like land or characters within the virtual world.

The earned coins/tokens can hold value within the game's ecosystem, allowing players to purchase in-game items or upgrades. They can also be traded on external marketplaces for real-world value, potentially turning playtime into a source of income.

Beyond Play-to-Earn

Whilst earning rewards is a core aspect, GameFi goes beyond just P2E mechanics as it often integrates other DeFi elements, such as:

- **NFT-based in-game assets**: GameFi titles might leverage **Non-Fungible Tokens (NFTs)**, covered in Chapter 5, to represent ownership of in-game items or characters which players can then trade on decentralised marketplaces.
- **Decentralised marketplaces**: these platforms, built on blockchain technology, enable players to buy, sell, and trade their NFT-based in-game assets.
- **Yield farming**: some GameFi projects allow players to stake their earned tokens or NFTs to generate additional rewards, similar to DeFi yield farming. This incentivises players to hold onto their in-game assets and participate more actively in the game's economy.

The future of gaming?

GameFi presents a glimpse into a potential future for gaming when entertainment merges with financial opportunity. It empowers players through ownership of in-game assets and creates a more dynamic and potentially lucrative gaming experience. As both DeFi and GameFi continue to evolve, we can expect even more innovative ways for players to interact with these evolving digital economies.

What next?

Well, that's the end of our ecosystem section. There are of course more players that I yet have to introduce properly, such as wallets, crypto exchanges, and marketplaces, but these are not needed in this chapter, and we'll look at them in Chapter 6, *Transacting in a decentralised world*.

Next, we'll look at technologies and service providers supporting this ecosystem, as well as how to build blockchains and applications. If you're not interested in the details, jump to the duck in each subsection, and you may want to jump to *What about traditional payments?* where terms covered in the technical sections will be highlighted in bold, and then you can jump back if you want to know more.

Programming languages (Java jive)

Ah. This brings me back years to the time when I was an analyst programmer in financial services. In those heady nerdy days, most core banking systems were developed in COBOL, but if you wanted to be funky and cool, you could use Fortran, and those more IBM-bound might have used RPG. If you wanted to be completely "out there" and "progressive", your boss might even let you use Pascal… (Can you guess how old I am now? 😉).

Today, every day, "3 trillion dollars' worth of transactions are handled by a 64-year-old programming language that hardly anybody knows anymore"[28] and you guessed it, it's COBOL. It's no longer taught in schools. 43% of all banking systems rely on it, handling USD3 trillion of daily transactions including 95% of all ATM activity in the US, and 80% of all face-to-face card transactions. Experienced COBOL programmers who had long retired or moved on to other things are now coming back to help with maintaining this vast estate of legacy systems (sometimes driving Ferraris, as my friend Chris Skinner highlighted in his article "Anyone want to hire an old man who knows COBOL?"[29]).

Obviously, blockchains are not built using COBOL, but they still use mature programming languages, as well as newer ones. I won't bother ordering them by popularity, because such matters are always subjective, but you can look at some references which offer different rankings according to their own criteria.[30,31,32,33] I will, however, give you two tables for the most mature and less mature languages so you can decide for yourself.

Mature programming languages

Table 2.3 offers a glimpse into how mature programming languages are used in blockchain projects.

Emerging programming languages

Table 2.4 gives you a list of new or emerging programming languages popular with blockchain developers.

Note 1: yes, you read right! Libra, the now-defunct Facebook stablecoin project (later renamed Diem), was built using the Move language. The Diem Association closed its doors in 2022, but some members formed Aptos Labs[35] to continue developing blockchain technology based on Move.

The names of programming languages are so much cooler today!

Table 2.3 Mature programming languages used in blockchain projects. © 2024 Neira Jones

Language	Main Characteristics	Main Focus	Best Suited For	Example
SQL	First used in the 1970s, a mature interpreted standard language for relational databases, used for interacting with blockchain data stored in databases	Data management, analytics	Data management, analytics	The Graph[34]
C++	First used in 1979, a mature compiled object-oriented language with a large developer community offering high performance and low-level control	Performance, security	Performance-critical blockchain systems	Bitcoin, EOS, Litecoin, Ripple, Stellar
Python	First used in 1991, a mature interpreted general-purpose language, easy to learn, with a large community, popular for blockchain development tools	Ease of use, versatility	Back-end development, scripting, data analysis	Ethereum development tools, Algorand
PHP	First used in 1994, a mature interpreted general-purpose language, with limited use in core blockchain development but used in some frameworks for blockchain integration	Ease of use, web development	Back-end development (niche)	Hyperledger Composer

Language	Main Characteristics	Main Focus	Best Suited For	Example
Java	First used in 1995, a mature compiled object-oriented language with a large developer community, popular for permissioned blockchains	Performance, versatility	Enterprise blockchains, back-end development	IOTA, NEO, Corda, Hyperledger Fabric
Ruby	First used in 1995, a mature interpreted general-purpose language, known for developer productivity but with limited use in core blockchain development	Ease of use, developer productivity	Back-end development, smart contracts (niche)	Ethereum Rubies smart contracts
Javascript	First used in 1995, a mature interpreted ubiquitous language for web development, used for building user interfaces for dApps and mobile applications	Ease of use, web development	Front-end development, dApp interaction	Uniswap
C#	First used in 2000, a mature compiled object-oriented language similar to Java, primarily used for Microsoft's .NET blockchain frameworks	Performance, versatility	Back-end development, smart contracts (niche)	NEO blockchain

Table 2.4 Emerging programming languages used in blockchain projects. © 2024 Neira Jones

Language	**Main Characteristics**	**Main Focus**	**Best Suited For**	**Examples**
Go (Golang)	Developed by Google in 2009, this compiled language is gaining popularity	Performance, concurrency	Back-end development, high-performance systems	Hyperledger Fabric, Cosmos
Rust	This modern compiled language appeared in 2010 has strong memory safety features and is gaining traction in blockchain circles due to increased security focus	Performance, security, concurrency	High-performance systems, security-critical applications	Solana, Polkadot, Near Protocol, Filecoin, Cosmos
Solidity	Created in 2014 for the Ethereum Virtual Machine, this compiled language is very popular with the Ethereum ecosystem	Security, Ethereum-specific	Smart contract development (dApps)	Ethereum (smart contracts) Cryptokitties, Aave, Uniswap
Plutus	This Cardano-specific compiled functional language emerged in 2016 and focuses on security and formal verification	Security, verifiability	Smart contract development	Cardano
Kotlin	Created in 2016. A compiled language	Security, scalability, interoperability	Smart contract development	R3 Corda, Lisk, Tezos, Cosmos

Language	Main Characteristics	Main Focus	Best Suited For	Examples
Scilla	This compiled language emerged in 2017 and is designed for security and formal verification on the Zilliqa blockchain	Security, scalability	Smart contract development (Zilliqa)	Zilliqa
CX	A secure, compiled and interpreted functional language launched in 2017 designed for smart contracts with a focus on formal verification. Linked to the Skycoin blockchain	Security, verifiability	Research & experimentation	Likely defunct, limited information available
Simplicity	A compiled language that emerged in 2017 designed for safety and ease of reasoning	Security, simplicity	Smart contract development	Kadena blockchain
Rholang	A compiled language that emerged in 2017 designed for formal verification of smart contracts specific to the RChain blockchain	Security, concurrency	Smart contract development (RChain)	RChain
Move	Developed by Facebook in 2017, this compiled language focused on safety and resource management on the Libra blockchain	Security, resource management	Smart contract development (Libra)	Aptos, Sui, Starcoin, Libra (see note 1)
Vyper	A compiled language (subset of Python) launched in 2018 designed to address security vulnerabilities on Ethereum. Similar to solidity	Security	Smart contract development (Ethereum)	Ethereum

Choosing a programming language

There is a lot of choice in blockchain programming languages, and **professionals starting a blockchain project should compare their properties, characteristics, and pros and cons depending on the planned application.**

- Traditional languages as shown in Table 2.3 are still relevant and their value shouldn't be underestimated. C++ may be used for performance-critical blockchain components, and SQL remains important for interacting with blockchain data stored in relational databases. For less mature blockchain languages (see Table 2.4), Solidity remains the most popular for Ethereum and EVM-compatible blockchains, whilst Java remains a prominent framework.
- Beyond the familiarity of the established stalwarts, newer languages are emerging with unique strengths: Rust has gained popularity for high-performance blockchain applications, whilst security-focused projects may prefer Move and Simplicity, although these languages may have smaller developer communities.
- Ultimately, the best language choice will depend on the project's needs. The blockchain landscape continues to evolve at pace and the trick is to keep up-to-date with new developments.

Blockchain development environments (with a little help from my friends)

In traditional development environments, you may be familiar with frameworks such as React or Express.js for Javascript, Django for Python, Ruby on Rails for Ruby, Flutter for mobile applications, or ASP.NET MVC for C#. They provide developers with a coding workspace (i.e. a virtual workshop) with a set of tools such as code editors, debuggers, APIs, and libraries of pre-built components.

Development frameworks provide an abstraction layer that acts as an intermediary between the developer and the complexities of the programming language, operating system, or specific underlying infrastructure. They allow developers to focus on application logic rather than getting bogged down in low-level details.

Blockchain development frameworks or platforms fulfil the same function as traditional development frameworks, the only difference is that they are **specific to blockchain developments**. For developers, choosing the right framework or platform will depend on several factors, including the project needs, such as whether the blockchain is public or permissioned (see Chapter 1, *Blockchain types*), the performance required of the application, the development team's programming language expertise, and the range and types of tools offered by the framework.

Public blockchain frameworks

A **public blockchain development framework** provides a development environment for public, open networks for businesses looking to leverage the potential of blockchain technology for **general-purpose applications**.

First, they offer **pre-built modules and tools for common blockchain development tasks** including consensus mechanism interaction, smart contract development, and identity management for an open network of participants.

Second, they offer an **abstraction layer** to hide the complexities of the underlying blockchain protocol (see Chapter 1, Box 1.5), allowing developers to focus on application logic.

Finally, these frameworks often **prioritise security** due to the nature of blockchain applications.

Some well-known examples of permissionless blockchain platforms include Truffle (Ethereum), Anchor (Solana), and Dapper Network (multi-chain).

Table 2.5 gives you examples of the most commonly used public blockchain frameworks in context.

Table 2.5 lists the most common frameworks (albeit not exhaustively), but as research and development in this space continues, new frameworks are emerging, and Table 2.6 gives you some examples:

If your project requires a permissioned, or hybrid, blockchain, you might want to look at permissioned blockchain development platforms.

Table 2.5 Common public blockchain development frameworks. © 2024 Neira Jones

Blockchain Framework	Creator	Features	Applicable Blockchains	Programming Languages
Truffle	Metamask	Simplifies smart contract compilation, deployment, testing and debugging	Ethereum	Solidity (smart contracts), JavaScript (development environment)
Cosmos SDK	Tendermint	A modular framework providing building blocks to create custom blockchains. It offers functionalities like staking, governance, and interoperability with other Cosmos-based blockchains. Can be used to develop side chains for the Cosmos network	Cosmos	Go (primary), other languages possible for custom modules
Embark	Embark Labs	A full-stack Ethereum framework for smart contracts, user interfaces development, and deployment	Ethereum	Solidity (smart contracts), JavaScript (full-stack development), Typescript (optional)
Eosio	Block one	A high-performance framework built for scalability allowing developers to build scalable decentralised applications and smart contracts	EOS	C++ (smart contracts), WebAssembly (alternative for smart contracts)

Table 2.6 Emerging public blockchain development frameworks. © 2024 Neira Jones

Blockchain Framework	**Creator**	**Main Features**	**Applicable Blockchains**	**Programming Languages**
Substrate	Parity Technologies	Modular framework for building custom blockchains with interoperability and on-chain governance. Can be used to develop side chains for the Polkadot network	Custom blockchains (on top of Polkadot)	Rust, AssemblyScript (optional)
Anchor	Solana Labs	Framework built on Solana offering a comprehensive suite of tools including wallet and token management but focusing on developing secure and scalable smart contracts	Solana	Rust
Dapper Network	Dapper Labs	Framework for simplifying development of interoperable blockchain applications, particularly for NFTs and gaming	Blockchain-agnostic (works with various chains)	Go, Solidity (for interacting with other blockchains)

Permissioned blockchain platforms

This can get confusing, as nuances can muddy the waters of our understanding of what a "platform" is and isn't. The development frameworks listed in the previous section are specific to public blockchains. If you want to develop a permissioned blockchain or a blockchain-enabled enterprise solution, these frameworks aren't suitable as they are designed with the core principles of public blockchains in mind (See Chapter 1, *What is a blockchain?*).

Permissioned blockchains (see Chapter 1, *Blockchain types*) have different requirements as they need to control access, maintain privacy, and use consensus mechanisms suited for smaller groups of known participants, features which are often absent in frameworks built for open access and transparency.

A **permissioned blockchain platform** provides a development environment for private, controlled networks. For businesses looking to leverage the potential of blockchain technology for specific applications, this restricted access offers several advantages.

First, they offer **restricted access** as organisations have control over who can participate in the network, ensuring only authorised participants can see and contribute data. This controlled environment enhances privacy and confidentiality within the network, which can be crucial for sensitive business information.

Second, permissioned blockchain platforms are often **designed with specific use cases in mind** and may cater to industries like supply chain management, trade finance, or healthcare data management. This focus allows for customisation of the platform to address the specific challenges and requirements of these industries.

Finally, these platforms offer a degree of **customisation** as participating organisations can tailor the network to meet their specific needs. This might involve features like alternative consensus mechanisms for improved performance within the private network, or privacy functionalities for handling sensitive data.

Some well-known examples of permissioned blockchain platforms include Hyperledger Fabric, R3 Corda, and Quorum.

Permissioned blockchain platforms are specifically designed to address the needs of permissioned blockchain development, and the most common ones are shown in Table 2.7, with examples of deployments in financial services.

Table 2.7 Permissioned blockchain development platforms. © 2024 Neira Jones

Permissioned Blockchain Platform	Creator	Main Features	Financial Services Deployments
R3 Corda[36]	R3 Consortium	Designed for interoperable business networks with a focus on financial services Programming language: Kotlin The R3 consortium has major financial institutions members including ABN AMRO, Bank of America, Barclays, BBVA, Goldman Sachs, HSBC, J.P. Morgan, Société Générale, Standard Chartered, and others	Contour[37]: A trade finance platform used by institutions like BNP Paribas and Standard Chartered for streamlining trade finance processes TradeTrust[38]: The Singapore Trade Finance Platform facilitates secure and efficient trade finance for businesses in Singapore
Hyperledger Fabric[39]	Linux Foundation	Designed for building permissioned blockchains with a focus on scalability and security. Often used in enterprise settings Programming language: Java	Not as popular as R3 Corda in financial services Confidential Consortium Framework[40] (CCF): an initiative exploring Hyperledger Fabric for building permissioned blockchains to address confidentiality needs in financial services. This showcases the platform's potential for financial applications, though not a specific deployment
Quorum[41]	Enterprise Ethereum Alliance initially, Consensys is now the leading developer	Permissioned version of the Ethereum blockchain, offering a familiar environment for Ethereum developers with focus on privacy controls with features specifically designed for enterprise use cases in consortium blockchain networks Programming language: Solidity	Limited publicly available information about Quorum deployments, which is likely due to the private nature of many enterprise blockchain projects. JP Morgan Chase, a founding member of the EEA may be using it, and Consensys offers enterprise support for Quorum, suggesting that deployments may exist, although not publicly disclosed

Table 2.7 only gives deployment examples in financial services, but these environments have been used for other use cases (e.g. supply chain management, healthcare data management). In addition, it is challenging to find information on private enterprise blockchain deployments because of their very nature, hence the scarcity of examples.

Choosing a development environment

Developers have a choice of blockchain frameworks or platforms and **professionals should decide carefully:**

- See Chapter 1, Do you really need a blockchain?
- Assuming you do, understanding your project needs is crucial as blockchain frameworks or platforms may be applicable to some use cases more than others.
- Some blockchain development environments are network-specific (e.g. Ethereum only, Solana only), some are multi-chain, some are for permissioned blockchains (e.g. Hyperledger Fabric). If the project requires a specific blockchain, make sure the framework is compatible.
- Understand the blockchain development environment's characteristics so that it can support your development team's skill set. Some frameworks focus on ease of use whilst others may offer more granular control which requires a steeper learning curve. You need to understand the trade-offs between ease of use and the levels of customisation offered by different blockchain development environments.
- As with traditional development environments, support is crucial, and developers should evaluate the developer community for a given environment. A large and active developer community can be invaluable when facing challenges during development.
- Security is always (or should be) an area of focus for blockchains, it is therefore crucial for developers to ensure that their chosen development environment has a good security track record and has undergone thorough security audits.
- Cost may be a consideration, as some environments may have licensing fees or require specific hardware, which may impact overall project costs.
- Choosing a framework or development platform is not a decision that should be taken lightly because you're usually in it for the long run.

It is therefore important to understand whether the framework will be able to cater to the expected transaction volumes and anticipated growth and to be aware of the framework's development roadmap. Performance might be an important consideration.
- Stay up-to-date as the blockchain landscape is rapidly evolving, and what is here today might not be here tomorrow...

So now we've got the software development environment sorted out, we need the infrastructure on which to run our blockchain project.

Blockchain infrastructure and services providers (with a little help from my friends)

I've already covered the hardware resources (and the services around this) necessary for nodes to participate in blockchain networks (see Chapter 1, *Who can do what?*). Now, these participants need to connect to a blockchain network.

As you may imagine, most blockchain projects run in the cloud. This is because cloud providers manage infrastructure, provide elasticity of resources, and may also provide additional services like security and integration tools.

Some organisations may choose to run all or part of their blockchain networks on their own hardware infrastructure, which may happen in heavily regulated industries (e.g. data residency, infrastructure control), or for security reasons, which requires significant technical expertise and makes scaling more complex.

Cloud infrastructure providers

Cloud infrastructure providers are the unsung heroes of blockchain development, offering on-demand computing resources that streamline the entire process, from building to deploying blockchain applications. Major players include Amazon Web Services (AWS), Microsoft Azure, and Google Cloud Platform (GCP). Here's how they help:

- **Virtual Machine (VM) management**: a VM is a software abstraction layer providing an isolated environment for running various operating

systems and applications, independent of the underlying physical hardware. Cloud providers offer VMs to run blockchain nodes as well as tools to efficiently launch and manage these VMs. Examples include AWS EC2 (Elastic Compute Cloud), Azure Virtual Machines, and Google Compute Engine.
- **Storage solutions**: blockchain data can be bulky. Cloud providers offer various storage solutions to securely store this data, ensuring its accessibility and integrity. Examples include AWS S3 (Simple Storage Service), and Azure Blob Storage,
- **Secure network environments**: for enhanced security, cloud providers offer Virtual Private Cloud (VPC) solutions. These create isolated network environments specifically for blockchain nodes. Examples include AWS VPC, Azure Virtual Network, and Google Cloud VPC.
- **Monitoring and logging**: keeping an eye on the health and performance of a blockchain network is crucial. Cloud providers offer comprehensive monitoring and logging services that seamlessly integrate with blockchain infrastructure. Examples include AWS Cloud Watch, AWS Cloud Trail, Azure Monitor, Azure Log Analytics, Google Cloud Monitoring, and Google Stackdriver.

It's also worth noting that whilst the centralised cloud providers mentioned earlier offer robust solutions, some projects may explore decentralised cloud storage providers. Whilst still an emerging field compared to established providers, decentralised cloud storage is gaining traction due to its potential benefits of data privacy, security, and censorship resistance. An example is Filecoin,[42] a P2P network where users can store data on a global network of computers, offering a decentralised alternative to traditional cloud storage.

Choosing the right cloud provider for a blockchain project requires careful consideration of factors including the specific features offered, pricing models, and the level of security and compliance required. It's also worth noting that some cloud providers might offer additional blockchain-specific tools or services beyond the general infrastructure resources already mentioned. By leveraging cloud infrastructure providers, blockchain developers can focus on building their applications, leaving the complexities of managing underlying infrastructure behind.

Security services providers

You know by now that security is crucial to blockchain infrastructures. There are numerous services that project developers may use, ranging from dedicated services to fulfil a specific need, to full-stack security firms. These firms specialise in identifying and mitigating security vulnerabilities within blockchain infrastructures or projects. The list of services they may provide includes:

- **Penetration testing**: simulating real-world attacks on blockchain infrastructures and applications to uncover weaknesses and vulnerabilities.
- **Threat intelligence**: providing insights to clients by gathering and analysing data on existing and emerging blockchain security threats to help them mitigate potential attacks.
- **Security monitoring**: ongoing monitoring of blockchain infrastructures and applications to detect suspicious activity and potential breaches. This may include security information and event management (SIEM), vulnerability scanning, and patching.
- **KYC/AML services**: some firms may offer services such as **know your customer (KYC)** and **anti-money laundering (AML)** checks to enhance compliance with applicable regulations.
- **Smart contract audit and formal verification**: conducting thorough reviews of smart contract code to identify vulnerabilities that could lead to malicious attacks. Some firms may also offer formal verification of smart contracts using mathematical proofs to guarantee the absence of vulnerabilities.

Service providers include Hacken,[43] Trail of Bits,[44] Quantstamp,[45] Peckshield,[46] SlowMist,[47] Certik,[48] Consensys Diligence[49] (a security arm of Consensys), OpenZeppelin,[50] and ChainSecurity.[51] This is not an exhaustive list (and not a recommendation either 😉), and it is advisable to research individual companies to understand their specific services and areas of expertise as some may even tailor their services to specific project requirements. If you have an enterprise project, professional services firms such as Deloitte, EY, and PwC also provide services.

Blockchain testing services

Rigorous testing ensures the stability and functionality of the blockchain network under various conditions. Whilst open-source libraries are available (e.g. JMeter,[52] libFuzzer,[53] American Fuzzy Lop (AFL),[54] Locust,[55] and Mythril[56]), commercial service providers, such as BlazeMeter[57] and Testfort,[58] may offer several services:

- **Stress testing** to assess network capacity and identify bottlenecks, ensuring that the infrastructure can work with drastic load increases.
- **Fuzz testing**, where invalid or unexpected data inputs are used to uncover vulnerabilities in the code.
- **Block and chain size testing** to ensure that the block size and chain size adheres to the blockchain protocol.
- **Data encryption and decryption testing** to ensure that the encryption mechanisms used are operating properly.
- **Performance testing** where system performance metrics are defined to ensure that the project is ready for release.
- **Penetration testing**: simulating real-world attacks on blockchain infrastructures and applications to uncover weaknesses and vulnerabilities.

In addition, blockchain-specific tools such as Truffle (see Table 2.5), whilst primarily used for blockchain development, also offer testing functionality.

This is not an exhaustive list (and not a recommendation either 😉), and it is advisable to research individual companies to understand their specific services and areas of expertise as some may even tailor their services to specific project requirements. The security service providers mentioned in the previous sections may also offer these services.

Blockchain-as-as-Service (BaaS)

The term **Blockchain-as-a-Service (BaaS)** started growing in popularity around 2017–2018 after cloud providers started to offer basic blockchain services. In the blockchain world, the term BaaS (not to be confused with the traditional financial services term **Banking-as-a-Service**, also BaaS) encompasses cloud-based services offering a complete package for blockchain development, and at the time of writing, most BaaS offerings concentrate on Ethereum support, although there is a growing trend towards BaaS supporting other blockchains. For the remainder of this chapter, I will use BaaS as short for Blockchain-as-a-Service (not the other one).

BaaS offers a pre-built blockchain infrastructure consisting of:

- a managed network of nodes,
- the implementation of a specific consensus mechanism,
- development tools such as programming languages, APIs, and SDKs. BaaS providers may also choose to support established blockchain development frameworks,
- various security features (e.g. encryption, access management, intrusion detection).

BaaS platforms offer tools and services that simplify the process of building decentralised applications (dApps) on existing blockchains, most commonly Ethereum. They don't provide the infrastructure or functionalities to create entirely new blockchains. Key functionalities of BaaS include:

- **Development tools**: BaaS platforms offer SDKs and APIs that streamline development for dApps. These tools allow developers to interact with the underlying blockchain network (e.g. Ethereum) without needing to write low-level code.
- **Security**: BaaS providers will include security features including encryption for data at rest and in transit and access control mechanisms.
- **Network management**: BaaS providers often handle tasks like node management, transaction fee payment (gas fees), and network security, allowing developers to focus on application logic.
- **Scalability and performance**: Some BaaS solutions offer features that can improve the scalability and performance of dApps compared to directly developing on the mainnet (see Chapter 1, Box 1.6).

The potential benefits of BaaS include:

- **Reduced development time and cost**: BaaS simplifies and accelerates the development process for dApps.
- **Focus on application logic**: Developers can concentrate on building the core functionalities of their dApp without worrying about blockchain infrastructure.
- **Accessibility**: BaaS makes blockchain technology more accessible to developers with less experience in core blockchain development and as such introduces a layer of abstraction.

Examples of BaaS providers include Alchemy,[59] Infura,[60] Amazon Managed Blockchain,[61] IBM, Oracle Blockchain,[62] and IBM Blockchain Platform.[63] Microsoft used to provide the Azure Blockchain Service, but this shut down in 2021[64] and they seem to have replaced this with their hybrid Web3 developer platform.[65] Please note that this is not an exhaustive list and some BaaS providers will concentrate on permissioned enterprise applications (e.g. R3 Corda), whilst others focus on non-enterprise services. In addition, a large majority of BaaS providers focus on Ethereum, but there is a growing trend towards supporting other blockchains. It is advisable to research individual companies to understand their specific services.

BaaS has the potential of offering valuable services for developers to build applications on established blockchains and may streamline development, reduce costs, and make blockchain technology more accessible.

A special kind of BaaS: payments

BaaS providers who offer cloud-based infrastructures specifically designed to streamline and secure blockchain-based payment applications are emerging. They build on the standard features of BaaS shown earlier, with added functionalities to help developers build payment applications:

- **Secure custody solutions**: secure storage and management of digital assets used for payments, often complying with regulatory requirements (see Box 2.7).
- **Fiat integration**: integration with traditional financial systems to enable seamless conversion between fiat currencies and cryptocurrencies. This allows users to easily move funds into (on-ramp), and out of (off-ramp) the blockchain network used for the payments (see Box 2.8).
- **High throughput processing**: these BaaS solutions focus on scalability and performance as they can handle large volumes of payment transactions efficiently, which is crucial for real-world payment applications.
- **Regulatory compliance**: features like KYC/AML integration and compliance with applicable regulations should be provided.

Exhibiting the same potential benefits as standard BaaS solutions, BaaS for payments should be able to handle high throughputs and streamline regulatory compliance for developers of blockchain-based payment applications.

Examples of providers include Fireblocks,[66] BitGo,[67] Paxos,[68] R3 Corda,[69] and Anchorage Digital.[70] Please note that this is not an exhaustive list and specific features and functionalities might differ between providers. It's always recommended that individual BaaS providers be explored to understand their offerings tailored for payment applications.

BOX 2.7 WHAT IS CUSTODY?

Imagine having a valuable piece of jewellery. If you want to keep it safe, you might either keep it in a safe at home (self-custody), or you might decide to entrust it to a bank's safe deposit vault (custody service).

It's the same with financial instruments, traditional or decentralised. If you have some cryptocurrency, you might decide to safeguard the cryptocurrency yourself (e.g. through a self-custodial wallet), or you might entrust it to a custodian (e.g. a centralised crypto exchange or custody provider). In a blockchain context, custody services are similar to traditional financial institutions that hold your assets securely. They aim to ensure the safety of the assets whilst users relinquish some control over their assets to the custodian (who manages the keys).

BOX 2.8 ABOUT RAMPS

For centralised payment ecosystems, we often use the word "rails", as in bank rails or card rails, representing the network infrastructure. We access these rails through various payment gateways. In blockchain infrastructures, we have ramps, and these act as gateways to allow us to move money into (on-ramp) and out of (off-ramp) the blockchain network for payments.

On-ramp refers to the process of converting traditional currency (fiat) into cryptocurrency. In the context of payments, it means users can easily deposit their regular money (e.g. US dollars, British Pound, Euros) to be used for payments on the blockchain network.

Off-ramp is the opposite: it refers to converting cryptocurrency back into fiat currency, allowing users to take their funds out of the blockchain system and convert them back to regular (fiat) currency after making payments.

Crypto payment processors

These services look very similar to BaaS payment providers as they offer functionalities specifically designed to streamline and secure the acceptance of cryptocurrency payments. But unlike BaaS, they target businesses and individuals wanting to accept or use cryptocurrencies for payments (not application developers). Like BaaS, they leverage cloud-based infrastructures to provide user-friendly features, for integrating crypto payments into existing business workflows, with an emphasis on payment-related needs and may offer the following features:

- **Secure custody solutions**: secure storage and management of digital assets used for payments, often adhering to regulatory requirements to ensure the safekeeping of cryptocurrency holdings used for transactions (see Box 2.7).
- **Fiat integration**: integration with traditional financial systems to enable seamless conversion between fiat currencies and cryptocurrencies. This allows users to easily move funds into (on-ramp) and out of (off-ramp) the blockchain network used for the payments (see Box 2.8). Some providers may offer crypto exchange functionality for P2P transactions.
- **High throughput processing**: these solutions focus on scalability and performance as they can handle large volumes of payment transactions efficiently, which is crucial for real-world payment applications.
- **Regulatory compliance**: features like KYC/AML integration and compliance with applicable regulations should be provided.

Crypto payment processors are a special type of BaaS provider specifically geared towards the usage of cryptocurrency payments.

Examples of providers include (at the time of writing) BitPay,[71] CoinPayments,[72] NOWPayments,[73] MoonPay,[74] and ForumPay.[75] Please note that this is not an exhaustive list and specific features and functionalities might differ between providers. It's always recommended to explore individual providers to understand their specific offerings.

Choosing infrastructure and service providers

When choosing service providers, **professionals should consider their options carefully:**

- **Cloud infrastructure providers**: consider factors such as features, services, pricing models and security:
  - **Features**: evaluate virtual machine (VM) types, storage solutions, and security tools.
  - **Pricing models**: compare pricing models to find the most cost-effective option for your needs.
  - **Security and compliance**: evaluate the provider's security practices and compliance with applicable regulations.
  - **Blockchain-specific services**: providers may offer additional blockchain-focused tools or services that may benefit your project.
- **Security services providers**: consider factors such as services, expertise, and reputation:
  - **Services offered**: Identify the specific security services required (e.g. penetration testing, smart contract audits).
  - **Expertise**: choose a provider with expertise in the type of blockchain you're using.
  - **Reputation and track record**: research the provider's reputation and experience in the blockchain security space.
- **Blockchain testing services**: consider factors such as testing scope, whether you're interested in open source, and expertise:
  - **Testing scope**: determine the types of testing needed (e.g. stress testing, fuzz, testing, security testing).
  - **Open source vs. commercial**: evaluate the benefits of open-source testing tools versus features offered by commercial providers.
  - **Provider expertise**: consider the provider's experience in testing similar blockchain projects.
- **Blockchain-as-a-Service (BaaS)**: developers should consider factors such as the blockchains and development tools supported, security features, and performance:
  - **Supported blockchains**: choose a BaaS platform that supports the blockchain you plan to use.
  - **Development tools**: evaluate the development tools (SDKs, APIs) offered by the BaaS provider and whether your development team has the appropriate skills.
  - **Security features**: ensure the BaaS platform offers adequate security features for your application.
  - **Scalability and performance**: consider the BaaS platform's ability to handle your expected transaction volume.

- **BaaS for payments**: like generic BaaS platforms, these focus on developers and whilst the generic considerations for BaaS platforms will apply, consider additional factors such as the specific focus on payments, custody solutions, fiat integration, and regulations:
  - **Focus on payments**: look for BaaS providers specifically designed for building blockchain-based payment applications.
  - **Secure custody solutions**: evaluate the provider's secure storage solutions for digital assets used in payments (see Box 2.7).
  - **Fiat integration**: consider the BaaS provider's capabilities for integrating with traditional financial systems.
  - **Regulatory compliance**: ensure the BaaS platform adheres to applicable regulations.
- **Crypto payment processors**: consider factors such as your target audience as crypto payment processors offer functionalities similar to Baas for payments (i.e. secure custody, fiat integration, and performance) but focus on businesses or individuals wanting to accept/use crypto for payments, not developers.

The blockchain space is constantly evolving and it is therefore important to keep up-to-date with current developments.

Now that we understand the building blocks at our disposal, let's build something.

How do you build a blockchain? (think twice)

First things first: the white paper

When developing a blockchain, one of the first things you need to decide is which consensus protocol it will use (see Chapter 1, *How are transactions validated and settled?*) In Chapter 1, *Who can do what?* I introduced the hardware technologies (e.g. mining rigs) and other infrastructure services available to the various types of nodes to enable them to participate in blockchain ecosystems. Once you've decided on the blockchain project, its consensus, its purpose, its utility, and various other factors, you've got to put all this down in writing in what is essentially a project proposal called a "white paper". I briefly introduced the Bitcoin white paper in Chapter 1, *How did blockchains come about?*

BOX 2.9 WHAT IS A BLOCKCHAIN WHITE PAPER?

A blockchain **white paper** is a document explaining the primary purpose, technology, current state, and plans for a blockchain project. It should also give information about its participants, utility, and all the potential factors that might give its underlying coin/token economic value (see Chapter 4, *Tokenomics and metrics*).

It is meant as a high-level guide that enables investors to ascertain whether a project has future potential and to raise the interest of potential users and other stakeholders.

The oldest white paper is the Bitcoin white paper, entitled "Bitcoin: A Peer-to-Peer Electronic Cash System", and was written under the pseudonym of Satoshi Nakamoto in October 2008. Bitcoin was intended to give users an alternative payment system free of central control, but otherwise operating just like any other currency. As such, we can say that the primary purpose of Bitcoin was to be a cryptocurrency (more on this in Chapter 5). More recently, the 2014 white paper "Zerocash: Decentralised Anonymous Payments from Bitcoin"[76] that described zk-proofs (see Chapter 1, *Zero-knowledge proof*), a cryptographic technique used by many layer 2 scaling solutions, received the IEEE "Test of Time" award for its "broad and lasting impact on both research and practice in computer security and privacy".

Blockchain utility

If you're thinking of a blockchain project, it needs to solve a problem and be useful for something (see Chapter 1, *Do you need a blockchain?*), in other words, it needs to have "utility", which is a word often used in blockchain circles.

BOX 2.10 WHAT IS BLOCKCHAIN UTILITY?

The **utility** of a blockchain refers to its practical usefulness beyond the fact that it has an underlying coin/token. Simply put, we're talking about how the core properties and characteristics of a blockchain (See *What is a blockchain?*) make them useful for various use cases where the technology can be used to solve real-world problems or improve existing processes.

The more utility a blockchain has, the more chances it has to succeed. Some examples include supply chain management, record-keeping, voting systems, DeFi, data provenance, digital identity, gaming, virtual worlds, and micro-payments.

We mustn't, however, fall into the trap of believing the promises of some blockchain projects with wishful thinking utility (i.e. theoretical utility, or vapour-ware marketing) and mistake them for real-world adoption.

Many factors affect utility, such as scalability, security, interoperability, and of course, regulations. Similar to services and solutions using centralised infrastructures, the utility of a blockchain will be determined by its ability to solve a specific problem or improve an existing process in a way that is better, more efficient, secure, or transparent than what can be achieved using traditional technologies.

So you've now got your white paper, and you think your blockchain project has utility, it's time to build it... As per traditional systems, you can build it from scratch, or you can use services that help you speed up the process.

Building a blockchain from scratch

Building a new blockchain from scratch is a significant undertaking, but there are tools and frameworks available to support development, as shown in the previous sections.

The process will be different depending on whether you want to build a permissionless or permissioned blockchain.

Building a permissionless blockchain

Developing a completely new blockchain is a complex and time-consuming endeavour and you have to think it through carefully. First, see Chapter 1, *Do you need a blockchain?* Then, you must ask yourself the same question again, because whilst building a blockchain from scratch offers more control and flexibility, it's a resource-intensive process. If leveraging blockchain technology without the burden of building your own infrastructure is all you really need, then you may want to consider BaaS, as covered in the previous section. If you're still not deterred, Figure 2.7 illustrates a possible approach.

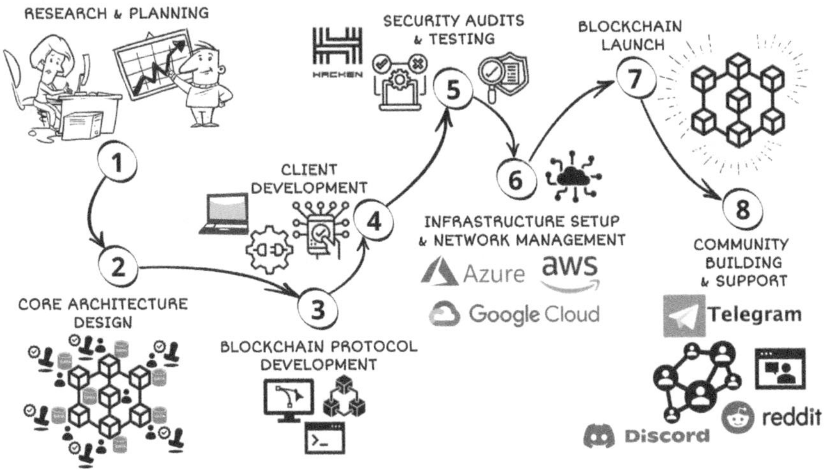

Figure 2.7 Building a permissionless blockchain. © 2024 Neira Jones.

For those interested in these steps in more detail, read on, for the others, you can just jump to the next duck for a quick summary.

1. **Research and planning**: Conduct thorough research on existing permissionless blockchain solutions like Ethereum, Solana, and Cardano. Online resources are available for documentation and tutorials to understand their functionalities, features, consensus mechanisms, utility, and limitations. This will help define the problem your blockchain aims to solve and the target audience. This stage generally involves the production of a white paper (see Box 2.9) or technical specification outlining the goals, governance model, and technical roadmap. Several online sources offering blockchain white paper templates are readily available.

2. **Core architecture design**: This is a fundamental step as it determines the core components of your blockchain:
   a. **Data structure**: This involves deciding on the block structure and header (see Chapter 1, Table 1.5) and other blockchain metadata (e.g. transaction metadata such as timestamps, fees, addresses), and off-chain data links if appropriate (see Chapter 1, *Layer 2 scaling solutions*). You'll essentially be developing a database, and you may explore open-source options (e.g. LevelDB,[77] RocksDB,[78] LMDB,[79] BadgerDB,[80] BoltDB[81]) considering factors such as performance, scalability, and community support, or custom data structures depending on your data storage requirements, however, the latter is complex and requires a deep understanding of storage systems. At this stage, you may also have to define other elements, including consensus-specific data (e.g. difficulty target, staking information), data related to smart contract storage (if used), and chain-specific data (see Chapter 1, Table 1.5).
   b. **Consensus mechanism**: this stage involves researching existing consensus mechanisms like PoW or PoS (see Chapter 1, Figure 1.13 for a comprehensive list of consensus protocols and their applicability) and careful evaluation of the requirements for security, scalability, and decentralisation. Online resources are available to help with this (e.g. whitepapers, online forums).
   c. **Coin design**: (see Chapter 1, Box 1.11) in most permissionless blockchains the native coin plays an essential role in incentivising network participation, and you'll need to decide its purpose (e.g. transaction fees, rewards), supply, and distribution. You may also consider alternative mechanisms such as reputation systems.
   d. **Smart contract functionality**: if you decide that your blockchain needs to support smart contracts (see *Smart contracts*), this step involves the selection of a programming language for smart contract development (see Tables 2.5 and 2.6 for a comprehensive list). Focus on well-established languages with strong communities and security best practices. If you feel brave, you may consider developing a **custom virtual machine (CVM)** to accommodate your specific blockchain or to accommodate a specific language not supported by existing **VMs**. Warning: this is complex, and you may

sacrifice compatibility with other blockchains and should only be considered for niche use cases.

e. **Cryptography**: cryptography is a cornerstone of blockchain security, making use of techniques such as hashing functions, digital signatures, and asymmetric encryption (see Chapter 1 for details). Leverage well-established cryptographic libraries like OpenSSL,[82] BouncyCastle,[83] and libsodium[84] to ensure secure implementation of these operations.

3. **Blockchain protocol development**: This is the most complex and technical part of the process. With the chosen programming languages (see Tables 2.1 and 2.2), you'll need to develop the communication protocols for nodes to interact and share information on the blockchain network. This involves programming the logic for block formation, validation, and implementing the chosen consensus mechanism (See Chapter 1, *How are transactions validated?*). Tools are available to help streamline the process, such as protocol-specific libraries, as well as libp2p[85] which may be helpful for building the peer-to-peer (P2P) communication aspects.
4. **Client development**: This stage involves crafting the tools and APIs that empower users and applications to seamlessly interact with the network. Here, you'll need to consider leveraging language-specific blockchain libraries, often available for popular languages like Javascript. If your blockchain has a unique consensus mechanism, open-source protocol implementations might offer built-in libraries or APIs suitable for client development. There is also the option of building custom client-side libraries or APIs, but this approach requires deep technical expertise. Carefully evaluate your options to choose the most efficient path for building your permissionless blockchain's user interface.
5. **Security audits and testing**: Security is the bedrock of any blockchain infrastructure. To ensure your creation has the best chance of surviving, multiple lines of defence are available:
   a. **Security audits**: see *Security service providers* for examples.
   b. **Testing**: implement a multi-pronged and rigorous testing strategy to ensure your blockchain functions as expected under various conditions. This might involve stress testing to simulate heavy network traffic to identify potential bottlenecks and assess

the overall network capacity and fuzz testing where invalid or unexpected data inputs are used to uncover vulnerabilities in the code. You may consider open-source libraries, commercial testing solutions, and blockchain-specific tools. See *Blockchain testing services* for examples.

By combining professional security audits with a robust testing strategy, you can significantly increase the confidence in the security and stability of your permissionless blockchain network. Please note that the security companies listed are just a starting point and project developers should conduct a thorough research to identify the providers best suited for their project's specific needs.

6. **Infrastructure setup and network management**: before launching your blockchain, you need to establish the infrastructure for running your validator nodes. Decide whether you want to deploy your blockchain in the cloud, or whether part of it must be on-premise due to regulatory requirements (e.g. data residency). See *Cloud infrastructure providers* for more details.
7. **Launching the blockchain**: It's time to take your creation from blueprint to reality! Launching your permissionless blockchain involves two key steps:
   a. **Genesis block**: the foundation stone of your blockchain, the very first page of the ledger, will contain crucial information including initial network parameters and, most importantly, the coinbase transaction (see Chapter 1, *Block formation*). This special transaction acts as a reward for the miners (in PoW systems) or validators (in PoS systems) who create the Genesis block and kick-start the block creation process.
   b. **Network seeding**: unlike permissioned blockchains with a known set of validators, permissionless networks rely on anyone to join and validate transactions. Network seeding jumpstarts the network by attracting these validators in the early stages by running initial validator nodes yourself or collaborating with early adopters. This initial group helps establish a minimal viable network, proving the concept and attracting more validators to secure the network over time.
8. **Community building and support**: This step is about building a community around your blockchain to attract users, developers, and

potential collaborators. This usually involves the use of online forums, developer communities, chat channels (e.g. Telegram, Discord, Reddit), and social media to spread awareness about your project. It is also crucial to develop a clear strategy to encourage participation in your network, which may involve catering for regional variations, incentives (see Chapter 4, *Tokenomics and metrics*), or other reward mechanisms to attract users, developers, and validators. It is also advisable to monitor all engagement channels to assess the success of your community-building strategy.

Embarking on the development of a permissionless blockchain is a significant and complex endeavour, and **professionals should consider the following:**

- Building a new blockchain requires a team with strong skills in cryptography, distributed systems, software development, and security.
- This is a time-consuming and resource-intensive undertaking, and the financial and development resources needed for the project's long-term sustainability must be assessed carefully.
- For permissionless blockchains, building a user base and critical mass for a new blockchain can be challenging. Develop a clear strategy to attract users and incentivise participation in your network.
- Careful planning, security audits, testing, and ongoing maintenance remain essential for a successful permissionless blockchain network.
- Leveraging established tools and services simplifies development by providing core infrastructure and functionalities.
- Building a new blockchain can be a significant financial undertaking, and contributing factors include team size and expertise, tools and services required, security audits and testing, ongoing maintenance, and upgrades.
- Scalability is always a concern in blockchain projects, especially for permissionless blockchains, and planning for a growing number of users and transactions is advisable. Considering layer 2 scaling solutions may help (see Chapter 1, *Layer 2 scaling solutions*).
- Depending on the aim of the blockchain project, a possible (generally quicker) alternative to building a completely new permissionless blockchain from scratch would be to develop a layer 2 solution, leveraging many features from the underlying layer 1 blockchain (see

Chapter 1, *Layer 2 scaling solutions*). The steps will in principle be largely the same as those for developing a permissionless blockchain, with added layer 1 integration elements.

Building a permissioned blockchain

This quick guide is not intended to be taken as gospel, but to help readers understand the main steps involved and tools that may be used. Building a permissioned blockchain from scratch is less complex than building a public blockchain (but it's still no mean feat!). First, see Chapter 1, *Do you need a blockchain?* If you still do, Figure 2.8 illustrates a possible approach.

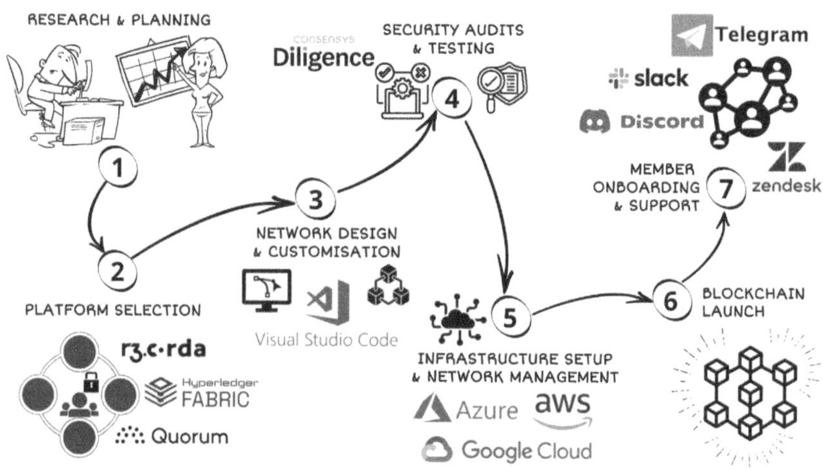

Figure 2.8 Building a permissioned blockchain. © 2024 Neira Jones.

For those interested in these steps in more detail, read on, for the others, you can just jump to the next duck for a quick summary.

1. **Research and planning**: this stage is about defining the requirements, use case(s) for the project, the specific problem(s) the permissioned blockchain is trying to solve, and the pre-defined participating organisations or departments that will form the consortium.
   a. This stage generally involves the production of a white paper (see Box 2.9) or technical specification outlining the goals, governance model, and technical roadmap. Several online sources offering

blockchain white paper templates are readily available. It is also advisable to research existing permissioned blockchain platforms such as Hyperledger Fabric, Quorum, or R3 Corda (see Table 2.7) to understand their functionalities, limitations, and inherent security features.

   b. In addition to defining the use case and identifying initial participating organisations, this stage should also involve refining the specific set of pre-defined participants. This could include specific departments within organisations, or different organisations.
   c. Based on the information identified in planning, the specific content of the genesis block and the coinbase transaction should be defined to specify what data it will contain.
   d. Whilst permissioned blockchains are generally less expensive than public blockchains, building one still requires investment. Factor in team size and expertise required (blockchain developers familiar with security best practices), platform licensing (if applicable), tools and services needed, security audits and testing, ongoing maintenance, and potential future upgrades.
2. **Permissioned blockchain platform selection**: this step involves evaluating the different platforms (see Table 2.7) based on features, scalability, performance, and community support. This means considering factors such as the community size, regulatory requirements, and the desired level of customisation. This also involves configuration choices, such as the deployment options (e.g. cloud-based, on-premise, hybrid) offered by the chosen platform. If cloud is the preferred choice, compare the deployment features of the various providers (see *Cloud services providers*).
3. **Blockchain network design and customisation**: this is the architecture development stage which primarily involves designing the network architecture and defining the roles and permission levels for the different participants. It also involves:
   a. Using the chosen platform's SDKs and tools to build and manage the business logic with the network which may take the form of custom smart contracts (e.g. Quorum), chaincode (Hyperledger Fabric) or flows (R3 Corda) to manage business logic within the network. In addition to this, client-side applications that interact with the network are also developed using the platform's SDKs.

b. This stage also involves defining the overall network structure, including the number and types of nodes (e.g. ordering service nodes, validator nodes) and how they interact.
c. Additionally, different roles are established for participants (e.g., validator, auditor) and permission levels are assigned to control access to specific network functionalities.
d. Then, the consensus mechanism (e.g. Raft in Hyperledger Fabric) and privacy features (e.g. access control lists) offered by the chosen platform are configured to align with the project's requirements.
e. Selecting a development environment for developing the code (smart contract or other) means understanding the permissioned blockchain platform-specific features as these environments should support the programming languages used by the platform (see Tables 2.3–2.6). Such environments include Visual Studio Code (VS Code), Truffle (see Table 2.5, whilst Truffle is primarily used for Ethereum development, it can also be used with Quorum (see Table 2.7) due to its shared Solidity language base), IntelliJ IDEA, WebStorm, and specific **Integrated Development Environments (IDEs)** such as Hyperledger Fabric Studio (a web-based IDE for developing chaincode). Choosing the right development environment will depend on the development team's expertise, the project requirements, and the platform support (e.g. extensions, plug-ins).

An integrated development environment **(IDE)** is a software application combining a variety of tools to help programmers develop software efficiently. IDEs may include features such as code editors, debuggers, compilers or build automation tools, version control, graphical user interface builders, testing tools, etc. They aim to improve productivity, reduce errors, increase code quality, and simplify collaboration.

4. **Security audits and testing**: security is fundamental to blockchain infrastructures, and it is, therefore, crucial to conduct thorough security audits of the code to identify and address vulnerabilities. Performing rigorous testing serves to ensure the stability and functionality of the permissioned blockchain network under various conditions. It is

also advisable to leverage both blockchain security audit companies and the platform's own testing frameworks. See *Security services providers* and *Blockchain testing services* for more details.

5. **Infrastructure setup and network management**: depending on the chosen platform and deployment options, this stage focuses on deploying the infrastructure that forms the backbone of your blockchain. One option is to **leverage cloud services providers** (see *Cloud infrastructure providers* for more details) but if you require greater control over your environment and network security, you can choose an **on-premise deployment**, which requires you to set up your own infrastructure for VM management, data storage, and network security. Regardless of your deployment choice, (cloud or on-premise), remember to leverage the monitoring and logging functionalities offered by your cloud provider or platform-specific management tools (e.g. Hyperledger Fabric Certificate Authority, Quorum Explorer, Corda Network Node Manager). These tools are essential for keeping your network healthy and functioning optimally.
6. **Launching the blockchain**: this stage marks the transition from development and configuration to the live operation of your permissioned blockchain network. Unlike permissionless blockchains that require network seeding, launching a permissioned blockchain focuses on a set of pre-defined participants and involves the **Genesis block creation** and **network initialisation**. The Genesis block, the foundation block of your blockchain, is created using the information defined during the planning stage (Step 1) and will typically contain critical data such as the network name, initial configuration settings, and a timestamp. The pre-defined participants in the consortium might be involved in the creation and signing of the genesis block. Concurrently, these participants are invited to join the network and configure their nodes according to the predefined settings.
7. **Member onboarding and support**: at this point, the members' onboarding procedures (e.g. consortium) must be established, and the ongoing network maintenance and monitoring practices must be defined. This will include:
   a. **Joining procedures**: establish clear procedures for additional members to join your permissioned blockchain. This might involve applications, identity verification, or permission-level assignments.

b. **Training**: develop training materials and workshops to educate new members on using the blockchain network effectively. This could involve online resources, interactive tutorials, or even hands-on workshops.
c. **Support channels**: this involves creating ongoing support channels for members to address any technical issues or questions. This may involve using team communication platforms (e.g. Slack, Discord, Telegram), the creation of dedicated forums, the usage of documentation platforms (e.g. Read the Docs, Google Docs), and for projects with large user bases, it may also involve the usage of ticketing systems (e.g. Zendesk, OsTicket, Freshdesk, Help Scout, Gitcoin Helpdesk, LayerHQ).

By providing a smooth onboarding process and ongoing support, you'll foster a strong and engaged community around your permissioned blockchain network.

There are a lot of spinning plates to keep up in the air when embarking on the development of a permissioned blockchain, and **professionals should consider the following:**

- **Planning is crucial**: whilst developing a permissioned blockchain from scratch involves fewer steps when compared to a public blockchain, thorough planning is crucial.
- **Expertise required**: whilst less complex than a public blockchain, developing a permissioned blockchain still requires a team with blockchain development skills and an understanding of distributed systems.
- **Platform choice can significantly impact development**: the specific tools and steps might vary depending on the chosen permissioned blockchain platform. Carefully evaluate different platforms based on features, scalability, community support, and how well they align with your project's requirements.
- **Security audits and testing are paramount**: rigorous security audits, testing, and ongoing maintenance remain essential for a successful permissioned blockchain network.
- **Leveraging platforms**: leveraging established permissioned blockchain platforms simplifies development by providing core infrastructure and functionalities.

- **Financial investment**: building a new blockchain can be a significant financial undertaking, and contributing factors include team size and expertise, tools and services required, security audits and testing, ongoing maintenance, and upgrades.
- **Member onboarding and support are crucial**: clear member onboarding procedures (e.g. applications, identity verification, and permission level assignments) and ongoing support (e.g. training, workshops, dedicated channels) are crucial for fostering a strong and engaged member community.

Building blockchain applications

This section will show, at a high level how to build the various types of blockchain applications introduced earlier (smart contracts, dApps, CApps, blockchain-enabled applications). The world of blockchain technology offers possibilities for a wide range of applications, some of which rely on tokens (see Chapter 1, Box 1.11) to function.

Token development

When new blockchain projects are launched, they will usually do so on an existing blockchain. This is why projects will usually start with a token, as developing a blockchain from scratch takes time and effort. These tokens can represent a variety of things within a blockchain ecosystem, creating unique functionalities and economic models. As the project gets more traction (e.g. investors, users), it may eventually develop its own blockchain and have its own coin. The process of migrating tokens to coins is called "token migration".

Developing a new token based on an existing blockchain means following the token standards for that blockchain, and these include:

- **Ethereum**: ERC-20, the most widely used token standard for fungible tokens (see Chapter 4, *Fungibility*), ERC-721 for non-fungible tokens (see Chapter 5, *Non-Fungible Tokens*), and ERC-1155, a multi-token standard that can represent both fungible and non-fungible tokens.
- **Binance Smart Chain**: BEP-20, the main token standard for this blockchain, which is compatible with ERC-20.

- **TRON blockchain**: TRC-20, which is TRON's equivalent for ERC-20.
- **Polygon**: uses ERC standards
- **Solana**: SPL is the native standard for creating and managing tokens on the Solana network. It is designed for high performance and scalability.
- **Cardano**: Cardano supports the creation and management of custom tokens natively on its blockchain, without the need for smart contracts.
- **Algorand**: Algorand Standard Asset (ASA) is the native token standard for creating and managing tokens on the Algorand blockchain. It supports a wide range of asset types, including fungible and non-fungible tokens, and like Cardano, doesn't need smart contracts.

Ethereum and compatible blockchains typically require smart contracts to define the token's behaviour, including issuance, transfer, and other functionalities, whilst others (Cardano, Algorand) offer native token support, simplifying the process of token creation and management. The choice of blockchain and token standard depends on the specific needs of the blockchain project (see Chapter 4, *Tokenomics*).

The following sections will delve into the core processes involved in building blockchain applications, equipping you with the foundational knowledge to navigate the landscape. We'll explore the steps required to bring your blockchain-powered ideas to life, from clearly defining your project's purpose to crafting secure and well-structured smart contracts. Whether you envision a centralised application leveraging blockchain elements, a general-purpose blockchain solution, or a dApp, this guide will equip you with the essential steps to embark on your blockchain development journey, including considerations for incorporating tokens (covered in more detail in Chapter 4, *Tokenomics*).

Building smart contracts

And now for some more exciting stuff... So we've laid down the foundation for our new blockchain ecosystem, either by building a new blockchain or by choosing an existing one that we like. It's time to grow the ecosystem by building applications on it, and this starts with smart contracts (Figure 2.9).

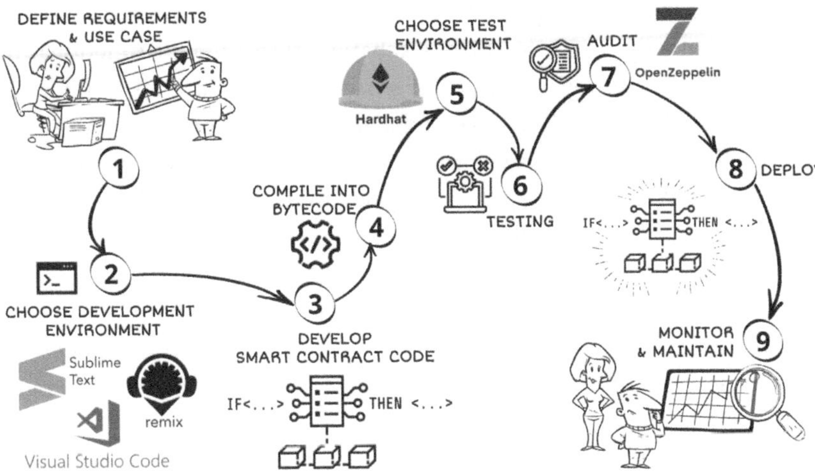

Figure 2.9 Building a smart contract. © 2024 Neira Jones.

For those interested in these steps in more detail, read on, for the others, you can just jump to the next duck for a quick summary.

Whilst the specific steps may vary depending on the chosen blockchain and desired functionality, here's a general breakdown of the process for building a smart contract, including relevant tools and services:

1. **Define the requirements and use case**: clearly define the purpose and functionality of your smart contract. You need to be thorough and consider the following:
   a. Laying down the purpose of the smart contract, articulating the problem it is trying to solve, and the processes it aims to automate.
   b. Identifying the parties involved, their roles and responsibilities, and how they will interact with the smart contract.
   c. Determining the desired outcomes and the actions that the smart contract should trigger under specific conditions.
   d. If your smart contract is intended to manage and interact with tokens (see Chapter 1, Box 1.11), you'll need to decide on your token design (type, total supply, initial distribution), function (minting, transfer, burning), and security best practices (preventing unauthorised minting, ensuring proper ownership transfer, mitigating vulnerabilities. (See Chapter 4, *Tokenomics*).

2. **Choose your development environment**: the previous section should help with that as different blockchains offer different functionalities and programming languages for smart contracts, as well as Tables 2.3 and 2.4. You should also consider factors including transaction fees, scalability, and existing developer communities when making your choice. Many of the public blockchain frameworks introduced in Tables 2.3 and 2.4 will include development environments for smart contracts, as well as the permissioned blockchain platforms included in Table 2.7, and that might just do the job for you. But there are also development environments that specifically focus on smart contract development (i.e. compile, deploy, debug), such as Remix for Ethereum. Table 2.8 gives the most popular options:

   How do you choose between what is offered by a full-stack blockchain platform and a smart contract-specific IDE? Table 2.9 gives you some clues.
3. **Develop your smart contract code**: the earlier section on *Programming languages* (and Tables 2.3–2.6) should help with this. You have to ensure that your development team has the right skills as each blockchain platform has its own language (e.g. Solidity for Ethereum). Plenty of online resources are available, including Solidity tutorials,[86] Solana documentation,[87] and Hyperledger Fabric Smart Contract Development Guide.[88] Once you've decided you should consider factors including:
   a. Structuring your code logic, which involves defining variables, functions, and events to represent the desired functionalities of your smart contract.
   b. Implementing security best practices to guard against common vulnerabilities including **reentrancy attacks** and **integer overflow**. Here also, plenty of online resources are available.[89]
4. **Compiling your smart contract**: whilst the specific steps involved might be handled within your development environment behind the scenes, compilation is a crucial process for most blockchain platforms. It's not dissimilar to using a traditional programming language (like COBOL 😉) which gives you an abstraction layer from the underlying hardware (say, IBM). Your COBOL programme has to be translated into machine code by a compiler specific to that hardware platform (assembly language). Similarly, for blockchain environments, your code has

Table 2.8 Smart contract-specific IDEs. © 2024 Neira Jones

IDE Name	Creator	Features	Supported Blockchains	Languages
Remix	Ethereum Community (Open-source project)	Web-based IDE for smart contract development lifecycle (compile, deploy, debug). Supports injection points for various blockchain networks	Multiple (Ethereum, Hyperledger Fabric, custom blockchains)	Solidity, JavaScript
Sublime Text (with extensions)	Sublime Text HQ	Customizable code editor with plugins for smart contract development (Solidity)	Multiple (Ethereum, permissioned blockchains)	Solidity
Visual Studio Code (with extensions)	Microsoft	Popular code editor with various blockchain extensions for smart contract development (Solidity, Vyper, Chaincode)	Multiple (Ethereum, permissioned blockchains)	Depends on extensions (e.g. Solidity, Vyper, Chaincode)

Table 2.9 Smart contract-specific IDEs vs. full-stack blockchain platforms/frameworks with IDE functionality. © 2024 Neira Jones

	Smart Contract-Specific IDE	**Full-Stack Blockchain Platform/Framework with IDE Functionality**
Focus	Smart contract development lifecycle (compile, debug, deploy)	Comprehensive blockchain development (smart contracts, UI, back-end)
Features	Tailored for smart contracts (syntax highlighting, debuggers, network interaction)	May include some smart contract features, but also broader functionalities (e.g. token management, front-end development)
Resource consumption	Lightweight, efficient and resource-friendly	Might have larger resource footprint due to broader scope
Flexibility	Standalone, integrates with various tools	More integrated approach, might require adapting to framework structure
Customisation	Extensive extensions and plugins from communities	More limited extension options compared to dedicated smart contract IDEs
Learning curve	Lower as focused on smart contract development	Steeper, as more functionalities to learn
Examples	Remix, Visual Studio Code with extensions	Truffle, Hyperledger Composer

to be translated into a machine-readable format called **bytecode**. Many popular smart contract development environments (like Remix or Truffle for Ethereum) and some IDEs automate the compilation process in the background when you deploy your smart contract. However, it's important to understand that compilation is still happening behind the scenes to generate the necessary bytecode for deployment. In some instances, manual compilation may be necessary if you have a complex process that is beyond the development environment's capabilities, or when security auditors request the source code and compiled bytecode for separate analysis. In addition, some blockchain environments may have off-chain compilation options which might be used for security or performance reasons.

Bytecode is a machine-readable instruction set similar to assembly code in traditional systems. However, unlike assembly language, it is not targeted at specific hardware due to the distributed nature of blockchains where it is impossible to know which hardware the code will run on (as each node can choose its own hardware). This is why the abstraction layer from the underlying hardware provided by a VM is necessary. Essentially, the code developed in your chosen programming language will be compiled to run on a VM (e.g. the EVM), which gives you code portability and interoperability across environments.

5. **Choose your test environment**: this crucial step involves deploying your smart contract bytecode into a test environment, and you have two options:
   a. **Use a local development environment**: many development environments allow you to simulate a blockchain node on your machine. This facilitates initial testing and debugging in an isolated environment without interacting with a real network or incurring fees. Popular options include Remix (built-in local node simulator for testing), Truffle (with Ganache for local Ethereum testing), and Hardhat[90] (for local Ethereum testing).
   b. **Use a testnet:** this is a copy of the main blockchain with fake data or tokens which allows you to test its interaction with a simulated blockchain environment that closely resembles the real world. Testnet environments may involve fees and popular examples include Ethereum Rinkeby Testnet, Solana Devnet, and Hyperledger Fabric Testnet.
6. **Test your smart contract**: at this point, you should write unit tests as they allow you to isolate and test individual functions of your smart

contract to ensure they behave as expected under various conditions. Many frameworks and libraries are available for unit testing smart contracts depending on the chosen platform and language. You should also simulate different scenarios, including smart contract behaviour under edge cases and unexpected user inputs to identify potential vulnerabilities. This may involve manually interacting with the smart contract through your development environment or writing automated test scripts.

7. **Audit your smart contract**: consider engaging a security audit company (see *Security services providers*) as professional audits can help identify and address potential security vulnerabilities in your code. This is highly recommended for critical smart contracts handling significant funds or assets.
8. **Deploy your smart contract**: once you're confident in your smart contract functionality and security, it can be deployed to the mainnet (see Chapter 1, Box 1.6) for real-world use. Be aware of the transaction fees associated with deploying your smart contract to the mainnet as these fees will vary depending on the blockchain and network conditions.

   CAUTION: Deploying to the mainnet is a permanent step as deployed smart contracts are typically immutable (see Box 2.11).

   Since changes to smart contracts on the mainnet are typically not possible, ensure that steps 6 and 7 (testing and auditing) are completed thoroughly.

   Once you're confident that your smart contract is ready to go, you will require two elements:

   a. **A wallet with funds**: a crypto wallet compatible with your chosen blockchain is required to hold the cryptocurrency required to pay transaction fees for deployment on your chosen blockchain.
   b. **Deployment tools**: whilst some development environments offer built-in deployment functionalities, you might need to use separate deployment tools. These tools bridge the gaps between your development environment and the live blockchain network and may offer functionalities including wallet connectivity, transaction submission, and monitoring. Popular examples include Infura (for Ethereum), and Alchemy (multi-chain). Javascript libraries can also be used (e.g. Web3.js).

The deployment process starts with connecting your wallet to the blockchain, specifying your smart contract bytecode, setting the fee (e.g. gas price, gas limit), and initiating the **deployment transaction** through the deployment tool (this is the equivalent of the coinbase transaction when launching a new blockchain). This transaction will broadcast your smart contract to the blockchain network for validating nodes to process before it is permanently added to the blockchain ledger, and henceforth the smart contract is immutable (see Chapter 1, *How are transactions validated*).

It is advisable to monitor the deployment of your smart contract, and some deployment tools may offer functionalities to help ensure the transaction is successfully submitted. As explained in Chapter 1, the confirmation time can vary depending on network congestion and fees.

After this, your smart contract is live.

BOX 2.11 CAN YOU KILL A SMART CONTRACT POST-DEPLOYMENT?

You know that anything deployed on a blockchain ledger becomes immutable, and this applies to smart contracts. This means that **you can't directly modify or "kill" a smart contract after deployment**, hence the importance of testing and auditing prior to deployment. However, depending on the specific functionality, built into the smart contract itself, there might be mitigation strategies:

- **Upgradeable contracts** (if designed for upgradability): some smart contracts are designed with the ability to be upgraded to a new version. This upgrade process typically involves deploying a new contract and migrating functionality or data from the original contract. However, this approach requires careful planning and implementation during the initial development phase.
- **Self-destruct mechanism** (if included): in rare cases, a smart contract might be designed with a "self-destruct" mechanism that allows it to be destroyed under specific conditions. This is a complex approach and should be used with extreme caution due to the permanent nature of the deletion.

9. **Monitor and maintain your smart contract**: this is where you track the success of your smart contract and monitor its performance through key metrics like gas consumption and user interactions to identify potential issues or areas for optimisation (see Chapter 4, *Smart contract and DeFi metrics*). Finally, you need to stay up-to-date with the latest security best practices and updates for your chosen blockchain platform to ensure your smart contract remains secure.

Building a smart contract is a complex endeavour, and **professionals should consider the following:**

- **Define your project clearly**: before coding, meticulously outline your smart contract's purpose, functionalities, and involved parties. Decisions you make at this stage will typically be irreversible after deployment (remember immutability…).
- **Align platform and tools**: choose a blockchain that suits your project's needs (fees, scalability, and developer community). Then, select a compatible development environment, and consider the skills of your team and potential learning curve.
- **Security is crucial**: consider engaging a security audit company for critical smart contracts to identify and address potential vulnerabilities before deployment and use all the tools available in your arsenal. Also, ensure your team has the necessary programming skills and prioritise robust security practices throughout the development process.
- **Thorough testing is essential**: extensively test your smart contract in a test environment (local or testnet) using unit tests, various scenarios, and edge cases to identify and fix issues before deployment.
- **Deployment is immutable**: deploying your smart contract to the mainnet makes it live and deployed contracts are typically unchangeable. Rigorous testing and auditing are crucial beforehand. Also, be aware of transaction fees and ensure you have a compatible crypto wallet with sufficient funds to cover deployment costs. Deployment tools can streamline the process.
- **Monitor and maintain your smart contract**: track key metrics like gas consumption and user interactions to identify potential issues or areas for optimisation. Stay updated with security best practices for your chosen platform to maintain your smart contract.

Building dApps

Whilst it is technically possible to build dApps on PoW blockchains, by now you hopefully understand that it's perhaps not desirable, given their scalability limitations (see Chapter 1, *Are blockchains scalable?*), although it's technically possible, albeit complex, to build dApps using PoW layer 2 scaling solutions. It is therefore unsurprising that PoS blockchains are preferred for building dApps, Ethereum and EVM-compatible blockchains remaining the most popular. Figure 2.10 gives a possible approach.

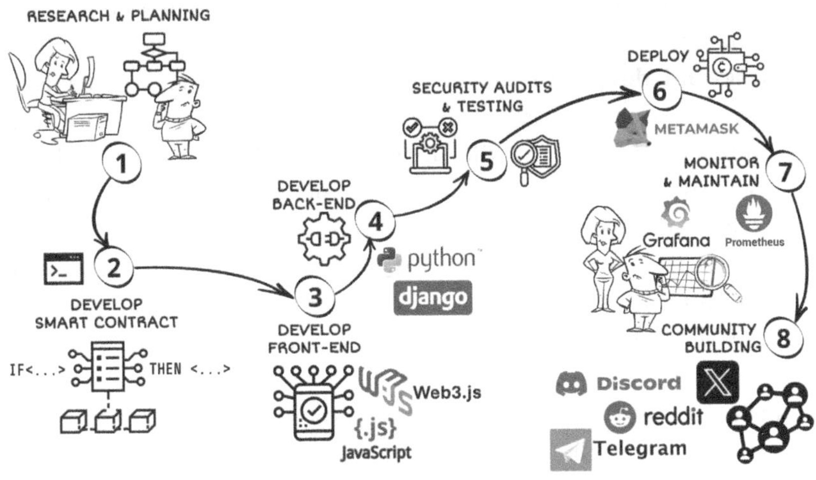

Figure 2.10 Building a dApp. © 2024 Neira Jones.

For those interested in these steps in more detail, read on, for the others, you can just jump to the next duck for a quick summary.

1. **Research and planning**: this involves defining the problem and audience, choosing a blockchain, exploring existing dApps to understand how similar dApps function (blockchain explorers can help with this, see Table 1.10), and creating a project roadmap. This stage of course involves choosing your blockchain, considering factors such as scalability, security, whether it supports the smart contract features you require, its associated fees, and whether its developer community is thriving. Chapter 1 should help you with this, as well as Chapter 4

where metrics are defined. If your dApp might benefit from a tokenised economy, you should also research existing dApps that use tokens to understand best practices and potential pitfalls.

2. **Smart contract development**: See *Building smart contracts.*
3. **Front-end development**: as this stage is about designing the front-end user interface (see *dApps* and Figure 2.5), I won't dwell on traditional front-end technologies (e.g. HTML, CSS, Javascript, React Vue.js), but once the UI is built, it needs to integrate with the chosen blockchain. In order to do this, you may want to use platform-specific libraries such as Web3.js library[91] for Ethereum, Solana Web3.js library for Solana, or platform-specific SDKs like the AvalancheJS library[92] for Avalanche.
4. **Back-end development**: this stage is optional and depends on whether your dApp requires functionality beyond what the smart contract and UI can handle alone. You may leverage back-end technologies for this, and popular options include Python[93] (with Django framework), Java[94] (with Spring framework), or Node.js[95] (with Express framework). You may also have to develop APIs to facilitate communication between your front-end and back-end components. Tools for designing and testing APIs, such as Postman[96] can help with this.
5. **Security audits and testing**: this is a crucial stage and involves auditing and testing the smart contract (see *Building smart contracts*) and the front end and back-end (if applicable). For Ethereum, you may leverage frameworks like Truffle (see Table 2.5), and for general Javascript applications you may use Mocha.[97] Testnets provided by your chosen blockchain are ideal for testing.
6. **Deployment**: once your dApp is fully developed and tested, it's time to deploy it to the mainnet. This makes your dApp accessible to the public and allows users to interact with it. Different blockchains have varying deployment processes, but the general steps involve:
   a. **Choosing a wallet**: you'll need a crypto wallet compatible with your chosen blockchain platform. Popular options include MetaMask wallet for Ethereum, Phantom wallet for Solana, or Avalanche Wallet for Avalanche. These wallets allow you to interact with the blockchain and pay any necessary fees associated with deployment. See Chapter 6, *Crypto wallets* for more details.

   b. **Interacting with the blockchain**: using your chosen wallet, you'll initiate a transaction on the blockchain network to deploy your smart contract code. This transaction typically requires a fee.
7. **Monitoring and maintenance**: just like any traditional application, dApps require ongoing monitoring and maintenance. By proactively monitoring and maintaining your dApp, you can ensure its continued functionality, security, and positive user experience. Here are some key aspects to consider:
   a. **System monitoring and data visualisation**: tools like Prometheus[98] can be used to collect data on various system metrics related to the performance of your dApp. This data can include smart contract execution times, transaction volume, and resource usage on the blockchain. Tools like Grafana[99] can help visualise the data collected by Prometheus, allowing you to identify trends, troubleshoot potential issues, and ensure your dApp operates efficiently.
   b. **Security updates**: whilst smart contracts are immutable once deployed, the surrounding environment (oracles, front-end code) might require updates to address security vulnerabilities or introduce new features.
   c. **Community engagement**: monitor user feedback and engage with your dApp's community to identify areas for improvement and address any bugs or usability issues.
8. **Community building**: a thriving community is essential for the success of your dApp. A strong community can provide valuable feedback, help identify bugs, promote your dApp, and contribute to its long-term growth. Here are some key strategies for building a strong dApp community:
   a. **Choose the right platforms**: identify where your target audience spends their time online and choose accordingly (e.g. Discord, Telegram, Reddit, X): Subreddits like r/dapps[100]) may be a good place to connect with potential users. Regardless of the platform chosen, you have to be present in your chosen platforms, answer questions, address concerns, and actively participate in discussions. Use social media to promote your dApp and provide valuable content (e.g. blogs, tutorials).
   b. **Organise events, contests, and incentives**: you may choose to host AMAs (Ask Me Anything) sessions with your team, and run

hackathons or bug bounty programs to incentivise participation. You may also consider offering rewards for early adopters, community members who contribute to bug bounty programs, or those who create valuable content or tutorials for your dApp.

Ultimately, it's about maintaining clear communication channels with your community, being honest about challenges, and providing updates on development progress. Building a strong community takes time and effort, but it's a crucial element for the long-term success of your dApp.

Building a dApp is a complex endeavour, and **professionals should consider the following:**

- **Build solid foundations**: clearly define your dApp's purpose and target audience and the problem it is trying to solve. Research existing dApps for inspiration.
- **Choose the right blockchain**: choose a blockchain that aligns with your needs and consider factors like scalability, security, the developer community, and the availability of smart contract features you require. Be aware of transaction fees. You may have to avoid PoW blockchains due to scalability limitations.
- **Security is paramount**: prioritise robust security practices throughout the entire development lifecycle of your dApp. Ensure your development team has the necessary programming skills and prioritise secure smart contract coding. Thorough testing and security audits are crucial before deployment to identify and fix vulnerabilities that could compromise your dApp (and remember, a smart contract is immutable).
- **Focus on user experience**: design a user-friendly front end that integrates seamlessly with the chosen blockchain. If needed, leverage secure back-end technologies for functionalities beyond the smart contract and UI capabilities. Ensure your APIs are designed to ensure effective communication between front-end and back-end components.
- **Deployment and beyond**: deploy your dApp to the mainnet using a compatible crypto wallet and be aware of associated fees. Proactively monitor your dApp's performance, security, and user experience. Use tools to identify potential issues.

- **Community matters**: building a thriving community is instrumental for the long-term success of your dApp. Use online platforms, organise events, incentivise participation to gather feedback, and address issues to foster a vibrant community.

Building CApps and blockchain-based applications

As covered earlier, dApps embody the decentralised and distributed characteristics not generally found in traditional payment systems. These new characteristics can easily be transposed to CApps and blockchain-enabled applications, in conjunction with traditional programming techniques, far be it from me to teach grandmother to suck eggs! 😉 (I know, this is a very British expression[101]).

What about traditional payments? (fear of missing out)

Inevitably, the industry reacts, or acts, in the best way it can. Some, once detractors of everything decentralised and crypto, are revisiting their positions and entering the fray. Others withdraw to take time to consider their options. This section gives you some real-life examples of deployments, but in no way suggests that these deployments will last. This will remain a very fluid situation for some time yet...

In any instance, now that you understand the mechanics, perhaps the news headlines around the decentralised world may not be as enigmatic as they once were...

- **December 2017**: UK fintech firm Revolut launched their crypto service to enable users to buy Bitcoin, Litecoin, and Ethereum. Revolut is known for building its own financial infrastructure in-house whenever possible, it is therefore likely that it might have used a combination of internal development and external resources (like crypto exchanges or liquidity providers) to launch its service.[102]
- **September 2021**: Mastercard acquired **blockchain analytics** (see Chapter 1, Table 1.10) company Ciphertrace, signalling a potential future move into KYC/AML blockchain compliance services.[103]
- **June 2022**: acquirer checkout.com partnered with **BaaS** provider Fireblocks to allow merchants to accept payments in USDC around the clock.[104]

- **October 2022**: WorldPay (FIS) joined the Fireblocks network to enable digital asset settlements for their merchants.[105]
- **February 2023**: Visa announced its crypto settlement solutions for acquirers and issuers, focusing on interbank settlement with stablecoin USDC over Solana and Ethereum, allowing acquirers and issuers to settle transactions in USDC instead of fiat currencies, delivering faster settlement times, improving operational efficiency, and lowering costs.[106]
- **April 2023**: Fashion brand Ralph Lauren's new Miami store started accepting cryptocurrency payments, using BitPay as their **crypto payment processor.**[107]
- **May 2023**: Visa partnered with BaaS provider Consensys to help central bank digital currency (CBCD) networks to bridge the gap with financial services institutions.[108]
- **July 2023**: Solana Pay plugin for Shopify launched, offering Shopify users to accept USDC payments at the checkout.[109]
- **March 2024**: Ingenico partnered with crypto exchange Binance and **BaaS** provider Nilos to allow customers to make in-store payments using cryptocurrencies.[110]
- **March 2024**: Mastercard-owned CipherTrace informed clients that it was pulling some of its products, a story linked to a criminal court case and controversy over data quality. Mastercard confirmed this, whilst stating that they remained "convinced of the long-term potential of crypto analytics and crypto intelligence".[111]
- **March 2024**: UK fintech Revolut launches its Revolut Ramp service to allow its 40 million users to buy cryptocurrencies and deposit them directly into MetaMask wallets. Crypto contributes to a significant proportion of Revolut's revenue.[112]
- **April 2024**: Stripe announced that it would start accepting the USDC stablecoin at checkout on the Ethereum, Solana, and Polygon blockchains, enabling merchants using Stripe's technology to accept payments made in USDC.[113]
- **April 2024**: WorldPay announced that it achieved 50% faster payment processing using the Fireblocks Payments Engine.[114]
- **May 2024**: Mastercard announced that it will enable blockchain transactions between Latin America and European corridors, marking the first real-world application of its Crypto Credential solution designed to facilitate and verify interactions between consumers and businesses.[115]

- **May 2024**: telco Vodafone announced its plan to integrate mobile phone SIM cards into digital wallets, identity, and blockchains, using the SIM card cryptography for blockchain integration.[116]
- **May 2024**: **Crypto payment processor** MoonPay announced its collaboration with PayPal to allow MoonPay users in the US to buy cryptocurrency using their PayPal account.[117]
- **May 2024**: Commonwealth Bank of Australia launched its NameCheck solution in 2023, leveraging bank account data, for verifying the accuracy of account details when making payments. This solution aims to protect people and businesses from scams and mistaken payments. In May 2024, CBA announced the start of a pilot to run NameCheck on Liink, a private blockchain developed by JP Morgan's Onyx division.[118]
- **July 2024**: Nuvei partnered with Mastercard to launch an off-ramping solution in Europe that allows consumers to convert digital assets into fiat currency on Mastercard debit, credit, and prepaid cards. This integration enables near real-time transfers without third-party exchanges, facilitating seamless transactions between digital and traditional finance. The solution aligns with Nuvei's goal of enhancing digital economy engagement and Mastercard's strategy for secure digital asset interactions.[119]

There are many more examples than just those I have presented here, but at least they give you a flavour. The traditional rails are flexing and changing, and incumbent players are getting ready, or at least hedging their bets. You shouldn't, however, be surprised that all the given in this section are either CeFi or CeDeFi… Centralised governance still rules in the payments world.

Building blockchains and applications – conclusion (where do we go from here?)

In this whistle-stop tour of blockchain fundamentals, we covered:

- The ecosystem, introducing smart contracts, dApps, and comparing TradFi, CeFi, CeDeFi, and CeFi.
- The technologies and services behind blockchain infrastructures
- How to build blockchains and blockchain applications
- Implementations in the payments world

I have tried to explain the jargon and debunk a few myths. I have given you my opinion on some aspects of the ecosystem, offered classifications and analogies, but feel free to disagree, I always welcome a good debate! A few years from now, things will have moved on, and I will have to revisit this chapter.

In any instance, I hope I have clarified the types of applications that can be built using blockchain technology, whether these are centralised or decentralised, and why building a blockchain from scratch is as significant an endeavour as building a payment rail from scratch. I also hope I have demystified the technologies, and you may now ponder on some of the pitfalls as well as the opportunities that blockchain infrastructures present. Ultimately, a lot of it depends on faith. There's nothing wrong with that. Faith can move mountains, or at least, rebuild infrastructures 😉. Innovation depends on faith. For example, it took seven years for Wise to become profitable. That's a whole load of faith from the founders and their investors. But that wasn't blind faith, which is fundamentally wrong in this context. Of course, successful, and lasting, deployments – especially in payments – will all depend on the effectiveness of the available governance frameworks and a thorough understanding of the potential risks – some of which were introduced here and in the previous chapter.

To complete our understanding of blockchains, we must examine the operation, economics, risks, and governance frameworks of blockchain infrastructures.

Let's go on the third leg of our trip.

Notes

1 "How Vitalik Buterin Co-Founded Ethereum at the Age of 19 as a Developer" Nodeflair website. Available at: https://nodeflair.com/blog/vitalik-buterin-co-founded-ethereum-at-the-age-of-19-heres-what-he-did-as-a-developer (Accessed 16 June 2024).

2 Buterin, V. (2014). "A Next-Generation Smart Contract and Decentralized Application Platform" *White Paper*, 3(37), 2–1. Available at: https://finpedia.vn/wp-content/uploads/2022/02/Ethereum_white_paper-a_next_generation_smart_contract_and_decentralized_application_platform-vitalik-buterin.pdf (Accessed 16 June 2024).

3 Band Protocol website. Available at: https://www.bandprotocol.com/ (Accessed 21 June 2024).

4 Nest Oracle website. Available at: https://www.nestprotocol.org/oracle (Accessed 21 June 2024).
5 Pyth Network website. Available at: https://pyth.network/ (Accessed 21 June 2024).
6 "The Oracle Problem and the Future of DeFi" BIS, 7 September 2023. Available at: https://www.bis.org/publ/bisbull76.pdf (Accessed 21 June 2024).
7 Chainlink website: Available at: https://chain.link/ (Accessed 21 June 2024).
8 "Swift, Chainlink Tokenization Experiment Successfully Transfers Value across Multiple Blockchains" Coindesk, 31 August 2023. Available at: https://www.coindesk.com/tech/2023/08/31/swift-chainlink-tokenization-experiment-successfully-transfers-value-across-multiple-blockchains/ (Accessed 21 June 2024).
9 "Bringing Capital Markets Onchain with DTCC and Chainlink" DTCC, 21 September 2023. Available at: https://www.dtcc.com/dtcc-connection/articles/2023/september/21/bringing-capital-markets-onchain-with-dtcc-and-chainlink (Accessed 21 June 2024).
10 UMA website. Available at: https://uma.xyz/ (Accessed 30 August 2024).
11 "De Beers Group Introduces World's First Blockchain-backed Diamond Source Platform at Scale" De Beers Group website, 5 May 2022. Available at: https://www.debeersgroup.com/media/company-news/2022/de-beers-group-introduces-worlds-first-blockchain-backed-diamond-source-platform-at-scale (Accessed 30 June 2024).
12 "Tracker and Sarine to Collaborate on Diamond Traceability Solution" De Beers Group website, 9 October 2023. Available at: https://www.debeersgroup.com/media/company-news/2023/tracr-and-sarine-to-collaborate-on-diamond-traceability-solution (Accessed 30 June 2024).
13 Livepeer website. Available at: https://livepeer.org/ (Accessed 30 June 2024).
14 Securitize website. Available at: https://www.securitize.io/ (Accessed 16 June 2024).
15 Compound website. Available at: https://compound.finance/ (Accessed 16 June 2024).
16 Provenance website. Available at: https://provenance.io/ (Accessed 17 June 2024).
17 TradeIX website. Available at: https://www.tradeix.com/ (Accessed 17 June 2024).
18 Fnality International website. Available at: https://www.fnality.org/home (Accessed 17 June 2024).

19 "Reviewing Access to RTGS Accounts for Settlement" Bank of England, 8 February 2024. Available at: https://www.bankofengland.co.uk/paper/2024/dp/reviewing-access-to-rtgs-accounts-for-settlement (Accessed 17 June 2024).
20 "Fnality Completes 'World's First' Blockchain Payments at Bank of England" *Reuters*, 14 December 2023. Available at: https://www.reuters.com/world/uk/fnality-completes-worlds-first-blockchain-payments-bank-england-2023-12-14/ (Accessed 17 June 2024).
21 IBM Food Trust. IBM website. Available at: https://www.ibm.com/products/supply-chain-intelligence-suite/food-trust (Accessed 17 June 2024).
22 "Pancake Bunny Exploit: $44 Million Stolen as BUNNY Token Crashed 99% in Seconds" *Cryptopotato*, 20 May 2021. Available at: https://cryptopotato.com/pancake-bunny-exploit-44-million-stolen-as-bunny-token-crashed-99-in-seconds/ (Accessed 30 August 2024).
23 "Meerkat Finance: Anatomy of a $31 Million DeFi Rug Pull on Binance Smart Chain" Vidma, 14 July 2023. Available at: https://www.vidma.io/blog/meerkat-finance-anatomy-of-a-31-million-defi-rug-pull-on-binance-smart-chain (Accessed 30 August 2024).
24 "How The DAO Hack Changed Ethereum and Crypto" CoinDesk, 9 May 2023. Available at: https://www.coindesk.com/consensus-magazine/2023/05/09/coindesk-turns-10-how-the-dao-hack-changed-ethereum-and-crypto/ (Accessed 30 August 2024).
25 "DeFi Trading Platform Mango Markets Loses $117 Million in Hack" Investopedia, 12 October 2022. Available at: https://www.investopedia.com/mango-markets-got-hacked-6750070 (Accessed 30 August 2024).
26 "Deus Finance Loses $6M Following Stablecoin Hack" *CoinTelegraph*, 6 May 2023. Available at: https://cointelegraph.com/news/deus-finance-loses-6m-following-stablecoin-hack (Accessed 30 August 2024).
27 "Radiant Capital appears to suffer $51 million exploit on its BNB Chain and Arbitrum instances" *The Block*, 16 October 2024. Available at: https://www.theblock.co/post/321606/radiant-capital-appears-to-suffer-51-million-exploit-on-its-bnb-chain-and-arbitrum-instances (Accessed 29 November 2024).
28 "The World Depends on 60-Year-Old Code No One Knows Anymore" PC Mag, 1 December 2023. Available at: https://www.pcmag.com/articles/ibms-plan-to-update-cobol-with-watson (Accessed 24 May 2024).
29 Chris Skinner. "Anyone Want to Hire an Old Man Who Knows COBOL?" *The Finanser*, 22 January 2024. Available at: https://thefinanser.com/2024/01/anyone-want-to-hire-a-cobol-programmer (Accessed 24 May 2024).

30 "Top Programming Languages for Blockchain Development" *Medium*, 14 December 2023. Available at: https://medium.com/@fyattani/top-programming-languages-for-blockchain-development-b4c6a2a7e1b8 (Accessed 24 May 2024).
31 "The Best Programming Language for Blockchain in 2024" 4IRE, 15 November 2023. Available at: https://4irelabs.com/articles/top-blockchain-programming-languages/ (Accessed 24 May 2024).
32 "Top 5 Blockchain Programming Languages" *Ignite*, 1 February 2022, last edited 21 May 2024. Available at: https://ignite.com/blog/top-5-blockchain-programming-languages (Accessed 24 May 2024).
33 "Top 15 Blockchain Programming Languages in 2024" Techvify Software, 4 May 2024. Available at: https://techvify-software.com/blockchain-programming-languages/ (Accessed 24 May 2024).
34 The Graph website. Available at: https://thegraph.com/ (Accessed 24 May 2024).
35 Aptos Labs website. Available at: https://aptoslabs.com/ (Accessed 24 May 2024).
36 R3 Consortium website. Available at: https://r3.com/ (Accessed 16 June 2024).
37 Contour website. Available at: https://www.contour.network/ (Accessed 24 May 2024).
38 TradeTrust website. Available at: https://www.tradetrust.io/ (Accessed 24 May 2024).
39 Hyperledger Foundation website, Hyperledger Fabric. Available at: https://www.hyperledger.org/projects/fabric (Accessed 16 June 2024).
40 Confidential Consortium Framework website. Available at: https://ccf.microsoft.com/ (Accessed 25 May 2024).
41 Quorum on GitHub. Available at: https://github.com/Consensys/quorum (Accessed 16 June 2024).
42 Filecoin website. Available at: https://filecoin.io/ (Accessed 16 June 2024).
43 Hacken website. Available at: https://hacken.io/audits/ (Accessed 1 June 2024).
44 Trail of Bits website. Available at: https://www.trailofbits.com/ (Accessed 1 June 2024).
45 Quantstamp website. Available at: https://quantstamp.com/ (Accessed 1 June 2024).
46 Peckshield website. Available at: https://peckshield.com/ (Accessed 1 June 2024).
47 Slowmist website. Available at: https://www.slowmist.com/ (Accessed 1 June 2024).

48 Certik website. Available at: https://www.certik.com/ (Accessed 1 June 2024).
49 Consensys Diligence website. Available at: https://consensys.io/diligence/ (Accessed 1 June 2024).
50 OpenZeppelin website. Available at: https://www.openzeppelin.com/ (Accessed 20 June 2024).
51 ChainSecurity website. Available at: https://chainsecurity.com/ (Accessed 2 June 2024).
52 Jmeter on GitHub. Available at: https://github.com/apache/jmeter (Accessed 3 June 2024).
53 LLVM Compiler Infrastructure website, liFfuzzer library. Available at: https://llvm.org/docs/LibFuzzer.html (Accessed 2 June 2024).
54 American Fuzzy Lop on GitHub. Available at: https://github.com/google/AFL (Accessed 2 June 2024).
55 Locust website. Available at: https://locust.io/ (Accessed 3 June 2024).
56 Mythril on GitHub. Available at: https://github.com/Consensys/mythril (Accessed 21 June 2024).
57 BlazeMeter website. Available at: https://www.blazemeter.com/ (Accessed 3 June 2024).
58 Testfort website. Available at: https://testfort.com/blockchain-testing (Accessed 3 June 2024).
59 Alchemy website. Available at: https://www.alchemy.com/defi (Accessed 3 June 2024).
60 Infura website. Available at: https://www.infura.io/ (Accessed 3 June 2024).
61 Amazon Managed Blockchain website. Available at: https://aws.amazon.com/managed-blockchain/ (Accessed 3 June 2024).
62 Oracle Blockchain website. Available at: https://www.oracle.com/uk/blockchain/ (Accessed 3 June 2024).
63 "IBM Support for Hyperledger Fabric" IBM website. Available at: https://www.ibm.com/products/blockchain-platform-hyperledger-fabric (Accessed 3 June 2024).
64 "Microsoft Is Shutting Down Its Azure Blockchain Service" ZDNet, 12 May 2021. Available at: https://www.zdnet.com/finance/blockchain/microsoft-is-shutting-down-its-azure-blockchain-service/ (Accessed 3 June 2024).
65 Azure Web3 website. Available at: https://azure.microsoft.com/en-us/solutions/web3 (Accessed 3 June 2024).
66 Fireblocks website. Available at: https://www.fireblocks.com/ (Accessed 3 June 2024).
67 BitGo website. Available at: https://www.bitgo.uk/ (Accessed 3 June 2024).

68 Paxos website. Available at: https://paxos.com/ (Accessed 3 June 2024).
69 Corda website. Available at: https://corda.net/ (Accessed 23 June 2024).
70 Anchorage Digital website. Available at: https://www.anchorage.com/ (Accessed 3 June 2024).
71 Bitpay website. Available at: https://bitpay.com/retail/ (Accessed 25 March 2024).
72 "Merchant Tools" CoinPayments website. Available at: https://www.coinpayments.net/merchant-tools (Accessed 25 March 2024).
73 NOWPayments website. Available at: https://nowpayments.io/pos (Accessed 25 March 2024).
74 Moonpay website. Available at: https://www.moonpay.com/en-gb/business/onramps (Accessed 3 June 2024).
75 ForumPay website. Available at: https://forumpay.com/payments (Accessed 25 March 2024).
76 "White Paper That Birthed Crypto ZK-proofs Receives IEEE 'Test of Time' Award" *Cointelegraph*, 20 May 2024. Available at: https://cointelegraph.com/news/whitepaper-birthed-crypto-zk-proofs-receives-ieee-test-of-time-award (Accessed 24 May 2024).
77 LevelDB on GitHub. Available at: https://github.com/google/leveldb (Accessed 2 June 2024).
78 RockDB on GitHub. Available at: https://github.com/facebook/rocksdb (Accessed 2 June 2024).
79 LMDB on GitHub. Available at: https://github.com/LMDB (Accessed 2 June 2024).
80 BadgerDB on GitHub. Available at: https://github.com/dgraph-io/badger (Accessed 2 June 2024).
81 BoltDB on GitHub. Available at: https://github.com/boltdb/bolt (Accessed 2 June 2024).
82 OpenSSL website. Available at: https://www.openssl.org/ (Accessed 2 June 2024).
83 BouncyCastle website. Available at: https://www.bouncycastle.org/download/bouncy-castle-java/ (Accessed 2 June 2024).
84 Libsodium website. Available at: https://doc.libsodium.org/ (Accessed 2 June 2024).
85 Libp2p website. Available at: https://www.libp2p.io/ (Accessed 2 June 2024).
86 "Introduction to Smart Contracts" Ethereum.org website. Available at: https://ethereum.org/en/developers/docs/smart-contracts/ (Accessed 18 June 2024).
87 "Developing with Rust" Solana website. Available at: https://solana.com/docs/programs/lang-rust (Accessed 18 June 2024).

88 "Chaincode for Developers" Hyperledger Fabric website. Available at: https://hyperledger-fabric.readthedocs.io/en/release-1.4/chaincode4ade.html (Accessed 18 June 2024).
89 "How to Write Robust and Sustainable Smart Contracts" Consensys Diligence, 19 September 2023. Available at: https://consensys.io/diligence/categories/best-practice/ (Accessed 18 June 2024).
90 Hardhat website. Available at: https://hardhat.org/ (Accessed 19 June 2024).
91 Web3.js library. Available at: https://web3js.readthedocs.io/en/v1.10.0/ (Accessed 22 June 2024).
92 AvalancheJS on GitHub. Available at: https://github.com/ava-labs/avalanchejs (Accessed 21 June 2024).
93 Django framework. Available at: https://docs.djangoproject.com/en/5.0/ (Accessed 21 June 2024).
94 Spring framework. Available at: https://spring.io/ (Accessed 21 June 2024).
95 Express framework. Available at: https://expressjs.com/ (Accessed 21 June 2024).
96 Postman website. Available at: https://www.postman.com/ (Accessed 21 June 2024).
97 Mocha website. Available at: https://mochajs.org/ (Accessed 21 June 2024).
98 Prometheus website. Available at: https://prometheus.io/ (Accessed 22 June 2024).
99 Grafana website. Available at: https://grafana.com/ (Accessed 22 June 2024).
100 Reddit, r/dapps. Available at: https://www.reddit.com/r/dapps/ (Accessed 20 June 2024).
101 "Teach Your Grandmother to Suck Eggs" Cambridge Dictionary. Available at: https://dictionary.cambridge.org/dictionary/english/teach-your-grandmother-to-suck-eggs (Accessed 4 June 2024).
102 "Revolut Lets Customers Buy Bitcoin, Litecoin and Ethereum" *Finextra*, 5 December 2017. Available at: https://www.finextra.com/newsarticle/31413/revolut-lets-customers-buy-bitcoin-litecoin-and-ethereum (Accessed 3 June 2024).
103 "Mastercard Makes a Big Bet on Crypto, Buying Blockchain Analytics Start-up CipherTrace" *CNBC*, 9 September 2021. Available at: https://www.cnbc.com/2021/09/09/mastercard-to-buy-blockchain-analytics-start-up-ciphertrace.html (Accessed 3 June 2024).
104 "Checkout.com Launches 24/7 Stablecoin Settlement in Partnership with Fireblocks" *Cointelegraph*, 7 June 2022. Available at: https://cointelegraph.com/news/checkout-com-launches-24–7-stablecoin-settlement-in-partnership-with-fireblocks (Accessed 3 June 2024).

105 "Crypto: Fireblocks Onboards Fis Amid Launch of Payments Engine for Businesses" *Finance Feeds*, 24 October 2022. Available at: https://financefeeds.com/crypto-fireblocks-onboards-fis-amid-launch-of-payments-engine-for-businesses/ (Accessed 3 June 2024).

106 "Visa Expands Stablecoin Settlement Capabilities to Merchant Acquirers" Visa, 9 May 2023. Available at: https://usa.visa.com/about-visa/newsroom/press-releases.releaseId.19881.html (Accessed 3 June 2024).

107 "Ralph Lauren's New Web3-centric Miami Store Accepts Crypto" Vogue Business, 4 April 2023. Available at: https://www.voguebusiness.com/technology/ralph-laurens-new-web3-centric-miami-store-accepts-crypto (Accessed 3 June 2024).

108 "Visa Partners with ConsenSys to Help Bridge CBDCs With Traditional Finance" *CoinDesk*, 13 January 2022. Available at: https://www.coindesk.com/business/2022/01/13/visa-partners-with-consensys-to-help-bridge-cbdcs-with-traditional-finance/ (Accessed 3 June 2024).

109 Solana Pay. Shopify app store. Available at: https://apps.shopify.com/solana-pay (Accessed 3 June 2024).

110 "Ingenico, Binance and Nilos Join Forces to Facilitate Cryptocurrency Acceptance" Ingenico, 21 March 2024. Available at: https://ingenico.com/en/newsroom/press-releases/ingenico-binance-and-nilos-join-forces-facilitate-cryptocurrency-acceptance (Accessed 3 June 2024).

111 "Mastercard-owned CipherTrace Tells Clients It Is Shutting Down Key Products" *Yahoo! Finance*, 13 March 2024. Available at: https://finance.yahoo.com/news/mastercard-owned-ciphertrace-tells-clients-220438951.html (Accessed 3 June 2024).

112 "Revolut Teams Up with MetaMask in Latest Example of Fintech's Crypto Creep" *DL News*, 6 March 2024. Available at: https://www.dlnews.com/articles/fintech/revolut-deepens-crypto-push-with-metamask-collaboration/ (Accessed 3 June 2024).

113 "Stripe Adds Support for Stablecoin Payments" *Ledger Insights*, 26 April 2024. Available at: https://www.ledgerinsights.com/stripe-adds-support-for-stablecoin-payments/ (Accessed 3 June 2024).

114 "How Worldpay Achieves 50% Faster Payment Processing with the Fireblocks Payments Engine" Fireblocks, 11 April 2024. Available at: https://www.fireblocks.com/resources/how-worldpay-achieves-50-percent-faster-payment-processing-with-the-fireblocks-payments-engine/ (Accessed 29 November 2024).

115 "Mastercard Issues New Crypto Announcement: Key Details Revealed" *U Today*, 29 May 2024. Available at: https://u.today/mastercard-issues-new-crypto-announcement-key-details-revealed (Accessed 3 June 2024).

116 "Vodafone Plans Crypto Integration into Mobile Phones via Sim Card" *Crypto News Australia*, 6 May 2024. Available at: https://cryptonews.com.au/news/vodafone-plans-crypto-integration-into-mobile-phones-via-sim-card-120498/ (Accessed 3 June 2024).

117 "MoonPay Expands Crypto Options with PayPal Integration" *IBS Intelligence*, 6 May 2024. Available at: https://ibsintelligence.com/ibsi-news/moonpay-expands-crypto-options-with-paypal-integration/ (Accessed 3 June 2024).

118 "Commonwealth Bank of Australia to Pilot NameCheck Solution on JP Morgan's Liink Network" *Fintech Futures*, 30 May 2024. Available at: https://www.fintechfutures.com/2024/05/commonwealth-bank-of-australia-to-pilot-namecheck-solution-on-jp-morgans-liink-network/ (Accessed 4 June 2024).

119 "Nuvei Introduces Off-ramping of Digital Assets to Cards via Mastercard Move in Europe" *PR Newswire*, 11 July 2024. Available at: https://www.prnewswire.com/news-releases/nuvei-introduces-off-ramping-of-digital-assets-to-cards-via-mastercard-move-in-europe-302194809.html (Accessed 30 August 2024).

3

BLOCKCHAIN OPERATIONS AND GOVERNANCE

Blockchain operations (a little less conversation, a little more action)

Drawing parallels

To my knowledge, there is no specific classification that defines what blockchain operations consist of, but I'll attempt one here by drawing a parallel with traditional payment systems, where the operational categories consist of:

- **A settlement infrastructure**: the centralised infrastructure facilitating the transfer of funds between parties (e.g. a card scheme such as Visa or Mastercard, a payment scheme such as UK Faster Payment Systems, US FedNow, and Brazil Pix).
- **Participants**: regulated financial services institutions, technology and services providers (supervised or regulated).

DOI: 10.4324/9781003480761-4

- **Regulations**: payment regulations, financial services regulations, data protection regulations, anti-money laundering regulations, security regulations, etc.
- **Regulators**: government bodies overseeing and regulating financial institutions and markets to maintain financial stability, protect consumers, and prevent fraudulent activity.
- **Governance models**: the set of rules and procedures governing the operation of the payment system (e.g. card scheme rules), agreements between financial institutions, participation models (e.g. directly connected settling participant), corporate governance, applicable standards (e.g. EMV, ISO 20022), market practices, codes of conduct, legal and accounting frameworks, etc.
- **Payment services and instruments**: mobile payments, digital wallets, P2P payment apps, cards, overlay services (e.g. verification of payee), etc.

Fundamentally, these operational categories can be applied to blockchain infrastructures, although their constituents may differ slightly from one blockchain model to another. The specific components (e.g. ledger, nodes, and smart contracts) were covered in Chapters 1 and 2, and Table 3.1 puts it all into context.

I will cover the concept of "The Code is Law" in the *Blockchain governance* section later on in this chapter.

Operational components

You'll be pleased to know that we've covered the details of the core operational components in the previous chapters, and these are common to permissionless and permissioned blockchains:

- Blockchain ledger (see Chapter 1, *Distributed Ledger Technology* and *What is a blockchain?*)
- Blockchain nodes (see Chapter 1, *Who can do what?*)
- Blockchain protocol (see Chapter 1, Box 1.5)
- Smart contracts (where applicable, see Chapter 2, *What is a smart contract?*)

Blockchain operations encompass the multifaceted activities involved in developing, maintaining, and governing blockchain networks and

Table 3.1 Blockchain operations. © 2024 Neira Jones

Components	Permissionless Blockchain	Permissioned Blockchain
Participation	Open access	Restricted access
Settlement infrastructure	Blockchain ledger	
Participants	Validating nodes, full nodes, light nodes, governance nodes, pools, farms, etc.	Consensus nodes, authority nodes, ordering service nodes, governance nodes, etc.
Regulations	Blockchain protocol (see Chapter 1, Box 1.5)	
	The code is law	The code is only law within applicable regulations, depending on industry
Regulators	No single entity can change the blockchain network outside of the blockchain protocol No single entity can make changes to the blockchain protocol	A single entity, or consortium, controls the blockchain protocol and therefore changes to the blockchain network Governing bodies for applicable regulations
Governance models	Decentralised governance, including on-chain governance (e.g. voting on upgrades or rule changes), off-chain governance (i.e. community involvement), incentive/penalty models, tokenomics	Consortium-based governance, voting mechanisms, reputation systems, identity management, leadership structures Regulatory compliance and reporting, corporate governance, applicable standards, certifications and codes of conduct
Services	Wallets, dApps, smart contracts, information services, marketplaces, decentralised games, prediction markets, oracles, decentralised file storage, layer 2 solutions, interoperability solutions, privacy-enhancing technologies, regulatory compliance tools, etc.	Supply chain management (e.g. provenance tracking), smart contracts for automation, trade finance, identity management, data sharing and auditable data collaboration, regulatory compliance, etc.

applications. Effective operational management of these core components should aim to ensure the smooth functioning and growth of a blockchain project and will typically include:

- **Security and risk management**: implementing robust security measures to protect against hacks, vulnerabilities, and malicious attacks (see Chapter 1, *How are transactions validated and settled?*).
- **Scalability solutions**: addressing the challenges of scalability to handle increased transaction volumes without compromising speed or cost-effectiveness (see Chapter 1, *Are blockchains scalable?*).
- **Partnerships and ecosystem development**: collaborating with industry partners, integrating with other blockchain projects, and fostering ecosystem growth through strategic alliances (see Chapter 2, *Building blockchains and applications*).
- **Compliance and regulatory considerations**: navigating legal frameworks, tax implications, and regulatory requirements across jurisdictions to ensure compliance and mitigate legal risks.

Regarding the core operational components, these activities are crucial for ensuring the functionality, security, and sustainability of these decentralised networks and the applications and services that run on them. But whilst these components are essential to blockchain operations for maintaining the technical infrastructure (e.g. validation, consensus, nodes), which were covered extensively in earlier chapters, blockchain operations also include:

- **Blockchain governance**: this refers to the decision-making processes and structures or a range of activities such as blockchain protocol upgrades, network parameters, and community initiatives. Governance models can be on-chain (decisions made through voting mechanisms embedded in the blockchain protocol), or off-chain (decisions are made through informal discussions, forums, or external governance structures that influence protocol development and community decisions). As per Table 3.1, governance structures will vary across permissionless and permissioned blockchains.
- **Blockchain economics**: this refers to the design and structure of a blockchain's economic system, similar to a monetary policy in centralised financial systems. This may be referred to as **tokenomics**

(see Chapter 4, *Tokenomics and metrics*) for permissionless blockchains, whilst permissioned blockchains may adopt different economic models including membership and user fees, subscription or shared revenue models, or other consortium-defined structures and integration with existing financial systems.

Blockchain operations integrate all these components with the aim to create decentralised systems that offer transparency, security, and efficiency across various industries. Success is of course contingent on effectively managing the technical infrastructure, governance mechanisms, economics, funding strategies, and operational challenges. Many blockchain projects claim to revolutionise traditional business processes, enhance financial inclusion, and drive innovation in global economies.

In this chapter, I will cover the various aspects of blockchain governance, and present only some aspects of blockchain economics as this is covered extensively in Chapter 4 (it was worth a whole chapter 😉).

Blockchain governance (playin' by the rules)

The Code is Law

"The Code is Law" is a fundamental principle in blockchain governance, particularly in permissionless blockchains, as highlighted in Table 3.1. This concept isn't formally defined within a blockchain and nor does blockchain code explicitly state it, but it's a widely used expression that emphasises the immutability and binding nature of blockchain protocols and smart contract code, fostering autonomy and trustlessness, specifically:

- **Immutability**: once deployed on the blockchain, smart contracts are typically immutable, meaning they can't be altered or stopped by any single party, including their creators (see Chapter 2, Box 2.11). This immutability ensures that the terms defined in the smart contract are enforced **autonomously** and **automatically**, without relying on centralised authorities.
- **Decentralised decision-making**: blockchain governance often operates under decentralised principles, where decisions about upgrades, changes, or disputes are made collectively by network participants.

The concept of "The Code is Law" implies that governance decisions should respect the integrity and immutability of existing blockchain protocols and smart contracts.

The concept of **The Code is Law** has its roots in early discussions about digital technology and its impact on governance. Legal scholar Lawrence Lessig used the phrase "Code and Other Laws of Cyberspace" in his 2000 book[1] to explore how code embedded in online platforms shapes user behaviour and interactions. Lessig's work helped set the stage for the ongoing debate about the role of code in regulating online environments. Supporters see the code as a way to create predictable and self-enforcing systems, claiming that transparency in the code fosters trust and eliminates ambiguity in the rules. Critics argue that the code can't adapt to unforeseen circumstances and may lead to rigid systems that are difficult to change. Questions also arise about who controls the code and the potential for biases within it. Whilst the concept is evocative, it's crucial to recognise the limitations of the phrase "The Code is Law" in a legal sense. Blockchain networks often operate on a global scale, and the code itself doesn't have the power to supersede national or international laws (although, as we know, the nature of decentralised systems makes them an enabler to circumvent these very laws[2]). Legal frameworks and regulations established by governments can still apply to blockchain activities, and code can't override them (although enforcement may be a challenge). The code only lays out the rules for the blockchain network itself, but it doesn't have the authority of a legal system. It can't enforce penalties or hold anyone accountable in the traditional legal sense (but does so within the network itself).

"The Code is Law" aims to provide the foundation for a self-governed system. As you will realise by now, this can only be truly applied to permissionless blockchains, as their permissioned counterparts, with their varying degrees of centralisation, can decide how much of a "law" the code will be, and they can always change it to suit their needs 😉.

In essence, "The Code is Law" underscores the foundational principle of trustlessness and autonomy in blockchain governance, emphasising the importance of transparent and predictable outcomes based on immutable rules encoded in blockchain protocols and smart contracts (if applicable).

However, it also necessitates careful consideration of risks and the need for governance mechanisms that can address unforeseen challenges (e.g. how are disagreements and disputes resolved?) whilst preserving the integrity of the decentralised ecosystem.

Blockchain governance refers to the processes and mechanisms through which decisions about the protocol, network upgrades, and operational parameters are made. Governance ensures that the blockchain network evolves, adapts, and resolves conflicts in a transparent and efficient manner, within the framework set by the code. In order to participate in governance, stakeholders must have a mechanism by which they are able to speak their minds and influence decisions. Think of it as "having the talking stick" when in a large crowd, where everyone knows that they can speak when they have the "stick". Blockchains operate in a similar way, and the "talking stick" mechanism of the large crowd (the blockchain community) may be implemented through on-chain or off-chain governance (or a combination of both).

On-chain governance

On-chain governance refers to decision-making processes that occur directly on the blockchain itself. In this model, stakeholders participate in proposing, debating, and voting on changes or upgrades to the blockchain network using native on-chain mechanisms which may be facilitated by the blockchain's coin (see Chapter 1, Box 1.11).

Whilst "The Code is Law" establishes the core rules and principles of the immutable blockchain, the outcomes of on-chain governance allow for some adaptation and evolution leading to modifications of the code over time.

Key features of on-chain governance include:

- **Proposal submission**: coin holders with a stake in the network can submit proposals for changes or improvements to the blockchain protocol.
- **Voting**: coin holders may vote on proposed changes. The weight of each stakeholder's vote typically corresponds to the number of coins/tokens they hold or stake in the network, although other mechanisms may be used (e.g. reputation systems).

- **Execution**: once a proposal is approved through voting, the changes are automatically executed through smart contracts or protocol rules embedded in the blockchain.
- **Transparency and immutability**: decisions and voting outcomes are transparent and verifiable on the blockchain, ensuring immutability and reducing the risk of manipulation.
- **Decentralisation**: on-chain governance aims to decentralise decision-making power, distributing it among network participants rather than relying on a central authority.

Examples of blockchains using on-chain governance include:

- **Tezos**[3]: uses a self-amendment process where stakeholders holding the Tezos native coin XTZ (pronounced "tez") can vote on proposed amendments to the protocol.
- **Decred**[4]: employs a hybrid Proof of Work (PoW) and Proof of Stake (PoS) system where stakeholders holding the Decred native DCR coin can vote on proposals directly affecting the network. Decred positions itself as having "a strong focus on community input, open governance, and sustainable funding for development".
- **Cosmos**[5]: a hybrid PoS blockchain designed for interoperability, where holders of the native coin, ATOM, can vote on network upgrades and parameter adjustments.

On-chain governance is more prevalent in PoS and hybrid protocol blockchains (see Chapter 1, Table 1.4) because these protocols often have a more streamlined decision-making process due to the inherent features of staking mechanisms. Stakeholders who hold and stake their coins have a vested interest in the long-term health and security of the network, making them more likely to participate in on-chain governance. Additionally, PoS and hybrid blockchains often have smaller validator sets compared to PoW networks, facilitating better coordination and faster voting processes on the blockchain itself.

By contrast, PoW blockchains, like Bitcoin, have a vast number of miners participating in the network. Implementing on-chain governance mechanisms for such a large and geographically dispersed group can be complex and inefficient as reaching consensus on proposals could be slow and cumbersome. In addition, PoW miners are primarily incentivised by transaction fees and block rewards, making participating in potential on-chain governance a lower priority compared to allocating computational resources for mining in view of earning rewards.

Finally, introducing complex on-chain voting mechanisms could potentially introduce new vulnerabilities or attack vectors to the PoW blockchain (e.g. manipulation by miners with a large amount of hash power, slow decision-making, and increased blockchain size). Therefore, PoW blockchains often primarily rely on off-chain governance models.

Off-chain governance

Off-chain governance refers to decision-making processes that occur outside the blockchain protocol itself, typically involving discussions, debates, and decision-making through informal or formal mechanisms that are not enforced by the blockchain protocol directly. Similarly to on-chain governance, the outcomes of off-chain governance allow for some adaptation and evolution leading to modifications of the code over time.

Characteristics

This model usually features:

- **Discussion forums**: community discussions and debates about proposed changes often take place on public platforms. Social media platforms like X, Telegram or Discord are popular for real-time discussions and quick feedback. Dedicated blockchain forums (e.g. Bitcointalk,[6] Ethereum Stack Exchange[7]) or Reddit subreddits (e.g. r/Bitcoin,[8] r/ethereum,[9] r/solana[10]) often provide in-depth analysis and technical discussions about proposed changes. Blockchain projects may also create dedicated platforms for their communities to exchange ideas and proposals.
- **Governance proposals**: stakeholders (e.g. developers, token holders, community members) may propose changes or upgrades through off-chain channels. These proposed changes may then be submitted through formal proposal systems (which are then considered by the development team or a designated governance body) or discussion forums to gather community feedback.

- **Decision-making**: the actual decision-making process, such as finalising proposals or adopting changes, may involve core developers, elected community representatives, or community-wide consensus-based voting through off-chain mechanisms (e.g. Snapshot,[11] Tally[12]).
- **Implementation**: once decisions are made, changes are implemented through updates to the software or protocol. This typically involves developer teams, and when changes require network upgrades, node operators (e.g. full nodes, miners, validators, see Chapter 1, *Who can do what?* for more details) may also be involved.
- **Trust and reputation**: off-chain governance relies heavily on trust and reputation within the community, as decisions are not enforced by protocol rules but rather by the consensus and cooperation of stakeholders. Successful change implementation hinges on stakeholders' willingness to cooperate and abide by the agreed-upon changes.

Examples of blockchains using off-chain governance include:

- **Bitcoin**: Changes and upgrades to the Bitcoin protocol are proposed and discussed extensively in forums and developer communities, although final decisions are made by developers.
- **Ethereum**: Ethereum's governance primarily relies on off-chain discussions and proposals.[13] Whilst the Ethereum Foundation plays a significant role, community discussions on platforms like Reddit and Discord influence key decisions. Although Ethereum transitioned from PoW to PoS in 2022, its governance structure remains largely off-chain. However, some improvement proposals reaching an advanced stage in off-chain discussions may be implemented through a limited on-chain governance mechanism.

For successful off-chain governance, transparency throughout the process is crucial. This includes clear communication of proposed changes, rationale behind decisions, and how community feedback is incorporated. Additionally, some projects explore incentive mechanisms to encourage active participation in discussions and proposal creation.

It's also important to note that the decision-making power within off-chain governance can vary significantly between projects and trade-offs exist between:

- **Centralised control**: where the project's core team or a designated governing body might have the final say on proposals, with a defined improvement proposal process, even if community discussions occur beforehand.
- **Decentralised ideals**: where the project strives for a more democratic approach, and community voting, or consensus voting mechanisms, hold greater weight in final decisions.

If you're interested in knowing how off-chain governance improvement proposals work in practice, read on, otherwise, you can skip the next section and move on to *On-chain vs. off-chain governance* (and there's always the duck…).

In practice: improvement proposals

With off-chain governance, the project team, essentially developers, have to agree to code changes. But as democratic as blockchains claim to be, not all developers are created equal (in terms of change proposals at least)… How the process works is described at a high level in Figure 3.1.

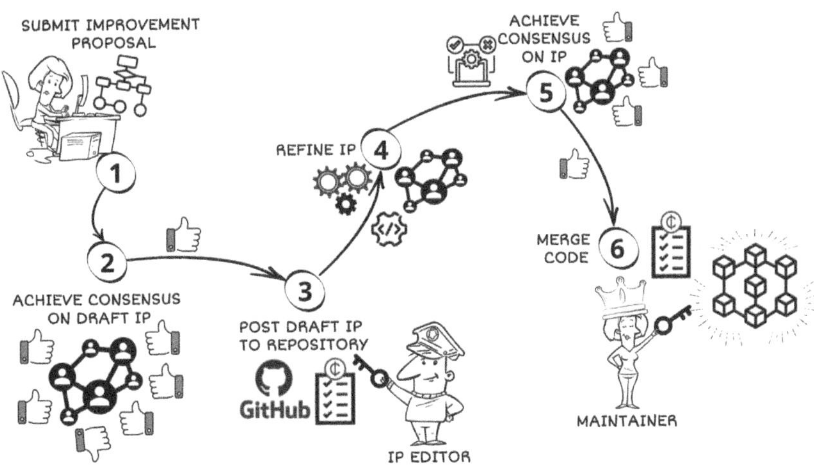

Figure 3.1 The blockchain improvement proposal process. © 2024 Neira Jones.

Here are the steps:

1. Any developer can submit a draft **improvement proposal (IP)** through the blockchain improvement process. Each blockchain

has its own improvement proposal process: **Bitcoin Improvement Proposal (BIP)**[14] process, **Ethereum Improvement Proposal (EIP)**[15] process, **Binance Evolution Proposal (BEP)**,[16] **Solana IMprovement Documents (SIMD)**,[17] etc.

2. **Achieving consensus on the draft IP**: this is not a formal process. The IP author must convince the community that the IP is worth it, which involves marketing, lobbying, or any other informal communication mechanisms. Consensus on an IP doesn't need to be unanimous as it's essentially based on the lack of disagreement.
3. **Submitting the IP to the repository**: a special type of developer, the **IP editor**, will decide if the draft IP is posted to the repository for formal community review.
4. **Refining the IP**: If the IP is accepted, the developer community gives feedback, and the author updates the IP if required.
5. **Achieving consensus on the IP**: Once consensus is achieved in the developer community (i.e. no strong objections), the IP code is ready to be merged with the blockchain source code.
6. **Merging the code**: Only a few people can authorise a change to the blockchain source code, and these are special developers called **maintainers**. When IP source code is authorised by a maintainer, it is merged with the blockchain source code and included in the next update released to the public.

Essentially, there is a power hierarchy in the blockchain community: at the top of the tree, you have the maintainers who will commit the changes to the blockchain, then you have the IP editors, who decide if an IP is posted to the open repository (e.g. GitHub) for community review and makes any changes to it depending on community feedback, and then you have the developer community who propose IPs and participate in informal consensus for IP inclusion to the blockchain code. I'll let you decide if this is a truly decentralised process 😉.

On-chain vs. off-chain governance

Both on-chain and off-chain governance models have their strengths and weaknesses, and many blockchain projects may use a combination of both approaches depending on their specific needs, community dynamics, and technological capabilities. Usually, this would include the following considerations:

- **Flexibility**: on-chain governance provides more immediate and transparent decision-making processes, whereas off-chain governance allows for broader discussions and considerations.
- **Security and efficiency**: on-chain governance ensures decisions are enforced by blockchain consensus mechanisms through offers transparent and verifiable decision-making, enhancing security and reducing the risk of manipulation, whilst speed of decision-making may be a challenge. By contrast, off-chain governance can be more flexible as it allows for broader participation and iterative discussion before proposals are formalised but may require more trust and coordination among participants.

Professionals should remember the following:

- Whilst "**The Code is Law**" emphasises trustless and immutable operations within a blockchain, it's **not a legal concept** and can't adapt to unforeseen circumstances. Be mindful of these limitations when designing governance rules.
- **Choose a governance model that best suits your project**. On-chain governance offers transparency and secure enforcement but can be complex for large communities. Off-chain governance is more flexible for discussions but relies on trust and may lack automatic enforcement. Consider your community's dynamics and the technical capabilities of your blockchain. Avoid overly complex on-chain voting mechanisms, especially for PoW blockchains where large numbers of participants can make voting cumbersome.
- **Establish clear and transparent decision-making processes** within your chosen governance model. This fosters trust and ensures everyone understands how decisions are made. Open communication and active stakeholder participation are crucial for effective blockchain governance. Encourage discussion and input from all relevant parties.
- **In off-chain governance, ensure a strong foundation of trust and coordination** among stakeholders to mitigate the risk of decisions not being implemented.

- **Consider a hybrid approach** that combines on-chain and off-chain mechanisms. This can leverage the strengths of both models for optimal decision-making and enforcement.
- **Beware of centralised control within a seemingly decentralised governance structure**. True decentralisation distributes decision-making power, not concentrates it.
- **Don't overlook the limitations of "The Code is Law" and potential legal implications**. Real-world laws still apply, and the code itself can't supersede them.

Operational tokens

In Chapter 1, *Rewards and incentives*, I introduced the concept of coins and tokens (Box 1.11), and their crucial role in blockchain ecosystems. Tokens power blockchain operations for both permissionless and permissioned blockchains and also shape governance aspects.

Utility tokens

Utility tokens act as digital keys or coupons that may be used for various purposes, such as paying for transaction fees (see Chapter 1, *Submitting transactions* and *Transaction fees*), accessing exclusive features, and paying for other network fees (e.g. fees for deploying smart contracts, interacting with dApps, oracle fees, name registration fees). Utility tokens are found in both PoS and PoW blockchains, however, their role can differ slightly.

In PoS blockchains, utility tokens are often used for a wider range of purposes as the native coin's primary function is to secure the network through staking rewards, whereas PoW blockchains prioritise security through mining and miners get rewarded in the native coin.

The core characteristics of utility tokens are:

- **Native**: a utility token is native to its specific blockchain platform. It's created and operates on that blockchain and can't be transferred to another blockchain without additional steps.
- **Unit of account within its ecosystem**: the utility token serves as the primary unit of account for measuring the value of services offered. This means prices, rewards, incentives, penalties, and grants are

all denominated in the token. For example, with Decentraland – a 3D virtual world platform – the MANA token can be used to purchase virtual plots of land within their metaverse as this system functions as a mini-economy with internal goods and services.

- **Facilitates access and use**: the primary purpose of a utility token is to grant users access to specific functionalities, products, or services within the associated blockchain platform. This could include things like:
  - Paying transaction fees on the network.
  - **Access specific functionalities and benefits**. For example, Binance Coin (BNB) holders receive discounts on trading fees on the Binance exchange.
  - **Purchasing digital goods or services** within a platform (e.g. games, storage). For example, the FIL token on the Filecoin decentralised storage network can be used to pay for storage and storage providers earn FIL tokens.
  - **Donations** to developers.
  - **Staking** the token to earn rewards or unlock features.

In addition, some utility tokens are often tradeable on crypto exchanges, allowing users to buy, sell, or hold them based on their value and utility within the ecosystem. However, their primary purpose is not as a speculative investment but to facilitate actions within the platform. Regardless, many utility tokens have a capped or limited total supply, which can influence their value and incentivise users to hold them.

Utility tokens typically don't confer voting rights (unlike governance tokens, which are covered next), unless a blockchain implementation (typically PoS) has implemented a coin voting mechanism where the underlying coin – used for staking – also functions as a governance token. Coin voting systems create a situation where the token's utility (staking for security) becomes intertwined with its governance function (voting rights). In essence, the utility token becomes a governance token for those who choose to stake their holdings to participate in governance.

Overall, the defining characteristic of a utility token is its role in providing access and utility within a specific blockchain ecosystem. Their primary function revolves around facilitating actions within a particular platform, not necessarily functioning as a global medium of exchange or store of value.

Most public blockchain projects will implement a utility token for operations. Permissioned blockchains, with their controlled access, might theoretically explore alternative fee structures besides utility tokens, including:

- **Subscription fees**: instead of a token, users pay a subscription fee to access the network and its functionalities.
- **Validator fees paid in fiat**: validators who secure the network may be compensated directly in fiat currency, eliminating the need for a utility token.

This space is constantly evolving and there may be other alternative examples. However, due to the private nature of permissioned blockchains, it's challenging to find specific real-world examples of these models in operation. After all, their implementations are, well, private ☺, and it's advisable to consult the specific platform's documentation to understand their token implementation.

Utility tokens may evolve alongside the blockchain's utility (see Chapter 2, *Blockchain utility*), and they may evolve into governance tokens, or other types of tokens as the blockchain project evolves.

BOX 3.1 THE CURIOUS CASE OF BITCOIN

Bitcoin BTC can be viewed as a special case when considering the definition of a utility token. it is important to note that Bitcoin wasn't initially created to function as a utility token within its own ecosystem. Its primary purpose was to serve as a peer-to-peer electronic cash system, independent of financial institutions. However, like all utility tokens, BTC serves as:

- **A unit of account**: prices within the Bitcoin network (e.g. transaction fees) were denominated in BTC.

- **A medium of exchange**: users needed BTC to pay for transactions on the network.
- **An incentive for miners**: miners were rewarded in BTC for securing the network.

Over time, Bitcoin's adoption and network effects transformed BTC's role and transcended its initial purpose as a decentralised digital currency to become:

- **A store of value**: investors began seeing Bitcoin as a potential hedge against inflation and a valuable asset class.
- **A speculative instrument**: BTC's price volatility attracted speculation, further propelling its value beyond its utility within the network.

Today, Bitcoin BTC's primary function is not solely focused on facilitating transactions within its own ecosystem. Whilst it is still used for those purposes, its role as a store of value and speculative asset has become more prominent, and its original aim to become a universal peer-to-peer electronic cash system was never realised. Depending on which side of the fence you sit on, some may see its potential as "digital gold", as Deutsche Bank[18] suggests, or as definitely "not digital gold" as the US Securities and Exchange Commission ascertains.[19] This case highlights the evolving nature of tokens and how their function can change over time.

As you may imagine, there are ongoing debates as to what Bitcoin's BTC is or isn't.

Finally, you might have heard the term "exchange token", and this simply refers to a utility token that is specific to a crypto exchange (see Chapter 6, *Crypto exchanges*). It is issued by the exchange and provides users with various benefits on the platform, including reduced trading fees, access to exclusive features, participation in token sales, and rewards for holding the token. Exchange tokens are typically used to incentivise user engagement and loyalty within the exchange ecosystem. Prominent examples are Binance Coin (BNB) and Kucoin Token (KCS).

Governance tokens

Governance tokens give holders **voting rights** on proposals that affect the future of the blockchain (a "talking stick"). Think of them as an upgraded version of utility tokens. The number of governance tokens held often determines the voting weight of the holder as more tokens usually translate into greater influence over protocol upgrades, fee structures, blockchain upgrades, etc. They empower holders to participate in shaping the project's future direction through a decentralised governance process similar to shares in a company, but instead of dividends, they offer a say in how the project evolves.

The core characteristics of governance tokens are:

- **Native**: governance tokens are native to their specific blockchain platform. They are created and operate on that blockchain and can't be easily transferred to other blockchains without additional steps.
- **Confer voting rights**: token holders can vote on proposals that affect the blockchain protocol. The number of governance tokens a user holds often determines their voting weight. More tokens typically translate into greater influence over the voting outcome, which creates a system where users with a larger stake potentially have a more significant voice in decision-making. The process for submitting and voting on proposals can vary depending on the governance model (e.g. some models allow any token holder to submit proposals, whilst others might require a minimum token holding or community consensus before a proposal goes to a vote). What token holders may vote on includes:
    - **Protocol upgrades**: changes to the underlying blockchain technology or consensus mechanism (e.g. switching from PoW to PoS).
    - **Fee structures**: adjustments to transaction fees within the network, potentially impacting user costs and project revenue.
    - **Treasury management**: proposals for allocating funds from the project's treasury, which might involve funding development initiatives, marketing campaigns, or community rewards programs.
    - **New feature implementation**: ideas for adding new functionalities to the platform, potentially expanding its capabilities and user base.

- **Enable decentralised governance**: governance tokens facilitate a decentralised approach to managing and evolving the blockchain protocol. Decisions are made collectively by token holders, fostering community ownership and participation.

Token evolution

Both governance and utility tokens incentivise user participation in the blockchain project, contributing to the development and growth of blockchain ecosystems by attracting users and fostering a sense of community involvement.

Whilst utility tokens are used for operations and primarily reward users for engaging with the platform, they may be used for governance purposes in blockchains that have implemented a coin voting system.

Governance tokens give users a stake in the blockchain's future by facilitating a more decentralised approach to managing and growing blockchain protocols, fostering community ownership.

In practical terms, whilst utility tokens are typical in layer 1 public blockchains, pure governance tokens (as far as I can tell) are a rare breed there and, where implemented, they will incorporate some utility, making them hybrid tokens. The reason for this is simple: if a token lacks utility, users might be less motivated to hold it and participate in governance, making it difficult to generate revenue for ongoing network development and operations.

For layer 1 blockchains, utility tokens may evolve to incorporate governance features over time. An example is Algorand,[20] which launched in 2019 with their ALGO utility token (transaction fees, staking rewards), and introduced governance features in 2021 to allow holders to vote on proposals by staking an amount of ALGO. At the time of writing, ALGO functions as both a utility and governance token.

In addition, whilst utility tokens form the basis of operations for layer 1 public blockchains, blockchain applications may at the outset use governance tokens which generally evolve to incorporate utility. For example, COMP, initially a governance token for the Compound DeFi lending protocol,[21] evolved into being used as collateral within the platform. Similarly, MakerDAO,[22] a Decentralised Autonomous Organisation (see later section) that manages the decentralised borrowing and lending DeFi platform

Maker, uses MKR as their governance token, but MKR also incentivises token holders through staking rewards.

Professionals should remember the following:

- To ensure effective use of tokens, professionals should **clearly distinguish between utility tokens**, which facilitate access within a platform, **and governance tokens**, which offer voting rights on the project's future.
- Professionals should **stay informed** about how a token's role within an ecosystem might evolve over time to incorporate both utility and governance features.
- Professionals should **consider the layer context when evaluating tokens**. Utility tokens are more common in public layer 1 blockchains, whilst applications built on top might initially use governance tokens that later gain utility. Permissioned blockchains may use alternative mechanisms, and it's important to consult the specific platform's documentation to understand their token or fee structures.
- When encountering a new token, it's valuable for professionals to **assess its primary function and utility** within its specific ecosystem. Not all tokens function in the same way and it's important to understand the specific purpose (utility, governance, or hybrid) and practical use cases within the platform.

Smart contracts

I've covered various aspects of smart contracts in Chapter 2 and how they automate transactions and agreements. Here, I'll add to this picture by showing the crucial roles they play in blockchain governance by establishing a set of transparent and immutable rules.

On-chain and off-chain governance

Smart contracts may be used to facilitate both on-chain and off-chain governance, including:

- **Automating on-chain governance**: smart contracts can encode governance rules on-chain, eliminating the need for manual intervention or centralised control. Pre-defined parameters within the smart contract enable automated decision-making and ensure transparent and unbiased execution of governance processes.

- **Facilitating decentralised voting**: smart contracts can be used in on-chain governance to create secure and verifiable voting systems for proposals, upgrades, or other community decisions within a blockchain network.
- **Off-chain governance and smart contract interaction**: whilst smart contracts are suited to automating on-chain governance processes, off-chain discussions and consensus-building often play a crucial role in blockchain governance. Here, smart contracts can be designed to integrate with off-chain processes, including where a proposal debated and agreed upon off-chain could be encoded into a smart contract for subsequent on-chain voting and execution.
- **Treasury management and fund distribution**: smart contracts can automate the distribution of funds from a blockchain project's treasury based on pre-defined rules. This eliminates the risk of misappropriation and provides a transparent record of fund allocation, contributing to both on-chain and off-chain governance by ensuring responsible financial management.
- **Parameter changes and protocol upgrades**: smart contracts can be used to govern the process of implementing upgrades or changes to the blockchain protocol. Specific conditions within the smart contract can trigger upgrades automatically upon reaching a consensus within the community, streamlining the on-chain governance process.

Smart contract governance use cases

The applicability of smart contract functionality for blockchain governance depends on the type of blockchain.

- **Permissionless blockchains**: here, core governance processes like proposal discussions and voting, often occur off-chain due to scalability limitations but smart contracts might be used to facilitate voting mechanisms or execute actions based on off-chain decisions.
- **Permissioned blockchains**: with their pre-defined set of participants, these may use alternative governance models that rely less on smart contracts and focus on off-chain consensus mechanisms among trusted participants.

In addition to facilitating on-chain and off-chain governance processes, smart contracts may also be used for governance of blockchain applications by automating pre-defined rules and enforcing agreements transparently:

- **Payment channels**: smart contracts may be used to create **state channels** (see Chapter 1, *Layer 2 scaling solutions, State channels*) for micropayments. They enable fast and efficient off-chain transactions between trusted parties, with smart contracts governing the rules for adding and withdrawing funds. The final settlement happens on-chain, but the governance of day-to-day transactions lies within the channel's smart contract. This creates a separate governance layer for managing micropayments without relying on the main chain. The Lightning Network,[23] a layer 2 solution for Bitcoin, uses payment channels to conduct off-chain transactions governed by smart contracts.
- **Recurring payments**: smart contracts can automate recurring payments for subscriptions or services, empowering a self-governing system. Users define the payment terms within the smart contract, and subsequent payments are automatically deducted from their wallets upon reaching designated intervals. This eliminates the need for manual intervention and central oversight, establishing a decentralised governance model for recurring billing. Livepeer,[24] a decentralised video streaming service, is an example.
- **Cross-chain bridges**: secure and verifiable cross-chain transactions for payments or token transfers rely heavily on smart contract governance. These contracts manage the locking and releasing of assets on one chain based on the corresponding asset creation on the other. This enforces pre-defined rules for cross-chain transfers, ensuring a trustless governance framework for transactions across different blockchain ecosystems. An example is Ren,[25] a cross-chain bridge (RenBridge) that allows users to transfer BTC to other blockchains, governed by smart contracts. When a user locks BTC in a Ren vault, a corresponding amount of wrapped BTC (wBTC) is minted on the target chain. The smart contract ensures the locked BTC remains locked until the wBTC is burned for redemption, allowing users to leverage their BTC across different blockchain ecosystems.

BOX 3.2 THE CURIOUS CASE OF CROSS-CHAIN BRIDGES

Whilst cross-chain bridges offer valuable interoperability in the blockchain ecosystem, they also present unique risks and challenges in terms of security and regulatory compliance. For example, RenBridge has been widely used for processing a significant volume of cross-chain transfers, including both legitimate and unfortunately, illicit activities. RenBridge became a popular tool for money laundering and other illicit activities and analysis shows that at least $540 million in cryptoassets originating from theft, fraud, ransomware, and various other criminal activities were laundered through RenBridge since 2020.[26] This included over $153 million in ransomware proceeds, at least $267.2 million in assets stolen from exchanges and DeFi services, and funds allegedly linked to North Korean hacking groups. The bridge's decentralised nature made it an attractive option for criminals seeking to evade regulated exchanges that require customer identification (e.g. KYC). It's therefore no surprise that cross-chain bridges like Ren's have faced increased regulatory scrutiny due to their potential for facilitating financial crime.

The case of Ren highlights the need for improved security measures and potentially new regulatory approaches to address the use of DeFi tools for illicit purposes.

- **Decentralised exchanges (DEXs)**: (covered in Chapter 6, *Transacting in a decentralised world*) whilst DEXs might use off-chain governance for parameter adjustments, smart contracts form the backbone of their core functionalities as they automate the trading logic and order matching within the exchange, ensuring fair and transparent exchange processes. This exemplifies how smart contracts play a crucial role within a dApp's governance framework, even when core decision-making happens off-chain. Uniswap[27] is an example.
- **DeFi**: (see Chapter 2, *Lifting the veil on DeFi*) smart contracts are crucial to DeFi, and they automate core functionalities, acting as self-governing protocols. They enforce loan terms, manage collateral, and set interest rates based on pre-defined rules within peer-to-peer lending platforms. This eliminates the need for intermediaries like banks and fosters trustless financial governance.

- **Escrow services**: smart contracts can act as self-governing escrow agents, securely holding funds or assets until predetermined conditions are met. This eliminates the need for a trusted third party and establishes a transparent governance framework for transactions in marketplaces or freelance platforms. Users can be confident that funds are released only when pre-defined criteria are fulfilled. The XRP Ledger implements smart contracts through its escrow feature, which is particularly useful for facilitating secure cross-border transactions.[28]

Smart contract governance, whilst innovative, presents challenges. The immutability of deployed smart contract code can create issues if errors or vulnerabilities are discovered post-deployment. Patching or altering a smart contract is difficult (see Chapter 2, Box 2.11), and exploits could potentially lead to loss of funds or unintended consequences. Additionally, their decentralised nature can make dispute resolution challenging, as there's no central arbitrating authority.

Aside from financial services, smart contracts may also be applied to governance for other use cases such as identity management, supply chain management, and voting systems. Smart contracts also play a crucial role in Decentralised Autonomous Organisations (DAOs) to create self-governing online communities.

Decentralised Autonomous Organisation (DAO)

What is a DAO?

A **Decentralised Autonomous Organisation (DAO)** is a blockchain application that uses smart contracts for rule enforcement and aims to promote oversight and management of an entity similar to a corporation. DAOs intend to give every member a voice, vote, and opportunity to propose initiatives and members typically buy their way in by acquiring the DAO's governance token. DAOs are typically implemented using a collection of smart contracts and may incorporate multiple dApps.

How is a DAO set up?

A DAO is typically set up using a governance token as a way of distributing voting rights and decision-making power among their members, but there are alternative governance structures (e.g. share-based DAOs where shares are used to represent voting power instead of tokens). Since governance tokens are the most popular method, I will concentrate on this model for the purpose of this section, but references are provided at the end of this chapter for alternative models.[29,30,31]

A DAO initially raises capital by trading fiat for its governance token which confers investors voting power and may grant ownership proportion. If a DAO is successful, the value of the native token will increase, enabling the DAO to issue future tokens at a greater value to raise more capital. If the members approve, this capital can be used to invest in assets, including companies, real-world assets, or other digital assets. The value of the DAO will increase if the value of those assets appreciates.

DAOs are technically interesting structures as a way of managing a company. Of course, the exact rights and responsibilities associated with holding DAO governance tokens may vary significantly across implementations. Some DAOs may primarily focus on voting, whilst others may focus more on ownership or profit-sharing mechanisms. These specific details would be included in the DAO smart contract and governance documents.

Practical considerations

When assessing DAOs, several factors should be considered:

- **Voting rights and influence**: governance tokens generally give holders the ability to vote on proposals and decisions within the DAO. The weight of a token holder's vote usually depends on how many tokens they have. In many cases, the voting power is directly proportional to the number of tokens held (i.e. 1 token = 1 vote), where an individual's voting power is directly proportional to the number of tokens they hold. In other cases, DAOs may use a "1 authorised wallet = 1 vote" system, where each approved wallet has equal voting power regardless of token holdings.

- **Decision-making power**: token holders may influence various aspects of the DAO, including protocol changes, budget structures, partnerships, and other strategic decisions.
- **Ownership representation**: governance tokens may signify ownership in a decentralised protocol. They can be seen as similar to shares in a traditional company, representing a stake in the organisation.
- **Potential financial benefits**: whilst not explicitly stated in all cases, governance tokens may also entitle holders to a share of the DAO's profits or value, similar to how shareholders might benefit from a company's success.
- **Liability considerations**: in some legal interpretations, governance token holders might be considered partners in a general partnership, potentially exposing them to liability for the DAO's actions, including losses suffered (e.g. in security incidents), debts, or obligations. The lack of a formal legal entity structure for many DAOs contributes to the uncertainty around liability.
- **Tax implications**: receiving governance tokens may be considered a taxable event, and any profits from DAO activities distributed to token holders could be subject to income tax. The specific tax treatment may vary depending on the jurisdiction and the nature of the DAO's activities.

Example implementations and evolution

DAOs have a chequered history:

- In April 2016, the DAO was formed as a venture capital fund and raised more than $150 million in a few weeks. In June 2016, a user exploited a software vulnerability in the smart contract (underscoring the importance of thorough security audits) and was able to siphon out millions of dollars' worth of ETH out of the DAO repeatedly.[32] This led to major disagreements in the Ethereum community splitting those in favour of immutability, and those in favour of refunding investors (and therefore breaking immutability). The DAO was delisted from major exchanges a few months later.
- In 2021, ConstitutionDAO[33] was formed as a single-purpose DAO by like-minded individuals in an attempt to buy a rare copy of the U.S.

Constitution. They raised capital, bid at Sotheby's, and didn't win the auction. ConstitutionDAO only lasted one month, and they promptly offered refunds to their members. You can check the performance of their governance token (PEOPLE) on blockchain explorers and may realise that it is highly likely that members didn't get back all the money they put in, as Ethereum transaction fees could have been substantial at the time, and for those that didn't initiate a refund promptly, the value of their token holding might have dropped substantially due to market fluctuations.

However, not all is doom and gloom:

- **Uniswap**, a decentralised crypto exchange (see Chapter 6, *Transacting in a decentralised world*), launched in 2018 and its market capitalisation at the time of writing was $5 billion.
- **MakerDAO**, also a DeFi lending and borrowing platform, launched in 2017, and at the time of writing has a market capitalisation of $2.5 billion.
- **AAVE**, a DeFi lending and borrowing platform launched in 2020 and, at the time of writing, its market capitalisation was $1.5 billion.

Let's have a quick bifurcation from the flow of this section as I think it may be useful… Those familiar with traditional metrics are probably wondering if the term "market capitalisation" is the same here as for traditional businesses. It's very similar. Whilst I cover metrics extensively in Chapter 4, it's worth clarifying the difference.

The use of the term **market capitalisation** refers to the total market value of an entity. It is a metric calculated by multiplying the current price of a unit (share for companies, token for blockchain platforms) by the total number of units outstanding (outstanding shares for companies, circulating supply for blockchain platforms), and reflects the size and potential value of the organisation or project. The market capitalisation of a blockchain project will fluctuate according to the volatility of its token.

In DeFi circles, market capitalisation is often used alongside another indicator: **Total Value Locked (TVL)** (see *DeFi specific metrics*). TVL aims to reflect the level of user engagement and activity within the platform (see Chapter 2, *Lifting the veil on DeFi*) as it represents the total amount of tokens users have committed to it.

Blockchain explorers typically list both market capitalisation and TVL, and some also include a market capitalisation to TVL ratio, which is a helpful indicator: a ratio below 1 may suggest a potentially undervalued token, whilst a ratio above 1 may suggest market hype. For more detail on metrics, see Chapter 4, *Tokenomics and metrics*.

DAOs are a relatively new concept and the way they operate and are used is constantly evolving, including ongoing advancements in DAO governance, where new models are emerging to facilitate decision-making and member participation.

DAOs represent a new approach to organisational structure, with potential applications in DeFi, blockchain protocol governance, and community-driven projects. However, they face significant challenges, including regulatory uncertainty, scalability issues in decision-making processes, and security vulnerabilities as demonstrated by past incidents. DAOs are considered relevant to the blockchain ecosystem as they align with principles of decentralisation and community governance. Whilst they offer a framework for transparent and autonomous management of resources, their effectiveness and long-term viability remain subjects of debate, although innovation continues.

As DAOs evolve, they may influence traditional organisational structures, but their impact and adoption across industries are yet to be fully determined, and as regulatory scrutiny increases, potential token holders may be discouraged.

The role of DAOs in blockchain governance

Blockchain governance encompasses a spectrum of approaches, including both on-chain and off-chain mechanisms. Within this landscape, DAOs are emerging as a tool for on-chain governance, fostering community-driven decision-making and promoting a more distributed power dynamic. DAOs could play a number of roles in on-chain governance, including:

- **Decentralised decision-making**: as DAOs leverage smart contracts to automate governance processes, proposals for protocol upgrades, treasury allocation, and other strategic decisions may be submitted and voted on by token holders, ensuring a transparent and community-driven approach. This empowers participants to have a direct say in the future of the project.
- **Enhanced transparency**: DAO operations are typically recorded on a public blockchain, providing increased visibility into decision-making processes. This fosters trust and accountability among token holders as they can track proposals, voting results, and the execution of actions.
- **Community-driven development**: DAOs can facilitate governance participation for a wider range of stakeholders as token holders can not only vote on proposals but also submit their own ideas for protocol improvements or feature development. This fosters a collaborative environment where the community plays an active role in shaping the project's direction.
- **Alignment of incentives**: governance tokens often grant voting rights and potentially a share of the DAO's value or profits, which in turn incentivises token holders to make decisions that benefit the long-term health of the project, as their own stake is directly tied to its success.
- **Flexibility and experimentation**: as DAOs may be created with diverse governance structures, this enables experimentation with different voting mechanisms, reputation systems, and other approaches to distributed decision-making, fostering innovation in blockchain governance.

However, it's important to acknowledge that DAO governance is still a nascent field that presents its own challenges, including:

- **Scalability**: as the number of DAO token holders increases, reaching consensus on decisions may become inefficient.
- **Security risks**: smart contracts governing DAOs may be vulnerable to hacks or exploits, potentially leading to loss of funds or manipulation of governance processes.
- **Regulatory uncertainty**: the legal status of DAOs and their governance tokens remains unclear in many jurisdictions.

Despite these challenges, DAOs present an interesting facet of blockchain governance.

Upgrades, challenges, and disagreements

An introduction to blockchain forks

Operating a blockchain also means evolving it. The immutability of blockchain code and the distributed nature of blockchains can make it difficult to implement upgrades or bug fixes. Unlike traditional software, blockchain changes require a more complex process.

Whilst "The Code is Law" promotes transparency, trustlessness, and autonomy in blockchain governance, it also presents challenges in adapting to changing circumstances and resolving unforeseen issues.

In the previous section, I've explained the various ways that changes can be implemented, but what if a change proposal divides the community and participants don't all agree to the change? This is where I must introduce the concept of forks.

BOX 3.3 WHAT IS A FORK?

A fork is a technical event when a blockchain diverges into two separate paths forward. Forks can be **accidental**, in which case they should be resolved by the blockchain protocol relatively quickly making the split temporary, or **intentional**, with the purpose of implementing new rules, reversing the effects of hacking, or resolving disagreements within the community. Forks are classified as either soft forks (backwards-compatible changes, which shouldn't result in a permanent split) or hard forks (non-backwards-compatible changes that may result in two distinct blockchains). How forks are resolved depends on the blockchain implementation and the intent.

Blockchain forks may occur for a variety of reasons and can have a significant impact on the overall health and stability of a blockchain network and Figure 3.2 illustrates this.

Blockchain forks come in three types:

- **Accidental fork**: these are brief glitches in blockchains where near-simultaneous block creation (PoW) or validator selection (PoS) splits the transaction history. Network delays can cause temporary ledger

Figure 3.2 Why do forks happen? © 2024 Neira Jones.

divergence, but these forks self-resolve by following the chain with the most weight (longest in PoW, highest stake in PoS). Orphan blocks from the shorter chain are eventually discarded. A natural byproduct of distributed systems. Think of it as the equivalent of a "race condition" in traditional programming (or a "deadly embrace" as I prefer to call it 😉).

- **Intentional fork**: these come in two types. The first type is the **soft fork**, which is designed to be compatible with the original blockchain and primarily used to implement minor fixes and additional features. The intent of the soft fork is to maintain unity in the community through gradual implementation and these don't end up in a chain split. The second type is the **hard fork**, which is incompatible with the original blockchain and is used for major upgrades or when disagreements or serious incidents happen. These forks are major technical events, and they create a new blockchain.
- **Codebase fork**: this term is accepted in blockchain circles, but they are not, in my opinion, true "forks". They are more a testimony to the original blockchain rather than a "split" from it. A codebase fork is merely a copy of the code of the original blockchain which is then used to develop a completely new project, or test ideas. Codebase forks could have been introduced in Chapter 2 under *How do you build a blockchain?* but that would have been too confusing... If you research forks, you may come across fork classifications that don't include this category.

I propose a classification in Figure 3.3.

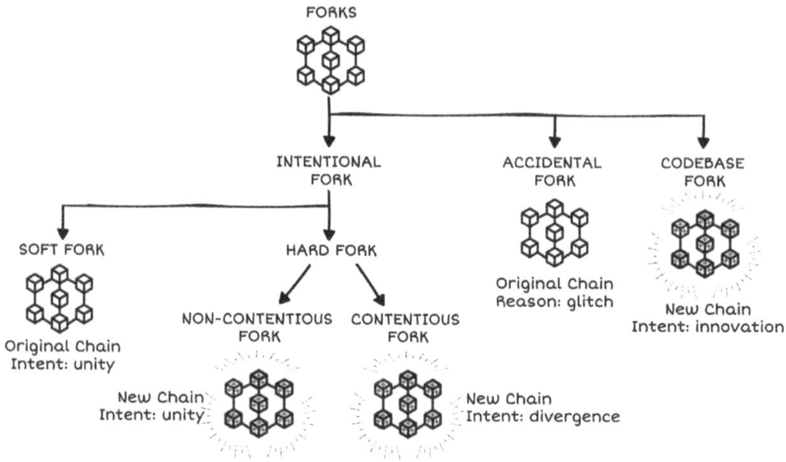

Figure 3.3 Blockchain forks. © 2024 Neira Jones.

If you're not interested in the specific details of forks, you can jump straight to Table 3.2 in the *Recap on forks* section, otherwise, read on.

Codebase forks

Codebase forks are not related to upgrades or philosophical disagreements but merely copying the code of an existing blockchain. As such they might have been better placed in Chapter 2, where I detail software development, however, I include them here for completeness as we are exploring all "forks" in this chapter.

> A **codebase fork** is a software development practice mostly used in public blockchains that creates a new blockchain project based on the source code of an existing one. Think of it as modifying a publicly available recipe to create your own dish. A codebase fork is sometimes called a "standard fork".

There are two main reasons why developers might use codebase forks:

- **Create a new project**: by copying the codebase, developers can create a completely new project with their own direction and features, essentially getting a kick-start with code already written. This can be useful for creating specialised versions of the base software or for exploring new functionalities.

- **Propose improvements**: whilst improvements may be dealt with through established processes (see *In practice, improvement proposals*), developers may choose to use a codebase fork for urgent fixes or highly complex changes as this allows them to test changes and implement them independently without waiting for approval from the original project's maintainers. If they gain enough consensus from the community, they may submit a "pull request" back to the original project's maintainers for merging with the original code. This allows for collaboration and innovation but may also lead to fragmentation if consensus on the benefits is not reached (and may lead to another type of fork).

As an example, Litecoin[34] was a codebase fork of the Bitcoin blockchain (and the Litecoin token was created).

Accidental forks

These are temporary disruptions, sometimes referred to as "chain splits", that may mostly occur in PoW blockchains due to the competitive nature of mining. Where two or more miners find a block at nearly the same time (see Chapter 1, *How are transactions validated and settled*), this simultaneous mining leads to a temporary divergence in the ledger's transaction history, creating different versions of the blockchains across full nodes as illustrated in Figure 3.4.

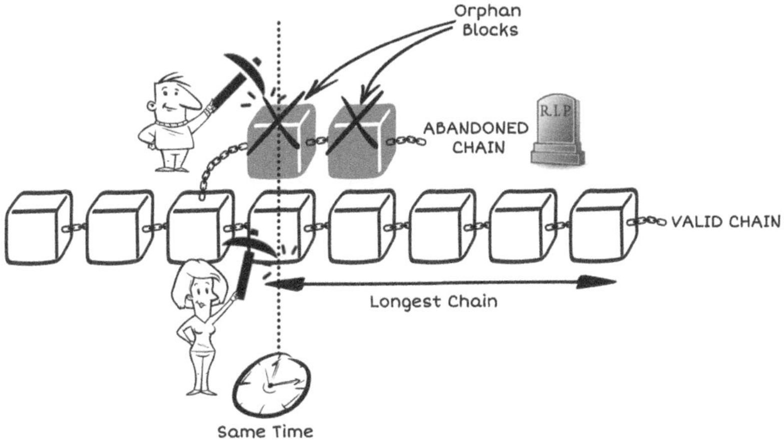

Figure 3.4 An accidental fork. © 2024 Neira Jones.

Because of network latency in PoW, miners may not be immediately aware of each other's blocks. This temporary split is resolved automatically as the network continues to add blocks. Blockchains are typically designed to follow the "longest chain" (considered the valid chain), and the blocks on the shorter chain (orphan blocks[35]) are eventually abandoned as only the valid chain will be used.

Accidental forks are less frequent in PoS blockchains because the validator selection process is more deterministic and there's less competition compared to PoW. However, similar to PoW, accidental forks in PoS are resolved by following the chain with the "highest total stake" instead of the "longest chain".

As you realise by now, accidental forks are a feature of distributed systems and would happen extremely rarely in centralised systems (i.e. coding errors resulting in a race condition), where concurrency issues are largely resolved by centralised systems only allowing one update at any point in time.

Soft forks

Soft forks represent backwards-compatible upgrades to the underlying blockchain protocol. This means that after the soft fork is implemented, two key things happen: new rules are introduced, and existing nodes can still function. The introduction of new rules with a soft fork allows the protocol to evolve and address minor issues or even introduce new functionalities (e.g. improved efficiency, and bug fixes).

However, the key aspect is that these new rules are designed in a way that older software versions, the ones running on existing nodes, can still recognise and validate blocks created according to the old rules. This backward compatibility is what makes soft forks a smoother and less disruptive upgrade path compared to other options.

There are several advantages to using soft forks for upgrades. First, they enable a gradual adoption process because older nodes remain functional, and miners and users have the flexibility to upgrade to the new software at their own pace, avoiding the potential for a network split or disruption that can occur with other upgrade methods (which may result in an entirely new blockchain). Second, the backward-compatibility aspect encourages wider participation in the upgrade process, ultimately leading to faster and more widespread adoption of the new features or bug fixes. Soft forks also offer a level of flexibility, allowing for incremental improvements to the blockchain protocol over time. After a soft fork activation, blocks mined under the old rules (e.g. miners that haven't upgraded to the new software) will be rejected by the network in some sort of democratic upgrade enforcement process.

However, because soft forks are typically suited for minor changes or bug fixes, they have limitations. The process typically includes a proposal, a signalling period (in which miners show their support and start using the new rules, coexisting with old rules), and activation (where the new rules become the norm as a sufficient percentage of miners support it), after which (post-activation) blocks validated with the old rules will be rejected by the network (this may sometimes result in accidental forks). If a more fundamental alteration to the protocol is needed, a soft fork might not be sufficient, and the activation mechanism used for soft forks can sometimes concentrate power in the hands of miners or large stakeholders who can influence the adoption of the upgrade.

A successful example of a soft fork is SegWit[36] on the Bitcoin blockchain, which aimed to increase transaction capacity (block structure), efficiency, privacy, and scalability. SegWit signalling started on 15 November 2016, and after sufficient miner support, activation took place on 24 August 2017. At the time of writing, most Bitcoin transactions are conducted using the SegWit format (this can be easily checked using blockchain explorers).

A soft fork is illustrated in Figure 3.5.

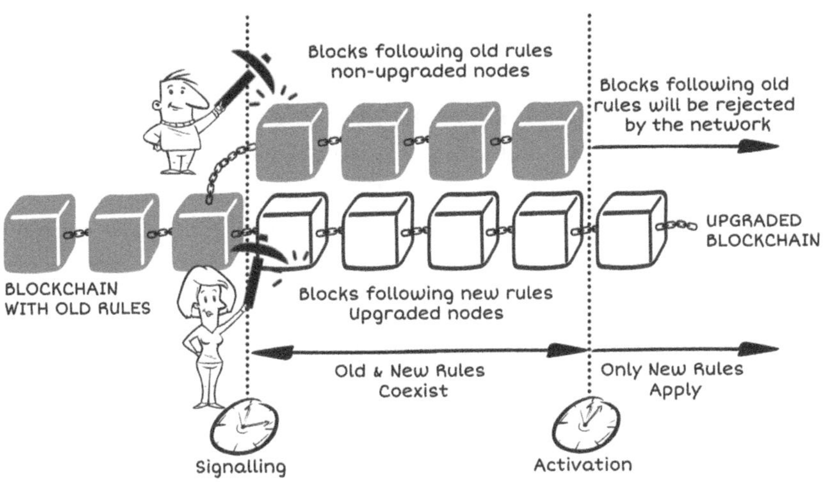

Figure 3.5 A soft fork. © 2024 Neira Jones.

Soft fork risks and challenges

COMMUNITY, ADOPTION, AND GOVERNANCE CHALLENGES

Soft forks can create a fragmented network where some users can't access new features, leading to a two-tiered system, causing confusion and operational issues. User experience may suffer as many don't understand the upgrade implications, risking feature loss or unexpected behaviour. Governance challenges arise from community disagreements over fork necessity and implementation. Coordinating stakeholders and managing the adoption process becomes critical, requiring a balance between pushing upgrades and maintaining network cohesion.

TECHNICAL, SECURITY, AND SCALABILITY RISKS

Soft forks can introduce subtle vulnerabilities and consensus risks (e.g. accidental forks), especially if miners don't upgrade. Implementation requires meticulous coding to avoid bugs and unintended consequences. Long-term scalability is constrained by backward compatibility requirements, potentially leading to technical debt. Additionally, the limited scope of changes possible through soft forks may hinder the blockchain's ability to adapt to future needs, impacting its competitiveness.

ECONOMIC AND INCENTIVE RISKS

Soft forks can alter economic incentives within the network. New features or rule changes might affect mining profitability or token economics (see *Chapter 4, Tokenomics and metrics*), potentially leading to shifts in network participation. There's a risk of creating perverse incentives if the soft fork isn't carefully designed, which could negatively impact network security or decentralisation. Users and businesses may face uncertainty about the value and utility of their assets during the transition period.

REGULATORY AND LEGAL UNCERTAINTIES

Soft forks can potentially alter the regulatory status of a cryptocurrency or blockchain. There's a risk that new features introduced through a soft fork could trigger additional regulatory scrutiny or compliance requirements. Legal uncertainties may arise regarding the interpretation of smart contracts or agreements that were established before the soft fork but continue to operate under new rules.

Hard forks

Unlike the other forks, hard forks are major technical events. As shown in Figure 3.3, there are fundamentally two types of hard forks:

- **Non-contentious hard forks**: these are intended to implement significant improvements, such as protocol upgrades and improvements, addition of new features, or response to critical issues (e.g. major hacks or bugs). These are usually planned in advance and their intent is to enhance or protect the existing blockchain, maintain network consensus and community unity so as not to result in a lasting blockchain split.
- **Contentious hard fork**: these happen as a result of fundamental disagreements in the community such as philosophical divergences on protocol rules or responses to critical issues, and always result in a blockchain split.

It is important to point out an important aspect of blockchain governance: a non-contentious hard fork intended as an upgrade or fix can evolve into a contentious hard fork if significant disagreement arises within the community (and therefore a lasting blockchain split that results in an entirely new blockchain and a new coin). This transition may occur for several reasons:

- **Unforeseen consequences**: as the implications of a proposed upgrade become clearer, some community members may object to its implementation.
- **Competing visions**: different factions within the community may have divergent views on the best path forward for the blockchain.
- **Economic interests**: some stakeholders might oppose changes that could affect their economic position within the ecosystem.
- **Technical disagreements**: developers and node operators might disagree on the technical merits or risks of a proposed upgrade.

A prime example is the Ethereum Classic (ETC) hard fork on Ethereum which was originally planned as a soft fork to implement security fixes to reverse transactions in response to The DAO hack (to reimburse token holders).[37] It eventually materialised into a contentious hard fork because part of the community fundamentally disagreed with the prospect of breaking immutability.

Whilst hard forks can address critical issues or introduce major improvements, they can also be divisive within the community and harm network stability.

Hard fork risks and challenges

Hard forks are significant technical events for blockchains and it's worth exploring the challenges they present.

ECONOMIC RISKS

Hard forks can lead to significant economic uncertainties as the value of tokens may experience extreme volatility as the market reacts to the fork, which can affect the overall market capitalisation and investor confidence. Asset duplication can occur, with token holders potentially receiving tokens on both the original and new chains, complicating portfolio management and potentially leading to confusion or missed opportunities. Market fragmentation may result in the dilution of market capitalisation across multiple chains, reducing the overall value proposition. Liquidity issues may arise as trading volume gets distributed across different markets, making it harder to execute large trades without significant price impact.

TECHNICAL, SECURITY, AND INFRASTRUCTURE RISKS

Blockchain networks become more vulnerable after a hard fork due to divided computational resources or staking power, putting both the original and new chains at a higher risk of **51% attacks**. Transaction integrity is threatened by potential **replay attacks**, as transactions on one chain may be replicated on the other, and **double-spending** risks are heightened during the transition period. Smart contracts and dApps may face compatibility issues or behave unexpectedly on the new chain, requiring modifications and additional testing.

Network stability and performance can suffer, with reduced hash rates or staking power potentially compromising overall security. Nodes may struggle with synchronisation, potentially leading to accidental forks. Infrastructure challenges multiply as operators need to maintain multiple versions of the software, potentially rendering some hardware obsolete. Increased maintenance requirements can strain resources and operational efficiency. Cryptographic risks emerge if algorithm changes are implemented, necessitating careful key management across chains to prevent vulnerabilities.

Data integrity and availability face increased challenges post-hard fork. The blockchain may experience accidental forks, potentially leading to conflicting transaction histories. Ensuring consistent access to historical data across all versions of the chain can become problematic. In addition, interoperability between the original and forked chains may be compromised, complicating cross-chain communication. This can introduce new security risks, particularly for bridge mechanisms designed to facilitate interactions between the separate chains.

OPERATIONAL RISKS

Operationally, hard forks present numerous challenges for exchanges, wallet providers, and service providers (see Chapter 6, *Transacting in a decentralised world*). Exchanges may delay or inconsistently support new tokens, potentially limiting user access to funds and affecting liquidity. Wallet compatibility issues can arise, making it difficult for users to access their assets on new chains and potentially leading to loss of funds. Service providers face increased operational complexity in supporting multiple chains, requiring additional resources, expertise, and infrastructure. Asset management becomes more challenging, with users and custodians needing to properly claim and secure forked assets to avoid potential losses and ensure the safety of their holdings.

REGULATORY AND LEGAL RISKS

Hard forks can attract increased regulatory scrutiny, potentially leading to new compliance requirements or legal challenges. Service providers may face liability issues if they mishandle forked assets or fail to provide adequate support to users, leading to potential legal disputes. Compliance becomes more complex as organisations may need to adhere to different regulations across multiple chains, especially if the hard fork results in assets being classified differently from a regulatory perspective. This can increase the burden on legal and compliance teams and create uncertainty in the regulatory landscape.

COMMUNITY, GOVERNANCE, AND ECOSYSTEM RISKS

The community and ecosystem face significant challenges during a hard fork. The blockchain community may experience a permanent split, leading to ideological divisions and reduced network effects as different factions support different chains. Governance processes become more complicated, with decision-making challenges arising from competing visions for the project's future and potential disagreements on protocol changes. The development roadmap may face uncertainty, potentially slowing innovation as resources and talent are divided between competing chains, hindering the overall progress of the project.

Users may experience confusion about the implications of the fork and face difficulties in accessing or managing their assets across different chains, leading to reduced confidence in the project. The broader ecosystem risks fragmentation, with multiple competing chains potentially slowing overall growth and adoption. Resources and community efforts may be diluted across chains, and the project's brand may suffer from the existence of multiple versions, confusing new users and potentially slowing the development and adoption of new features. Innovation challenges may arise, with the potential slowdown in the development and implementation of new features and improvements due to divided focus and resources.

Recap on forks

Table 3.2 aims to put all forks in context.

Forks play a crucial role in blockchain governance by providing a mechanism for adaptation and evolution. Blockchains, by their very nature, are resistant to change, and forks offer a way to introduce new features, address critical security vulnerabilities, or fundamentally alter the project's direction. It's also important to remember that forks can be divisive and lead to instability within a blockchain ecosystem. Finding the right balance between stability and innovation is a continuous challenge in blockchain governance.

Table 3.2 Comparing blockchain forks. © 2024 Neira Jones

Fork Type	Description/Intention	Token & Genesis Block Implications	Compatibility	Node Implications	Occurrence	Examples
Codebase fork	A copy of an existing codebase that allows for independent development Propose improvements, fix bugs, experiment with new features	May result in new token creation (and new genesis block) if the new code is not merged with the original chain	Depends on the intent	Nodes need to choose which chain (original or forked) to follow	Common	Litecoin (LTC) from Bitcoin blockchain
Accidental fork	An unintended creation of a separate codebase due to network issues or errors in version control systems	No new token creation, same genesis block as the original chain	Unintended and often temporary. Compatibility depends on the nature of the accident	Nodes may be confused and end up on the wrong chain unintentionally. The protocol usually resolves the accidental fork by directing nodes back to the main chain	Depends on the blockchain implementation	N/A

(Continued)

Table 3.2 (Continued)

Fork Type	Description/Intention	Token & Genesis Block Implications	Compatibility	Node Implications	Occurrence	Examples
Soft fork	A planned change to the codebase that introduces new functionalities but still allows older versions to interact with the new one Address scalability issues, implement new features without disrupting existing users	No new token creation, same genesis block as the original chain	Maintains backward compatibility with older versions	Nodes need to update their software to comply with the new rules. Older nodes might still be able to function in a limited capacity until new chain becomes only valid chain	Common	SegWit for Bitcoin blockchain
Hard fork	A deliberate change to the codebase that creates permanent incompatibility with older versions Pursue a radically different vision for the project's future or address critical security vulnerabilities that cannot be patched with a soft fork	New token creation, new genesis block	Incompatibility with original chain	Nodes must upgrade to the new version of the software to interact with the forked chain. Older versions become incompatible with the forked chain	Less common than soft forks	Bitcoin Cash (BCH) from Bitcoin blockchain Bitcoin Satoshi Vision (BSV) from Bitcoin Cash blockchain Ethereum Classic (ETC) from Ethereum blockchain

BOX 3.4 THE INTERESTING CASE OF THE ETHEREUM MERGE

The Ethereum Merge in 2022 was technically a planned hard fork. It was a major network upgrade that transitioned the Ethereum blockchain from a PoW to a PoS consensus protocol. The intent was to bring the community together in supporting the upgrade and to avoid:

- **A permanent split in the blockchain**: the Ethereum Merge aimed for a single chain continuing under the new PoS model (no new coin, same genesis block).
- **Discontinuity**: the Ethereum Merge aimed for chain continuity. Whilst there were concerns about potential temporary forks during the upgrade process, the goal was to have all nodes eventually converge on the upgraded PoS chain.

Some miners who opposed the switch to PoS continued running the PoW version of the chain, creating a hard fork (and at the time, the blockchain community was asking "Will the community follow?"[38]). The resulting split PoW chain is known as EthereumPoW (ETHW) and blockchain explorers show, at the time of writing, that this is not very popular.

Therefore, the Ethereum Merge can be classified as a successful major network upgrade, the first of its kind in the blockchain world, and a well-planned hard fork that didn't result in a permanent chain split. Overall, the Ethereum Merge stands out as a unique instance where a major network upgrade transitioned the consensus mechanism without a permanent blockchain split.

Evolution of governance models

Blockchain governance models have undergone significant evolution since Bitcoin. This evolution reflects the growing understanding of the challenges and opportunities presented by decentralised systems, as well as the need to balance autonomy, security, and adaptability.

Early blockchain networks like Bitcoin adopted a highly decentralised approach, relying on consensus among miners and off-chain governance. This model, whilst emphasising decentralisation, often led to slow decision-making processes and difficulties in implementing changes.

As the blockchain ecosystem matured, more structured governance models emerged:

- **On-chain governance**: platforms like Tezos introduced on-chain governance, allowing token holders to vote directly on protocol changes.
- **Delegated governance**: some networks, such as EOS, implemented a delegated PoS consensus where token holders elect representatives to make decisions on their behalf. This model attempts to balance decentralisation with efficient decision-making.
- **Hybrid models**: many blockchain projects now employ hybrid governance models that combine on-chain and off-chain elements. For example, Polkadot[39] uses a combination of on-chain voting and off-chain discussions to guide its development.

Over time, blockchain networks have explored hybrid governance models that balance the autonomy of smart contracts with the flexibility needed to adapt to changing circumstances. This includes mechanisms for upgrading smart contracts or adjusting protocol parameters without compromising the integrity of existing transactions or contracts.

Recent developments in blockchain governance include:

- **Quadratic voting**: some projects are experimenting with quadratic voting systems, which aim to give more weight to individuals who care deeply about specific issues. For example, Gitcoin Grants, a platform for funding open-source projects, uses quadratic voting to distribute funds.[40] In this system, the more an individual votes on a project, the less weight each additional contribution carries, preventing wealthy participants from dominating the voting process.

Quadratic voting is a voting system designed to balance efficient governance and inclusive participation whilst protecting minority interests. In this system, the number of actual votes cast is calculated as the square root of tokens held:

1 token = 1 vote
4 tokens = 2 votes

9 tokens = 3 votes
25 tokens = 5 votes

This quadratic relationship between the number of tokens held and votes is what gives the system its name.

- **Futarchy**: this governance model, proposed by economist Robin Hanson ("Shall We Vote on Values, But Bet on Beliefs?"[41]), uses prediction markets to guide decision-making. Whilst still largely theoretical in the blockchain space, it has garnered interest for its potential to align incentives. Augur, a decentralised prediction market platform, incorporates elements of futarchy by allowing users to create and trade on the outcomes of future events, potentially informing governance decisions.
- **Liquid democracy**: this model allows participants to either vote directly on issues or delegate their voting power to others, potentially combining the benefits of direct and representative democracy. The DPOS (Delegated PoS) system, used by EOS and others, implements a form of liquid democracy,[42] where token holders can vote for block producers directly or delegate their voting power to others.

As blockchain technology continues to evolve, governance models are also adapting to address new challenges. For instance, the rise of the metaverse and cross-chain interactions has led to discussions about governance across virtual worlds and different blockchain networks.

The need for governance in these new digital realms is highlighted by initiatives like INTERPOL's launch of the first global police metaverse.[43] As reported by INTERPOL, "The Metaverse has the potential to transform every aspect of our daily lives with enormous implications for law enforcement… But in order for police to understand the Metaverse, we need to experience it". As criminals increasingly exploit the metaverse, the World Economic Forum, in partnership with INTERPOL, Meta, Microsoft and others launched an initiative to define and govern the Metaverse.[44]

In payments, with AML/KYC and fraud challenges, many have argued that a virtual version of INTERPOL will be needed if we want to avoid the expanding metaverse becoming a fertile new ground for the next generation of cybercriminals and fraudsters.[45]

This development underscores the growing recognition that as blockchain technology and its applications expand into new domains, governance models will need to evolve to address novel challenges related to security, identity, and cross-platform interactions.

The evolution of blockchain governance models reflects an ongoing effort to balance decentralisation, efficiency, and adaptability. As the technology continues to mature and find new applications, we can expect further innovations in governance approaches to address emerging challenges and opportunities.

Blockchain operations and governance – conclusion (where do we go from here?)

In this whistle-stop tour of blockchain operations and governance, we covered:

- The various aspects of blockchain operations
- The fundamental aspects of on-chain and off-chain governance
- The importance of utility and governance tokens in blockchain operations
- The governance aspects of smart contracts
- Decentralised Autonomous Organisations (DAOs)
- How upgrades challenges, and disagreements are managed, including forks and other mechanisms, and the risks and challenges they present
- How governance models are evolving

I have tried to explain the jargon, debunk a few myths, and present a balanced view. I have given you my opinion on some aspects of the ecosystem, but feel free to disagree, I always welcome a good debate!

If you read this book a few years from now, more innovation will have happened, new governance models will have emerged, innovative technologies will be used, and behaviours will have evolved. Some blockchains will grow, others won't, and some will even disappear. Bitcoin and Ethereum will still dominate the market. We will continue to see vulnerabilities in blockchain infrastructure services leading to serious hacks, but governance models will evolve as a result, as well as regulations. The ecosystem will benefit from this.

All the terms introduced in this chapter can be found in the glossary, and references at the end of this chapter will also help.

I hope you've enjoyed this journey into blockchain governance and operations.

To complete our understanding of blockchains, we must examine the economics of this fascinating ecosystem.

Let's go on the fourth leg of our trip.

Notes

1 Lessig, L. (2000). *Code and Other Laws of Cyberspace*. New York: Basic Books. ISBN: 0-465-03999-7.

2 "5 Biggest Crypto Money Laundering Schemes of All Time | 2024 Updated" Techopedia, 29 April 2024. Available at: https://www.techopedia.com/biggest-crypto-money-laundering-cases-of-all-time (Accessed 19 July 2024).

3 Tezos website. Available at: https://tezos.com/ (Accessed 17 July 2024).

4 "Introduction to Decred" Decred website. Available at: https://docs.decred.org/ (Accessed 17 July 2024).

5 Cosmos website. Available at: https://cosmos.network/ (Accessed 17 July 2024).

6 Bitcoin Forum, Bitcointalk website. Available at: https://bitcointalk.org/ (Accessed 17 July 2024).

7 Ethereum Stack Exchange website. Available at: https://ethereum.stackexchange.com/ (Accessed 17 July 2024).

8 r/Bitcoin subreddit. Reddit. Available at: https://www.reddit.com/r/Bitcoin/ (Accessed 19 July 2024).

9 r/ethereum subreddit. Reddit. Available at: https://www.reddit.com/r/ethereum/ (Accessed 19 July 2024).

10 r/solana subreddit. Reddit. Available at: https://www.reddit.com/r/solana/ (Accessed 19 July 2024).

11 Snapshot website. Available at: https://docs.snapshot.org/introduction (Accessed 17 July 2024).

12 Tally website. Available at: https://www.tally.xyz/ (Accessed 17 July 2024).

13 "Introduction to Ethereum Governance" Ethereum website. Available at: https://ethereum.org/en/governance/ (Accessed 16 July 2024).

14 Bips.dev bitcoin improvement proposals website. Available at: https://bips.dev/ (Accessed 19 July 2024).

15 "Ethereum Improvement Proposals" Ethereum.org website. Available at: https://eips.ethereum.org/ (Accessed 19 July 2024).
16 "BEP 1: Purpose and Guidelines" GitHub. Available at: https://github.com/bnb-chain/BEPs/blob/master/BEPs/BEP1.md (Accessed 19 July 2024).
17 "Solana Improvement Documents" GitHub. Available at: https://github.com/solana-foundation/solana-improvement-documents/blob/main/proposals/0001-simd-process.md (Accessed 19 July 2024).
18 "I Could Potentially see Bitcoin to Become the 21st Century Gold" Deutsche Bank website. Available at: https://www.db.com/what-next/digital-disruption/dossier-payments/i-could-potentially-see-bitcoin-to-become-the-21st-century-gold (Accessed 19 July 2024).
19 "Why Is Bitcoin Not a Digital Gold?" Securities and Exchange Commission website. Available at: https://www.sec.gov/comments/sr-cboebzx-2021-019/srcboebzx2021019–8857582-239811.pdf (Accessed 19 July).
20 "Participate in Algorand Governance" Algorand website. Available at: https://governance.algorand.foundation/governance-period-12 (Accessed 17 July 2024).
21 Compound website. Available at: https://compound.finance/ (Accessed 17 July 2024).
22 "MKR Governance 101" MakerDAO website. Available at: https://makerdao.com/en/governance (Accessed 17 July 2024).
23 Lightning Network website. Available at: https://lightning.network/ (Accessed 16 July 2024).
24 Livepeer website. Available at: https://livepeer.org/ (Accessed 16 July 2024).
25 Ren protocol website. Available at: https://renprotocol.org/ (Accessed 17 July 2024).
26 "Cross-chain Crime: Over Half a Billion Dollars Laundered through a Cross-chain Bridge" Elliptic, 10 August 2022. Available at: https://www.elliptic.co/blog/analysis/cross-chain-crime-more-than-half-a-billion-dollars-has-been-laundered-through-a-cross-chain-bridge (Accessed 17 July 2024).
27 "Process" Uniswap website. Available at: https://docs.uniswap.org/concepts/governance/process (Accessed 16 July 2024).
28 "Use an Escrow as a Smart Contract" XRP Ledger website. Available at: https://xrpl.org/docs/tutorials/how-tos/use-specialized-payment-types/use-escrows/use-an-escrow-as-a-smart-contract/ (Accessed 16 July 2024).
29 "How DAO Frameworks Can Facilitate DeFi Governance" Gemini, 16 October 2023. Available at: https://www.gemini.com/cryptopedia/dao-crypto-decentralized-governance-blockchain-governance (Accessed 17 July 2024).

30 "Guide to DAOs (Part II): Understanding Different Models and How to Launch Your Own DAO" Kaironlabs, October 2022. Available at: https://kaironlabs.com/blog/guide-to-decentralized-autonomous-organizations-part-2 (Accessed 17 July 2024).

31 "DAOs and Governance: Managing Tokenised Product Development" Zerocap, 31 March 2023. Available at: https://zerocap.com/insights/research-lab/daos-and-governance-tokenised-product-development-quantblock/ (Accessed 17 July 2024).

32 "What Was the DAO?" Gemini, 5 October 2023. Available at: https://www.gemini.com/cryptopedia/the-dao-hack-makerdao (Accessed 15 July 2024).

33 ConstitutionDAO website. Available at: https://www.constitutiondao.com/ (Accessed 15 July 2024).

34 "What Is Litecoin?" Trade Finance Global website. Available at: https://www.tradefinanceglobal.com/blockchain/litecoin/ (Accessed 18 July 2024).

35 "Blockchain Forks: Navigating Orphan Blocks in Cryptocurrency Networks" Faster Capital, 1 June 2024. Available at: https://fastercapital.com/content/Blockchain-Forks--Navigating-Orphan-Blocks-in-Cryptocurrency-Networks.html (Accessed 7 July 2024).

36 "Segregated Witness (SegWit): Definition" Investopedia, 29 August 2023. Available at: https://www.investopedia.com/terms/s/SegWit-segregated-witness.asp (Accessed 7 July 2024).

37 "What Was the DAO?" Cryptopedia, 5 October 2023. Available at: https://www.gemini.com/cryptopedia/the-dao-hack-makerdao (Accessed 18 July 2024).

38 "Ethereum Merge: What You Need to Know" *Coindesk*, 7 September 2022. Available at: https://www.coindesk.com/tech/2022/09/07/ethereum-merge-what-you-need-to-know/ (Accessed 16 July 2024).

39 "Introduction to Polkadot OpenGov" Polkadot Wiki. Available at: https://wiki.polkadot.network/docs/learn-polkadot-opengov (Accessed 18 July 2024).

40 "Gitcoin Grants Quadratic Funding Implementation" GitHub. Available at: https://github.com/gitcoinco/quadratic-funding (Accessed 16 July 2024).

41 Hanson, R. (2013). "Shall We Vote on Values, But Bet on Beliefs?" *Journal of Political Philosophy*, 21(2), 151–178. https://doi.org/10.1111/jopp.12008.

42 "Delegated Voting: Empowering Decentralized Decision-Making" Colony blog. Available at: https://blog.colony.io/delegated-voting-empowering-decentralized-decision-making/ (Accessed 16 July 2024).

43 "INTERPOL Launches First Global Police Metaverse" INTERPOL website, 20 October 2022. Available at: https://www.interpol.int/en/News-and-Events/News/2022/INTERPOL-launches-first-global-police-Metaverse (Accessed 16 July 2024).

44 "Defining and Building the Metaverse" World Economic Forum website. Available at: https://initiatives.weforum.org/defining-and-building-the-metaverse/home (Accessed 16 July 2024).

45 "The Metaverse Will Need Its Own INTERPOL to Police Payments Crossing between Virtual, Real Worlds" Pymnts.com, 30 November 2021. Available at: https://www.pymnts.com/safety-and-security/2021/metaverse-will-need-its-own-interpol-police-payments-crossing-virtual-real-worlds/ (Accessed 16 July 2024).

4

TOKENOMICS AND METRICS

Tokenomics (money makes the world go round)

A contraction of "token" and "economics", **tokenomics** is a term used to describe the economic model used by a blockchain ecosystem, focusing on the design and management of coins or tokens. This includes token/coin supply (e.g. mining, staking, burning, inflationary and deflationary measures, etc.), distribution (e.g. airdrop, initial coin offering, etc.), utility (e.g. function, access, benefits, etc.), and governance (e.g. voting, upgrades, incentives structures, etc.). To draw a parallel with centralised payment ecosystems, tokenomics encompasses rules and processes related to a particular payment scheme, the applicable regulations, and the monetary policy under which the blockchain operates.

Tokenomics primarily applies to permissionless blockchains with coins and plays a crucial role in the economic functioning of these open, public networks. Tokenomics analyses the design, distribution, and utility of these tokens to understand their impact on the overall health and sustainability of the blockchain ecosystem.

DOI: 10.4324/9781003480761-5

There is limited applicability of tokenomics to permissioned blockchains, as these are designed for specific use cases within a closed network of pre-approved participants. They often don't require a coin in the traditional sense. In private blockchains, other incentive structures might be implemented to encourage participation which could involve access control mechanisms, reputation systems, or even direct payments between authorised users.

Figure 4.1 Tokenomics. © 2024 Neira Jones.

Supply and distribution: value creation

This section delves deeper into the world of tokenomics, placing a particular emphasis on supply and distribution. Understanding these concepts is crucial for evaluating the potential of any blockchain project and the overall health of its ecosystem. We'll explore the various factors that influence token value, including how the total supply (capped or uncapped) impacts scarcity and inflation within the project. We'll also examine how the initial supply is distributed through fixed or gradual release models. The circulating supply, a dynamic figure representing active tokens, will be analysed in light of mining, staking, and burning mechanisms. Finally, we'll explore the diverse strategies employed for allocating tokens at launch, such as public sales, venture capital (VC) funding, airdrops, and team allocations. By equipping ourselves with a thorough understanding of these concepts, we'll be well positioned to assess the health and potential of any blockchain project we encounter.

Total supply

This represents the absolute maximum number of tokens that will ever exist. It dictates the project's monetary policy, potentially setting a cap (limited supply) on the number of tokens ever created, similar to scarcity in traditional economics. Conversely, an uncapped supply can lead to inflationary pressures, potentially diluting the value of existing coins/tokens. Here are some examples:

- **Limited supply**: Bitcoin (BTC)'s total supply is capped at 21 million coins, designed to mimic the scarcity of precious metals like gold. Ethereum (ETH)'s total supply is capped at 1 billion ETH. This is sometimes referred to as "maximum supply".
- **Uncapped supply**: Ripple (XRP) has an uncapped total supply, with the creators arguing it facilitates its use as a global settlement currency.

Initial supply

This refers to the number of tokens created and distributed at the project's launch. It establishes the starting point for the circulating supply and doesn't necessarily reflect the total supply. Here are some issuance models for initial supply:

- **Fixed initial supply**: a predetermined number of tokens are created at launch. This often coincides with a capped total supply.
- **Gradual release**: an initial portion of tokens are distributed at launch, with the remaining tokens released over time according to a predefined schedule. This can occur with either a capped (ETH) or uncapped total supply [dash digital cash (DASH)].

Note: Bitcoin's BTC is a unique case as there wasn't a true "fixed initial supply" and no BTCs were pre-created and distributed at launch (meaning the initial supply was zero). Instead, all BTC are created and released through the mining process (see Chapter 1, *How are transactions validated and settled?*, *Proof of work*).

Circulating supply

This dynamic figure represents the number of tokens currently active in the ecosystem, available for trading or use. It's constantly in flux as new tokens are released through mechanisms like mining, staking rewards, minting, burning, or governance decisions (if the total supply is not fixed), whilst existing tokens might be locked up in staking contracts or burned through specific protocols.

Transaction fee burning: some protocols implement mechanisms that burn a portion of the transaction fees collected from network activity. This effectively reduces the circulating supply of tokens, potentially increasing the relative value of remaining tokens (i.e. a long-term value proposition for token holders).

BOX 4.1 MINTING AND BURNING

Minting and **burning** tokens are essentially inflationary and deflationary measures, respectively. Minting is sometimes referred to as **seigniorage**, which is a broad economic term referring to the difference between the production cost of a currency and its face value and is generally associated with governments minting physical currency. The concept of minting applies equally to crypto assets where it refers to the creation of new tokens which can be distributed to developers, investors, or users as a reward or incentive.

Burning tokens, on the other hand, is the process of permanently removing tokens from circulation by sending them to a designated burn address. This reduces the total supply of tokens, potentially increasing the value of the remaining tokens. Token burning is often used as a deflationary mechanism to control supply, increase scarcity, or as part of a project's tokenomics strategy to reward long-term holders. Some tokens implement automatic burning mechanisms [Binance with its Build and Build (BNB) token], whilst others conduct periodic burns based on specific conditions or community decisions (e.g. ETH, XRP).

Distribution models: initial funds allocation

This roadmap outlines the initial token allocation strategy, which may encompass a combination of:

- **Public sales**: these fundraising mechanisms raise capital by offering tokens to the general public, or defined sets of investors, in exchange for fiat currencies or other cryptocurrencies. These may include Initial Coin Offerings (ICOs), Initial Exchange Offerings (IEOs), Initial DEX Offerings (IDOs), Security Token Offerings (STOs). See Box 4.2 for more details.
- **Venture Capital (VC) funding**: traditional investment from VC firms in exchange for equity or tokens. VC funding provides crucial support for blockchain startups in the early stages, offering not only financial resources but also expertise and network connections. Pantera Capital and Andreesen Horowitz are well-known examples, and many analysts rank VC firms from time to time. A reference is provided at the end of this chapter.[1]
- **Airdrops**: free token distributions aimed at promoting awareness and attracting users to the project's ecosystem. Airdrops can be a cost-effective way to bootstrap a user base and generate initial interest and many publications rank airdrops, and a reference is provided at the end of this chapter.[2]
- **Team and advisor allocations**: tokens reserved for the project's development team and advisors to incentivise long-term commitment and expertise. A well-defined distribution model fosters transparency and trust in the project's legitimacy.

BOX 4.2 WHAT ARE ICOS, IEOS, IDOS, AND STOS?

These are public funding events with specific characteristics depending on the platform used or assets covered.

Initial Coin Offering (ICO): this is the public blockchain version of **crowdfunding** or even an Initial Public Offering (IPO) in traditional finance. During an ICO, a blockchain project seeking to raise capital for development creates a new coin(usually a utility token, see Chapter 3, *Operational tokens*) and offers it for sale to the public through the project's website or a dedicated platform. Investors contribute funds (typically in fiat currency like USD or EUR, or established cryptocurrencies like BTC or ETH) in exchange for newly minted coins from the project. ICOs often involve producing a white paper (see Chapter 2, Box 2.9) detailing the project's goals, tokenomics, and roadmap. Regulations surrounding ICOs vary by jurisdiction.

Initial Exchange Offering (IEO): this is very similar to an ICO, the only difference being that the process is facilitated by a centralised crypto exchange (see Chapter 6, *Transacting in a decentralised world*). Unlike ICOs where sales are open to the general public, IEOs are only open to crypto exchange customers. The crypto exchange vets the project thoroughly before offering the token to its user base. This vetting process can potentially enhance security and perceived legitimacy for investors compared to both ICOs and Initial DEX Offerings (IDOs). As IEOs often involve **Know Your Customer (KYC)** and **Anti-Money Laundering (AML)** compliance, this can limit participation for some users who prefer anonymity. Additionally, centralised exchanges may have stricter regulatory compliance obligations, potentially impacting the types of projects they list.

Initial DEX Offering (IDO): similar to an IEO but orchestrated by a decentralised crypto exchange (DEX) (see Chapter 6, *Decentralised crypto exchanges*). IDOs generally offer greater anonymity for participants as decentralised crypto exchanges are Decentralised Finance (DeFi) services (see Chapter 2, *Lifting the veil on DeFi*) that typically don't enforce KYC/AML checks (although due diligence processes will depend on the exchange). This can be attractive to a wider range of users who value privacy. IDOs potentially offer a wider list of projects compared to IEOs; however, the lack of a centralised authority vetting projects on decentralised exchanges can introduce increased risk for investors as malicious projects might more easily exploit the platform.

Security Token Offering (STO): the most regulated of public token sales. An STO is a regulated fundraising mechanism similar in principle to an ICO (sale of new tokens), but unlike ICOs, STOs list tokens that function as securities (see Chapter 5, *Security tokens*). This means they represent ownership or investment rights in an underlying asset, such as real estate, intellectual property, or even shares in the issuing company itself. Due to assets sold being generally classified as securities, STOs are subject to strict regulations and participation might be limited to accredited investors who meet specific financial requirements set by regulators. This contrasts with ICOs which are often open to the general public. In addition, STOs can be used for a variety of fundraising purposes throughout a project's lifecycle, not just the initial launch phase. This allows for more flexibility in securing capital for ongoing development or expansion.

There are specific services used to launch ICOs, IEOs, and IDOs, and these are referred to as token launch platforms or launchpads (see Chapter 6, *Token launch platforms*).

Ongoing funding mechanisms

Sustaining development is a critical aspect of blockchain operations. Strategies include:

- **Treasury funding**: projects may allocate a portion of their initial supply to a treasury that can be used for ongoing development, marketing, and operational expenses. This allocation typically happens during the initial funds allocation phase.
- **Transaction fees**: some blockchain protocols generate revenue through transaction fees collected from network activity (see *Under the hood: transaction fees* later on in this chapter). A portion of these fees might be used to fund ongoing development or distributed to token holders through staking rewards, creating a self-sustaining economic model.
- **Grants**: blockchain foundations [e.g. Ethereum Foundation,[3] Solana Foundation,[4] Interchain Foundation[5] (for Cosmos ecosystem), Hyperledger Foundation,[6] Aave Grants DAO[7]] and VC firms might offer grants (although this is not their primary focus) to support development efforts or specific initiatives aligned with their goals. Grants can be a valuable source of ongoing funding for innovative or socially impactful projects.
- **Private Equity funding**: similar to VC funding, private equity firms might invest in established blockchain projects with a strong track record, offering capital in exchange for equity or tokenised securities (see Chapter 5, *Security tokens*). Private equity funding can help accelerate growth and expansion for projects beyond the initial startup phase.
- **Community engagement**: building a strong community may facilitate alternative fundraising mechanisms. For example, projects might leverage community fundraising campaigns in exchange for coins/tokens or other project-related rewards or introduce donation mechanisms where users can donate funds or resources in exchange for coins/tokens, exclusive access to features, or simply because they have faith 😉. Building and engaging a strong community through social media, forums, and events to attract early adopters, contributors, and supporters.

- **Play-to-Earn (P2E) and GameFi**: as covered in Chapter 2, *GameFi: revolutionising gaming with DeFi*, these models allow users to earn coins/tokens or cryptocurrencies through gameplay, potentially generating revenue for the project and attracting a user base. A portion of the in-game currency earned by players could be used to fund ongoing development.

On-chain and off-chain governance

Supply and distribution are fundamental cornerstones of tokenomics, shaping the perceived value and the overall health of a blockchain project. The interplay between on-chain and off-chain governance mechanisms defines how token holders and project teams can influence decisions regarding total supply, circulating supply, distribution models, funding mechanisms, and the inherent benefits and challenges associated with each approach.

Table 4.1 shows the difference between on-chain and off-chain governance as they apply to token supply and distribution.

Table 4.2 shows the benefits of both on-chain and off-chain governance.

Whilst on-chain and off-chain governance each offer benefits, they also present challenges and limitations, which are highlighted in Table 4.3.

Information asymmetry is a general economic term describing unequal access to information between parties in a transaction. In blockchain and tokenomics, it applies where there's a significant imbalance in knowledge between project teams/founders and token holders (on-chain governance) or the community (off-chain governance). Information asymmetry may lead to uninformed decisions, manipulation, and erosion of trust. This risk can be mitigated through transparency, independent audits, and effective community engagement.

Recap on supply and distribution

Supply and distribution are the cornerstones of tokenomics, shaping a blockchain project's perceived value and long-term viability. The interplay between on-chain and off-chain governance mechanisms determines how token holders and project teams influence decisions around these

Table 4.1 On-chain and off-chain governance for supply and distribution. © 2024 Neira Jones

Supply & Distribution	On-chain Governance	Off-chain Governance
Total supply	Token holders vote on proposals to change the total supply	The project's core team or a central authority decides the total supply
Initial supply	Not implemented in practice	The project team or founders determine the initial supply before the launch
Circulating supply	Token holders may vote on mechanisms that affect the circulating supply (e.g. burning, treasury management, staking reward rate)	The project team or blockchain protocol rules determine how new tokens are released or burned
Distribution models – initial allocation	For some distribution models using on-chain smart contracts, token holders may directly vote on proposals to modify vesting schedules for team tokens. This could involve extending the lockup period for team tokens, with the final decision made through on-chain voting	The project team typically designs the initial allocation strategy considering factors like fundraising needs and community incentives
Funding mechanisms	Some protocols allow on-chain voting for proposals related to treasury management or fee distribution	The project team or relevant entities decide on the specific ongoing funding mechanisms implemented (e.g. treasury allocation size, fee distribution)

Table 4.2 Benefits of on-chain and off-chain governance for supply and distribution. © 2024 Neira Jones

Benefits	On-chain Governance	Off-chain Governance
Transparency	Token holders may vote on proposals, ensuring transparency around details and voting records for any supply-related changes	A clear and well-defined distribution model fosters trust in the project
Community building	Token holders may vote on proposals for community reward programmes or airdrop distributions	Off-chain governance decisions by the project team might involve setting aside tokens for community initiatives or developer grants
Ongoing funding	Token holders may vote on proposals related to treasury management or fee distribution, promoting on-going funding for some protocols	The project team or relevant entities (e.g. foundations) design and implement the specific funding mechanisms (e.g. treasury allocation size or grant programs)

critical aspects. On-chain governance offers transparency and community involvement, whilst off-chain governance prioritises clarity and control by the project team. Both approaches have their advantages and disadvantages, and the optimal choice depends on the specific project and its goals.

Professionals should remember the following:

- **Token supply should be considered carefully**: token supply should align with the project's long-term goals. A capped total supply (like BTC) is used to limit inflation, whilst an uncapped supply may be suitable for specific use cases (like Ripple).
- **The token initial distribution is a strategic choice**: whether the choice is a fixed initial supply or a gradual release schedule, a balanced allocation strategy for public sales, VC funding, airdrops, and team/advisor token allocation should incentivise project development and community participation.

Table 4.3 On-chain and off-chain governance risks for supply and distribution. © 2024 Neira Jones

Risks	On-chain governance	Off-chain governance
Market volatility	Token holders have limited mitigation strategies (e.g. token burning)	Project team's initial decisions on the total supply and distribution model might not adapt well to changing market conditions
Decision-making challenges	• Complex voting processes and participation thresholds • Potential delays due to consensus mechanisms	• Lack of transparency in decision-making by project team/founders • Limited avenues for community input
Security risks	• Smart contract vulnerabilities • Manipulation of voting mechanisms (e.g. vote buying, Sybil attacks) • Technical barriers for some token holders to participate securely (e.g. understanding wallets, interacting with smart contracts, authentication, etc.)	• Security breaches with partners chosen by the project team/founders • Inadequate security protocols throughout distribution
Regulatory uncertainty	Evolving regulations around on-chain governance and tokenomics can create challenges	Project teams might struggle to adapt their off-chain strategies to comply with evolving regulations
Community risks	Low voter participation could undermine the effectiveness of on-chain governance	Centralised decision-making might not reflect community interests
Incentive alignment	Whilst the initial allocation strategy is off chain, token holders may vote on proposals to modify vesting schedules or staking rewards, aligning incentives with community sentiment	The initial allocation strategy is typically determined off chain by the project team, which may not necessarily align with community sentiment
Information asymmetry	Limited access to complex technical information for some token holders may hinder effective voting	Project team may withhold crucial information about financials, token lockup periods, or conflicts of interest, leading to uninformed decisions and potential manipulation

- **Not all governance approaches are suitable for every project**: whilst token holder voting promotes on-chain transparency and community involvement in supply-related decisions, it may introduce potential complexities and delays in decision-making. Whilst off-chain governance gives more control to the project team, it may result in alienating the community, and clear communication is essential to address information asymmetry risks to maintain trust.
- **Security is crucial:** the potential vulnerabilities of smart contracts (see Chapter 2, *Building smart contracts*), and the risk of manipulation of voting mechanisms in on-chain governance, make security-focused design and token holder education (e.g. secure wallet management, best practice) fundamental.
- **On-going funding is a challenge**: funding mechanisms should extend beyond the initial launch to ensure the growth of the project. This could involve treasury allocation models, transaction fee distribution (where applicable), or exploring alternative fundraising methods fostered by a strong community.
- **Regulatory compliance is still applicable**: regulations around tokenomics evolve all the time and this may affect any supply and distribution strategy. This is especially crucial for projects relying on off-chain governance models and particularly relevant to financial services and the payments industry specifically.

Now that we understand token supply and distribution, it's time to look at the purpose of these tokens, and what would make them valuable to the ecosystem.

Token utility

The token utility is a similar concept to blockchain utility (see Chapter 2, Box 2.10) and represents the purpose and function of tokens, such as payment for services, rewards and incentives, access to decentralised applications (dApps), or governance rights. Tokenomics defines the overall token design, including its utility and core functionality (e.g. utility, governance, hybrid) within the project's ecosystem. Understanding token utility is essential for navigating the ever-evolving blockchain landscape. By assigning specific purposes to tokens within a project's ecosystem, projects can create valuable incentives for user participation.

"Token utility" should not be confused with "utility tokens" (see Chapter 3, *Operational tokens – Utility tokens*) which are a type of token, as "token utility" is a characteristic of any token. Even when looking at utility tokens (which by definition should have "utility"), you will find projects dying due to their token not having much utility (as community interest dies overtime)... This is the case for the Bancor protocol, which initially raised $153 million. The value of its BNT token declined dramatically from its all-time high of over $21 in June 2017 to around $0.48 at the time of writing, a drop of nearly 98%. Whilst Bancor hasn't completely died, its dramatic value reduction due to utility issues makes it a relevant example.[8]

Token utility is the lifeblood of a successful blockchain project. By carefully defining the purpose and function of tokens, projects can incentivise user participation and foster a thriving ecosystem. Understanding the various use cases, governance models, and potential pitfalls associated with token utility empowers project creators to design a robust tokenomic framework. This framework should prioritise long-term value creation, transparent communication, and a balance between decentralisation and efficiency. Ultimately, a well-designed token utility creates a win-win scenario, attracting users, fostering community engagement, and propelling the project towards its long-term goals.

Fungibility

The concept of fungibility plays a crucial role in this ecosystem. All tokens (utility, governance, hybrid) within an ecosystem that functions are fungible, meaning one unit is identical to another. **Fungibility** is one aspect of token utility, and it allows tokens to function seamlessly as units of account or mediums of exchange.

BOX 4.3 WHAT IS FUNGIBILITY?

Fungibility refers to the interchangeability of a particular token. A bank note, whether it is worn or brand new, whether it came from an ATM or your friend's wallet – as long as it's not a forgery – holds the same value and can be used for the same purposes. A bank note is fungible. Each bank note stands in for any other bank note and is readily accepted in transactions because of their identical value and function. Similarly, fungibility allows coins/tokens to act as a reliable unit of exchange within a blockchain ecosystem. However, not all coins/tokens are fungible.

The Mona Lisa, a one-of-a-kind masterpiece, is irreplaceable and holds a value far beyond its physical materials. Unlike interchangeable bank notes, the Mona Lisa possesses unique qualities that make it irreplaceable. You can't exchange the Mona Lisa for any other piece of art, no matter how valuable it is. In the world of crypto, certain tokens might have special characteristics, functionalities, or values that distinguish them from others, making them non-fungible and therefore unsuitable as a unit of account. An example is a **Non-Fungible Token (NFT)**, and these are covered in Chapter 5.

Fungibility, in essence, is about interchangeability. It's what allows specific coins/tokens to act as equal substitutes within a system, facilitating smooth transactions and operations, in view of building a digital economy where value can be readily exchanged.

Fungibility, as described here, is about interchangeability within a blockchain ecosystem, but there is an additional nuance to it. Some tokens offer a way to achieve similar fungibility across different blockchains and these are called "wrapped tokens". A **wrapped token** essentially takes an existing token from one blockchain and "wraps" it in a new token on a different blockchain. This wrapped token inherits the value and core functionality of the original token, but with the added benefit of being usable within the new blockchain environment. For example, a wrapped Bitcoin (WBTC) allows users to hold and use BTC on the Ethereum blockchain, unlocking functionalities that native BTC wouldn't have on Ethereum. Wrapped tokens are a significant innovation in DeFi, promoting interoperability between blockchains and expanding the reach and potential use cases of various tokens.

For blockchain projects, deciding which types of token to use is a fundamental part of tokenomics, and token utility is equally fundamental to the success of a blockchain project. There are many ways in which a token can have utility, including payments, rewards and incentives, voting rights, discounts and benefits, access to dApps, and specific use cases (e.g. identity management, data access, and monetisation).

On-chain and off-chain governance

It's almost impossible to give a comprehensive list of what token utility could be, as this is a fast-moving landscape, and how governance models may impact it. Across all token types, on-chain governance may be achieved through governance tokens, coin-voting systems, reputation-based systems, or hybrid mechanisms. On-chain governance empowers users to participate in shaping the token's value proposition through voting on proposals impacting both the governance and utility aspects of the ecosystem's token(s). By contrast with off-chain governance, the project team retains control over the token's roadmap and value proposition ensuring alignment with their overall vision for the ecosystem.

Table 4.4 shows the impact of on-chain and off-chain governance on common examples of token utility.

Table 4.5 shows the impact of both on-chain and off-chain governance on blockchain principles such as community alignment, transparency, flexibility, and decentralisation.

Table 4.4 On-chain and off-chain governance impact on token utility. © 2024 Neira Jones

Token utility	**On-chain governance**	**Off-chain governance**
Payments	• Voting on proposals to integrate the token with new payment gateways or platforms • Deciding on transaction fee structures for using the token within the ecosystem	• Project team determines which merchants or platforms will accept the token for payment • Project team sets initial transaction fee structures
Rewards & incentives	• Voting on distribution models for staking or liquidity provision rewards • Deciding on burning mechanisms to potentially increase the value of tokens earned as rewards	• Project team designs initial reward structures for staking, liquidity provision, or other incentive programmes • Project team may retain control over burning mechanisms, though some off-chain governance models might allow for proposals on burning strategies

(Continued)

Table 4.4 (Continued)

Token utility	On-chain governance	Off-chain governance
Discounts & benefits	• Voting on proposals to offer token holders discounts on services or products within the ecosystem • Deciding on loyalty programmes rewarding token holders with exclusive benefits	• Project team sets initial discount structures and loyalty programmes • May introduce new programmes without community voting depending on the governance model
Staking & collaterals	• Voting on proposals to adjust staking requirements or rewards • Deciding on using the token as collateral for loans within a DeFi ecosystem	• Project team designs initial staking requirements and rewards • Project team may decide on using the token as collateral without community involvement, though some models might allow voting on such integrations
Voting rights (governance)	• Deciding on mechanisms for on-chain voting, such as minimum token holding requirements or tiered voting structures based on token holdings • May also involve proposals to integrate off-chain voting mechanisms for specific decisions	• Project team retains control over the project's roadmap and token value proposition
Data access & monetisation	• Voting on proposals regarding data access protocols or how users can monetise their data through token ownership	• Project team designs initial data access and monetisation mechanisms • May require community involvement for changes depending on the project's vision for data governance

Table 4.4 (Continued)

Token utility	**On-chain governance**	**Off-chain governance**
Fundraising & donations	• Voting on proposals for allocating funds raised through token issuance or determining charitable causes to support	• Project team might have more control over initial fundraising allocation but could integrate on-chain voting for future fundraising initiatives or community-driven donations
Identity management	• Voting on proposals regarding how identity credentials are stored and managed on the blockchain through token ownership	• Project team designs initial identity management framework • May integrate on-chain voting for future changes to the identity management system depending on the project's commitment to decentralisation
Social governance	• Voting on proposals to influence community development, content moderation, or feature implementation within a social platform	• Project team may have more control over social governance aspects but could also explore integrating on-chain voting mechanisms for specific decisions
Access to dApps	• Voting on proposals to expand access to dApp features or functionalities tied to token ownership • Deciding on membership tiers within a dApp based on token holdings	• Project team determines initial access levels for dApp features based on token ownership • Project team may introduce new membership tiers in the future, though some models might involve community voting on such changes

Table 4.5 Impact of on-chain and off-chain governance on blockchain principles. © 2024 Neira Jones

Principle	**On-chain governance**	**Off-chain governance**
Community alignment	Community shapes token utility based on their needs and interests, fostering a more engaged user base with a stronger stake in the project's success	Project team shapes a clear vision for token utility, but they need to clearly communicate their vision to attract users who align with that vision
Transparency	Publicly verifiable voting records ensure transparency and accountability in governance, building trust with the community, but may lead to slower decision-making	Off-chain governance offers faster decision-making through streamlined communication channels within the project team but may lead to information asymmetry within the community
Innovation	Community voting can encourage proposals for expanding token utility, fostering a dynamic and user-driven environment that adapts to changing needs, but knowledge disparity across the community may lead to uninformed decisions	The project team should have a clear vision for token utility and subsequent improvements, but community sentiment may not always align. Community voting may be used to encourage proposals for expanding token utility to address this
Flexibility vs. decentralisation	On-chain governance mechanisms allow for ongoing adjustments to token utility based on community feedback and market trends (decentralisation) but may require more time due to voting procedures (less flexibility)	Project team may be agile enough to adapt the token's utility roadmap based on their continuous evaluation of user feedback and market trends (flexibility). However, depending on the project structure, changes may require team consensus and may not be as responsive to community input as on-chain governance (less decentralised)

Whilst on-chain and off-chain governance each offer benefits (as well as trade-offs), they also present some risks, which are highlighted in Table 4.6.

Table 4.6 On-chain and off-chain governance risks. © 2024 Neira Jones

Risks	**On-chain governance**	**Off-chain governance**
Market adoption & speculation	Voters may prioritise short-term utility benefits over proposals with long-term value creation for the ecosystem, hindering long-term token adoption	Project team may prioritise features that attract short-term speculation over features that drive long-term utility and adoption
Decision-making	• Complex voting processes and participation thresholds can lead to delays in implementing utility changes • Low voter turnout for utility-related proposals could lead to decisions that don't reflect the long-term needs of the ecosystem • Voters might prioritise short-term benefits over proposals with long-term utility gains • Vulnerability to manipulation of voting mechanisms (e.g. vote buying) can erode trust in the governance process	• Project team decision-making processes may not be responsive to community needs and market changes, potentially diminishing the token's core purpose of empowering the community • Without a formal voting mechanism, users might have limited influence on the token's utility evolution • Lack of transparency may lead to decreased adoption, slow adaptation to changing market conditions, and a stagnant ecosystem
Interest alignment	A small group of token holders with high voting power could prioritise their interests over the broader community, potentially leading to decisions that don't reflect the overall ecosystem's needs	Project team's interests may not always be perfectly aligned with the long-term interests of the community, potentially leading to utility features that benefit the project team more than the community

(Continued)

Table 4.6 (Continued)

Risks	On-chain governance	Off-chain governance
Security risks	• Vulnerabilities in the voting system itself could be exploited (e.g. hacking, smart contract bugs) • Gaming the system through vote buying or manipulation could be a concern, especially for tokens with low market capitalisation • Potential for Sybil attacks where a single actor impersonates multiple voters to sway voting outcomes • Social engineering and phishing attacks targeting voters with misleading information or fake proposals	• Security breaches with partners chosen by the project team for integrations or other functionalities related to token utility • Inadequate security protocols throughout the system managing token utility
Information asymmetry	• Proposals for integrating the token with other platforms or adding complex functionalities (e.g. hybrid tokens) might be difficult for the average token holder to understand. This could lead to uninformed voting decisions as proposals might require careful design to ensure clarity and avoid confusion amongst voters • Complex technical details within proposals could further exacerbate information asymmetry	Project team may withhold crucial information about the token's utility roadmap, potential limitations, or technical specifications, hindering informed community engagement and potentially leading to manipulation

Table 4.6 (Continued)

Risks	**On-chain governance**	**Off-chain governance**
Regulatory uncertainty	• Uncertainty around how regulators may classify tokens and their associated activities can make it difficult to design effective on-chain proposals • Without clear regulatory guidelines, the community might struggle to propose and vote on utility features that fall within acceptable boundaries	• The project team's interpretation of the regulatory landscape might limit the scope of token utility features, which may stifle innovation and restrict the token's potential use cases • Regulatory changes could force the project team to make sudden adjustments to the token's utility, potentially leading to delays, disruptions in the ecosystem, and community disagreements

Table 4.6 shows us that on-chain governance fosters decentralisation but faces complexity and security risks, whilst off-chain governance offers efficiency but may lack transparency and community empowerment.

Recap on token utility

Professionals should remember the following:

- **Token utility should align with project goals**: token design should include clear purposes as this will drive user engagement and contribute to the project's long-term success.
- **Balancing short-term vs. long-term benefits is crucial**: if short-term gains are prioritised over features that create lasting value for the ecosystem, the project's long-term viability may be affected.
- **There are trade-offs associated with each governance model**: on-chain governance focuses on decentralisation (complex but transparent), whilst

off-chain governance prioritises efficiency (flexible but potentially less transparent). A balanced and considered approach is advisable.

- **Clear communications are essential to community engagement**: regardless of governance models, without easy-to-understand information about token utility proposals, voters and the community may not be able to make informed decisions. In any instance, the community should be actively involved in discussions and decision-making processes around token utility evolution in order to avoid disagreements with serious consequences (see Chapter 3, *Upgrades, challenges and disagreements – An introduction to blockchain forks*).
- **Maintain transparency**: clearly communicating the project's vision for token utility, and avoiding withholding crucial information from the community, may mitigate information asymmetry risks.
- **Strong security is crucial**: without robust security measures to protect against vulnerabilities in voting systems, smart contracts, informal governance processes, and token utility integrations, the project may face challenges that could eventually lead to its demise.
- **Regulatory compliance is still applicable**: regulations around tokenomics evolve all the time and this may affect how token utility evolves and new token utility features should comply with evolving legal frameworks.

Incentives and penalties

The mechanics of incentives and penalties are covered in detail in *Under the hood: incentives and penalties*; I will however introduce at a high level the fundamental aspects of this crucial aspect of tokenomics.

Incentives

Incentives are mechanisms used to align stakeholder behaviours with network goals, such as staking rewards, transaction fee burning, or token buybacks. This motivates users to hold or actively use the token. It creates a feedback loop that fosters network growth and token adoption. Examples include:

- **Staking rewards**: in proof-of-stake (PoS) blockchains, this is used to reward users who lock up their tokens for a specific period, contributing to network security or stability. The Binance blockchain

(BNB chain) offers staking rewards to users who lock up their BNB tokens to validate transactions on the network.[9]

- **Liquidity mining**: in DeFi systems, this is used to incentivise users to provide liquidity to decentralised exchanges (see Chapter 6, *Transacting in a decentralised world*) by depositing their tokens into liquidity pools, facilitating smooth token trading. SushiSwap (SUSHI) offers liquidity mining rewards to users who contribute to liquidity pools for various token pairs on their decentralised exchange platform.[10]
- **Burning mechanisms**: this is a deflationary measure and involves removing tokens from circulation to reduce the overall supply and potentially increase the relative value of remaining tokens. The BNB token uses a burn mechanism, where Binance allocates a portion of its profits to buy back and burn BNB tokens quarterly.[11]
- **Discounts and benefits**: a feature of token utility, this is used to provide users with discounts on fees, exclusive access to features, or early participation opportunities for holding or using the token within the ecosystem.

Penalties

Unlike traditional financial systems with established legal frameworks for enforcing penalties, blockchain ecosystems rely on a combination of economic penalties and protocol-level mechanisms to discourage malicious behaviour. Here's a breakdown of some key approaches:

Slashing: this is a penalty mechanism used in PoS blockchains to penalise validators for misconduct. Examples of misconduct include going offline for extended periods, providing incorrect information, or attempting to double-sign transactions. Slashing mechanisms result in a validator temporarily or permanently losing a portion of their stake. This discourages validators from acting dishonestly as it directly impacts their potential rewards.

Reputation systems: these systems are primarily seen in PoS blockchains (see Chapter 1, *Blockchain types*) due to their inherent design and focus on validator trust [whilst Proof of Work (PoW) focuses on computing power], although some hybrid and permissioned blockchains make use of them. Validators with a history of malicious behaviour can develop a negative reputation within the network. This negative reputation is recorded on-chain (e.g. uptime, accuracy, adherence to consensus) and a scoring system would translate the recorded data into a reputation score, which in turn can influence a validator's ability to participate in the network. For example, this may limit their ability to participate in future consensus rounds or force them to stake a higher amount to participate, thus affecting their income. Validators with lower scores may also receive fewer staking rewards, and they may even be the subject of community sanctions as a bad reputation may lead to a validator being ostracised, making difficult to find stake delegators (see Chapter 1, *PoS staking resources and services*), limiting their income further. Reputation systems incentivise good behaviour by associating negative consequences with malicious activities.

In PoW blockchains, there is less reliance on penalty systems when compared to other models. This is because PoW blockchains are inherently designed for security, and the blockchain protocols inherently enforces good behaviour, especially in mature PoW blockchains (i.e. large number of miners), where the network will automatically reject invalid blocks. The protocol may also increase the difficulty target (see Chapter 1, Table 1.5) if malicious activity reaches an unacceptable threshold and may even penalise miners that support an invalid fork (see Chapter 3, *Upgrades, challenges and disagreements – An introduction to blockchain forks*).

On-chain and off-chain governance

Both on-chain and off-chain governance play a role in shaping the incentive and penalty structures within tokenomics and Table 4.7 shows this.

For a comprehensive account of incentives and penalties, please jump to the later section. In the meantime, to complete our tour of tokenomics, we must look at market dynamics.

Market dynamics

There are many factors at play when assessing market dynamics, and this section aims to cover the most common ones. These factors may influence token price and liquidity, including trading volume, exchange listings, and market sentiment. In the previous sections, we covered the effects of on-chain and off-chain governance on supply and demand and token utility. For the other factors that may influence market dynamics, on-chain and off-chain governance have a more limited effect, but it may be helpful to understand where they may play a role.

Table 4.7 On-chain and off-chain governance for incentives and penalties. © 2024 Neira Jones

Impact	On-chain governance	Off-chain governance
Incentives	Token holders wield direct voting power on proposals, including: • Adjustments to staking reward rates to maintain validator engagement and network security • Introducing new functionalities or use cases for the token within the ecosystem to incentivise broader adoption and increase its value proposition • Distribution of tokens through liquidity mining programmes to incentivise market participation • Allocation of tokens for developer grants or funding initiatives to spur innovation and ecosystem development • Automatic distribution of staking rewards to validators and token holders, motivating participation • Programmatic allocation of transaction fees to ecosystem participants, incentivising various roles • On-chain reputation systems that unlock additional benefits for consistently good actors	Discussions will take place on off-chain channels (e.g. social media, forums), including: • Provide valuable feedback to project teams on proposed incentive structures, ensuring community alignment • Social recognition and status within the community for active participation • Potential for off-chain rewards (e.g. airdrops, exclusive access) based on participation metrics • Building relationships and networking opportunities within the ecosystem, which can lead to career advancement and informal influence on future developments • Community-driven grant programmes for ecosystem development • Shape the direction of future on-chain governance proposals based on community needs and project goals

(Continued)

Table 4.7 (Continued)

Impact	On-chain governance	Off-chain governance
Penalties	Token holders can vote on proposals to: • Introduce new penalty structures for undesirable behaviours not currently addressed by the protocol. This can deter activities that threaten network security or integrity • Adjust the severity of existing penalties like slashing deductions or limitations on participation based on reputation score. This allows the community to calibrate the appropriate level of deterrence • Create a framework for dispute resolution related to penalties through a community voting process. This fosters fairness and transparency in handling penalty disputes • Automated slashing of staked tokens for validator misbehaviour, discouraging harmful actions • Temporary or permanent loss of voting rights for malicious actors, penalising bad behaviour • Smart contract-enforced lockup periods for unstaking to prevent network attacks	Off-chain discussions to identity and deter undesirable behaviour, including: • Community pressure and negative sentiment expressed through off-chain channels can incentivise developers or project teams to implement penalties or adjust the protocol to address these issues. This indirect form of social pressure can be a powerful deterrent • Soft governance mechanisms like off-chain reputational systems or blacklisting mechanisms might be employed for minor offenses. Social ostracism or loss of reputation can deter undesirable behaviour • Public callouts and criticism on community forums, creating social pressure • Exclusion from informal decision-making processes, reducing the influence of bad actors • Potential blacklisting from off-chain services or partnerships, limiting ecosystem access

Table 4.7 (Continued)

Impact	On-chain governance	Off-chain governance
Benefits	Direct community control • Transparent and immutable record of all governance actions ensures accountability for both incentives and penalties • Immediate execution of approved proposals without intermediaries allows for timely implementation of incentives and penalties • Cryptographic verification of voting power and results prevents manipulation, ensuring fair distribution of incentives and enforcement of penalties • Ability to create complex, multi-step governance processes enforced by smart contracts allows for nuanced and effective incentive and penalty structures • Direct community control over economic policies and token distribution aligns incentives with stakeholder interests and ensures penalties are community driven	Collaborative exploration • Flexibility to adapt governance processes quickly allows for responsive adjustments to incentives and penalties • Opportunity for in-depth discussions and iterative proposal refinement helps in designing effective incentive and penalty structures • Easier inclusion of non-token-holding stakeholders broadens the perspective on incentives and penalties, ensuring they are well-rounded and community focussed • Ability to quickly respond to emerging issues or opportunities ensures that incentives and penalties remain relevant and effective • Fostering community engagement and education improves understanding and participation in governance, leading to better-designed incentives and penalties

(*Continued*)

Table 4.7 (Continued)

Impact	On-chain governance	Off-chain governance
Challenges & limitations	The distributed nature of on-chain governance may lead to: • Voter apathy and low participation rates can hinder the effectiveness of incentive and penalty mechanisms, leading to poorly informed decisions • Varying skill levels within the community can slow decision-making and affect the quality of incentive and penalty proposals • Complex voting mechanisms or proposals might lead to difficulty in understanding or reaching consensus on incentives and penalties • Potential for "tyranny of the majority" in token-weighted voting systems can skew incentive structures and penalty enforcement • Risk of governance attacks through token accumulation or flash loans can undermine the integrity of incentive and penalty systems • Difficulty in upgrading governance mechanisms once deployed can limit the adaptability of incentive and penalty structures • Limited ability to handle subjective or nuanced decisions can challenge the design of effective incentives and penalties	The lack of formality of off-chain governance may lead to: • Decisions or penalties made off chain rely on community pressure and project team willingness, potentially weakening their effectiveness • Off-chain discussions might not be publicly accessible or transparent, hindering community participation and accountability in incentive and penalty decisions • Potential for centralisation around influential community members can bias incentive structures and penalty enforcement • Difficulty in achieving clear consensus can complicate the design and acceptance of incentives and penalties • Risk of decisions being influenced by vocal minorities rather than true majority opinion can misalign incentives and penalties with broader community needs • Challenges in maintaining consistent engagement can affect the ongoing refinement and effectiveness of incentives and penalties

- **Supply and distribution**: tokenomics analyses how the supply and distribution model (as covered in earlier section), coupled with the token's utility and perceived value, affects its overall demand in the market. This interplay of forces ultimately influences the token's price. A well-designed tokenomics model fosters a healthy balance between supply and demand, promoting sustainable price growth. See Tables 4.1–4.3 for the impact both on-chain and off-chain governance may have on supply and distribution.
- **Token utility**: as covered in the previous section, the token's utility within the project's ecosystem significantly influences its value proposition. Tokens with a clear and valuable use case tend to attract more users and drive demand. See Tables 4.4–4.6 for the impact both on-chain and off-chain governance may have on token utility.
- **Liquidity**: the availability of a token on major crypto exchanges and the overall level of trading activity directly affect its liquidity. High liquidity facilitates smoother trading and potentially reduces price volatility.

Both on-chain and off-chain governance mechanisms can influence liquidity by incentivising users to provide liquidity for the token. On-chain proposals might offer rewards for liquidity providers, allocate funds for crypto exchange listings, or adjust tokenomics to improve exchange appeal. Off-chain discussions can explore potential integrations with crypto exchanges and identify suitable partners.

- **Network effects**: this concept explores how the token's design and use contribute to the overall growth and value of the project's network. A high token utility that attracts more users creates a positive feedback loop. Increased network activity and adoption can lead to a rise in token value as demand for the token's functionality grows.

Both on-chain and off-chain governance mechanisms play a crucial role in shaping network effects by fostering innovative token use cases and expanding the token's utility within the project's ecosystem. This ultimately drives network growth and user adoption.

- **Market sentiment**: overall market sentiment towards cryptocurrencies can play a major role in token price fluctuations.

Positive industry news, well-reasoned on-chain proposals with clear communication (often informed by prior off-chain discussions), and a responsive development team engaging with the community all contribute to bullish sentiment and increased token demand. Conversely, negative news, rushed or poorly communicated on-chain votes, or lack of communication from the project team can trigger bearish sentiment and price drops.

- **Competition**: the presence of competing blockchain projects offering similar functionalities or tokens with overlapping utilities can influence market dynamics. A well-established competitor can pose a challenge to a new project's token value. On-chain or off-chain governance have limited effect on this.
- **Regulations**: evolving government regulations and legal frameworks surrounding cryptocurrencies can significantly impact market dynamics. Uncertainty or restrictive regulations can dampen investor confidence and token adoption. On-chain or off-chain governance have limited effect on this.

Professionals should remember the following:

- Market dynamics factors such as supply and demand, token utility, liquidity, network effects, and market sentiment can all **influence the token's price and overall health**, and careful assessment is advisable as these might affect network viability.
- Both **on-chain governance proposals and off-chain discussions can incentivise positive outcomes** for these factors (e.g. liquidity rewards, fostering innovative use cases, clear communication) and carefully balancing choices in governance model is crucial to network health.
- Focusing solely on short-term price fluctuations and neglecting the long-term impact of market dynamics **may lead to unsustainable tokenomics and hinder long-term growth**. Token design often involves balancing the need for initial user acquisition (through

incentives) with fostering long-term token value. Governance models should incorporate mechanisms that encourage both participation and responsible token use.

- Underestimating the importance of **building a strong and engaged community** through effective on-chain and off-chain governance practices may lead to decreased token adoption and lower network effects.
- Ignoring the influence of external factors like **competition and regulations** on market dynamics may lead to **missed opportunities or unpreparedness** for changing market conditions.

Beyond tokenomics fundamentals

Whilst understanding supply and distribution, token utility, incentives, penalties, and market dynamics form the core of tokenomics analysis, there's more to consider for a project's long-term success. Here are some emerging trends and considerations:

- **Evolving regulatory landscape**: regulations surrounding cryptocurrencies are constantly evolving. Staying adaptable and compliant is crucial for long-term viability.
- **Deflationary mechanisms vs. continuous inflation**: some projects implement token burning or other mechanisms to reduce the overall supply over time, potentially increasing token value in the long run. Conversely, some projects have ongoing token issuance. Carefully considering the impact of these opposing approaches is an important part of long-term tokenomics strategies.
- **Evolving DAOs**: whilst basic Decentralised Autonomous Organisation (DAO) structures empower communities, future tokenomics might explore more sophisticated DAO models. This could involve exploring concepts like quadratic voting (where voting power is based on the square root of total tokens committed) or exploring reputation-based systems for enhanced governance participation. Considering how these models can be integrated into tokenomics design may lead to a more engaged and effective governance system.
- **Social impact and ESG considerations**: a growing number of projects are weaving social impact or environmental, social, and governance

(ESG) factors into their tokenomics. This may attract investors seeking purpose-driven projects.

- **Interoperability and the metaverse**: the ability for tokens to function across different blockchain ecosystems and potentially within the **metaverse** is becoming increasingly important. Consider how your tokenomics integrates with these evolving trends.

By staying informed about these ongoing developments and tailoring tokenomics accordingly, projects can position themselves for sustainable growth in the ever-changing crypto landscape. As the blockchain space matures, we can expect advancements in tokenomics where more sophisticated incentive structures may be developed to incentivise participation and promote desired behaviours within blockchain networks. We may also see an evolution towards more interoperability between public and private blockchains to facilitate interaction and value transfer. We may even see projects with a social focus that might use tokenomics to promote behaviours contributing to positive social change.

Whilst tokenomics primarily focuses on public blockchains with coins, it's important to be aware of potential applications in permissioned and hybrid blockchain models, especially as the technology continues to develop.

By understanding the multifaceted aspects of tokenomics, stakeholders and users gain valuable insights into the potential value proposition and long-term sustainability of a blockchain project. It helps assess whether the token's design creates a healthy economic ecosystem that fosters long-term growth and an engaged community. Remember, tokenomics is a dynamic field, constantly evolving alongside the blockchain landscape. As always, the trick is to keep up to date with the latest developments.

BOX 4.4 THE CURIOUS CASE OF XRP

Ripple Labs's RippleNet is a private blockchain specifically designed for financial institutions to facilitate faster and more cost-effective cross-border transactions. Their XRP utility token acts as a bridge currency to provide liquidity for transactions within the private network. When a bank needs to convert one currency to another, XRP can be used as an intermediary, facilitating a smoother and faster exchange process.

XRP isn't the main currency used for settling transactions on RippleNet, and financial institutions can choose to settle transactions in any currency they prefer.

However, XRP has a secondary market where it can be traded on crypto exchanges independent of RippleNet. This trading activity and speculation around XRP's value create a market for liquidity.

Whilst not the primary driver of RippleNet, XRP's design, distribution, and utility within the Ripple ecosystem are still relevant for tokenomics analysis as a significant portion of XRP is held in escrow by Ripple Labs, with controlled releases to ensure market stability. The use of XRP for liquidity purposes incentivises some financial institutions to hold XRP, potentially influencing its market value (XRP value on 31 August 2024 = $57). The existence of a secondary market for XRP adds another layer of complexity to the tokenomics analysis.

Ripple has faced numerous challenges and the most prominent is probably the US Securities and Exchange Commission (SEC) lawsuit filed in 2020. The SEC-increased scrutiny over the cryptocurrency industry led to this lawsuit and cast a shadow over XRP, impacting its price and trading volume, leading to the delisting of XRP from major US crypto exchanges, increasing price volatility, and damaging investor confidence, as well as creating significant legal and financial burdens for Ripple. In any case, it seems, in my opinion, that the SEC's motto is "if in doubt, it's a security" 😉, regardless of whether the asset passes the **Howey Test** or not... Ripple has vigorously defended itself in court, arguing that XRP is a currency and not a security (see Chapter 5, *About money*). The case is ongoing, with significant implications for the cryptocurrency industry as a whole.[12] In response to market challenges, Ripple has focused on building partnerships with financial institutions, educating the market, growing XRP's utility to reduce dependence on price speculation, expanding its product offerings, and emphasising XRP's unique features, as well as continuing to work on improving the XRP ledger's scalability through various technical upgrades and optimisations.

The case of Ripple and XRP demonstrates that tokenomics can extend beyond just public blockchains. Even in private networks, tokens can play a role in facilitating specific functionalities and influencing the overall ecosystem's dynamics. XRP's unique use case as a token with liquidity within a private network highlights the evolving nature of tokenomics and its potential applications in various blockchain models.

Under the hood: incentives and penalties (you can't always get what you want)

In Chapter 1, we covered the stages at which validating nodes may receive economic rewards and other incentives (including non-economic) for their contribution to the community (see Chapter 1, *Reaching consensus*). Here, we'll examine in detail economic and non-economic incentives, as well as penalties.

Economic incentives

Rewards and incentives can get confusing as the rules and terminology may vary across blockchains.

(Note from the author: well, what do you expect? It's hard enough having to understand the differences between the card scheme operating regulations for Visa and Mastercard, despite the existence of regulatory frameworks within which these private entities operate. Unlike centralised systems, blockchain infrastructures have no globally accepted regulations or pricing frameworks – other than their own rules – giving us globally accepted terminology and processes. At least, when we talk about **interchange** or **merchant service charge (MSC)** on the card rails, we all know what we mean! I will attempt to give this some structure in the context of blockchains. 😉).

Whilst the term **block reward** is commonly used to describe the economic incentive, in some blockchains, it combines newly minted coins and transaction fees, such as in the Bitcoin blockchain.

In other blockchains, such as Ethereum, the block reward consists only of the newly minted coins, and transaction fees are a distinct component treated as additional incentives.

Consequently, because it's a moot point, and for the purpose of clarity, I will separate the two components, and Table 4.8 compares potential economic incentives for PoW and PoS blockchains. It is however important to remember that technology evolves and changes to incentive structures may happen as part of tokenomics and other economic systems, making it advisable to refer to the latest rules for each specific blockchain.

When allocating new coins/tokens as rewards, a blockchain protocol should behave similarly to a **central bank** or monetary authority and

Table 4.8 Comparing PoW and PoS economic rewards. © 2024 Neira Jones

Economic incentives	**Proof of Work (PoW)**		**Proof of Stake (PoS)**
	Miner	**Full node**	**Validator**
New coins	Yes	No	Yes
Transaction fees	Yes	No	Yes
Other economic rewards	Mining pool rewards Secondary market for mining equipment	Fees for services provided (e.g. access to historical data, blockchain analytics)	Delegation rewards Staking pool rewards Validator fees Validator network rewards Staking derivatives and financial products
	Community rewards Educational and consulting services		
Indirect economic incentive	Participants may indirectly benefit from protocol improvements as a well-functioning blockchain attracts users, developers, and businesses, leading to increased demand and value for the native coin/token		

enforce a "monetary policy", because, after all, they must equally worry about things like inflation and deflation... Minting new coins is a bit like printing money, so careful economic design is crucial (see *Tokenomics*). In any instance, new coin issuance varies across blockchain implementations and may change over time, but fundamentally, participants (e.g. PoW miners, PoS validators, full nodes) will receive economic rewards for their contribution to the ecosystem.

Full nodes' economic incentives

Full nodes (if they don't fulfil other roles) don't receive transaction fees (validating nodes do) but may get other rewards. These include economic rewards for participation in the evolution of the blockchain, **fees for**

services they may provide by capitalising on the fact that they hold a full copy of the blockchain ledger, and for their role as an essential participant in maintaining the integrity and security of the blockchain network. Services that may be provided by full nodes include:

- Providing access to data.
- Offering blockchain analytics.
- Consensus monitoring [e.g. real-time updates on block height, number of active nodes, hashrate, Total Value Locked (TVL), etc.].
- Node hosting and maintenance, including cloud-based hosting and managed node services.
- Providing Application Programming Interface (API) or infrastructure services to developers, exchanges, or other projects.
- Providing services on Layer 2 solutions (see Chapter 1, *Are blockchains scalable?*).
- Providing educational and consulting services.

PoW economic incentives

PoW blockchain **miners** may get both new coins/tokens and transaction fees for successfully mining blocks, but how this is done will depend on the specific blockchain implementation.

Most PoW blockchains implement a halving mechanism to reduce the block reward of newly minted coins by a specific percentage at regular intervals in order to combat inflation and maintain the value of existing coins. This is why most PoW blockchains start with a high initial block reward to encourage mining activity.

For example, Bitcoin originally offered 50 BTC per block reward (2009), 6.25 BTC in May 2020, and reduced this by half to 3.125 BTC in April 2024. The Bitcoin blockchain has halving events every four years, and the last one will occur in 2140, after which time there will be 21 million BTC in circulation and no more BTC will be created (see *Supply and distribution value creation – total supply*). At that point, transaction fees will be the primary source of income for miners. (Note from the author: in June 2024, 1 BTC = £54,900).

In addition to new coins and transaction fees, and depending on the blockchain, miners may benefit from other economic rewards such as:

- **Mining pool rewards**: whilst mining pools may charge a fee for participation, they may offer incentives (e.g. bonus) to miners for their contribution to the pool's mining efforts.
- **Secondary market for mining equipment**: as technology advances, miners need to upgrade their mining rigs to remain in the game. They may sell their old mining rigs on the secondary market.
- **Community rewards**: depending on the blockchain, these are incentives that may be given by the blockchain protocol, the community or project sponsors in the form of grants, funding, voluntary donations, or tips to participants for contributions to the development and growth of the blockchain ecosystem. Activities that may attract community rewards include writing and maintaining code, developing applications to enhance the blockchain, participating in bug bounties, community support and education, promoting the adoption of the blockchain, and creating high-quality content (e.g. tutorials, reviews, analysis).
- **Educational and consulting services**: miners may capitalise on their expertise in blockchain technology, mining, and network operations to offer educational or consulting services to other participants, projects, or organisations.

Professionals should remember the following:

- **Miners may benefit financially from their activities** as they receive new coins and transaction fees if they mine blocks successfully, but this is resource intensive and competitive and may not be accessible to everyone (solo mining).
- **Mining in PoW blockchains can be accessible** to those who have little or no resources (or just want to maximise their chances of successfully mining blocks) as they may join mining pools or use MaaS providers (although due diligence is advised before engaging with these entities). Miners may derive passive income as a result.
- **Mining in PoW blockchains can also be lucrative for investors** who can afford to launch or invest in mining farms, most of which are publicly listed entities. Investors may derive passive income.
- **Full nodes may get economic benefits** through community rewards and from fees for services they provide (e.g. data access, research and analytics, APIs, etc.).

- **Indirect economic benefits may be derived** from a well-operated blockchain as it attracts stakeholders, leading to increased demand and value for the native cryptocurrency. Participants may benefit from market speculation and price appreciation of the cryptocurrency they mine (caveats on volatility apply).
- The way rewards are designed and distributed depends on the specific blockchain.

PoS economic incentives

Similar to miners in PoW blockchains, **validators** in PoS blockchains may get new coins/tokens and transaction fees for being selected to propose a new block for inclusion in the blockchain (solo staking). The incentive process is dictated by the blockchain protocol. We've already ascertained that PoS blockchains select validators depending on their stake (e.g. amount, length of time held), rather than their computing power they have (see Chapter 1, *Reaching consensus*). As such, the bigger the stake and the longer it is held, the more the chance a validator has to be selected to propose a new block and earn the block reward and transaction fees.

In addition to new coins and transaction fees (the staking reward), and depending on the blockchain, validators may benefit from **other economic rewards** such as:

- **Delegation rewards**: validators may delegate their stake and therefore earn additional staking rewards based on the delegated stake, thus increasing the overall staking reward beyond what they would earn from their own stake.
- **Staking pool rewards**: whilst validators who operate staking pools may charge a fee for participation, they may offer incentives (e.g. bonus, grant) to validators who delegate their coins/tokens to the pool's validating efforts.
- **Validator fees**: validators may charge a fee for their validation services, which can be paid by users who delegate their coins/tokens to the validator. The validator can set these fees according to factors such as the level of service provided, reputation, and competition in the network.
- **Validator network rewards**: validators may be rewarded by the blockchain protocol or through dedicated reward pools for uptime,

performance, voting participation, contribution to network security or data availability, and adherence to protocol rules. The size and frequency of these rewards are dependent on the specific blockchain protocol.

- **Staking derivatives and financial products**: validators may have opportunities to participate in or benefit from financial products and derivatives tied to staking rewards, such as staking pools, staking derivatives, or staking-as-a-service offerings. These products can provide additional income streams or investment opportunities for validators.
- **Community rewards**: these are the same as those for miners in PoW blockchains and apply to multiple participants, not just validators.
- **Educational and consulting services**: validators may capitalise on their expertise in blockchain technology, validating, staking, and network operations to offer educational or consulting services to other participants, projects, or organisations.

BFT economic incentives

Similar to PoW and PoS validators, BFT validators will earn transaction fees, and in some implementations, they may also get staking and reputation-based rewards.

However, as BFT is mostly used in permissioned blockchains, where validators are pre-selected (i.e. trusted) and should have **shared objectives** (e.g. same industry or consortium), the need to economically motivate validators to collaborate and maintain network integrity is lessened due to reduced competition and less reliance on economic incentives when compared to PoW or PoS.

Indirect economic incentives

All blockchain participants may derive indirect economic benefits from their contribution to maintaining the integrity and security of the network as a well-operated blockchain attracts users, developers, and businesses. Successful blockchain ecosystems will foster applications, products, and services development on their platform, in turn potentially leading to increased demand and value for the native coin/token, thus **maximising investment** for all.

In addition, contributors who maintain a strong reputation and history may also increase their own value to the network through reputation points or other forms of recognition they may obtain, in turn leading to **commercial opportunities**. For example, partnership opportunities with developers, projects, or service providers may bring economic benefits through collaborations or revenue-sharing agreements.

Other aspects of indirect economic incentives are related to **network effects** which play an important role in blockchain ecosystems. We can draw a parallel with a well-run public transport network that expands its infrastructure as more people use it, increasing the number of routes and becoming more efficient, potentially leading to shorter travel times and lower fees. Similarly, with blockchain networks, as more participants join, the infrastructure becomes more secure (e.g. more validators) and new developments and innovations may enhance scalability, usability, and **utility** (see Chapter 2, Box 2.10). These efficiency improvements may potentially lead to faster transactions and lower fees, attracting more users in a self-reinforcing cycle. Of course, indirect economic incentives will vary across blockchain implementations, but network effects play an important part as they may lead to a stronger ecosystem that will attract both users and participants beyond sentiment and market speculation. Young blockchains rely on network effects as those participating early are betting on the potential future growth of the ecosystem rather than the token/coin value.

Non-economic incentives

Several non-economic incentives are common to all blockchains, although how they are derived depends on the specific blockchain. These include:

- **Increasing network security, integrity, and stability**: regardless of the blockchain, ensuring that the network remains secure (e.g. validation, consensus) benefits all participants through a sense of collective responsibility which encourages honest behaviour as dishonest behaviour harms the network reputation and value.
- **Increasing network influence and reputation**: participants who build a positive reputation in the community may gain long-term benefits, such as influencing decisions, having access to exclusive services, or attracting business opportunities. Different blockchains may emphasise

this aspect differently: for example, BFT emphasises reputation and collaboration within the validator network, whereas both PoW and PoS have more open competitive dynamics.

- **Encouraging social responsibility**: participants often gain a sense of contributing to a wider social good by promoting decentralisation, transparency, and independence from censorship (in public blockchains). In addition, both PoS and BFT blockchains emphasise their lower energy consumption when compared to PoW.
- **Early adoption**: in PoS, early staking may lead to higher potential rewards as the network grows and the coin/token value increases. In PoW, early mining may lead to higher mining rewards. In BFT, early participation may lead to more community connections and business opportunities.

In addition, other non-economic incentives will be specific to the various blockchains, including:

- **POW**: miners may be motivated by the **technical and intellectual challenges** that PoW blockchains present, and satisfaction may be derived by contributing to the decentralised system with computing power and expertise.
- **PoS**: validators are allowed to participate in **governance decisions** through their stake and, therefore, can influence the future direction of the blockchain.
- **BFT**: participants may have **access to exclusive services or data** depending on their reputation and performance. The selected group of validators may also sometimes participate in governance and decision-making. In addition, depending on the blockchain (especially in financial services), validators may be motivated to **comply with applicable laws and regulations** to avoid penalties.

Penalties

Similar to rewards and incentives, penalties can be economic and non-economic, but it is important to understand that the ways penalties will be applied depend on the blockchain implementation.

Table 4.9 explains at a high level how participants may be penalised, economically or otherwise.

Table 4.9 Comparing PoW, PoS, and BFT: validating node penalties. © 2024 Neira Jones

Proof of Work (PoW)	Proof of Stake (PoS)	Byzantine Fault Tolerance (BFT)
Some PoW blockchains penalise miners for supporting invalid forks by reducing rewards or excluding miners from block creation Unacceptable levels of malicious activity may lead the network to adjust the difficulty target, making mining less profitable Malicious attempts to create invalid blocks result in network rejection and therefore loss of the block reward In rare cases, a valid block might be orphaned if another valid block is built on top of a different chain (see Chapter 3, *Soft forks*). This wastes computational resources Malicious miners may develop a bad reputation in the community and even be blacklisted by mining pools, making it harder for them to participate profitably	**Slashing**: malicious behaviour or inactivity may cause a validator's stake to be slashed partially or fully, resulting in reduced rewards Validators who consistently make mistakes or go offline may receive **reduced staking rewards** Participation in malicious activity diverts attention from validating legitimate transactions (opportunity cost) **Validators may be excluded from other rewards** (e.g. reputation, governance) for unacceptable behaviour Validators who repeatedly violate the blockchain protocol rules can be **temporarily or permanently disqualified from participating in consensus** Validators with a history of bad behaviour might **lose the trust** of those who delegate stakes to them, making it harder for them to earn staking rewards	In extreme cases, validators who act maliciously can be **temporarily (jailing) or permanently excluded** from the validator set, thus affecting their income In some BFT implementations, a high number of faulty validators can **slow the network down or even stall it** Validators with poor performance or malicious behaviour may **have their blocks rejected** Validators with a history of bad behaviour can have their **reputation score reduced**, making them less likely to be chosen as leaders in future rounds Some BFT implementations may implement **a form of slashing**, although this is not as severe as in PoS networks Validators must often stake several coins as collateral (the bond) to participate. BFT blockchains may penalise badly behaved validators by **increasing their bond size**

Table 4.9 doesn't give an exhaustive list of potential penalties, and these will depend on the specific blockchain implementation. In PoW and PoS permissionless networks, economic penalties are seen as an effective way of discouraging bad behaviour. In contrast, BFT networks, typically smaller and usually permissioned, with known validators, can implement stricter penalties (and the BFT network is designed to operate even in the presence of faulty participants, see Chapter 1, *The Byzantine's general problem*).

Ultimately, the choice of penalties is a fine balance between security and validator participation: harsh penalties might discourage participation, whilst lenient ones might not deter bad behaviour effectively. At the same time, the optimal balance between security and participation can vary depending on the blockchain type.

Recap on incentives and penalties

Understanding how blockchains incentivise good behaviour and penalise bad actors is crucial for all stakeholders, from developers crafting new applications to regulators shaping the industry's future.

Professionals should remember the following:

- **Demystifying rewards and penalties**: across PoW, PoS, and BFT blockchains, it is important to grasp the economic incentives (block rewards, transaction fees) that stimulate participation and the non-economic benefits (security, reputation) that motivate responsible behaviour. Rewards and risks should be factored into project planning, investment decisions (e.g. investors prioritising network stability and established protocols, whilst monitoring Maximum Extractable Value (MEV) – covered later in *Validating nodes and transaction fees* – for informed strategies), and application design focusing on cost efficiency for a smooth user experience.
- **Transparency builds trust**: staying informed about the latest fee structures and penalties across various blockchains is vital for everyone. Developers should prioritise transparency by making fees and penalties clear within their applications. This empowers users and fosters trust within the entire ecosystem.

- **Participation with responsibility**: remember, bad behaviour comes with consequences. Economic penalties (reduced rewards, slashing) and non-economic ones (reputation loss, exclusion) exist for all blockchain types. This knowledge is vital in any strategy aiming to ensure responsible participation and a healthy network as well as for informed investment decisions.
- **Validator performance**: for validators in PoS and BFT blockchains, consistent participation, reliable performance, and a positive reputation are the keys to maximising staking rewards. Ultimately, these factors contribute to a secure and healthy network environment for everyone.
- **Considering validator pools** (PoS): validators may pool their stake with others in order to boost influence and potentially increase rewards, but pool selection should be made wisely, carefully assessing the pool's reputation and fees.
- **Investing wisely**: investors should consider how penalties can impact validator behaviour and the overall network stability. Monitoring MEV (covered later under *Validating nodes and transaction fees*) can inform investment strategies, whilst prioritising well-established protocols with robust incentive structures and a proven track record helps mitigate potential risks.
- **The role of regulators**: evaluating how incentives influence network behaviour and participant actions is crucial for regulators. Developing frameworks that promote responsible participation, user protection through transparency requirements, and fostering secure and sustainable blockchain development whilst encouraging innovation should be key priorities.

Under the hood: transaction fees (ticket to ride)

Any ecosystem, especially when relating to funds movement, relies on fees to incentivise stakeholders. In traditional card payments, there are numerous transactional fees, and these may be paid by ecosystem stakeholders for functions performed or services rendered by other ecosystem stakeholders (e.g. authorisation fee, interchange). The same applies to blockchains, but with added decentralisation and peer-to-peerness.

Transaction fee structure

PoW transaction fees

The transaction fee is the total amount a user pays to have their transaction validated by the network and included in a block.

In PoW blockchains, the protocol sets a minimum recommended fee – the **base fee** – to have a transaction processed within a reasonable time frame and ensures that miners are fairly rewarded. The blockchain protocol may adjust the base fee gradually over time or at specific intervals. The base fee may decrease during periods of low activity to prevent excessive fee hikes, and it may increase during congestion periods, although these adjustments are not generally immediately sensitive to network activity due to their scheduled nature.

This may lead users who want their transactions to be processed faster during congestion to engage in bidding wars by offering a higher fee – the **user-defined fee** – as miners may be incentivised to prioritise transactions that are more lucrative.[13] One major consequence of excessively high fees is the potential rise of "dust",[14] representing small account balances that become unusable (hence dust) because the fees exceed their value.

In a nutshell, the transaction fee in PoW blockchains consists of the base fee and the user-defined fee where applicable.

Transaction fee = base fee + user-defined fee

PoS transaction fees for Ethereum and Ethereum Virtual Machine (EVM)-compatible blockchains

Similar to PoW blockchains, the transaction fee represents the total amount a user pays to have their transaction validated and included in a block on the blockchain. However, Ethereum and EVM-compatible blockchains use the concept of "gas" and "gas price".

Gas is the unit that measures the computational effort required to execute a specific transaction on the network and different transactions have varying gas requirements (gas used) depending on their complexity.

The **gas price** is the amount a user is willing to pay per unit of gas to have a transaction processed on the blockchain.

Therefore, the transaction fee is calculated as:

$$\text{Transaction fee} = \text{gas used} \times \text{gas price}$$

Unlike PoW blockchains where users pay a fee on top of a set base fee which is adjusted on a scheduled basis, Ethereum and EVM-compatible blockchains have a different approach. They use a **dynamic base fee** automatically adjusted by the blockchain protocol based on network congestion. This dynamic base fee plays a critical role in managing network throughput and transaction inclusion. In periods of congestion, the base fee automatically increases, making transactions more expensive, which discourages unnecessary activity and helps maintain network efficiency.

However, users still have some influence over transaction speed through the gas price they offer. A higher gas price signifies the user's willingness to pay more per unit of gas, incentivising validators to prioritise their transactions for faster processing during congested periods. A gas price below the base fee will result in the transaction not being processed by the network.

As such, **the gas price is market-driven**, and users must strike the right balance to ensure timely processing whilst avoiding overpaying and transaction failure. Blockchain networks may experience price fluctuations based on demand, congestion, and overall network activity, sometimes leading to the gas price being far more expensive than the transaction amount itself. In extreme congestion scenarios, users may even engage in "gas wars"[15] by setting excessively high gas limits to outbid others, which may introduce bottlenecks for low-value transactions.

Ultimately, high fees can deter users from making transactions, hindering network usage. However, whilst low fees may attract users and increase network usage, this might not sufficiently incentivise network participants or create a sustainable economic model.

As a cost control mechanism, users may set a **gas limit**, which specifies the maximum amount of gas they are willing to pay for a specific transaction. This means that the user has to estimate the amount of gas they will likely require for that transaction. If the transaction is processed successfully and the gas used is less than the gas limit, the user will only pay for the gas used. If the gas used is more than the gas limit, the transaction will fail and no gas is used, but the user may still be charged a small fee for attempted execution. The ideal scenario is when the gas used matches the gas limit and signals that the user's estimate was accurate. Some crypto wallets and other services (see Chapter 6, *Transacting in a decentralised world*) may provide users with estimation tools to enable them to decide which price is appropriate depending on blockchain network congestion and transaction speed.[16]

Because technology evolves fast in this space, it is advisable to look at each blockchain protocol to understand its pricing structure.

PoS transaction fees for non-EVM-compatible blockchains

Transaction fees on blockchains not compatible with Ethereum (e.g. Cardano, Tezos) share the same core concept of paying fees for transaction processing. However, unlike EVM-compatible blockchains, they typically don't involve a gas concept, and their fee determination might be influenced by factors like staking, network parameters, or a combination of market forces and fixed fee structures. It is advisable to look at each blockchain's specifications to understand their pricing structures.

Transaction fee units

The **denomination unit** for transaction fees or gas is the smallest divisible unit of the native **coin** or **token** for a blockchain, as shown in Table 4.10 for some popular blockchains.

Table 4.10 Unit of measurement for transaction fees. © 2024 Neira Jones

Blockchain	**Type**	**Unit of Measurement for Transaction Fee**
Bitcoin	PoW	**Satoshi** 1 BTC = 100,000,000 Satoshis
Ethereum and EVM compatible	PoS	**Gwei** 1 Gwei = 1,000,000,000 wei 1 ETH = 1,000,000,000 Gwei
Solana	PoS	**Lamport** 1 SOL = 1,000,000,000 Lamports
Cardano	PoS	**Lovelace** 1 ADA = 1,000,000 Lovelace
Litecoin	PoW	**Litoshi** 1 LTC = 100,000,000 Litoshis (lit)

Ultimately, whilst the transaction cost represents an expenditure of the native coin/token, users will be interested in the transaction cost expressed in **fiat currency**, such as the dollar (USD), pound (GBP), or euro (EUR). This will involve the conversion of value, and two additional elements are needed:

- **The native coin/token price**: this is determined by the market and is readily available on crypto exchanges (e.g. Binance[17]) or market data websites (e.g. coinmarketcap.com[18] or cryptoslate.com[19]).
- **The exchange rate provider**: no single entity sets the exchange rate as this is determined by supply, demand, and market forces. Service providers, including crypto exchanges, online converters, market data APIs, may provide this facility.

Recap on transaction fee structure

Professionals should remember the following:

- **Users pay fees to get transactions validated and included in a block** on a blockchain. These fees vary depending on the type of blockchain and how busy the network is.
- **In PoW blockchains, transaction fees typically consist of a base fee (minimum recommended) and an optional user-defined fee** (tip for miners). High fees in PoW systems can lead to "dust," where small account balances become unusable due to fees exceeding their value.
- **For Ethereum and EVM-compatible blockchains, transaction fees are calculated by multiplying gas (computational effort) by the gas price (user's offer per unit of gas).** Unlike PoW, these blockchains have a dynamic base fee that automatically adjusts based on network congestion. Users can also set a gas limit to control their maximum spend on a transaction. High gas prices during congestion can lead to "gas wars" where users compete by offering even higher fees to get their transactions processed faster.
- Other non-EVM PoS blockchains determine fees differently, considering factors like staking, network parameters, or a combination of market forces and fixed fees. It's important to consult individual blockchain specifications for details on their fee structures.
- **Transaction fees are typically denominated in the smallest unit of the native cryptocurrency** for that blockchain (e.g. Satoshi for BTC, Gwei for ETH).

- To convert transaction fees to a fiat currency (e.g. USD, EUR, etc.), you'll need the current price of the native token and the prevailing exchange rate.

Validating nodes and transaction fees

Transaction fee evaluation

When prioritising transactions (see Chapter 1, *Validating transactions*), validating nodes will check if the transaction fee is included in the transaction, and whether it meets the **minimum fee requirement**, where required by the blockchain protocol (e.g. base fee). The base fee itself is not used to reward validating nodes (they get the amount users pay above the base fee), and this mechanism helps the blockchain network to control the overall supply of the underlying cryptocurrency and discourages spam transactions.

This means that once the transaction is recorded on the ledger, the base fee is "burned" (i.e. removed from circulation). Think of it as a kind of network fee that encourages users to only submit legitimate transactions, but instead of rewarding validating nodes, it regulates network usage (e.g. a bit like card scheme fees on the card rails, although for blockchains, the base fee is not given to anyone, it just disappears).

Validators may also prioritise transactions based on the transaction fee offered by the user, and as they are rewarded for their effort with a portion of the transaction fee, this directly affects their earnings. Transactions with higher fees may take priority over those with lower fees, which means the latter may remain pending (aka unspent) for a long time. However, lower fee transactions may be prioritised by validating nodes depending on network conditions, block size, or protocol-specific rules.

In addition, the transaction will fail if it takes more resources than the specified gas limit (e.g. it runs out of "gas").

As you may imagine, validating nodes are likely to implement strategies to maximise revenue.

Maximum Extractable Value (MEV)

Maximum Extractable Value (MEV) refers to the maximum value block producers (miners or validators) can obtain by including, reordering, or excluding transactions when producing a new block.

- **In PoW blockchains**, since miners may prioritise faster block creation for higher rewards, they're less likely to engage in extensive MEV extraction as it might slow down block creation.
- **In PoS blockchains**, as validators' computational effort is not as intensive as in PoW, there is more time and incentive to engage in MEV extraction strategies.

The act of manipulating transaction order for MEV can have both positive and negative consequences and it's a complex issue. Whether it's a dubious practice depends on your perspective:

- **Positive**: MEV can incentivise validators to be more efficient, potentially leading to faster transaction processing.
- **Negative**: MEV can lead to unfair advantages for certain users willing to pay extra for prioritised transactions, potentially hindering the overall fairness and efficiency of the network. MEV can also contribute to network disruption such as significant transaction delays or high fees.

Table 4.11 gives a breakdown of the arguments for and against MEV.

MEV manipulation attacks include:

- **Front-running**, where a validating node observes a pending transaction and then inserts its own transaction before the user's, buying the same token at a slightly higher price. This drives the price up before the user's original transaction executes, allowing the miner to profit from the price difference.
- **Back-running** is the opposite of front-running, where a validating node inserts its transaction after a user's transaction, but strategically placed to benefit from the user's action. Imagine a user placing a large buy order for a token, driving its price up. The miner can then insert their own buy order after the user's but before the price adjusts to reflect the new market conditions, profiting from the inflated price caused by the initial purchase.
- **Sandwich attacks** combine both front-running and back-running. The validating node inserts two transactions, one before and one after a user's transaction, to manipulate the price and capture profits in the middle.

Table 4.11 For or against MEV? © 2024 Neira Jones

	Arguments for MEV	Arguments against MEV
Market	**Market efficiency**: MEV may improve market efficiency by ensuring that transactions with the highest value are included in blocks first. This can benefit users who are willing to pay higher fees for faster transaction confirmation	**Unfair advantage**: MEV can give miners or validators an unfair advantage by allowing them to prioritise certain transactions for their own benefit, potentially leading to higher fees for regular users. This can be seen as a form of rent-seeking behaviour
Security	**Security incentive**: MEV can incentivise miners or validators to participate in the network and secure it. The additional revenue they can earn from MEV can contribute to the overall health and security of the blockchain	**Market manipulation**: MEV may involve dubious practices (e.g. front-running, back-running, sandwich attacks) which can be detrimental to fair market competition
Technical	**Innovation**: MEV research and tools may lead to innovative solutions, such as block builders that help users optimise their transaction fees and avoid manipulation attacks	**Network congestion**: MEV strategies often involve bidding wars for block space, leading to network congestion and increased transaction fees for everyone **Complexity**: MEV extraction techniques can be complex and require advanced knowledge, potentially creating an uneven playing field for users

In blockchain networks, understanding MEV is crucial as it highlights the complexities involved in maintaining a decentralised and secure system whilst acknowledging the potential for manipulation within the block creation process. Developers are exploring ways to mitigate the negative aspects of MEV whilst preserving its potential benefits. Some proposed solutions include block scheduling, making transaction ordering less predictable – reducing potential MEV exploitation – and separation of transaction selection from validation.

It's important to remember that MEV isn't inherently bad. It's a natural consequence of the economic incentives built into blockchain protocols. Whilst MEV can incentivise efficient block production, it's potential downsides may be addressed through:

- **Blockchain protocol design** to mitigate the negative impacts of MEV, such as by implementing mechanisms to prevent manipulation attacks or by fairer block space allocation methods.
- **Transparency and education**: increased transparency about MEV and its potential impacts can help users make informed decisions about their transactions.
- **Community collaboration** between developers, researchers, and users can lead to the development of tools and solutions that address the challenges of MEV whilst preserving the benefits.

The fee structure lays the foundation for a secure and functioning blockchain system, and MEV is a natural consequence of the economic model, with both positive and negative aspects. Developers are constantly working to refine the way transactions are processed to ensure fairness and efficiency. This ongoing effort is crucial for maintaining a healthy blockchain ecosystem.

Recap on transaction fees

Professionals should remember the following:

- **Transaction fees are crucial**: it is important to grasp the fee structures of PoW (base fee + user fee) and PoS (gas * gas price) blockchains to navigate network costs effectively. Transaction fees should be factored into project planning, investment decisions, and user experience design, especially for microtransactions.
- **Beware the pitfalls**: high fees can create unusable "dust" in PoW systems and gas wars during PoS network congestion. For PoW, the impact of fees on user adoption and network scalability is an important consideration. PoS blockchains should be mindful of MEV and its potential to manipulate transaction fees and create an uneven playing field.

- **Cost optimisation**: on PoS blockchains, gas limits may be used to control spending and tools for gas price estimation may be leveraged. Layer-2 solutions or alternative blockchains with lower fees for cost-sensitive transactions may offer alternative mechanisms. Developers should explore code efficiency to minimise gas usage and optimise transaction throughput.
- **User education**: to avoid surprises and ensure a smooth user experience, blockchain projects should clearly explain their transaction fee structures, optimal transaction speeds, and be aware of users' needs. Tools and resources are available for fee estimation. Regulators should consider user protection measures regarding potential fee volatility and transparency of MEV practices.
- **Stay informed, stay ahead**: blockchain fee structures are dynamic and it is always advisable to consult individual blockchain protocols for up-to-date fee details. For investors and developers, monitoring trends in transaction fees to assess network health and potential future costs help with informed decision-making.
- **Plan for MEV**: it is important to understand how MEV can impact transaction fees and to mitigate its negative effects; blockchain projects may deploy strategies to prevent MEV manipulation (e.g. front-running) or ensure fair block space allocation. Regulators may need to evaluate the potential need for regulations to address MEV and promote fair market competition.
- **Embrace transparency**: transparency around transaction fees and MEV practices fosters trust within the ecosystem and empowers users to make informed decisions. Open discussions and collaboration within the developer community help to find solutions that optimise transaction fees and mitigate MEV's negative aspects.

Blockchain metrics (think twice)

In Chapters 1 and 2, we covered fundamental blockchain mechanics and introduced some metrics (e.g. transaction speed, block interval). We introduced some more metrics throughout this chapter (e.g. total supply, circulating supply). We understand the characteristics of blockchains, their various types, how transactions are validated, and who the main ecosystem actors are, but we now also need to understand how well (or badly) these network infrastructures perform. Ecosystem actors, and stakeholders in general, should be able to assess the security, decentralisation, and scalability (amongst other factors) of any project they may be involved with. An understanding of available metrics will enable us to assess and monitor aspects of interest.

With centralised payment ecosystems, we are familiar with performance measures such as transactions/second (TPS), number of active users, fraud ratios, resilience, or market capitalisation, to name but a few, and these indicators are generally easily verifiable.

For blockchains, we also have metrics, but these are a bit more complicated, and not always easily verifiable from a single trusted source. To this effect, I'll attempt to demystify blockchain metrics by classifying them into those that are common to most blockchains and those that are specific to only some blockchains. You may, if you're never going to be involved or interested in assessing blockchains, skip this section for now and go straight to the duck, or even to the conclusion, but trust me, understanding metrics helps in the long run... You can look at Table 4.12 for a comprehensive list of metrics and decide whether you want to delve further.

In general, blockchain metrics can either be set by the blockchain protocol itself, determined by network conditions and participation, or by market activity. Table 4.12 gives a summary of blockchain metrics that may be used to assess security, decentralisation, scalability, and other factors, either directly or indirectly. You will recognise the various elements as most of them were introduced in previous chapters and this one.

The metrics listed in Table 4.12 will be explained in the next sections.

Common metrics set by the blockchain protocol

This first set of common metrics is directly set by the blockchain protocol and may help with assessing various blockchain factors, such as scalability and network health as illustrated in Table 4.13:

For details on these metrics, please read on, otherwise skip to the next set.

Block size limit: expressed in bytes, this specifies the maximum amount of data allowed in a block. A large block size indicates increased transaction capacity, whilst a smaller block size indicates faster block creation but may raise concerns over scalability. It is used by developers, researchers, and users. PoW blockchains usually have a fixed block size

Table 4.12 Useful blockchain metrics. © 2024 Neira Jones

Metrics	POW & PoS Common Metrics	PoW Specific	PoS Specific
Set by blockchain protocol	Block size limit Block interval Maximum supply Minimum transaction fees (where implemented)	Difficulty target Difficulty adjustment frequency	Minimum stake requirement Slashing rate Epoch length
Determined by network conditions & participation	Average block creation time Average block size Node count Node response time Mempool size Throughput Network uptime Confirmation time Fees Developer count Total supply Developer tools and resources Security audits and bug bounties	Hashrate Chainwork Miner distribution Mining pool distribution Mining pool uptime	Total stake Active validators Average validator uptime Validator distribution Validator uptime distribution Staking pool distribution Staking ratio Active staking wallets Momentum
Market driven	DAU On-chain transaction volumes Active wallet addresses Circulating supply Exchange listings Trading volumes Social media & community engagement		

limit (e.g. Bitcoin, Litecoin), as do some PoS blockchains (e.g. Cardano, Tezos, Cosmos). Some PoS blockchains implement dynamic adjustments to the block size limit to optimise network capacity according to activity

Table 4.13 Common blockchain metrics determined by the blockchain protocol. © 2024 Neira Jones

Metrics	Description	Used By	Indicator
Block size limit	Maximum amount of data allowed in a block (bytes)	Developers, researchers, users	**Large**: increased transaction capacity but potential scalability concerns. **Small**: faster block creation but limited scalability
Block interval	Target time between creating consecutive blocks (seconds)	Developers, researchers, users	**Longer**: enhanced security but slower transaction processing. **Shorter**: faster transaction processing but potential security implications
Maximum supply	Maximum number of coins/ tokens that will ever exist	Investors, users, researchers	**Fixed**: predictable inflation, potentially higher long-term value. **Unlimited**: concerns about continuous inflation impacting value
Minimum transaction fees	Minimum fee required for a transaction to be processed (if applicable)	Network developers, users	Used with other metrics to assess scalability and network health. High fees due to congestion may disadvantage some users

(e.g. EOS, Algorand, Solana). These block size limits are typically set by the consensus mechanism of the blockchain protocol.

Block interval: expressed in seconds, this specifies the target time between the creation of consecutive blocks. A longer block interval may indicate enhanced security, whilst a shorter interval may indicate faster transaction processing. Developers, researchers, and users may use the block interval in conjunction with other metrics (e.g. average block creation time, confirmation time, throughput) to assess potential scalability bottlenecks.

BOX 4.5 WHAT IS THE BLOCK INTERVAL?

The **block interval** is a measure representing the "expected" or target time it takes to add a new block (i.e. a batch of transactions) to a blockchain. This predetermined value is set by the blockchain protocol and is usually represented in seconds or minutes. To draw a parallel with centralised infrastructure, this is the rough equivalent of the expected settlement cycle (transaction initiation to finality), but for blockchains, this is also the rough equivalent of transaction speed (e.g. what the user experiences when they make a card payment, settlement happening much later), but bearing in mind that there are several transactions in a block, this is also not an absolute proxy. It must also be clarified that the "actual" time it takes to create a new block is usually referred to as "block creation time" and this may vary depending on network conditions. Ideally, the block creation time should be close to the block interval as this would mean that blocks are created consistently, but they may not always be the same, again depending on network conditions. Beware: whilst some blockchains clearly differentiate between "block interval" and "block creation time", others will use the terms interchangeably and therefore context must be understood.

Maximum supply: this represents the maximum number of coins/tokens that will ever exist and is fixed after the launch of the blockchain project. A fixed supply indicates predictable inflation and potentially higher long-term value. For example, there is a maximum supply of 21 million BTC. Some blockchains have an unlimited supply (uncapped systems) which may raise concerns about continuous inflation, ultimately impacting value. Investors, users, and researchers may use this indicator to gain insight into potential coin/token value, inflation control, network economics, monetary policy analysis, and overall investment considerations.

Minimum transaction fees: in blockchains where this measure is implemented (see *Under the hood: transaction fees*), this can be used as an indirect measure, alongside other metrics, to assess scalability and other factors. For example, transactions with fees below the set minimum wouldn't be processed, freeing up block space for other valid transactions. In addition, network congestion may cause transaction fees to rise above the set minimum which may incentivise users to offer higher fees in exchange for prioritisation, but this may also disadvantage users who can't afford high fees, hindering scalability for low-value transactions.

Common metrics determined by network conditions and participation

This second set of common metrics is determined by network conditions and participation and may help with assessing various blockchain factors, such as decentralisation, scalability security, and network health. This is illustrated in Table 4.14:

For details on these metrics, please read on, otherwise skip to the next set.

Average block creation time: expressed in seconds, it measures the average time it takes to mine or validate a block and is influenced by hashrate and difficulty target (PoW) or validator selection process (PoS). It helps understand transaction processing speed and confirmation times. A high value may indicate network congestion, slower transaction, potentially impacting the user experience, and this can be a sign of scalability limitations. A low value may indicate faster transaction processing but may mean increased network resource usage or centralisation. This metric is used by developers, users, and investors to understand transaction processing speed and confirmation times.

Average block size: expressed in bytes and determined by validation activity, this indicates the average amount of data stored in each block and affects mining/staking efficiency as it has an impact on transaction throughput and storage requirements. In PoW blockchains, a large average block size indicates miners are using block space efficiently and this can increase transaction throughput, thus improving user experience but

Table 4.14 Common blockchain metrics determined by network conditions. © 2024 Neira Jones

Metrics	Description	Used By	Indicator
Average block creation time	Time to mine/validate a block	Developers, users, investors	High values indicate potential congestion and scalability limitations
Average block size	Amount of data stored in each block	Developers, users	High values approaching the block size limit may indicate congestion
Node count	Total number of computers running the network	Developers, researchers	a high node count indicates better decentralisation
Node response time	Time a node takes to respond to a request	Developers, users	Slow response times may indicate congestion or inefficient infrastructure
Mempool size	Number of transactions waiting to be included in a block	Developers, users	Large size suggests congestion and potentially slower processing times
Throughput	Transactions processed per second	Developers, investors, users	A high throughput indicates an efficient network and potential for scalability
Network uptime	Duration for which the network is operational, relevant to PoS	Developers	Important for assessing network reliability and security

(*Continued*)

Table 4.14 (Continued)

Metrics	**Description**	**Used By**	**Indicator**
Confirmation time	Time for a transaction to be considered final	Stakeholders	Can be impacted by scalability limitations
Fees	Transaction processing costs	Developers, investors, users	High fees due to congestion can be a sign of scalability limitations
Developer count	Number of active developers	Investors	A high or growing number suggests continuous innovation
Governance participation rate	Percentage of token holders involved in governance (where used)	Investors, researchers	A high rate indicates a strong and engaged community
Developer tools and resources	Availability and quality of developer resources	Developers	Comprehensive resources can attract developers and foster a thriving ecosystem
Security audits and bug bounties	Frequency and results of security audits	Stakeholders	Regular audits and well-established bug bounty programmes demonstrate a strong security commitment

may raise concerns about scalability (as larger blocks are more resource intensive to process) and centralisation (if only powerful nodes are able to process blocks efficiently). For PoW and PoS, very high values approaching the block size limit may indicate network congestion. In PoS blockchains. a larger average block size may optimise validator efficiency and network performance. Whilst average block size is often more critical in PoW due to its influence on mining, this indicator is still relevant for PoS network optimisation and potential future functionality. For both PoW and PoS, a small average block size may limit transaction throughput and network adoption but may improve scalability. This metric is used by developers, users, and those interested in blockchain scalability and efficiency.

Node count: expressed in the number of nodes and determined by network participation, the node count is the total number of computers running and validating transactions on the network. A high node count indicates greater blockchain decentralisation and potential resilience, whilst a low number of nodes may raise concerns about centralisation and potential security risks. Blockchain developers use the node count to assess the overall decentralisation and health of a network, as well as potential issues with performance and scalability by tracking node count over time. They may also use the node count for testing and development to monitor the deployment of new features and upgrades. Researchers may use the node count to analyse the distribution and location of nodes to gain insights into network efficiency, topology, centralisation risks, security threats (e.g. Denial of Service attacks), as well as for protocol design and improvements. For completeness purposes, I must mention that node count is not the only metric used to measure decentralisation. The **Herfindahl index** measures the concentration of hashrate (PoW) or stake distribution (PoS) across different nodes. A lower Herfindahl index indicates a more even distribution and greater decentralisation, whilst a higher index suggests a more concentrated distribution and potential centralisation risks. Similarly, the **Gini coefficient** measures the inequality of hashrate or stake distribution. A value closer to zero indicates a more equal distribution and greater decentralisation, whilst a value closer to one indicates a more unequal distribution and potential centralisation risks.

Node response time: expressed in milliseconds and determined by the network infrastructure and hardware, this represents the average time a node takes to respond to a request. A faster response time indicates efficient network performance and a potentially smoother user experience, whilst a slower response time may suggest network congestion or an inefficient infrastructure, ultimately impacting the user experience. Blockchain developers use the node response time to assess the overall performance and responsiveness of a network, as well as during debugging and troubleshooting where it helps with pinpointing the source of a problem (e.g. slow response time from specific nodes might indicate software issues or hardware constraints). They may also use the node response time for network scalability testing of new features and upgrades. Researchers may use the node count to analyse network performance to gain insights into network efficiency, scalability, and potential bottlenecks, as well as for network optimisation research and protocol design and improvements. For users, whilst the node response time is not a direct measure of transaction confirmation times, it gives a general indication of how quickly their transactions might be processed.

Mempool size: expressed in number of transactions, it is determined by user activity and network capacity and represents the number of transactions waiting to be included in a block. A large number of transactions in the mempool may suggest network congestion and potentially slower transaction processing times, whilst a low number indicates that the network is processing transactions efficiently. Blockchain developers use the mempool size to assess network congestion, as well as during debugging and troubleshooting where it helps with pinpointing the source of a problem (e.g. slow response time from specific nodes might indicate software issues or hardware constraints). They may also use the node response time for network scalability testing of new features and upgrades. Researchers may use the node count to analyse network performance to gain insights into network efficiency, scalability, and potential bottlenecks, as well as for network optimisation research and protocol design and improvements. For users, whilst the node response time is not a direct measure of transaction confirmation times, it gives a general indication of how quickly their transactions might be processed.

Throughput: expressed in transactions per second, it is dynamically influenced by network activity and the network's capacity to process transactions in a given timeframe and helps with assessing network scalability and performance. A high transaction throughput indicates the network can handle a larger volume of transactions efficiently, potentially improving user experience and scalability. A low transaction throughput may lead to transaction delays and backlogs, impacting the user experience and potentially hindering network adoption. Blockchain developers use throughput to monitor network performance, and by analysing throughput trends, they can identify bottlenecks and make improvements, as well as plan for future network scalability. Investors may use the throughput as an indicator of network adoption and usage as a consistently high throughput and a clear scalability roadmap is viewed favourably. They may also use the throughput to compare different blockchains for different purposes (e.g. standard transactions, niche applications). For users, whilst the throughput is not a direct measure of transaction confirmation times, it gives a general indication of how quickly their transactions might be processed.

Network uptime: this metric plays a crucial role in PoS blockchains because block production relies on active validators. Downtime signifies a lack of validator participation, potentially hindering transaction processing and network security. Measuring and analysing network uptime is particularly relevant for assessing the reliability and health of PoS networks. Whilst not so crucial as in PoS, network uptime is still important for PoW blockchains as downtime can disrupt mining operations, slow down transaction processing, and potentially impact network security if it persists for extended periods. However, the focus in PoW often shifts towards hashrate, as a primary indicator of network security and resilience.

Confirmation time: transaction mechanics were covered in Chapter 1, *When can a transaction be considered final?* Stakeholders use this metric alongside others to understand network performance, usability, and to identify potential scalability bottlenecks.

Fees: as covered earlier, whilst some blockchains may implement dynamic or minimum fee structures, network activity dynamically influences the fees (e.g. gas limit). Developers may consider high fees caused by network congestion as an indicator of scalability limitations and explore ways of handling more transactions without high fee increases. Investors may consider high fees as an indicator of network value (i.e. high demand, congestion), but excessively high fees may deter users.

Governance participation rate: this measures the percentage of token holders actively participating in on-chain governance processes and varies depending on the specific blockchain governance system. This can indicate the level of community engagement and decentralisation within the blockchain ecosystem and is used by investors, researchers, and those interested in the decision-making processes and level of community involvement. A high participation rate suggests a strong and engaged community actively involved in shaping the network's future, whilst a low value raise concerns about community apathy, potential centralisation of decision-making power, or flaws in the governance mechanisms.

Developer count: this is a dynamic value representing the total number of developers which is a rough proxy for the development activity and future innovation potential of a blockchain. A high or growing number of active developers indicates a potential for continuous innovation, whilst a low or stagnant number of developers may raise concerns about the blockchain's long-term sustainability. Investors may look at this indicator to assess a blockchain project's growth potential as a strong developer base suggests continuous innovation, bug fixes, new features, etc. However, a growing developer base could put pressure on the scalability of the network, and researchers may analyse how the network is handling increased activity and explore potential scalability solutions. But this metric comes with a warning: whilst a large number of developers can be considered a positive factor, the quality and experience of developers matters as a smaller team of highly skilled developers can be just as valuable as a large team with less experience.

Developer tools and resources: understanding the availability and quality of developer tools, documentation, and educational resources offered by the blockchain project may influence developer adoption, innovation, and blockchain project sustainability as a comprehensive and user-friendly set of developer tools and resources can attract developers and foster a thriving blockchain ecosystem. Conversely, a limited or outdated set of resources may hinder developer adoption and limit the network's growth and adoption potential, which may be a red flag for investors. Of course, similar to the developer count, the quality and scope of the developer tools and resources are perhaps more important than just the quantity. Whilst not directly related to scalability, this metric can however help with assessing a blockchain's long-term viability.

Security audits and bug bounties: the frequency and results of independent security audits and bug bounty programmes may indicate a blockchain project's commitment to security. Stakeholders use this metric to assess the potential risk of blockchain vulnerabilities. Project developers or independent security firms may perform audits, and the project team may instigate bug bounty programmes. Regular security audits, well-established bug bounty programmes, and a project's track record of promptly addressing identified vulnerabilities all demonstrate a project's strong commitment to security and a proactive approach to risk management. Conversely, the lack of independent security audits, limited or inactive bug bounty programmes, and consistently unaddressed vulnerabilities may raise concerns about potential security weaknesses and the project's commitment to addressing them. Whilst not directly related to scalability, this metric can however help with assessing a blockchain's long-term viability.

Common metrics determined by market activity

The metrics in this third set of common metrics are determined by market dynamics and interactions and may help with assessing various factors, including community interest, viability, and liquidity. Table 4.15 illustrates this.

For details on these metrics, please read on, otherwise skip to the next set.

Daily Active Users (DAU): this measures the number of unique individual users who interact with the blockchain network on a given day, including sending, receiving, trading cryptocurrencies, using dApps, participating in DeFi protocols, or staking. This may be more challenging to measure in permissionless blockchains (see Chapter 1, *Blockchain types*) and privacy-focussed blockchains (see Chapter 1, *Are blockchains private and anonymous?*), especially for users interacting through crypto wallets that don't reveal user's identities (see Chapter 6, *Transacting in a decentralised world*). Stakeholders may use this metric to gauge the overall user engagement with a blockchain network as a significant surge in DAU may have an impact on scalability and performance, whilst a consistently declining DAU may indicate waning user interest or potential issues with the blockchain's usability or functionality. This metric comes with a warning and should be considered alongside others as it doesn't necessarily reflect the quality of user engagement (e.g. a project may have a high DAU, but users may only be interacting minimally or for speculative purposes). It's also important to consider that privacy regulations and user preferences for data anonymity may make it challenging to accurately measure DAU on some blockchains.

On-chain transaction volumes: this represents the actual usage of the blockchain network for its core purpose (e.g. trading cryptocurrencies, using dApps, executing smart contracts) and is most commonly measured daily, but can also be weekly. It doesn't include off-chain transactions (i.e. those that happen outside of the main blockchain ledger) and shouldn't include speculative or manipulative activities (although, this is very difficult to achieve because these involve actual on-chain transactions). Several

Table 4.15 Common blockchain metrics determined by market activity. © 2024 Neira Jones

Metrics	Description	Used By	Indicator
Daily Active Users (DAU)	Number of unique users interacting with the network per day	Developers, users	**High DAU** can strain network resources. **Low DAU** might indicate waning interest
On-chain transaction volumes	Total daily (or weekly) volume of transactions happening on the blockchain	Developers, validators, users, investors	**High volume** may indicate broader adoption but could stress scalability. **Low volume** suggests low user activity or potential scalability issues
Active wallet addresses	Number of unique wallets interacting with the network within a timeframe	Developers, validators, security auditors	Surge in active addresses suggests increased adoption but may impact scalability. Decline signifies decreasing user engagement
Circulating supply	Total number of coins/tokens currently in circulation	Investors, traders, users	Unequal distribution could raise concerns about price manipulation. Not directly related to scalability but helps assess project viability with other metrics
Exchange listings	Number of exchanges where a coin/token is traded	Investors, traders, users	May influence liquidity, accessibility, and adoption, potentially impacting scalability if high
Trading volume	Total amount of a cryptocurrency traded on exchanges within a period	Investors, traders, users	High volume can impact transaction processing efficiency
Social media & community engagement	Level of activity and sentiment on social media platforms and developer forums	Developers, project managers, marketing teams	**Strong engagement** suggests community support and potential network growth. **Limited engagement** raises concerns about declining interest or potential project risks

stakeholders may provide this data, such as full nodes, blockchain explorers, blockchain monitoring and analytics service providers (see Chapter 1, Table 1.9), as well as crypto exchanges and marketplaces (see Chapter 6, *Transacting in a decentralised world*). Like others, this indicator shouldn't be used on its own but in conjunction with other metrics, and it may help stakeholders gauge the actual usage of a blockchain as a high value may indicate broader adoption and potential for future growth (whilst this might stress a blockchain's scalability), whilst a significant decline might raise concerns about user interest or potential issues with scalability or transaction fees (which may inform prioritisation of blockchain development efforts).

Active wallet addresses: this measures the number of unique blockchain wallet addresses that have interacted with the blockchain in a specific time frame (e.g. sending, receiving, or swapping coins/tokens, interacting with DeFi applications, etc.). Unlike DAU, it gives a clear picture of on-chain activity, but it has some limitations. For example, one wallet doesn't necessarily equate to one individual user, one single user can control multiple wallets, and activities that don't involve on-chain transactions will not be captured (e.g. custodial wallet, see Chapter 7). Stakeholders may use this metric to gauge overall user engagement with a blockchain network as a significant surge in the number of active wallet addresses, whilst signifying increased adoption, may have an impact on scalability and performance, whilst a consistently declining number of active wallet addresses may indicate decreasing user engagement potentially impacting the project's value proposition and viability. In addition, project teams may use this metric to identify where user adoption is lagging and therefore focus their product development efforts.

Circulating supply: an important part of tokenomics, this is a dynamic value representing the total number of coins/tokens that are currently in circulation and consists of the total number of coins/tokens that have already been issued (or mined), those that are currently locked in circulation (e.g. staked coins), excluding any that have been permanently removed from circulation (e.g. burned). Whilst this metric is not directly related to scalability, it helps assess, in conjunction with other metrics, the viability of a blockchain project. For example, investors might use it to understand coin/token distribution in order to determine whether an unequal or unfair distribution could be a worry. This may happen if a large allocation is made to developers and founders without a vesting schedule, potentially raising concerns about pump-and-dump schemes where the team might sell their tokens early at an inflated price. In addition, coin/token distribution helps investors understand the dynamics of supply and demand, and whether their interests align with those of other holders. Ultimately, a larger allocation to development and marketing may suggest a focus on long-term growth (indicating potential scarcity and possible long-term value appreciation), whilst a larger public allocation may indicate a desire for wider adoption (more readily available supply may impact the price in the short term). Stakeholders may use this metric to assess current market activity as a higher circulating supply may indicate greater liquidity and user adoption, whilst a low value may indicate lower liquidity but doesn't necessarily imply lower value. Whilst this metric is not directly used to assess blockchain scalability, it can, in conjunction with other metrics, help identify potential bottlenecks as a sudden or sustained decline in circulating supply could indicate a decrease in user activity, which may potentially suggest underlying scalability issues.

Exchange listings: this represents the number of crypto exchanges where a particular coin/token is available for trading and stakeholders may use this metric to assess the tradability and potential market value of the blockchain's token/coin as this may influence liquidity, accessibility, adoption levels, and volatility. Whilst this metric is not directly used to assess blockchain scalability, it can, in conjunction with other metrics, help identify whether a high number of exchange listings could lead to increased network activity which may impact scalability, or whether the activity is primarily for speculative trading (which doesn't necessarily translate in actual network usage).

Trading volume: representing the total amount of a token/coin being traded on crypto exchanges within a specific period of time (e.g. daily, weekly, monthly), this metric may be used by stakeholders to assess market activity, liquidity, and volatility of the asset. Whilst this metric is not directly used to assess blockchain scalability, it can, in conjunction with other metrics (e.g. throughput, block size, average block creation time), help identify whether high trading volumes are impacting the blockchain network's capacity to process transactions efficiently and identify areas for improvement.

Social media and community engagement: this evaluates the level of activity and sentiment on social media platforms and developer forums related to the blockchain project and may be used by stakeholders to gauge the health and potential of a blockchain project. This is difficult to measure, but stakeholders may use social media platforms and basic engagement metrics (e.g. follower count, shares, comments, reposts, mentions) as well as social listening tools to gather data (e.g. volume of conversations, sentiment, reach) and assess community health (e.g. helpfulness of community members, constructive criticism, quality of discussions). Strong community engagement can indicate community support, network growth potential, and a collaborative development environment, whilst a limited or negative community engagement could raise concerns about declining interest, potential project risks, or a lack of transparency. Whilst this metric is not directly used to assess blockchain scalability, it can, in conjunction with other metrics, be an indicator of future demand (i.e. an active community could lead to network growth potentially impacting scalability), potential bottlenecks (e.g. community discussions may reveal limitations related to scalability), and a well-engaged community may participate more actively in the blockchain goals and development roadmap if scalability is a stated goal.

Common metrics for privacy-focused blockchains

Typically, these metrics may be useful for those privacy-focused stakeholders and will depend on the type of cryptographic technique used (see Chapter 1, *Privacy-focused blockchains*):

- **Percentage of transactions shielded**: this indicates the proportion of transactions where transactions details such as sender, receiver, and amount are obfuscated.
- **Ring signature size**: this indicates the number of senders in the anonymity set, and the higher it is the more difficult it is to identify the true sender.
- **Number of zk-SNARK proofs**: the number of proofs generated can be an indicator of the overall privacy although this metric has limitations as a standalone metric (e.g. an increase in proofs could indicate network congestion rather than a surge in privacy-focused transactions) and should be used in conjunction with other metrics.

Recap on common metrics

Professionals should remember that blockchain metrics are complicated, but here's a quick guide on common metrics:

- **Analyse trade-offs, not silos**: when evaluating protocol settings like block size and block interval, the balance between transaction capacity, security, and scalability must be understood. It is important to investigate how these settings impact blockchain-protocol-determined metrics like block creation time and throughput, and holistic metrics analysis helps identify potential bottlenecks before they become roadblocks.
- **Decentralisation demands a holistic view**: node count is a good starting point for measuring decentralisation, but it's just one piece of the puzzle. For a more comprehensive picture, metrics like the **Herfindahl index** or **Gini coefficient** can be considered. Additionally, throughput trends can be analysed alongside node count to proactively plan for future network growth and scalability needs.
- **Network efficiency is all about harmony**: to diagnose potential congestion and optimise network efficiency, average block size, mempool size, and confirmation times should be monitored in unison. Node response time could be leveraged for network scalability testing, pinpointing performance issues before they disrupt user experience.
- **Tokenomics shapes the future**: don't underestimate the power of tokenomics! Maximum supply (if applicable) and minimum transaction fees (if implemented) may influence long-term token valuation and network economics. Understanding token distribution models may help provide valuable insights into network adoption and token value.
- **Network uptime, the bedrock of trust**: regardless of the consensus mechanism, consistently monitoring network uptime is crucial. Uptime directly impacts the overall reliability and security – a critical factor for building user trust.
- **Privacy matters – a balancing act**: when evaluating any blockchain, the interplay between user privacy and network transparency reflected in various metrics must be understood. Whilst privacy-focused blockchains have specific anonymity metrics (like ring size), public

blockchains may raise privacy concerns. For example, DAU might be a less accurate measure of user engagement if users are actively trying to obscure their activity. It's crucial to understand how a blockchain's core design and privacy features influence the interpretation of common metrics.

- **Look at the Big Picture**: a single metric can't tell the whole story. Considering a combination of relevant metrics helps with getting a complete picture of a blockchain's performance and health.
- **Stay ahead of the curve**: the blockchain industry is constantly evolving keeping up to date with the best practices, and emerging metrics helps.

After this tour of common metrics, we'll examine other metrics as they apply specifically to PoW, PoS, smart contracts, and DeFi.

PoW-blockchain-specific metrics

All the common metrics described in the previous sections may be used to assess PoW blockchains, but these will also have metrics specific to their architecture.

Metrics set by the PoW protocol

As more miners join a PoW blockchain, or as their mining hardware becomes more powerful (through upgrades), the total computational power of the network increases (increasing the ability for miners to perform more cryptographic hash functions, aka solve the puzzles). The blockchain protocol therefore needs to ensure that the network remains stable, and has some tools at its disposal, as summarised in Table 4.16.

For details on these metrics, please read on, otherwise skip to the next set.

Difficulty target: expressed as a hexadecimal number, this represents the mining difficulty level that miners have to achieve when mining the block (i.e. find a hash that is below the difficulty target). Whilst the primary users are miners, full nodes will also verify that submitted blocks comply with it. By adjusting the difficulty target, the blockchain can ensure network stability (i.e. predictable block time leading to predictable transaction confirmation) regardless of the fluctuating collective computing power of miners, as well as ensuring network security. A high value

Table 4.16 Metrics set by the PoW protocol. © 2024 Neira Jones

Metrics	Description	Used By	Indicator
Difficulty target	Difficulty level for miners to solve the cryptographic hash	Miners	**High**: more difficult mining, slower block production (potentially increased security). **Low**: easier mining, faster block production (potential security concerns)
Difficulty adjustment frequency	Frequency of adjusting the difficulty target (blocks or time interval)	Miners, investors, security/ stability stakeholders	**High**: maintains block creation time near target, network stability. **Low**: block creation time deviates from target, potential security/user experience impact

means a more difficult mining process and slower block production, but potentially increased security. A low value indicates an easier mining process and could potentially raise concerns about security. By setting a difficulty target, PoW blockchains aim to ensure fair competition amongst miners as it prevents a single entity from dominating block production and predictability of transaction throughput. Blockchain developers will set the initial difficulty target and define the adjustment parameters. A sudden drop in difficulty could raise concerns about a potential security breach or a decline in the blockchain's available computational power.

Difficulty adjustment frequency: expressed either in the number of blocks (e.g. after every 2,016 blocks in Bitcoin) or time interval (e.g. Dash, Zcash), this indicates the frequency at which the blockchain adjusts the difficulty target. A high frequency helps maintain the block creation time close to the target block interval as mining activity fluctuates, contributing to network stability. A lower frequency may lead to the block creation time deviating too much from the target block interval, potentially impacting network security or user experience. This metric is used by miners, investors, and those interested in blockchain security and stability. Caution is advised if the difficulty adjustment mechanism seems erratic.

Metrics determined by network conditions and participation

The second set of metrics is directly influenced by mining activity and summarised in Table 4.17.

For details on these metrics, please read on, otherwise skip to the next set.

Hashrate: This is a dynamic measure of the blockchain's **current computational power** dedicated to validating transactions and securing the network. The hashrate is expressed in hashes per second (H/s) or in larger units (e.g. kilohash/s, megahash/s, gigahash/s, etc.), and the higher it is, the more difficult it is for malicious actors to successfully attack the network.

A higher hashrate may also mean a faster average block creation time (i.e. faster transaction processing) and greater decentralisation (no single entity or group can control the network), potentially leading to an average block creation time faster than the block interval (see Box 4.5).

As the block interval is set by the blockchain protocol to ensure predictable and stable network operations, a higher average block creation time may have negative consequences for the blockchain network, such as reduced security (i.e. more blocks added quicker making it easier for malicious actors to attack the network), increased centralisation (i.e. a central entity or large mining pool could control a large portion of the hashrate and gain substantial influence), or instability (i.e. straining the network infrastructure and leading to delays).

To avoid this, blockchains will adjust the difficulty target (see Table 4.16) upward (puzzles more difficult to solve) or downward (puzzles easier to solve) to keep the block creation time as close as possible to the block interval. Miners, investors, and security researchers use the hashrate to assess network security and mining profitability.

Chainwork: this important PoW concept is a **historical and cumulative measure of the total computational power** that has been invested in maintaining the blockchain's integrity from its first block (the genesis block) to the present. It is calculated by adding all the difficulty targets of

Table 4.17 PoW metrics determined by network conditions. © 2024 Neira Jones

Metrics	**Description**	**Used By**	**Indicator**
Hashrate	Current computational power dedicated to validating transactions (hashes/second)	Miners, investors, security researchers	**High**: more secure network, potentially faster block creation (may require difficulty adjustment). **Low**: less secure network, potentially slower block creation
Chainwork	Total computational power invested in securing the blockchain (hash or larger units)	Security researchers, advanced users	**High**: more secure blockchain, potentially indicates successful operation. **Low/stable/declining**: raises concerns about security and viability
Miner distribution	Geographic and mining pool spread of miners (percentage of hashrate)	Security researchers, investors, developers, users	**High geographic and pool distribution**: stronger security, better scalability, resists censorship. **Low distribution or high concentration**: potential security and decentralisation risks
Mining pool distribution	Distribution of hashrate across mining pools (percentage)	Investors, developers, users	**Moderate concentration** (around 50%): potential decentralisation concerns. Low concentration: may reduce efficiency. **High concentration** (>50%): significant decentralisation risks
Mining pool uptime	Percentage of time a mining pool is operational (contributing to hashrate)	Investors, developers, users	**High uptime with good pool distribution**: minimal impact on scalability. **High concentration with low uptime**: potential scalability & resilience issues

all blocks in the blockchain and is expressed in in hash (H) or in larger units (e.g. kilohash, megahash, gigahash, etc.). The higher the chainwork, the more computational effort has been invested in the blockchain and the more secure the blockchain. For example, the Bitcoin chainwork was 736 exahash (EH) – 736 quintillion hashes – in March 2024, whilst the Litecoin and Zcash chainwork was 172 EH and 15.5 EH, respectively, at the time. It's also interesting to note that Ethereum Classic, a fork of the Ethereum blockchain that remained on PoW after Ethereum transitioned to PoS (The Merge), had a chainwork of 102 terahashes (TH) – 102 trillion hashes – in March 2024. Whilst the chainwork is not used during the validation process, miners use it as an indicator of profitability: if the chainwork is particularly high on a given PoW blockchain, it could mean that rewards would be less profitable given the computing power (hashrate) they would have to dedicate to mining blocks. Security researchers and advanced users use the chainwork to assess network security and future potential as a continuously increasing chainwork indicates the blockchain has been operating successfully over time, whilst a stable or declining chainwork raises concerns about blockchain security and viability.

Miner distribution: this refers to the spread of miners across geographies and mining pools and can be expressed as a percentage of hashrate (more useful) or a number of miners per region (less useful as it doesn't take computing power into account). This is a difficult metric to track as miner location may not always be identifiable. Stakeholders may use this metric, in conjunction with others, to assess security (good distribution strengthens security and censorship resistance), scalability (as geographically dispersed miners can help distribute the load across the network), and centralisation (as a high concentration of miners in one geography or mining pool may lead to blockchain manipulation by dominant groups).

Mining pool distribution: expressed as percentage of the hashrate, it is directly determined by miners joining or leaving mining pools (see *Who can do what?*) and is therefore a dynamic metric that analyses the distribution of computing power across mining pools when compared to the total hashrate. If the mining pool concentration is over 50% of the hashrate, it could raise concerns over decentralisation (e.g. a single pool controlling a large proportion of the hashrate could disrupt governance decisions or even raise security concerns about potential manipulation), but whilst low pool concentration could be considered ideal for decentralisation, a very fragmented mining pool landscape across small pools may reduce efficiency as these would have a smaller chance of earning rewards. Investors may look at this metric to assess the sustainability of the blockchain in the long run, whilst developers and users may be concerned about large mining pools controlling large portions of the hashrate which may influence upgrades or protocol changes which may impact scalability decisions. For example, as of 8 April 2024, Bitcoin exhibited a moderately high concentration, with the top three mining pools controlling around 50% of the hashrate, raising potential concerns over decentralisation.[20] Similarly, Dogecoin showed a more balanced distribution with the top mining pool controlling around 20% of the hashrate.

Mining pool uptime: expressed as a percentage of time over a defined monitoring period where a mining pool is operational and allowing miners to contribute hashrate to block production (i.e. the total operational time divided by the monitoring time, which may be hourly, daily, or weekly). When considered alongside mining pool distribution, this metric can give additional insights into network scalability: whilst a high mining pool uptime across a well-distributed pool landscape has minimal impact on scalability, high mining pool concentration with low uptime may have disastrous effects on hashrate and therefore scalability and resilience.

Recap on PoW-specific metrics

Professionals should remember that hashrate, chainwork, and security are interlinked:

- **Monitor hashrate trends**: a steady increase in hashrate indicates a growing and potentially more secure network. Sudden drops in hashrate could signal technical issues or a decline in network security, prompting further investigation.
- **Consider chainwork alongside hashrate**: don't solely rely on hashrate, also analyse chainwork to understand the cumulative computational effort invested in securing the blockchain. A continuously increasing chainwork is a positive sign, whereas a stagnant or declining chainwork might raise concerns about network health.

- **Analyse difficulty target and adjustment frequency**: a consistently high difficulty target may indicate a very secure network, but it can also lead to slow block times and potentially discourage some miners. Conversely, a consistently low difficulty target may speed up block times but raise concerns about security.
- **Monitor difficulty adjustment frequency**: whilst a highly frequent adjustment may help maintain the target block time, it can also introduce unnecessary volatility for miners. Conversely, infrequent adjustments may lead to block times deviating significantly from the target, leading to increased transaction confirmation times and potential network instability.
- **Evaluate miner distribution for decentralisation**: a geographically dispersed and well-distributed miner base strengthens network security and censorship resistance. Conversely, a high concentration of miners in a single region or mining pool can increase centralisation risks. Tools and services can help track miner distribution trends.
- **Track mining pool distribution and uptime**: monitor the distribution of hashrate across mining pools. Whilst some concentration is normal, excessive control by a single pool (over 50% hashrate) raises decentralisation concerns. Additionally, ensure chosen mining pools maintain high uptime to minimise disruptions to hashrate and network stability.
- **Use hashrate and chainwork for informed investment decisions**: investors can leverage hashrate and chainwork to assess the potential security and future viability of PoW blockchains. A strong and growing hashrate alongside a continuously increasing chainwork suggests a potentially more secure and sustainable network.

Remember, a holistic approach is vital. These metrics, alongside others like transaction volume and fees, provide valuable insights for informed decision-making within a PoW blockchain ecosystem.

PoS-blockchain-specific metrics

All the metrics described in the "common metrics" sections may be used to assess PoS blockchains, but these will also have metrics specific to their architecture.

Metrics set by the PoS protocol

There are metrics that are set by the blockchain protocol (either hardcoded, or agreed through on-chain governance, see *Blockchain governance*), and are summarised in Table 4.18.

Table 4.18 Metrics determined by the PoS protocol. © 2024 Neira Jones

Metrics	**Description**	**Used By**	**Indicator**
Minimum stake requirement	The minimum number of coins/tokens required to become a validator	Investors, developers, users	**High**: potentially more security, less decentralisation (fewer validators). **Low**: more decentralisation (more validators), potentially less security
Slashing rate	Percentage of a validator's stake deducted for misbehaviour	Security researchers, developers	**Low**: validators behaving honestly, strong network security. **High**: potential validator misbehaviour, security concerns
Epoch length	Time interval (seconds, days, blocks) defining a validation cycle	Developers, investors	**Shorter**: faster block finality (potentially unstable). **Longer**: slower confirmation, potentially more secure

For details on these metrics, please read on, otherwise skip to the next set.

Minimum Stake Requirement: this depends on the specific blockchain and is usually expressed in the blockchain's coin/token and may optionally be displayed as the equivalent in fiat currency at the current market value. The minimum stake requirement specifies the minimum number of coins/tokens that a validator needs to stake (see Tables 1.6 and 1.7) to be eligible to participate in transaction and block validation. It is an important metric as it enables stakeholders to assess, in conjunction with other metrics and design choices, the security, decentralisation, and scalability of a blockchain network. A high minimum stake requirement might negatively impact scalability and decentralisation as it limits validator participation and potentially impacts transaction speed but could offer stronger security guarantees. A low minimum stake requirement may be more attractive to validators, potentially positively contributing to decentralisation and scalability (although validators with low stakes may have limited computing resources to keep up with the demand, which in turn could hinder scalability instead of improving it) but could raise concerns about security if it becomes too easy to engage in malicious activities.

Slashing rate: expressed as a percentage of a validator's stake, it represents, where implemented, the percentage of staked tokens that will be taken away (slashed) from a misbehaving validator and is a PoS blockchain incentive system aimed at maintaining validator honesty. A low slashing rate indicates that validators are generally behaving honestly, contributing to network security and stability, whereas a high value suggests potential issues with validator misbehaviour, raising concerns about the security and reliability of the network. Therefore, stakeholders can use this metric in conjunction with other metrics and design choices to gain insights into the blockchain's ability to maintain security and validator performance whilst handling increasing transaction volumes.

Epoch length: typically expressed in time intervals, it can range from seconds (Cosmos, Solana) to days (Cardano), but can also be measured in the number of blocks (Algorand) and represents a blockchain operational cycle. It is difficult to give a generic definition as its implementation varies across PoS blockchains, but it's fair to say the start of an epoch begins with the creation of a particular block designated as the "epoch boundary block" which signals that the network is now in active validation stage, corresponding to steps 3–6 in Chapter 1, Figure 1.14, including block formation to finalisation. For some PoS blockchains, the cycle may also include reward distribution to validators at the end of an epoch, but others may distribute staking rewards more or less frequently. An epoch typically ends with the creation of a new epoch boundary block (when the epoch length is reached), signalling the next cycle. This metric, in conjunction with others, is important to developers and blockchain designers as they use the epoch length to achieve a balance between scalability (shorter epochs may lead to faster block finality but might also introduce more frequent fluctuations and potential instability, and very short epochs may increase validator workload and network congestion), security (longer epochs may allow for more security, but also lead to slower transaction confirmations), and efficiency (epoch length should ensure that validators have enough time to process blocks). It is also important to investors who may want to get further insights into the user experience and the overall network performance and scalability. In addition, blockchain explorers and blockchain monitoring and analytics service providers (see Chapter 1, Table 1.10) may use this to organise PoS blockchain data for visualisation purposes or for tracking network activity.

Metrics determined by network conditions and participation

The second set of metrics is directly influenced by staking activity and summarised in Table 4.19.

Table 4.19 PoS metrics determined by network conditions. © 2024 Neira Jones

Metrics	Description	Used By	Indicator
Total stake	Total amount of coins/tokens staked by validators and delegators (e.g. ETH for Ethereum)	Investors, developers	**High**: increased participation, potentially stronger security. **Low**: lower security concerns
Active validators	Number of validators currently participating in consensus	Investors, developers	**High**: more secure and stable network, potentially less scalable. **Low**: less secure and stable network, potentially more scalable
Average validator uptime	Percentage of time validators are online over a period	Investors, developers	**High**: more secure, stable, and resistant network. **Low**: less secure, stable, and resistant network

Table 4.19 (Continued)

Metrics	Description	Used By	Indicator
Validator distribution	Spread of validators across geographies and entities (anonymous vs. known)	Investors, developers	**Well distributed**: more secure and decentralised. **Poorly distributed**: less secure and decentralised
Validator uptime distribution	Consistency of validator participation over a period	Investors, developers	**Well distributed**: more secure network. **Poorly distributed**: less secure network
Staking pool distribution	Distribution of stake across staking pools	Investors, developers	**Well distributed**: more decentralised network. **Poorly distributed**: more centralised network
Staking ratio	Percentage of total supply staked for consensus	Investors, developers	**High**: more coins securing the network, potentially stronger security. **Low**: fewer coins securing the network, not necessarily weaker security (depends on context)
Momentum	Growth or decline in staking activities	Investors, developers	**Positive**: healthy growing network. **Negative**: lower engagement, potential centralisation
Active staking wallets	Number of wallets currently delegating tokens to validators	Investors, developers	**High**: more coins contributing to validation, potentially more secure network. **Low**: fewer coins contributing to validation, potentially less secure network

For details on these metrics, please read on, otherwise skip to the next set.

Total stake: typically expressed in the blockchain's coin/token (e.g. ETH for Ethereum, ADA for Cardano), it refers to the total amount currently staked by validators and delegators to secure the network. Investors may use this indicator to assess network activity and reward yields, whilst blockchain developers use it to gauge network security and overall health as a growing total stake indicates increased participation and potentially stronger security, whilst a significantly declining or stagnant number may raise concerns.

Active validators: expressed as a snapshot of the number of active validators at a particular point in time, it should be distinguished from the number of total validators on the network, as some may be registered but temporarily inactive due to maintenance or technical issues. Used in conjunction with other metrics, the number of active validators gives insight into security and stability (the more the validators, the more secure and stable the blockchain), scalability and growth (a balance must be sought between too high a number which could introduce overheads and slow down the network, and too few validators which might limit processing capacity), and competition (more validators potentially means more competition and lower rewards).

Average validator uptime: expressed as the percentage of time validators are online and actively participating in the consensus process over a specific period of time (e.g. weekly, monthly), this can in conjunction with other metrics, give insights into security and stability (the more active validators, the more secure, stable, and resistant to attacks the blockchain is). It may also indirectly influence scalability as a blockchain with consistently available validators may have the potential for faster transaction processing, and therefore future growth and adoption.

Validator distribution: this is a metric that can be used to assess the health and security of a PoS blockchain beyond what the number of validators can give us as it gives us insights into two key aspects: geographic distribution and entity distribution. With geographic distribution, this will be expressed as a percentage of validators concentrated across geographies or regions. With entity distribution, this will be expressed as a percentage of validators spread across anonymous entities (e.g. solo validators or staking services utilising self-custody services where user identities remain hidden) and known entities (e.g. cryptocurrency exchanges, infrastructure providers, or reputable staking services). A well-distributed validator base across and entities gives greater confidence in the blockchain's security and decentralisation, whilst lack of distribution may concentrate power across a few dominant players and raise security concerns. Whilst validator distribution doesn't directly influence scalability, it may, for some implementations, help reduce latency for geographically dispersed users. Some caveats apply, such as where there is a high concentration across anonymous entities, making this metric unreliable. In any instance, it should be used, where available, in conjunction with other metrics, depending on the assessment criteria.

Validator uptime distribution: this is an important metric to assess the reliability and health of a PoS blockchain as it measures how consistently validators are online and participating in the consensus process. It may be expressed as the percentage of time a single validator is online and participating over a specified period (e.g. a day, a week, a month), or as a percentage of validators falling within specified uptime ranges (e.g. 90%–100% uptime, 80%–90% uptime). This metric is important for assessing security as a well-distributed uptime distribution, with a majority of validators consistently online and participating, indicates a more secure network environment.

Staking pool distribution: this metric is key to determining the level of centralisation in a PoS network and may be expressed as either a percentage of the overall network stake that is delegated to a specific staking pool or as a percentage of staking pools falling within specified stake ranges (e.g. 0%–10% or total stake, 10%–20% of total stake). A well-distributed staking pool landscape, where no single player controls a significant share of the stake, promotes decentralisation and hardens the network to attacks or manipulation. Investors may look at this indicator for centralisation risks (high concentration may impact the network and therefore the coin/token value) to help inform a diversification strategy (understanding the pool landscape) or to identify high-reward opportunities (smaller staking pools within a well-distributed landscape may generate higher returns). Network developers may look at this indicator to make protocol design choices to achieve optimal distribution, such as offering incentives to smaller staking pools or capping pool stake size.

Staking ratio: sometimes referred to as the "staking participation rate", it is expressed as a percentage and calculated as the total stake divided by the total supply (aka circulating supply), and therefore the higher the ratio the more coins/tokens are committed to network security through consensus (validation). You have to look at this metric in conjunction with many others, as whilst, in theory, a higher staking ratio may indicate stronger network security, decentralisation, or decreased rewards, a lower staking ratio may not always indicate the opposite (e.g. early-stage blockchains, blockchains implementing slashing mechanisms or alternative security mechanisms, high transaction volumes and active user engagement, etc.). However, investors may use this metric to assess the overall network activity and potential staking reward, as well as staking yield levels or liquidity, whilst blockchain developers may use it to gauge network health and security as a high staking ratio may indicate strong commitment from coin/token holders, whereas a significant fall in the staking ratio may indicate reduced security or potential loss of confidence. Blockchain information services (e.g. explorers) may monitor various metrics for multiple blockchains.[21] You must also be aware of the context when looking at the term "staking ratio" as it sometimes refers to an individual validator's ratio. In this latter context, the validator's staking ratio is the proportion of the total tokens that a specific validator has staked relative to the total stake. This ratio is important because it can influence the likelihood of the validator being selected to validate new blocks and earn rewards. Validators with higher staking ratios have a greater chance of being chosen to validate transactions and secure the network, thus earning more rewards in the process.

Active staking wallets: not to be confused with the number of active wallets, this metric represents the number of unique wallet addresses that have currently delegated their tokens to validators (see Chapter 1, *Who can do what? – PoS specifics*). It may be used to assess staking participation and network security as a high number of active staking wallets shows that a large proportion of the coin/token supply is contributing to validation, potentially indicating a more secure network.

Momentum: sometimes referred to as "staking activity" or "staking velocity", this metric is a bit of a catch-all aimed at assessing the dynamism (growth or decline) in staking activities. It may measure the change in staked coins/tokens over time, the change in the number of active wallets over time, or validator churn. It may be used in conjunction with other metrics such as the number of validators and the number of active staking wallets. For example, a high number of validators combined with a high number of staking wallets and positive momentum indicates a healthy growing network, whereas a low number of validators and/or staking wallets with negative momentum may indicate lower engagement levels and potential centralisation.

Recap on PoS-specific metrics

Professionals should remember the following:

- **Monitor key security metrics**: track both the total stake and the number of active validators as a rising total stake and a healthy number of active validators suggest strong security on the network. Additionally, a well-distributed validator base (across geography and entity type) enhances both security and decentralisation. Consistent validator uptime, measured as individual validator uptime or overall distribution, strengthens the network environment.
- **Evaluate decentralisation**: consider validator distribution again, as this same metric promotes decentralisation by preventing any single entity from wielding excessive control. Monitor staking pool distribution to avoid relying on a dominant pool, which could centralise control.
- **Scalability considerations**: epoch length may indirectly impact scalability as shorter epochs may lead to faster block finality (quicker transaction confirmations) but potentially introduce instability. Conversely, longer epochs enhance security (more time for validation) but slow down confirmations.
- **Staking considerations**: staking may impact all stakeholders. Investors should research minimum stake requirements and potential rewards to see if they align with their investment goals. Staking pools allow participation with smaller amounts and can contribute to network security whilst offering potential rewards, but pool selection should assess the reputation and how they prioritise security to minimise risks. Developers and researchers can analyse staking metrics to understand network health and security.
- **Network health**: a high number of active staking wallets contributes to a potentially more secure network. However, the staking ratio should be analysed cautiously as a high ratio may suggest stronger security (more coins are actively participating in validation), whilst a very low ratio in a mature blockchain might raise decentralisation concerns as it indicates a smaller portion of coins are actively staked, potentially concentrating power in the hands of a few. Context is important, as for early-stage blockchains, where a large portion of coins might still be locked in distribution or development, a low ratio may indicate healthy accumulation by users who haven't yet started staking, whilst a high ratio may indicate significant initial investor participation in securing the network.

Remember, a holistic approach is crucial. Analyse these metrics alongside others (transaction volume, fees) to make informed decisions within a PoS blockchain ecosystem.

Smart contract and DeFi metrics

Smart contracts and DeFi have revolutionised blockchain capabilities. To assess the health and activity of these ecosystems, various metrics provide valuable insights. This section provides a breakdown of key metrics, including their units of expression, how they are measured, and which stakeholders would use them.

Smart contract metrics

In platforms that support smart contracts (e.g. Ethereum), the verification process includes executing the smart contract code to validate its logic and ensure it does not lead to any unintended consequences. We covered the best practices for the development and validation of smart contracts in Chapter 2 (e.g. testing, audits), but specific metrics are also available to assess the health of any implementation to include smart contract activity, usage, and economic factors, as illustrated in Table 4.20.

Table 4.20 Smart contract metrics. © 2024 Neira Jones

Metrics	Description	Used By	Indicator
Deployed smart contracts	Total deployed contracts on blockchain	Developers, investors, researchers	**High**: active ecosystem, **Low**: limited dApp/ DeFi potential
Number of interactions	User interaction frequency with smart contracts	Defi users, developers, investors	**High**: active DeFi adoption, **Low**: limited user engagement
Active smart contracts	Identifies actively used contracts	Defi users, developers, investors	**High**: mature DeFi ecosystem, **Low**: less user engagement
Gas used per transaction	Gas expenditure for smart contract interactions	Developers	**High**: less efficient contracts, **Low**: more efficient interactions

For details on these metrics, please read on, otherwise skip to the next set.

- **Deployed smart contracts**: this tracks the total number of smart contracts deployed on the blockchain and is measured by querying the blockchain ledger for all deployed smart contract addresses. Developers, investors, and researchers can use this metric to gauge developer activity and potential for dApp and DeFi services on the network. High numbers suggest an active ecosystem, whilst low numbers might indicate limitations for dApps.
- **Number of interactions**: this measures the frequency of users interacting with deployed smart contracts and tracks on-chain transactions that interact with specific smart contract addresses. DeFi users, developers, and investors can use this metric to assess user adoption of DeFi services built on the blockchain. High interaction indicates active usage and a potentially thriving DeFi ecosystem.
- **Active smart contracts**: depending on the blockchain, this can be tracked daily, weekly, or monthly and goes beyond total deployment figures as it identifies actively used contracts. In traditional financial systems, think of it as a banking app measured by the total number of downloads (deployed smart contracts) compared to active issuers of the app (active smart contracts) and these two measures can vary widely. The number of active smart contracts is measured by analysing user interactions with smart contract addresses over a specific period of time. DeFi users, developers, and investors can use this metric to assess DeFi ecosystem maturity and user engagement. A high number of active contracts suggests a robust and engaged user base.
- **Gas used per transaction**: measured by the gas units (see Table 4.10) consumed during a transaction on the blockchain, it tracks the gas expenditure associated with smart contract interactions. Developers use this metric to optimise their smart contracts for cost-effectiveness. Lower gas usage per transaction translates into cheaper and more efficient smart contract interactions. DeFi users may also be interested in gas costs to understand transaction fees associated with DeFi services.

These metrics can be relevant for assessing the network's utility and potential for supporting dApps and DeFi services. They are used by developers, investors, and those interested in the potential use cases and innovation on the blockchain. High smart contract activity (e.g. deployed smart contracts, number of interactions, active smart contracts) suggests an active developer community and potential for innovative applications built on the blockchain, whilst limited smart contract activity could indicate a lack of developer interest or suggest the network might not be suitable for dApp or DeFi development.

DeFi-specific metrics

Smart contract metrics provide valuable insights into DeFi; however, to understand the health and potential of DeFi systems built on these smart contracts, we need to explore additional DeFi-specific metrics. This section will examine key metrics used to gauge the size, adoption, and overall performance of DeFi ecosystems. Table 4.21 illustrates this.

For details on these metrics, please read on, otherwise skip to the recap.

- **Total Value Locked (TVL)**: expressed in the fiat currency equivalent (usually USD) of the total value of assets deposited in DeFi protocols (lending, borrowing, staking, etc.). It is measured by aggregating the value of various cryptocurrencies locked within DeFi smart contracts. Investors, researchers, and DeFi users use TVL to gauge the overall health and attractiveness of a DeFi ecosystem. High TVL suggests a robust and potentially lucrative DeFi space, attracting new users and capital. However, TVL alone doesn't guarantee stability, and further analysis is needed.
- **Market capitalisation**: expressed in the fiat currency equivalent (usually USD) of the total market value of all DeFi tokens within the ecosystem, it is measured by multiplying the current price of each DeFi token by its circulating supply and summing the total value. Investors and researchers use market capitalisation to assess the overall size and potential of the DeFi market. A high market capitalisation suggests a mature and potentially lucrative DeFi space. Beware: this is not true market capitalisation as we understand it in traditional centralised environments due to the volatile nature of tokens.
- **Number of DeFi protocols**: this tracks the total number of DeFi protocols (lending platforms, decentralised exchanges, etc.) operating on the blockchain and is measured by identifying and counting unique DeFi

Table 4.21 DeFi metrics. © 2024 Neira Jones

Metrics	Description	Used By	Indicator
Total Value Locked (TVL)	Total value of assets deposited in DeFi protocols (fiat equivalent)	Investors, researchers, DeFi users	**High**: potentially lucrative DeFi space, **Low**: less capital locked
Market capitalisation	Total market value of all DeFi tokens (fiat equivalent)	Investors, researchers	**High**: large DeFi market, **Low**: smaller DeFi market size
Number of DeFi protocols	Total number of DeFi protocols operating on the blockchain	Developers, investors, researchers	**High**: diverse and evolving DeFi landscape, **Low**: limited DeFi innovation
DeFi protocol revenue	Total income generated by DeFi protocols (fiat equivalent)	Investors, researchers	**High**: sustainable and potentially self-sustaining ecosystem, **Low**: less revenue generation
Protocol risk scores	Risk assessment of DeFi protocols (varies by provider)	Investors, DeFi users	**Low**: potentially more secure protocol, **High**: exercise caution

applications deployed on the blockchain. Developers, investors, and researchers can use this metric to gauge the diversity and innovation within the DeFi ecosystem. A growing number of protocols suggests a dynamic and evolving DeFi landscape.

- **DeFi protocol revenue**: expressed in the fiat currency equivalent (usually USD) of the total income generated by DeFi protocols through fees, interest earned on loaned assets, or other revenue streams, it is measured by analysing on-chain transactions and protocol data. Investors and researchers can use this metric to assess the sustainability and profitability of DeFi protocols. High and growing revenue suggests a healthy and potentially self-sustaining ecosystem.

- **Protocol risk scores**: the unit of expression varies as several analytics platforms provide risk scores for DeFi protocols, considering factors like smart contract security audits, code quality, and potential vulnerabilities. Investors and DeFi users can leverage these scores to assess the potential risks associated with interacting with specific DeFi protocols. Lower risk scores generally indicate a more secure protocol.

Recap on smart contract and DeFi metrics

Of course, the specific metrics highlighted here are not, on their own, sufficient for a useful assessment as no single metric provides a complete picture of a smart contract or DeFi ecosystem's health. Other metrics covered earlier (e.g. active wallet addresses, transaction volumes, developer activity) must be used, and a comprehensive analysis should consider a combination of all relevant metrics along with qualitative factors like the overall market sentiment, regulatory landscape, and the reputation of the blockchain platform itself.

Professionals should remember the following:

- **Don't rely on a single metric**: whilst smart contract activity metrics (deployed contracts, interactions, active contracts) provide valuable insights, a holistic understanding of DeFi health requires looking beyond. Consider metrics like active wallet addresses, transaction volumes, and developer activity covered earlier in this document. Additionally, qualitative factors like market sentiment, regulations, and blockchain platform reputation play a crucial role.
- **Understand the stakeholders and their needs**: investors may use metrics like TVL and market capitalisation to assess DeFi market size and potential. DeFi users are interested in metrics like gas used per transaction to understand transaction fees. Developers leverage DeFi protocol revenue to gauge the sustainability of these protocols. By understanding these stakeholder needs, you can effectively target relevant metrics for informed decision-making.

- **Look beyond headline numbers**: a high TVL might suggest a thriving DeFi ecosystem, but it doesn't guarantee stability. Similarly, a high number of deployed smart contracts doesn't necessarily translate to a robust developer community. Always delve deeper and consider factors like the composition of TVL (e.g. stablecoins vs. volatile assets) or analyse active smart contracts versus total deployments.
- **Context is key**: metrics like protocol risk scores require context. A lower score from a reputable analytics platform generally indicates a more secure protocol. However, it's crucial to understand the specific factors considered in the scoring and the potential limitations of any single provider.
- **Combine quantitative and qualitative analysis**: don't get bogged down by numbers alone and consider the bigger picture. For example, market sentiment shifts, or regulatory changes, may impact the metrics. A comprehensive assessment should leverage both quantitative metrics and qualitative factors for a well-rounded understanding of the DeFi ecosystem's health.

Beyond metrics

After this tour of blockchain metrics, we mustn't lose sight of the fact that things evolve rapidly in this space, improvements will be made, some blockchain projects will disappear, and what you measure today might be very different tomorrow. Consequently, there are always other factors that must be considered when assessing blockchains, and one of them is its utility (see Chapter 2, Box 2.10) as well as token utility, covered earlier in this chapter.

Utility and real-world applications

Whilst metrics provide quantitative measures of a blockchain's performance, they don't capture the full picture. The utility of a blockchain – how it is used in real-world applications – plays a crucial role in its long-term success. For instance, a blockchain designed for supply chain management might prioritise different features compared to one focussed on financial transactions. The ability of a blockchain to solve real-world problems, integrate with existing systems, and provide tangible benefits to its users is a key determinant of its value.

Community and ecosystem

The strength and engagement of a blockchain's community can significantly impact its development and adoption. An active community contributes to the growth of the ecosystem by developing new applications, providing support, and fostering innovation. Projects with strong communities often have better resilience and adaptability, as they can leverage collective knowledge and resources to overcome challenges.

Governance and decentralisation

Effective governance mechanisms are essential for the sustainable development of blockchain projects. Decentralised governance models, such as those employed by DAOs, allow stakeholders to participate in decision-making processes. This can enhance transparency, reduce the risk of centralisation, and ensure that the project evolves in line with the community's interests. However, governance models must also balance efficiency and inclusivity to avoid decision-making paralysis.

Security and regulatory compliance

Security is a fundamental aspect of any blockchain network. Whilst metrics like hashrate and the number of validators can provide insights into a network's security, they do not account for all potential vulnerabilities. Continuous security audits, robust consensus mechanisms, and proactive threat mitigation strategies are essential to safeguard the network.

Additionally, regulatory compliance is becoming increasingly important as governments around the world develop frameworks for blockchain technology. Projects that proactively address regulatory requirements are more likely to gain institutional support and achieve mainstream adoption.

Interoperability and scalability

As the blockchain ecosystem grows, the ability of different blockchains to interact and transact with each other becomes increasingly important. Projects like Polkadot and Cosmos are pioneering solutions to enable seamless cross-chain communication. Scalability remains a critical challenge, but layer-1 and layer-2 solutions (see Chapter 1, *Are blockchains scalable?*), as well as new consensus mechanisms developments, aim to address this issue.

Environmental impact

The environmental impact of blockchain technology, particularly energy consumption, is a growing concern. PoW blockchains like Bitcoin are often criticised for their high energy usage. In response, many projects are exploring more energy-efficient consensus mechanisms, such as PoS and Proof of Authority (PoA) (see Chapter 1, Table 1.4), as well as hybrid models. Assessing the environmental footprint of a blockchain project is becoming an important factor for both developers and users.

Future outlook

The blockchain space is dynamic, with continuous innovations and emerging trends. Technologies such as zero-knowledge proofs, DeFi, NFTs, and the integration of artificial intelligence are expanding the horizons of what blockchain technology can achieve. Staying informed about these trends and understanding their potential impact is crucial for anyone involved in the blockchain ecosystem.

Whilst blockchain metrics provide valuable insights into the performance and health of a network, they are only one piece of the puzzle. A holistic assessment of a blockchain project requires considering its utility, community strength, governance, security, regulatory compliance, interoperability, scalability, environmental impact, and future trends. By looking beyond metrics, stakeholders can make more informed decisions and contribute to the sustainable growth of the blockchain ecosystem.

In this section, I aimed to provide a balanced view of the importance of metrics whilst highlighting the broader context in which blockchain projects operate. I hope I have achieved this goal, but if you want to explore further, valuable references are included at the end of this chapter.[22,23,24,25]

Tokenomics and metrics – conclusion (where do we go from here?)

In this (not so) whistle-stop tour of tokenomics and metrics, we explored:

- The fundamental aspects of tokenomics: supply and distribution, token utility, incentive and penalty structures, and market dynamics,
- A detailed account of economic and non-economic incentives and penalties,

- A detailed account of transaction fees, and
- A comprehensive coverage of blockchain metrics, ranging from common metrics to protocol-specific ones, as well as smart contract and DeFi metrics.

I know it was a long chapter, but I hope it wasn't too cumbersome. I have tried to explain the jargon, debunk a few myths, and present a balanced view. I have given you my opinion on some aspects of the ecosystem, but feel free to disagree, I always welcome a good debate!

If you read this book a few years from now, more innovation will have happened, tokenomics will evolve, innovative technologies will be used, behaviours will have changed. Economics is a complex subject at the best of times, tokenomics introduces even more complexity and uncertainty, and who knows how this space will move on.

I hope all the concepts introduced in this chapter have now become a bit clearer, as they will be fundamental to understanding the dynamics of blockchain ecosystems, why crypto assets work in the way they work, and the transactional processes and services around them, which are covered in the next chapters.

All the important terms introduced in this chapter can be found in the glossary. To complete our understanding of blockchain ecosystems, we must examine the assets that exist on these infrastructures.

Let's go on the fifth leg of our trip.

Notes

1 "30 Best Crypto Venture Capital Funds & Investment Firms for 2024" Ninja, 19 April 2024. Available at: https://ninjapromo.io/top-30-crypto-vc-investment-funds (Accessed 19 July 2024).
2 "50 Biggest Crypto Airdrops: $26.6B in 'Free Money'" CoinGecko, 5 March 2024. Available at: https://www.coingecko.com/research/publications/biggest-crypto-airdrops (Accessed 19 July 2024).
3 Ethereum Foundation website. Available at: https://ethereum.foundation/ (Accessed 9 July 2024).
4 Solana Foundation website. Available at: https://solana.org/ (Accessed 9 July 2024).
5 Interchain Foundation website. Available at: https://interchain.io/ (Accessed 9 July 2024).

6 Hyperledger Foundation website. Available at: https://www.hyperledger.org/ (Accessed 9 July 2024).

7 Aave Grants DAO website. Available at: https://aavegrants.org/ (Accessed 9 July 2024).

8 "The Ugly Side of DeFi; The Bancor & Solend Controversy Explained" chaindebrief, 20 June 2022. Available at: https://chaindebrief.com/the-ugly-side-of-defi-the-bancor-solend-controversy-explained/ (Accessed 18 August 2024).

9 "BNB Chain Staking" bnbchain.org website. Available at: https://www.bnbchain.org/en/bnb-staking (Accessed 19 July 2024).

10 "Put Your Funds to Work by Providing Liquidity" Sushi.com website. Available at: https://www.sushi.com/pool (Accessed 19 July 2024).

11 "BNB Auto-Burn: Mechanisms and Impacts Explored" Binance website, 8 May 2024. Available at: https://www.binance.com/en/square/post/7732625721697 (Accessed 19 July 2024).

12 "Ripple (XRP) Community Speculates on Upcoming SEC Meeting Today" *CryptoPotato*, 25 July 2024. Available at: https://cryptopotato.com/ripple-xrp-community-speculates-on-upcoming-sec-meeting-today/ (Accessed 24 July 2024).

13 "Bitcoin Fees Hit ATH Post Halving: Are Users Getting Priced Out?" *DailyCoin*, 20 April 2024. Available at: https://dailycoin.com/bitcoin-fees-hit-ath-post-halving-are-users-getting-priced-out/ (Accessed 13 June 2024).

14 "Dusting Attacks: What Is Crypto Dust?" Tangem website, 18 April 2024. Available at: https://tangem.com/en/blog/post/dusting-attack-explained/ (Accessed 19 July 2024).

15 "Inscriptions: The Viral Craze Causing Gas Wars & Network Outages" *Blockonomi*, 21 December 2023. Available at: https://blockonomi.com/inscriptions-the-viral-craze-causing-gas-wars-network-outages/ (Accessed 7 April 2024).

16 "Ethereum Gas Tracker" Etherscan website. Available at: https://etherscan.io/gastracker (Accessed 13 June 2024).

17 Binance website. Available at: https://www.binance.com/ (Accessed 3 March 2024).

18 Coinmarketcap.com website. Available at: https://coinmarketcap.com/ (Accessed 3 March 2024).

19 Cryptoslate.com website. Available at: https://cryptoslate.com/ (Accessed 3 March 2024).

20 Blockchain.com website. Bitcoin hashrate distribution. Available at: https://www.blockchain.com/explorer/charts/pools (Accessed 8 April 2024).

21 Stakingrewards.com website. Available at: https://www.stakingrewards.com/ (Accessed 21 April 2024).

22 "Blockchain Interoperability Solutions and Challenges: Where Are We Now?" *Finextra*, 30 October 2023. Available at: https://www.finextra.com/blogposting/25112/blockchain-interoperability-solutions-and-challenges-where-are-we-now (Accessed 17 July 2024).

23 Zheng, Z., Xie, S., Dai, H., Chen, X., and Wang, H. (2017). "An Overview of Blockchain Technology: Architecture, Consensus, and Future Trends" In *IEEE International Congress on Big Data (BigData Congress)*. Honolulu, HI, USA, 25–30 June 2017, pp. 557–564.

24 Bellini, E., Iraqi, Y., and Damiani, E. (2020). "Blockchain-Based Distributed Trust and Reputation Management Systems: A Survey" *IEEE Access*, 8, 21127–21151.

25 Sunyaev, A. (2020). "Distributed Ledger Technology" In *Internet Computing*. Berlin/Heidelberg: Springer, pp. 265–299.

5

DIGITAL AND VIRTUAL ASSETS

About money (money makes the world go round)

Why are we here?

Picture this: you're standing in line at your favourite coffee shop, fumbling through your pockets for loose change. The person behind you whips out their phone, taps it on a reader, and walks away with their steaming latte. Meanwhile, your tech-savvy friend is bragging about buying a digital artwork for some Ethereum (ETH). And just when you thought you had a handle on things, your nephew starts talking about earning "V-Bucks" in some online game.

Welcome to the wild, wacky, and occasionally baffling world of modern money and assets. Gone are the days when a shiny coin or crisp banknote was the height of financial sophistication. Today, we're navigating a landscape filled with cryptocurrencies, virtual assets, NFTs, and other digital wonders that would make our grandparents' heads spin faster than a Bitcoin miner's cooling fan 😉.

DOI: 10.4324/9781003480761-6

In this chapter, we'll embark on a journey through the evolving concept of value exchange, from the humble beginnings of traditional money to the dizzying heights of Decentralised Finance (DeFi). We'll explore why your favourite cryptocurrency might not be considered "real" money or "digital gold" (despite what that enthusiastic YouTuber tells you); dive into the virtual realms where digital coins reign supreme and attempt to demystify the alphabet soup of crypto-assets (NFTs, anyone?).

So grab your digital wallet, put on your cryptographic thinking cap, and let's dive into the fascinating, perplexing, and occasionally hilarious world of digital and virtual assets. Who knows? By the end of this chapter, you might just be ready to explain to your confused aunt why that JPEG of a bored ape is worth more than her car (or even her house!).

Let's have some definitions first.

Currency

Before we dive into the deep end of the financial pool, let's start with the basics: currency. It's the foundation of our economic system, the universal language of commerce that keeps the world spinning (and shopping 😉).

Currency, in its simplest form, is any medium of exchange that's widely accepted for goods and services. It's what allows us to trade without resorting to a complicated barter system – because let's face it, trying to buy a car with a truckload of chickens would be messy in more ways than one.

The concept of currency has been around for millennia, evolving from shells and beads to coins, paper notes, and now digital forms. I won't indulge in giving you a history of money, it's already been done very well, including by my friend David Birch in his excellent "Before Babylon, Beyond Bitcoin: From Money We Understand to Money that Understands Us".[1] Since then, currency's been on quite the journey, as illustrated in Figure 5.1.

Modern currencies come in various flavours. Historically, there were commodity currencies (also called "representative currencies"), directly backed by and exchangeable for physical goods like gold or silver. However, in today's global economy, true commodity currencies no longer exist. Modern currencies are primarily fiat currencies, not backed by or directly exchangeable for physical commodities. We dive into these in the next section.

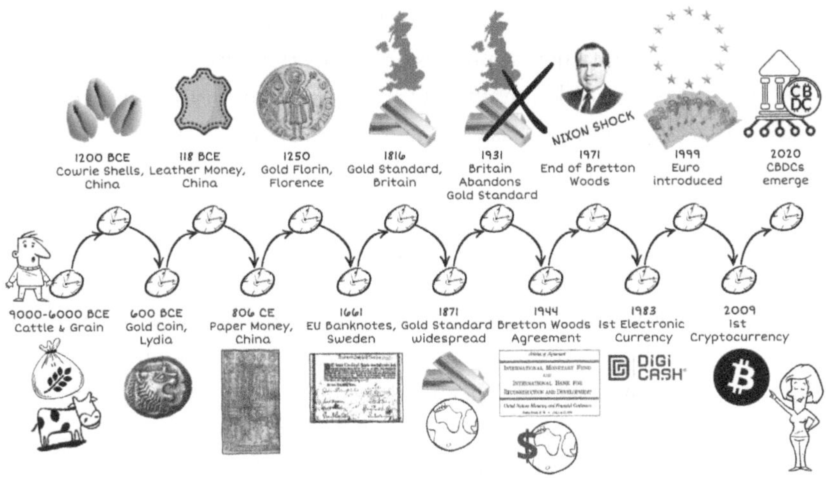

Figure 5.1 Evolution of currency. © 2024 Neira Jones.

The value of a currency is determined by a complex dance of factors, including economic conditions, political stability, and international trade. It's like a financial soap opera, with plot twists driven by central banks, governments, and global markets.

One key feature of a successful currency is its **stability**. Wild fluctuations in value can lead to economic chaos faster than you can say "hyperinflation". That's why central banks often play a game of economic Jenga, carefully adjusting interest rates and money supply to keep the currency stable (and at the time of writing, don't we know it!).

Interestingly, whilst we often think of currency as something issued by governments, that's not always the case. Community-issued, or local, currencies popped up as alternatives in support of local economies and are pegged at a 1:1 ratio to the national currency. Examples include the Bristol Pound, which launched in the UK in 2012, and BerkShares[2] in the US, which launched in 2006. Whilst their intent is noble, competition from modern digital payment methods presents serious challenges for these systems. The Bristol Pound ceased operating in 2021, and at the time of writing, whilst BerkShares still exist, more than 90% of Berkshire businesses don't accept them as payment.

So, whether it's jingling in your pocket, folded in your wallet, or existing as ones and zeros in your bank account, the currency continues to be the lifeblood of our economic system. It's come a long way from seashells and salt, but its fundamental purpose remains the same: to make sure you can buy that overpriced latte without having to trade your firstborn for it.

Now that we've got the basics down, let's move on to the most common form of currency in today's world: **fiat currency**.

Fiat money

We already know that "money", in the traditional sense, is what people consider to be the accepted medium of exchange for the payment of goods and services, as well as the repayment of debt. Fiat money, a term I have used several times in the previous chapters, is a government-issued currency that is not backed by a physical commodity, such as gold or silver, but rather by the government that issued it. It derives its value from supply and demand, and the stability of the issuing government. Fiat money gives central banks greater control over the economy, as they can adjust how much money is printed through their monetary policy, giving them more flexibility to respond to economic crises.

As such, fiat money has no intrinsic value, which is why it is often referred to as "paper money". The US dollar before 1971 and the British pound before 1931 were representative currencies (i.e. backed by gold) before they became fiat currencies. Governments have to make fiat currency **legal tender** by setting it as the standard for debt repayment, and most modern currencies are fiat money. I covered this aspect in my first book "Understanding Payments", but for completeness, I reproduce in Figure 5.2 a figure I used there to show that fiat money has been around for a while.

Figure 5.2 Fiat money, a trust-based currency in a complex world.

Before 1931, the British pound was backed by gold, which means that it could be exchanged for a fixed amount of gold. The UK temporarily suspended this equivalence during World War I but reinstated it in 1925. In 1931, during The Great Depression, the UK permanently abandoned the gold standard, effectively making the British pound a fiat currency.

In July 1944, at a conference in Bretton Woods, New Hampshire, with delegates from 44 countries, a new international monetary system was established aiming to promote economic growth after World War II, stable exchange rates, and prevent competitive currency devaluations. At that point, the US dollar was pegged to gold at $35 per ounce, and other currencies were pegged to the US dollar. This essentially created an indirect gold standard system dubbed the Bretton Woods system, which led to the formation of the International Monetary Fund (IMF) and the World Bank. Whilst agreed upon in 1944, the Bretton Woods system didn't become fully operational until 1958 and came under pressure in the 1960s due to increased circulation of the US dollar and economic growth in other countries. In 1971, President Richard Nixon announced the suspension of the US dollar convertibility into gold, effectively ending the Bretton Woods system, in a move commonly dubbed as the "Nixon Shock". Since then, the US dollar has been a fiat currency.

The euro was designed to be a modern currency for the EU and created fiat. It was introduced in January 1999 as an accounting currency for the participating states and became physical (notes and coins) in January 2002, where it replaced the national currencies for participating countries. The Euro is backed by the economic strength and policies of the participating nations.

Why am I telling you this?

Simply, whilst e-money is a fiat substitute and therefore money, a cryptocurrency is not money, nor is it a fiat.

Let's explore these various types.

e-Money

Comparing e-money with other digital assets

Whilst I cover the concept of **e-money** in detail in my first book, we'll begin by revisiting relevant aspects of e-money, this well-established electronic representation of traditional currencies that has been part of our financial ecosystem for decades. Unlike the novel and often volatile world of cryptocurrencies, e-money operates within existing regulatory frameworks, providing a bridge between physical cash and digital transactions.

E-money is a type of virtual asset functioning as an electronic store of value that acts as a cash substitute and is issued by regulated entities (e.g. an e-money institution in the EU, an entity operating under the US Special Purpose National Bank Charter, or a "Payments Bank" in India, or banks in general). E-money may be used for making payments to entities other than the issuer (unlike a virtual currency). Types of e-money include prepaid cards, electronic prepaid accounts, and virtual payment accounts for use online. Also spelled "eMoney", "e-Money", "e-money", and "emoney". A notable example is Alipay (see Chapter 6, Figure 6.1).

E-money is like your regular money decided to get a trendy makeover and move into your smartphone. E-money is a digital representation of cold, hard cash, usually stored on electronic devices, and has become part of our daily lives. It's perfect for when you want to buy something online or send money to a friend without the hassle of digging through your couch cushions for loose change. Popular applications like Venmo, swish or Cash App have even become verbs (e.g. "I'll Cash App you", "swish me").

We'll examine e-money in more detail in the next section, but in the meantime, let's compare the various types of assets (for now, I exclude security tokens from Table 5.1 as these are not used for payments).

Bank vs. non-bank issuers

Table 5.1 summarises the key features and characteristics of e-money, which is always issued by a centralised issuer which may or may not be a bank.

And just because a picture speaks a thousand words in Figure 1.3.

In Figure 5.3, I have tried to be as generic as possible to cater to the different collateralisation ratios and jurisdictions. In addition, commercial banks don't require additional permissions to issue e-money as their

Table 5.1 Comparing cryptocurrencies, stablecoins, e-money, and fiat currencies. © 2024 Neira Jones

Feature	**Cryptocurrencies**	**Crypto-Backed Stablecoins**	**Algorithmic Stablecoins**	**NFTS**	**Commodity-Backed Stablecoins**	**Fiat-Backed Stablecoins**	**e-Money**	**Fiat Currencies**
Backing asset	None	Other cryptocurrencies	Algorithmically controlled supply	Digital or physical assets (e.g. art, collectibles)	Physical commodities (e.g. gold, oil)	Fiat currency	Issuer reserves (e.g. safeguarded funds and other reserves)	Government trust
Decentralisation	High	High	High	Variable (depends on the platform)	Low to moderate	Low (centralised issuer)	Low (centralised issuer)	None
Collateral ratio	N/A	Over-collateralised (e.g. 1.5:1 or more)	No collateral, but soft peg to fiat.	N/A	1:1 or variable	1:1 ratio	Variable (jurisdiction dependent)	Bank reserves
Redeemability against underlying asset	N/A	Redeemable for crypto collateral	Not directly redeemable	Not directly redeemable	Often redeemable for physical commodity	Usually redeemable for fiat	Fiat substitute	N/A
Usability for goods and services	Limited	No	No	No	No	Limited	High	High
Markets	Cryptocurrency exchanges, over-the-counter (OTC) markets	Cryptocurrency exchanges, DeFi platforms	Cryptocurrency exchanges, DeFi platforms	NFT marketplaces (e.g. OpenSea, Rarible)	Specialised commodity exchanges, cryptocurrency exchanges	Cryptocurrency exchanges, OTC markets, some forex platforms	Banks, financial institutions, e-money platforms	Banks, forex markets
Use case	Store of value, speculation, payments	DeFi applications, stable trading pair	Experimental stable medium of exchange	Digital collectibles, art, gaming assets	Hedge against inflation, stable store of value	Stable medium of exchange, crypto on/off ramp	Digital payments, remittances, loyalty, gift cards, micro-payments	Medium of exchange, store of value, payments
Scalability	Variable	Variable	Variable	Variable (depends on the platform)	Variable	Variable	High	High

(Continued)

Table 5.1 (Continued)

Feature	**Cryptocurrencies**	**Crypto-Backed Stablecoins**	**Algorithmic Stablecoins**	**NFTS**	**Commodity-Backed Stablecoins**	**Fiat-Backed Stablecoins**	**e-Money**	**Fiat Currencies**
Smart contract usage	Variable	Extensive	Extensive	Extensive	Limited	Limited	None	None
Yield generation	Through staking or lending	Through over-collateralisation and DeFi	Through algorithmic mechanisms	Through resale, royalties	Through lending or commodity appreciation	Through lending or reserve management	None	Interest (savings accounts, bonds)
Price stability	Highly volatile	Moderate-to-high volatility	Can be volatile (soft peg to fiat)	Highly volatile	Relatively stable (tied to commodity prices)	Stable (hard peg to fiat)	Stable (regulated and backed by issuer reserves)	Stable (controlled by central banks)
Risk profile	High	High	High	High	Moderate (tied to commodity market)	Low (if properly backed and regulated)	Low (regulated, but depends on issuer stability)	Low (unstable economies)
Issuance	Decentralised (mining, staking)	Decentralised (smart contracts)	Decentralised (algorithmic)	Decentralised (various platforms)	Centralised issuer	Centralised issuer	Centralised issuer	Centralised (central bank)
Regulatory oversight	Limited	Limited	Limited	Limited to moderate	Moderate to high	High	High	High
KYC/AML requirements	Depends on crypto exchange (see Note 1)	Depends on platform	Depends on platform	Depends on platform	Yes	Yes	Yes	No for everyday transactions (see Note 2)
Governance	Often community driven	Often DAO based	Often DAO based	Decentralised or platform based	Centralised or semi-decentralised	Centralised (oversight depends on jurisdiction)	Centralised (regulated by financial authorities)	Centralised (government and central bank)
Transparency	Variable (blockchain dependent)	High (on-chain collateral)	High (algorithm visible)	Variable (depends on the platform)	Depends on issuer (regular audits)	Depends on issuer (regular audits)	Moderate to high (depends on regulatory requirements)	Moderate (central bank policies)

Note 1: Yes, for centralised exchange (CEX), No for decentralised exchange (DEX).
Note 2: No for everyday cash transactions, Yes for large cash transactions and interactions with financial institutions.

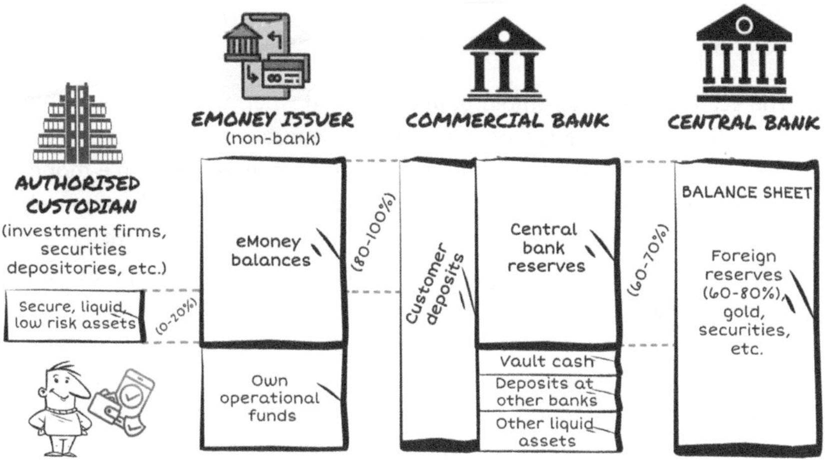

Figure 5.3 How e-money issuers operate. © 2024 Neira Jones.

banking permissions give them the right to do so, hence the difference between banks and non-bank issuers in terms of the reserves they hold to back their customer balances. I won't delve further into the technicalities as this is covered in my first book, but it's worth highlighting that non-bank e-money issuers rely on third party custodians that can be commercial banks or other authorised financial services institutions (e.g. investment firms) to secure their customers' funds.

This reliance on third party-custodians creates its own set of challenges, as evidenced by the collapse of Silicon Valley Bank (SVB) and the impact it had on many crypto businesses and other fintech-focused firms[3] (see *Fiat-collateralised stablecoins*).

The Wirecard scandal and its impact on e-money

Crypto businesses haven't got a monopoly on financial risks and scandals, and one significant event was the catalyst for increased regulatory oversight of e-money institutions.

BOX 6.1 THE WIRECARD SCANDAL

The scandal began to unfold publicly in 2019 when the Financial Times (FT) published a series of investigative reports[4] alleging accounting irregularities at Wirecard, a German payment processor with an e-money licence (the types of payment processing licences are covered extensively in my first book *Understanding Payments*), the then darling of the fintech industry. Despite these allegations, Wirecard continued to operate and even expanded its business.

The company's dramatic fall began in June 2020 when Wirecard announced that €1.9 billion was missing from its balance sheet. This revelation led to a rapid collapse of the company's stock price and the arrest of its CEO, Markus Braun, on suspicion of falsifying accounts.[5]

Several key failures in regulatory oversight and corporate governance were exposed:

- **Regulatory oversight failure**: Germany's financial regulator, BaFin, came under intense scrutiny for its handling of the situation. Instead of thoroughly investigating the allegations against Wirecard, BaFin temporarily banned short-selling of Wirecard stock and filed a criminal complaint against two FT journalists who had reported on the company's irregularities[6] (so much for whistleblower protection!). This raised questions about the regulator's ability to detect and prevent financial fraud.
- **Corporate governance failures**: the scandal revealed critical weaknesses in Wirecard's internal controls and the supervisory board's oversight. A central issue was the board's failure to properly scrutinise the company's claimed cash reserves, particularly the €1.9 billion supposedly held in custodian accounts in Asia, which ultimately proved non-existent.[7] The board's lack of due diligence on Wirecard's international operations and third-party acquirers, coupled with ineffective risk management processes, allowed fraudulent activities to persist undetected. Potential conflicts of interest among board members further compromised independent oversight.[8]
- **Auditing failures**: EY, Wirecard's long-time auditor, failed to detect the accounting irregularities that had persisted for years. This raised serious questions about the quality and effectiveness of external audits.[9]

- **Financial reporting enforcement failures**: the case exposed weaknesses in Germany's two-step enforcement procedure for financial reporting. The Financial Reporting Enforcement Panel (FREP), tasked with investigating violations of accounting requirements, was found to be ineffective.[10]

The impact of the Wirecard scandal on e-money institutions, and the fintech industry in general, was significant:

- **Increased regulatory scrutiny**: the scandal led to calls for stricter regulation of fintech companies and electronic money institutions across Europe. Regulators across Europe began reassessing their approach to overseeing innovative financial services firms. There have been calls for more stringent licensing and ongoing supervision of equated monthly instalments (EMIs) and payment institutions. This heightened regulatory focus aims to prevent similar scandals and ensure the stability and integrity of the rapidly evolving fintech sector. Whilst the immediate regulatory impact was most pronounced in Europe, the scandal has influenced discussions on corporate governance and financial oversight globally. It has prompted regulators in other jurisdictions to review their own systems for potential vulnerabilities. The case has been used as an example in international discussions on improving cross-border cooperation in financial supervision, highlighting the need for enhanced collaboration among regulatory bodies worldwide to address the challenges posed by multinational financial entities.
- **Loss of trust**: the collapse of Wirecard, once considered a fintech success story, eroded trust in the sector and raised concerns about the stability and reliability of e-money institutions. This caused regulators and policymakers to place increased emphasis on the importance of corporate culture and governance in preventing fraud, leading to more holistic approaches to oversight.
- **Regulatory reforms**: the European Commission launched a consultation on strengthening the quality of corporate reporting and its enforcement, directly influenced by the Wirecard scandal. This initiative aimed to enhance the reliability of corporate reporting across the EU and improve investor protection. Notably, the introduction of the Payment Services Directive 3 (PSD3) and the payment services

regulation (PSR) were key developments. Specifically, PSD3 and PSR introduced enhanced safeguarding requirements for customer funds, stricter operational resilience standards, improved transparency, and expanded supervisory powers, all aimed at mitigating risks associated with e-money institutions. Germany, being at the epicentre of the scandal, implemented several regulatory changes. BaFin, the German financial regulator, was given expanded powers to investigate companies directly, rather than relying on other bodies like FREP. The government proposed reforms to strengthen BaFin's independence and investigative capabilities.

- **Re-evaluation of governance structures**: the scandal prompted a re-evaluation of corporate governance structures, particularly in Germany and other EU countries, with a focus on strengthening internal controls and supervisory board effectiveness. The case also exposed weaknesses in Germany's two-step enforcement procedure for financial reporting, leading to proposals for a more centralised and empowered enforcement mechanism. There have also been calls for creating a European Single Capital Market Supervisor (ESCMS) to address cross-border issues and ensure consistent oversight across the EU.
- **Audit reforms**: the scandal highlighted the need for more robust auditing practices. There have been discussions about mandatory rotation of auditors and stricter separation of audit and non-audit services. The European Commission considered reforms to enhance auditor independence and promote a greater level of professional scepticism, ensuring that auditors critically evaluate financial statements and challenge management assertions more rigorously.
- **Whistleblower protection**: the scandal underscored the importance of whistleblowing mechanisms, leading to suggestions for strengthening whistleblower protection and creating more effective reporting channels.

These regulatory developments aimed to address the systemic weaknesses exposed by the Wirecard scandal, with a focus on strengthening oversight, improving auditing practices, enhancing corporate governance, and protecting investors. The ongoing reforms underscore the far-reaching impact of the scandal on the regulatory landscape for financial services and corporate oversight, not just in Europe but globally.[11]

At the time of writing, Jan Marsalek, Wirecard's former COO, remained a fugitive and is believed to be in Russia under the protection of Russian intelligence services. Interpol has issued a red notice for his arrest.[12] Meanwhile, the trial of former Wirecard CEO Markus Braun and two other executives began in Munich in December 2022, with charges including fraud, breach of trust, and market manipulation. This is still ongoing, and his legal funds have dried up.[13] In August 2024, two more Wirecard executives were charged with embezzlement.[14]

The Wirecard scandal had devastating consequences for both investors and customers. Investors, including retail and institutional shareholders, suffered massive financial losses as Wirecard's stock price plummeted from over €100 to less than €2 within days. Many pension funds and investment firms were heavily exposed, leading to significant write-downs. Customers, particularly small businesses relying on Wirecard's payment processing services, faced operational disruptions and potential loss of funds.[15] The scandal eroded trust in fintech companies and payment processors, making it more difficult for legitimate businesses in the sector to attract investment and customers. The fallout also highlighted the need for stronger investor protection measures and more rigorous due diligence in the rapidly evolving fintech industry.[16]

We have since moved on from the Wirecard scandal, and it is undeniable that regulatory oversight over e-money institutions has increased globally.

e-Money and innovation

Despite the challenges, we mustn't forget that e-money institutions are a significant driver for innovation in the payments industry for several reasons:

- **Agility and flexibility**: e-money institutions can quickly adapt to changing market conditions and technology advancements. Unlike incumbent banks, they can implement new technologies and processes rapidly, such as quicker customer onboarding or the issuance of virtual accounts in a few steps. It is no wonder that most neo-banks at the time of writing started life as e-money institutions before they obtained their banking licences (e.g. Monzo, Starling, and Revolut in the UK; N26 in Germany).

- **Cost efficiency**: e-money institutions typically operate with a lower and more flexible cost base when compared to traditional banks, allowing them to offer lower fees and more competitive pricing for their services.
- **Technology innovation**: unincumbered by legacy systems, e-money institutions are typically digitally native, able to leverage cloud computing, artificial intelligence, and other technologies to enhance their services and customer experiences. This agility makes them particularly appealing to younger, digitally savvy demographics, and increasingly to older generations. In fact, in the UK, neo-banks (which started as e-money institutions) are set to outpace legacy banks for the first time by Q1 2025.[17]
- **Market disruption**: e-money institutions are often seen as disruptors in the financial services industry. They challenge traditional banks by offering innovative payment solutions that cater to the needs of modern consumers and businesses. This disruption fosters competition and drives the entire industry towards more customer-centric and technologically advanced solutions.

Of course, this wouldn't be possible without a conducive regulatory environment. In Europe, regulations support innovation by providing a clear legal framework for the issuance and management of e-money. The EU's E-Money Directive (Directive 2009/110/EC) and subsequent regulations, including the Payment Services Directive (PSD2) and the upcoming PSD3/PSR, ensure that EMIs operate under stringent safeguards to protect customer funds whilst allowing them to offer a wide range of payment services. This regulatory support encourages the growth and innovation of EMIs within a secure and compliant environment, but this might not be the case everywhere. In addition, looking back at Figure 5.3, e-money institutions, in Europe at least, can't offer lending services from customer balances as these funds must be safeguarded at authorised custodians, which can make them less capital efficient compared to traditional banks that can use customer deposits for lending purposes. Traditional banks still have the upper hand on that front.

Recap on e-money

Professionals should be aware of the opportunities that e-money may offer:

- **Enhanced efficiency**: e-money can significantly streamline payment processes by reducing transaction times, lowering costs, and minimising errors compared to traditional payment methods. It can enable real-time payments, instant settlements, and cross-border transfers with greater ease and speed.
- **Financial inclusion**: by providing accessible and affordable financial services, e-money can help bridge the gap between the banked and unbanked, or under-banked, populations. It can facilitate payments, remittances, and savings for those who previously lacked access to formal banking services.
- **Innovation catalyst**: e-money can serve as a catalyst for innovation in the broader financial ecosystem. It can enable the development of new payment products and services, such as peer-to-peer payments, micropayments, and subscription-based models. Additionally, it can support the growth of emerging technologies like blockchain and artificial intelligence within the financial industry.
- **Competitive advantage**: businesses of all sizes can leverage e-money to gain a competitive edge. For instance, retailers can offer faster checkout times and loyalty programmes, fintech companies can develop innovative payment solutions, and remittance services can provide cheaper and faster cross-border transfers.

Professionals should also consider the challenges associated with e-money:

- **Regulatory landscape**: the rapidly evolving regulatory environment for e-money can create uncertainty for businesses and consumers alike. Compliance costs can be high, and inconsistent regulations across different jurisdictions can hinder innovation and market growth.
- **Consumer protection**: protecting consumers from fraud, scams, and data breaches is essential for building trust in e-money systems. Implementing robust security measures, clear dispute resolution processes, and consumer education programmes are vital.

- **Operational resilience**: ensuring the security and resilience of e-money systems is paramount to protect against cyberattacks, fraud, system failures, and other operational risks. Robust security measures, contingency planning, and incident response capabilities are essential.
- **Trust and reputation**: building and maintaining trust in e-money is crucial for widespread adoption. Negative incidents, such as data breaches, fraud, or operational failures, can erode consumer confidence and damage the reputation of the entire industry.
- **Competition with traditional banking**: e-money firms face stiff competition from established banks and other financial institutions. Differentiating e-money services and offering unique value propositions is essential for gaining market share.
- **Interoperability**: ensuring seamless interoperability between different e-money systems and traditional payment methods is essential for widespread adoption. Promoting open standards and collaboration among industry players can facilitate interoperability.
- **Talent acquisition**: finding and retaining skilled professionals with expertise in e-money, payments, modern technology, and financial services can be challenging. Investing in talent development and building a strong talent pipeline is crucial for the growth of the e-money industry.

E-money has undoubtedly reshaped the way we transact, serving as a bridge between traditional cash and the digital age. Its flexibility and efficiency have paved the way for innovative payment solutions. But the evolution of digital currency doesn't stop there. CBDCs are emerging as a potential game changer. These government-backed digital assets could alter the financial landscape, and it's likely that existing e-money institutions will play a pivotal role in their development and implementation. We'll cover CBDCs in Chapter 7 as they warrant a chapter of their own.

Let's look at cryptocurrency.

Cryptocurrency

Ah, **cryptocurrency** – the rebellious teenager of the financial world. It bursts onto the scene in 2009 with Bitcoin, promising to revolutionise money as we know it and become the universal and democratic medium of exchange, giving power back to the people by eliminating the need for banks. But what exactly is this digital upstart that has central bankers clutching their pearls and tech bros singing its praises?

> A **cryptocurrency** is a type of digital or virtual currency that uses cryptography for security. Cryptocurrencies are typically decentralised and operate on blockchain technology, ensuring transparency and security by recording all transactions on a public blockchain ledger.

It's like the cool, enigmatic new kid in school who speaks in code and doesn't play by the traditional rules. Unlike fiat currency, cryptocurrencies are typically decentralised systems based on blockchain technology. But before you start thinking that cryptocurrency is just magic internet money (though some might argue it is), let's break it down a bit:

- **Cryptocurrencies operate on blockchain networks**, which are decentralised by design. However, the degree of decentralisation in terms of operational control and influence can vary significantly among different cryptocurrencies. Blockchain technology is the backbone of most cryptocurrencies. (see Chapter 1, *What is a blockchain* for a refresher).

  Note from the author: I should really say "operate on distributed ledger technology", as not all distributed ledger technology (DLT) platforms are blockchains, but for the purpose of simplicity, I will use "blockchain" throughout and apologise to the purists in advance 😉.
- **Some cryptocurrencies are created through mining [Proof of Work (PoW)], whilst others are created and distributed as rewards for validators [Proof of Stake (PoS)]** (see Chapter 4, *Validating nodes and transaction fees*). There are other ways of creating cryptocurrencies (which are essentially coins or tokens), such as pre-mining at project launch (see Chapter 4, *Supply and distribution; value creation*), through a hard fork (see Chapter 3, *Hard forks*). An additional way of creating cryptocurrencies is through algorithmic processes that don't involve mining or staking but rather use algorithms to maintain their **peg** to a fiat currency by minting or burning tokens based on demand (see *Stablecoins*).

- **Cryptocurrencies are stored in digital wallets** specifically designed for that purpose (see Chapter 6, *Transacting in a decentralised world*).
- Looking at world economies, if fiat currencies are a merry-go-round, cryptocurrencies are a rollercoaster. There are typically **characterised by their volatility** as their value can skyrocket or plummet faster than you can say "HODL".

The term **HODL** is derived from a misspelling of "hold". It means retaining crypto-assets that you own for an extended period of time, even during highly volatile market movements. It entered the crypto scene when an enthusiastic BitcoinTalk forum user, going by the name of GameKyuubi, posted a semi-intelligible tirade (possibly after a few drinks) after making an unfortunate Bitcoin trade during a volatile price rally in December 2013. In his post, he wrote: "I AM HODLING" in an effort to convey that from that point on, he would simply hold his Bitcoin rather than sell it, regardless of market conditions. Within hours, the typo found its way onto every Bitcoin community channel in the form of memes and GIFs, catapulting HODLing into crypto vernacular. It must be noted that there is an alternative explanation which states that "HODL" stands for "Hold On for Dear Life" and conveys the same sentiment, but I personally prefer the first version...

Cryptocurrencies are quite different from traditional money as they aren't widely accepted in exchange for goods and services (sorry, you can't buy a car with Dogecoin (DOGE), despite what Elon Musk might like to see[18]), **and their value can be wildly unpredictable**. Central banks and governments are still figuring out how to regulate them. (Note from the author: whilst I mention applicable regulations in context within each chapter, I don't extensively cover crypto-related regulations in a dedicated chapter of this book. This will be covered extensively in my next book, "Payments Unbound - Navigating through the perils and potential of decentralised markets").

But there's more to cryptocurrency than just buying and selling. It's spawned the entire DeFi ecosystem (see Chapter 2, *Lifting the veil on DeFi*), NFTs (see *Non-Fungible Tokens*) and blockchain-based applications (see Chapter 2, *Blockchain application types*). It's like the financial world decided to have a wild house party, and cryptocurrency brought all its eccentric friends.

So, whether you see cryptocurrency as the future of finance or as a kind of digital **tulip mania**,[19] one thing's for sure: it's shaken up the financial world in more ways than one.

First, let's put things into perspective.

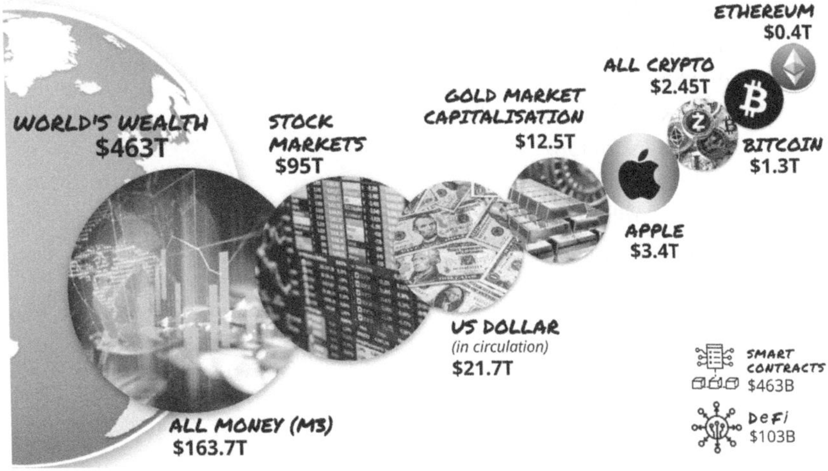

Figure 5.4 Positioning cryptocurrencies. © 2024 Neira Jones.

When I was researching data sources for Figure 5.4, I did a lot of reading, so I'll indulge in sharing the answer to a question I was asking myself.

BOX 5.1 HOW DO YOU DETERMINE THE TOTAL AMOUNT OF MONEY IN THE WORLD?

Well, it's not an easy task. You first have to identify key data sources, such as the IMF, the Bank for International Settlements (BIS), the World Bank and the central banks of major economies. Then you have to gather data for M3 **money** for the largest economies. Gross Domestic Product (GDP) rankings are readily available and usually list nominal GDP,[20] or Purchasing Power Parity (PPP), which is adjusted GDP in current international dollars[21] as an alternative way of comparing GDP across countries, based on what basket of goods they could buy in those countries rather than currency exchange rates. Here's the list using nominal GDP:

- United States: $28.8 trillion
- China: $18.5 trillion
- Germany: $4.6 trillion
- Japan: $4.1 trillion
- India: $3.9 trillion
- United Kingdom: $3.5 trillion
- France: $3.1 trillion
- Brazil: $2.3 trillion
- Italy: $2.3 trillion
- Canada: $2.2 trillion
- Russia: $2.1 trillion
- Mexico: $2 trillion
- Australia: $1.8 trillion
- South Korea: $1.8 trillion
- Spain: $1.7 trillion
- Indonesia: $1.5 trillion
- Saudi Arabia: $1.1 trillion
- Netherlands: $1.1 trillion
- Türkiye: $1.1 trillion
- Switzerland: $0.9 trillion

The IMF calculates the total GDP worldwide to be $109.53 trillion. When we aggregate the data for these 20 major economies, we come up with a total base figure of $88.4 trillion or 81% of global GDP. If we assume that the average M3 to GDP ratio for these economies is 1.5%, it gives us $132.6 trillion total M3 money. If we use the same 81% proportion, these give us a global M3 money total of $163.7 trillion, which is the figure I have shown in Figure 5.4.

It's important to note that this is still an estimate, and the actual figure could vary due to factors such as the differences between countries when they define M3 money, the fluctuations in exchange rates, and the rapid pace of change in global financial markets, but it gives you an idea.

The reason why I wanted to spend a bit of time on this is to show that even with traditional, centralised, and heavily regulated financial infrastructures, where data are readily available and transparent and where accuracy and reporting are crucial, statistics is still a challenge. Imagine how difficult it is to perform the same exercise for decentralised financial systems...

Looking at Figure 5.4, we soon realise that the whole crypto ecosystem is still very small in the context of money; this, however, doesn't mean that it can't have an impact on the world's economy, as we will see later.

In any instance, aside from their volatility and limited utility as a medium of exchange when compared to traditional money, **cryptocurrencies are generally not accepted as legal tender**. That is unless you live in El Salvador.

Bizarre experiments

In a peculiar move spearheaded by President Nayib Bukele, **El Salvador made Bitcoin legal tender in September 2021**, making it an official currency alongside the US dollar.[22] Users were incentivised to download the digital wallet Chivo with a $30 joining reward and, by October 2021, three million Salvadorians had downloaded it. A study conducted by the National Bureau of Economic Research and published in April 2022[23] found that only 20% of those who downloaded the wallet continued to use it after spending the $30, and by the end of 2022, less than 20% of businesses in El Salvador were accepting Bitcoin payments[24] due to technical challenges; infrastructure limitations; lack of education; and of course, volatility.

The IMF has been critical of El Salvador's move, citing risks to financial stability and consumer protection, and as of late 2023, Bitcoin investments didn't yield the expected returns for the government, despite their mining of nearly 474 Bitcoin (31 August 2024, 1BTC = $58,929) between 2021 and May 2024.[25] El Salvador continues with hopes to make the country a crypto haven – including a vision to build a volcano-powered Bitcoin-dedicated city (I guess you need geothermics to power those mining rigs 😉) – hurting its chances to get a quick cash injection from the IMF, in a country where extreme poverty has doubled since 2019 and almost half the population lives with food insecurity.[26]

El Salvador is not alone in such an experiment. The second poorest economy in the world, the Central African Republic (CAR), made Bitcoin legal tender on 27 April 2022[27] by launching the Sango Project aiming to create a crypto hub and attract investment. Plans included creating a "Crypto Island" and issuing Sango Coin, a national digital currency, but limited infrastructure and internet access hindered adoption, and merchant adoption lacked for the same reasons as in El Salvador. Again here, the IMF, and other international organisations, expressed concerns. On 24 March 2023, the government's constitutional court ruled that the purchase of "e-residency" and land using cryptocurrencies were unconstitutional, invalidating key portions of the law that made Bitcoin legal tender, effectively ending CAR's experiment.[28]

Both El Salvador's and CAR's Bitcoin experiments highlight the challenges of implementing cryptocurrencies as legal tender, especially in countries with limited technology infrastructures and complex economic situations. Time will tell.

Recap

Professionals should remember a few things:

In the world of crypto, the only constant is change.

- **Currency is any widely accepted medium of exchange for goods and services**, evolving from commodity-based forms to modern digital currencies. It's crucial for facilitating trade and avoiding the complexities of barter systems.
- **Fiat money is government-issued currency not backed by physical commodities**. It derives value from supply and demand and the stability of the issuing government. Central banks control fiat money supply through monetary policy.
- **Cryptocurrencies are decentralised digital currencies**. They offer the potential for revolutionising money but face challenges including volatility and regulatory issues.
- **Cryptocurrencies operate on blockchain networks**, ensuring transparency and security through public ledger systems. They can be created through various methods including mining (Proof of Work) and staking (Proof of Stake).
- Cryptocurrencies have spawned a broader ecosystem including DeFi, NFTs, and blockchain-based applications.
- Whilst cryptocurrencies have shaken up the financial world, they are **not widely accepted for goods and services and their value can be highly unpredictable**.
- **Cryptocurrencies represent a small fraction of the global financial system** compared to traditional forms of money and stock markets.

The journey through the history and evolution of money sets the stage for a detailed exploration of digital and virtual assets. As we move forward, we will delve deeper into the complexities of digital and virtual assets, including cryptocurrencies, whilst the emerging role of CBDCs will be covered in Chapter 7.This chapter aims to demystify these modern financial innovations, providing a comprehensive understanding of their impact on the global economy and whether they have the potential to reshape the future of money.

Digital and virtual assets (just an illusion)

What is a virtual asset?

Good question. The answer depends on who you talk to. Sometimes the term digital/virtual asset refers to cryptocurrencies, other times it refers to e-money or virtual currencies used on a popular gaming platform. It all depends on context. And regulations.

The terms "digital asset" and "virtual asset" are used interchangeably, and it's difficult to pinpoint a globally agreed definition. Let's examine this.

Defining digital assets: US, UK, Germany

In my struggle to find a generally accepted definition, I examined three markets:

United States: "Digital asset.--Except as otherwise provided by the Secretary, the term 'digital asset' means any digital representation of value which is recorded on a cryptographically secured distributed ledger or any similar technology as specified by the Secretary." Source: Infrastructure Investment and Jobs Act 2021, Public Law No: 117-58, Section 80603.

What does it mean? According to this, a digital asset is a representation of value that is recorded on a cryptographically secured distributed ledger (which may or may not be a blockchain), but we don't know what we may be allowed to do with it (e.g. payments, trading, investment). The broad nature of the definition may encompass a wide range of digital assets beyond cryptocurrencies. Whilst the definition gives regulatory authorities (the Secretary) the power to specify what constitutes "similar technology", it does not address the functional aspects of digital assets or their economic roles. The lack of specificity – apart from the fact that it concentrates on unspecified types of crypto-assets – regarding uses and types of technologies could lead to potential regulatory ambiguity and may require further clarification in the future.

United Kingdom: "The term "digital asset" includes a cryptographically secured digital representation of value or contractual rights that uses a form of distributed ledger technology and can be transferred, stored, or traded electronically." Source: Financial Services and Markets Act 2023, Part 6, Section 104.

What does it mean? Similar to the US definition, a digital asset is a representation of value that is recorded on a cryptographically secured distributed ledger (which may or may not be a blockchain) and therefore concentrates on crypto-assets. However, now we get added purpose inasmuch as it may be transferred, stored, or traded electronically. We also have the new use case of representing contractual rights which encompasses a range of crypto-assets beyond just cryptocurrencies.

Germany: "[...] Crypto-assets shall mean digital representations of value that are not issued or guaranteed by any central bank or public authority and do not have the legal status of currency or money but are accepted by natural or legal persons as a means of exchange or payment or serve investment purposes by virtue of an agreement or actual practice, and which can be transferred, stored and traded electronically." Source: German Banking Act (Kreditwesengesetz – KWG), amended by the Act Implementing the Amending Directive on the Fourth EU Anti-Money Laundering Directive, 2020, Section 1 (11) Sentence 4.

What does it mean? This definition sits somewhere across the US and UK definitions. It also concentrates on crypto-assets as representations of value but excludes assets that are not issued by a central bank or monetary and those that are otherwise regulated (currency or money). These assets may be transferred, stored, or traded electronically and may be used for payments or investment purposes.

Whilst all the definitions agree that a virtual asset exists purely in a digital form, you'd be forgiven for being confused! Table 5.2 puts all of this in context.

Table 5.2 Comparing US, UK, and Germany digital asset definitions. © 2024 Neira Jones

Aspect	United States	United Kingdom	Germany
Term used	Digital asset	Crypto-asset	
Definition source	Infrastructure Investment and Jobs Act 2021	Financial Services and Markets Act 2023	German Banking Act (Kreditwesengesetz – KWG), amended 2020
Representation of value	Yes		
Representation of rights	Not mentioned	Contractual rights	Not mentioned
Means of exchange	Not specified	Yes	
Economic role	Not addressed	Not addressed	Payments, investments
Usage	Not specified	Transfer, store, trade electronically	
Issuer exclusion	Not specified		Excludes assets issued or guaranteed by central banks or public authorities
Technology mentioned	Digital representation of value stored on a cryptographically secured distributed ledger or similar technology	Digital representations of value recorded on a cryptographically secured distributed ledger	
Potential ambiguities	Broad definition, unspecified uses, regulatory ambiguity	Broad but specifies uses, includes contractual rights	Excludes central-bank-issued assets, specifies uses, broader scope but more detailed

Table 5.2 highlights the varying approaches and regulatory frameworks adopted by each jurisdiction, which underscores the complexity and evolving nature of digital asset regulation. This led me to look outside of national regulations to the **Financial Action Task Force (FATF)**, because its work has worldwide applicability. The FATF offers us this definition in their 2021 "Updated Guidance for a Risk-Based Approach to Virtual Assets and Virtual Asset Service Providers"[29]:

"**Virtual asset**: A virtual asset is a digital representation of value that can be digitally traded, or transferred, and can be used for payment or investment purposes. Virtual assets do not include digital representations of fiat currencies, securities, and other financial assets that are already covered elsewhere in the FATF Recommendations."

The FATF, by definition, aims to prevent financial crime worldwide. This is why both the digital representation of fiat currencies, which is already regulated (e.g. e-money, CBDC), and closed-loop systems (e.g. gaming currencies) are excluded from the FATF definition of a virtual asset.

Considering this, I finally get to propose a definition for digital or virtual assets in an attempt to cover the whole spectrum. I will also stick to the term "virtual asset", but "digital asset" is equally applicable.

A proposed definition

A virtual asset refers to any digital representation of value that can be digitally traded, transferred, or used for payment, investment, utility, governance, or ownership purposes.

This definition covers all potential use cases, some of which were introduced in previous chapters; it covers all types of assets, whether regulated or unregulated; remains technology neutral; and allows for centralised and decentralised implementations. It remains broad enough to encompass current and potential future forms of virtual assets, whilst still providing a clear framework for understanding what constitutes a virtual asset.

Figure 5.5 offers a classification framework.

Phew! It took more than 5,000 words to get to this definition, but I think it was worth it!

We covered e-money in detail earlier, let's continue with what we set out to do and define these categories a bit more in the next section.

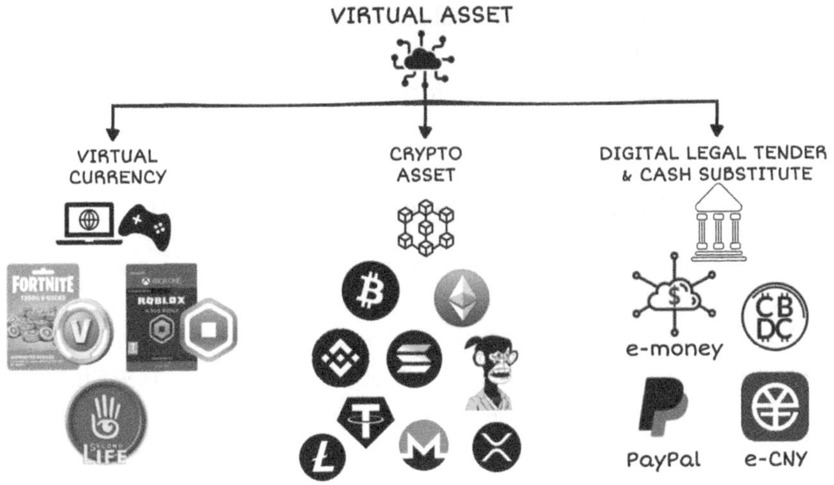

Figure 5.5 Classifying virtual assets. © 2024 Neira Jones.

Virtual currencies (money for nothing)

The examples of virtual currencies given in Figure 5.5 are well established within traditional gaming communities.

Virtual currencies are issued, managed, and controlled by private issuers, developers, or the founding organisation. They are used in a specific community as a medium of exchange to obtain in-game assets and incentives or participate in activities. Traditional games, such as Fortnite, Roblox, or Second Life, are centralised environments. Their gaming virtual currencies (e.g. Linden Dollar for Second Life, V-Bucks for Fortnite, Robucks for Roblox) are **closed loop** systems, meaning the virtual currencies can only be used for transfer or exchange of value within those environments and are therefore not portable to other games. Another notable example outside of gaming is the Amazon Coin, which launched in 2013, and was designed to be used primarily for purchasing apps, games, and in-app items from the Amazon Appstore, particularly on Kindle Fire devices. This virtual currency was pegged to the US dollar. Amazon aimed to make it easier for customers to buy digital content and to encourage app developers by providing a new revenue stream. Whilst Amazon coins are still in use, they haven't expanded significantly and remain a niche payment method within the Amazon ecosystem.[30]

There's really not much more to say about that, other than you might find the term "virtual currency" to apply to "cryptocurrency", where the terms may be used interchangeably. Context is important, and for the purpose of this book, I will use the term "virtual currency" only in the context of centralised gaming platforms (or other similar environments).

Crypto-assets (everybody's jumpin')

This is where it gets interesting, and even more confusing, as we have seen earlier when trying to define virtual assets.

You'll be pleased to know that we already started introducing crypto-assets in earlier sections, where we talked about coins and tokens (see Chapter 1, Box 1.11), as well as utility and governance tokens (see Chapter 3, *Operational tokens*). The reason I introduced these particular crypto-assets in earlier sections is because they fulfil a primary purpose that was relevant to that section (e.g. utility, governance). From these sections, you may have already realised that assets with an operational primary purpose may evolve in time to fulfil other purposes as the project gains traction and popularity, such as with Bitcoin's BTC (see Chapter 3, Box 3.1) and Ripple's XRP, a utility token that can also be traded on exchanges (see Chapter 4, Box 4.3).

This variability of purpose is what makes classifying crypto-assets challenging. For the purpose of this chapter, I will follow one rule: I will use the crypto-asset's **primary purpose**, as specified in the white paper (or specification) for the project, to classify new/emerging assets, or the **current main purpose** for established crypto-assets. This will, of course, evolve over time, but the model can adapt to this.

Classifying crypto-assets

Crypto-assets come in various forms, and these are shown in context in Figure 5.6.

Operational tokens

We covered operational tokens in Chapter 3, and they come in the form of utility tokens, governance tokens, or hybrid forms. I list some examples in Figure 5.6, and the only thing to add from the earlier detailed coverage is that these tokens, with a primary purpose of utility and/or governance,

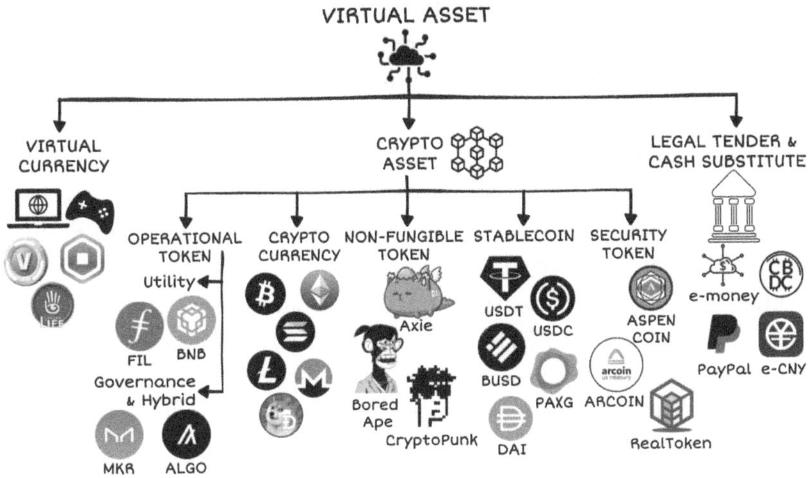

Figure 5.6 Classifying crypto-assets. © 2024 Neira Jones.

may also be traded on crypto exchanges as the ecosystems become more established, evolving them into cryptocurrencies. At the time of writing, looking at blockchain explorers, both utility tokens Binance's BNB and Solana's SOL are in the top ten ranking of cryptocurrencies by market capitalisation, which illustrates my point.

Cryptocurrencies

Definitions and types

A cryptocurrency is a type of crypto-asset intended to be a medium of exchange and that uses cryptography for security. Cryptocurrencies are typically decentralised and operate on distributed ledger technology (e.g. a blockchain), ensuring transparency and security by recording all transactions on a public ledger. This was the original purpose of Bitcoin (BTC), but over the years, BTC has morphed into a store of value used for speculative purposes. Some even refer to BTC as "digital gold", which is a misnomer since gold is a stable asset and cryptocurrencies are highly volatile. To this day, no cryptocurrency can claim to be a true medium of exchange. Also spelled "crypto currency".

This definition shows the evolving nature of cryptocurrencies, and nowadays, people view cryptocurrencies more as speculative assets or stores of value, rather than as a medium of exchange. The only constant in the crypto world is change.

Cryptocurrencies come in various forms, and the first and most well-known is BTC, created in 2009 at the same time as the Bitcoin blockchain. It was designed as a peer-to-peer electronic cash system to enable online payments without the need for a trusted central authority.

After BTC came **altcoins** (a contraction of "alternative" and "coin"), and the first was Ethereum's ETH, soon followed by Litecoin's LTC, Cardano's ADA, and many others. We can draw a parallel between the cards industry and the creation of terms such as "alternative payment methods" which was coined by the card world, meaning any payment form that is not traditional cards, regardless of their popularity or dominance. For cryptocurrencies, whilst BTC dominates, ETH is still pretty popular, but an altcoin, nevertheless.

Altcoin types are illustrated in Figure 5.8.

Then came cryptocurrencies inspired by internet memes and jokes, which often gain popularity through social media and online communities, and sometimes acquire significant market value due to community interest and speculative trading. The first widely recognised **meme coin** is DOGE, initially created in 2013 as a joke, based on the popular "Doge" meme featuring a Shiba Inu dog. Despite its origin as a parody, DOGE has gained popularity over time, especially after Elon Musk's endorsement. Many other meme coins followed, including Shiba Inu (SHIB), Pepe (PEPE), dogwifhat (WIF), and many others, as illustrated in Figure 5.7.

These coins, often not meant to be taken seriously, can gain momentum if the community wants to be in on the joke and buys the coin. If it gets popular and spikes in value, investors may also jump in, as well as celebrities. As a result, meme coins are generally considered high-risk investments due to their volatile nature and lack of fundamental value or utility.

Another type of cryptocurrency is the **privacy coin**, which is designed to provide enhanced privacy and anonymity for transactions as they focus on protecting user identities and transaction details. Examples are Monero (XMR), Zcash (ZEC), and Dash (DASH). These have gained media, and regulatory, attention due to the fact that they are favoured by criminals and scammers and used as the requested means of payment for **ransomware** attacks and similar.

Figure 5.7 Meme coins. © 2024 Neira Jones.

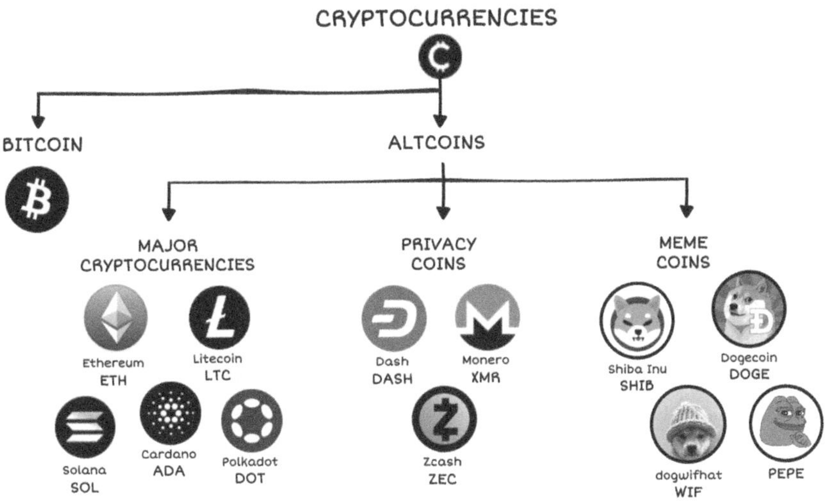

Figure 5.8 Cryptocurrencies. © 2024 Neira Jones.

I offer Figure 5.8 as a potential classification of cryptocurrencies based on volumes traded and market capitalisation at the time of writing. This is of course a stake in the ground, and those familiar with the industry mainly argue that many tokens/coins are missing. I didn't include prominent tokens you may be familiar with because their primary purpose is different (e.g. USDT), and these will be covered in the following sections. Hopefully, all will make sense as you read on.

How are cryptocurrencies created?

New cryptocurrencies can be created in several ways, and they may start with utility or governance properties, and you're already familiar with the mechanisms, which include:

- **Creating a new blockchain**: (see Chapter 2, *Building a blockchain from scratch*), such as with Bitcoin and Ethereum.
- **Forking an existing blockchain**: (see Chapter 3, *An introduction to blockchain forks*), such as with Bitcoin Cash (BCH) a fork of Bitcoin, and Ethereum Classic (ETC), a fork of Ethereum.
- **Creating tokens on existing blockchains**: here, developers may create new tokens using smart contract-capable blockchains like Ethereum or EVM-compatible blockchains. These tokens use the existing blockchain's infrastructure, and for this to work, the token must be developed using the specific token standard for that blockchain (e.g. ERC-20 for Ethereum). Examples are Chainlink (LINK), Tether (USDT), and Uniswap (UNI). Developers may also use blockchains that support token development natively without the need for smart contracts such as with Cardano [e.g. World Mobile Token (WMT), MELD], Algorand with Yieldly (YLDY), and Algomint (goETH, goBTC) (see Chapter 2, *Token development*).
- **Layer-2 solutions**: (see Chapter 1, *Layer 2 scaling solutions*) As Layer 2 solutions are built on top of existing blockchains to improve scalability or add functionality, they may introduce new tokens within their ecosystem, such as with Polygon (MATIC), Optimism (OP), and Arbitrum (ARB).

New cryptocurrencies can be created through various methods, including developing new blockchains, forking existing ones, creating tokens on existing platforms, and building Layer-2 solutions. Each method has its own technical requirements and considerations, and the choice depends on the project's goals and desired features.

Recap on cryptocurrencies

Professionals should remember a few things about cryptocurrencies:

- **Volatility**: cryptocurrencies are known for extreme price fluctuations, making them high-risk investments.
- **Regulatory challenges**: the regulatory landscape for cryptocurrencies varies globally and is still evolving, creating uncertainty for users and investors.
- **Security concerns**: whilst blockchain technology is secure, cryptocurrency exchanges and wallets can be vulnerable to hacks and theft (see Chapter 6, *Transacting in a decentralised world*).
- **Scalability issues**: many cryptocurrencies face challenges in handling large transaction volumes efficiently.
- **Environmental impact**: PoW cryptocurrencies like Bitcoin's BTC have been criticised for their high energy consumption.
- **Adoption hurdles**: widespread adoption for everyday transactions remains limited.
- **Technological complexity**: the technical nature of cryptocurrencies can be a barrier for many potential users.
- **Market manipulation**: the cryptocurrency market is susceptible to manipulation due to its relatively small size and lack of regulation (see Figure 5.4).
- **Interoperability**: different cryptocurrencies often operate on separate networks, limiting their ability to interact with each other.
- **Privacy concerns**: whilst offering some level of anonymity, most cryptocurrencies are not fully private, and transactions can potentially be traced. Privacy coins were designed to address this concern.

Cryptocurrencies offer new ways to store and transfer value, but they come with a unique set of challenges and considerations that must be addressed as the industry continues to evolve. Understanding the various types of cryptocurrencies and their respective roles within the broader ecosystem is crucial for anyone looking to navigate this rapidly changing landscape.

Non-fungible tokens (NFTs)

What is an NFT?

A non-fungible token (NFT) is a type of crypto-asset that represents ownership or proof of authenticity of a unique item or piece of content, often digital in nature. Unlike fungible tokens such as BTC or ETH, which are identical and can be exchanged on a one-to-one basis, NFTs are unique and cannot be exchanged on a like-for-like basis. NFTs are typically used to represent digital art, collectibles, music, videos, and other digital assets, ensuring provenance and ownership through blockchain technology. The most popular blockchain for NFTs is Ethereum, using the ERC-721 and ERC-1155 token standards (also used by Ethereum Virtual Machine (EVM)-compatible blockchains). NFTs have gained significant attention for their potential to revolutionise the digital content and art markets, despite debates over their environmental impact and speculative nature.

This definition highlights the unique nature of NFTs and their role in the digital economy. NFTs have emerged as a new way to own, trade, and monetise digital assets, offering a level of authenticity and provenance previously difficult to achieve in the digital realm.

Now, you're probably wondering how NFTs can "represent" any kind of unique asset, and that's a legitimate question. What we first have to understand is that whilst an NFT "represents" the asset, it is not the asset in and by itself. This representation is achieved through a process called **minting** whereby NFTs are created and where the NFT information is recorded on a blockchain (essentially making this a form of tokenisation).

When an NFT is minted, its information is validated (e.g. owner, ownership history, description, link, etc.), a new block is added to the chain in the usual way (see Chapter 1, *How are transactions validated and settled?*), and the token is created. Each token has an owner, and ownership and transferability are usually managed through smart contracts. Even if 1,000 NFTs of the same item are minted, each token is unique and distinguishable from all the others, a bit like limited edition prints of an original painting, or tickets to an event or a film, as shown in Figure 5.9.

Figure 5.9 Minting an NFT. © 2024 Neira Jones.

Whilst Ethereum and EVM-compatible blockchains are the most popular for NFTs, other blockchains enable NFT creation (e.g. Tezos with TZIP-12). These NFT standards enable features such as copyright, ownership, royalties, transaction history, etc.

So, in a nutshell, an NFT records who owns a digital item and its history, but it doesn't store the item itself.

BOX 5.2 CREATING AN NFT

Creating (aka **minting**) NFTs involves several steps, often using blockchain platforms that support smart contracts. The first step will of course be to choose a blockchain, and the most popular blockchain for NFTs is Ethereum, but other blockchains like Binance Chain, Flow, and Tezos also support NFT creation, as well as Bitcoin with Ordinals.

The second step will be to choose a token standard, and here, developers will use specific token standards to create NFTs. The most common standards are ERC-721 and ERC 1155 for Ethereum and EVM-compatible blockchains (see Chapter 2, *Token development*).

Minting an NFT involves creating a new token on the blockchain. This process includes:

- **Metadata**: adding metadata to the token, which includes details about the asset, such as its name, description, and a link to the digital file if required.
- **Smart contract**: deploying a smart contract that governs the NFT's properties and behaviour, such as transferability and royalties (see Chapter 2, *Building blockchain applications*).
- **Marketplace listing**: once minted, NFTs can be listed on various marketplaces for sale or auction. Popular NFT marketplaces include OpenSea, Rarible, and Foundation. (see Chapter 6 for more details).

Visa produced a good white paper on creating NFTs.[31]

What do you actually own?

Good question. When you browse for NFTs, you could very well right-click on the image and download the JPEG… This very fact generated a lot of scepticism and puzzlement. The token holder might have paid a serious amount of money for that NFT you just downloaded.

And yes, this is a minefield, and I won't even try to explain what can be copyrighted or not (I'm not sure I even can!), but Professor Bryan Frye at the University of Kentucky wrote the excellent and eminently readable "Are CryptoPunks Copyrightable?"[32] if you want to delve further into the subject. And if you want a full account of the legal implications, The Cambridge Handbook of Law and Policy for NFTs, edited by Nizan Geslevich Packin,[33] gives a comprehensive account.

Note from the author: the way I look at it is that NFTs are good for digital creators as, from what I observe, they usually retain copyright and reproduction rights. The creator can sell their original artwork as an NFT, but they can also sell "prints" afterwards, and because NFTs rely on smart contracts, they can be programmed to pay royalties to the creator for each sale. The NFT holder owns the original digital artwork, and as far as I can tell, all this gives them is "bragging rights" and, overtime, if the artwork's appreciates in value, they could make a lot of money by reselling it (of course, the reverse is also true as the price is demand driven).

Evolution and use cases

It all started in 2012–2013 with the creation of Bitcoin-based coloured coins representing a tiny fraction of a BTC that could represent ownership of real-world assets on the blockchain. Although this concept remained mostly theoretical, it laid the groundwork for future developments of such digital tokens.[34]

In May 2014, the first NFT, "Quantum", was minted by digital artist Kevin McCoy on the Namecoin blockchain (the first fork of the Bitcoin blockchain in 2011) and this marked the beginning of NFTs, although it didn't gain widespread attention at the time.[35] Sotheby's sold Quantum for $1.47 million in 2021 as the first of its kind.[36] The Bitcoin blockchain was however never designed for recording asset ownership, and Ethereum later became the home of NFTs.

The craze really started in 2017, where notable projects emerged, starting with CryptoPunks, a collection of 10,000 unique pixelated characters, and CryptoKitties, a blockchain game that allowed players to breed and trade (cute) virtual cats. The hype continued in 2021, a year generally acknowledged as the NFT Boom, where the COVID-19 pandemic was a significant driver for digital activity. During this period and through 2022, we saw new popular NFT collections, such as Art Blocks, VeeFriends, Bored Ape Yacht Club (BAYC), Pudgy Penguins, Mutant Ape Yacht Club, and Azuki, as illustrated in Figure 5.10.

Figure 5.10 Popular NFT collections. © 2024 Neira Jones.

Two of the most significant NFT events happened in 2021, both involving digital artist Beeple. In October 2020, Beeple sold the NFT of a 10-second video depicting a giant Donald Trump collapsed on the ground, with his body covered in slogans and set in an otherwise idyllic landscape, for $67,000 to Miami-based art collector Pablo Rodriguez-Fraile. Fraile sold the NFT in February 2021 for $6.6 million[37] (yes, you read that right). Then, in March 2021, Beeple's digital artwork "Everydays: The First 5000 Days", a digital collage consisting of 5,000 images created daily by Beeple over more than 13 years, sold for $69 million at Christie's auction house,[38] highlighting the potential of NFTs in the art world and attracting significant attention from both artists and investors.

Following the 2021 boom, the NFT market continued to evolve and diversify. New platforms and standards emerged on various blockchains beyond Ethereum, including Cardano, Solana, Flow, and Tezos. These blockchains developed their own NFT platforms and standards to support the growing demand for unique digital assets. NFT applications expanded beyond digital art:

- **Collectibles**: NFTs are popular in the world of digital collectibles, where they can represent unique items such as virtual trading cards, in-game assets, and more. Examples include NBA Top Shot,[39] which allows fans to buy, sell, and trade officially licensed NBA collectible highlights, and Axie Infinity,[40] a game where players collect and battle with cute fantasy creatures called Axies.
- **Music and entertainment**: artists are using NFTs to sell unique digital content, such as exclusive tracks, albums, and concert tickets. Kings of Leon released their album "When You See Yourself" as an NFT, offering special perks to buyers.[41]
- **Virtual real estate**: NFTs are used to represent ownership of virtual land and properties in digital worlds. Platforms like Decentraland and The Sandbox allow users to buy, sell, and develop virtual real estate using NFTs.
- **Domain names**: NFTs can represent ownership of blockchain-based domain names, providing a decentralised alternative to traditional domain name systems. Examples include Ethereum Name Service (ENS) and Unstoppable Domains. 2023 brought further innovation with the launch of **Ordinals**,[42] a project that leveraged the 2021 Bitcoin

Taproot soft fork[43] (see Chapter 3, *An introduction to blockchain forks*) to create NFTs on the Bitcoin blockchain. This development showcased the ongoing experimentation and expansion of NFTs across different blockchain ecosystems.

A **Bitcoin Ordinal** is a unique digital asset created by attaching data to individual Satoshis (see Chapter 4, Table 4.10) on the Bitcoin blockchain. They share similarities with traditional NFTs, representing unique, tradable digital items like art or collectibles. However, Ordinals differ in key ways: they're native to the Bitcoin blockchain, store data directly on chain, and don't require a separate token standard. Unlike many NFTs, Ordinals don't use smart contracts, as Bitcoin's scripting capabilities are more limited than platforms like Ethereum. This makes Ordinals simpler but less programmable, leveraging Bitcoin's security and decentralisation for digital assets in a more straightforward manner.

Some Bitcoin community members object to Ordinals primarily due to scalability concerns. Critics argue that Ordinals increase block sizes, potentially causing network congestion and higher fees. There are also concerns about deviating from Bitcoin's core function as a currency and the long-term impact of storing non-financial data on the blockchain. These objections reflect the ongoing debate about balancing innovation with preserving Bitcoin's original vision and functionality.

What now?

As always, markets move on. The initial hype was followed by market consolidation. Dapper Labs, Larva Labs, and Yuga Labs are prominent brands in the NFT space, each known for their NFT collections. Dapper Labs, founded in 2018, created CryptoKitties and developed the Flow blockchain. At its peak in December 2017, some rare CryptoKitties sold for over \$100,000, with one fetching \$170,000. However, by 2024, the average price had plummeted to around \$70 (and the lowest price at about \$5), with weekly trading volumes of only about \$4,470. Dapper Labs has faced significant challenges since its initial success. The company underwent multiple rounds of layoffs, with 51 staff members let go in July 2023, following previous cuts in November 2022 and February 2023. These reductions came amidst a prolonged downturn in the NFT market, with NBA Top Shot experiencing a dramatic decrease in sales volume and user activity since its peak in early 2021. Dapper Labs also faced legal troubles, including a Security and Exchanges Commission (SEC) investigation and a class-action lawsuit over NBA Top Shot Moments, which they settled for $4 million in 2024.[44]

Larva Labs, established in 2005, gained fame for creating the CryptoPunks and Meebits collections. At their height in 2021, some CryptoPunks sold for millions, with CryptoPunk #7523 fetching $11.8 million.[45] At the time of writing, the lowest price (aka floor price) for a CryptoPunk is around 15.8 ETH (approximately $51,000).

On March 11, 2022, Yuga Labs, known for the Bored Ape Yacht Club (BAYC), acquired the intellectual property rights of CryptoPunks and Meebits from Larva Labs. This acquisition included all IP, trademarks, copyrights, and NFT holdings related to these projects. Yuga Labs subsequently granted commercial rights to individual token holders of both CryptoPunks and Meebits. BAYC NFTs saw their peak in April 2022, with a floor price of around 150 ETH (over $400,000 at the time). However, by 2024, the floor price had dropped to about ten to 15 ETH (approximately $30,000–$45,000), representing a decline of over 90% from its peak.

Caveat emptor.

Commercial use cases

You might think NFTs are just a bit of fun, or something reserved for the more speculative minds among us, but there are some notable use cases:

- **Adidas** started experiencing with NFTs to expand **brand engagement** and launched their "Into the Metaverse" collection of 30,000 NFTs in December 2021, which sold out within hours of launch and made $22 million at the time. The NFTs would grant holders early access to exclusive physical products and virtual experiences. Adidas continues to be involved with NFT and launched several NFT collections since (14 of them), for which there is a secondary market on various NFT marketplaces (e.g. OpenSea). Their latest collection, ALTS by Adidas, launched in April 2023, and has a floor price of 0.073 ETH (~$3,200) at the time of writing. Holders of the original "Into the Metaverse" tokens can burn them in exchange for the new ones, only paying for gas fees, giving them access to new perks. At the time of writing, the collection is still going.[46]

- **Visa** explored NFTs since 2021, where they acquired CryptoPunk #7610 for approximately $150,000,[47] signalling their endorsement of NFTs, and their intent to understand the infrastructure required for brands to purchase, store, and leverage NFTs. They since launched the Visa Creator Program to **support artists, musicians, fashion designers, and filmmakers**[48] with educational resources and community access. In addition, Visa partnered with crypto payment processor Moonpay[49] to enable NFT purchases using Visa cards, allowing users to buy NFTs directly with their Visa credit or debit cards, **simplifying the purchasing process** for those unfamiliar with cryptocurrency transactions.
- In June 2022, **Mastercard** announced partnerships with several NFT marketplaces[50] and exchanges[51] to enable cardholders to purchase NFTs directly using their Mastercard, without needing to buy cryptocurrency first. This initiative aimed to **simplify the NFT purchasing process**, making it more accessible to a broader audience and integrating it into mainstream financial services. In April 2023, Mastercard, in partnership with Polygon, launched a free limited-edition Mastercard Music Pass NFT as the key to unlock their Mastercard Artist Accelerator programme. The Web 3 platform gives free access to educational materials, unique AI tools, and experiences to boost creativity for music artists. Mastercard stated that their Web 3 investments led to a positive impact on revenue, especially among Gen Z audiences who showed a preference for selecting Mastercard when making purchasing decisions.
- In November 2022, **Macy's** launched its third NFT collection tied to its annual Thanksgiving Day Parade[52] to **extend the reach of its traditional event to a new younger, digitally savvy audience**. This collection included 10,000 free NFTs, each featuring parade-themed artwork, which were distributed on a first-come, first-served basis. 9,500 NFTs were made available to the public and 500 reserved for Macy's employees. Previous years' NFT holders were given early access to the new collection in a wish to engage customers digitally and create a new tradition around the iconic parade. The initiative lent support to Make-A-Wish[53] by donating 10% of every NFT sale.

- In September 2022, **Starbucks** launched their Web-3-based **loyalty programme**, Starbucks Odyssey, to a selected group of waitlist members, including employees and customers.[54] This program combines the existing Starbucks Rewards with NFT collecting and gamified elements where members can engage in interactive "Journeys" to earn "Journey Stamps" (NFTs) and "Odyssey Points," which unlock new benefits and experiences. These experiences range from virtual coffee-making classes to exclusive events and trips to Starbucks roasteries and coffee farms. Starbucks has two types of NFTs: activity-based NFTs and limited-edition NFTs. Members may earn activity-based NFTs (i.e. the equivalent of a "stamp" on a traditional loyalty card) by completing various activities, such as playing virtual games or participating in coffee-related challenges. These NFTs offer benefits like bonus points, access to coffee-making courses, or invitations to exclusive events, all based on stamp rarity, essentially making activity-based NFTs a kind of "utility NFT" (see Chapter 3, *Utility tokens*). Limited-edition NFTs aim to attract collectors and can be purchased by members using credit cards but are also sold on secondary markets (e.g. NFT marketplaces). Starbucks Odyssey could have significant implications for loyalty programmes across industries.[55]
- In March 2023, the online site of luxury South Korean department store **Shinsegae**, **SSG.com**, began issuing digital guarantees minted as NFTs for luxury products.[56] These NFTs provide blockchain warranties for luxury items, giving customers additional peace of mind regarding authenticity. These digital warranties, sent to the customer's smart phone, help **fight counterfeit goods** and include detailed information including the item's serial number, product history, and warranty period.

After the crypto market crash following the Terra/Luna collapse (see Box 5.4) and the FTX (Futures Exchange) demise[57](see Chapter 6, *The FTX scandal*), NFTs fell out of favour, but it seems that they experienced a revival in 2024, with new use cases emerging.[58]

NFT coins

NFT coins emerged during the explosive growth of the NFT market in 2021 and were developed to facilitate transactions within NFT ecosystems, allowing users to buy, sell, and trade NFTs. Unlike NFTs, NFT coins are fungible, and their primary purpose is to serve as the utility, governance, or hybrid token for specific NFT platforms. As such, they are not a new category of token (e.g. utility, governance), but they are operational tokens specific to NFT ecosystems.

The earliest notable example came in 2018 with Web 3 game **Axie Infinity** and their **AXS** (Axie Infinity Shards) and **SLP** (Smooth Love Potion) tokens. Together, these tokens form the backbone of Axie Infinity's Play-to-Earn (P2E) model, allowing players to earn cryptocurrency through gameplay, participate in governance, and engage in various economic activities within and outside the game ecosystem (e.g. trading on exchanges, providing liquidity using AXS or SLP). AXS is a governance token with a capped supply of 270 million, used for voting on game decisions, staking, and some in-game transactions. AXS is designed for long-term value appreciation. SLP, conversely, is a utility token with an unlimited supply primarily used for breeding Axies (see Figure 5.6). Players earn SLP through gameplay, and it's continuously minted and burned to manage supply (see Chapter 4, *Tokenomics and metrics*). Both tokens can be traded on exchanges, allowing players to convert in-game earnings to real-world value. The key differences are in their supply dynamics, governance roles, and primary in-game functions.

Since then, many NFT tokens appeared, with varying functionality: GALA (Gala Games, 2020), IMX (ImmutableX, 2021), FLUF (FLUF World, 2021), ApeCoin (Bored Ape Yacht Club, 2022). (Note from the author: in 2022, 25-year-old NFT collector Nathan Head earned $75,000 the day of the ApeCoin airdrop after selling the 10,950 tokens he received.[59] At the time, ApeCoin was trading at around $6.80 per token. As of July 2024, ApeCoin traded at around $0.78.)

Other notable NFT coins include those launched by Web 3 platforms such as MANA (Decentraland, 2017); SAND (The Sandbox, 2020); and NFT marketplaces, such as RARI (Rarible, 2020), RARE (SuperRare, 2021), LOOKS (LooksRare, 2022), X2Y2 (X2Y2, 2022), and BLUR (Blur, 2023). (Note from the author: it's worth noting that OpenSea, despite being one of the largest NFT marketplace, has chosen, at the time of writing, not to issue its own token. This sets it apart from many of its competitors who have used token launches as a way to incentivise usage and distribute governance rights to their users.)

NFT coins are primarily operational tokens (utility or governance) aimed to support the growing NFT ecosystem, whilst also being traded on exchanges (in the hope of value appreciation). A word of warning, there is confusion with the term "NFT coin" and misuse of terminology is common: some may refer to cryptocurrencies used to purchase NFTs (e.g. ETH) to refer to cryptocurrencies commonly used to buy NFTs; others might incorrectly use "NFT coin" when they mean an actual NFT. Context is important.

In any instance, as the NFT space continues to evolve, they have the potential to play a role in shaping the future of digital ownership and asset management.

Considerations for NFTs

Professionals and enthusiasts should be aware of several considerations when dealing with NFTs:

- **Volatility**: like other crypto-assets, NFTs can be highly volatile, with prices subject to rapid fluctuations based on market demand and speculation.
- **Environmental impact**: the minting and transaction processes for NFTs were originally considered resource intensive. But since Ethereum's transition to PoS, and Ethereum's dominance for NFTs, this concern seems to have been alleviated for now. Bitcoin Ordinals and similar NFT-like assets on PoW blockchains may still be an issue.
- **Regulatory challenges**: the regulatory landscape for NFTs is still evolving, with potential implications for intellectual property rights, taxation, and securities laws.
- **Security concerns**: whilst blockchain technology provides a degree of security, NFTs are still vulnerable to theft, fraud, and losses if not properly managed. Additionally, third-party services, smart contracts, and applications associated with NFTs can also be susceptible to vulnerabilities.
- **Market manipulation**: the NFT market can be susceptible to manipulation, including **wash trading** and price inflation by creators or collectors.
- **Interoperability**: different blockchains and platforms may have varying levels of interoperability, affecting the transfer and use of NFTs across ecosystems.

- **Adoption hurdles**: despite growing interest, mainstream adoption of NFTs faces challenges, including technical complexity and public scepticism.

NFTs represent a significant innovation in the digital asset space, offering new ways to own, trade, and monetise digital content. However, they come with unique challenges and considerations that must be addressed as the market matures. Understanding the various applications and implications of NFTs is crucial for anyone looking to understand this fast-paced digital environment.

Stablecoins

A **stablecoin** is a type of cryptocurrency designed to maintain a stable value by pegging its value to a reserve of assets, such as fiat currencies or commodities. This stability reduces the volatility typically associated with cryptocurrencies, making stablecoins suitable for transactions and as a medium of exchange in the digital economy. They can be backed by fiat, other cryptocurrencies, commodities, or use algorithms to manage supply and demand.

Stablecoins are a type of cryptocurrency that were initially designed to address the volatility risks associated with traditional cryptocurrencies. The concept of stablecoins was first introduced in 2014, with Tether (USDT) being one of the earliest examples. The stablecoin market has grown significantly since then, expanding from a market capitalisation of less than $1 billion in 2017 to over $170 billion at the time of writing, driven by the growing adoption of blockchain technology, smart contracts, and DeFi applications.

The main characteristics of stablecoins are:

- **Price stability and store of value**: stablecoins are designed to maintain stable prices by pegging their values to underlying assets through careful tokenomic design. As such, stablecoins are not speculative instruments.
- **Accessibility and storage**: stablecoins are accessible to anyone with an internet connection.

- **Geography agnostic**: stablecoins have no geographical boundary limitations.
- **Smart contract integration**: stablecoins can engage with smart contracts in the blockchain ecosystem.
- **Lower costs on cross-border transfers**: stablecoin can facilitate international transfers without foreign exchange (FX) fees, potentially lowering costs when compared to traditional banking.

There are four main types of stablecoins:

- **Fiat-collateralised stablecoins**: these are backed by reserves of traditional fiat currencies, such as the US dollar or the British pound. The issuer holds the reserves in a bank account or custody service and the ratio of fiat to stablecoin should be 1:1 (the hard peg), which should ensure that the value of the stablecoin is pegged to the underlying fiat currency at all times.
- **Commodity-collateralised stablecoins**: these are backed by reserves of tangible assets, such as gold or silver (but may be real estate or other tangible assets). The issuer holds a certain quantity of the commodity in reserve for each stablecoin in circulation.
- **Crypto-collateralised stablecoins**: these are backed by reserves of other cryptocurrencies, such as BTC or ETH. These stablecoins use smart contracts to lock in cryptocurrency stock and the ratio of cryptocurrency to stablecoin is usually over-collateralised (e.g. 2:1) to account for the volatility of the underlying cryptocurrency.
- **Algorithmic stablecoins**: these are not backed by fiat, commodity, or cryptocurrency collateral, rather, they use algorithms and smart contracts to achieve price stability through minting (when the price goes up) and burning (when the price goes down). They use a fiat currency, usually the US dollar, as a benchmark, and this is referred to as a "soft peg".

The classification given in Figure 5.11 is what most blockchain enthusiasts will recognise, however, the innovative nature of DeFi has led to the emergence of hybrid models and new types, of which "synthetic stablecoins" are a prime example. The latter are not backed by fiat, commodities, or other cryptocurrencies, and whilst they use algorithms for price stabilisation, their mechanisms differ significantly from algorithmic stablecoins. New types of stablecoins continue to emerge as developers continue to explore algorithmic mechanisms.

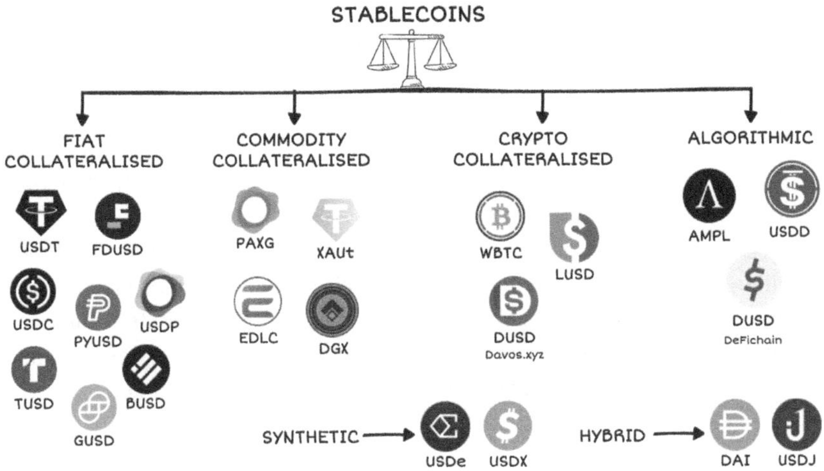

Figure 5.11 Main types of stablecoins. © 2024 Neira Jones.

On **collateralisation and pegs**. I will use the terms "collateralisation" and "peg" quite a lot in this section, so let's clarify them.

Collateralisation: in the context of stablecoins, collateralisation refers to the practice of backing the value of a stablecoin with reserve assets. These assets can be fiat currencies, cryptocurrencies, or other valuable commodities. For example, fiat-collateralised stablecoins are backed by fiat currencies held in reserve. Crypto-collateralised stablecoins often employ over-collateralisation, where the value of the collateral exceeds the value of the stablecoins issued. This approach provides a buffer against the high volatility of cryptocurrencies, ensuring the stablecoin maintains its peg even during significant price fluctuations of the crypto collateral. Collateralisation is measured by the "collateralisation ratio" expressed as "collateral:stablecoin", such as "1:1" (used for fiat-backed stablecoins), or, for example, "1.5:1" (over-collateralised). The processes of minting and burning are integral to maintaining this balance (see Chapter 4, *Tokenomics and metrics*).

Peg: a peg refers to the fixed exchange rate between a stablecoin and its target asset. Stablecoins can have either a "hard peg" or a "soft peg". A hard peg, as used by fiat-collateralised stablecoins, maintains a strict 1:1 collateralisation ratio with the target asset. For instance, USDT, a fiat-backed stablecoin, aims to maintain a hard peg of 1 USDT = 1 USD. A soft peg, often employed by algorithmic or crypto-backed stablecoins, allows for slight fluctuations around the target value. These stablecoins use algorithms or collateral management systems to adjust supply and demand, aiming to keep the price close to the peg. The minting and burning processes are also critical here; stablecoins may mint new coins when the price is above the peg and burn coins when the price is below the peg to stabilise the value.

Understanding collateralisation and pegs is crucial for grasping how different types of stablecoins maintain their stability. Whilst collateralisation provides backing for the stablecoin's value, the peg determines its target price. These mechanisms work together with the intent of creating a more stable digital asset in the volatile cryptocurrency market.

The next sections will explore the main types of stablecoins with prominent examples (i.e. where substantial market capitalisation exists).

Fiat-collateralised stablecoins

Fiat-collateralised stablecoins are the most common type, where each token is backed by an equivalent amount of fiat currency held in reserve (a 1:1 collateralisation ratio). This model seeks to provide a high degree of stability by directly linking the stablecoin's value to a well-established national currency. Fiat-collateralised stablecoins are **typically centralised**, as they rely on a trusted custodian to hold the fiat reserves backing the stablecoin. This centralisation is necessary to ensure the integrity of the peg and to prevent fraudulent issuance of tokens. However, it also introduces counterparty risks and potential regulatory challenges. This was famously evidenced in March 2023 by the collapse of Silicon Valley Bank (SVB) in the first major bank run fuelled and accelerated by social media.[60] Before its collapse, SVB was a custodian of several crypto businesses and stablecoins. Pantera Capital, a prominent crypto-focused venture capital firm, listed SVB as one of its custodians alongside BitGo and Coinbase's custodial service. Additionally, SVB provided business banking services to a significant number of crypto firms, including Circle, the issuer of the stablecoin USDC. Circle had \$3.3 billion deposited with SVB, which represented about 8% of the reserves backing USDC, causing it to lose its peg to the US dollar.[61] SVB was also known for its crypto-friendly stance, serving various digital asset firms, and contributing to the broader crypto ecosystem.[62]

Prominent examples of fiat-backed stablecoins include:

- **USDT**: issued by Tether Limited, USDT is pegged to the USD and has the largest trading volume among stablecoin offerings. However, Tether has faced controversy regarding its reserves. On 15 October 2021, Tether was fined $41 million by the US Commodity Futures Trading Commission (CFTC) for deceiving consumers about its reserves.[63] Specifically, Tether claimed to maintain "100% reserves at all times" but failed to disclose that a significant portion of these reserves were not held in cash and included unsecured receivables and other non-fiat assets.
- **USDC**: issued by Circle, USDC is fully backed by assets in reserve and exchangeable for USD on a 1:1 basis. Whilst USDC has generally been seen as a more transparent and regulated stablecoin compared to its competitors, it has not been entirely without controversy. In March 2023, USDC briefly lost its peg to the US dollar following the collapse of SVB,[64] where a significant portion of Circle's reserves were held, raising concerns about the stability and risk management of USDC. Like other cryptocurrencies, USDC has faced increasing regulatory scrutiny and although it has been more transparent about its reserves than some other stablecoins, questions have been raised about the specific composition of those reserves and their liquidity.[65] The US SEC has classified some stablecoins, including USDC, as securities, which could have significant implications for the industry.
- **FDUSD**: issued by First Digital Trust, First Digital USD (FDUSD) is pegged to the US dollar and aims to provide a stable and secure digital currency option. FDUSD is designed to maintain a 1:1 reserve ratio with the US dollar, ensuring that each token is backed by one dollar in reserve. First Digital Trust emphasises transparency and regular audits to verify the reserves backing FDUSD. The stablecoin is intended to facilitate seamless transactions and provide stability in the volatile cryptocurrency market.
- **PYUSD**: Paypal is the issuer of PYUSD, but they partnered with Paxos Trust Company to issue the stablecoin, whilst PayPal is the primary entity responsible for its development, marketing, and integration into

its platform. PYUSD is fully backed by US dollar deposits, short-term US Treasury bonds, and similar cash equivalents, maintaining a 1:1 reserve ratio. The stablecoin is subject to regulatory oversight by the New York Department of Financial Services (NYDFS) and emphasises transparency through monthly reserve reports and third-party audits.

- **TUSD (TrueUSD)**: issued by TrustToken, TUSD is pegged to the US dollar and aims to provide a transparent and reliable stablecoin option. TUSD maintains a 1:1 reserve ratio with the US dollar, with its reserves held in FDIC-insured bank accounts. The stablecoin undergoes regular audits to verify its backing and emphasises real-time attestation of its reserves. TUSD is designed to facilitate seamless transactions in the cryptocurrency ecosystem whilst maintaining stability and trust.
- **GUSD (Gemini Dollar)**: issued by the Gemini Trust, founded by Cameron and Tyler Winklevoss, who also operates the Gemini cryptocurrency exchange. GUSD is pegged 1:1 to the US dollar and backed by funds held by State Street Bank. GUSD has generally been regarded as a stablecoin with a strong track record of maintaining its 1:1 peg. Gemini Trust seems to have adhered to strict regulatory standards and has regularly undergone audits to ensure the backing of GUSD.
- **USDP (Pax Dollar)**: issued by Paxos Trust Company, USDP is fully backed by US dollar reserves, including cash and cash equivalents, maintaining a 1:1 reserve ratio. The stablecoin is regulated by the New York State Department of Financial Services (NYSDFS) and undergoes monthly attestations to verify its reserves.
- **BUSD (Binance USD)**: a 1:1 USD-backed stable coin issued by Binance (in partnership with Paxos) and regulated by the NYSDFS. Launched on 5 September 2019, BUSD only lasted until February 2023 as Paxos Trust Company was ordered by the NYSDFS to stop minting BUSD. The NYSDFS found issues with Paxos' due diligence and oversight processes with Binance, as well as with their monitoring and reporting obligations. Investors were encouraged to convert their tokens to other stablecoins.[66]

Note from the author: Paxos is unique in its role as a stablecoin issuer. Not only do they issue their own token Pax Dollar (USDP), but they also issue tokens on behalf of other entities, such as Paypal for PYUSD, and Binance with BUSD. The practice of a regulated entity like Paxos issuing stablecoins for other companies is not common in the industry. Think of is as "Stablecoin-Issuing-as-a-Service". With this model, Paxos issues stablecoins for others, whilst maintaining regulatory compliance and reserve management. As a parallel, this is a bit like a **BIN sponsorship** arrangement in the cards world.

Commodity-collateralised stablecoins

Commodity-collateralised stablecoins are backed by tangible assets, primarily precious metals like gold or silver. This approach aims to provide a store of value that is independent of government-issued currencies. However, the valuation of **commodities** can fluctuate, and the physical storage and management of these assets introduce operational complexities. Similar to fiat-collateralised stablecoins, commodity-collateralised stablecoins often **exhibit a degree of centralisation** due to the need for secure storage and management of the underlying commodities. Whilst the physical nature of these assets can provide a tangible backing, the centralisation inherent in their custody can impact the overall decentralisation of the system.

These stablecoins use blockchain technology to create a digital representation of ownership in precious metals, primarily gold. Primarily operating on the Ethereum network as ERC-20 tokens (although there are other implementations), they seamlessly integrate into the broader crypto ecosystem. They provide investors with a practical way to access commodity markets whilst ensuring transparency through regular audits. The assets are stored securely in reputable vaults, and many of these stablecoins are regulated by financial authorities, which enhances their trustworthiness.

The following are prominent examples of commodity-collateralised stablecoins by market capitalisation at the time of writing:

- **PAXG (Paxos Gold)**: issued by Paxos Trust Company, PAXG is a gold-backed cryptocurrency pegged to the price of one fine troy ounce of a London Good Delivery gold bar. Each PAXG token represents ownership of physical gold stored in Brink's vaults in London. PAXG emphasises transparency through regular audits and is regulated by the NYSDFS.
- **XAUt (Tether Gold)**: issued by TG Commodities Limited, XAUt is a digital asset that represents ownership of one troy fine ounce of physical

gold on a London Good Delivery gold bar. Each XAUt token corresponds to a specific allocated gold bar, identifiable by a unique serial number.

- **EDLC (Edelcoin)**: issued by Edelcoin AG, EDLC is a stablecoin backed by a diversified basket of precious and base metals, including copper and nickel. This unique hybrid token is designed to provide stability and minimise volatility, serving as a reliable store of wealth independent of inflationary fiat currencies and monetary policies. Each Edelcoin is over-collateralised by pre-existing metals, with reserves totalling 125% of the actual metal value, ensuring robust backing and security. The reserves undergo regular independent verification and transparent disclosure. Issued as an ERC-20 token on the Ethereum blockchain, Edelcoin is also planned for expansion to additional EVM-compatible chains and is tradable on both centralised and decentralised crypto exchanges, enhancing its accessibility and liquidity.
- **DGX (Digix)**: issued by DigixGlobal, DGX is a gold-backed cryptocurrency where each token represents 1 gram of 99.99% London Bullion Market Association (LBMA) standard gold. The physical gold backing the tokens is stored in secure vaults in Singapore and Canada, with custodians that are fully insured members of the Bullion Association.

Crypto-collateralised stablecoins

Crypto-collateralised stablecoins can **range from semi-centralised to decentralised**, depending on the governance structure and management of the collateral. Whilst the underlying cryptocurrencies are typically decentralised, the platforms or protocols used to manage the collateral and issue stablecoins can introduce elements of centralisation. As the value of the underlying cryptocurrencies can fluctuate, the complex mechanisms involved in maintaining over-collateralisation and managing **liquidation risks** can introduce operational challenges potentially impacting stability, and challenges related to security and scalability remain.

There are very few examples of pure crypto-backed stablecoins, but prominent examples include:

- **WBTC (Wrapped Bitcoin)**: issued by BitGo, WBTC is an ERC-20 token soft pegged 1:1 to BTC on the Ethereum blockchain. It aims to bring

BTC's liquidity to the Ethereum ecosystem, enabling BTC holders to participate in DeFi applications. WBTC is fully backed by BTC, with proof of reserves published daily. The minting and burning processes are transparent and verifiable on chain, enhancing trust in the token's backing.

- **LUSD (Liquidity USD)**: issued by the Liquity Protocol, LUSD is an ERC-20 stablecoin soft-pegged 1:1 to the US dollar on the Ethereum blockchain. It aims to provide a decentralised, over-collateralised stablecoin backed solely by ETH. LUSD is minted when users deposit ETH as collateral into Liquity's smart contract-based "Troves", with a minimum collateralisation ratio of 110%. The protocol is governance free and censorship resistant, with no admin keys or centralised control. LUSD's stability is maintained through various mechanisms, including redemptions, liquidations, and the Stability Pool, all of which are transparent and verifiable on chain, enhancing trust in the token's backing and peg.
- **DUSD (Davos.xyz USD)**: issued by the Davos Protocol, DUSD is an omni-chain stablecoin soft pegged 1:1 to the US dollar and operates across multiple blockchains. It aims to provide a decentralised, over-collateralised stablecoin backed by various yield-generating crypto-assets. DUSD is minted when users deposit these assets as collateral into the Davos Protocol's smart contracts, allowing users to retain the rewards and staking advantages of their collateral. DUSD's stability is maintained through mechanisms such as over-collateralisation, arbitrage opportunities, and a reserve pool funded by a portion of the yield from the collateral. These mechanisms are designed to be transparent and verifiable on chain, aiming to enhance trust in the token's backing and peg whilst facilitating various DeFi strategies.

The scarcity of pure crypto-collateralised stablecoins is due to several factors. First is the volatility risk associated with using cryptocurrencies as collateral, which necessitates over-collateralisation to maintain stability (making this capital inefficient). Additionally, managing these stablecoins requires sophisticated risk management and liquidation mechanisms, adding complexity. Secondly, market dominance by fiat-backed stablecoins like USDT and USDC, which offer more perceived stability and easier regulatory compliance, has also contributed to the decline in pure crypto-collateralised stablecoins. Indeed, regulatory scrutiny has further pushed projects towards hybrid models, which combine crypto collateral with other assets and mechanisms to enhance stability and reduce risks.

This is why hybrid models, which offer greater flexibility and stability, are perceived to be more attractive to users and investors. These models can incorporate real-world assets and fiat-backed stablecoins, providing a more balanced approach to managing collaterals and risks. As a result, the stablecoin ecosystem has largely shifted towards fiat-backed, commodity-backed, or hybrid models to address the challenges associated with pure crypto collateralisation.

Algorithmic stablecoins

Arguably the most decentralised, algorithmic stablecoins rely either on mathematical formulas and smart contracts to maintain price stability (via minting and burning, aka seigniorage, see Box 5.3), or on **arbitrage**. They also need oracles (see Chapter 2, *Oracles*) for accurate real-world price data to determine when and how much to mint or burn tokens, as well as to assess broader market conditions that may influence their stabilisation mechanisms.

The benchmark for stability is generally a fiat currency, most likely the US dollar, and this is referred to as a "soft peg" compared to the "hard peg" of a fiat-collateralised stablecoin (i.e. 1:1). By eliminating the need for a centralised authority or collateral, these stablecoins aim to achieve a high degree of autonomy and resistance to censorship. However, the complexity of these algorithms and the potential for unforeseen vulnerabilities have led to high-profile failures, highlighting the risks associated with this approach.

BOX 5.3 SEIGNIORAGE AND ARBITRAGE

Seigniorage determines when to mint and burn tokens to regulate supply based on the stablecoin's price deviation from the peg, how many tokens must be burned to achieve the desired price correction, as well as other parameters such as reserve ratios. Seigniorage is under the control of the stablecoin issuer and implemented through algorithms and is not an immediate process.

Arbitrage is a market-driven process where arbitrageurs (e.g. traders, automated trading bots) capitalise on price differences between exchanges. When a stablecoin's price deviates from its peg, arbitrageurs buy the undervalued token on one exchange and sell it on another where it's overvalued. In essence, the incentive to maintain the peg is not altruistic but purely profit driven, and this rapid market activity helps to stabilise the price almost instantly. Unlike seigniorage, arbitrage occurs naturally without requiring any action from the stablecoin issuer.

Notable algorithmic stablecoins by market capitalisation at the time of writing include:

- **USDD**: issued by Tron DAO on the TRON network, USD Digital (USDD) is a decentralised stablecoin with a soft peg to the US dollar, launched on May 5, 2022. It operates across multiple blockchains, including BNB Chain, Ethereum and TRON. USDD is generated through a mechanism similar to other algorithmic stablecoins, using collateralised debt positions (CDPs) where users can lock cryptocurrencies as collateral. The stablecoin aims to maintain its peg through over-collateralisation and algorithmic adjustments. It faced controversy when it lost its peg in June 2022, dropping as low as 93 cents. This led to concerns that USDD might suffer a fate similar to TerraUSD (UST), which had collapsed dramatically in May 2022. However, USDD is much smaller in scale than UST was, and it aims to be over-collateralised, which may reduce the risk of a total collapse. The project, backed by TRON founder Justin Sun, has offered high annual percentage yields (APY) of up to 30% to attract users, though such high returns may pose risks to the stablecoin's long-term stability. At the time of writing, USDD was maintaining its peg.
- **DUSD (Decentralised USD)**: issued by DeFiChain, DUSD is an algorithmic stablecoin pegged to the US dollar. It is minted by locking cryptocurrencies as collateral in vaults on the DeFiChain network. DUSD employs various mechanisms to maintain its peg, including

over-collateralisation and algorithmic adjustments. Whilst it offers a decentralised stablecoin option, its stability can be influenced by market conditions and the overall health of the DeFiChain ecosystem. At the time of writing, DUSD had been experiencing continuing issues and its price was $0.024.

- **AMPL (Ampleforth)**: issued by the Ampleforth Foundation, AMPL is an algorithmic stablecoin designed to maintain a target price around $1. It uses an elastic supply mechanism that automatically adjusts the total token supply based on market demand. AMPL employs daily rebases to increase or decrease the supply, affecting all holders' balances proportionally. The protocol relies on oracles to provide price data for its supply adjustments. Whilst it aims for price stability, AMPL's value can be influenced by market conditions and the effectiveness of its supply adjustment algorithm. The stability and adoption of AMPL depend on the overall health of its ecosystem and user participation in the rebase mechanism.

Algorithmic stablecoins are technically very interesting, but they present challenges, and one particular event shook the industry.

BOX 5.4 THE CATASTROPHIC COLLAPSE OF TerraUSD

Algorithmic stablecoins entered public consciousness in May 2022 when the $18.7 billion TerraUSD (UST) and its $20 billion backing token Luna experienced a catastrophic collapse. Similar to other algorithmic stablecoins, UST was designed to maintain a 1:1 soft peg with the US dollar, using LUNA as part of its price stabilisation mechanism rather than traditional backing. The protocol allowed users to mint 1 UST by burning $1 worth of LUNA, and conversely, 1 UST could be redeemed for $1 worth of LUNA, creating arbitrage opportunities to help maintain the peg. The supply of LUNA was managed algorithmically, with tokens minted or burned as needed based on market conditions, and oracles monitored the price of the US dollar to ensure stability. This system relied entirely on market confidence in the algorithm and the value of LUNA, which ultimately proved vulnerable. During the period of market stress, the system failed to maintain the peg as it proved vulnerable to a "death spiral" scenario, where a loss of confidence in UST led to massive selling pressure, causing both UST and LUNA to collapse. The collapse was attributed to flaws in the design, such as volatility in Luna, inaccuracies in the price oracle, and high redemption fees, which impeded the price stabilisation mechanism. This had far-reaching consequences.

The failure of UST and Luna erased nearly $60 billion in value within days, affecting thousands of investors, including many retail participants who lost significant portions of their savings.[67] This event triggered a wider sell-off in the cryptocurrency market, exacerbating existing liquidity issues and contributing to a broader crypto market downturn.

The collapse raised serious concerns about the stability and reliability of stablecoins in general, prompting regulators and financial authorities worldwide to scrutinise the crypto sector more closely. The IMF commented on the incident in its Global Financial Stability Report, emphasising the need for comprehensive regulation of crypto-assets. The report stated that "Failures in the crypto space – including the fall of TerraUSD and the FTX debacle – have sparked calls for strengthening countries' policy frameworks for crypto-assets, including by enhanced regulation and supervision".[68]

The **contagion risks** associated with the UST collapse were significant. Other stablecoins, including those backed by traditional assets, experienced temporary deviations from their pegs. For instance, Tether (USDT), the largest stablecoin by market capitalisation, briefly dipped below its $1 peg, causing further market panic, and signalling impending doom for algorithmic stablecoins.[69] This instability in stablecoins, which are crucial for liquidity in the crypto ecosystem, led to increased volatility across various cryptocurrencies.

The aftermath of the UST collapse had lasting effects on the cryptocurrency market and regulatory landscape. It accelerated the decline in overall crypto market capitalisation, contributing to what some termed a "crypto winter." The incident also prompted increased scrutiny from regulators globally, with many calling for stricter oversight of stablecoins and the broader crypto market.

In response to the crisis, several jurisdictions began developing or accelerating plans for stablecoin regulation. For example, the European Union incorporated specific provisions for stablecoins in its Markets in Crypto-Assets (MiCA) regulation[70] (I cover this in more detail in my next book "Payments Unbound"). In the United States, the collapse reinvigorated discussions about the need for comprehensive crypto regulation, with lawmakers and regulators emphasising the importance of investor protection.[71]

The UST collapse also led to a re-evaluation of risk within the crypto industry itself. Many projects and investors became more cautious about algorithmic stablecoins, leading to a shift in focus towards more traditional, collateralised stablecoin models. This event served as a stark reminder of the experimental nature of many crypto projects and the potential for rapid, catastrophic failures in the space.

Following this, many algorithmic stablecoins were on the brink of collapse, and some have since recovered, but not to the dizzying heights of pre-crash market capitalisation (e.g. Fei Protocol's FEI).

One notable example of relative health is DAI, which, at the time of writing, is third by market capitalisation behind USDT (fiat backed) and USDC (also fiat backed).

BOX 5.5 THE INTERESTING CASE OF DAI

The DAI token, managed by the MakerDAO and generated through the Maker Protocol, doesn't fit neatly into a single stablecoin category because it is:

- **Crypto-collateralised**: DAI is primarily backed by a basket of cryptocurrencies and other digital assets as collateral. Users can generate DAI by depositing supported cryptocurrencies like ETH, WBTC, and others into smart contracts called "vaults" which ensure over-collateralisation, typically at 1.5:1 or more.
- **Algorithmically controlled**: DAI uses algorithmic mechanisms to help maintain its peg, including an automated system for liquidating under-collateralised positions, the DAI Savings Rate (DSR) which can be adjusted to influence demand, and the Maker (MKR) token mechanism for token minting and burning to recapitalise the system if needed.

Whilst originally backed solely by crypto-assets, DAI now incorporates centralised stablecoins like USDC as part of its collateral. DAI is backed by over 20 different cryptocurrencies and stablecoins, with USDC and USDP providing the largest share of collateral, followed by ETH and WBTC.

DAI is best characterised as a hybrid, multi-collateral stablecoin that uses both crypto-collateralisation and algorithmic mechanisms to maintain its peg. It aims to combine the stability advantages of asset backing with the decentralisation benefits of algorithmic approaches.

Another example similar to DAI is USDJ[72] which is issued on the Tron blockchain.

All in all, hybrid models may be an interesting evolution of algorithmic stablecoins.

Synthetic stablecoins

As briefly mentioned in the introduction, synthetic stablecoins are unique enough to be considered a distinct category as they don't fit neatly in any of the existing four main categories: they are not fiat backed, not commodity backed, they involve crypto-assets but are not directly backed by them, and whilst they use algorithms for price stabilisation, their mechanism differs significantly from algorithmic stablecoins. But like algorithmic stablecoins, they are **decentralised**, and rely on oracles for asset pricing and to assess the overall risk profile of the portfolio, enabling appropriate hedging strategies.

In essence, a synthetic stablecoin derives its value from a complex algorithm and a portfolio of assets, primarily other cryptocurrencies. Synthetic stablecoins maintain their soft peg to a target currency (usually the US dollar) through a process called **delta hedging**, which involves continuously adjusting the portfolio of assets to offset price fluctuations. Whilst the algorithms used in synthetic stablecoins are generally less complex than those employed by traditional algorithmic stablecoins, they still involve sophisticated mathematical models and require careful management.

Synthetic stablecoins are designed to offer the stability of a traditional stablecoin whilst leveraging the decentralised nature of cryptocurrencies. However, they also introduce new complexities and risks, as their value is dependent on the performance of the underlying asset portfolio, the effectiveness of the hedging algorithm, and broader market conditions.

Whilst synthetic stablecoins have the potential to offer innovative solutions to the challenges faced by traditional stablecoins, they are still a relatively new concept, and their long-term viability and regulatory landscape remain uncertain.

Prominent examples, according to market capitalisation at the time of writing, include:

- **USDe (Ethena USDe)**: issued by Ethena Labs, USDe is a synthetic stablecoin with a soft peg to the US dollar. It is fully backed by crypto-assets and maintained via automated delta-hedging trading operations. USDe is minted by providing staked Ethereum (stETH) as collateral, with the protocol opening corresponding short perpetual positions to hedge against price changes. The stability of USDe is ensured through delta-hedging derivatives positions and a mint/redeem arbitrage mechanism. Whilst USDe offers a scalable and censorship-resistant form of money, it is exposed to various risks, including smart contract risk, liquidity risk, and market risk.
- **USDX**: issued by the Kava Protocol, USDX is a synthetic stablecoin designed to maintain a soft peg to the US dollar. It is minted by users who deposit accepted cryptocurrencies as collateral into the Kava platform. USDX employs an over-collateralisation mechanism and algorithmic adjustments to maintain its peg. The stability of USDX is ensured through various risk parameters, liquidation processes, and a mint/burn mechanism that responds to market demand. Whilst USDX offers a decentralised stablecoin option within the Kava ecosystem, its stability can be influenced by market conditions, collateral values, and the overall health of the Kava network.

It's important to remember that synthetic stablecoin are still nascent.

Comparing stablecoins

Trying to understand stablecoins can be a bit confusing, and Table 5.3 aims to shed some light:

After this tour of stablecoins, let's examine what we can do with them.

Table 5.3 Comparing stablecoins. © 2024 Neira Jones

Feature	Fiat-Collateralised	Commodity Collateralised	Crypto-Collateralised	Algorithmic	Synthetic
Backing asset	Fiat currencies (e.g. USD)	Tangible assets (e.g. gold)	Cryptocurrencies (e.g. ETH)	None (algorithmically managed)	Various assets (derivatives, other stablecoins)
Collateralisation	Yes, 1:1 with fiat	Yes, 1:1 with commodity	Yes, often over-collateralised (e.g. 1.5:1 or more)	None	Varies (can be multiple assets)
Peg type	Hard peg	Hard peg	Soft peg with fiat	Soft peg with fiat	Soft peg with fiat
Redeemability against the underlying asset	Usually redeemable for fiat	Often redeemable for physical commodity	Redeemable for crypto collateral	Not directly redeemable	Redeemable based on mechanism (e.g. derivatives, other stablecoins)
Reliance on oracles	Low to none	Moderate	High	High	High
Stabilisation mechanism	Fiat reserves, minting/burning. Arbitrage plays a minor role	Commodity reserves, minting/burning. Arbitrage plays a minor role	Over-collateralisation, liquidations. High reliance on arbitrage	Algorithmic supply adjustment. High reliance on arbitrage	Delta-hedging, derivatives, collateral management. High reliance on arbitrage
Issuer	Centralised entity	Centralised entity	Decentralised protocols	Decentralised protocols	Decentralised protocols
Governance	Centralised	Centralised	Often DAO-based or community governance	DAO-based or algorithmic governance	DAO-based or hybrid governance
Transparency	High, regular audits	High, regular audits	On-chain verification	Algorithmic transparency	Complex, often on chain
Regulation	Typically regulated	Typically regulated	Varies, often less regulated	Typically unregulated	Typically unregulated

(Continued)

Table 5.3 (Continued)

Feature	**Fiat-Collateralised**	**Commodity Collateralised**	**Crypto-Collateralised**	**Algorithmic**	**Synthetic**
Market capitalisation	Largest	Moderate	Moderate	Smaller	Emerging
Liquidity	Generally high, especially for major stablecoins	Moderate, depends on the specific commodity and issuer	Varies, can be high for well-established projects	Often lower due to complexity and perceived risk	Typically lower due to complexity and newer market presence
Risk factors	Counterparty risk, regulatory risk, lack of transparency in reserves, bank run risk, smart contract risks (for blockchain interactions)	Counterparty risk, price volatility of underlying commodity, storage and insurance costs, regulatory risk, smart contract risks (for blockchain interactions)	High volatility of collateral, smart contract vulnerabilities, liquidation cascades during market stress, over-collateralisation inefficiency	Depegging risk during market stress, complex mechanisms may fail, lack of intrinsic value, vulnerability to speculative attacks, smart contract vulnerabilities	Smart contract vulnerabilities, complex mechanisms may be opaque, interdependence on other crypto-assets, potential for cascading failures in linked systems
Use cases	Payments, remittances, trading pair on exchanges, store of value	Store of value, commodity exposure in crypto markets, trading	DeFi applications, lending, borrowing, yield farming	DeFi applications, experimental finance models	Complex DeFi strategies, derivatives trading, risk management
Examples	USDT, USDC, PYUSD	PAXG, XAUt	WBTC, LUSD, DUSD (Davos.xyz)	USDD, DUSD (Defichain), AMPL	Ethena USDe, USDX

Payments and cross-border transaction use cases

Stablecoins enable efficient remittances, international business payments, merchant transactions, and peer-to-peer payments, potentially offering a faster and more cost-effective alternative to traditional systems. Here are some examples:

- **Remittances**: stablecoins provide a quick and low-cost method for sending money across borders as they reduce the need for intermediaries and potentially lower transaction fees. This is particularly beneficial for individuals in countries with limited access to banking services. For example, Moneygram used USDC to distribute United Nations High Commissioner of Refugees (UNHCR) donations in Ukraine,[73] demonstrating how stablecoins can streamline remittances and support humanitarian efforts.
- **Cross-border business payments**: businesses can use stablecoins for cross-border transactions, reducing the time and cost associated with traditional methods. For example, SAP is testing cross-border payments for businesses using stablecoins,[74] showcasing their potential to improve transaction processes and reduce costs.
- **Merchant payments**: stablecoins allow businesses to accept digital payments without the volatility of traditional cryptocurrencies, and also avoiding centralised systems' longer settlement cycles. For example, both Worldpay and Checkout.com offer merchant settlement in USDC in partnership with Fireblocks, enabling merchants to receive payments in a stable digital currency around the clock.[75,76]
- **Peer-to-peer transactions**: individuals can use stablecoins for direct transactions, bypassing traditional banking fees. For example, in August 2023, PayPal launched PayPal USD (PYUSD),[77] allowing users to send and receive stablecoins seamlessly, enhancing the speed and efficiency of transactions.

Financial trading and exchange operations use cases

Stablecoins have found a place in crypto trading and exchange operations. Their stability and ease of use make them valuable tools for traders and exchanges alike, offering solutions to some of the challenges posed by the volatility of traditional cryptocurrencies, including:

- **Facilitating trades on cryptocurrency exchanges**: stablecoins are widely used on cryptocurrency exchanges to facilitate trading as they provide a stable medium of exchange and a safe haven during periods of high volatility. Traders can quickly move in and out of positions without converting to fiat, maintaining liquidity, and reducing transaction costs.

- **Providing market liquidity**: stablecoins provide liquidity in the crypto markets, acting as a stable trading pair against other cryptocurrencies, helping traders hedge against volatility and maintain the value of their assets without converting to fiat.
- **Hedging against volatility**: stablecoins are used as a hedge against market volatility as traders and investors can park their funds in stablecoins during periods of high volatility to preserve value and avoid losses. For example, Binance, one of the largest cryptocurrency exchanges, used their stablecoin BUSD as a trading pair for many cryptocurrencies, although BUSD has been phased out in favour of FDUSD.

Corporate finance use cases for stablecoins

Stablecoins are increasingly finding applications in corporate finance, offering businesses new tools for managing their financial operations. These digital assets provide stability and efficiency in various aspects of corporate financial management, from treasury operations to international trade, including:

- **Treasury management**: companies can hold stablecoins as part of their treasury to mitigate risk. For example, Ramp, a corporate credit card issuer and expenses management firm, allocated a significant portion of its corporate treasury into Circle's USDC stablecoin through the Circle Yield product.[78] This allowed Ramp to generate higher returns compared to traditional treasury management options. The company found stablecoins to be efficient, rapid, and cost-effective for transactions, providing an alternative to traditional bank transfers. In June 2022, Checkout.com discussed the potential for stablecoins in corporate treasury, emphasising their utility for immediate settlements and the need for widespread adoption at the wholesale level.[79]
- **FX**: stablecoins can simplify FX transactions by providing a stable, digital medium for currency conversions. For example, stablecoins can help fund managers complete their FX trades in time to meet the

shorter settlement cycle required in some jurisdictions. This involves using stablecoins to facilitate instantaneous **Delivery-versus-Payment (DvP)** for digital assets, thus addressing the challenges posed by a T+1 settlement cycle.

- **Trade finance**: stablecoins are being explored for trade finance operations, allowing for faster and more transparent international trade transactions. For example, Australian Digital Dollar (AUDD), a stablecoin pegged 1:1 to the Australian dollar, is used on the Stellar network for trade finance.[80] By leveraging blockchain technology, AUDD facilitates faster and more compliant transactions, creating permanent records on a public ledger. This stablecoin helps streamline the trade financing process, from transaction origination and documentation to approvals and disbursements. AUDD also ensures compliance with counter-terrorism financing and anti-money laundering requirements through the SEP-12 protocol (a Know Your Customer KYC API on Stellar), making it a suitable medium for trade finance operations.

DeFi use cases for stablecoins

DeFi has emerged as a significant frontier for stablecoin applications, extending beyond basic lending and borrowing. Stablecoins serve as the backbone for many DeFi protocols, enabling a wide range of financial services without the need for traditional intermediaries. The following are some notable DeFi use cases for stablecoins:

- **Savings**: stablecoins can be used as a stable store of value, offering a way to hold savings without the volatility associated with other cryptocurrencies, protecting savings from inflation. For example, Aave, a DeFi lending protocol, allows users to deposit stablecoins like USDC to earn interest, providing a stable way to grow savings.
- **Lending, borrowing, and staking**: stablecoins are commonly used in DeFi applications where users can lend their stablecoins to earn interest or stake them in various protocols to earn rewards, providing a passive income stream. Stablecoins can also be used as collateral in DeFi lending platforms, allowing users to borrow against their stablecoin holdings. For instance, Aave, a popular DeFi lending protocol, uses

stablecoins like USDC and DAI as lending and borrowing assets. Other examples include Aave, MakerDAO (Oasis), and Compound.

- **Yield farming**: investors can use stablecoins to participate in yield farming strategies. This involves providing liquidity to DeFi protocols in exchange for rewards, often in the form of the protocol's native tokens. For instance, users might deposit stablecoins into a liquidity pool on Uniswap and earn trading fees and UNI tokens as rewards.
- **Liquidity provision**: stablecoins are often used to provide liquidity in various DeFi protocols. For example, Curve Finance specialises in stablecoin liquidity pools, allowing for efficient swaps between different stablecoins.
- **Cross-border transactions**: DeFi protocols and stablecoins are increasingly enabling cross-border transactions, offering faster settlements and lower costs by eliminating intermediaries. Transactions can be completed in minutes and are transparent, as they are recorded on public blockchains. Users typically convert fiat to stablecoins, transfer them via blockchain, and then convert back to fiat. Whilst promising, this method still faces regulatory and adoption challenges.
- **Decentralised exchanges (DEX)**: Stablecoins are popular trading pairs on DEXs (see Chapter 6, *Transacting in a decentralised world*), enabling trading without fiat on-ramps. DEXs operate on a peer-to-peer basis, allowing users to trade directly without intermediaries. Platforms like Uniswap and SushiSwap use stablecoin pairs to provide liquidity and facilitate seamless transactions. Stablecoins help maintain price stability and enhance price discovery, making them essential for efficient trading. This decentralised approach also improves security and privacy, as users retain control over their funds throughout the trading process.

It's important to note that whilst many of these opportunities can provide passive income, they also come with risks. DeFi platforms may have smart contract vulnerabilities, and the decentralised nature of these platforms can make them more difficult for new users to navigate. Additionally, yields and interest rates will fluctuate based on market conditions and demand.

Emerging stablecoin use cases

As the adoption of stablecoins continues to grow, new and innovative use cases are emerging across various sectors. These potential applications showcase the versatility of stablecoins and their potential to revolutionise different aspects of finance, technology, and everyday transactions, including:

- **Facilitating fund raising and ICOs**: stablecoins are increasingly being used in fundraising efforts and Initial Coin Offerings (ICOs). Businesses can enhance transparency, attract global participation, and offer investors a stable value proposition by accepting stablecoins. It could widen the investor base and facilitate the liquidity of tokenised assets. The concept of using stablecoins in fundraising is still evolving, and many of the purported benefits (enhanced transparency, global participation, stable value proposition) are theoretical or in the early stages of implementation. As the cryptocurrency and blockchain space continues to develop, we may see more innovative uses of stablecoins in fundraising efforts.
- **CBDCs**: stablecoins could serve as a model for CBDCs (see Chapter 7), offering a digital alternative to traditional fiat currencies with the benefits of blockchain technology.
- **Potential integration into the Internet of Things (IoT)**: stablecoins can facilitate transactions in the IoT ecosystem for machine-to-machine transactions by providing a stable, programmable currency for micro-transactions between connected devices.
- **Tokenised markets**: asset tokenisation (see *Security tokens, Asset tokenisation* later in this chapter) presents a significant opportunity to transform traditional financial markets by creating new, more accessible, and efficient ways of trading assets. Stablecoins can enhance asset tokenisation by providing a stable unit of account for pricing tokenised assets and facilitating efficient, low-cost settlements in these markets. Tokenised bank deposits are an example of a fusion between traditional banking and blockchain technology of which the Regulated Liability Network (RLN)[81] initiative is an example (See Chapter 7, *The Regulated Liability Network*). The RLN is a blockchain-based system designed to handle regulated liabilities intended to provide on-chain, 24×7, programmable, final settlement in sovereign currencies, consisting of the liabilities of both public- and private-regulated financial institutions. Stablecoins could support tokenised regulated liabilities enabling them to serve as digital stand-ins for conventional deposit holdings, stored within a wallet rather than a traditional bank account.

- **Virtual marketplaces**: stablecoins could be used as a medium of exchange in virtual marketplaces for digital goods, ensuring price stability for buyers and sellers. They could also facilitate cross-platform transactions without the need for complex currency conversions as virtual economies often span multiple platforms, games, and virtual worlds.
- **Gaming**: stablecoins may have a variety of applications in gaming,[82] as exemplified by the Microsoft EY partnership to introduce a blockchain-based platform to enable Microsoft Xbox developers to track and manage payments and royalty contracts.[83] Potential gaming use cases include:
  - **In-game currency**: stablecoins could serve as a stable in-game currency, providing a consistent value for virtual goods and services within games, potentially replacing closed-loop virtual currencies.
  - **Cross-game asset transfers**: stablecoins could facilitate the transfer of value between different games or virtual worlds, allowing players to move their assets more easily, thus increasing asset portability.
  - **Esports prizes and payments**: stablecoins could be used for esports tournament prizes and player payments, providing a stable and easily transferable form of value.
  - **Microtransactions**: stablecoins could enable efficient microtransactions within games, allowing for small purchases without the volatility associated with other cryptocurrencies.

Recap on stablecoins

Stablecoins have emerged as a significant innovation in the cryptocurrency landscape, offering a degree of stability and utility that traditional cryptocurrencies lack. By pegging their value to underlying assets or using algorithmic mechanisms, stablecoins aim to mitigate the volatility associated with cryptocurrencies whilst leveraging the benefits of blockchain technology.

The evolution of stablecoins has significantly impacted the cryptocurrency landscape, addressing the volatility that often characterises traditional cryptocurrencies. Initially introduced in 2014, stablecoins have grown to a market capitalisation exceeding $170 billion, driven by their utility in DeFi and blockchain applications.

The rise and fall of various stablecoins underscore the need for regulatory oversight to ensure market stability and protect investors. As the market continues to evolve, the future of stablecoins will likely hinge on balancing innovation with the necessary safeguards to mitigate risks.

Professionals should be aware of the opportunities that stablecoins may offer:

- **Enhanced efficiency**: stablecoins have the potential to revolutionise payment systems by offering faster, cheaper, and more secure transactions compared to traditional methods. They could facilitate cross-border payments, remittances, and micropayments.
- **Financial inclusion**: by providing access to financial services without the need for traditional bank accounts, stablecoins can help bridge the financial divide. They can empower unbanked and underbanked populations by enabling them to participate in the global economy.
- **New investment avenues**: stablecoins can unlock a range of investment opportunities within the DeFi ecosystem, offering higher yields and greater liquidity compared to traditional savings accounts. They can also serve as a bridge between traditional finance and the decentralised world.
- **Innovation in existing financial mechanisms**: stablecoins have the potential to enhance the operations of payment firms and e-money institutions. By providing a stable digital asset, they can improve transaction processing speeds, reduce costs, and expand the range of services offered. For instance, stablecoins can enable real-time payments, instant settlements, and cross-border transfers with greater efficiency.
- **Innovative use cases**: beyond optimising existing financial services, stablecoins have the potential to unlock entirely new business models and applications. For example, they can facilitate the development of tokenised assets, DEX, and programmable money. Moreover, stablecoins can play a crucial role in emerging technologies like the IoT and supply chain management.
- **Strengthened macroeconomic stability**: by providing a stable digital medium of exchange, stablecoins can contribute to macroeconomic stability, especially in countries with high inflation rates. They can also serve as a hedge against currency devaluation. However, they might not

be ideal in deflationary environments where the value of the pegged asset is increasing.

Professionals should also be aware of the risks that stablecoins may present:

- **Regulatory uncertainty**: the regulatory landscape for stablecoins is evolving rapidly, and a lack of clear guidelines can create challenges for issuers, investors, and consumers. This uncertainty can hinder innovation and investment in the stablecoin market.
- **Consumer protection**: if stablecoins gain wider adoption, ensuring consumer protection becomes increasingly important. Issues such as fraud, scams, and loss of funds due to technical glitches will need to be addressed.
- **Operational risks**: complex mechanisms, such as those used in algorithmic stablecoins, can introduce operational risks and vulnerabilities. Smart contract bugs, oracle failures, and other technical issues can lead to significant losses. The collapses of TerraUSD and SVB serve as stark reminders of the potential consequences of systemic failures in stablecoin systems.
- **Inherent volatility**: whilst designed to be stable, crypto-collateralised and algorithmic stablecoins are inherently more susceptible to market fluctuations compared to fiat-backed or commodity-backed stablecoins. This volatility can impact the trust and confidence of users.
- **Centralisation**: many stablecoins, especially fiat-collateralised and commodity-collateralised ones, rely on centralised entities for custody and management, introducing counterparty risk. This can undermine the core principles of decentralisation often associated with cryptocurrencies.
- **Environmental impact**: the energy consumption associated with some blockchain networks, including those used for stablecoin issuance, has raised concerns about environmental sustainability. This can impact the public perception of stablecoins and their long-term viability.

It's important to remember that the stablecoin landscape is rapidly evolving, and new opportunities and challenges may arise. As a constant theme throughout this book, the trick is to keep up to date.

Security tokens

A security token is a digital representation of ownership in a real-world asset, partial or otherwise. The asset may be a piece of the project itself. Security tokens are a developing area with regulatory considerations as they function similarly to traditional securities but leverage blockchain technology for issuance, trading, and record keeping. Security tokens are sometimes called "investment tokens".

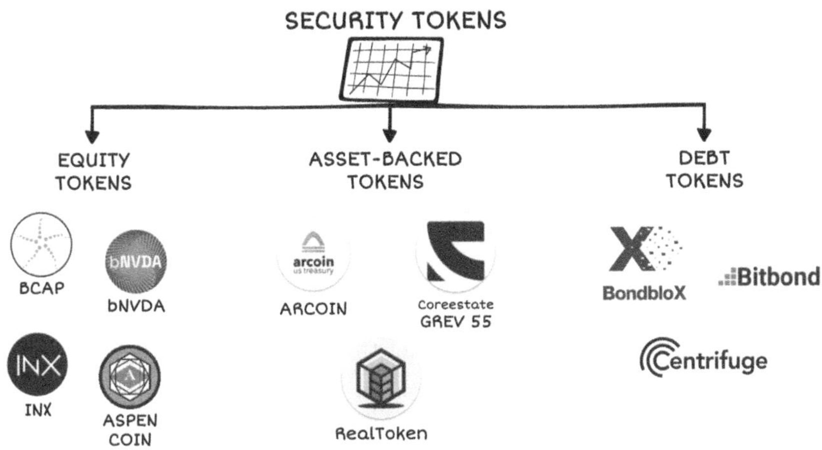

Figure 5.12 Security tokens. © 2024 Neira Jones.

The different types of security tokens are illustrated in Figure 5.12.

Security tokens involve tangible things (e.g. equity, debt, gold, real estate), and for these goods to be traded on blockchain ecosystems, they must be transformed into tokens, and this process is called tokenisation. What many don't realise is that when they invest in tokens, they're not really buying real estate, works of art, or cars. They merely own fractions of a tokenised security.

I include security tokens in this chapter as they are an important part of blockchain ecosystems, although they are not strictly related to "payments". Payments professionals may be interested in the tokenisation aspects of security tokens, which is why I cover this first. If you're not interested in the specific types of tokenised securities, just jump to the recap (and the duck 😉).

Asset tokenisation

Asset tokenisation breaks down illiquid assets into their smallest shares. It makes them tradable without intermediaries and thus opens up asset classes with traditionally high access barriers to small investors, who can now invest in a wide variety of assets – from real estate to vintage cars, art, and wine to diamonds.

Any item can be tokenised in its entirety too, giving the token holder full ownership of the asset. Items like agricultural assets can be tokenised for trading, and artworks, luxury goods and legal documentation can be tokenised for security and traceability. Once the value is tokenised, it is then stored in a secure digital "safe," able to be traded or sold at any time to anyone around the world. But the governance frameworks and legalities of owning fractions of real-world assets are more or less non-existent (e.g. support, maintenance, storage, etc.).

In any instance, tokenisation is the process of converting rights to an asset into a digital token on a blockchain. This process involves several steps:

- **Asset identification**: determining the asset to be tokenised, such as real estate, art, or equity.
- **Legal structuring**: ensuring the tokenisation process complies with relevant securities laws and regulations.
- **Smart contract development**: creating smart contracts (see Chapter 2, *Building smart contracts and applications*) that define the terms and conditions of the token, including ownership rights, transferability, and compliance with regulations.
- **Token issuance**: distributing the tokens to investors through a security token offering (STO) or other means (see Chapter 4, Box 4.1).
- **Trading and settlement**: enabling tokens to be traded on regulated exchanges or secondary markets (see Chapter 6, *Transacting in a decentralised world*).

Tokenisation provides several benefits, including increased liquidity, **fractional ownership**, and enhanced transparency. By converting physical or traditional assets into digital tokens, tokenisation may allow for easier transfer and trading of these assets, opening up new investment opportunities.

BOX 5.6 WHAT IS FRACTIONAL OWNERSHIP?

Fractional ownership is a method of shared ownership where multiple parties each own a portion of an asset. This allows investors to purchase a share of high-value assets that might otherwise be unaffordable, such as real estate, art, or luxury items. In the context of security tokens, fractional ownership is achieved through tokenisation by dividing an asset into smaller, tradable digital tokens, each representing partial ownership of the underlying asset.

Fractional ownership via security tokens offers benefits such as lower entry barriers, portfolio diversification, increased liquidity, and transparency. However, it also comes with risks including regulatory uncertainty, market volatility, technical risks, and lack of physical control. Security tokens have the potential to increase liquidity in traditionally illiquid markets like real estate and fine art. This could lead to more efficient price discovery and potentially reduce illiquidity premiums, resulting in more efficient markets and possibly higher valuations.

Asset tokenisation presents interesting potential use cases:

- **Environmental assets**: natural resources, carbon credits, or renewable energy projects can be tokenised, creating new markets for environmental investments. For instance, the World Bank issued bond-i, the world's first blockchain-operated bond, which could pave the way for tokenised green bonds.[84]
- **Real estate**: large commercial properties or luxury real estate can be tokenised, allowing investors to purchase small fractions of these assets. For instance, the St. Regis Aspen Resort in Colorado tokenised ownership stakes on the Ethereum blockchain, allowing investors to buy fractional ownership for as little as $1.[85]
- **Fine art and collectibles**: valuable artworks or rare collectibles can be tokenised, allowing multiple investors to own a share of these typically illiquid assets.
- **Private equity and venture capital**: tokenisation can make it possible for smaller investors to participate in private equity deals or venture capital investments that traditionally require large minimum investments.

- **Increased liquidity**: tokenisation can significantly enhance the liquidity of traditionally illiquid assets:
  - **24/7 trading**: tokenised assets can be traded around the clock on digital platforms, unlike traditional markets with limited trading hours.
  - **Global access**: tokenised markets can be accessed globally, increasing the pool of potential investors, and enhancing liquidity.
  - **Automated market making**: smart contracts can facilitate automated trading and market making, potentially improving liquidity in secondary markets.
- **Reduced operational costs**: tokenisation can streamline many aspects of asset management and trading:
  - **Automated compliance**: smart contracts can encode regulatory requirements and automate compliance processes, reducing administrative overhead.
  - **Efficient settlement**: blockchain-based systems can enable near-instantaneous settlement of trades, reducing counterparty risk and freeing up capital.
  - **Transparent record keeping**: the immutable nature of blockchain provides a transparent and auditable record of all transactions, potentially reducing the need for intermediaries and associated costs.
- **New asset classes**: tokenisation enables the creation of entirely new asset classes and investment products:
  - **Synthetic assets**: tokens can represent synthetic assets that derive their value from underlying assets or indices, creating new investment opportunities.
  - **Tokenised funds**: investment funds can be tokenised, allowing for more efficient management and potentially lower fees for investors. For example, Invesco and Elwood Asset Management launched a blockchain ETF that tracks the Elwood Blockchain Global Equity Index.[86]

Asset tokenisation platforms

Asset tokenisation platforms come in various shapes, including:

- **Real estate tokenisation platforms**: RealT offers tokenised ownership in real estate properties, allowing fractional investment in properties.
- **Art and collectible tokenisation platforms**: Masterworks[87] offers fractional ownership in fine art through tokenisation.

- **Enterprise tokenisation platforms**: Polymath,[88] Consensys Codefi Assets,[89] and DTCC[90] all provide technology to create, issue, and manage security tokens on the blockchain for various assets.
- **Commodity tokenisation platforms**: Atomyze[91] provides tokenisation for various commodities including precious metals.
- **Equity tokenisation platforms**: Securitize[92] provides a platform for the tokenisation of various assets, including private company shares.

These platforms can also work with regulated crypto exchanges, and some exchanges may even offer tokenisation services to the token issuer.

In addition, you're probably wondering why you can't track the prices of security tokens on platforms like coinmarketcap.com or cryptoslate.com. This is because these platforms primarily track cryptocurrencies and tokens traded on public crypto exchanges; whilst security tokens are traded on specialised platforms designed for regulated securities, data availability is subject to regulations, and performance and valuation metrics are different. As a result, the trading data necessary for listing on these tracking sites are not publicly available, but there are dedicated platforms that offer information and analytics services for security tokens, such as Security Token Market.[93]

Now that we understand tokenisation, let's have a look at what types of security tokens are available.

Security token types

As per Figure 5.12, they typically fall into three main categories:

- **Equity tokens**: these represent ownership in an asset (e.g. a company), similar to traditional stocks. An example is Aspen Coin,[94] which represents fractional ownership in the equity of the entity that owns the St. Regis Aspen Resort, rather than direct ownership of the physical property itself. It was one of the first major real estate assets to be tokenised, allowing investors to have an equity stake in a luxury hotel property. Another example is Blockchain Capital (BCAP),[95] representing shares in a venture capital fund, allowing investors to gain exposure to a portfolio of blockchain and crypto investments. For an example of ownership in a platform, the INX Token[96] represents ownership in the INX trading platform, allowing token holders to share in the company's profits. Interestingly, INX also has utility as token holders benefit from reduced trading fees on the platform (effectively having the secondary purpose of a utility token). Also, in July 2024, INX launched tokenised Nvidia shares (bNVDA) on their platform.[97] Holders of bNVDA have the claim to the collateral value – Nvidia stock (NVDA) – held by a licensed custodian under an account control agreement and are entitled to all shareholder rights, including NVDA dividends. Equity token holders have voting rights, maintain the right to get a share of the profits in the form of dividends, are entitled to the losses. The value of the token is usually not linked to its demand on the crypto market but rather to the performance of the issuing company.

- **Asset-backed tokens**: these represent tokenised ownership in physical assets like real estate or commodities. Investors can purchase tokens representing fractional ownership in specific assets, allowing them, to benefit from the asset appreciation in value. Examples include RealT[98] and Coreestate,[99] where investors can purchase tokens representing fractional ownership in specific properties, receiving rental income proportional to their token holdings. Arca Labs[100] is another example and they provides tokenised investment products, consisting primarily of US Treasury securities in a tokenised format. In the fine arts space, Maecenas, a blockchain-based art investment platform, tokenised a $5.6 million Andy Warhol painting "14 Small Electric Chairs (1980)",[101] allowing fractional ownership as early as 2018.
- **Debt tokens**: these represent debt instruments, similar to bonds. These are short-term loans with an interest rate provided by the company's investors (e.g. mortgages, company bonds, etc.), and the terms are secured by smart contracts. Token holders don't own any part of the underlying asset (e.g. a property), just shares in the "tokenised debt security". For example, Centrifuge[102] is a decentralised platform that allows businesses to finance their real-world assets by issuing tokens backed by those assets, including invoices, real estate, and other forms of debt. Other examples include BondbloX[103] and Bitbond,[104] which offer fractional bond ownership allowing investors to buy and sell fractions of bonds in smaller denominations.

Regulatory considerations

Security tokens are subject to securities laws in most jurisdictions. Key regulatory aspects include:

- **Registration**: most security tokens must be registered with appropriate regulatory bodies (e.g. the SEC in the US) unless they qualify for an exemption.
- **Investor accreditation**: many offerings are limited to accredited investors, though some platforms are working to expand access to retail investors.
- **Compliance**: issuers must comply with ongoing reporting and disclosure requirements.
- **Cross-border regulations**: international offerings must navigate complex cross-border securities laws.
- **Smart contracts** play a crucial role in automating security token management. They can enforce compliance measures such as KYC/AML checks and investor accreditation, automate dividend distribution, manage voting rights, and handle cap table management. Smart contracts can also streamline corporate actions like stock splits or mergers. These automations can reduce administrative costs, minimise human error, and increase transparency. However, it's crucial to thoroughly audit smart contracts to ensure they function as intended (see Chapter 2, *Building smart contracts*).

Tokenising real-world assets is a complex process, and tokenised securities are probably the most regulated of crypto-assets. This is still a nascent field, but it has the potential to disrupt traditional financial markets by increasing liquidity in traditionally illiquid assets and democratising access to high-value investments. They could also streamline capital-raising processes for companies, potentially reducing costs and time associated with public offerings. However, challenges remain, including the need for evolving regulatory frameworks and for traditional financial institutions to adapt their systems.

Recap on security tokens

This section only touched the surface of security tokens, and for those wanting to learn more about it, there are plenty of good books on the subject.[105,106]

Professionals should remember a few things:

- **Regulatory compliance**: security tokens are subject to securities laws, requiring registration with regulatory bodies and adherence to ongoing reporting requirements.
- **Investor accreditation**: access to Security Token Offerings (STOs) may be restricted for retail investors who don't meet accredited investor requirements.
- **Smart contract reliance**: security tokens heavily depend on smart contracts for automating compliance, dividend distribution, and voting rights management, which may introduce new risks such as coding errors, vulnerabilities to hacks, or unforeseen issues in contract execution. The complexity of these smart contracts could also lead to challenges in auditing and regulatory oversight, potentially creating gaps in investor protection or compliance assurance.
- **Liquidity challenges**: whilst tokenisation aims to increase liquidity, the market for security tokens is still developing and may face liquidity constraints.
- **Cross-border complexities**: international offerings of security tokens must navigate complex and varying securities laws across jurisdictions.
- **Valuation uncertainties**: traditional valuation methods may not always apply to tokenised assets, creating challenges in price discovery and market efficiency.
- **Custody and security risks**: proper storage and management of both security tokens and underlying assets are crucial. This involves secure digital wallets for tokens and appropriate physical security for tangible assets, introducing complexities in reconciliation, auditing, and regulatory compliance.
- **Market immaturity**: the security token market is still in its early stages, potentially leading to volatility and unpredictable market behaviour.
- **Technological barriers**: understanding and interacting with blockchain technology may present challenges for traditional investors and institutions.
- **Integration with traditional finance**: the adoption of security tokens requires adaptation of existing financial systems and processes, which may face resistance or technical hurdles.

Security tokens represent a significant innovation in asset tokenisation and investment, offering new opportunities for fractional ownership and increased liquidity. However, they come with unique challenges and considerations that must be addressed as the market evolves. Understanding the regulatory landscape, technological implications, and market dynamics is crucial for anyone looking to engage with security tokens in this rapidly developing field.

In any instance, it's probably quite confusing, and you may still be wondering, for example, what the differences are between a commodity-collateralised stablecoin and an asset-backed security token… Table 5.4, in the next section, aims to give a comparative analysis and clarify a few points.

And now that we've rounded up crypto-assets, let's tie this all up.

Virtual assets vs. fiat currencies (would it make any difference to you?)

Figure 5.13 revisits and expands on the virtual asset classification given earlier in Figure 5.5:

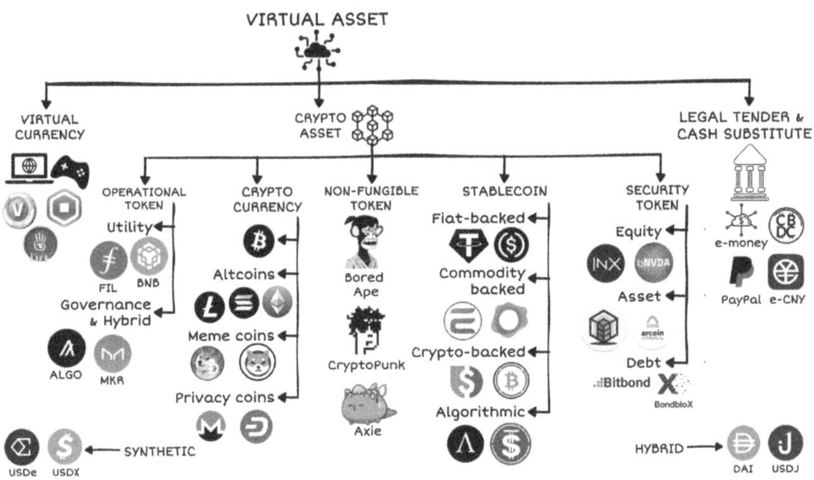

Figure 5.13 Classifying virtual assets. © 2024 Neira Jones.

Table 5.4 aims to clarify the whole picture even further. I decided not to include virtual currencies in the table because these are simply closed-loop mediums of exchange applicable only to the issuing platform (e.g. a gaming platform) and e-money as the table was already too large. However, you can easily derive their comparative properties from Table 5.1 and other assets listed in the table.

Table 5.4 Comparing crypto-assets and fiat currencies. © 2024 Neira Jones

Feature	Cryptocurrencies	Crypto-Backed Stablecoins	Algorithmic Stablecoins	NFTs	Commodity-Backed Stablecoins	Equity Tokens	Asset-Backed Security Tokens	Debt Security Tokens	Fiat-Backed Stablecoins	Fiat Currencies
Backing asset	None	Other cryptocurrencies	Algorithm-controlled supply	Digital or physical assets (e.g. art, collectibles)	Physical commodities (e.g. gold, oil)	Company equity	Real-world assets (e.g. real estate, art)	Debt instruments	Fiat currency	Government trust
Decentralisation	High	High	High	Variable (depends on the platform)	Low to moderate	Low to moderate	Low to moderate	Low to moderate	Low (centralised issuer)	None
Collateral ratio	N/A	Over-c ollateralised (e.g. 1.5:1 or more)	No collateral, but soft peg to fiat.	N/A	1:1 or variable	N/A	Variable	Variable	1:1 ratio	Bank reserves
Redeemability against the underlying asset	N/A	Redeemable for crypto collateral	Not directly redeemable	Not directly redeemable	Often redeemable for physical commodity	Not directly redeemable	May be redeemable for underlying asset	Redeemable at maturity	Usually redeemable for fiat	N/A
Usability for goods and services	Limited	No	No	No	No	No	No	No	Limited	High
Markets	Cryptocurrency exchanges, OTC markets	Cryptocurrency exchanges, DeFi platforms	Cryptocurrency exchanges, DeFi platforms	NFT marketplaces (e.g. OpenSea, Rarible)	Specialised commodity exchanges, cryptocurrency exchanges	Security token exchanges, specialised marketplaces	Security token exchanges, specialised marketplaces	Security token exchanges, specialised debt markets	Cryptocurrency exchanges, OTC markets, some forex platforms	Banks, forex markets
Use case	Store of value, speculation, payments	DeFi applications, stable trading pair	Experimental stable medium of exchange	Digital collectibles, art, gaming assets	Hedge against inflation, stable store of value	Investment in company growth	Fractional ownership of assets	Debt financing	Stable medium of exchange, crypto on/off ramp	Medium of exchange, store of value, payments
Scalability	Variable	Variable	Variable	Variable (depends on the platform)	Variable	Moderate	Moderate	Moderate	Variable	High
Smart contract usage	Variable	Extensive	Extensive	Extensive	Limited	Extensive	Extensive	Extensive	Limited	None
Yield generation	Through staking or lending	Through over-collateralisation and DeFi	Through algorithmic mechanisms	Through resale, royalties	Through lending or commodity appreciation	Through company profits/dividends	Through asset appreciation/revenue	Through interest payments	Through lending or reserve management	Interest (savings accounts, bonds)

Feature	Cryptocurrencies	Crypto-Backed Stablecoins	Algorithmic Stablecoins	NFTs	Commodity-Backed Stablecoins	Equity Tokens	Asset-Backed Security Tokens	Debt Security Tokens	Fiat-Backed Stablecoins	Fiat Currencies
Price stability	Highly volatile	Moderate-to-high volatility	Can be volatile (soft peg to fiat)	Highly volatile	Relatively stable (tied to commodity prices)	Volatile (based on company performance)	Relatively stable (based on underlying asset)	Relatively stable (based on debt terms)	Stable (hard peg to fiat)	Stable (controlled by central banks)
Risk profile	High	High	High	High	Moderate (tied to commodity market)	High	Moderate	Low to moderate	Low (if properly backed and regulated)	Low (unstable economies)
Issuance	Decentralised (mining, staking)	Decentralised (smart contracts)	Decentralised (algorithmic)	Decentralised (various platforms)	Centralised issuer	Centralised (company issuance)	Centralised or semi-centralised	Centralised or semi-centralised	Centralised issuer	Centralised (central bank)
Regulatory oversight	Limited	Limited	Limited	Limited to moderate	Moderate to high	High	High	High	High	High
KYC/AML requirements	Depends on crypto exchange (see Note 1)	Depends on platform	Depends on platform	Depends on platform	Yes	Yes	Yes	Yes	Yes	No for everyday transactions (see Note 2)
Governance	Often community- riven	Often DAO based	Often DAO based	Decentralised or platform-based	Centralised or semi-decentralised	Typically centralised (corporate governance)	Variable (depends on structure)	Typically centralised (debt governance)	Centralised	Centralised (government and central bank)
Transparency	Variable (blockchain dependent)	High (on-chain collateral)	High (algorithm visible)	Variable (depends on the platform)	Depends on issuer (regular audits)	Moderate to high	Moderate to high	Moderate to high	Depends on issuer (regular audits)	Moderate (central bank policies)
Risk factors	High volatility, regulatory uncertainty, security threats (e.g., hacking), counterparty risk, lack of transparency in reserves, smart contract risks	High volatility, collateral risk, regulatory challenges, counterparty risk, smart contract vulnerabilities, liquidation cascades during market stress	Depegging risk during market stress, potential failure of algorithm, lack of intrinsic value, vulnerability to speculative attacks, smart contract vulnerabilities	Market volatility, illiquidity, copyright issues, lack of intrinsic value, vulnerability to speculative attacks	Commodity price risk, storage and insurance costs, regulatory risk, counterparty risk, smart contract risks	Market volatility, regulatory scrutiny, company performance risk, counterparty risk	Asset valuation risk, regulatory compliance, liquidity risk, counterparty risk	Credit risk, interest rate risk, regulatory compliance, counterparty risk	Redemption risk, regulatory scrutiny, counterparty risk, lack of transparency in reserves, bank-run risk	Inflation risk, monetary policy changes, geopolitical risks

Note 1: Yes, for centralised exchange (C0EX), No for decentralised exchange (DEX).

Note 2: No for everyday cash transactions, Yes for large cash transactions and interactions with financial institutions.

Phew! Table 5.4 took me a long time to produce, especially as the industry, technology, and regulations evolve so fast. I have no doubt that in a few years' time, I will have to revisit this table. In the meantime, I hope you find it a useful tool.

But wait, there's more! You will have noticed that I haven't yet covered an important category: CBDCs. There has been much attention given to CBDCs over the past few years, and whilst these should have rightly been covered in this chapter, they are worth one of their own. In Chapter 7, we'll peek into the evolution of CBDCs, because apparently, even governments and central banks want in on this digital asset party.

Digital and virtual assets – conclusion (what next?)

In this whistle-stop tour of digital and virtual assets, we covered several concepts:

- The various types of money, including currency, fiat money, e-money, cryptocurrency, and their history,
- A proposed definition of virtual assets,
- Virtual currencies, and
- Crypto-assets including cryptocurrencies, NFTs, stablecoins, and security tokens.

I have tried to explain the jargon and debunk a few myths, and you'll find the key terms in the glossary for future reference. I have given you my opinion on some aspects of the characteristics of virtual and crypto-assets.

In the absence of universally approved classifications, I offered categorisation frameworks, and I hope they go some way into clearing out misconceptions and misunderstandings. I will watch with interest if this gets adopted.

If you read this book a few years from now, new crypto-asset models will emerge (as many have already done with hybrid versions), traditional businesses may incorporate aspects of crypto-assets within their operations, and regulatory pressure will increase. The use of NFTs for loyalty programmes may catch on, as may the integration of stablecoins for faster B2B settlements. Maybe traditional gaming platforms will rethink their virtual currencies to consider stablecoins, and maybe they will incorporate

NFTs for in-game items (as Web 3.0 games already do), but many major gaming companies are still cautious due to regulatory uncertainties, environmental concerns, and mixed player reactions.

In any instance, I hope I have offered a balanced overview of the whole space and debunked the myth that everything is completely unregulated. To this effect, I go back to the principle I introduced in my first book:

> **The Regulations at the Edges Principle.**
> When something unregulated starts touching something regulated, regulations will soon affect the unregulated thing, until, in time, what is unregulated becomes regulated.
>
> Neira Jones, August 2023

I think this chapter demonstrates this.

To complete our understanding of virtual assets, we must understand the trading facilities and markets available to users, and we'll look at this next in Chapter 6, before we delve into CBDCs in Chapter 7.

Let's go on the sixth leg of our trip.

Notes

1 Birch, D. (2017). *Before Babylon, Beyond Bitcoin: From Money that We Understand to Money that Understands Us*. London: London Publishing Partnership.

2 BerkShares website. Available at: https://berkshares.org/ (Accessed 22 July 2024).

3 "How the Collapse of Silicon Valley Bank Could Shape Fintech" *Finextra*, 21 April 2023. Available at: https://www.finextra.com/blogposting/24095/how-the-collapse-of-silicon-valley-bank-could-shape-fintech (Accessed 31 August 2024).

4 "Wirecard: Inside an Accounting Scandal" *Financial Times*, 7 February 2019. Available at: https://www.ft.com/content/d51a012e-1d6f-11e9-b126-46fc3ad87c65 (Accessed 5 August 2024).

5 "Wirecard: The Timeline" *Financial Times*, 25 June 2020. Available at: https://www.ft.com/content/284fb1ad-ddc0-45df-a075-0709b36868db (Accessed 5 August 2024).

6 "German Regulator Files Complaint on Alleged Wirecard Manipulation" *Financial Times*, 16 April 2019. Available at: https://www.ft.com/content/8e1948be-6060-11e9-b285-3acd5d43599e (Accessed 5 August 2024).
7 "Wirecard Scandal: Singapore Fines Financial Firms over Breaches" *BBC*, 22 June 2023. Available at: https://www.bbc.co.uk/news/business-65981701 (Accessed 5 August 2024).
8 "Wirecard Scandal: When All Lines of Defense against Corporate Fraud Fail" Oxford Business Law Blog, 23 November 2020. Available at: https://blogs.law.ox.ac.uk/business-law-blog/blog/2020/11/wirecard-scandal-when-all-lines-defense-against-corporate-fraud-fail (Accessed 5 August 2024).
9 "EY Fraud Expert: 'Incomprehensible' That Wirecard 'Red Flags' Were Ignored" *Financial Times*, 6 May 2021. Available at: https://www.ft.com/content/0288d7b1-1e52-4a3d-a9e1-6850afaed26 (Accessed 5 August 2024).
10 "Germany to Sever Ties with Accounting Watchdog after Wirecard Scandal" *Reuters*, 28 June 2020. Available at: https://www.reuters.com/article/technology/germany-to-sever-ties-with-accounting-watchdog-after-wirecard-scandal-idUSKBN23Z0J2/ (Accessed 5 August 2024).
11 European Parliament. (2020). What Are the Wider Supervisory Implications of the Wirecard Case? Available at: https://www.europarl.europa.eu/RegData/etudes/STUD/2020/651385/IPOL_STU(2020)651385_EN.pdf (Accessed 5 August 2024).
12 "The Double Life of Former Wirecard Executive Jan Marsalek" Spigel International, 5 March 2024. Available at: https://www.spiegel.de/international/business/jan-marsalek-an-agent-for-russia-the-double-life-of-the-former-wirecard-executive-a-7e667c03-6690-41e6-92ad-583d94ba97e0 (Accessed 5 August 2024).
13 "Wirecard ex-CEO Braun Loses Lawyer as Legal Funds Dry Up" *Reuters*, 5 Junes 2024. Available at: https://www.reuters.com/business/finance/wirecard-ex-ceo-braun-loses-lawyer-legal-funds-dry-up-2024-06-05/ (Accessed 5 August 2024).
14 "Two More Wirecard Executives Implicated in Widening Financial Scandal" *Finextra*, 6 August 2024. Available at: https://www.finextra.com/newsarticle/44552/two-more-wirecard-executives-implicated-in-widening-financial-scandal (Accessed 6 August 2024).
15 "Wirecard Asset Freeze Leaves Vulnerable People without Cash" *The Guardian*, 29 June 2020. Available at: https://www.theguardian.com/business/2020/jun/29/wirecard-asset-freeze-leaves-vulnerable-people-without-cash (Accessed 5 August 2024).

16 "The Wirecard Scandal: What Went Wrong?" *Investors Chronicle*, 1 July 2020. Available at: https://www.investorschronicle.co.uk/content/57f770af-4a9e-5f81-a5da-c4bb29d8b408 (Accessed 5 August 2024).

17 "UK Neobanks Set to Outpace Incumbents in Mobile Arms Race" *Finextra*, 25 July 2024. Available at: https://www.finextra.com/newsarticle/44496/uk-neobanks-set-to-outpace-incumbents-in-mobile-arms-race (Accessed 5 August 2024).

18 "Elon Musk Hints Dogecoin Payment for Teslas 'At Some Point'—Meme Currency Soars" *Forbes*, 14 March 2024. Available at: https://www.forbes.com/sites/roberthart/2024/03/14/elon-musk-hints-dogecoin-payment-for-teslas-at-some-point-meme-currency-soars/ (Accessed 21 July 2024).

19 "The Real Story Behind the 17th-Century 'Tulip Mania' Financial Crash" *History*, 16 March 2020. Available at: https://www.history.com/news/tulip-mania-financial-crash-holland (Accessed 21 July 2024).

20 "GDP, Current Prices" International Monetary Fund. Available at: https://www.imf.org/external/datamapper/NGDPD@WEO/OEMDC/ADVEC/WEOWORLD (Accessed 3 August 2024).

21 "GDP, Current Prices, Purchasing Power Parity" International Monetary Fund. Available at: https://www.imf.org/external/datamapper/PPPGDP@WEO/OEMDC/ADVEC/WEOWORLD (Accessed 3 August 2024).

22 "El Salvador Sees Greener Crypto-currency Mining in Its Future" *Reuters*, 15 October 2021. Available at: https://www.reuters.com/business/el-salvador-sees-greener-crypto-currency-mining-its-future-2021-10-15/ (Accessed 22 July 2024).

23 "Are Cryptocurrencies Currencies? Bitcoin as Legal Tender in El Salvador" April 2022, revised February 2023. Available at: https://www.nber.org/system/files/working_papers/w29968/w29968.pdf (Accessed 22 July 2024).

24 "A Year on, El Salvador's Bitcoin Experiment Is Stumbling" *Reuters*, 8 September 2022. Available at: https://www.reuters.com/technology/year-el-salvadors-bitcoin-experiment-is-stumbling-2022-09-07/ (Accessed 22 July 2024).

25 "El Salvador Mined Nearly 474 Bitcoins, Adding to State Crypto Holding, in Last Three Years" *Reuters*, 15 May 2024. Available at: https://www.reuters.com/world/americas/el-salvador-mined-nearly-474-bitcoins-adding-state-crypto-holding-last-three-2024-05-14/ (Accessed 22 July 2024).

26 "Short on Cash, El Salvador Doubles Down on Bitcoin Dream" *US News*, 2 February 2024. Available at: https://www.usnews.com/news/world/articles/2024-02-02/short-on-cash-el-salvador-doubles-down-on-bitcoin-dream (Accessed 22 July 2024).

27 "Central African Republic Adopts Bitcoin as an Official Currency" *Reuters*, 28 April 2024. Available at: https://www.reuters.com/world/africa/central-african-republic-adopts-bitcoin-an-official-currency-2022-04-27/ (Accessed 22 July 2024).
28 "CAR to Drop Crypto as Legal Tender" Central Banking, 27 March 2023. Available at: https://www.centralbanking.com/central-banks/currency/digital-currencies/7956294/car-to-drop-crypto-as-legal-tender (Accessed 22 July 2024).
29 Financial Action Task Force (FATF). (2021). Updated Guidance for a Risk-Based Approach to Virtual Assets and Virtual Asset Service Providers. Available at: https://www.fatf-gafi.org/media/fatf/documents/recommendations/RBA-VA-VASPs.pdf (Accessed 23 July 2024).
30 Amazon Coin Listing on Amazon UK: https://www.amazon.co.uk/coins (Accessed 30 July 2024).
31 "NFTs Engaging Today's Fans in Crypto and Commerce" Visa, 2022. Available at: https://usa.visa.com/content/dam/VCOM/regional/na/us/Solutions/documents/visa-nft-whitepaper.pdf (Accessed 30 July 2024).
32 "Are CryptoPunks Copyrightable? Are CryptoPunks Copyrightable?" Brian L. Frye, 2022. Available at: https://uknowledge.uky.edu/cgi/viewcontent.cgi?article=1725&context=law_facpub (Accessed 30 July 2024).
33 Packin, N.G. (ed.) (2024) *The Cambridge Handbook of Law and Policy for NFTs*. Cambridge: Cambridge University Press.
34 "Who Invented NFTs?: A Brief History of Nonfungible Tokens" *Cointelegraph*, 20 May 2023. Available at: https://cointelegraph.com/explained/who-invented-nfts-a-brief-history-of-nonfungible-tokens (Accessed 25 July 2024).
35 "Quantum: The Story Behind the World's First NFT" NFT Now, 21 March 2023. Available at: https://nftnow.com/art/quantum-the-first-piece-of-nft-art-ever-created/ (Accesses 3 August 2024).
36 "First Ever NFT Goes up for Auction at Sothebys" yahoo!finance 5 June 2021. Available at: https://finance.yahoo.com/news/first-ever-nft-goes-auction-164000957.html (Accessed 28 December 2024).
37 "Insight: How a 10-Second Video Clip Sold for $6.6 million" *Reuters*, 1 March 2021. Available at: https://www.reuters.com/business/media-telecom/how-10-second-video-clip-sold-66-million-2021-03-01/ (Accessed 25 July 2024).
38 "Online Auction 20447, Beeple | The First 5000 days" Christie's website. Available at: https://onlineonly.christies.com/s/beeple-first-5000-days/beeple-b-1981-1/112924 (Accessed 25 July 2024).
39 NBA Top Shot website. Available at: https://nbatopshot.com/ (Accessed 31 August 2024).

40 Axie Infinity website. Available at: https://axieinfinity.com/ (Accessed 31 August 2024).
41 "Kings of Leon Will Be the First Band to Release an Album as an NFT" *Rolling Stone*, 3 March 2021. Available at: https://www.rollingstone.com/pro/news/kings-of-leon-when-you-see-yourself-album-nft-crypto-1135192/ (Accessed 3 August 2024).
42 "Bitcoin Ordinal NFT: Everything You Need to Know" Investopedia, 8 December 2023. Available at: https://www.investopedia.com/what-are-bitcoin-ordinals-7486436 (Accessed 26 July 2024).
43 "What Is Bitcoin's Taproot Upgrade?" *The Block*, 13 February 2024. Available at: https://www.theblock.co/learn/271535/what-is-bitcoins-taproot-upgrade (Accessed 26 July 2024).
44 "Dapper Labs Settles NBA Top Shot NFT Lawsuit for US$4 mln" *Yahoo! Finance*, 4 June 2024. Available at: https://finance.yahoo.com/news/dapper-labs-settles-nba-top-090101761.html (Accessed 3 August 2024).
45 "'CryptoPunk' NFT Sells for $11.8 Million at Sotheby's" *Reuters*, 10 June 2021. Available at: https://www.reuters.com/technology/cryptopunk-nft-sells-118-million-sothebys-2021-06-10/ (Accessed 3 August 2024).
46 Adidas collect website. Available at: https://collect.adidas.com/ (Accessed 3 August 2024).
47 "Visa Steps into the Metaverse with First NFT Purchase" Blockworks, 2021. Available at: https://blockworks.co/news/visa-steps-into-the-metaverse-with-first-nft-purchase (Accessed 30 July 2024).
48 Visa NFT Creator Program. Visa website. Available at: https://usa.visa.com/partner-with-us/info-for-partners/visa-creator-program.html (Accessed 30 July 2024).
49 "MoonPay's Supported Payment Methods" Moonpay website. Available at: https://support.moonpay.com/customers/docs/moonpays-supported-payment-methods-1 (Accessed 30 July 2024).
50 "Mastercard Brings Its Payments Network to Web3 and NFTs" Mastercard, 9 June 2022. Available at: https://www.mastercard.com/news/perspectives/2022/simple-nft-purchasing-on-nft-marketplaces/ (Accessed 30 July 2024).
51 "Mastercard to Allow 2.9B Cardholders to Make Direct NFT Purchases" *Cointelegraph*, 10 June 2022. Available at: https://cointelegraph.com/news/mastercard-to-allow-2-9b-cardholders-to-make-direct-nft-purchases (Accessed 30 June 2024).
52 "Parade NFT" Macy's website. Available at: https://www.macys.com/social/macys-parade-nft/?cache=1722255659866 (Accessed 30 July 2024).
53 Make-A-Wish website. Available at: https://wish.org/ (Accessed 30 July 2024).

54 "Starbucks Brewing Revolutionary Web3 Experience for Its Starbucks Rewards Members" Starbucks, 12 September 2022. Available at: https://stories.starbucks.com/press/2022/starbucks-brewing-revolutionary-web3-experience-for-its-starbucks-rewards-members/ (Accessed 30 July 2024).

55 "Transitioning from Web2 to Web3 Loyalty Programs: Enhancing Customer Loyalty with NFTs" *Medium*, 7 August 2023. Available at: https://medium.com/@kristina.hayhoe/transitioning-from-web2-to-web3-loyalty-programs-enhancing-customer-loyalty-with-nfts-39aad002b5d7 (Accessed 30 July 2024).

56 "Korean Retailer Issues Blockchain Warranties as NFTs for Luxury Items" *Ledger Insights*, 25 August 2021. Available at: https://www.ledgerinsights.com/korean-retailer-shinsegae-blockchain-warranty-as-nft-for-luxury-items/ (Accessed 29 July 2024).

57 "The Collapse of FTX: What Went Wrong with the Crypto Exchange?" Investopedia, 6 June 2024. Available at: https://www.investopedia.com/what-went-wrong-with-ftx-6828447 (Accessed 3 August 2024).

58 "Top NFT Business Models for 2024" GamesPad website. Available at: https://gamespad.io/top-nft-business-models-for-2024/ (Accessed 30 July 2024).

59 "Meet a 25-Year-Old NFT Collector Who Earned $75,000 the Day of the ApeCoin Airdrop—Before the Bored Ape Token Surged 90%" *Yahoo! Finance*, 18 March 2022. Available at: https://finance.yahoo.com/news/meet-25-old-nft-collector-142922500.html (Accessed 30 July 2024).

60 "SVB Collapse Was Driven by 'The First Twitter-Fueled Bank Run'" *CNN*, 14 March 2023. Available at: https://edition.cnn.com/2023/03/14/tech/viral-bank-run/index.html (Accessed 3 August 2024).

61 "Here's What On-Chain Data Tells Us about Crypto's Reaction to the Demise of Silicon Valley Bank and Its Impact on USDC" Chainalysis, 16 March 2023. Available at: https://www.chainalysis.com/blog/crypto-market-usdc-silicon-valley-bank/ (Accessed 3 August 2024).

62 "Silvergate, Silicon Valley Bank, Signature and the "Unbanking" of U.S. Crypto" Linklaters, 17 March 2023. Available at: https://www.linklaters.com/en/insights/blogs/fintechlinks/2023/march/silvergate-silicon-valley-bank-signature-and-the-unbanking-of-us-crypto (Accessed 3 August 2024).

63 Commodity Futures Trading Commission. (2021). *In the Matter of: Tether Holdings Limited, Tether Operations Limited, Tether International Limited, and Tether Limited*. Washington, DC: CFTC.

64 "The Silicon Valley Bank Collapse Explained" University of Washington, School of Law, 24 March 2023. Available at: https://www.law.uw.edu/news-events/news/2023/svb-collapse (Accessed 1 August 2024).

65 "SEC's Scrutiny of USDC Could Derail Circle IPO Plan: Barron's" *Crypto Briefing*, 19 June 2024. Available at: https://cryptobriefing.com/secs-scrutiny-usdc-security-circle-ipo-plan/ (Accessed 1 August 2024).

66 Paxos website, BUSD. Available at: https://paxos.com/busd/ (Accessed 7 August 2024).

67 Rostova, N., Klinova, A., and Klinova, A. (2023). How Algorithmic Stablecoins Fail. Swiss National Bank. Available at: https://www.snb.ch/dam/jcr:5140cb30-3c8c-433d-8619-0354b8f1036e/sem_2023_05_26_rostova.n.pdf (Accessed 1 August 2024).

68 International Monetary Fund. (2023). Assessing Macrofinancial Risks from Crypto Assets. Available at: https://www.imf.org/-/media/Files/Publications/WP/2023/English/wpiea2023214-print-pdf.ashx (Accessed 1 August 2024).

69 CNBC. (2022). UST Debacle Will 'Probably be the End' of Algorithmic Stablecoins. Available at: https://www.cnbc.com/2022/06/02/ust-debacle-will-probably-be-the-end-of-algorithmic-stablecoins.html (Accessed 1 August 2024).

70 "Regulation (EU) 2023/1114 of The European Parliament and of The Council" EUR-LEX. Available at: https://eur-lex.europa.eu/legal-content/EN/TXT/?uri=CELEX%3A32023R1114 (Accessed 7 August 2024).

71 "Terra Crash Sharpens Washington's Attention on Crypto Regulations" MarketWatch, 18 May 2022. Available at: https://www.marketwatch.com/story/terra-crash-sharpens-washingtons-attention-on-crypto-regulations-11652800609 (Accessed 7 August 2024).

72 USDJ on coinmarketcap.com. Available at: https://coinmarketcap.com/currencies/usdj/ (Accessed 1 August 2024).

73 "Circle, Stellar, MoneyGram and the UNHCR Convene to Advance Humanitarian Aid" *Circle*, 13 April 2023. Available at: https://www.circle.com/blog/circle-stellar-moneygram-and-the-unhcr-convene-to-advance-humanitarian-aid (Accessed 31 July 2024).

74 "Cross-border Payments Made Easy with Digital Money: Experience the Future – Today" SAP, 25 June 2023. Available at: https://community.sap.com/t5/technology-blogs-by-sap/cross-border-payments-made-easy-with-digital-money-experience-the-future/ba-p/13560384 (Accessed 31 July 2024).

75 "$40 Billion Payments Giant Checkout.com Leaps into Crypto with Stablecoin Payments Feature" *CNBC*, 29 June 2022. Available at: https://www.cnbc.com/2022/06/07/checkoutcom-jumps-into-crypto-with-stablecoin-payments-feature.html (Accessed 31 July 2024).

76 "Worldpay from FIS Becomes First Global Merchant Acquirer to Offer Direct USDC Settlement, Driving Digital Currency Adoption to

Businesses" FIS, 6 April 2022. Available at: https://www.fisglobal.com/about-us/media-room/press-release/2022/worldpay-from-fis-becomes-first-global-merchant-acquirer-to-offer-direct-usdc-settlement (Accessed 31 July 2024).

77 "PayPal Launches U.S. Dollar Stablecoin" Paypal, 7 August 2023. Available at: https://newsroom.paypal-corp.com/2023-08-07-PayPal-Launches-U-S-Dollar-Stablecoin (Accessed 31 July 2024).

78 "The Briefing: How Ramp's Early Adoption of Stablecoins Increased Our Corporate Treasury Returns" Ramp, 13 January 2022. Available at: https://ramp.com/blog/how-stablecoins-increased-our-corporate-treasury-returns (Accessed 1 August 2024).

79 "The Stablecoin Opportunity and How to Make It a Reality" Checkout.com, 20 June 2022. Available at: https://www.checkout.com/blog/the-stablecoin-opportunity-and-how-to-make-it-a-reality (Accessed 1 August 2024).

80 "The Role of Stablecoins in Making Trade Financing More Responsive" AUDD, 22 August 2023. Available at: https://www.audd.digital/the-role-of-stablecoins-in-making-trade-financing-more-responsive/ (Accessed 1 August 224).

81 "The Regulated Liability Network – Digital Sovereign Currency" The Regulated Liability Network, 15 November 2022. Available at: https://regulatedliabilitynetwork.org/ (Accessed 31 July 2024).

82 "Stablecoin Use Cases: Gaming" PoundToken, 13 June 2023. Available at: https://poundtoken.io/blogs/stablecoin-use-cases-gaming/ (Accessed 31 July 2024).

83 "How Blockchain Helped a Gaming Platform Become a Game Changer" EY website. Available at: https://www.ey.com/en_uk/consulting/how-digital-transformation-opened-new-channels-for-growth (Accessed 31 July 2024).

84 "World Bank Prices First Global Blockchain Bond, Raising A$110 Million" World Bank, 23 August 2028. Available at: https://www.worldbank.org/en/news/press-release/2018/08/23/world-bank-prices-first-global-blockchain-bond-raising-a110-million (Accessed 1 August 2024).

85 "In $18 Million Deal, Nearly One-fifth of St. Regis Aspen Sells through Digital Tokens" *The Aspen Times*, 9 October 2018. Available at: https://www.aspentimes.com/trending/in-18-million-deal-nearly-one-fifth-of-st-regis-aspen-sells-through-digital-tokens/ (Accessed 1 August 2024).

86 "Invesco Launches Blockchain ETF with Elwood Asset Management" *Finextra*, 11 March 2019. Available at: https://www.finextra.com/pressarticle/77587/invesco-launches-blockchain-etf-with-elwood-asset-management (Accessed 1 August 2024).

87 Masterworks website. Available at: https://www.masterworks.io (Accessed: 23 July 2024).
88 Polymath website. Available at: https://polymath.network/ (Accessed: 23 July 2024).
89 ConsensysCodefiAssetswebsite.Availableat:https://consensys.io/staking/assets (Accessed 24 July 2024).
90 DTCC website. Available at: https://www.dtcc.com/dtcc-digital-assets/solutions/tokenization (Accessed 24 July 2024).
91 Atomyze website. Available at: https://atomyze.us/ (Accessed: 23 July 2024).
92 Securitize website. Available at: https://securitize.io/ (Accessed: 23 July 2024).
93 Security Token Market website. Available at: https://stomarket.com/ (Accessed 24 July 2024).
94 Aspen Coin token trading. Security Token Market website. Available at: https://stomarket.com/sto/aspencoin-st-regis-aspd/trading (Accessed: 30 November 2024).
95 Blockchain Capital Token BCAP. Available at: https://stomarket.com/sto/blockchain-capital-bcap (Accessed: 23 July 2024).
96 INX. (2023). INX Token. Available at: https://www.inx.co/inx-token/ (Accessed: 23 July 2024).
97 "INX Launches On-Chain Tokenized NVIDIA Share Trading" *Business Insider*, 11 July 2024. Available at: https://markets.businessinsider.com/news/currencies/inx-launches-on-chain-tokenized-nvidia-share-trading-1033548327 (Accessed 24 July 2024).
98 RealT. (2023). Tokenized Real Estate. Available at: https://realt.co/ (Accessed: 23 July 2024).
99 Coreestate website. Available at: https://coreestate.io/ (Accessed 2 August 2024).
100 Arca Labs website. Available at: https://www.arcalabs.com/ (Accessed: 23 July 2024).
101 "Maecenas Successfully Tokenises First Multi-million Dollar Artwork on the Blockchain" Maecenas website, 6 September 2018. Available at: https://blog.maecenas.co/blockchain-art-auction-andy-warhol/ (Accessed 30 November 2024).
102 Centrifuge website. Available at: https://centrifuge.io/ (Accessed: 23 July 2024).
103 BondbloX website. Available at: https://www.bondblox.com/ (Accessed: 23 July 2024).

104 Bitbond STO website. Available at: https://www.bitbondsto.com/ (Accessed 2 August 2024).

105 Sun, W., Wu, X. (Brian), and Kwok, A. (2019). *Security Tokens and Stablecoins Quick Start Guide: Learn How to Build STO and Stablecoin Decentralized Applications*. Birmingham: Packt Publishing, Limited.

106 Hines, B. and Wiley, J. (2021). *Digital Finance: Security Tokens and Unlocking the Real Potential of Blockchain*. Hoboken, NJ: John Wiley & Sons, Inc.

6

TRANSACTING IN A DECENTRALISED WORLD

Introduction

The way we interact with money has undergone a dramatic transformation. From tangible coins and paper bills, it has evolved into a complex digital ecosystem. Once confined to physical wallets and bank vaults, the ways we use financial assets now unfold primarily in the digital realm. This shift has brought unprecedented convenience and opportunity, but it has also introduced new challenges and risks.

This chapter explores how traditional finance has adapted to the digital age, examining the various types of traditional digital wallets and how they function. We'll then journey into the dynamic landscape of crypto-asset interactions, further expand the concepts of public and private keys, introduce custodial and non-custodial wallets, and the distinctions between hot and cold storage.

Beyond wallets, we'll examine the marketplaces where crypto-assets are traded. From centralised crypto exchanges to decentralised platforms,

DOI: 10.4324/9781003480761-7

we'll uncover the intricacies of these trading venues and the factors that influence their popularity. This includes exploring both the successes and failures of prominent exchanges, such as the cautionary tales of Mt. Gox and futures exchange (FTX).

As we navigate this complex terrain, we'll uncover the convergence of traditional and digital payment systems and explore the potential impact on our financial future. By the end of this chapter, you'll have a comprehensive understanding of how money is evolving and the opportunities and challenges that lie ahead.

Digital wallets (where does all the money go?)

At a high level, digital wallets are secure platforms that provide a user-friendly interface for storing, managing, sending, receiving, and trading digital assets.

In this chapter, we'll look at the two main types of digital wallets:

- **Traditional digital wallets**: centralised digital facilities that enable wallet holders to interact with their money using centralised banking or payment systems.
- **Crypto wallets**: digital facilities that enable wallet holders to interact with their crypto-assets that are stored on blockchains.

To delve deeper into this evolving landscape, we'll begin by examining traditional digital wallets, understanding their structure, functionalities, and how they've shaped our digital financial lives.

Traditional digital wallets

These wallets are part of our everyday lives and may be used for a wide variety of purposes. They are sometimes classified into two categories:

- **e-wallet**: a hardware-agnostic digital wallet accessible via desktop, mobile, or other devices.
- **Mobile wallet**: a type of e-wallet specifically designed for smartphones.

But this classification is not very helpful if we want to understand how digital wallets operate. We have to categorise them further as shown in Figure 6.1:

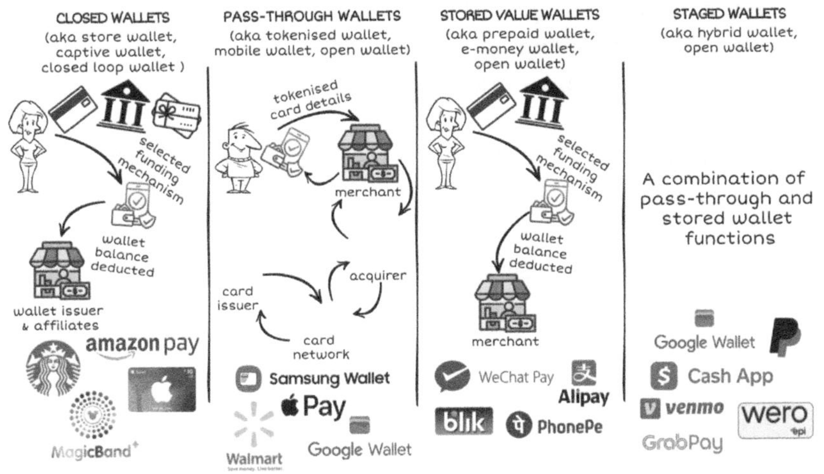

Figure 6.1 Traditional digital wallets. © 2024 Neira Jones.

As this can be a bit overwhelming (e.g. Do they store funds? Do they not? How do they work?), we'll go over these in the next sections. For those already familiar with the different types of wallets presented in Figure 6.1, just skip to the recap.

Closed wallets

A closed wallet is a digital wallet restricted to transactions within a specific ecosystem, brand, store, service provider, or merchant network. These wallets often include elements such as loyalty programmes, tailored rewards, as well as a recognisable brand experience.

- **Issuer**: the ecosystem owner, typically operating as a payment institution in the EU, or equivalent in other geographies. Because of the limited network (wallet used at issuer only), issuers typically don't need an e-money licence or similar.
- **Funding sources**: a user's linked bank account, credit/ debit card, gift cards/vouchers, etc.
- **Asset stored**: the wallet holds customer funds issued by the wallet provider, similar to e-money.
- **User fees**: typically, there are no direct user fees for using closed wallets, but users may encounter inactivity fees if the wallet is not used for a certain period.

- **Merchant fees**: not applicable as transactions occur within the wallet issuer's own ecosystem.
- **Payment rail used**: proprietary payment system.
- **Process**:
  - The user links a bank account or credit card to the wallet.
  - When a user makes a purchase, the wallet deducts funds from the user's balance.
  - The merchant receives payment from the wallet issuer.
- **Other names**: store wallet, captive wallet, closed-loop wallet.
- **Examples**: Amazon Pay, Starbucks app, Apple Gift Card, Disney MagicBands.

The fact that these wallet are "closed loop" is no indication of limited size or market share. For example, for fiscal year 2023, Starbucks reported $1.5 billion in revenue for their stored value cards (Starbucks app) and linked loyalty programme (Starbucks Rewards), with more than $210 million in customer unspent balances (aka "breakage", or as I like to call it "free money for the issuer").[1]

Closed wallets are ideal for loyal customers of a specific brand or store, offering exclusive perks and rewards but may feel restrictive for those who shop across different brands. In addition, they benefit merchants by fostering customer loyalty and ensuring transactions remain within their ecosystem, but they limit merchant exposure to a broader customer base outside the closed network.

Pass-through wallets

A pass-through wallet stores payment card information for quick and secure transactions but doesn't hold funds. Think of it as a convenient digital wrapper for your physical payment cards.

- **Issuer**: technology companies or financial institutions (often with payment institution license).
- **Funding sources**: linked credit or debit cards.
- **Asset stored**: the wallet doesn't store customer funds.
- **User fees**: generally, there are no direct fees for users when using pass-through wallets.

- **Merchant fees**: pass-through wallets don't impose fees on merchants.
- **Payment rail used**: card networks (e.g. Visa, Mastercard)
- **Process**:
  - User adds their credit or debit card information to the wallet.
  - When a user makes a purchase, the wallet generates a token representing the card information.
  - The token is sent to the merchant for payment processing.
  - The merchant sends a payment request to the card issuer.
  - If authorised, the card issuer approves the transaction.
- **Other names**: tokenised wallet, mobile wallet, open wallet.
- **Examples**: Apple Pay, Google Wallet (for pass-through functions), Samsung Wallet, Walmart Pay.

Pass-through wallets provide the convenience of having your credit or debit card information securely stored on your phone, allowing quick and secure payments without the need for physical cards, a bit like the 21st-century version of a leather wallet. In addition, they offer merchants a seamless and secure payment process without additional fees, but they rely on existing card networks which already impose transaction fees.

Whilst pass-through wallet providers themselves don't directly profit from transaction fees, they can generate revenue through other means, such as data analytics, value-added services, or partnerships with financial institutions. For instance, partnerships with card issuers can provide pass-through wallets with valuable customer data, enabling them to offer targeted marketing and financial products. In return, card issuers may share a portion of fees or other revenue streams with the wallet provider, incentivising their participation in the payment ecosystem.

Stored value wallets

A stored value wallet primarily focuses on storing value for transactions, rather than acting as a payment intermediary.

- **Issuer**: financial institutions or technology companies, often with an e-money license (EU) or equivalent.

- **Funding sources**: cards, bank accounts, other wallets, P2P transfers, over-the-counter (OTC) payments, cash deposits, vouchers, payroll deposits, government benefits, cryptocurrency (emerging), etc.
- **Asset stored**: the wallet holds customer funds as e-money issued by the wallet provider.
- **User fees**: users might face fees for loading and withdrawing funds, for expedited transfers, account maintenance, or currency conversion
- **Merchant fees**: merchants are typically not charged a fee by the wallet issuer (other than potential, and optional, premium services not directly tied to transaction processing, such as analytics and loyalty).
- **Payment rail used**: proprietary payment systems, local payment schemes.
- **Process**:
  - User loads funds into the wallet, typically through a linked bank account, credit card, or cash deposit (depending on the provider).
  - When a user makes a purchase, funds are deducted from the wallet balance.
- **Other names**: prepaid wallet, e-money wallet, open wallet.
- **Examples**: Alipay (China), WeChat Pay (China), Vanilla Prepaid Card (United States), Green Dot MoneyPak (United States), Blik (Poland), PhonePe (India), and Paytm (India).

Stored value wallets are well suited for individuals who prefer to manage their spending by preloading funds, offering ease of use across multiple currencies and funding sources. In addition, they allow merchants to accept preloaded funds without incurring transaction fees, though they may require investment in wallet integration to facilitate seamless transactions.

Stored value wallet providers often adopt a fee-free model for merchants to attract a larger merchant base and encourage wider acceptance of the wallet. By eliminating transaction fees, these wallets become a more attractive payment option for businesses, especially small merchants. This can lead to increased usage of the wallet, which in turn can generate revenue through various means, such as user fees, interest on stored funds (where allowed by regulations), and the sale of additional financial services (e.g. loans, insurance products, investment opportunities, money transfer services to their user base). Additionally, a vast user base can provide valuable data for targeted marketing and partnerships, further contributing to the wallet provider's profitability.

Staged wallets

A staged wallet combines elements of both pass-through and stored value wallets, allowing users to store funds and/or use payment card information, or facilitate fund transfers between bank accounts.

- **Issuer**: financial institutions or technology companies, often with an e-money license (EU) or equivalent for stored value elements.
- **Process**:
  - A user can either link a payment card or load funds into the wallet, or link bank accounts for direct transfers.
  - When a user makes a purchase, funds can be deducted from the wallet balance, charged to the linked card, or transferred directly between bank accounts.
- **Funding sources**: linked bank accounts, credit cards, debit cards, prepaid balance, other wallets, cash deposits (in some cases), loyalty points (in some cases), cryptocurrency (in some cases).
- **Asset stored**: the wallet may hold customer funds as e-money for peer-to-peer (P2P) transactions or as a float for transaction processing.
- **User fees**: users might face fees for transferring funds to a bank account, currency conversion, withdrawals, or expedited transfers.
- **Merchant fees**: merchants may incur specific transaction fees imposed by the wallet issuer, but these are not typical for stored value transactions.
- **Payment rail used**: card networks (e.g. Visa, Mastercard), bank transfers, proprietary payment systems.
- **Other names**: hybrid wallet, open wallet.
- **Examples**: Google Wallet (for stored value or pass-through functions using Visa, Mastercard, or local payment schemes), PayPal (for stored value and pass-through functions, using Visa, Mastercard, PayPal network, bank transfers), GrabPay (Singapore, Malaysia, Philippines, Indonesia), Cash App (primarily US), Venmo (primarily US), Zelle (bank transfers, primarily US), Wero (bank transfers, European Union).

Staged wallets offer a versatile solution by combining the ability to store funds and link payment cards, providing flexibility but requiring careful management of various funding options. In addition, they provide merchants with the flexibility to accommodate various payment methods and funding sources, but they may involve specific transaction fees imposed by the wallet issuer, which can impact the merchant's cost structure.

Recap on traditional digital wallets

Traditional digital wallets have truly changed the game in how we manage our money, bringing a level of convenience and flexibility that makes everyday transactions a breeze. Each type of wallet is designed to fit different lifestyles and needs. In some geographies, like China, digital wallets have been the preferred payment method for a long time. Table 6.1 gives a useful summary.

Here's a quick recap:

- **Closed wallets** are great if you're loyal to a particular brand or store, offering perks and rewards that make shopping more enjoyable. However, they can feel a bit restrictive if you like to shop around.
- **Pass-through wallets** are like having your credit or debit card on your phone, making payments quick and secure without the hassle of carrying physical cards. They keep your card details safe through tokenisation, which helps reduce the risk of fraud.
- **Stored value wallets** are perfect for those who like to plan their spending by loading funds in advance from potentially multiple sources. They can also make it easier to handle transactions in different currencies. Selecting a reputable wallet provider is advisable, as there's always a risk of losing access to your funds if something goes wrong with the provider.
- **Staged wallets** offer a flexible approach by letting you store funds and link cards, giving you the best of both worlds. They're versatile but can get a bit tricky to manage with all the different funding options.

Whilst these digital wallets offer plenty of benefits like enhanced security and convenience, they also come with some downsides, such as tech dependency and potential fees that users or merchants may incur.

Table 6.1 Comparing traditional digital wallets. © 2024 Neira Jones

Feature	**Closed Wallet**	**Pass-Through Wallet**	**Stored Value Wallet**	**Staged Wallet**
Issuer	Ecosystem owner	Technology companies or financial institutions	Financial institutions or technology companies	Financial institutions or technology companies
Funding source	Linked bank account, credit/debit card, gift cards/vouchers	Linked credit or debit cards	Cards, bank accounts, other wallets, P2P transfers, OTC payments, cash, vouchers, government benefits, payroll deposits, cryptocurrency	Linked bank accounts, credit cards, debit cards, prepaid balance, other wallets, cash deposits, loyalty points, cryptocurrency
Assets stored	Customer funds similar to e-money	Does not store customer funds	Customer funds as e-money	May hold customer funds as e-money
User fees	Typically no direct user fees, possible inactivity fees	Generally no direct fees	Possible fees for loading, withdrawing, expedited transfers, account maintenance, currency conversion	Possible fees for transferring funds to a bank account, currency conversion, withdrawals, expedited transfers
Merchant fees	Not applicable within issuer's ecosystem	No fees imposed by wallet issuer	Typically no fees, except for optional services	Possible transaction fees, not typical for stored value
Payment rails	Proprietary payment system	Card networks (e.g., Visa, Mastercard)	Proprietary systems, local payment schemes	Card networks, bank transfers, proprietary systems
Other names	Store wallet, captive wallet, closed-loop wallet	Tokenised wallet, mobile wallet, open wallet	Prepaid wallet, e-money wallet, open wallet	Hybrid wallet, open wallet
Examples	Amazon Pay, Starbucks app, Apple Gift Card, Disney MagicBands	Apple Pay, Google Wallet, Samsung Wallet, Walmart Pay	Alipay, WeChat Pay, Vanilla Prepaid Card, Green Dot MoneyPak, Blik, PhonePe, Paytm	Google Wallet, PayPal, GrabPay, Cash App, Venmo, Zelle, Wero

As we transition into the world of crypto wallets, we'll explore how they offer different approaches to managing digital assets. What unique features do crypto wallets bring to the table, and how do they compare to traditional digital wallets in terms of security and functionality? Let's delve into this evolving, alternate landscape, and find out.

Crypto wallets

A crypto wallet is a digital wallet that enables users to manage their cryptocurrencies and other crypto-assets by storing the private and public keys necessary to access and interact with blockchain networks. It doesn't store the cryptocurrencies themselves, which are recorded on the blockchain, but provides the interface for users to send, receive, and track their assets.

Unlike traditional assets like money or money substitutes, stocks, and bonds, which are stored in traditional financial accounts or wallets, crypto-assets are recorded on blockchains or other distributed ledger technology. Crypto wallets provide the user interface between blockchains, where crypto-assets are stored, and users who need to prove that they own crypto-assets. This involves cryptographic keys, more specifically public and private keys.

Public and private keys

We covered this concept in Chapter 1 (see Figure 1.15). Crypto wallets store these keys:

- **Public key**: allows users to receive crypto transactions and can be freely shared. Anyone can send transactions to a public key.
- **Private key**: proves that the user owns the crypto-asset. A user needs the private key to "unlock" a transaction and prove that they own the crypto-asset received in the transaction. This key, stored in the crypto

wallet, must be kept secure as losing a private key means losing access to the crypto-asset.

You can have any number of public keys connected to a private key. Public and private keys fit together and are known as key pairs. Users will submit transactions by digitally signing them (see Chapter 1, *Submitting transactions*), which means that the transaction will be encrypted using the public key and signed with the private key, which proves that the transaction hasn't been altered. Nodes will then validate transactions as explained in Chapter 1, *Validating transactions.*

Crypto wallets can be categorised into several types, including software wallets (mobile and desktop applications), hardware wallets (physical devices designed for secure storage), and paper wallets (printed documents containing public and private keys). Each type offers different levels of security and convenience for managing digital assets The types of crypto wallets are shown in Figure 6.2.

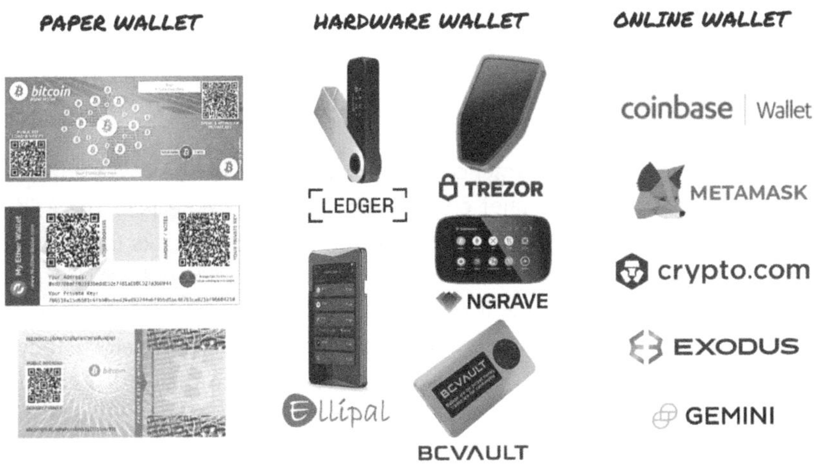

Figure 6.2 Crypto wallets. © 2024 Neira Jones.

In the cryptographically enabled blockchain world, keys are important, and understanding the implications of key management is equally important. This is why crypto wallets are further categorised according to who manages the keys.

Custodial vs. non-custodial wallets

The phrase "Not you keys… Not your crypto" is a fundamental mantra in the crypto community, and it emphasises the importance of controlling one's private keys to truly prove ownership of crypto-assets.

BOX 6.1 NOT YOUR KEYS... NOT YOUR CRYPTO

The phrase is often attributed to Andreas Antonopoulos, a prominent figure in the crypto space. He popularised the saying "Your keys, your Bitcoin. Not your keys, not your Bitcoin" during a Bloktex event in Kuala Lumpur, Malaysia, in 2017.[2] Antonopoulos is known for advocating the importance of self-custody and educating people about the risks of relying on centralised exchanges (CEX) to hold their proof of ownership of cryptocurrencies (see later section in this chapter).

Following Antonopoulos's use of the phrase, it gained traction within the crypto community, especially on platforms like Reddit and Twitter, where users frequently discussed the importance of controlling private keys to ensure true ownership of crypto- assets. Overtime, several variations of the saying have been used to express this sentiment, such as "Not your keys... Not your crypto", or "Not your keys... Not your coins".

The phrase saw a resurgence in popularity in November 2022 during the collapse of FTX, a major crypto exchange at the time (see *The FTX scandal* later in this section). The event highlighted the risks of storing keys on CEX, as many users lost access to their funds when the exchange went bankrupt. This incident reinforced the message behind "Not your keys, not your coins", as users realised the importance of self-custody in protecting their assets. The saying underscores a critical aspect of cryptocurrency ownership: if you do not hold the private keys to your wallet, you do not have full control over your coins. This concept is crucial for crypto users to understand, as it directly relates to the security and autonomy of their digital assets.

Consequently, we can further classify wallets into custodial and non-custodial, and the main differences are shown in Table 6.2.

Table 6.2 Comparing custodial and non-custodial wallets. © 2024 Neira Jones

Features	**Custodial Wallet**	**Non-Custodial Wallet**
Access to funds	The private keys are controlled by the wallet issuer	The private keys are controlled by the wallet user
Account creation	Involves KYC and AML checks, which potentially makes account creation slower	No KYC or AML checks, making account creation fast
Access	Online	Online, offline
Recovery of funds	Options are available to recover access to login credentials since accounts are centrally managed by the wallet issuer	Varies depending on the wallet type. Some hardware wallets offer backup options
Security	Depends on the wallet issuer security processes and technologies deployed	Depends on the wallet user's ability to manage the security of their private keys
Convenience	Generally more user friendly, with active interfaces	Technical knowledge required
Crypto-assets supported	Typically supports major cryptocurrencies like BTC, Ethereum, and the top 20–50 altcoins by market capitalisation. NFT support is limited, often only available on selected platforms The range of supported assets is determined by the wallet provider and may change based on regulatory considerations. Adding new assets requires provider approval and implementation	Generally supports a wider range of cryptocurrencies, including less common altcoins and tokens. Many non-custodial wallets, especially those Ethereum-based (like MetaMask), allow users to add custom ERC-20 tokens. NFT support is more common, particularly in Ethereum-based wallets which can display and manage ERC-721 and ERC-1155 tokens. Some wallets may be dedicated to one crypto, such as Trezor with their Trezor Safe 5 Bitcoin-Only The range of supported assets is determined by the wallet's underlying blockchain support and the user's ability to add custom tokens

(Continued)

Table 6.2 (Continued)

Features	Custodial Wallet	Non-Custodial Wallet
Access to dApps	No direct access	Full and direct access to a wide range of dApps and services across various blockchain networks. Users can interact with dApps directly from their wallet interface
DeFi SUPPORT	No direct support	Extensive support for DeFi services. Users can directly interact with DeFi protocols for lending, borrowing, yield farming, liquidity provision, and more Provides full access to the DeFi ecosystem with no restrictions from the wallet provider
Interoperability	Limited to the platforms and services integrated by the wallet provider Typically operates within a single blockchain ecosystem	Some wallets support multiple blockchain networks, increasing the variety of supported assets, enabling cross-chain transactions and asset transfers
Transaction finality	The transaction is not reflected on chain in real-time Finality depends on the wallet provider's internal processes and may not be immediate	The transaction is reflected on chain in real time, but true finality can vary depending on the blockchain. For example, BTC transactions typically require multiple confirmations for finality, whilst some other chains offer faster finality
Examples	Coinbase Wallet, Binance, Kraken	MetaMask, Ledger, Trezor, MEW

Professionals should remember the following:

- **Custodial wallets** offer a more user-friendly experience with simplified account management and recovery processes. The security of users' funds is primarily reliant on the wallet provider's systems. Whilst this can be convenient, it also means that users relinquish control over their private keys. This trade-off in security for ease of use is a key consideration.
- **Non-custodial wallets**, on the other hand, place full control of crypto-assets in the user's hands through the management of private keys. This provides a higher level of security but demands a greater understanding of crypto-assets and associated risks. Whilst these wallets offer more flexibility and access to the broader crypto ecosystem, they also require more technical knowledge and careful management to prevent potential loss of funds.

Note from the author: of course, this space evolves rapidly, and whilst the information provided in Table 6.2 is current at the time of writing, this may evolve in many areas, including assets and services supported.

In addition, you'll often hear about two main types of wallets: hot wallets and cold wallets. Each has its perks, and understanding their differences can help determine the right mix of convenience and security.

Hot and cold wallets

Hot wallets are a bit like traditional digital wallets. They are connected to the internet, which makes them convenient for quick transactions and frequent trading. This means that users can easily access their funds whenever needed. Hot wallets typically come in the form of software applications or mobile apps, such as MetaMask and Coinbase Wallet. However, because they are always online, they are more vulnerable to potential hacks and online threats. So, whilst they are perfect for day-to-day crypto use, caution is advised. For these reasons, hot wallet providers implement several security measures to protect users, such as encryption, **two-factor authentication**, IP address and device whitelisting (allowing users to restrict access to their accounts from specific trusted devices or locations), or multi-signature (multi-sig) technology which requires multiple private keys to authorise a transaction. In addition, reputable wallet providers often store users' data in offline storage (aka "cold storage"), keeping only a small portion of data online for immediate transactions. Many providers also conduct regular security audits and penetration testing to identify and address potential vulnerabilities. Hot wallets are often referred to as "hot storage".

On the other hand, **cold wallets** are a bit like a safe deposit box. These wallets are offline, which makes them more secure against online threats. Cold wallets usually take the form of physical devices that resemble USB sticks, although in the early days, paper wallets (the original cold wallets) were popular. They are ideal for long-term safekeeping of private keys associated with larger amounts of cryptocurrency, keeping these assets safe from potential cyberattacks. The physical devices may implement specific security features such as PIN protection, backup, or hardware security modules. Examples of cold wallets include hardware wallets (e.g. Ledger, Trezor) and paper wallets. Whilst they offer enhanced security, they are less convenient for frequent transactions since most hardware wallets need to be physically connected to a computer or smartphone to sign transactions. In addition, some "ultra cold" wallets have no physical connection capability at all (e.g. Ellipal) and use **QR codes** to transfer signed transactions to an internet-connected device for broadcasting to the network of validators. The latter are often referred to as "air-gapped" wallets. I guess paper wallets can also be classified as "ultra cold", but their usage has waned in favour of hardware devices.

Figure 6.3 classifies crypto wallets according to their temperature.

Figure 6.3 Hot and cold wallets. © 2024 Neira Jones.

Many crypto enthusiasts find it beneficial to use a combination of both hot and cold storage. Hot wallets are better for everyday transactions involving smaller amounts, but because they are always online, they are more vulnerable to hacking attempts and online threats. By contrast, cold wallets are more suited to transactions involving larger amounts or infrequent use. By keeping private keys offline, cold wallets protect against online attacks and unauthorised access. Ultimately, the key is to find the right balance between security and convenience to suit specific needs.

We'll go over these in a bit more detail.

Paper wallets

First introduced and popularised around 2010–2011, paper wallets provide offline (aka "cold") storage of crypto-assets. These ultra-cold wallets are printed on paper where QR codes are associated with the private and public key pair. Just like cash, the paper itself could be lost, stolen, burned, faded, or be washed with your favourite pair of jeans on laundry day. Paper wallets are the cheapest options for controlling and managing access keys. Paper wallets acted like homemade credit or debit cards, letting users swipe or scan the paper document to disperse the private and public keys on any device connected to the blockchain. There are no setup fees, monthly subscriptions, or other charges commonly associated with a crypto wallet.

Paper wallets were an essential part of the cryptocurrency development journey. Like any other fledgling industry, this invention became popular and swiftly faded once the market found a better alternative in the form of hardware wallets. Whilst it doesn't make much sense to use them today, paper wallets were massive contributors to progressing the industry forward and introducing a concept of cold storage in crypto. Paper wallets have claimed their rightful place in the history of cryptocurrencies.

Hardware wallets

With hardware wallets, the modern crypto world introduced a much better alternative for cold storage than paper wallets. Now, users can simply purchase a cold wallet device that is much more resilient; has private key backups; and, unlike paper wallets, will not lead to losses if damaged. You may be wondering why, because you still might inadvertently stomp on it or drive over it, or indeed put it in the washing machine with your favourite pair of jeans. This is because hardware wallets come with extra security features like robust physical construction, tamper-evident seals, and secure chipsets. Additionally, they often offer multiple layers of encryption and backup options such as recovery phrases or seed words, allowing you to restore your wallet on a new device if the original is damaged beyond repair. Hardware wallets may have other security features like two-factor authentication, fingerprint scanners, and other redundancies. This way, hardware wallets can't be accessed even if they fall into the hands of malicious individuals.

Hardware wallets are usually designed to manage keys associated with multiple crypto-assets, although some hardware wallets can be specific to one cryptocurrency (e.g. Trezor Safe 5 for Bitcoin). Another specialised type of hardware wallet is the central bank digital currency (CBDC) wallet, commonly referred to as a "bearer wallet", which is specifically designed to store CBDCs (see Chapter 7, *Hybrid infrastructure* and *Table 7.2*).

Online crypto wallets

Online crypto wallets encompass a range of digital solutions that are connected to the internet. These are hot wallets that can be broadly categorised into several types, each with its own characteristics and use cases:

- **Web-based crypto wallets** are accessed through a web browser and can be either custodial or non-custodial. Custodial web wallets, often provided by exchanges or other trading venues, manage the private keys on behalf of the user. This offers convenience but requires trusting the platform with your assets. For example, Coinbase Wallet (when used through the Coinbase exchange platform) and Binance Web Wallet are popular custodial web wallets. Non-custodial web wallets, on the other hand, allow users to maintain control of their private keys whilst still offering the convenience of online access. MyEtherWallet (MEW)[3] and MyCrypto[4] are well-known examples of non-custodial web-based wallets.
- **Mobile crypto wallets** are smartphone applications that allow users to manage access to their crypto-assets on the go. These can also be custodial or non-custodial, with varying levels of security features such as biometric authentication. The portability of mobile wallets makes

them popular for day-to-day transactions. Custodial mobile wallets include the mobile apps of major exchanges like Coinbase, Binance, and Kraken. For non-custodial options, Trust Wallet (owned by Binance but operated independently) and Exodus are popular choices that support multiple cryptocurrencies.

- **Desktop crypto wallets** are software applications installed on a computer. These are typically non-custodial and offer more control to the user but require proper security measures on the device. They're often favoured by users who prefer managing their assets from their personal computers. Exodus also offers a desktop version, which is a non-custodial wallet that can be installed on a computer. Electrum is another well-known desktop wallet, primarily used for Bitcoin (BTC).
- **Browser extensions** are wallet interfaces that integrate directly with web browsers, allowing for easy interaction with decentralised applications (dApps). They are usually non-custodial and have gained popularity due to their seamless integration with web-based blockchain services. MetaMask is one of the most widely used browser extension wallets, primarily for Ethereum and ERC-20 tokens. Phantom is a popular browser extension wallet for the Solana ecosystem.

Each type of online wallet offers different balances of convenience, security, and functionality. Online wallets generally offer high accessibility, allowing users to manage their assets from various devices and locations. However, their constant internet connection makes them more vulnerable to potential cyberattacks compared to offline storage methods. This presents a significant challenge for regulators in terms of ensuring the security of users' assets whilst not stifling innovation in the space.

Professionals should remember the following:

- **DeFi access**: non-custodial crypto wallets offer direct integration with Decentralised Finance (DeFi) platforms and other blockchain-based services. This functionality has made them increasingly popular amongst users who frequently interact with various blockchain applications. For regulators and policymakers, the integration of wallets with DeFi platforms raises important questions about financial stability, consumer protection, and the potential for systemic risk in decentralised financial systems. Custodial wallets don't offer access to DeFi services, and they are by nature more regulated.

- **Blurred lines**: it's worth noting that the lines between these categories can blur, as some wallets offer multiple access methods. For example, a wallet might provide both web and mobile interfaces. Additionally, the level of security and control can vary significantly within each category, depending on the specific implementation and provider. This complexity presents challenges to regulators in terms of categorising and overseeing different wallet types.
- **Understand trade-offs**: when choosing an online wallet, users should carefully consider their needs, technical expertise, and risk tolerance. They need to weigh the trade-offs between convenience, security, and functionality. For substantial holdings, many experts recommend using online wallets in conjunction with offline storage methods for enhanced security. Professionals in the financial sector should be aware of these considerations when advising clients or developing crypto-related products.
- **Governance must evolve**: regulators and policymakers should consider the global nature of cryptocurrency transactions when developing frameworks for crypto wallet oversight. The borderless nature of these transactions can complicate jurisdictional issues and may require international cooperation to effectively regulate. Furthermore, the rapid pace of innovation in the crypto space means that regulations need to be flexible enough to accommodate new technologies and use cases as they emerge. This might involve principles-based regulation rather than prescriptive rules that could quickly become outdated.

As the crypto ecosystem continues to evolve, online wallets are likely to play a crucial role in making blockchain technology more accessible to a wider audience. However, their development will need to address ongoing challenges in security, user experience, governance, and regulatory compliance. For policymakers, this presents an opportunity to shape the future of digital asset management through thoughtful regulation that balances innovation with consumer protection.

Online crypto wallets present a complex and rapidly evolving aspect of the crypto ecosystem. For professionals, regulators, and policymakers, understanding the technical aspects, security considerations, and user behaviours associated with these wallets is crucial for developing effective strategies and policies. As the technology continues to mature, a balanced approach that fosters innovation whilst protecting consumers and maintaining financial stability will be key to the future of the crypto industry.

Risks and regulations

I don't plan to cover either topic in any great detail as this will be extensively covered in my next book "Payments Unbound", but here's a taster.

BOX 6.2 CRYPTO WALLET RISKS EXAMPLES

To illustrate the potential risks of different wallet types, consider the following real-world examples:

- **Hardware wallet security**: Ledger, a prominent hardware wallet manufacturer, experienced a data breach in July 2020 where the information of 270,000 customers, including email addresses, phone numbers, and shipping addresses, was compromised.[5] Whilst the breach did not affect private keys or cryptocurrency holdings, it highlighted the importance of selecting reputable hardware wallet providers with robust security measures. And if you thought that was the end of that, think again. The compromised credentials were posted on a prominent hacking forum in December 2020.[6] Immediately following the breach, Ledger owners began receiving numerous phishing emails pointing them to fake Ledger applications designed to trick them into entering their wallet's recovery phrases. In June 2021, scammers sent fake replacement devices (used to steal users' keys) to Ledger customers using those leaked credentials.[7] Luckily, Ledger were aware of this scam and had warned customers, but some may have fallen for it.
- **Custodial wallet risks**: Coinbase, a major cryptocurrency exchange offering custodial wallets, has faced customer criticism regarding account accessibility and withdrawal processes. One major complaint was poor customer service, delayed transactions, and a pattern of **account takeover fraud** to steal funds.[8]
- **Non-custodial wallet risks**: the 2023 Atomic Wallet hack resulted in the loss of over $100 million in cryptocurrency for about 5,500 users.[9]

The incident highlighted the importance of maintaining strong security practices, such as using strong passwords, enabling two-factor authentication, and regularly backing up wallet data.

- **Phishing attacks**: these remain a prevalent threat to crypto wallet users. A notable example is the 2022 phishing campaign targeting MetaMask users, where scammers posed as legitimate support representatives to steal user credentials.[10]

Ultimately, similarly to centralised payment systems, it all comes down to cyber hygiene, information security best practice, and effective governance. But crypto wallets have additional challenges associated with their decentralised nature.

BOX 6.3 CRYPTO WALLET: REGULATORY CONSIDERATIONS

The regulatory environment for cryptocurrencies, including wallets, is rapidly evolving. Some jurisdictions have been more proactive than others:

- **Japan**: known for its early adoption of cryptocurrency regulations, Japan recognised Bitcoin as legal property under the Payment Services Act (PSA) in 2017. This paved the way for regulating crypto wallet providers as virtual currency exchange service providers. In 2020, Japan established the Japanese Virtual Currency Exchange Association (JVCEA), of which all crypto exchanges are members. The Financial Services Agency (FSA) oversees the industry and requires licensing for crypto wallet operators.
- **United States**: the US regulatory landscape is complex and fragmented. Whilst there's no specific federal law governing crypto wallets, the Securities and Exchange Commission (SEC) has asserted jurisdiction over certain crypto-assets and related activities, whilst the Commodity Futures Trading Commission (CFTC), the Consumer Financial Protection Bureau (CFPB), and the Federal Trade Commission (FTC) are encouraged by the White House to get involved.[11] The Financial Crimes Enforcement Network (FinCEN) also has regulations in place for anti-money laundering (AML) and Know-Your-Customer (KYC) compliance for cryptocurrency businesses, including wallet providers.

- **China**: China has imposed a blanket ban on cryptocurrency trading and mining, effectively outlawing cryptocurrencies, and related activities, including crypto wallets.[12] They state that they facilitate public financing without approval (they'd much rather concentrate on their central bank digital currency, but more on that in Chapter 7).
- **United Kingdom**: The Financial Services and Markets bill became an act (law) in June of 2023 and extended existing laws regarding crypto-assets, services, and providers. This included custodial wallet providers and primarily concentrated on AML obligations.[13]
- **Singapore**: Singapore has implemented the PSA to regulate cryptocurrency service providers, including crypto wallet providers. The Monetary Authority of Singapore (MAS) requires licensing for businesses providing digital payment token services.[14]
- **European Union**: The Markets in Crypto-Assets (MiCA) regulation entered into force in June 2023,[15] establishing a comprehensive regulatory framework for crypto-assets, including licensing requirements, consumer protection measures, and market abuse rules.
- **Financial Action Task Force (FATF)**: in 2021, the FATF issued its updated guidance on virtual assets and virtual asset service providers (VASPs)[16] and has been since providing regular updates on its implementation worldwide. The guidelines outline standards for AML and counter-terrorist financing (AML/CFT) in the cryptocurrency industry.

Ultimately, whilst regulations for crypto wallets are evolving rapidly across the globe, a consistent theme is the focus on consumer protection, AML, and combating financial crime.

The cryptocurrency landscape is still evolving rapidly, presenting both opportunities and challenges. Whilst the potential for financial gain is undeniable, it's essential to approach the space with caution. The lack of comprehensive regulations in many jurisdictions means that investors and businesses face a higher degree of risk, including the threat of fraud, hacking, and market volatility. As the industry matures, regulatory frameworks are gradually being established to protect consumers and maintain market integrity. Staying informed about the latest developments in both technology and regulation is crucial for navigating this dynamic environment successfully.

Recap on crypto wallets

Crypto wallets serve as interfaces for managing private keys that prove ownership and enable interactions with blockchain networks. For professionals, regulators, and policymakers, understanding these tools is essential in navigating the complex landscape of digital assets.

Anyone assessing crypto wallets should remember the following:

- **Crypto wallets don't store crypto-assets** (see Chapter 5): crypto wallets serve as interfaces for managing private keys that prove ownership and enable interactions with blockchain networks. For professionals, regulators, and policymakers, understanding these tools is essential in navigating the complex landscape of crypto-assets.
- **There are numerous types of crypto wallets**: the variety of crypto wallet types reflects diverse user needs and the ongoing challenge of balancing security with convenience. Hardware wallets are often praised for their security features but can be cumbersome for frequent transactions and require technical knowledge. Software wallets aim to balance security and usability, making them popular for regular crypto management, but there are security trade-offs.
- **The balance between security and convenience must be understood**: custodial wallets offer high accessibility and ease of use, as the service provider manages the private keys. However, this reliance on a third party raises significant questions about key security and user control. Non-custodial wallets, on the other hand, give users full ownership of their private keys, enhancing security and autonomy but placing the responsibility of key management entirely on the user. This tension between user experience and the protection of access credentials is a central issue for wallet developers, users, and regulators alike. As the crypto ecosystem evolves, addressing this balance will be crucial.
- **Perspective is important**: when comparing crypto wallets to traditional digital payment methods, it's important to recognise the significant differences in their current utility and adoption. Traditional digital wallets and payment platforms, such as those prevalent in China, have achieved widespread adoption and integration into daily financial activities. They offer seamless user experiences and broad

merchant acceptance. In addition, traditional digital payment methods typically provide robust consumer protections and dispute resolution mechanisms, which are often lacking or less developed in the crypto space. This is an important consideration for both users and regulators trying to understand crypto wallets.

- **Understanding practical applicability is crucial**: crypto wallets, whilst innovative, have more limited practical applications for everyday transactions in most regions. They can offer increased user control over crypto-assets and potential benefits for specific use cases like cross-border transfers. However, they often come with higher technical barriers and may present security risks if not managed properly. The cost-effectiveness of crypto transactions can vary widely depending on network congestion and fee structures, sometimes offering advantages over traditional methods, but not consistently.
- **Reputation is important**: for those new to crypto, whether individuals or institutions, starting with a well-established software wallet can introduce the technology. As users become more familiar with the space, they often consider hardware wallets for long-term key storage. This progression underscores the need for solutions that can adapt to varying levels of user expertise and changing needs.
- **Security is always important**: robust security practices are crucial regardless of wallet type. Strong passwords, two-factor authentication, and regular backups of recovery phrases are important, but they also highlight the need for ongoing user education. For professionals and policymakers, understanding these security considerations is vital in developing balanced frameworks that address both protection and innovation.

In conclusion, whilst crypto wallets play an increasingly important role in the blockchain ecosystem, their current utility and adoption are still limited compared to traditional digital payment methods in most markets. As the technology matures, approaches to using, developing, and regulating these tools must evolve as well. The challenge lies in fostering an environment that encourages innovation whilst addressing security concerns, usability issues, and responsible use of these emerging technologies, all the whilst recognising the strengths and established position of traditional digital payment systems.

Cryptocurrency tumblers

Now that we've covered crypto wallets, I must introduce another type of service that was originally introduced to address privacy concerns. Think of it as an "overlay service" that works in conjunction with crypto wallets.

Imagine a large pool of coins from various users. When a user wants to enhance their transaction privacy, they can send their coins to a cryptocurrency tumbler, which is a service that will combine these coins with funds from other users before sending them out to the intended recipients. This process disrupts the link between the original source of the funds and the final destination, making it more difficult to track the flow of specific coins.

The term **cryptocurrency tumbler** is primarily used in the context of privacy-focused cryptocurrencies. It refers to a voluntary service offered by some blockchains or third-party providers that allows users to obfuscate the origin and destination of their cryptocurrency transactions. Other terms used to refer to this service include "cryptocurrency mixing service", "mixing service", "crypto mixer", "mixing pool", and "Bitcoin mixer".

There are two types of cryptocurrency tumblers:

- **Centralised tumblers**: these are services managed by a single entity that handles the mixing process. Users send their coins to the tumbler, which then mixes them with coins from other users and redistributes them to the specified addresses. Users can use any type of wallet, but they often use custodial wallets to interact with centralised tumblers since the tumbler itself temporarily holds the funds. Examples include UniJoin and Yo!Mix Mixer.
- **Decentralised tumblers**: also known as non-custodial mixers, these services operate without a central authority. Users must use non-custodial wallets to participate in a P2P network where they contribute to a pool, and the mixing is done collaboratively. Examples include Tornado Cash, Mixero, Wasabi Wallet, Samourai Wallet's Whirlpool, and BNB mixer.[17]

The main characteristics of cryptocurrency tumblers are:

- **Anonymity**: tumblers enhance privacy by breaking the link between the sender and recipient of funds. This is achieved by pooling coins from multiple users and redistributing them in a way that makes it difficult to trace the transactions. Users typically receive different coins than those they deposited in the tumbler, severing the direct link to their original wallet. They can then use these "tumbled", and therefore "clean", coins to perform onwards transactions.

- **Regulation**: the use of cryptocurrency tumblers is subject to significant regulatory scrutiny due to their potential use in illicit activities such as money laundering and terrorism financing.
  - **United States**: under the Bank Secrecy Act (BSA), services that act as money transmitters, including mixers and tumblers, must comply with AML regulations and register as money service businesses. In 2019, FinCEN issued guidance that mixer or tumbler service providers must comply with these regulations. Notably, the US Department of the Treasury has sanctioned services like Blender.io[18] and Tornado Cash,[19] making it illegal for US citizens and entities to use them. Additionally, FinCEN has proposed new regulations under Section 311 of the USA Patriot Act, classifying the mixing of convertible virtual currencies as a primary money laundering concern.
  - **United Kingdom**: in the UK, cryptocurrency exchanges and mixing services are required to register with the Financial Conduct Authority (FCA). The FCA has issued guidelines that require these services to comply with AML regulations, including conducting customer due diligence and reporting suspicious activities. The UK government has expressed intentions to regulate the cryptocurrency space more comprehensively, particularly in light of concerns about financial crime.
  - **European Union**: The EU has established a comprehensive regulatory framework for crypto-asset service providers, which includes mixing services. The European Banking Authority (EBA) has highlighted the risks associated with privacy-enhancing tools like mixers and has mandated that crypto service providers implement strict monitoring measures. Regulation 2023/1113 requires crypto-asset service providers to collect and make information available about the sender and beneficiary of transfers, regardless of the amount transacted. These rules are applicable from December 30, 2024.
  - **Global perspective**: the FATF has noted the increased use of tumblers for obfuscating illicit funds and recommends that transactions involving these services be flagged as suspicious. Some jurisdictions have banned or restricted the use of mixing services entirely.

  - **Enforcement actions**: authorities have acted against operators of mixing services, such as the arrest of the founder of Bitcoin Fog and the seizure of ChipMixer assets. These actions underscore the regulatory challenges and legal risks associated with operating or using tumblers.
- **Assets mixed**: primarily cryptocurrencies, including Bitcoin and other privacy-focused coins. Tumblers do not typically handle stablecoins, focusing instead on enhancing the privacy of common cryptocurrencies.
- **How users mix coins**: users will deposit coins by initiating a transaction from their wallet to a unique wallet address provided by the tumbler. Think of this unique tumbler address as a staging area for "recognisable" coins prior to them being "tumbled". This intermediary address is generated specifically for their use, ensuring that their deposit is correctly attributed to their account within the tumbler's system. Users will specify the details of the transaction (e.g. recipient, preference for delay, or distribution pattern) and send the correct amount and type of cryptocurrency as specified by the tumbler. After the mixing process, the specified recipient receives the mixed (clean) coins from the temporary tumbler address. The process may take some time, depending on the service and the desired level of anonymity. Mixing services often charge fees which can vary depending on the desired level of anonymisation.
- **Benefits**: these services attract users who value financial privacy and don't want their transaction history publicly viewable on the blockchain. These services may be beneficial for:
  - Privacy-conscious users who deal with sensitive information or engage in activities where financial privacy is important, or
  - Users who want to protect themselves from targeted surveillance or financial profiling.
- **Risks**:
  - **Security**: users must trust the tumbler to handle their funds securely, as there is a risk of theft or loss if the service is compromised. Reputable mixing services are crucial, as malicious actors could potentially exploit vulnerabilities within a mixing pool to steal funds.
  - **Regulatory**: the legal status of tumblers varies by jurisdiction, and using them may expose users to legal risks, especially if associated with illicit activities.

- **Criminal activity**: mixers are often used to facilitate criminal activities such as money laundering, fraud, and the financing of illegal goods and activities. They enable criminals to obscure the origins of illicit funds by mixing them with legitimate transactions.
- **Tainted coins**: mixed coins may be flagged as "tainted" by some exchanges, affecting their usability. Users should be aware that some platforms might refuse to accept coins that have been mixed, as exchanges often determine whether coins are "tainted" by analysing transaction patterns and comparing them against known mixing service addresses or other suspicious activity indicators.

I covered metrics in Chapter 4, *Tokenomics and metrics*, and there is an additional metric for tumblers commonly referred to as the "mixing pool size". This refers to the total amount of cryptocurrency currently held within a mixing pool, and it can influence the effectiveness of the anonymisation process. A larger mixing pool offers a higher degree of anonymity for users. With more coins in the pool, it becomes increasingly difficult to trace individual transactions because each user's coins are mixed with a larger pool of anonymous funds. Conversely, a smaller mixing pool offers less effective anonymisation, as, with fewer coins, the chances of identifying the source and destination of specific funds increase.

Professionals should remember the following:

- **Regulations are important**: tumblers should be examined under the lens of local and international AML regulations. Be aware of the regulatory landscape, including potential sanctions and enforcement actions against certain mixing services. Regulatory developments may affect the operation and use of tumblers.
- **Security and compliance risks are real**: potential users must carefully select tumblers to handle funds securely, as there is a risk of theft or loss if the service is compromised. Reputable mixing services are crucial to prevent exploitation by malicious actors. Additionally, tumblers may lack identity verification tools required by financial institutions, such as KYC checks, which can create compliance issues.
- **Understanding tumbler types and characteristics is important**: the differences between centralised and decentralised tumblers may affect usability, flexibility, and convenience. Not all crypto wallets work with

all tumblers (e.g. non-custodial wallets require technical knowledge). In addition, the transparency of tumbler operations should be assessed, including fee structures and transaction processes, to ensure they meet professional standards. Staying informed about new technologies and protocols that could improve tumbler security and privacy or enhance tracking capabilities is advisable.

- **Usability is not guaranteed**: mixed coins may be flagged as "tainted" by some exchanges, affecting their usability and acceptance. In addition. tumblers are often associated with money laundering, which can impact their reputation and acceptance in the crypto community, as well as posing legal risks. Professionals should balance privacy needs with compliance requirements.
- **Complete anonymisation is not guaranteed**: consider the mixing pool size to assess this. A larger mixing pool increases anonymity, making it harder to trace transactions, whilst a smaller pool may offer less effective anonymisation.
- **Technology advancements may affect tumbler operations**: advancements in blockchain analysis and tracking technologies could affect the future use of tumblers and their effectiveness in providing anonymity.

Cryptocurrency tumblers present both opportunities and challenges in the evolving landscape of digital finance. For users, they offer enhanced privacy and anonymity, but these benefits come with significant risks and regulatory considerations. Professionals must navigate these complexities to ensure secure and compliant operations, whilst policymakers face the task of balancing innovation with the need for oversight and regulation. As the technology and regulatory environments continue to evolve, staying informed and adaptable will be crucial for all stakeholders involved in the use and governance of cryptocurrency tumblers.

Recap on digital wallets

Digital wallets have fundamentally transformed how we manage and transact with money, offering unprecedented convenience and flexibility.

For professionals, these wallets present opportunities to enhance customer engagement and streamline payment processes, but they also require adaptation to new technologies and regulatory landscapes.

Users benefit from the ease of making transactions but must navigate a complex ecosystem with varying levels of security and functionality. For crypto wallets, the shift from custodial to non-custodial empowers users with greater control over their assets, but also places more responsibility on them for security and key management. Education and awareness are crucial for users to make informed choices and protect their assets effectively.

Regulators and policymakers face the challenge of balancing innovation with consumer protection and financial stability. The decentralised nature of some crypto wallets presents unique regulatory challenges, particularly in areas of AML/KYC compliance and cross-border transactions. As the line between traditional and crypto finance blurs, developing flexible yet robust regulatory frameworks becomes increasingly important.

As digital wallets continue to evolve, collaboration amongst all stakeholders will be essential to address security concerns, enhance user experience, and establish effective regulatory guidelines.

Now that we've covered traditional digital wallets, crypto wallets, and tumblers, it's time to trade.

Trading places (shop around)

We covered closed-loop virtual currencies in Chapter 5, and I will omit how these are traded from this section as they are tied to their specific platforms and use traditional payment mechanisms, as does e-money, which was covered earlier.

Crypto-assets, by contrast, can be traded in many places, from crypto exchanges to specialist marketplaces. To access these markets, the crypto wallets we covered earlier, as well as other services, are available. Similarly to traditional payments, where traditional digital wallets are used to perform transactions at merchants using specific payment networks, crypto wallets give their users the ability to access trading venues. Let's examine these services.

On ramp and off ramp

I introduced the concepts of "on-ramp" and "off-ramp" in Chapter 2, Box 2.8, and these are essentially services that facilitate the conversion of fiat currency into cryptocurrency and vice-versa. These include:

- **Custodial wallets** such as Binance or Coinbase (we covered these earlier).

- **Non-custodial wallets with integrated services**: wallets like MetaMask and Trust Wallet are not on ramp or off ramp themselves but integrate third-party services (e.g. MoonPay) to enable users to purchase cryptocurrencies with fiat currency directly within the wallet.
- **Traditional payment platforms**: Payment service providers (PSPs) like PayPal, Block (formerly Square), Revolut, and Cash App offer integrated crypto trading features (in partnership with third-party services), providing on-ramp and off-ramp capabilities (albeit indirectly).
- **Banking services with crypto features**: Some banks and financial institutions allow customers to buy, sell, or hold cryptocurrencies directly through their banking apps in a similar way to PSPs. Examples include, at the time of writing, N26 and Fidor Bank.
- **Brokerage services**: these companies offer brokerage services that allow users to buy and sell cryptocurrencies using fiat currency, providing on-ramp and off-ramp capabilities. Examples include Robinhood, eToro, and SoFi.
- **Crypto payment processors**: these companies facilitate the purchase of cryptocurrencies using credit/debit cards or bank transfers, acting as on-ramp services. They integrate with various platforms and wallets to enable users to buy cryptocurrencies with fiat currency. Examples include Moonpay[20] and Simplex.[21] Wyre, another popular provider, wound down in 2023 as a result of the "crypto winter" following the FTX collapse and the Bolt Financial (a traditional PSP) cancellation of its planned $1.5 billion acquisition of Wyre[22] (see also *The FTX scandal*).

For those mostly interested in the retail trading of cryptocurrencies and non-fungible tokens (NFTs), the sections on *crypto exchanges*, *NFT marketplaces*, *gaming and metaverse marketplaces*, and *traditional payment platforms offering cryptocurrency trading* will be particularly relevant. The remaining sections after these will cover more specialised services (e.g. security token exchanges) and can be skipped if they are of less interest, and of course, there's always the ducks...

For those who can't wait, Table 6.4 gives a summary in *The comparison table you've been waiting for* in the *Recap on trading places* section.

Crypto exchanges

Crypto exchanges come into five main categories (as always, there will be hybrid models incorporating features from different models):

- **Centralised crypto exchanges (CEX)**: traditional exchanges operated by a central authority, offering a wide range of cryptocurrencies and trading options, but with associated counterparty risk.
- **Decentralised crypto exchanges (DEX)**: decentralised platforms that facilitate P2P trading without intermediaries, offering greater anonymity and (potentially) security but often with lower liquidity and user experience.
- **Hybrid crypto exchanges**: combine elements of both CEXs and DEXs, aiming to offer the best of both worlds.
- **P2P crypto exchanges**: direct trading platforms where individuals can buy and sell cryptocurrencies without intermediaries, offering flexibility but requiring caution due to potential scams.
- **Atomic swaps**: direct trading platforms where users can trade cryptocurrencies across blockchains, enabling cross-chain interoperability but often technically complex and with limited availability.

The various types of crypto exchanges are shown in Figure 6.4.

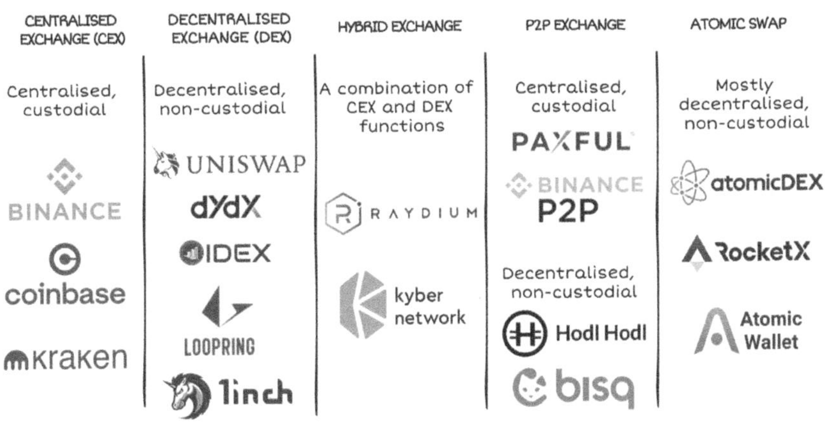

Figure 6.4 Crypto exchanges. © 2024 Neira Jones.

Centralised crypto exchanges (CEX)

A CEX is a trading platform where a central authority manages all transactions and account balances. These exchanges act as intermediaries between buyers and sellers, facilitating trades and maintaining custody of users' funds. Users trust the exchange to handle their assets securely and efficiently, as the exchange verifies transactions and manages the order book. Essentially, CEXs maintain control over the user's private key, which is why they are referred to as custodial exchanges.

The main characteristics of CEX are:

- **Custody**: the CEX holds custody of users keys, thus controlling the assets, which means that users deposit their proof of ownership of cryptocurrencies into the exchange's wallets, and the exchange is responsible for securing these assets. Whilst this provides convenience, it also means users must trust the exchange to protect their funds from hacks or mismanagement.
- **Regulation**: CEX are often subject to regulatory oversight depending on the jurisdiction in which they operate. In most countries, they are subject to AML and KYC regulations and may need to obtain licences or permissions to operate legally depending on the jurisdiction (e.g. money service businesses, payment institutions, specific crypto exchange licences). In the US, they may need to register with FinCEN and comply with the Bank Secrecy Act (BSA). In the EU, they fall under the 5th Anti-Money Laundering Directive (AMLD5). This can impact the types of services they offer and the cryptocurrencies they list.
- **Assets traded**: cryptocurrencies, stablecoins, fiat currencies.
- **How users can trade**: users create accounts on the exchange, deposit funds, and trade cryptocurrencies through the exchange's interface. They can place various types of orders, such as market orders (buy/sell at the current market price), limit orders (buy/sell at a specified price), or stop orders (trigger a buy/sell when a certain price is reached).
- **What users can do**: users can trade a wide range of cryptocurrencies and stablecoins, access advanced trading features like margin trading and futures contracts, and use fiat currency to buy crypto. They can also participate in staking, lending, and other financial services offered by the exchange.
- **Benefits**: high liquidity, user-friendly interfaces, and access to a wide range of trading pairs. CEX often provide customer support and security features like insurance against hacks.
- **Risks**:
    - **Security**: CEX are prime targets for hackers, and users must trust the platform to secure their funds.

- **Regulatory**: These platforms may face regulatory scrutiny, which can impact their operations and the availability of certain cryptocurrencies.
- **Custodial**: Users do not have control over their private keys, meaning they rely on the exchange to manage their funds.

Examples include Binance, Coinbase, and Kraken.

Historically, centralised crypto exchange are the oldest exchanges in operation. The first centralised crypto exchange was BitcoinMarket.com, but it didn't rise to any significant prominence (see *Peer-to-Peer (P2P) crypto exchanges*), which is why Mt. Gox, which famously rose to prominence in 2013, is generally acknowledged as being first.

Figure 6.5 gives a historical timeline of the rise and fall of Mt. Gox.

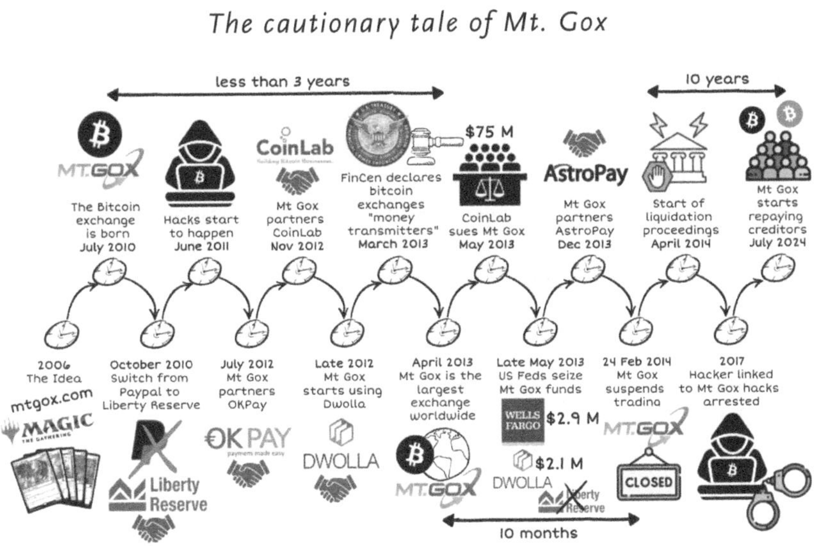

Figure 6.5 The rise and fall of Mt. Gox. © 2024 Neira Jones.

THE IDEA

In 2006, Jed McCaleb registered the domain "mtgox.com", originally intending to create a trading platform for Magic: The Gathering (MTG), a collectible cards game created by mathematician Richard Garfield and published by Wizards of the Coast in 1993. The name "Mt. Gox" was an acronym for "Magic: The Gathering Online eXchange".

THE BIRTH OF A CRYPTO EXCHANGE

In **July 2010**, McCaleb repurposed the dormant domain and launched Mt. Gox as a BTC exchange. On its first day of operation, Mt. Gox enabled the trading of just 20 BTCs, each selling for about 5 cents. Mt. Gox began to use **Paypal** as their payment processor. But in **October 2010**, Mt. Gox switched from Paypal to **Liberty Reserve** as its main funding option due to issues with chargeback fraud. Liberty Reserve ran its own private digital currency, a currency exchange, and an unregulated payment processing business that allowed you to send and receive funds.

Chargeback fraud was a prevalent issue for BTC exchanges, including Mt. Gox, in their early years. This type of fraud occurs when a customer purchases something with a credit or debit card and then disputes the charge with their card issuer, claiming unauthorised use or unsatisfactory goods or services. The issuer then initiates a chargeback, refunding the customer and the transaction amount will eventually be deducted from the merchant's account.

In the context of Bitcoin exchanges, chargeback fraud was particularly problematic because of the nature of the transactions. Customers would purchase BTC with their credit cards, then immediately cash out the BTC for fiat currency or transfer it to another wallet. Once they had access to the funds, they would initiate a chargeback, effectively reversing the original transaction and keeping both the BTC and the refunded fiat currency.

This practice was extremely damaging to Bitcoin exchanges, as it resulted in significant financial losses. As a result, many exchanges, including Mt. Gox, sought alternative payment methods to mitigate the risk of chargeback fraud. Liberty Reserve, despite its own issues, offered a degree of protection against chargebacks, which is why Mt. Gox switched to using it as its primary funding option.

It's important to note that whilst chargeback fraud was a significant problem for crypto exchanges in their early days, the industry has implemented various measures to reduce its impact. These include stricter verification processes, fraud prevention tools, and increased collaboration with financial institutions. However, the issue has not entirely disappeared and remains a challenge for some exchanges.

In **March 2011**, Mark Karpelès, a French developer living in Japan, acquired 88% of Mt. Gox from McCaleb and subsequently moved the company's headquarters to Tokyo, Japan, and began expanding its operations.

In **June 2011**, PayPal froze Mt. Gox's account due to concerns about the legality of Bitcoin transactions.

Throughout its operation, Mt. Gox partnered with several traditional payment processors to facilitate fiat currency transactions, including Paypal, Liberty Reserve, and Dwolla.

TEETHING PROBLEMS

Three months later, on **13 June 2011**, Mt. Gox reported that approximately 25,000 BTCs (valued at around $400,000 at the time) had been stolen from 478 accounts.

On **19 June 2011**, a hacker used compromised credentials to create a massive sell order of about 650 BTCs at an extremely low price, causing the price of BTC to drop to one cent on the Mt. Gox exchange. The price corrected itself within minutes, but accounts holding the equivalent of more than $8.75 million were affected. As a result of this hack Mt. Gox took a number of security measures, including arranging for a substantial amount of its BTCs to be taken offline and held in cold storage.

In **October 2011**, approximately 2,609 BTCs (approximately $8,300 at the time) were lost forever when Mark Karpelès accidentally sent these BTCs to an invalid address due to a bug in the Bitcoin Protocol. This wasn't seen as a big deal.

THE RISE OF MT. GOX

In **July 2012**, Mt. Gox began its partnership with **OKPay**, a global payment service provider based in the British Virgin Islands primarily serving Eastern Europe and Russia, allowing deposits and withdrawals in various currencies. The partnership with OKPay was significant for Mt. Gox as it provided an important payment channel, especially for customers in regions where other payment processors had limited reach or were unavailable.

In **November 2012, CoinLab** and Mt. Gox signed an agreement granting CoinLab the exclusive right to use Mt. Gox's technology to operate Bitcoin exchange services in the US and Canada. Mt. Gox was expected to transfer its American and Canadian customers to CoinLab who would bring financial and investment partnerships in the US.

In late 2012, Mt. Gox began using payment processor **Dwolla**[23] for US transactions.

In February 2013, Mt. Gox announced expanded support for OKPay, including instant deposits for USD, EUR, and RUB.

In **March 2013**, the US Treasury Department's FinCEN declared Bitcoin exchanges to be money transmitters, requiring them to register as money service businesses, formally comply with AML requirements, and report suspicious activity.[24]

Also, in March 2013, the new 0.8.0 version of Bitcoin Core temporarily forked off the main blockchain using differing rules on how transactions could be accepted. Mt. Gox briefly halted BTC deposits and BTCs prices briefly dipped by 23% to $37 as the event occurred[25] before recovering to their previous level in the following hours (~$48). (Note from the author: now you see the real-life implications of a soft fork 😉, see Chapter 3, *An introduction to blockchain forks* for a reminder).

By **April 2013**, despite earlier setbacks, Mt. Gox became the largest Bitcoin exchange, handling over 70% of all Bitcoin transactions worldwide, supporting various major trading pairs including BTC/USD, BTC/EUR, and BTC/JPY, amongst others. In spite of the hacks, by 2013, Mt. Gox had established itself as the largest Bitcoin exchange in the world, in part as a result of increased interest in Bitcoin as the price of the coins increased rapidly (jumping from $13 dollars in January 2013 to a peak of more than $1,200).

After this, it started to go bad.

THE SLIPPERY SLOPE

In **May 2013**, CoinLab sued Mt. Gox for $75 million, alleging a breach of contract. Peter Vessenes, CoinLab's CEO, stated that the lawsuit was filed with the hope that Mt. Gox would "do what's best for U.S. and Canadian customers and settle this matter quickly, allowing our customers to transact in the U.S. with a fully licensed and registered company that meets American standards for service quality".[26] This lawsuit was seen as a setback to efforts to bring a new level of legitimacy to Bitcoin trading, as CoinLab was working with Silicon Valley Bank and was registered and compliant with US regulations.

In the same month, US federal agents seized $2.1 million from Mt. Gox's account with payment processor Dwolla, and an additional $2.9 million was seized from Mt. Gox's **Wells Fargo** account, including $50,000 from CEO Mark Karpelès's personal account. When opening the Wells Fargo account, Karpelès had stated Mt. Gox was not engaged in the money services business, which investigators found to be false.[27] These seizures significantly impacted Mt. Gox's operations, leading to the temporary suspension of US dollar withdrawals in June 2013 and contributing to ongoing liquidity issues for the exchange. Mt. Gox then registered as a money service business[28] with the US Treasury Department and resumed withdrawals a couple of weeks after.[29]

On **28 May 2013**, OKPay suspended transactions with all Bitcoin exchanges, including Mt. Gox, citing pressure from its partners (who remained unnamed).[30] On the same day, Liberty Reserve was shut down by the US Government after its founders were charged with money laundering and operating an unlicensed money-transmitting business,[31] cutting off a key source of funds to Mt. Gox. US authorities alleged that Liberty Reserve had laundered more than $6 billion in criminal proceeds during its operation.

In **September 2013**, Mt. Gox countersued CoinLab for not being able to lawfully operate as its partner in the US for failing to register as a money service business[32] (ironic isn't it? Since Mt. Gox didn't have the required licence themselves until May 2013...)

In **December 2013**, Mt. Gox announced a partnership with payment processor **AstroPay**[33] to serve the Latin American market, allowing customers in countries like Brazil, Chile, Colombia, Mexico, Peru, and Uruguay to make deposits in USD to their Mt. Gox accounts.[34] This partnership facilitated faster transfer times and quicker account deposits.

By the end of 2013, the earlier legal and regulatory setbacks caused Mt. Gox to lose its place as the largest Bitcoin exchange in the world, falling behind Bitstamp[35] BTC-e, a crypto exchange founded by Alexander Vinnik primarily serving the Russian market, and possibly Coinbase (depending on the sources). But it was still in the top three to four exchanges.

THE SPECTACULARLY SWIFT COLLAPSE

On **7 February 2014**, Mt. Gox announced that they were temporarily halting all Bitcoin withdrawals "to obtain a clear technical view of the currency processes".[36] Customers were still able to trade, and the announcement led to a significant increase in trading volume on Mt. Gox in the 24 hours following the announcement.

On 24 February 2014, Mt. Gox suspended trading and closed its website, sending shockwaves through the Bitcoin community. It was revealed that approximately 850,000 BTCs, worth around $350 million at the time, belonging to customers and the company were missing, likely stolen. This amount represented about 7% of the total number of BTCs in existence at that point, which was estimated to be 12 million BTC, approximately $7.2 billion at the time. On 28 February, Mt. Gox filed for bankruptcy protection in Japan,[37] declaring liabilities of about $65 million against assets of $38 million. In the same month, a Tokyo court ordered OKPay to return $5.1 million in customer funds to Mt. Gox as part of the exchange's bankruptcy proceedings.

The fates seemed to turn when in **March 2014**, Mt. Gox reported finding 200,000 BTCs in old digital wallets, worth approximately $116 million at the time. This significant amount of money could potentially be used to partially compensate creditors, but the fact that Mt. Gox's management simply "forgot" about these BTCs raised questions about their management practices and governance. This also led to the revision of the total BTC losses from 850,000 to 650,000 BTCs (which were never recovered).

THE LIQUIDATION

In **April 2014**, Mt. Gox began liquidation proceedings. WizSec, a Tokyo-based security company, conducted investigations into the Mt. Gox theft over several years. Their findings, which were published in various blog posts and reports, indicated that most of the missing BTCs were stolen directly from Mt. Gox's hot crypto wallet over time, beginning in late 2011.[38] This was evidence that, as well as governance failures, Mt. Gox was riddled with security vulnerabilities that had been exploited by hackers for a long time. Furthermore, WizSec had identified Vinnik, BTC-e's founder, as the owner of the wallets into which the stolen BTCs had been transferred, many of which were sold on BTC-e (surprise!).

In **late 2014**, Kraken, an established CEX, was chosen to assist in processing claims and distributing the remaining Mt. Gox assets to creditors.[39]

In **2017**, Vinnik was arrested in Greece and indicted for laundering over $4 billion, including funds stolen from Mt. Gox in 2011. Vinnik had "obtained" funds from the hack of Mt. Gox and laundered them through BTC-e and Tradehill,[40] a San-Francisco-based crypto exchange that eventually shut down in August 2013 due to regulatory pressure. BTC-e went offline on 25 July 2017 following money laundering charges.[41]

In **June 2018**, the Tokyo District Court moved the Mt. Gox case from bankruptcy to civil rehabilitation, opening the possibility for creditors to receive their funds in BTC rather than fiat currency. The creditors eventually agreed to this.

In **2019**, Mark Karpelès was found guilty of falsifying data to inflate holdings but acquitted of the more serious charges of embezzlement and aggravated breach of trust.[42]

THE LATTER YEARS

In **June 2023**, the US Department of Justice charged two Russian nationals involved with Vinnik and BTC-e, Alexey Bilyuchenko and Aleksandr Verner, with conspiring to launder approximately 647,000 BTCs stolen from Mt. Gox over several years, leading up to its collapse in 2014.

In **May 2024**, Alexander Vinnik pleaded guilty to conspiracy to commit money laundering,[43] after serving a five-year prison sentence in France.[44]

On **5 July 2024**, Mt. Gox began repaying its creditors in BTC and Bitcoin Cash (BCH) under the legal rehabilitation plan.[45] The exchange had recovered approximately 140,000 BTC (worth about $9 billion at the time) following its bankruptcy. The creditor notices can be found in the references at the end of this chapter.[46] As of July 16, 2024, about 90,344 BTC (valued at $5.77 billion) remained in Mt. Gox's Bitcoin wallets, awaiting distribution to creditors over the following months. A number of CEX were designated to facilitate the repayments, including Bitbank, Kraken, Bitstamp, SBI VC Trade, and Bitgo. As you may imagine, the distribution of such a large amount of Bitcoin raised concern about market impact, but as long-term Bitcoin holders control about 46% of the market, this hodling (see Chapter 5, *Cryptocurrency*) behaviour has contributed to market stability. At the time of writing, the repayment deadline set by the trustee was 31 October 2024.

WHAT HAPPENED TO JED AND MARK?

Jed McCaleb, the original founder of Mt. Gox, went on to co-found Ripple in 2012 (initially called OpenCoin), left Ripple in July 2013, and co-founded Stellar in 2014 where he still serves as Chief Technology Officer (CTO). He distanced himself from Mt. Gox very early on.

He is worth $2.7 billion as of 14 August 2024[47] (the equivalent of the Winklevoss twins put together).[48]

Mark Karpelès, who acquired Mt. Gox from Jed McCaleb in 2011, served as CEO until the exchange's collapse in 2014. Following legal proceedings and a brief imprisonment in Japan, Karpelès joined London Trust Media, the provider of virtual private network service Private Internet Access,[49] as CTO in April 2018 but left in October 2019. He later became CEO of Karpelès Lab Inc.[50] (a technology consulting company) and CTO of Shells.com,[51] a cloud computing service. In 2023, Karpelès was appointed Minister of Technology for Joseon, a virtual nation-state focusing on cyber sovereignty and blockchain technology. Despite his controversial past, Karpelès has remained involved in the technology and cryptocurrency sectors, offering insights on industry events and security issues. Karpelès' stated intention not to profit from the bankruptcy[52] suggests that it's unlikely that he has retained the massive potential wealth that was initially possible from the Mt. Gox bankruptcy.

WHAT DID WE LEARN?

The Mt. Gox incident remains one of the most significant in crypto history, highlighting the importance of security, governance, and proper management in crypto exchanges. It led to increased regulatory scrutiny and efforts to improve security measures across the industry.

The collapse of Mt. Gox wasn't just a financial disaster; it was a personal one for many people. Beyond the staggering loss of millions of dollars in Bitcoin, countless individuals and businesses were deeply affected. Investors saw their hard-earned savings vanish overnight, causing significant financial hardship. For some, the loss of funds was devastating, leading to stress, anxiety, and even bankruptcy. It's important to remember that behind the numbers and statistics are real people whose lives were turned upside down by this event.

You would think that it would lead to more industry cooperation, sensible regulations, and accountability. Then, we had FTX, which I will cover later.

WHY DID I SPEND SO MUCH TIME ON THIS?

The answer is simple: this is a payments book, and I want to **dispel a myth** propagated by many: "The ultimate goal of the cryptocurrency industry is to create a decentralised, secure, and efficient global financial system that operates outside traditional banking structures and government control." Really? I'm sure you have heard this, or derivations thereof, proclaimed by enthusiasts and believers to whomever wants to listen.

Let's examine the facts objectively: Mt. Gox was one of the first crypto exchanges to come to market, and even at the start, when crypto was mostly for the faithful, it relied on Paypal for transactions. If we look at the chronological account, between 2010 and 2014, Mt. Gox relied on five payment processors (Paypal, Liberty Reserve, Dwolla, OKPay, and AstroPay) and two banks (Mizuho Bank and Wells Fargo). And I'm not counting the various entities involved in the repayment process.

Like it or not, **the crypto industry needs centralised payments to even exist**. Because frankly, why would you play in that pond if your efforts don't eventually translate into something tangible and beneficial in the real-world (i.e. money)? You might as well play a virtual game, it's less hassle, and certainly less risky. The Bitcoin whitepaper's title is "Bitcoin: A Peer-to-Peer Electronic Cash System", but 16 years later, that aim still hasn't been fulfilled. The intertwining of the crypto world with the traditional, centralised payments world, has been, is, and will continue to be inevitable (as Thanos would say, for all of you Marvel fans out there 😉).

In the meantime, let's continue to explore crypto exchanges.

Decentralised crypto exchanges (DEX)

A decentralised exchange is a P2P trading platform where users trade directly with each other from their wallets without a centralised authority. These DeFi services use smart contracts to automate transactions and eliminate the need for intermediaries, ensuring that users retain control over the access to their funds. DEXs can be categorised into several types based on their operational mechanisms (but please beware, many DEXs may fall into several categories at the same time depending on the features they offer):

- **Automated market makers (AMM)-based DEXs**: AMM DEXs (see Box 6.4) use smart contracts to create liquidity pools, allowing users to trade directly with these pools rather than through a traditional order book. This model removes the need for order matching by using algorithms to determine prices based on the ratio of assets in the pool.

Examples include Uniswap,[53] Curve,[54] Trader Joe XYZ,[55] SushiSwap,[56] and PancakeSwap.[57]

A **liquidity pool** is a collection of cryptocurrency tokens or assets locked in a smart contract on a DEX to facilitate trading. It provides the necessary liquidity for users to trade directly with the pool rather than waiting for a matching counterparty. In traditional forex markets, large banks act as market makers, holding reserves of various currencies to facilitate exchanges.

A liquidity pool in DeFi is similar to these bank reserves, but instead of being controlled by a central entity, it's managed by a smart contract and funded by multiple participants.

- **Order-book-based DEXs**: these DEXs operate similarly to CEX by maintaining an order book that records buy and sell orders. They can be further divided into:
  - **On-chain order books**: all orders and transactions are recorded on the blockchain, providing transparency but potentially leading to higher fees and slower speeds due to blockchain constraints. dYdX[58] is an example still operating at the time of writing, whilst, ZigZag, another example, was forced to shut down in April 2024 due to regulatory pressure.[59]
  - **Off-chain order books**: order matching and storage occur off chain, enhancing speed and reducing costs but introducing potential risks of centralisation. One example is IDEX[60] and 0x[61] is a platform that enables DEX building. Another example is EtherDelta, which launched in 2016 and shut down in 2018 due to regulatory pressure.[62] As you understand the immutable nature of smart contracts, you will also understand why EtherDelta's smart contracts still hold approximately $42 million in customer assets. Many of these customers may have forgotten about them due to the interface shut down.
- **Layer-2 DEXs**: these exchanges operate on layer-2 scaling solutions built on top of existing blockchain networks, primarily Ethereum. They aim to address scalability issues, reduce transaction costs, and improve the overall performance whilst maintaining the security guarantees of the underlying blockchain. Layer-2 DEXs use various technologies such as Optimistic Rollups, ZK-Rollups, or state channels (see Chapter 1, *Layer 2 scaling solutions*) to process transactions off chain and periodically settle them on the main chain. This approach allows for faster and cheaper

trades whilst still benefiting from the decentralisation and security of the base layer. Examples include Loopring (ZK-Rollups),[63] QuickSwap (on Polygon),[64] and dYdX (which as well as being an on-chain order book DEX, is also a Layer-2 DEX).

- **DEX Aggregators**: these platforms aggregate liquidity from multiple DEXs to offer users the best prices and reduced slippage. They facilitate transactions by routing them through the most efficient paths across various exchanges. Examples include 1inch Exchange,[65] Matcha,[66] ParaSwap,[67] OpenOcean,[68] Swapzone,[69] Defillama,[70] Swoop Exchange,[71] Atlas DEX,[72] XY Finance,[73] altFINS,[74] Rubic,[75] and OKX DEX.[76]

Each type of DEX offers unique benefits and trade-offs, catering to different trading preferences and strategies within the DeFi ecosystem and their main characteristics are:

- **Custody**: users retain custody of their funds as they connect their personal non-custodial wallets to the DEX and execute trades directly from their wallets. This means users have full control over their private keys and are responsible for their own security.
- **Regulation**: DEXs typically operate with less regulatory oversight compared to CEX, as they do not hold custody of user funds and often do not require user identification. However, they may still face regulatory challenges related to compliance with AML regulations and securities laws (where assets traded may be defined as securities) and may not be available in some regions.
- **Assets traded**: cryptocurrencies and stablecoins.
- **How users can trade**: users connect their wallets to the DEX platform and trade directly with other users through smart contracts. The trades are executed on chain, and users can see their transactions recorded on the blockchain.
- **What users can do**: Users can trade cryptocurrencies and stablecoins, participate in yield farming, and provide liquidity to earn fees. They can also engage in DeFi activities without relying on a central authority.
- **Benefits**: enhanced privacy and control, as users retain control of their funds. DEXs offer censorship resistance and eliminate the need for a central authority, reducing the risk of centralised hacks, though they are still susceptible to smart contract vulnerabilities.

- **Risks**:
  - **Smart contract vulnerabilities**: since DEXs rely on smart contracts to facilitate trades, any bugs or vulnerabilities in the smart contract code can be exploited by attackers, leading to the potential loss of funds.
  - **Phishing attacks**: users may be tricked into connecting their wallets to malicious DEX interfaces or fake websites, leading to unauthorised access to their funds.
  - **Front running and MEV (Maximum Extractable Value)**: DEXs can be susceptible to front running, where attackers manipulate transaction orders to their advantage, potentially leading to financial losses for users.
  - **Liquidity risks**: as they have a smaller user base, less efficient order matching due to their reliance on AMM, and limited market maker participation, DEXs may have lower liquidity compared to CEX, leading to higher slippage and less efficient trading.
  - **Impermanent loss**: a risk specific to liquidity providers in AMM protocols on DEXs. It occurs when the price ratio of deposited assets changes compared to when they were deposited, potentially resulting in less value than if the assets were simply held.
  - **User experience**: DEXs may be less intuitive for new users, requiring a better understanding of blockchain technology.

BOX 6.4 AUTOMATED MARKET MAKERS (AMMs)

In traditional finance, market makers are typically financial institutions or professional traders who provide liquidity by buying and selling assets from their own accounts. They profit from the spread between buy and sell prices and help maintain market stability by ensuring there are always counterparties available for trades. In traditional markets, market making is often limited to large institutions, whereas AMMs allow anyone to participate as a liquidity provider.

AMMs are decentralised protocols designed to facilitate trading on DEXs without relying on traditional order book systems. They achieve this by using liquidity pools, where users, known as liquidity providers, deposit funds. These pools enable continuous trading and liquidity, with algorithms determining asset prices based on their supply and demand within the pool. AMMs are DeFi services that allow users to become liquidity providers by depositing assets into pools in exchange for rewards.

Beyond DEXs, AMM principles can be applied in various contexts. Hybrid AMMs, like Balancer, combine features of traditional market making with automated algorithms, allowing liquidity pools with multiple tokens in varying ratios. Dynamic AMMs, such as Curve, adjust parameters based on market conditions to optimise stablecoin trading. Virtual AMMs are used in synthetic asset platforms like Synthetix,[77] where assets are traded through simulation rather than direct exchange. Some lending protocols, such as Aave and Compound, use AMM principles to manage interest rates and liquidity. In gaming and NFTs, platforms like Rarible and OpenSea facilitate the trading of digital assets using AMM-like mechanisms.

AMMs are largely unregulated, though some jurisdictions are considering how to apply existing market-making regulations or develop new ones. The decentralised nature of AMMs poses challenges to traditional regulatory approaches.

It has been widely reported that DeFi services are very much susceptible to hacks and cyberattacks and DEXs continue to have their fair share. Two recent examples at the time of writing include:

- **FixedFloat**, an order book-based DEX with off-chain order books focusing on cryptocurrency exchange with Lightning Network support, suffered two significant hacks in early 2024. The first occurred on 16–17 February 2024, resulting in a loss of $26.1 million, including 409 BTC and 1,728 ETH. The attackers exploited vulnerabilities in FixedFloat's security infrastructure, gaining access to sensitive functions within the protocol. A second hack followed on 31 March 2024, where the same attacker exploited a vulnerability in a third-party service (Time4VPS hosting) used by FixedFloat, leading to an additional loss of $2.8 million. In both cases, the hacker used compromised servers and multiple IP addresses to launch the attacks. FixedFloat has since implemented extensive security enhancements, but no significant fund recovery has been reported.

- **KyberSwap**, an AMM-based DEX that uses smart contracts to create liquidity pools for trading, experienced a hack on November 22, 2023, resulting in a loss of approximately $54–56 million. The attack exploited a vulnerability in KyberSwap's Elastic platform, specifically in the protocol's liquidity calculations. This flaw allowed the attacker to manipulate the system and artificially double the liquidity, which they were then able to drain. The exploit involved a series of precise calculations that bypassed a security check by less than 0.00000000001%, taking advantage of a small precision error in the protocol's arithmetic. In the aftermath, KyberSwap offered a 10% white hat bounty to the hacker for returning the funds, which was not accepted. However, the team managed to recover $4.7 million in drained funds that were taken by third-party MEV bots. The incident affected multiple networks, including Base, Polygon, Ethereum, Optimism, and Arbitrum.

DEXs have emerged as a transformative force in the crypto landscape, enabling P2P trading, furthering user control, enhancing privacy, and potentially democratising access to trading, they come with their own set of challenges. However, whilst DEXs provide benefits, including reduced reliance on intermediaries and the potential for lower fees, they also come with their own challenges.

Professionals should remember the following:

- **Driving innovation with risk in mind**: professionals and developers can leverage DEX technology to create innovative financial products such as decentralised derivatives, yield farming strategies, and tokenised assets. However, this shouldn't be done at the expense of strong security as DEXs rely on smart contracts (see Chapter 2, *Building smart contracts*) or robust tokenomics models that incentivise user participation and platform growth whilst avoiding inflationary pressures (see Chapter 4, *Tokenomics and metrics*). Failure to manage risks effectively can result in financial losses, reputational damage, and legal liabilities.
- **Assessing DEX platforms**: professionals involved in DEX evaluation, factors such as liquidity depth, trading volume, security audits, and the experience and reputation of the development team. Failure to do

so can lead to significant financial losses due to market manipulation, security breaches, or platform failures. Chapter 4, *Tokenomics and metrics* should help with this. Users should prioritise security by using reputable DEX platforms with proven track records and take precautions (e.g. two-factor authentication, hardware wallets) as neglecting security measures can result in the loss of funds due to hacking, theft, or unauthorised access. They should also diversify DEX usage across multiple platforms to reduce reliance on a single exchange and mitigate risks associated with platform failures or security breaches as concentrating funds on a single DEX increases exposure to platform-specific risks. In addition, the concept of **impermanent loss**, which can affect liquidity providers, must be understood as this can lead to unexpected financial losses when providing liquidity on DEXs.

- **Regulating DEX**: regulators face a unique challenge in overseeing DEXs due to their decentralised nature, where balancing innovation with consumer protection is paramount. A comprehensive regulatory framework should foster a thriving DEX ecosystem whilst mitigating risks, which requires a collaborative approach involving policymakers, industry stakeholders, and experts to develop effective rules and enforcement mechanisms. To protect the broader financial system, regulators must assess the systemic risks posed by DEXs, such as market manipulation and money laundering, as well as consider the impact of DEXs on traditional financial markets, which is essential to ensure fair competition and consumer protection. Professionals should stay ahead of regulatory trends by monitoring evolving compliance standards and adapting business models accordingly to ensure long-term sustainability.

Different types of DEXs, such as AMM based, order book based, Layer 2, and DEX aggregators, each offer unique advantages and trade-offs, catering to various trading preferences and strategies within the DeFi ecosystem.

For professionals in the field – whether users, payment specialists, regulators, or developers – understanding the nuances of DEXs is crucial. Users should be aware of the security measures necessary to protect their assets, whilst payment professionals can explore the efficiencies DEXs may bring to transactions. Regulators and policymakers face the task of ensuring consumer protection without stifling innovation, and developers have the opportunity to enhance the functionality and security of these platforms.

As DEXs continue to evolve, they hold the potential to reshape crypto-asset trading, making it essential for all stakeholders to stay informed and engaged in this dynamic space. The journey of DEXs is far from over, and their continued development promises to be an interesting chapter in the ongoing story of DeFi.

In the interim, let's continue or exploration of the world of crypto exchanges.

Hybrid crypto exchanges

Hybrid exchanges combine features of both CEX and DEX, aiming to offer the benefits of decentralised trading with the liquidity and convenience of CEX. They aim to provide flexibility and efficiency by decentralising certain aspects, such as order matching (e.g. AMM, order book models), whilst keeping other functions, like deposit and withdrawal, centralised.

The main characteristics of hybrid crypto exchanges are:

- **Custody**: hybrid exchanges may offer both centralised and decentralised custody options. Users can choose to hold their funds on the exchange for convenience or use decentralised features to retain control over their private keys.
- **Regulation**: hybrid exchanges may face complex regulatory requirements, as they incorporate elements of both centralised and decentralised models. They must navigate compliance with financial regulations whilst also addressing the challenges of decentralised governance.
- **Assets traded**: cryptocurrencies and stablecoins.
- **How users can trade**: users can trade through both centralised order books and decentralised protocols, depending on the specific features of the hybrid exchange. This allows users to choose their preferred method of trading based on their needs.
- **What users can do**: benefit from the liquidity of CEX whilst retaining some control over their funds through decentralised features. Users can participate in both traditional and decentralised financial services.
- **Benefits**: combines the security and control of DEXs with the liquidity and user experience of CEXs, allowing for a more versatile trading experience.

- **Risks**:
  - **Complexity**: The integration of centralised and decentralised features can create complex systems that are harder to secure and manage.
  - **Regulatory challenges**: balancing compliance with decentralised features can be difficult, potentially leading to regulatory issues.
  - **Security risks**: hybrid exchanges may inherit security risks from both CEXs and DEXs, such as vulnerabilities in smart contracts and centralised points of attack, requiring robust security measures.
  - **Liquidity risks**: achieving optimal liquidity can be challenging, as hybrid exchanges must effectively integrate liquidity from both centralised and decentralised sources, potentially leading to inefficiencies.
  - **Centralisation**: whilst hybrid exchanges aim to combine the benefits of both CEX and DEX, they may compromise some aspects of decentralisation. Users might find themselves relying on centralised components for certain operations, which can lead to a potential loss of control over their funds compared to pure DEXs.

Examples include Raydium[78] and Kyber Network.[79]

Peer-to-Peer (P2P) crypto exchanges

P2P exchanges enable users to trade directly with each other without an intermediary, often using an escrow service, usually provided by the platform, to ensure transaction security. These platforms facilitate direct transactions between users, allowing them to negotiate terms and payment methods.

The main characteristics of P2P crypto exchanges are:

- **Custody**: P2P exchanges can be either custodial or non-custodial in terms of key management. In non-custodial exchanges, users maintain full control of their private keys throughout the trading process. Custodial P2P exchanges manage users' private keys on their behalf. Regardless of the key management model, most P2P exchanges use escrow services to temporarily hold funds during transactions, ensuring security and trust between parties. The escrow service provides a form of temporary fund custody during the transaction process.

- **Regulation**: P2P exchanges may have varying levels of regulatory oversight depending on their structure and jurisdiction. Some may require KYC verification to comply with AML regulations, whilst others operate with minimal regulatory involvement.
- **Assets traded**: primarily cryptocurrencies, such as BTC and ETH, also some stablecoins may be available, with flexibility in payment methods.
- **How users can trade**: users post buy or sell offers, and the platform matches them with interested parties. Trades are completed directly between users, often with the platform providing an escrow service to hold funds until both parties fulfil their obligations.
- **What users can do**: users can trade cryptocurrencies directly with other users using various payment methods, such as bank transfers or digital wallets. Users can also negotiate prices and terms directly with their counterparts.
- **Benefits**: greater privacy and control over trades, flexible payment methods, and often lower fees compared to CEX.
- **Risks**:
  - **Counterparty risks**: whilst the escrow service provided by reputable P2P exchanges significantly reduces counterparty risk, there may still be some residual risks. For example, if a buyer claims to have made a payment when they haven't, or if a seller attempts to provide false proof of cryptocurrency transfer, it could lead to disputes. These situations, whilst mitigated by escrow, may still require resolution processes and could potentially result in delays or complications in completing transactions.
  - **Fraud and scams**: there is a potential for scams (e.g. fake listings, impersonation) or fraudulent activities, especially if the platform lacks robust security measures or appropriate governance. Users need to be vigilant and verify the credibility of their trading partners.
  - **Security risks**: P2P exchanges can be either custodial or non-custodial, which affects their security profile. Non-custodial P2P exchanges, where users retain control of their private keys, reduce the risk of large-scale hacks that could compromise user funds. However, they shift the responsibility of key management to users, introducing risks of key loss or theft. Custodial P2P exchanges, whilst offering easier key management for users, are vulnerable

to security breaches or hacking attempts on the platform itself, potentially putting users' funds at risk. In both cases, users' personal information and transaction data could be compromised if the exchange's security measures are breached.

- **Regulatory risks**: P2P exchanges may face varying levels of regulatory scrutiny depending on the jurisdiction. Changes in regulations can impact the operations of these platforms and the availability of certain cryptocurrencies.
- **Limited customer support**: P2P platforms may offer limited customer support, leaving users to resolve disputes on their own.
- **Liquidity risks**: P2P exchanges may have lower liquidity compared to CEX, leading to potential delays in finding trading partners and executing transactions.

Examples of custodial P2P exchanges include Paxful[80] and Binance P2P.[81] LocalBitcoins used to be popular, although it stopped trading in 2023 due to regulatory pressure.[82]

Examples of non-custodial P2P exchanges include Hodl Hodl[83] and Bisq.[84]

Whilst many think that the first crypto exchange was Mt. Gox, this is not the case, as that title goes to BitcoinMarket.com, which was a P2P crypto exchange.

BOX 6.5 THE CAUTIONARY TALE OF BITCOINMARKET.COM

BitcoinMarket.com was the world's first cryptocurrency exchange, launched on 17 March 2010 by a Bitcoin Talk forum user known as "dwdollar". It was created to address the growing need for a platform where users could trade BTC for fiat currencies as interest in BTC increased. It aimed to address a need for a platform where users could trade BTC for fiat currencies at known exchange rates because informal personal agreements were not efficient enough to meet the market needs of an increasing number of users who now purchased crypto on a daily basis. The exchange operated as a custodial P2P platform, allowing users to trade directly with each other whilst the exchange acted as an **escrow** service to ensure custody of funds until trade completion.

It implemented an order book system, a matchmaking algorithm that connects buyers with sellers and provides the mechanism for transactions to take place. It offered a floating exchange rate for BTC against fiat currencies and allowed trades using PayPal as a payment method, facilitating fiat-to-crypto transactions. The platform provided a graph of the BTC exchange rate in US Dollars, with data also offered in JSON format.

In March 2011, a major update took place reducing the minimum trade size, introducing 24/7 trading, and measures to ensure payment of executed trades.

In June 2011, BitcoinMarket.com discontinued Paypal trading due to fraud issues. It's worth noting that issues with fraud were a common problem for early Bitcoin exchanges using PayPal, as chargebacks and reversible payments posed risks when dealing with immutable Bitcoin transactions. The decision by BitcoinMarket.com to discontinue PayPal trading was likely a protective measure against these fraud risks, and Paypal later blacklisted BitcoinMarket.com. Subsequently, the exchange continued to face challenges typical of early cryptocurrency platforms, including fraud risks and the need for trust in the platform's custody of funds.

BitcoinMarket.com played a crucial role in the early days of cryptocurrency trading. Demonstrating the need for cryptocurrency exchanges, it paved the way for future platforms and moved from informal P2P transactions to a more structured, albeit still early-stage, trading environment. Its experiences, including the challenges with payment methods like PayPal, informed the development of future exchanges and highlighted the need for robust security measures in cryptocurrency trading platforms.

It all but disappeared without a noise and accounts of its closure are non-existent.

Atomic swaps

Oh, the hype. From what I observe, there is a lot of confusion as to what atomic swaps are and aren't. I'll attempt to clarify.

Atomic swaps, also known as atomic cross-chain trading, are a type of smart contract technology that enables the exchange of one cryptocurrency for another without the need for a centralised intermediary or exchange. The term "atomic" describes a process that is indivisible and complete, meaning the swap either happens entirely or not at all, ensuring that neither party can cheat or end up with an incomplete transaction. Think of it as the decentralised equivalent of **atomic settlement** in centralised financial systems. Both aim to mitigate **counterparty (settlement) risk**.

The key characteristics of atomic swaps include:

- **Cross-chain interoperability**: swaps can occur between different blockchain networks, enabling interoperability across various cryptocurrencies.
- **Regulation**: navigating the regulatory landscape for atomic swaps can be challenging due to the lack of clear guidelines. Whilst atomic swaps facilitate P2P transactions without intermediaries, they must still comply with AML and KYC regulations. This means that users and platforms may need to implement identity verification and transaction monitoring systems to prevent misuse or illicit activities.
- **Assets traded**: atomic swaps support a wide range of cryptocurrencies; however, not all cryptocurrencies are compatible with each other, as they must support the same cryptographic hashing algorithm.
- **How users can trade**: users can initiate atomic swaps by creating a smart contract that specifies the terms of the trade, including the amount, price, and duration. Both parties must agree to the terms before the swap can proceed. Atomic swaps can be conducted on various types of platforms and through different protocols that support this technology:
  - **DEXs**: AtomicDEX,[85] RocketX[86] are examples.
  - **Wallet-integrated swaps**: Atomic Wallet[87] is an example.
  - **Blockchain protocols with native atomic swap support**: these blockchain networks have built-in support for atomic swaps, allowing users to perform cross-chain exchanges directly on the blockchain. Decred's DCRDEX[88] is an example.
  - **Layer 2 solutions** (see Chapter 1, *Layer 2 scaling solutions*): some Layer 2 solutions support atomic swaps. The Lightning Network[89] facilitates atomic swaps between BTC and other cryptocurrencies that support the Lightning Network.
  - **Some centralised exchanges (CEX)**: whilst many CEX have explored atomic swap technology, it is not widely implemented. However, OKX has implemented atomic swap technology for

certain trading pairs through its DEX aggregator. Other CEX that support atomic swaps include Binance, HTX, and Poloniex, although they might be more limited in terms of trading pairs (e.g. those involving privacy coins like Monero).

- **What users can do**: users can trade cryptocurrencies directly with other users using various payment methods, such as bank transfers or digital wallets. Users can also negotiate prices and terms directly with their counterparts. However, the availability of trading pairs for atomic swaps can be limited and users should verify the availability of desired trading pairs on their chosen platforms. Availability of services will also depend on the jurisdiction.
- **Benefits**:
    - **Interoperability**: swaps enable direct trading between different cryptocurrencies across various blockchain networks.
    - **Efficiency**: swaps reduce the need for multiple transactions and intermediaries, potentially lowering costs and increasing transaction speeds.
    - **Privacy**: swaps may enhance privacy by eliminating the need to transfer assets to a CEX, which often requires KYC procedures.
    - **Reduced counterparty risk**: the smart contracts that ensure the exchange either completes fully for both parties or doesn't occur at all, eliminating the need to trust intermediaries or the other trading partner.
- **Risks**:
    - **Complexity**: atomic swaps can be complex and challenging for beginners. They require both parties to agree on transaction details such as the amount, price, time lock duration, and exchange data, which can make the process time consuming and difficult to navigate.
    - **Privacy concerns**: although atomic swaps aim to enhance privacy, they can take multiple blocks to complete, potentially alerting malicious actors who might track addresses and target traders. Implementations may not offer strong transaction privacy.
    - **Compatibility issues**: not all cryptocurrencies can be traded using atomic swaps. Both cryptocurrencies involved must support the same cryptographic hashing algorithm, which limits the range of possible swaps.

- **Liquidity challenges**: as atomic swaps are P2P, finding a match for a specific swap can be difficult, leading to potential liquidity issues.
- **Security risks**: whilst atomic swaps are designed to be secure, the complexity of the technology means that users must ensure they are dealing with trusted parties to avoid potential security threats.
- **Legal and regulatory risks**: engaging in atomic swaps without proper understanding can lead to legal issues, especially if the swapped coins are linked to illicit activities. This is particularly relevant when swapping between cryptocurrencies with varying levels of privacy, such as BTC and Monero.

Atomic swaps represent a significant advancement in the cryptocurrency space by enabling decentralised, trustless, and secure exchanges of digital assets across different blockchain networks. However, the technology also presents challenges, such as regulatory compliance, complexity, and limited compatibility with certain cryptocurrencies.

As the regulatory landscape evolves and technological solutions advance, atomic swaps are likely to become more integral to the cryptocurrency ecosystem. Collaboration between regulators and the crypto industry is essential to balance compliance with innovation, ensuring the long-term viability of atomic swaps. This will enable seamless P2P transactions whilst ensuring compliance with legal requirements, potentially fostering a more secure and accessible financial system.

Are atomic swaps DeFi services?

I refer you back to Chapter 2, Figure 2.6 for a definition of DeFi.

- Atomic swaps can be considered part of the DeFi ecosystem when they are conducted on decentralised platforms or protocols. This is because they align with the core principles of DeFi, such as decentralisation, trustlessness, and P2P transactions. However, atomic swaps are not exclusively DeFi because:
- Atomic swaps **can be integrated into centralised exchanges**, allowing users to swap cryptocurrencies directly without the need for a decentralised platform. In this context, they are not considered DeFi.

- Atomic swaps **can also be used for non-financial applications**, such as cross-chain data sharing or smart contract execution, which extends their utility beyond the financial domain.

Thus, whilst atomic swaps are a powerful tool within the DeFi space, their broader applicability means they are not exclusively classified as DeFi services.

Recap on crypto exchanges

Crypto exchanges serve as gateways for users to buy, sell, and trade various crypto-assets. These platforms have significantly contributed to the mainstream adoption of crypto by providing user-friendly interfaces and streamlining the trading process. However, the industry has faced its share of challenges and controversies.

Recent events, such as the collapse of major exchanges, have highlighted the importance of robust security measures, transparent operations, and regulatory compliance. Whilst many exchanges strive to maintain high standards, users – businesses or individuals – must remain vigilant and conduct thorough research before entrusting their assets to any platform.

The crypto exchange landscape is diverse, ranging from CEX that offer custodial services to DEXs that allow for P2P trading. Each type has its own set of advantages and risks, catering to different user preferences and needs.

As the industry matures, we're witnessing increased scrutiny from regulators worldwide. This has led to the implementation of stricter KYC and AML policies on many platforms. Whilst these measures can enhance security and legitimacy, they also raise questions about user privacy and the original ethos of cryptocurrency.

For professionals and policymakers, it's crucial to understand the nuances of different exchange models and their implications for the broader financial system. The integration of traditional finance with crypto markets, which continues to happen, presents both opportunities and challenges that require careful consideration.

Users should always prioritise security by employing best practices such as using strong passwords, enabling two-factor authentication, and considering the use of hardware wallets for long-term storage. It's also wise to diversify holdings across multiple platforms or self-custody solutions to mitigate risk.

As we move forward, the evolution of crypto exchanges will likely be shaped by technological advancements, regulatory developments, and changing user expectations. The industry's ability to address current shortcomings whilst fostering innovation will be key to its long-term success and wider acceptance.

And this concludes our tour of crypto exchanges (you can jump to Table 6.4 for a quick comparison of all models). Let's examine other trading venues.

NFT marketplaces

NFT marketplaces allow users to trade NFTs. These platforms provide a venue for artists, creators, and collectors to buy, sell, and auction digital collectibles.

The main characteristics of NFT marketplaces are:

- **Custody**: NFT marketplaces typically do not hold custody of NFTs. Instead, NFTs' proofs of ownership remain in users' wallets until a transaction is completed. Users connect their wallets to the marketplace to list, buy, or sell NFTs.
- **Regulation**: NFT marketplaces currently face limited regulatory oversight, but this is evolving. As the market grows, there may be increased scrutiny regarding intellectual property rights, fraud prevention, and compliance with financial regulations.
- **Assets traded**: NFTs.
- **How users can trade**: users connect their NFT-capable crypto wallets to the marketplace, browse available NFTs, and purchase or auction NFTs using cryptocurrencies. Transactions are recorded on the blockchain, ensuring transparency and provenance.
- **What users can do**: buy, sell, and create NFTs representing digital art, collectibles, and other unique items. Users can also participate in auctions and discover new artists and collections.
- **Benefits**: NFT marketplaces provide a platform for artists and creators to monetise digital content, with ownership and provenance recorded on the blockchain.

- **Risks**:
  - **Market volatility**: the value of NFTs can be highly volatile, with prices subject to significant fluctuations. This volatility can lead to substantial financial losses for buyers and sellers if the market value of an NFT changes rapidly.
  - **Intellectual property risks**: issues related to copyright and ownership can arise, especially as this is a (very) confusing space.
  - **Regulatory risks**: the regulatory environment for NFTs is still evolving, and changes in regulations could impact the operation of NFT marketplaces. This uncertainty can affect the legal status and taxation of NFTs.
  - **Security risks**: NFT marketplaces can be targets for scams and fraud, requiring users to exercise caution as users' digital wallets and personal information can be compromised if the platform's security measures are inadequate.

Examples include OpenSea,[90] which was the largest NFT marketplace for some time, but at the time of writing, it was overtaken by Blur.[91] Other NFT marketplaces include Foundation,[92] LooksRare,[93] Magic Eden,[94] Nifty Gateway,[95] Rarible,[96] Solanart,[97] SuperRare,[98] and X2Y2.[99]

Gaming and metaverse marketplaces

Gaming and metaverse marketplaces provide platforms where users can trade in-game assets, virtual real estate, and other digital items within blockchain-based games or virtual worlds. These marketplaces have characteristics similar to NFT marketplaces, but cater to gamers, developers, and collectors, offering a venue to buy, sell, and exchange virtual goods and experiences. These marketplaces often integrate with the games or metaverse platforms they serve, allowing seamless trading of assets that have utility within these virtual environments.

The main characteristics of gaming and metaverse marketplaces include:

- **Custody**: similar to NFT marketplaces, gaming and metaverse marketplaces typically don't hold custody of digital assets. Instead, proofs of ownership of assets remain in users' non-custodial wallets until a transaction is completed. Users connect their wallets to the marketplace to list, buy, or sell assets.

- **Regulation**: these marketplaces currently face limited regulatory oversight, but this is evolving. Some jurisdictions are considering how to apply existing gambling and gaming laws to these platforms. There are also considerations around virtual and intellectual property rights, taxation of virtual asset transactions, fraud prevention, compliance with financial regulations, and consumer protection in virtual economies.
- **Assets traded**: digital assets such as in-game items, virtual real estate, NFTs, and other collectibles.
- **How users can trade**: users connect their non-custodial crypto wallets to the marketplace, browse available assets, and purchase or trade using cryptocurrencies. Transactions are recorded on the blockchain, ensuring transparency and provenance.
- **What users can do**: users can buy, sell, and trade digital assets, participate in virtual experiences, and engage with virtual communities. They can also explore virtual galleries, attend presentations, and join live auctions or events.
- **Benefits**: these marketplaces provide a platform for creators and developers to monetise digital content and for users to engage with immersive experiences. They also offer a decentralised economy where users have control over their digital assets.
- **Risks**:
    - **Market volatility**: the value of digital assets can be highly volatile, with prices subject to significant fluctuations. This volatility can lead to substantial financial losses for buyers and sellers if the market value changes rapidly.
    - **Intellectual property risks**: issues related to copyright and ownership can arise, especially as this is a complex space.
    - **Regulatory risks**: the regulatory environment for digital assets is still evolving, and changes in regulations could impact the operation of these marketplaces. This uncertainty can affect the legal status and taxation of digital assets.
    - **Security risks**: these marketplaces can be targets for scams and fraud, requiring users to exercise caution as users' digital wallets and personal information can be compromised if the platform's security measures are inadequate.

Examples include Decentraland Marketplace,[100] The Sandbox,[101] Axie Infinity Marketplace[102]

Traditional payment platforms offering crypto trading

Numerous traditional PSPs, including traditional digital wallets, payment processors, and crypto-friendly banks, may offer crypto trading features, often integrated with their existing payment services. These platforms leverage their existing infrastructure to offer limited crypto services alongside traditional payment options, making it easier for users to access cryptocurrencies.

The main characteristics of these services include:

- **Custody**: PSPs, as centralised entities, will typically hold custody of their customers' crypto-assets. Users can buy, sell, and hold cryptocurrencies within their accounts on the platform, which manages the security and storage of these assets.
- **Regulation**: traditional PSPs are regulated entities and must comply with applicable laws, including AML and KYC requirements. They may also need to comply with specific regulations related to cryptocurrency trading, depending on the jurisdiction.
- **Assets traded**: major cryptocurrencies like BTC and Ethereum, and potentially major stablecoins, with the option to convert between crypto and fiat currencies.
- **What users can do**: users can buy, sell, and hold cryptocurrencies directly through their existing accounts on traditional payment platforms. These platforms integrate crypto transactions with other financial services, providing a seamless experience for managing both crypto and fiat assets.
- **How users can trade**: trading is facilitated through user-friendly interfaces that allow users to execute buy and sell orders. Transactions are processed within the platform's infrastructure, enabling easy conversions between cryptocurrencies and fiat currencies whilst allowing users to monitor their holdings.
- **Benefits**: easy entry point for new users into the crypto market, leveraging existing user bases and infrastructure to offer crypto services. These platforms provide a familiar interface and integrates with traditional financial services.
- **Risks**: traditional payment platforms may provide a limited selection of cryptocurrencies compared to dedicated crypto exchanges (due to

de-risking strategies), which can restrict user options and limit market engagement. Additionally, these platforms are centralised, meaning users depend on the platform to manage and secure their crypto holdings, introducing risks related to potential security breaches or mismanagement. Regulatory risks are also significant, as changes in regulations could impact the availability and legality of crypto services on these platforms, potentially affecting their operation and user access. These platforms usually respond to regulatory pressures much quicker than crypto businesses so as not to affect their existing regulatory permissions.

Examples include PSPs such as Paypal,[103] Block (Square),[104] eToro,[105]; neo-banks such as N26,[106] Revolut,[107] and Wirex,[108]; as well as traditional banks such as DBS Bank[109,110] and Sygnum Bank.[111]

Over The Counter (OTC) trading desks

OTC trading desks are specialised platforms that facilitate **large-volume cryptocurrency trades** directly between parties, often used by institutional investors to minimise market impact and maintain privacy. Unlike CEX, OTC desks do not use a public order book (where transaction details such as the price, quantity, and parties involved are visible to all market participants), allowing trades to occur without revealing information to the broader market. This approach helps prevent price slippage and market disruption that can occur with large trades on public exchanges.

On whales, dolphins, and minnows

You may have seen these terms used to describe crypto traders, as illustrated in Figure 6.6.

Whales refer to individuals or entities who **hold a substantial amount of cryptocurrency** and have the potential to influence market prices significantly through their trades. Whales often use OTC desks for their transactions to avoid impacting market prices directly and to maintain privacy. Whilst the specific details of OTC trades are private, the associated blockchain transactions, such as moving large sums to or from exchanges, can be tracked on platforms like CoinMarketCap.com or cryptoslate.com, providing insights into potential market shifts.

Figure 6.6 Whales, dolphins, and minnows. © 2024 Neira Jones.

Dolphins are traders who **hold moderately large amounts of cryptocurrency**. Whilst they don't have as much influence as whales, their activities can still impact market dynamics to some extent. They are often considered mid-tier holders in the crypto ecosystem.

At the other end of the spectrum are **minnows**, who **hold relatively small amounts of cryptocurrency**. These smaller holders have minimal impact on the market individually but collectively represent a significant portion of the crypto community.

The activities of these groups are closely monitored by traders and analysts, as they can provide valuable insights into market trends and potential price movements. Whale movements, in particular, are often seen as indicators of significant market activity, and tracking tools (e.g. Arkham Intelligence,[112] Debank[113]) are used to observe their transactions on the blockchain.

Main characteristics

The main characteristics of OTC trading desks are:

- **Transaction privacy**: OTC desks provide a private trading environment where large trades can be executed without public disclosure.

This confidentiality is crucial for institutional investors who want to avoid signalling their trading intentions to the market.

- **Price negotiation**: unlike CEX where prices are determined by market supply and demand, OTC desks allow for price negotiation. This flexibility can result in more favourable rates for large trades.
- **Regulation**: OTC desks are often regulated under financial services laws and must comply with AML and KYC regulations. In some jurisdictions, they may need to register as broker-dealers or obtain specific crypto trading licenses.
- **Assets traded**: OTC desks typically handle a wide range of cryptocurrencies and fiat currencies, catering to the needs of high-net-worth individuals and institutional clients.
- **How users can trade**: trades are conducted directly between the buyer and seller, often facilitated by a dedicated account representative. This personalised service ensures that large transactions are executed smoothly and efficiently.
- **What users can do**: users can engage in large-scale trades, access deep liquidity, and benefit from tailored trading solutions. OTC desks often offer additional services such as custody and lending.
- **Benefits**: the primary advantages of OTC trading include transactional privacy, reduced market impact, and the ability to negotiate prices. OTC desks also provide dedicated service and access to deep liquidity pools.
- **Risks**:
    - **Counterparty risk**: there is a risk of default by the counterparty, as trades are conducted directly between parties without the oversight of a central exchange.
    - **Regulatory compliance**: OTC desks must navigate complex regulatory environments, which can affect their operations and the services they offer.

Examples of prominent OTC trading desks include Cumberland,[114] Galaxy Digital,[115] and B2C2.[116]

Having said that, you're probably wondering what the differences are between OTC trading desks and atomic swaps given that the characteristics are somewhat similar… Wonder no more, Table 6.3 is here to help:

Table 6.3 Comparing atomic swaps and OTC trading desks. © 2024 Neira Jones

Feature	OTC Trading Desks	Atomic Swaps
Purpose	Facilitates direct trading between two parties without public exchange order books	Enables cross-chain cryptocurrency exchange between two parties
Transaction type	Crypto to crypto or fiat to crypto	Crypto to crypto only
Transparency	Opaque; details are not public	Transparent; uses smart contracts, but only transaction amounts and addresses are visible
Privacy	High; details of transactions are private	Moderate; pseudonymous due to blockchain transparency
Counterparty risk	Exists; risk of default by one party	Minimal; transaction only completes if both parties fulfil conditions
Market impact	Low; insulated from market fluctuations	None; does not affect market prices
Negotiation	Price can be negotiated	No negotiation: terms are predefined by smart contracts
Use case	Suitable for large trades requiring privacy and liquidity	Suitable for decentralised, cross-chain exchanges
Settlement time	Can be slow; depends on negotiation and legal agreements	Depends on blockchain confirmation time
Scalability	Limited by liquidity and counterparty availability	Depends on blockchain used
Users	Institutional investors, high-net-worth individuals, and large traders	Tech-savvy users and those interested in DeFi
Examples	Cumberland, Genesis Trading, Circle Trade	Komodo, Atomic Wallet, Liquality

Security token exchanges

Main characteristics

These platforms are specifically designed for the trading of tokenised securities, adhering to applicable regulatory requirements. These exchanges facilitate the buying and selling of security tokens, which represent ownership in real-world assets.

The main characteristics of security token exchanges are:

You may see the acronym RWA in the contact of crypto-assets. **Real-world assets (RWAs)** in the crypto industry are tokens that represent tangible or traditional assets from the physical world. These digital tokens can stand for a wide variety of assets, including physical items like real estate, precious metals, or artwork, as well as financial assets such as stocks, bonds, or commodities. It's similar to how a concert ticket represents your right to attend a show, but in this case, the "ticket" is a digital token, and the "show" could be anything from a piece of land to a share in a company.

- **Custody**: security token exchanges typically provide custodial services to ensure compliance with regulatory requirements. This may involve holding the security tokens in a regulated manner, ensuring that they are properly accounted for and protected.
- **Regulation**: security token exchanges are subject to stringent regulatory oversight, as they deal with tokenised securities. They must comply with securities laws, including registration and reporting requirements, to operate legally and protect investors.
- **Assets traded**: security tokens representing ownership in RWAs, such as stocks, real estate, and bonds.
- **How users can trade**: users must undergo extensive verification processes to comply with securities regulations before trading security tokens. Once verified, they can trade security tokens through the exchange's platform.
- **What users can do**: trade tokenised assets that represent ownership in RWAs. Users can also access investment opportunities that may not be available on traditional markets.

Benefits and risks

Security token exchanges provide access to a regulated environment for trading securities, offering transparency and compliance with legal standards:

- **Accessibility to illiquid assets**: security token exchanges enable the tokenisation of assets like real estate and private equity, increasing liquidity and ease of trading for traditionally illiquid assets.
- **Fractional ownership**: tokenisation allows investors to purchase smaller portions of assets, making investments more accessible to a broader audience.
- **Increased liquidity**: security token exchanges could potentially enhance liquidity compared to traditional markets. This could lead to more efficient pricing and greater market participation. However, the market for security tokens is still developing, and liquidity may be limited when compared to more established financial markets, which can affect trading volume and price stability.
- **Enhanced transparency**: blockchain technology ensures transactions are recorded on an immutable ledger, reducing fraud, and building investor trust.
- **Regulatory compliance**: these exchanges are designed to adhere to applicable regulations (e.g. securities laws), offering protection and assurance through features like identity verification and AML/KYC compliance.
- **Cost efficiency**: by leveraging blockchain, these exchanges can reduce transaction fees, minimising the need for intermediaries, and streamlining processes when compared to traditional securities trading.
- **Global reach**: security token exchanges can operate across borders, allowing international investor participation and increasing the potential investor pool, which in turn may increase liquidity.

Security token exchanges have their fair share of associated risks:

- **Regulatory compliance**: security token exchanges are subject to stringent regulatory oversight, as they deal with tokenised securities. Failure to comply can result in legal penalties and operational restrictions.

- **Market risks**: security tokens may be less liquid than traditional securities, leading to potential price volatility. The market for security tokens is still developing, which can result in limited trading volume and higher price fluctuations.
- **Valuation and pricing risks**: determining the accurate valuation of tokenised assets can be challenging, especially if the underlying assets are illiquid or difficult to appraise. Mispricing can lead to market inefficiencies and potential losses for investors.
- **Custodial risks**: security token exchanges often provide custodial services for tokenised assets. This introduces risks related to the safekeeping and management of digital tokens, similar to those faced by CEX.
- **Technological risks**: the underlying technology must be robust to handle the complexities of tokenised securities. Smart contract vulnerabilities, hacking, and technical failures can pose significant risks to the security and integrity of the exchange.
- **Counterparty risks**: as with any trading platform, there is a risk that the other party in a transaction may default or fail to fulfil their obligations, leading to potential financial losses.
- **Operational risks**: security token exchanges must maintain robust operational procedures to ensure the smooth functioning of the platform. This includes managing trading systems, customer support, and compliance processes, all of which can be susceptible to operational failures or inefficiencies.

Qualified investors may use security token exchanges to trade security tokens and prominent examples include tZERO,[117] Securitize,[118] and INX.[119]

Other security tokens trading venues

It is worth pausing here for a minute to explain where security tokens (see Chapter 5) can be traded, because whilst security token exchanges are the primary market, there are other trading venues:

- **Security Token Offerings (STOs)**: (see Chapter 4, Box 4.1) these are used for the initial sale of the security tokens.
- **Alternative trading venues**: security tokens, whilst primarily traded on security token exchanges, can also be traded on other compliant

venues, such as over-the-counter (OTC) trading desks. The regulatory framework of the jurisdiction in which these platforms operate will dictate their ability to trade security tokens.

Historically, some regulated CEX, such as Binance, offered tokenised stock on their platforms. Others followed in Binance's footsteps, and in June 2021, FTX, the centralised crypto exchange of Sam Bankman-Fried's fame – started to move into tokenised stocks[120] in partnership with Switzerland-based token issuer Digital Assets AG (DAAG).[121] Stocks of Facebook, Google, Netflix, Nvidia, PayPal, Square, and Tesla were amongst those available.

In July 2021, Binance announced it would cease offering tokenised stock services, and by October 2021, it had discontinued these services altogether in every jurisdiction. This decision was part of Binance's efforts to comply with regulatory requirements in various jurisdictions. But FTX continued, and this is a whole different story...

The FTX scandal

We covered the Wirecard scandal in Chapter 5 and how it affected the payments world. The FTX scandal was equally significant to the crypto world and financial markets at large. I could have covered FTX in the earlier section on CEX, but the concept of trading tokenised securities needed to be introduced first, as this is what FTX got into.

FTX was a centralised crypto exchange known for its focus on crypto derivatives, including futures, options, volatility products, and leveraged tokens, as well as spot trading of various digital assets. Despite its extensive offerings, FTX was not a security token exchange. The exchange gained prominence due to its innovative trading products and aggressive marketing strategies. At its peak in July 2021, the company had over one million users and was the third largest crypto exchange by volume,[122] with a valuation of $18 billion.

However, its rapid ascent was matched by an equally swift downfall, triggered by financial mismanagement and a lack of transparency. The following is a chronological account of the events leading to the collapse of FTX, highlighting key moments and repercussions that have had lasting impacts on the industry.

2022

- **November 2**: concerns about FTX's financial stability arose when CoinDesk reported that Alameda Research, affiliated with FTX and also owned by Sam Bankman-Fried, held a large amount of FTT, FTX's own utility token, raising questions about the financial health of both entities.[123] Essentially, Alameda rested on a foundation largely made up of a coin that a sister company invented, not an independent collateral (e.g. fiat, other reserves), and routinely borrowed the capital it needed from FTX's customer deposits. In addition, Bankman-Fried used FTX funds to buy personal luxury items, finance elaborate advertising campaigns, and make political donations. After these revelations, FTX began to unravel.
- **November 6**: Binance, a competing exchange, announced plans to liquidate its FTT holdings, causing a significant drop in the token's value and triggering mass withdrawals from FTX.
- **November 8–9**: FTX faced a severe liquidity crisis and blocked customers from taking money out of the platform. Binance initially considered acquiring FTX but withdrew after reviewing its financials, citing issues beyond its control (read into this that Binance is no stranger to regulatory scrutiny and didn't want to add to their own problems).
- **November 10**: The Bahamas froze the assets of FTX's local subsidiary. and BlockFi, a crypto lender, paused client withdrawals due to the fallout from FTX's collapse.
- **November 11**: FTX filed for Chapter 11 bankruptcy protection, and Sam Bankman-Fried resigned as CEO. John J. Ray III, known for handling Enron's bankruptcy, took over as CEO.
- **November 15**: investors filed a class action lawsuit against FTX and its celebrity endorsers which included Tom Brady, Gisele Bundchen, Stephen Curry, Golden State Warriors, and Naomi Osaka, amongst others.[124] The suit claimed "false representation and deceptive conduct" and accused FTX and Alameda of operating a Ponzi scheme between them.
- **December 12**: Bankman-Fried was arrested in the Bahamas, and U.S. authorities charged him with multiple counts of financial misconduct.

2023

- **January**: Sam Bankman-Fried pleaded not guilty to fraud and other charges in a US court on 3 January 2023. His trial was set to begin in October 2023. In January, it was reported that $5 billion in assets had been recovered in cash and liquid assets,[125] though the total assets missing were estimated at $8 billion.
- **November 3**: Bankman-Fried was convicted of defrauding customers and investors, with losses exceeding $10 billion.

2024

- **March 28**: Bankman-Fried was sentenced to 25 years in prison.
- **May 8**: FTX announced plans to reimburse most of its customers, marking a significant step in the aftermath of its collapse.
- **August 8**: the US CFTC obtains a $12.7 billion judgement against FTX and Alameda in monetary relief to FTX customers and victims of FTX's fraud.[126]

I could almost copy the text I wrote at the end of the Mt. Gox collapse earlier; I would only need to substitute "Mt Gox" with "FTX" as the lessons to be learned are exactly the same. The main difference is that FTX was substantially bigger and traded in fancier crypto-assets. And of course, we had the linked failures of Silicon Valley Bank and Silvergate as a typical example of contagion risk.[127,128,129]

The only thing I would add is that the International Monetary Fund (IMF) weighed in, mentioning both the Terra/Luna (see Chapter 5, Box 5.4) and FTX collapses, in their September 2023 report "Assessing Macrofinancial Risks from Crypto Assets".[130] They warned about the potential risks that cryptocurrencies can pose to the global financial system and pointed out that the wild price swings of crypto-assets and the growing trend of using borrowed money for trading could create serious financial stability issues. The IMF also emphasised the need for countries to strengthen their regulatory frameworks to better manage these risks and suggested developing tools to help assess and track the vulnerabilities associated with cryptocurrencies. Their goal is to ensure that the financial system remains safe and sound amid the evolving landscape of digital assets.

Like Mt. Gox, the FTX collapse underscored the interconnectedness of the crypto ecosystem with the traditional financial world. Like a row of dominoes, the fall of one major player threatened to topple others, revealing the fragility of a system that many had believed to be robust.

In the end, whilst the FTX debacle was undoubtedly a setback for the crypto industry, it may also serve as a catalyst for positive change. Like a forest fire that clears away dead wood and allows for new growth, this crisis could lead to a stronger, more transparent, and better-regulated crypto sector. The challenge now is to learn from these hard lessons and build a more resilient financial ecosystem that can harness the potential of crypto-assets whilst protecting the interests of investors and users.

Recap on security token exchanges

Security token exchanges represent a novel development in financial markets, potentially offering enhanced liquidity, transparency, and accessibility to a wider range of investors. However, the evolving regulatory landscape and inherent risks necessitate careful consideration by participants. The FTX scandal serves as a cautionary tale, underscoring the importance of robust regulatory compliance and transparent operations in the crypto industry. This is why centralised crypto exchanges no longer offer tokenised securities. As the market for security tokens continues to mature, it will be crucial for exchanges to address these challenges to foster trust and stability in this emerging sector.

Token launch platforms (Launchpads)

Token launch platforms, commonly referred to as launchpads, provide a structured environment for new cryptocurrency projects to raise capital and gain exposure. These platforms facilitate the initial distribution of tokens to investors, often through mechanisms like Initial Coin Offerings (ICOs), Initial Exchange Offerings (IEOs), and Initial DEX Offerings (IDOs) (see Chapter 4, Box 4.2). Launchpads are designed to streamline the fundraising process and offer project access to a broad investor base.

The main characteristics of token launch platforms are:

- **Project vetting and support**: launchpads typically have a rigorous selection process to ensure that only high-quality projects are featured. This vetting process helps reduce investment risks and increases the chances of project success by providing marketing and technical support.

- **Token allocation and distribution**: each launchpad has its own rules regarding token distribution, vesting schedules, and lock-ups. These rules govern how tokens are allocated between private and public investors, ensuring a fair distribution process.
- **Regulation**: launchpads often operate under varying regulatory frameworks depending on their jurisdiction, and some may be subjected to specific regulations regarding AML and KYC requirements. In the US, the SEC has taken a strict stance, requiring many token offerings to comply with securities regulations. Other jurisdictions have developed specific crypto-asset offering regulations, such as the EU's MiCA regulation. This regulatory oversight can enhance investor confidence but may also impose additional compliance burdens on the project launching tokens.
- **Access to investment opportunities**: launchpads offer investors the opportunity to participate in token sales with minimal effort, making it easier to invest in new cryptocurrencies. This accessibility allows investors to engage in early-stage projects with potential for high returns.
- **Liquidity and trading**: after a successful token launch, tokens are often listed on major cryptocurrency exchanges, increasing their liquidity, and allowing investors to trade them at current market prices.
- **Decentralisation and security**: many launchpads strive to enhance decentralisation and prioritise the security of investors' funds. They often use blockchain technology to provide transparency and decentralisation (e.g. Polkastarter,[131] Trustswap,[132] DAO Maker[133]). However, the level of decentralisation may vary, with some platforms retaining centralised elements, such as project selection and token distribution, which can impact decentralisation (e.g. Binance Launchpad,[134] Kucoin Spotlight,[135] Gate.io Startup[136]). Investors should assess each launchpad's governance model and security measures to understand their approach to decentralisation and security.
- **Benefits**: launchpads provide a simplified way for projects to raise funds and for investors to access new investment opportunities. They offer professional support, increase project visibility, and often result in higher marketing efficiency.

- **Risks**:
  - **Market volatility**: the value of tokens can be highly volatile, affecting the overall investment outcome.
  - **Regulatory challenges**: changes in regulatory frameworks can impact the operation and availability of launchpads and the projects they support.
  - **Project failure**: despite rigorous vetting, there is always a risk that a project may not succeed as planned.

Token launch platforms play a crucial role in the cryptocurrency ecosystem by providing a structured and efficient means for projects to raise capital and for investors to access promising new ventures, but they present inherent risks and regulatory challenges.

Crypto Exchange-Traded Funds (ETFs)

Because there's been so much hype in the media about ETFs in relation to crypto-assets,[137] I include these here for completeness, although they are not strictly related to payments.

Exchange Traded Funds (ETFs) are investment funds traded on stock exchanges, much like individual stocks. They hold a collection of securities such as stocks, bonds, commodities, or a mix of these. ETFs are designed to track the performance of a specific index, sector, commodity, or other assets, and their shares can be bought and sold throughout the trading day at market prices. They are investment vehicles that allow investors to gain exposure to a basket of assets or a specific market sector in a single trade. They are characterised by their liquidity, as they can be bought and sold easily on stock exchanges, and their transparency, as holdings are typically disclosed daily. They often have lower costs when compared to mutual funds.

Following this generic definition, crypto ETFs are ETFs that track the performance of one or more cryptocurrencies or crypto-asset. They allow investors to gain exposure to the crypto market without directly owning or managing the underlying crypto-assets. There are several types of crypto ETFs:

- **Direct crypto ETFs**: these hold actual cryptocurrencies (e.g. BTC, ETH). These are also referred to as "spot crypto ETFs".
- **Futures-based crypto ETFs**: these hold cryptocurrency futures contracts.
- **Crypto company ETFs**: these invest in companies involved in cryptocurrency and blockchain technology.

The main characteristics of crypto ETFs are:

- **Diversification**: crypto ETFs can include a single cryptocurrency, such as BTC, or a basket of different cryptocurrencies, providing diversification within the crypto market. This helps mitigate the risk associated with investing in individual cryptocurrencies.
- **Regulation**: whilst crypto ETFs are regulated financial products, the underlying crypto markets they invest in may lack oversight. In the US, the SEC has approved both futures-based and spot crypto ETFs, although spot ETFs face greater regulatory hurdles due to concerns about market manipulation and investor protection.
- **Assets traded**: these funds may invest in futures contracts on cryptocurrencies or the cryptocurrencies themselves. Futures-based ETFs track the prospective value of a cryptocurrency, whilst spot ETFs track the actual current value by holding the digital assets directly.
- **How users can invest**: investors can buy and sell shares of crypto ETFs through traditional brokerage accounts, similar to how they would trade stocks. This provides easy access to the crypto market without the need to manage digital wallets or navigate crypto exchanges.
- **What users can do**: by investing in a crypto ETF, users can gain exposure to cryptocurrency price movements without directly owning or managing digital assets, reducing the complexity and security concerns associated with direct crypto investments.
- **Benefits**: crypto ETFs simplify the investment process, offer liquidity through trading on stock exchanges, and can be included in traditional investment accounts (depending on jurisdiction). They also provide a regulated way to invest in cryptocurrencies, which can offer a sense of legitimacy and security for investors.

- **Risks**:
  - **Market volatility**: Crypto ETFs are subject to the high volatility of the cryptocurrency markets, which can lead to significant price swings.
  - **Tracking error**: there may be discrepancies between the ETF's performance and the actual price movements of the underlying cryptocurrencies, especially for futures-based ETFs.
  - **Lack of direct ownership**: investors don't own the underlying digital assets, which means they miss out on the decentralisation and anonymity benefits associated with cryptocurrencies.

As shown, crypto ETFs operate under the regulatory framework of traditional securities. They provide exposure to crypto through traditional brokerage accounts and offer a way to invest in crypto without dealing with wallets or exchanges. The availability of crypto ETFs varies by jurisdiction due to differing regulatory approaches, including:

- **United States**: the US SEC has approved both BTC and ETH ETFs. The approval for Bitcoin ETFs came in January 2024,[138] which included significant asset managers like BlackRock and Fidelity. Ethereum ETFs were subsequently approved in May 2024,[139] marking a significant shift in the regulatory stance towards cryptocurrency investment products.
- **Canada**: Canada was the first country to approve a Bitcoin ETF in February 2021.[140] The Purpose Bitcoin ETF, launched by Purpose Investments, was the world's first physically settled Bitcoin ETF and began trading on the Toronto Stock Exchange. This approval came from the Ontario Securities Commission (OSC), marking Canada as a pioneer in regulated crypto investment products.
- **Europe and UK**: In Europe, the MiCA framework aims for EU-wide harmonisation of crypto regulations, which has led to the approval of various crypto Exchange-Traded Products (ETPs). For instance, physically backed BTC and ETH ETPs are available in countries like Switzerland, Germany, and France.[141]

  In the UK, the regulatory approach is more cautious, and the FCA has implemented comprehensive regulations classifying BTC and other cryptocurrencies as "restricted mass market investments". These regulations include restrictions on offering derivatives or ETPs tied to specific crypto-assets to retail consumers. However, the FCA has recently shown some openness by announcing support for listing physically backed BTC and ETH exchange-traded notes (ETNs) for professional investors.[142]

- **Brazil**: Brazil approved its first Bitcoin ETF in March 2021.[143] QR Asset Management's ETF, known as QBTC11, began trading on the Brazilian Stock Exchange (B3) in June 2021. This made Brazil the first country in Latin America to offer a Bitcoin ETF.
- **Australia**: Australia has been open to crypto ETFs, with the first such funds launching in May 2022 as the Australian Securities and Investments Commission (ASIC) provided guidance on crypto-asset ETFs, outlining requirements for funds that wish to invest directly in cryptocurrencies.[144] The Australian Securities Exchange (ASX) has also added digital assets to the list of eligible underlying assets for funds listed on the exchange.[145]

It's important to note that the regulatory landscape for crypto ETFs is evolving rapidly. Investors should always check the current status and availability in their jurisdiction before investing. Additionally, they should be aware of the risks associated with crypto investments, including high volatility and regulatory uncertainties.

Crypto index fund marketplaces

If crypto ETFs are pre-packaged baskets of specific cryptocurrencies, then crypto index fund marketplaces are like shopping centres for different crypto investment options. ETFs offer a fixed set of cryptocurrencies, traded on traditional exchanges. In contrast, crypto index fund marketplaces provide various funds, each holding a different mix of cryptocurrencies. This allows investors to choose funds that align with their specific investment goals and risk tolerance, offering more flexibility and potential diversification compared to ETFs.

Crypto index fund marketplaces offer investors a way to gain diversified exposure to the cryptocurrency market through a single investment vehicle. These funds track a specific index of cryptocurrencies, usually based on market capitalisation, and are designed to provide a broad representation of the crypto market. Unlike individual cryptocurrency investments, index funds spread risk across multiple assets, making them an attractive option for those looking to invest in the crypto market without the volatility associated with single cryptocurrencies.

The main characteristics of crypto index fund marketplaces are:

- **Diversification**: crypto index funds typically include a selection of the top cryptocurrencies by market capitalisation, such as BTC and ETH, along with other leading digital assets. This diversification helps mitigate the risk associated with investing in a single cryptocurrency.
- **Regulation**: these funds are often subject to regulatory oversight, similar to traditional financial products. In the US, some crypto index funds are registered as investment companies under the Investment Company Act of 1940. In other jurisdictions, they may fall under existing collective investment scheme regulations or specific crypto-asset fund regulations.
- **Assets traded**: the funds invest in a basket of cryptocurrencies, which can include a mix of well-established coins and emerging digital assets. The composition of the fund is usually rebalanced periodically to reflect changes in the market.
- **How users can invest**: investors can purchase shares of crypto index funds through brokerage accounts, similar to how they would buy shares of a stock or traditional ETF. These funds are often available OTC, providing easy access for investors.
- **What users can do**: by investing in a crypto index fund, users can gain exposure to the cryptocurrency market without the need to manage individual crypto wallets or navigate the complexities of trading on crypto exchanges.
- **Benefits**: crypto index funds provide a simplified way to invest in the crypto market, offering diversification, professional management, and reduced volatility compared to direct cryptocurrency investments. They also eliminate the need for investors to manage private keys or deal with the security concerns of holding cryptocurrencies directly.
- **Risks**:
  - **Market volatility**: whilst diversification reduces risk, the overall value of the fund can still be affected by the inherent volatility of the cryptocurrency market.

- **Regulatory changes**: as with other crypto-related financial products, changes in regulatory frameworks can impact the operation and availability of crypto index funds.
- **Liquidity**: some funds may trade at a premium or discount to their net asset value, depending on market demand, which can affect the liquidity and pricing of the fund.

Examples of crypto index funds include the Bitwise 10 Crypto Index Fund,[146] which tracks the ten most highly valued cryptocurrencies and rebalances monthly to reflect market changes.

Prediction markets

Whilst centralised prediction markets exist (e.g. PredictIt,[147] Iowa Electronic Markets[148]), decentralised prediction markets offer participants a platform to trade contracts based on the outcomes of future events, leveraging blockchain technology for enhanced transparency and security. These markets, where users can speculate on the outcome of future events by buying and selling event shares, aggregate the beliefs of participants, with market prices reflecting the collective prediction of the likelihood of various outcomes, essentially capitalising on the wisdom of crowds. They are used in diverse areas, from political elections to sports events, and are valued for their ability to provide insights that can surpass traditional polling methods.

The main characteristics of decentralised prediction markets are:

- **Diversification**: decentralised prediction markets cover a wide range of topics, including politics, finance, sports, and entertainment, allowing participants to diversify their bets across different types of events. This diversification helps mitigate the risk associated with focusing on a single event type.
- **Regulation**: decentralised prediction markets often fall into a legal grey area. In some jurisdictions, they may be regulated as gambling or betting platforms. In others, they might be considered derivatives markets. Some regions will not even allow these markets to operate. The decentralised nature of many prediction markets poses challenges to regulatory enforcement.

- **Assets traded**: participants trade contracts that pay out based on the outcome of specific events. These contracts are typically denominated in cryptocurrencies and are managed through smart contracts on the blockchain.
- **How users can invest**: users can participate in decentralised prediction markets by buying and selling contracts through the platforms. This process is facilitated by smart contracts, which automate the execution of trades and payouts.
- **What users can do**: by participating in decentralised prediction markets, users can express their beliefs about future events and potentially profit from accurate predictions. This participation also contributes to the market's overall forecasting accuracy.
- **Benefits**: decentralised prediction markets provide a dynamic and real-time method for forecasting, leveraging the wisdom of crowds. They offer increased transparency, security, and resistance to manipulation compared to traditional markets. However, they may also face challenges such as lower liquidity, which can affect trading efficiency, and the potential for market manipulation, as participants can still attempt to influence outcomes.
- **Risks**:
    - **Market manipulation**: despite their decentralised nature, these markets can still be susceptible to manipulation, where participants may attempt to influence prices for personal gain.
    - **Regulatory challenges**: legal restrictions in various jurisdictions can limit the operation of decentralised prediction markets, affecting their accessibility and growth.
    - **Complexity**: the complexity of using blockchain technology may deter some users, impacting the overall participation.
    - **Liquidity concerns**: some decentralised prediction markets may experience low trading volumes, leading to difficulties in buying or selling contracts at desired prices.

Augur, launched in 2015, was a once prominent decentralised prediction market, but due to regulatory pressure,[149] all but shut up shop, and its REP token has declined 99.8% in value from its all-time high. Similarly, Gnosis, initially launched in 2015 as an Ethereum-based prediction market (Gnosis 1.0) shifted its focus away from operating as a prediction market platform and transitioned to Gnosis 3.0,[150] which emphasises decentralised payments. Other examples include, Polymarket[151] and Prosper,[152] which seem to be operational at the time of writing.

Other DeFi services

I don't plan to cover DeFi services in any great detail, but the following sections should give an appreciation of what's available.

Lending and borrowing platforms

These are decentralised protocols that enable users to lend and borrow cryptocurrencies without traditional intermediaries. These platforms use smart contracts to automate the lending process, determine interest rates algorithmically, and manage collateral.

These are generally unregulated in most jurisdictions, though this is changing. Some countries are beginning to consider them under existing lending laws or developing specific DeFi regulations. In the US, the SEC has shown interest in regulating these platforms, particularly concerning securities laws.

Prominent examples include Aave and Compound.

Yield farming platforms

These are protocols that allow users to earn rewards by providing liquidity to various DeFi applications. These platforms often involve complex strategies of depositing, borrowing, and lending across multiple protocols to maximise returns.

These are generally unregulated, though some jurisdictions are beginning to consider them under existing investment laws or developing specific DeFi regulations. The complexity of yield farming strategies poses challenges to regulators in terms of risk assessment and investor protection.

Yearn Finance[153] is a prominent example at the time of writing.

Decentralised derivatives platforms

These are protocols that enable the creation and trading of financial contracts whose value is derived from underlying assets, without centralised intermediaries. These can include options, futures, and perpetual contracts based on cryptocurrencies or other assets.

In many jurisdictions, these may fall under existing derivatives regulations. Some countries are developing specific crypto-derivatives regulations. In the US, the CFTC has asserted jurisdiction over crypto derivatives, whilst the SEC may also have oversight depending on the nature of the underlying asset.

Prominent examples include dYdX and Synthetix.

Recap on trading places

In the evolving landscape of crypto trading, understanding the various platforms and their roles is crucial for professionals, users, and regulators alike. Crypto trading venues, akin to bustling marketplaces, offer diverse opportunities and challenges, each with unique characteristics that cater to different needs and preferences.

For professionals in the financial sector, crypto exchanges represent a dynamic frontier of innovation and risk. CEX, much like traditional stock exchanges, provide high liquidity and user-friendly interfaces, making them attractive for those seeking efficient trading experiences. However, they also pose significant custodial and security risks, as users must trust the platform to safeguard their assets. This trust is a double-edged sword, as evidenced by historical events like the Mt. Gox and FTX collapses, which underscore the importance of robust security measures and transparent governance.

DEXs, on the other hand, offer a peer-to-peer trading environment that mirrors the open-air markets of old, where individuals trade directly without intermediaries. This model enhances privacy and potentially reduces counterparty risk but often at the cost of liquidity and ease of use. For users, navigating these platforms requires a certain level of technical proficiency and awareness of potential scams, akin to navigating a complex bazaar.

Regulators and policymakers face the intricate task of balancing innovation with protection. The regulatory landscape is as varied as the platforms themselves, with jurisdictions imposing different levels of oversight. CEX are often subject to stringent regulations, including AML and KYC requirements, which aim to prevent illicit activities but can also stifle innovation.

In contrast, the decentralised nature of DEXs presents regulatory challenges, as these platforms operate without a central authority to hold accountable.

For users, the choice of trading platform is akin to selecting a mode of transport for a journey. CEX offer the comfort and convenience of a high-speed train, with clear routes and schedules, but require trust in the operator. DEX resemble a bicycle ride through winding paths, offering freedom and control but demanding more effort and vigilance.

In conclusion, the landscape of trading places in the crypto world is as diverse and complex as the crypto-assets themselves. Each platform offers distinct advantages and challenges, and understanding these nuances is essential for all stakeholders. As the industry matures, collaboration between professionals, users, and regulators will be key to fostering a secure, efficient, and inclusive trading environment.

Now that we got that out of the way, let's complete the picture.

The comparison table you've been waiting for

Crypto trading places come in many forms, from crypto exchanges to NFT marketplaces, and specialised exchanges. Even traditional PSPs may offer crypto trading services. In the next sections, I will introduce each of these and follow the same structure for each trading place: definition, custody, regulation, assets traded, how users can trade, what users can do, benefits, risks, and examples.

Table 6.4 gives an at-a-glance summary comparison of the various markets where crypto-assets can be traded.

Note from the author: I don't include gaming and metaverse marketplaces in Table 6.4 as these are characteristically, if not functionally, similar to NFT marketplaces.

What does this mean?

The convergence of traditional payment systems and crypto services presents both opportunities and challenges to various stakeholders, as described in Figure 6.7.

Traditional payment systems and crypto platforms increasingly intertwine through strategic partnerships, mergers, acquisitions, and payment systems interlinkages. A notable example is Stripe's partnership with Coinbase, announced in March 2024,[154] which enables Coinbase users to purchase cryptocurrencies using Stripe's payment infrastructure. This collaboration allows users in over 30 countries to buy crypto-assets directly with their

Table 6.4 Comparing crypto trading platforms. © 2024 Neira Jones

Characteristics	**Decentralised Crypto Exchange (DEX)**	**P2P Crypto Exchange**	**Atomic Swaps**	**NFT Marketplace**	**Hybrid Crypto Exchange**	**Centralised Crypto Exchange (CEX)**	**Security Token Exchange**	**Traditional Payment or Banking Platforms Offering Crypto**
Custody	Users retain custody of their keys	Both custodial and non-custodial models available	Users retain custody of their keys	Users retain custody of their keys	Both custodial and non-custodial models available	CEX holds custody of users' keys	Custodial services provided	PSPs hold custody of users' keys
Regulation	Typically less regulatory oversight	Varies, some require KYC	Typically less regulatory oversight	Limited but evolving	Complex regulatory requirements	Subject to AML and KYC regulations	Stringent regulatory oversight	Regulated, must comply with AML and KYC
Assets traded	Cryptocurrencies and stablecoins	Primarily cryptocurrencies, some stablecoins	Cryptocurrencies across different blockchains	NFTs	Cryptocurrencies and stablecoins	Cryptocurrencies, stablecoins	Security tokens	Limited selection of cryptocurrencies, some stablecoins
On ramp	No	Yes	No	No	Yes	Yes	No	Yes
Off ramp	No	Yes	No	No	Yes	Yes	No	Yes
Direct user access	Non-custodial wallet	Account on platform, cryptocurrency or fiat, KYC may apply	Non-custodial wallet	NFT-capable non-custodial wallet, cryptocurrency	Account on platform, cryptocurrency or fiat, KYC may apply	Account on platform with KYC/AML checks, cryptocurrency, fiat	Verified/accredited account with KYC/AML checks	Account on platform with KYC/AML checks, fiat
How users can trade	Connect wallets to DEX platform and trade directly	Post buy/sell offers, matched by platform, often with escrow service	P2P using smart contracts	Connect NFT-capable wallets, browse, and purchase/auction NFTs	Trade through both centralised order books and decentralised protocols	Create accounts, deposit funds, and trade through the exchange's interface	Extensive verification, trade through platform	User-friendly interfaces for buy/sell orders

(Continued)

Table 6.4 (Continued)

Characteristics	Decentralised Crypto Exchange (DEX)	P2P Crypto Exchange	Atomic Swaps	NFT Marketplace	Hybrid Crypto Exchange	Centralised Crypto Exchange (CEX)	Security Token Exchange	Traditional Payment or Banking Platforms Offering Crypto
What users can do	Trade, yield farming, provide liquidity	Trade directly with other users, negotiate terms	Trade cryptocurrencies across blockchains without intermediaries	Buy, sell, and create NFTs, participate in auctions	Participate in both traditional and DeFi services	Trade, stake, lend, use fiat to buy crypto, withdraw to fiat	Trade tokenised assets, access investment opportunities	Buy, sell, and hold cryptocurrencies
Benefits	Enhanced privacy and control, censorship resistance	Greater privacy, flexible payment methods, lower fees, direct user-to-user transactions	Reduced counterparty risks, lower costs, increased privacy, and interoperability	Monetise digital content, ownership recorded on blockchain	Combines security and control of DEXs with liquidity of CEXs	High liquidity, user-friendly interfaces, wide range of trading pairs.	Regulated environment, increased liquidity, fractional ownership	Easy entry, familiar interface, integrates with traditional services
Risks	Smart contract vulnerabilities, phishing attacks, front-running, liquidity risks, user experience	Regulatory, liquidity, counterparty risks, frauds/ scams, security breaches, limited support	Technical complexities, privacy concerns, compatibility issues	Market volatility, intellectual property risks, regulatory risks, security risks	Complexity, regulatory challenges, security risks, liquidity risks	Security threats, regulatory scrutiny, custodial reliance	Regulation, market, valuation, custody, technology, counterparty, and operational risks	Limited selection of cryptocurrencies, centralised risks, regulatory risks
Examples	Uniswap, SushiSwap, PancakeSwap	Non-custodial: Hodl Hodl, Bisq Custodial: Paxful, Binance P2P	RocketX, Atomic Wallet, AtomicDEX	OpenSea, Blur, Rarible	Raydium Kyber Network	Binance, Coinbase, Kraken	tZero, Securitize, INX	Paypal, Block, eToro, N26

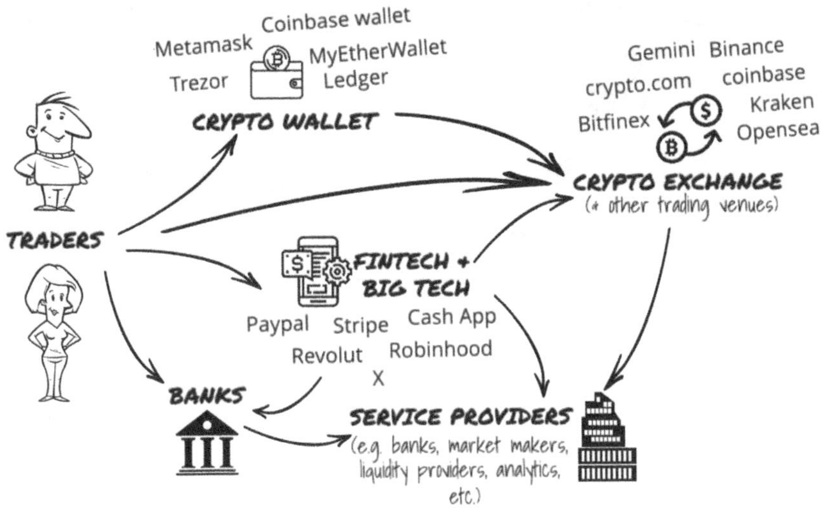

Figure 6.7 Transacting in a decentralised world. © 2024 Neira Jones.

local fiat currencies, leveraging Stripe's robust payment processing capabilities. Another significant use case is PayPal's development of its own stablecoin, PayPal USD (PYUSD), in partnership with Paxos, and companies like Triple-A are using it for cross-border payments,[155] further demonstrating the blending of traditional finance with innovative crypto services.

For professionals, this trend opens up new avenues for innovation in cross-border payments, remittances, and financial inclusion. However, it also requires a deep understanding of both traditional finance and blockchain technology to navigate this evolving landscape effectively.

For users, the integration of cryptocurrencies into mainstream payment systems offers increased choice and potentially faster and cheaper cross-border transactions, but the risks and volatilities associated with crypto-assets must be understood.

For regulators and policymakers, the convergence presents complex challenges in terms of consumer protection, financial stability, and preventing illicit activities. Regulators need to strike a balance between fostering innovation and ensuring the integrity of the financial system. This is exemplified by the increased regulatory pressure on virtual assets:

Figure 6.8 is another way of looking at Table 5.3 which was presented in Chapter 5. As you move from the left to the right of Figure 6.8, centralisation

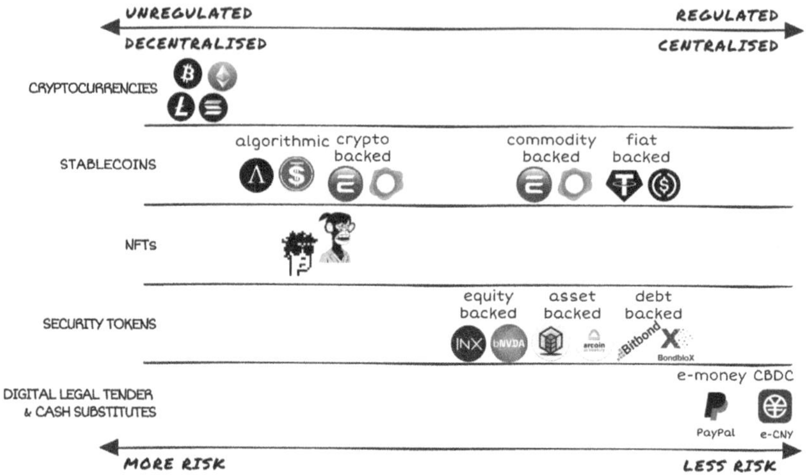

Figure 6.8 Regulatory pressure on virtual assets. © 2024 Neira Jones.

increases, and risks reduce, whilst regulations and oversight become more stringent. This tells us two things:

- Regulators and policymakers have been concentrating on the right-hand side of the chart because they can pinpoint the centralised entities responsible for the assets (e.g. a stablecoin or security token issuer).
- Decentralisation is a headache for regulators and policymakers, and more complex assets (e.g. algorithmic stablecoins, synthetic or hybrid tokens) are poorly understood. Their decentralised nature pose challenges to current regulatory models.

Central banks have been experimenting with the synchronisation of transactions across different financial infrastructures, specifically using central bank money within real-time gross settlement (RTGS) systems. Experiments have been conducted, such as the Bank of International Settlements (BIS) Innovation Hub London Centre and the Bank of England collaboration on Project Meridian stage 1,[156] which focused on the concept of synchronising transactions between RTGS and a digitised land registry, reducing settlement risk in real estate transactions by ensuring that funds are transferred only when a corresponding asset on another ledger is moved simultaneously. Project Meridian FX, the second phase of the project announced in June 2024,[157] a joint initiative for foreign exchange transactions with the Bank of England, the Eurosystem, and the London BIS Innovation Hub, aims to synchronise the transaction process between distributed ledger technology (DLT)-based systems and RTGS to address foreign exchange settlement risks.

As the intermingling of traditional finance and distributed ecosystems continues, we can expect to see further innovations that aim to blend the best aspects of both. This could lead to more efficient, transparent, and inclusive financial systems. However, it will require ongoing collaboration between traditional financial institutions, crypto companies, and regulators to ensure that these innovations serve the public interest whilst maintaining the integrity of the financial system.

Transacting in a decentralised world – conclusion (where do we go from here?)

In this chapter, we covered:

- The different types of digital wallets, from traditional payments to crypto services,
- The different types of crypto trading places, and
- How these services inevitably intermingle.

I have tried to explain the jargon and debunk a few myths, and the main terms introduced in this chapter will be found in the glossary. I shared some insights as to what the future might look like, supported by global market trends, tables, charts, and illustrations which I hope readers will find useful. The fundamental principles were covered, and I also gave you my opinion on some aspects of the industry. I know some may disagree with me, and I always welcome a good debate, but I hope I have equipped you to ask the right questions.

If you read this book a few years from now, new business models will emerge, and regulatory pressure will increase. Some businesses will thrive, some will pivot, and others will just disappear, as many have done even as I was writing. But the industry will continue to move on. As an example, following Apple's decision to open up access to its near-field communication

(NFC) chip and secure element (SE) technology in August 2024,[158] Circle, the issuer of the USD coin (USDC) stablecoin, didn't miss a beat and introduced USDC contactless payments on iPhones, enabling users to send USDC to NFC-enabled devices, such as point-of-sale payment terminals or other iPhones.[159]

To complete our understanding of these ecosystems, we must introduce the much-debated concept of CBDCs.

Let's go on the seventh leg of our trip.

Notes

1 "Starbucks Fiscal 2023 Annual Report" Starbucks, 2024. Available at: https://s203.q4cdn.com/326826266/files/doc_financials/2024/ar/fy23-annual-report.pdf (Accessed 12 August 2024).

2 "Not Your Keys, Not Your Coins" Stake Fish, 22 May 2020. Available at: https://blog.stake.fish/not-your-keys-not-your-coins/ (Accessed 13 August 2024).

3 MEW website. Available at: https://www.myetherwallet.com/ (Accessed 20 August 2024).

4 MyCrypto website. Available at: https://mycrypto.com/ (Accessed 20 August 2024).

5 "Addressing the July 2020 E-commerce and Marketing Data Breach — A Message from Ledger's Leadership" Ledger, 29 July 2020. Available at: https://www.ledger.com/addressing-the-july-2020-e-commerce-and-marketing-data-breach (Accessed 13 August 2024).

6 "Physical Addresses of 270K Ledger Owners Leaked on Hacker Forum" *Bleeping Computer*, 21 December 2020. Available at: https://www.bleepingcomputer.com/news/security/physical-addresses-of-270k-ledger-owners-leaked-on-hacker-forum/ (Accessed 13 August 2024).

7 "Criminals Are Mailing Altered Ledger Devices to Steal Cryptocurrency" *Bleeping Computer*, 16 June 2021. Available at: https://www.bleepingcomputer.com/news/cryptocurrency/criminals-are-mailing-altered-ledger-devices-to-steal-cryptocurrency/ (Accessed 13 August 2024).

8 "Is Coinbase in Trouble? 4 Reasons to Avoid Coinbase in 2024 (July Update)" Swanbitcoin, 21 June 2024. Available at: https://www.swanbitcoin.com/industry/is-coinbase-in-trouble/ (Accessed 13 August 2024).

9 "North Korean Hackers Swipe over $100M from Atomic Wallet Users" *CoinTelegraph*, 13 June 2023. Available at: https://cointelegraph.com/news/north-korean-hackers-swipe-over-100m-from-atomic-wallet-users (Accessed 13 August 2024).

10 "Warning: Active MetaMask Phishing Campaign" Halborn, 28 July 2022. Available at: https://www.halborn.com/blog/post/warning-active-metamask-phishing-campaign (Accessed 13 August 2024).

11 "FACT SHEET: White House Releases First-Ever Comprehensive Framework for Responsible Development of Digital Assets" The White House, 16 September 2022. Available at: https://www.whitehouse.gov/briefing-room/statements-releases/2022/09/16/fact-sheet-white-house-releases-first-ever-comprehensive-framework-for-responsible-development-of-digital-assets/ (Accessed 13 August 2024).

12 "Notice on Further Preventing and Resolving the Risks of Virtual Currency Trading and Speculation" The People Bank of China, 2021. Available at: http://www.pbc.gov.cn/en/3688110/3688172/4157443/4353814/index.html (Accessed 13 august 2024).

13 "Cryptoassets Manual" HMRC, 30 March 2021, updated 21 August 2023. Available at: https://www.gov.uk/hmrc-internal-manuals/cryptoassets-manual/crypto100350 (Accessed 13 August 2024).

14 "Licensing for Payment Service Providers" Monetary Authority of Singapore website. Available at: https://www.mas.gov.sg/regulation/payments/licensing-for-payment-service-providers/types-of-payment-services (Accessed 13 August 2024).

15 "MiCA regulation" EUR-Lex. Available at: https://eur-lex.europa.eu/eli/reg/2023/1114/oj (Accessed 13 August 2023).

16 "Updated Guidance for a Risk-Based Approach to Virtual Assets and Virtual Asset Service Providers" FATF, 28 October 2021. Available at: https://www.fatf-gafi.org/en/publications/Fatfrecommendations/Guidance-rba-virtual-assets-2021.html (Accessed 13 August 2024).

17 BNB mixer website. Available at: https://www.bnbmixer.com/ (Accessed 10 August 2024).

18 U.S. Treasury Issues First-Ever Sanctions on a Virtual Currency Mixer, Targets DPRK Cyber Threats. U.S Department of the Treasury. Available at: https://home.treasury.gov/news/press-releases/jy0768 (Accessed 30 November 2024).

19 U.S. Treasury Sanctions Notorious Virtual Currency Mixer Tornado Cash. U.S Department of The Treasury. Available at: https://home.treasury.gov/news/press-releases/jy0916 (Accessed 30 November 2024).

20 Moonpay website. Available at: https://www.moonpay.com/ (Accessed 16 August 2024).

21 Simplex website. Available at: https://www.simplex.com/ (Accessed 16 August 2024).

22 "Wyre Winding Down as Crypto Winter Bites" *Reuters*, 16 June 2023. Available at: https://www.reuters.com/technology/wyre-winding-down-crypto-winter-bites-2023–06–16/ (Accessed 16 August 2024).
23 Dwolla website. Available at: https://www.dwolla.com/ (Accessed 14 August 2024).
24 "FinCEN Issues Guidance on Virtual Currencies and Regulatory Responsibilities" FinCEN, 18 March 2023. Available at: https://www.fincen.gov/sites/default/files/shared/20130318.pdf (Accessed 14 August 2024).
25 "Major Glitch in Bitcoin Network Sparks Sell-Off; Price Temporarily Falls 23%" *Ars Technica*, 12 March 2013. Available at: https://arstechnica.com/information-technology/2013/03/major-glitch-in-bitcoin-network-sparks-sell-off-price-temporarily-falls-23/ (Accessed 14 August 2024).
26 "Bitcoin: CoinLab Files $75M Suit vs. Mt. Gox Exchange, Alleges Breach of Contract" *GeekWire*, 3 May 2013. Available at: https://www.geekwire.com/2013/bitcoin-seattles-coinlab-files-75m-suit-mt-gox-exchange-alleges-breach-contract/ (Accessed 14 August 2024).
27 "US Government Seized $5 Million from Bitcoin Behemoth Mt. Gox" *The Verge*, 23 August 2013. Available at: https://www.theverge.com/2013/8/23/4651926/us-government-seized-5-million-from-bitcoin-behemoth-mt-gox (Accessed 14 August 2024).
28 "Bitcoin Exchange Makes Apparent Move to Play by U.S. Money-Laundering Rules" *The Wall Street Journal*, 28 June 2013. Available at: https://www.wsj.com/articles/SB1000142412788732387390457857400957464468 (Accessed 14 August 2024).
29 "Bitcoin Operator Mt. Gox Resumes Withdrawals" *The Wall Street Journal*, 5 July 2013. Available at: https://www.wsj.com/articles/BL-MBB-4101 (Accessed 14 August 2024).
30 "OKPay Suspends Payment Processing to All Bitcoin Exchanges" *The Register*, 29 May 2013. Available at: https://www.theregister.com/2013/05/29/okpay_suspends_bitcoin_processing/ (Accessed 14 August 2024).
31 "U.S. Government Seizes LibertyReserve.com" KrebsonSecurity, 28 May 2013. Available at: https://krebsonsecurity.com/2013/05/u-s-government-seizes-libertyreserve-com/ (Accessed 14 August 2024).
32 "Mt. Gox Countersues Bitcoin Incubator CoinLab for $5.5 Million" *CoinDesk*, 16 September 2013. Available at: https://www.coindesk.com/markets/2013/09/16/mt-gox-countersues-bitcoin-incubator-coinlab-for-55-million/ (Accessed 14 August 2024).
33 AstroPay website. Available at: https://www.astropay.com/ (Accessed 14 August 2024).
34 "Mt. Gox and AstroPay Team Up for Faster Latin American Transfers" *CoinDesk*, 10 December 2023. Available at: https://www.coindesk.com/

markets/2013/12/10/mt-gox-and-astropay-team-up-for-faster-latin-american-transfers/ (Accessed 14 August 2024).

35 Bitstamp website. Available at: https://www.bitstamp.net/ (Accessed 14 August 2024).

36 "Mt. Gox Halts ALL Bitcoin Withdrawals, Price Drop Follows" *CoinDesk*, 7 February 2014. Available at: https://www.coindesk.com/markets/2014/02/07/mt-gox-halts-all-bitcoin-withdrawals-price-drop-follows/ (Accessed 14 August 2024).

37 "What Was Mt. Gox: From the Hack and Legal Battles to Repayment" Kucoin, 9 August 2024. Available at: https://www.kucoin.com/learn/crypto/what-was-mt-gox-from-the-hack-to-repayment (Accessed 14 August 2024).

38 "The 80,000 Stolen MtGox Bitcoins" WizSec, 19 June 2020. Available at: https://blog.wizsec.jp/2020/06/mtgox-march-2011-theft.html (Accessed 14 August 2024).

39 "Kraken Bitcoin Operator to Help Liquidate Mt. Gox" *The Wall Street Journal*, 25 November 2014. Available at: https://www.wsj.com/articles/BL-MBB-30183 (Accessed 14 August 2024).

40 "Tradehill Exchange: What It Was and History" Investopedia, 11 July 2024. Available at: https://www.investopedia.com/terms/t/tradehill-exchange.asp (Accessed 14 July 2024).

41 "Russian National and Bitcoin Exchange Charged in 21-Count Indictment for Operating Alleged International Money Laundering Scheme and Allegedly Laundering Funds from Hack of Mt. Gox" US DOJ, 26 July 2017. Available at: https://www.justice.gov/usao-ndca/pr/russian-national-and-bitcoin-exchange-charged-21-count-indictment-operating-alleged (Accessed 14 August 2024).

42 "Former Mt. Gox Chief Mark Karpeles Acquitted of Most Charges in Major Bitcoin Case" *CNN*, 14 March 2019. Available at: https://edition.cnn.com/2019/03/14/tech/mark-karpeles-mt-gox/index.html (Accessed 14 August 2024).

43 "BTC-e Operator Pleads Guilty to Money Laundering Conspiracy" US Department of Justice, 3 May 2024. Available at: https://www.justice.gov/opa/pr/btc-e-operator-pleads-guilty-money-laundering-conspiracy Accessed 14 August 2024).

44 "Appeal Denied: BTC-e's Alexander Vinnik Faces 5 Years in French Prison" *Finance Magnates*, 28 June 2021. Available at: https://www.financemagnates.com/cryptocurrency/news/appeal-denied-btc-es-alexander-vinnik-faces-5-years-in-french-prison/ (Accessed 14 August 2024).

45 "Mt. Gox Begins Repaying Bitcoin to Creditors a Decade after Exchange's Collapse. What It Means" *CNBC*, 5 July 2024. Available at: https://

www.cnbc.com/2024/07/05/mt-gox-begins-repaying-bitcoin-to-creditors-a-decade-on-from-collapse.html (Accessed 14 August 2024).

46 Mt Gox website, creditors notices. Available at: https://www.mtgox.com/ (Accessed 14 August 2024).

47 Forbes Profile, Jed McCaleb, 14 August 2024. Available at: https://www.forbes.com/profile/jed-mccaleb/ (Accessed 14 August 2024).

48 "Crypto Billionaires: 13 Richest People in Crypto in 2024" Techopedia, 15 March 2024. Available at: https://www.techopedia.com/crypto-billionaires-11-individuals-who-struck-it-rich-with-cryptocurrencies (Accessed 14 August 2024).

49 Private Internet Access website. Available at: https://www.privateinternetaccess.com/ (Accessed 14 August 2024).

50 Karpeles Lab website. Available at: https://klb.jp/l/en-US/ (Accessed 14 August 2024).

51 Shells.com website. Available at: https://www.shells.com/ (Accessed 14 August 2024).

52 "Former Mt. Gox CEO Doesn't Want His Billion Dollars" *WSJ*, 5 April 2018. Available at: https://www.wsj.com/articles/former-mt-gox-ceo-doesnt-want-his-billion-dollars-1522962084 (Accessed 15 August 2024).

53 Uniswap website. Available at: https://app.uniswap.org/swap (Accessed 15 August 2024).

54 Curve website. Available at: https://curve.fi/#/ethereum/swap (Accessed 15 August 2024).

55 Trader Joe XYZ website. Available at: https://traderjoexyz.com/avalanche (Accessed 15 August 2024).

56 SushiSwap website. Available at: https://www.sushi.com/swap (Accessed 15 August 2024).

57 PancakeSwap website. Available at: https://pancakeswap.finance/ (Accessed 15 August 2024).

58 dYdX website. Available at: https://dydx.exchange/ (Accessed 15 August 2024).

59 "US Regulatory Pressure Forces ZigZag Exchange Closure, zkSync Lite Emerges as Alternative!" *coincu*, 13 April 2024. Available at: https://coincu.com/254966-us-regulatory-zigzag-closure-zksync-lite/ (Accessed 15 August 2024).

60 IDEX website. Available at: https://idex.io/ (Accessed 15 August 2024).

61 0x website. Available at: https://0x.org/ (Accessed 15 August 2024).

62 "Defunct Crypto DEX Etherdelta Still Holds $42M in Customer Assets" Investing.com, 4 February 2023. Available at: https://www.investing.com/news/cryptocurrency-news/defunct-crypto-dex-etherdelta-still-holds-42m-in-customer-assets-2995398 (Accessed 15 August 2024).

63 Loopring website. Available at: https://loopring.io/#/pro (Accessed 15 August 2024).

64 Quickswap website. Available at: https://quickswap.exchange/#/ (Accessed 15 August 2024).

65 1Inch website. Available at: https://app.1inch.io/#/1/simple/swap/ETH (Accessed 15 August 2024).

66 Matcha website. Available at: https://matcha.xyz/ (Accessed 15 August 2024).

67 ParaSwap website available at: https://www.paraswap.io/ (Accessed 15 August 2024).

68 OpenOcean website: Available at: https://openocean.finance/ (Accessed 15 August 2024).

69 Swapzone website. Available at: https://swapzone.io/ (Accessed 15 August 2024).

70 Defillama website. Available at: https://swap.defillama.com/ (Accessed 15 August 2024).

71 Swoop Exchange website. Available at: https://swoop.exchange/ (Accessed 15 August 2024).

72 Atlas DEX website. Available at: https://atlasdex.finance/ (Accessed 15 August 2024).

73 XY Finance website. Available at: https://xy.finance/ (Accessed 15 August 2024).

74 altFINS website. Available at: https://xy.finance/ (Accessed 15 August 2024).

75 Rubic website. Available at: https://rubic.exchange/fr (Accessed 15 August 2024).

76 OKX DEX website. Available at: https://www.okx.com/web3/dex-swap (Accessed 15 August 2024).

77 Synthetix website. Available at: https://synthetix.io/ (Accessed 15 August 2024).

78 Raydium website. Available at: https://raydium.io/swap/ (Accessed 15 August 2024).

79 Kyber Network website. Available at: https://kyber.network/ (Accessed 15 August 2024).

80 Paxful website. Available at: https://paxful.com/ (Accessed 8 August 2024).

81 Binance P2P website. Available at: https://p2p.binance.com/ (Accessed 15 August 2024).

82 "LocalBitcoins has Been Closed" LocalBitcoins website. Available at: https://localbitcoins.com/ (Accessed 8 August 2024).

83 Hold Hodl website. Available at: https://hodlhodl.com/ (Accessed 15 August 2024).

84 Bisq website. Available at: https://hodlhodl.com/ (Accessed 15 August 2024).
85 AtomicDEX (Komodo) website. Available at: https://atomicdex.io/en/ (Accessed 15 August 2024).
86 RocketX website. Available at: https://www.rocketx.exchange/ (Accessed 15 August 2024).
87 Atomic Wallet website. Available at: https://atomicwallet.io/ (Accessed 15 August 2024).
88 Decred DCRDEX website. Available at: https://dex.decred.org/ (Accessed 15 August 2024).
89 Lightning Network website. Available at: https://lightning.network/ (Accessed 15 August 2024).
90 OpenSea website. Available at: https://opensea.io/ (Accessed 15 August 2024).
91 Blur website. Available at: https://blur.io/ (Accessed 15 August 2024).
92 Foundation website. Available at: https://foundation.app/ (Accessed 15 August 2024).
93 LooksRare website. Available at: https://looksrare.org/ (Accessed 15 August 2024).
94 Magic Eden website. Available at: https://magiceden.io/ (Accessed 15 August 2024).
95 Nifty Gateway website. Available at: https://www.niftygateway.com/explore/drops/ (Accessed 15 August 2024).
96 Rarible website. Available at: https://rarible.com/ (Accessed 15 August 2024).
97 Solanart website. Available at: https://solanart.io/ (Accessed 15 August 2024).
98 SuperRare website. Available at: https://superrare.com/ (Accessed 15 August 2024).
99 X2Y2 website. Available at: https://x2y2.io/fr (Accessed 15 August 2024).
100 Decentraland Marketplace website. Available at: https://decentraland.org/marketplace (Accessed 9 August 2024).
101 The Sandbox marketplace website. Available at: https://www.sandbox.game/en/shop/ (Accessed 9 August 2024).
102 Axie Infinity Marketplace website. Available at: https://app.axieinfinity.com/marketplace/ (Accessed 9 August 2024).
103 "Curious about Crypto? Get Confident with the App" Paypal website. Available at: https://www.paypal.com/us/digital-wallet/manage-money/crypto (Accessed 15 August 2024).
104 "Automatically Convert a Percentage of Square Sales into Bitcoin with Cash App" Square website. Available at: https://squareup.com/help/

us/en/article/7935-purchase-bitcoin-with-square (Accessed 15 August 2024).
105 eToro website. Available at: https://www.etoro.com/discover/markets/cryptocurrencies (Accessed 15 August 2024).
106 N26 website. Available at: https://n26.com/en-eu/crypto (Accessed 15 January 2024).
107 Revolut website. Available at: https://www.revolut.com/crypto/ (Accessed 15 August 2024).
108 Wirex website. Available at: https://wirexapp.com/ (Accessed 15 August 2024).
109 DBS Bank website, Digital Exchange. Available at: https://www.dbs.com.sg/corporate/solutions/capital-markets/dbs-digital-exchange (Accessed 15 August 2024).
110 DBS website, Digital Payment Token Exchange. Available at: https://www.dbs.com.sg/corporate/solutions/capital-markets/digital-payment-token (Accessed 15 August 2024).
111 Sygnum Bank website. Available at: https://www.sygnum.com/ (Accessed 15 August 2024).
112 Arkham Intelligence website. Available at: https://www.arkhamintelligence.com/ (Accessed 9 August 2024).
113 Debank website. Available at: https://debank.com/ (Accessed 9 August 2024).
114 Cumberland website. Available at: https://cumberland.io/ (Accessed 16 August 2024).
115 Galaxy Digital website. Available at: https://www.galaxy.com/trading/ (Accessed 16 August 2024).
116 B2C2 website. Available at: https://www.b2c2.com/solutions/product (Accessed 16 August 2024).
117 tZERO website. Available at: https://www.tzero.com/ (Accessed: 23 July 2024).
118 Securitize website. Available at: https://securitize.io/ (Accessed: 23 July 2024).
119 INX website. Available at: https://www.inx.co/ (Accessed: 23 July 2024).
120 "FTX Follows Binance's Lead with Move into Tokenized Stocks" *CoinDesk*, 24 June 2021. Available at: https://www.coindesk.com/markets/2021/06/24/ftx-follows-binances-lead-with-move-into-tokenized-stocks/ (Accessed 10 August 2024).
121 "Swiss-Based Digital Assets AG Launches Tokenized Stock Offerings on Solana" *CoinTelegraph*, 24 June 2021. Available at: https://cointelegraph.com/news/swiss-based-digital-assets-ag-launches-tokenized-stock-offerings-on-solana (Accessed 10 August 2024).

122 "Crypto Firm FTX Trading's Valuation Rises to $18 bln after $900 mln Investment" *Reuters*, 20 July 2021. Available at: https://www.reuters.com/technology/crypto-firm-ftx-trading-raises-900-mln-18-bln-valuation-2021–07–20/ (Accessed 10 August 2024).

123 "Divisions in Sam Bankman-Fried's Crypto Empire Blur on His Trading Titan Alameda's Balance Sheet" *CoinDesk*, 2 November 2022. Available at: https://www.coindesk.com/business/2022/11/02/divisions-in-sam-bankman-frieds-crypto-empire-blur-on-his-trading-titan-alamedas-balance-sheet/ (Accessed 10 August 2024).

124 "United States District Court Southern District of Florida Miami Division" Available at: https://docs-cdn-prod.news-engineering.aws.wapo.pub/publish_document/12afdf1a-a614–48a8–88e5-aa0e9e581c6f/published/12afdf1a-a614–48a8–88e5-aa0e9e581c6f.pdf (Accessed 10 August 2024).

125 "FTX Lawyers Say They Have Recovered $5 billion in Assets" *CNN* 11 January 2023. Available at: https://edition.cnn.com/2023/01/11/business/ftx-assets-recovered/index.html (Accessed 10 August 2024).

126 "CFTC Obtains $12.7 Billion Judgment against FTX and Alameda" CFTC, 8 August 2024. Available at: https://www.cftc.gov/PressRoom/PressReleases/8938-24 (Accessed 10 August 2024).

127 "The Crypto 'Contagion' That Helped Bring down SVB" Politico, 14 March 2023. Available at: https://www.politico.eu/article/crypto-help-bring-down-svb-silicon-valley-bank-ftx/ (Accessed 20 August 2024).

128 "The Role of Cryptocurrency in the Failures of Silvergate, Silicon Valley, and Signature Banks" Congressional Research Service, 25 April 2023. Available at: https://crsreports.congress.gov/product/pdf/IN/IN12148 (Accessed 20 August).

129 "How Silvergate's Crypto Collapse Differed from Silicon Valley Bank's: No Bailout" *CoinDesk*, 10 March 2023. Available at: https://www.coindesk.com/tech/2023/03/10/how-silvergates-crypto-collapse-differed-from-silicon-valley-banks-no-us-government-bailout/ (Accessed 20 August 2024).

130 "Assessing Macrofinancial Risks from Crypto Assets" International Monetary Fund, 29 September 2023. Available at: https://www.imf.org/en/Publications/WP/Issues/2023/09/30/Assessing-Macrofinancial-Risks-from-Crypto-Assets-539473 (Accessed 15 August 2024).

131 Polkastarter launchpad website. Available at: https://polkastarter.com/ (Accessed 9 August 2024).

132 TrustSwap launchpad website. Available at: https://trustswap.com/launchpads/ (Accessed 9 August 2024).

133 DAO Maker launchpad. Available at: https://app.daomaker.com/launchpad (Accessed 9 August 2024).

134 BinanceILaunchpad website. Available at: https://launchpad.binance.com/ (Accessed 9 August 2024).
135 Kucoin Spotlight launchpad website. Available at: https://www.kucoin.com/spotlight-center (Accessed 9 August 2024).
136 Gate.io Startup launchpad website. Available at: https://www.gate.io/startup (Accessed 9 August 2024).
137 "Coinbase Beats Revenue Estimates as Crypto Markets Ride ETF Euphoria" *Reuters*, 1 August 2024. Available at: https://www.reuters.com/technology/coinbases-second-quarter-revenue-surges-crypto-trading-resurgence-2024–08-01/ (Accessed 3 August 2024).
138 "US SEC Approves Bitcoin ETFs in Watershed for Crypto Market" *Reuters*, 11 January 2024. Available at: https://www.reuters.com/technology/bitcoin-etf-hopefuls-still-expect-sec-approval-despite-social-media-hack-2024-01-10/ (Accessed 3 August 2024).
139 "SEC Clears Path for Stake-Free Ethereum ETFs in Landmark Ruling" The Global Treasurer, 21 June 2024. Available at: https://www.theglobaltreasurer.com/2024/06/21/sec-ethereum-etfs-approval/ (Accessed 3 August 2024).
140 "Canadian Regulator Clears Launch of World's First Bitcoin ETF - Investment Manager" *Reuters*, 12 February 2021. Available at: https://www.reuters.com/world/americas/canadian-regulator-clears-launch-worlds-first-bitcoin-etf-investment-manager-2021–02–12/ (Accessed 3 August 2024).
141 "How European Investors Can Ride the Bitcoin ETF Wave" *Financial Times*, 25 March 2024. Available at: https://www.ft.com/content/6543416e-27f2–455a-b42b-7ae87eb9231d (Accessed 3 August 2024).
142 "FCA Updates Position on Cryptoasset Exchange Traded Notes for Professional Investors" Financial Conduct Authority, 11 March 2024. Available at: https://www.fca.org.uk/news/statements/fca-updates-position-cryptoasset-exchange-traded-notes-professional-investors (Accessed 3 August 2024).
143 "Brazil Bitcoin ETF Follows Similar Launches in Canada" *Blockworks*, 25 June 2021. Available at: https://blockworks.co/news/brazil-bitcoin-etf-follows-similar-launches-in-canada (Accessed 3 August 2024).
144 "Exchange Traded Products: Admission Guidelines" ASIC website. Available at: https://asic.gov.au/regulatory-resources/markets/market-supervision/exchange-traded-products-admission-guidelines/ (Accessed 3 August 2024).
145 "Australian Securities Exchange Gives Its First Approval of a Spot Bitcoin Listing to VanEck" *CoinDesk*, 17 June 2024. Available at: https://www.

coindesk.com/policy/2024/06/17/australian-securities-exchange-gives-its-first-approval-of-a-spot-bitcoin-listing-to-vaneck/ (Accessed 3 August 2024).

146 Bitwise website, Bitwise 10 Crypto Index Fund. Available at: https://bitwiseinvestments.com/crypto-funds/bitw (Accessed 9 August 2024).

147 PredictIt website. Available at: https://www.predictit.org/ (Accessed 9 August 2024).

148 Iowa Electronic Market website. Available at: https://iem.uiowa.edu/iem/ (Accessed 9 August 2024).

149 "Here's Why the US Gov't Always Shutters Prediction Markets" *Protos*, 26 September 2023. Available at: https://protos.com/heres-why-the-us-govt-always-shutters-prediction-markets/ (Accessed 9 August 2024).

150 Gnosis website. Available at: https://www.gnosis.io/ (Accessed 9 August 2024).

151 Polymarket website. Available at: https://polymarket.com/ (Accessed 9 August 2024).

152 Prosper website. Available at: https://prosper.so/ (Accessed 9 August 2024).

153 Yearn Finance website. Available at: https://yearn.fi/ (Accessed 15 August 2024).

154 "Stripe and Coinbase Integrate Crypto Services" Pymnts, 27 June 2024. Available at: https://www.pymnts.com/cryptocurrency/2024/stripe-and-coinbase-integrate-crypto-services/ (Accessed 17 August 2024).

155 "Triple-A Integrates PayPal USD for Cross-Border Payments" *The Paypers*, 29 May 2024. Available at: https://thepaypers.com/cryptocurrencies/triple-a-integrates-paypal-usd-for-cross-border-payments--1268321 (Accessed 17 August).

156 "Project Meridian: Innovating Transactions with Synchronisation" BIS, 19 April 2023. Available at: https://www.bis.org/about/bisih/topics/fmis/meridian.htm (Accessed 27 August 2024).

157 "English, European Central Bank to Trial FX, DLT Interoperability" *Ledger Insights*, 17 June 2024. Available at: https://www.ledgerinsights.com/english-european-central-bank-to-trial-fx-dlt-interoperability/ (Accessed 27 August 2024).

158 "Apple Finally Loosens Its Grip on NFC Payments in iOS 18: Why That Matters" SlashGear, 14 August 2024. Available at: https://www.slashgear.com/1643010/apple-opens-up-nfc-payments-ios-18/ (Accessed 19 August 2024).

159 "Circle Introduces USDC Contactless Payments on iPhones" *The Paypers*, 19 August 2024. Available at: https://thepaypers.com/cryptocurrencies/circle-introduces-usdc-contactless-payments-on-iphones--1269688 (Accessed 19 August 2024).

7

CENTRAL BANK DIGITAL CURRENCIES (CBDCS)

Introduction

In the previous two chapters, we delved into the world of cryptocurrencies, NFTs, stablecoins, and other crypto assets, as well as their varied trading facilities. These innovative but largely unregulated digital assets have sparked both excitement and controversy. We also covered the more established and regulated realm of electronic payments and e-money, the familiar digital payment solutions that are like the responsible older siblings of cryptocurrencies: they've got the digital savvy, but they're also backed by the full faith and credit of financial institutions and regulations.

Now, let's shift our focus to the intriguing and sometimes controversial world of Central Bank Digital Currencies (CBDCs). These are digital forms of a country's fiat currency, issued and regulated by a central bank or monetary authority. It's a bit like a central bank deciding to create its own version of Bitcoin but without all the volatility and mystery. CBDCs are like the James Bond of digital currencies: sophisticated, with a licence to bill, and potentially game-changing. Whilst some see them as a natural

DOI: 10.4324/9781003480761-8

evolution of money in the digital age, others raise concerns about privacy and government control.

As we explore this digital form of money, we'll examine how it's influencing the financial landscape, potentially making transactions faster, cheaper, and more accessible. We'll also consider the challenges and controversies surrounding their implementation and use.

Central bank digital currencies (CBDCs) (even better than the real thing)

What is a CBDC?

Oh, the hype. And yet, the definition of a CBDC is quite simple.

A Central Bank Digital Currency (**CBDC**) is a type of virtual asset functioning as an electronic store of value that is issued by a central bank, holds the status of legal tender, and is pegged to the value of that nation's fiat currency. It is the digital equivalent of notes and coins and therefore a direct claim on the central bank.

This is illustrated in Figure 7.1.

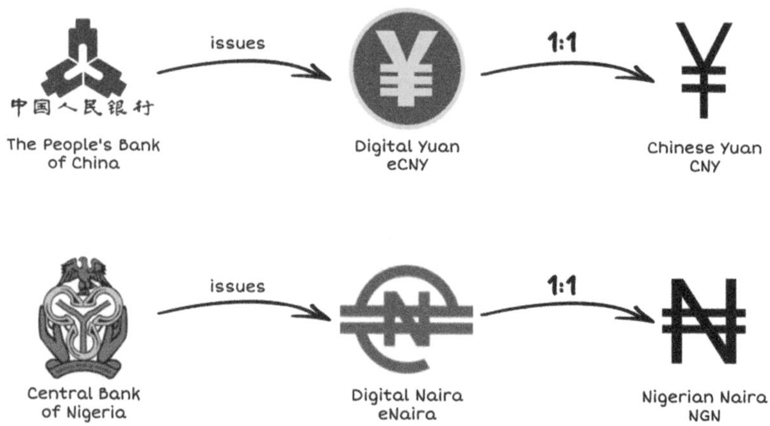

Figure 7.1 CBDCs. © 2024 Neira Jones.

As you may imagine, a CBDC represents a change to a nation's monetary system.

A **monetary system** is a framework established to manage a nation's currency, money supply, and interest rates, typically overseen by a central bank. It functions as a public good, serving the nation's interest by ensuring economic stability, facilitating trade, and promoting sustainable growth within the economy.

Note from the author: I used the word "typically" to indicate that whilst most monetary systems are indeed managed by a central bank, there are exceptions or variations in how different countries or regions structure their monetary systems. For instance, some economies rely on "currency boards" where the country's domestic currency is fully backed, at a fixed exchange rate, by a foreign reserve currency such as the US dollar (e.g. Hong Kong, Bermuda, Cayman Island, Djibouti), the Euro (e.g. Bulgaria, Bosnia and Herzegovina), the British Pound (e.g. Gibraltar, Falkland Islands), the Danish Krone (e.g. Faroe Islands), and the Singapore dollar (e.g. Brunei). You also know that monetary systems can be decentralised, such as those associated with blockchain infrastructures, where central banks are absent. This was covered extensively in Chapter 4, *Tokenomics and metrics*.

Given that a CBDC represents a potentially significant change to a nation's monetary system, why would you want to do that? I surmise that since a monetary system serves the public interest, any change to it must

- offer economic benefits beyond what is already available, and
- be carefully weighed against the need to maintain stability and public trust in the monetary system.

In addition, since a monetary system is a "public good" that permeates people's everyday lives and underpins the economy, the central bank must maintain the high quality of its governance arrangements and preserve fundamental rights.

A fine balance must be achieved, as shown in Figure 7.2.

For the economists amongst you wishing to delve further into the operational implications of CBDCs on monetary policy, the Bank of International Settlement has a good report.[1] I won't expand on this any further and will concentrate on payment implications.

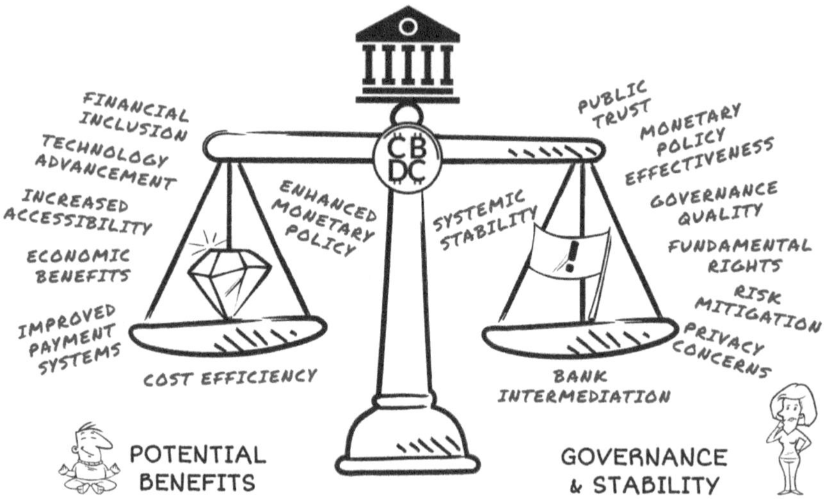

Figure 7.2 CBDCs, a central bank balancing act. © 2024 Neira Jones.

CBDC main characteristics

In his paper "Designing New Money – The Policy Trilemma of Central Bank Digital Currency",[2] sociologist Ole Bjerg outlines where a CBDC fits within today's financial ecosystem as shown in Figure 7.3.

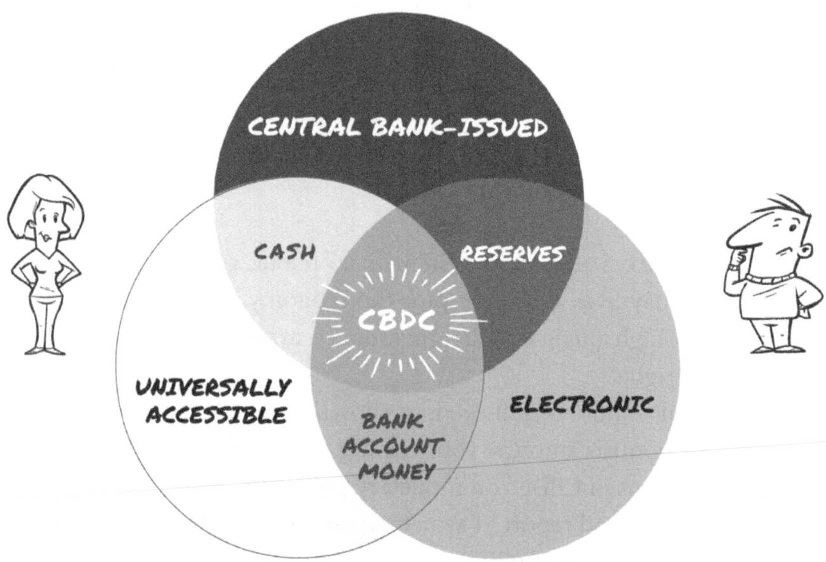

Figure 7.3 Ole Bjerg's CBDC policy trilemma. © 2024 Neira Jones.

CBDCs possess several key characteristics that distinguish them from other forms of digital currency and traditional fiat money, but they also share similarities:

- **Legal tender**: CBDCs, like fiat currencies, are recognised as legal tender by the issuing central bank, making them an official form of currency that must be accepted for payment of debts and transactions within the country.
- **Programmability**: one of the most significant features of CBDCs is their programmability. Distributed ledger technology (DLT)-based CBDCs allow for the implementation of smart contracts and automated processes, potentially enabling more efficient and innovative financial services. Even without DLT, programmability can be achieved through APIs and centralised systems that support conditional transactions and automation using traditional tools and techniques. In this way, they share similarities with e-money in terms of flexibility.
- **Security and privacy**: like cryptocurrencies, CBDCs are (or should be) designed with robust security measures to protect against fraud and cyber threats. They also aim to balance privacy with regulatory compliance, ensuring user data is protected whilst allowing for necessary oversight, unlike cryptocurrencies.
- **Interoperability**: CBDCs can be designed to seamlessly integrate with existing financial systems (unlike cryptocurrencies) and other digital currencies (like cryptocurrencies), facilitating cross-border transactions and enhancing the overall efficiency of the financial ecosystem. This will of course depend on the design choices.
- **Financial inclusion**: by providing a digital form of currency accessible to all citizens, CBDCs have the potential to enhance financial inclusion, particularly for unbanked and underbanked populations (which is the intent of cryptocurrencies, however as yet unrealised). This also depends on the design choices.
- **Monetary policy integration**: unlike cryptocurrencies, CBDCs can be integrated into a country's monetary policy framework, allowing central banks to manage money supply and interest rates more effectively. This also is contingent on design choices and policy decisions.
- **Resilience and reliability**: CBDCs should be designed to provide a stable and reliable form of digital currency, acting as a digital form of cash, reducing reliance on private payment systems and potentially enhancing the resilience of the national payment infrastructure.

These characteristics could make CBDCs a versatile and powerful tool for central banks, potentially enhancing the efficiency, security, and inclusiveness of the financial system. But there are a lot of "ifs" and "buts", and design choices are crucial.

In any instance, CBDCs can be broadly categorised into two main types: the retail CBDC and the wholesale CBDC. Each type serves different purposes and targets distinct user groups within the financial ecosystem:

- **Retail CBDCs** are designed for use by the general public and businesses for everyday transactions, essentially functioning as a digital version of cash. They may include **B2C**, **B2B**, **P2P**, and **G2C** interactions.
- **Wholesale CBDCs**, on the other hand, are intended for B2B use by financial institutions and are aimed at improving the efficiency of interbank settlements and large-value financial market transfers. These are usually aimed at financial firms holding reserve deposits with a central bank.

The choice between these types depends on the specific goals and priorities of the central bank implementing the CBDC. Additionally, there are various design choices within each type that can further differentiate CBDCs, including architecture, infrastructure, access, and interoperability considerations, as well as the degree of programmability incorporated into the currency. Both types of CBDCs are not mutually exclusive.

Ultimately, a CBDC is a claim on a central bank, and Figure 7.4 (expanding on Chapter 5, Figure 5.3) gives a comparison between cash, e-money, and CBDC.

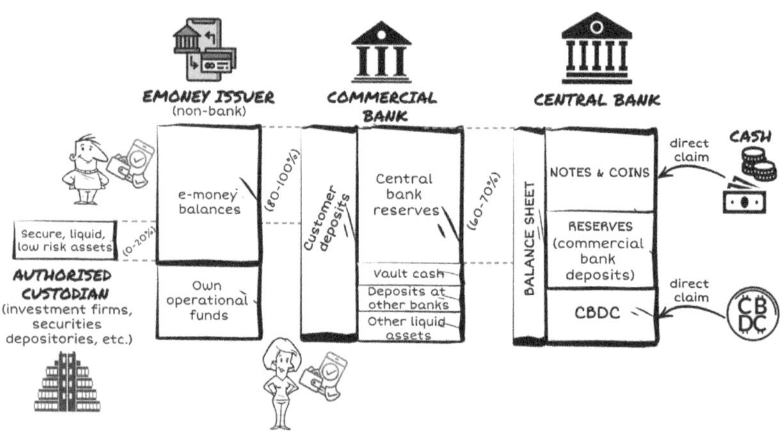

Figure 7.4 Cash vs. e-money vs. CBDC. © 2024 Neira Jones.

For those interested in delving down a bit further, the Bank for International Settlements (BIS) March 2021 paper entitled "Central bank digital currencies: putting a big idea into practice"[3] is a good read.

Let's delve a bit more into the two types of CBDCs.

Wholesale CBDC

Usage of a wholesale CBDC is similar to holding a **reserve account** in a central bank where an institution uses the account to deposit funds or settle interbank transfers (i.e. debiting the account of the bank that has net obligations to the rest of the system and crediting the account of the bank that has a net claim on the system). Wholesale CBDCS aim to improve the efficiency of large-scale, cross-border transactions and interbank settlements and are not for general purpose usage. With a wholesale CBDC, central banks can use their monetary policy tools, such as reserve requirements or interest on reserve balances, to influence lending and set interest rates.

An additional benefit of settlement in wholesale CBDCs is to potentially enable new forms of payment conditionality, where a payment only settles on the condition of delivery of another payment or an asset. Such conditional payment instructions could enhance the **Delivery-versus-Payment (DvP)** mechanism in **RTGS** systems (e.g. as used in a house purchase scenario).

Wholesale CBDCs benefited from renewed interest in recent years due to geopolitical factors. First, the **de-dollarisation** focus of the **BRICS** led participating countries to actively promote the development of an alternative payment system to the dollar. The founding members of BRICS are in the pilot phase of CBDC exploration, whilst Saudi Arabia, Iran, and the UAE are also exploring cross-border wholesale CBDCs. Secondly, since Russia's invasion of Ukraine and the resulting G7 sanctions, wholesale CBDC developments have doubled. At the time of writing, there were 13 cross-border wholesale CBDC projects, including mBridge, which connects China, Thailand, the UAE, and Hong Kong, and is planned, at the time of writing, to expand to 11 more countries by the end of 2024.

Retail CBDC

Usage of a **retail CBDC** extends beyond financial institutions to include the general public and businesses. A retail CBDC is a general-purpose digital currency which serves as a digital form of cash, accessible to everyone for everyday transactions. Retail CBDCs are designed to complement existing payment methods, aiming to offer a secure and convenient alternative to physical banknotes and coins. Central banks may use retail CBDCs to enhance financial inclusion, improve payment efficiency, and maintain monetary sovereignty in an increasingly digital economy.

Retail CBDCs operate on a much larger scale than their wholesale counterparts, requiring robust infrastructure to handle millions of transactions daily. They can be token-based or account-based (see *Access*), with the former resembling physical cash in its anonymity and the latter tied to user identities. Retail CBDCs can potentially offer programmable features, such as automatic tax payments or targeted stimulus distributions. However, their implementation also raises important considerations regarding privacy, cybersecurity, and the potential impact on commercial banks and monetary policy.

Retail CBDCs could offer an alternative to cash, and depending on the design choices, they could, unlike traditional digital payment methods, be usable offline, even when an internet connection isn't available, or a phone runs out of battery. Much research and development is being conducted on this[4] and many central banks are making CBDC offline capability a critical part of their work.

Wholesale vs. retail CBDC

As mentioned earlier, wholesale and retail CBDCs are not mutually exclusive. For example, whilst Jamaica's JAM-DEX is a retail CBDC only, both the Bahamas Sand Dollar and the Chinese eCNY operate as both wholesale and retail CBDCs.

The purpose of a CBDC will be decided by a central bank, and there are numerous design choices (e.g. architecture, infrastructure, access, interoperability).

Ultimately, whilst CBDCs may potentially offer efficiencies and improvements in financial transactions, their value is being questioned as traditional payment methods evolve. The balance between these new innovations and the continued modernisation of existing payment systems will be critical in determining the future landscape of financial transactions, and ultimately, the success of CBDCs.

CBDC vs. stablecoin

We covered stablecoins extensively in Chapter 5, but given some shared characteristics with CBDCs, it's worth revisiting them in context:

- **Issuance and backing**: CBDCs are issued directly by central banks and are considered legal tender, representing a direct claim on the central bank. Stablecoins, on the other hand, are typically issued by private entities and are pegged to a fiat currency or a basket of assets to maintain a stable value.
- **Regulation and control**: CBDCs are subject to strict regulatory oversight by central banks, which have full control over their issuance and management. Stablecoins may be regulated to varying degrees depending on the jurisdiction, but they often lack the same level of oversight and control as CBDCs.
- **Purpose and use cases**: CBDCs are designed to serve as a digital form of national currency, facilitating secure and efficient transactions within the economy, and integrated within a nation's financial ecosystem. Stablecoins are often used for cross-border transactions, remittances, and as a store of value in the cryptocurrency ecosystem.
- **Monetary policy**: CBDCs can be integrated into a country's monetary policy framework, allowing central banks to influence money supply and interest rates. Stablecoins do not have the same direct impact on monetary policy, as they are not issued by central banks.
- **Technological infrastructure**: CBDCs can be implemented using various technological infrastructures, including centralised, distributed, or hybrid models. Stablecoins are typically issued on blockchain platforms, leveraging blockchain and other forms of DLT.

Overall, whilst both CBDCs and stablecoins offer digital alternatives to traditional currency, they serve different roles within the financial system and are governed by distinct regulatory and operational frameworks. However, some argue that stablecoins present a viable and inclusive alternative to CBDCs. I'll let you decide.[5]

Could a central bank issue a stablecoin?

Yes, theoretically. Whilst stablecoins are typically associated with private issuers, central banks could issue stablecoins as part of their digital currency strategies. Here are some considerations:

- **Definition and purpose**: a stablecoin is a digital asset designed to maintain a stable value by being pegged to a reserve of assets, such as fiat currency (see Chapter 5, *Stablecoins*). Central banks could issue stablecoins to provide a stable digital currency option that is backed by central bank reserves, in a similar fashion to the USDF consortium of federally-insured US banks and their aim to issue a stablecoin.[6]

- **Regulatory framework**: for a central bank-issued stablecoin, a robust regulatory framework would be essential to ensure stability, transparency, and trust. This framework would likely involve strict oversight and requirements for asset backing, similar to those proposed for private stablecoins.[7,8]
- **Monetary policy integration**: central bank-issued stablecoins could be integrated into the existing monetary policy framework, allowing central banks to maintain control over money supply and implement monetary policy effectively. This would distinguish them from privately issued stablecoins, which typically operate outside central bank control.
- **Use cases and benefits**: a central bank-issued stablecoin could facilitate efficient cross-border payments, enhance financial inclusion, and provide a digital alternative to cash. It could also serve as a bridge between traditional fiat currency and digital assets.
- **Examples and exploration**: whilst no central bank has issued a stablecoin, discussions and explorations around this concept exist.

CBDC deployments

Developing a CBDC is a tough balancing act for central banks, and there's been much flip-flopping over the years:

- **United Kingdom**: in January 2022, the Economic Affairs Committee published the report "Central bank digital currencies: a solution in search of a problem?" concluding that

  > We have yet to hear a convincing case for why the UK needs a retail CBDC. Whilst a CBDC may provide some advantages on speed of settlement and cheaper and faster cross-border payments, it would present significant challenges for financial stability and the protection of privacy.[9]

  But in April 2023, the Bank of England started to create a team to oversee a proposed CBDC project, and in January 2024,[10] the Bank and HM Treasury published their answer to a consultation response on the digital pound,[11] stating that "Further work over the coming years during the design phase will explore the design and feasibility of a digital pound". Suffice to say, there are working groups aplenty, and lots of people thinking deep thoughts 😉.

- **Israel**: the Bank of Israel has been researching CBDCs since 2017, and in May 2021, it published a working paper to gauge public interest, stating that

  > in view of the rapid developments in the digital economy and in payments, and in view of the major central banks' work on the issue, the Bank of Israel is accelerating its research and preparation for the potential issuance of a digital shekel.[12]

  In the paper, the BoI stated, with regard to potential CBDC benefits, that "it may be possible to achieve those benefits by improving the existing payment systems". When finally, in July 2024, the Bank of Israel announced that it planned to "wait until another advanced economy launches a central bank digital currency (CBDC) before introducing one of its own"[13].
- **United States**: as far as I can tell, it's all a bit of a mishmash. I already mentioned, in the introduction to this book, the astounding outburst from Robert F. Kennedy Junior conflating FedNow (a real-time payment system) with a CBDC (!). In January 2024, we even had Donald Trump vouching to "Never Allow Central Bank Digital Currencies if Elected".[14] Is he being consistent? Well, who knows? Donald Trump capitalised on the NFT craze by issuing his own trading card collection depicting himself in various super-hero outfits (at $99 a pop),[15] and, in an attempt to appeal to the crypto crowd, positioned himself as a crypto enthusiast by headlining a big bitcoin conference in July 2024 in Nashville, supported by RFK, proposing a strategic national crypto stockpile to ensure that the federal government never sells off its bitcoin holdings, but stopped short of proposing a formal federal reserve of digital currency,[16] In any instance, the Federal Reserve is keeping a watching eye and issuing consultation papers,[17] adamant that any US CBDC would need to provide benefits that exceed the costs and risks, protect consumer privacy, safeguard against criminal activity, and have broad stakeholder support (thus kicking the CBDC ball into the long grass whilst appearing to line up the perfect shot 😉).

- No flip-flopping with **China**: whilst their eCNY initiative is generally referred to as a "pilot", former People's Bank of China (PBOC) governor Yi Gang said in July 2023 that total transactions had reached 950 million with a cumulative value of 1.8 trillion Yuan (US$249.9 billion) by the end of June, up from 100 billion Yuan (US$13.9 billion) the previous August.[18] Research started in 2014, and pilots in major cities started in late 2029. By 2021, more than 20.87 million personal wallets and over 3.51 million corporate wallets had been opened, performing a total of nearly 71 million transactions. The Chinese government is certainly committed to its CBDC and is regularly incentivising its usage through red packets, large lotteries, giveaways, and encouraging cities to pay municipal employees in eCNY and accept it for taxes and charges. Since 2022, it has been used for a variety of purposes, from transit and healthcare to buying crude oil. In 2024, the pilot is focused on encouraging overseas tourist use and expanding cross-border applications. Nothing "piloty" about that kind of scale, and certainly world-leading in terms of CBDC adoption. Why didn't the Chinese government formally launch it? There are various schools of thought: maybe pilot status allows for more flexibility in adjusting policies and regulations before a full-scale launch; perhaps the PBOC is still improving the user experience, and testing the security and resilience of the network before massively increasing adoption; or it could be that maintaining pilot status is a strategic decision allowing China to observe and react to international developments in the CBDC space; some observers even suggest that the only reason it's still called a pilot is because it hasn't taken off as much as expected. In any instance, in June 2024, the PBOC quietly removed the "pilot" label from the eCNY app,[19] I wonder why... But let's put things into perspective: by comparison, Alipay, China's leading mobile payments platform, had nearly 660 million monthly active users in China as of February 2024, and in June 2023, clocked a total of 1.8 trillion Yuan ($249.9 billion) cumulative transaction value.[20] These numbers highlight the significant gap between the adoption of eCNY and established payment platforms like Alipay. Despite lower-than-expected adoption rates, the Chinese government remains committed to the development and implementation of the e-CNY, viewing it as a potential way to increase resilience in China's payment ecosystem and possibly as a means to mitigate the dominance of the US dollar in international finance. I believe this is a long gameplay, not necessarily a fast-adoption one. Perhaps additional factors are at play, as detailed in the November 2022 Wired article "China's Digital Yuan Works Just Like Cash—With Added Surveillance",[21] exemplifying the concerns of other nations about privacy and programmability. The fact that China banned cryptocurrencies and associated activities (e.g. mining) since 2021 seems to add to the sentiment. I'll let you decide.

- **Europe**: the European Central Bank (ECB) wanted to address the fact that there was no digital payment option that covers the entire euro area other than international card schemes for card payments. A digital euro would be a European electronic means of payment accessible and accepted across the EU. The ECB launched the digital euro project in July 2021[22] and was, at the time of writing, in a two-year preparation phase, including finalising legislation, selecting private-sector partners, and some testing and experimentation.

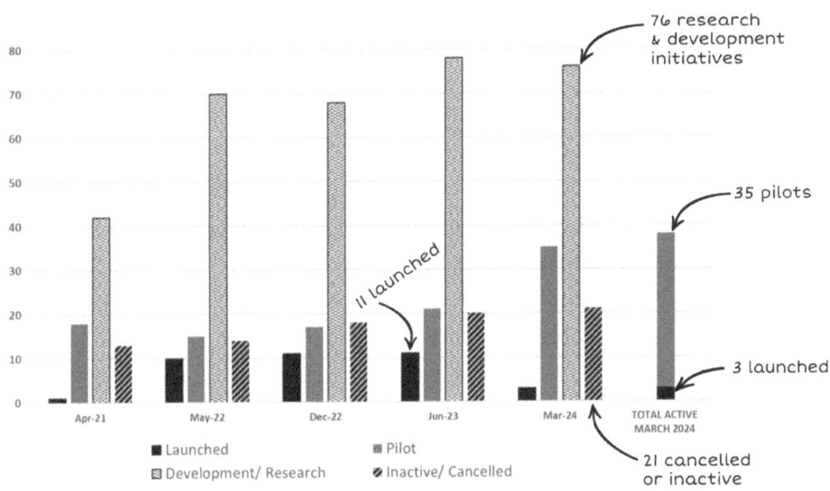

Figure 7.5 CBDC initiatives worldwide, April 2021–March 2024. © 2024 Neira Jones.

All I can say about Figure 7.5 is that there is a lot of talk (aka research and development 😉). For those interested in the state of CBDC adoption worldwide, the Atlantic Council have a tracker,[23] and at the time of writing, only three countries had launched: The Bahamas (2020, Sand Dollar, retail CBDC), Nigeria (2021, eNaira, retail CBDC), and Jamaica (2022, JAM-DEX, retail CBDC).

Recap on CBDC properties

- **Balance innovation with stability**: whilst CBDCs offer the potential for innovation in the financial system, it is crucial to balance these advancements with the need to maintain stability and public trust. Professionals should ensure that the introduction of a CBDC does not disrupt existing financial structures.
- **Consider privacy and security**: CBDCs must be designed with robust security measures to protect against fraud and cyber threats. At the same time, they should balance privacy concerns with regulatory requirements, ensuring that user data is protected whilst allowing for necessary oversight.
- **Enhance financial inclusion**: one of the key benefits of CBDCs is their potential to enhance financial inclusion, particularly for unbanked and underbanked populations. Policymakers should focus on ensuring that CBDCs are accessible to all citizens, regardless of their socioeconomic status.
- **Integrate with monetary policy**: CBDCs can be a powerful tool for central banks to manage monetary policy more effectively. Regulators should consider how CBDCs can be integrated into existing monetary frameworks to influence money supply and interest rates.
- **Leverage programmability**: DLT-based CBDCs may leverage programmability through smart contracts and automated processes, and whilst programmability is often associated with DLT-based CBDCs, programmability can also be achieved through centralised systems using APIs and other traditional technologies. Both options may enable more efficient and innovative financial services. Professionals should explore how this feature can be used to enhance the functionality of CBDCs.
- **Interoperability is key**: for CBDCs to be successful, they must be able to integrate seamlessly with existing financial systems and other digital currencies. This interoperability may facilitate cross-border transactions and enhance the overall efficiency of the financial ecosystem.
- **Address regulatory challenges**: the introduction of CBDCs presents several regulatory challenges, including ensuring compliance with existing laws and adapting to potentially new regulatory frameworks.

Regulators should work closely with stakeholders to address these challenges and ensure a smooth integration into the monetary system.

- **Monitor user impact**: the implementation of a CBDC will have a significant impact on users, including changes in how they interact with money and financial services. It is important to monitor this impact and address any concerns that arise to ensure a positive user experience.

As we conclude our exploration of CBDC properties, imagine a CBDC as a bridge connecting the traditional financial world with the digital future. This bridge must be robust enough to support the weight of innovation whilst flexible enough to adapt to the ever-changing financial landscape. It must also provide benefits that exceed those derived from improving existing payment infrastructures.

As we move forward to the next section on CBDC design choices, we'll delve into the architecture, infrastructure, access, and interoperability decisions that shape this bridge, ensuring it meets the needs of all stakeholders, from policymakers to end-users.

CBDC design choices (the choice is yours)

CBDC design choices apply to both retail and wholesale CBDCs and can be classified into four categories:

- **Architecture**: this relates to the choices regarding issuance and distribution of the CBDC (e.g. central bank, private issuers), ledger maintenance, accounts and services provision, and settlement.
- **Infrastructure**: encompasses the technical infrastructure choices (e.g. centralised, distributed, hybrid)
- **Access**: CBDCs can either be account-based (as in traditional bank and e-money accounts), token-based, or a combination of both depending on use.
- **Interoperability**: the decision on interoperability may include whether the CBDC would be for domestic use only, allow cross-border transactions, be available to non-residents, or a combination of these factors depending on usage.

We'll examine each category in turn.

Architecture

CBDC architecture choices ultimately come down to how much the central bank wants to be involved in all aspects of its operation. The three options are direct, intermediated, or hybrid, which are detailed in Table 7.1.

As shown in Table 7.1, each CBDC architecture model puts different responsibilities on the central bank, presents different opportunities for financial inclusion, and has varying implications on regulatory oversight.

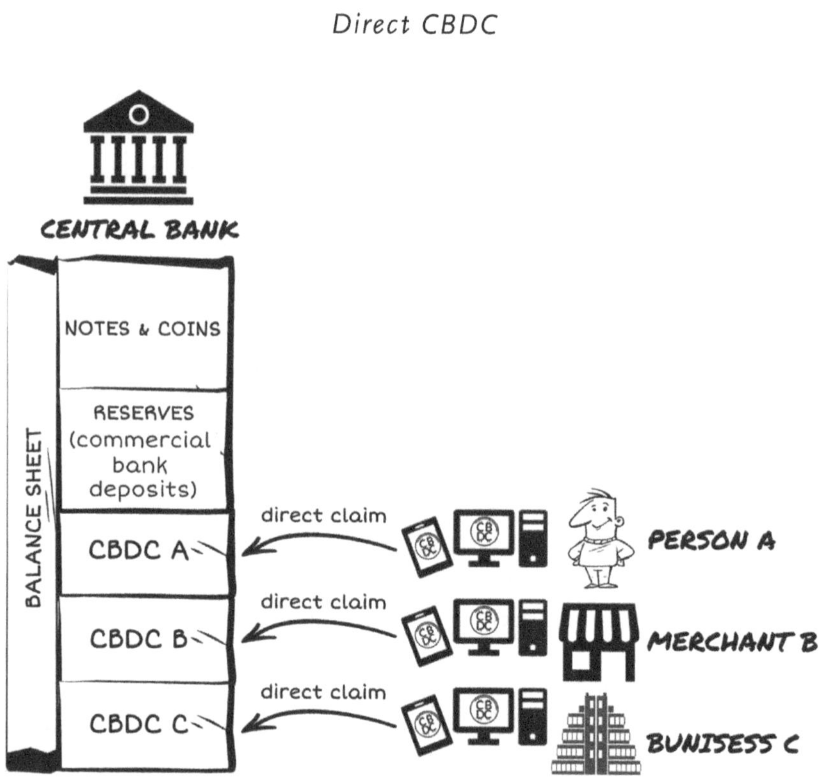

Figure 7.6 Direct CBDC. © 2024 Neira Jones.

The direct CBDC model places a significant operational burden on the central bank and distracts it from its main purpose of formulating monetary policy, being the banks to banks, acting as the lender of last resort, and regulating the domestic banking system as shown in Figure 7.6.

Table 7.1 Comparing CBDC architectures. © 2024 Neira Jones

Architecture Choices	**Direct CBDC**	**Intermediated CBDC (Synthetic, Indirect)**	**Hybrid CBCD**
Issuance	Central bank	Central bank	Central bank may issue one CBDC (for both wholesale and retail) or two CBDCs (one for wholesale, and one for retail)
Distribution (e.g. accounts & services)	Central bank	Financial institutions	Central bank (e.g. government agencies, large corporations) Financial institutions (retail customers, small businesses)
Liability	Central bank	Financial institutions	Central bank (e.g. government agencies, large corporations) or financial services institutions (retail customers, small businesses)
Wholesale ledger (settlement)	Central bank	Central bank	Central bank
Retail ledger (settlement)	Central bank	Financial institutions	Central bank (e.g. government agencies, large corporations) Financial institutions (e.g. retail customers, small businesses)
Systemic risk	Concentrates risk at central bank	Distributes risk across financial institutions	Distributes risk across financial institutions
Financial inclusion	High potential	Depends on financial institutions	Depends on financial institutions
Regulatory implications	Requires more extensive regulatory oversight and new regulations	Leverages existing banking regulations	Leverages existing banking regulations but may require new regulations due to dual-issuing

This is because this model means that the central bank not only issues the CBDC, but it also maintains the ledger of all retail transactions, performs retail settlement, and offers accounts and services directly to users (although KYC and authentication may be performed by third parties). In theory, "Business C" could also be a bank, which means that, in theory, this architecture could also be used for a wholesale CBDC, but the operational burden would remain the same for the central bank as the latter would need to maintain direct relationships with a large number of banks. It is therefore unsurprising that there are no known deployments or pilots, although Senegal briefly explored this option.

In addition, the direct CBDC may offer opportunities for financial inclusion as it provides access to a CBDC without the need for a bank account, just like cash.

However, the regulatory implications may be significant as this is a model where existing regulatory frameworks may not be sufficient.

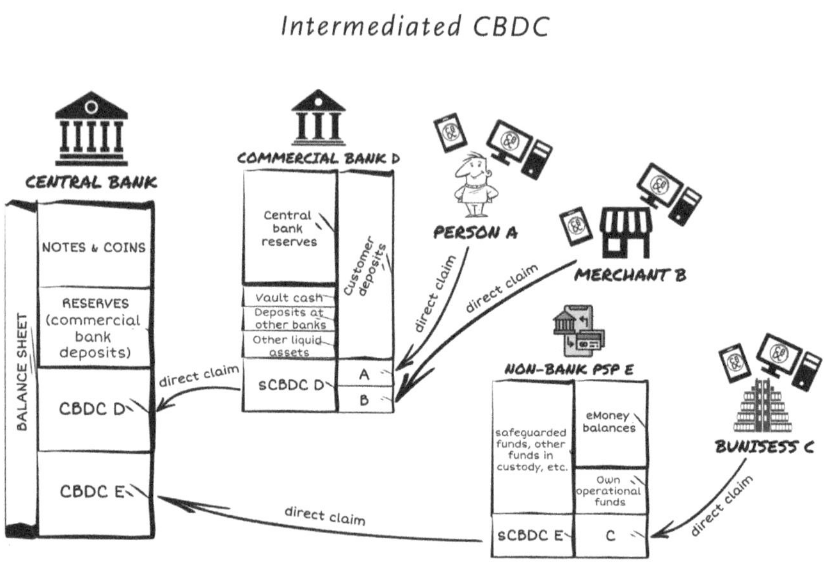

Figure 7.7 Intermediated CBDC. © 2024 Neira Jones.

In the intermediated CBDC model, sometimes referred to as "indirect" or "synthetic", and abbreviated as sCBDC, **the central bank issues the**

wholesale CBDC, maintains the wholesale ledger, performs wholesale settlement, and must honour claims of which it has theoretically no record as the financial institutions (e.g. commercial banks and non-bank PSPs) offer accounts and services to users and maintain the retail balances (sCBDC balance sheet liability). There is a variant of this model where the central bank would periodically record retail balances. Although the latter option would offer protection to businesses and consumers, it creates similar operational burdens for the central bank as in the direct model, with the addition of it having to rely on the intermediaries to consistently report the retail balances to the central bank.

This model may create opportunities for financial inclusion, but this will depend on the reach and capabilities of the distributing financial institutions.

In addition, this model may be easier to implement as it could largely rely on existing banking and financial services regulations. It is therefore unsurprising that the three CBDCs that have launched (The Bahamas, Jamaica, Nigeria) use this model, and 21 CBDC pilots, out of a total of 36, also use this model at the time of writing (the remaining pilots were still undecided on their architecture choice).

As shown in Figure 7.7, this model operates in a very similar fashion to the e-money model (see Chapter 5, Figure 5.3), with the difference that non-bank PSPs now have access to central bank CBDC reserves. Essentially, the retail balance (sCBDC) at the commercial bank or non-bank PSP is a special type of e-money, where the e-money issuer deposits the required reserves at the central bank, rather than at a commercial bank (as in Chapter 5, Figure 5.3), as in the typical e-money model.

However, as far as users are concerned, the liability of sCBDC still rests with the e-money issuer, not the central bank. The term "synthetic" means that the e-money replicates CBDC features, although it's not real CBDC (i.e. not issued by a central bank and lacks the risk-free nature of central bank money), as the purists often point out. However, sCBDC provides better safeguarding compared to typical e-money but credit risk still exists.

Nevertheless, intermediated CBDCs open up opportunities for innovation, but policymakers will need to take this new nuance into account and make sure regulations cater for this.

China's eCNY is an intermediated CBDC.

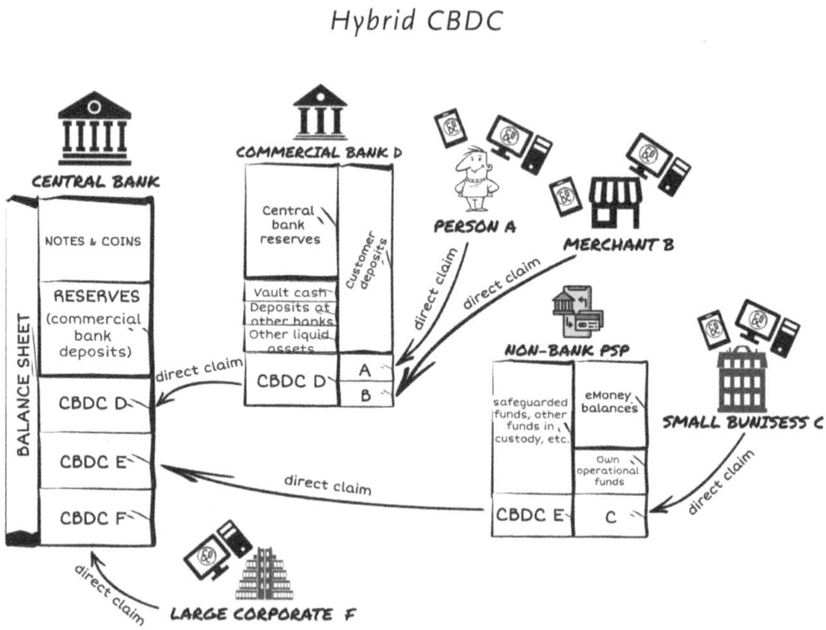

Figure 7.8 Hybrid CBDC. © 2024 Neira Jones.

The hybrid CBDC model represents a middle ground between direct and intermediated CBDCs, combining elements of both to create a versatile and adaptable system. In this model, the central bank may issue a single CBDC for both wholesale and retail purposes or separate ones for each, depending on the specific needs and goals, as shown in Figure 7.8.

Distribution may be handled by the central bank for larger organisations such as government agencies and large corporations, but the bulk or retail customers and small businesses would be primarily handled by financial institutions, allowing for a broad reach and the ability to cater to diverse user groups. This dual approach may enhance financial inclusion by making CBDCs accessible through various channels, but positive impact would depend on the distributing financial institutions' reach and capabilities, as in the intermediated CBDC model. Central bank CBDC distribution to large organisations (e.g. government agencies, large corporations) would be primarily aimed at improving efficiency, not financial inclusion (large organisations are already financially included, thank you 😉).

In terms of liability, the hybrid CBDC model may place responsibility on either the central bank or financial institutions, depending on the specific arrangements in place. This flexibility can help distribute systemic risk across the financial system, reducing the central bank's exposure. The central bank still maintains control over the wholesale ledger, ensuring consistency and reliability in settlements, whilst the retail ledger can be managed by either the central bank or financial institutions, depending on the context.

Regulatory implications for hybrid CBDCs involve leveraging existing banking regulations, but new regulations may be necessary due to the dual-issuing nature of this model. Overall, the hybrid CBDC offers a balanced approach, combining the benefits of direct and intermediated models whilst aiming to address their respective challenges. At the time of writing, there were 15 pilots remaining undecided on their architecture model and may be considering hybrid approaches (see Atlantic Council CBDC tracker).

Recap on CBDC architecture models

Understanding the pros and cons of each CBDC architecture model is a complex matter, and it is no wonder that there are still only three live CBDC deployments worldwide.

Professionals should remember the following:

- **Flexibility and control**: each CBDC architecture model offers varying degrees of flexibility and control for central banks, impacting how they manage issuance, distribution, and settlement processes. Regulators should assess which model aligns best with their strategic goals and operational capabilities.
- **Risk management**: the distribution of systemic risk differs across models. Direct CBDCs centralise risk within the central bank, whilst intermediated and hybrid models distribute risk across financial institutions. Policymakers should consider the risk appetite and resilience of their financial systems when choosing a model.
- **Financial inclusion**: direct CBDCs have the potential for enhancing financial inclusion by providing direct access to central bank money, just like cash. By contrast, intermediated and hybrid models depend on the reach and capabilities of financial institutions to achieve inclusion goals. Stakeholders should evaluate the existing financial landscape to determine which model best supports inclusion efforts.

- **Regulatory considerations**: direct CBDCs require extensive regulatory oversight, potentially new regulations, and place a significant operational burden on the central bank. Conversely, intermediated and hybrid models can leverage existing banking regulations, though hybrid models may still necessitate additional regulatory frameworks. Regulators must prepare for the regulatory demands each model imposes and ensure compliance mechanisms are robust.
- **Operational complexity**: the complexity of managing CBDC operations varies, with hybrid models potentially introducing more operational challenges due to their dual nature. Central banks and financial institutions should be prepared to invest in the necessary infrastructure and expertise to manage these complexities effectively.
- **User experience**: the choice of architecture affects user experience, with direct models offering direct interaction with the central bank (this still remains a theoretical model), whilst intermediated and hybrid models provide a more traditional payment experience through financial institutions. User-centric design should be prioritised to ensure ease of use and adoption.

In summary, the choice of CBDC architecture model involves balancing control, risk, inclusion, and regulatory implications. As we transition to discussing CBDC infrastructure choices, it's essential to consider how these architectural decisions will align with technological infrastructure options, such as centralised, distributed, and hybrid systems, to create a cohesive and efficient digital currency ecosystem. This next section will delve into the infrastructure choices that underpin these architecture models, highlighting how they can further influence the effectiveness and efficiency of CBDCs.

Infrastructure

Infrastructure choices will determine which technologies will be used for the development of the CBDC, and we'll examine these in some detail. But first, let's get one thing out of the way:

A CBDC doesn't need to use distributed ledger or blockchain technology.

Some readers may find this surprising, but the hype, controversy, and misunderstandings have led many to believe that all CBDCs are blockchain-based, or that they require DLT to function. Opinions on this are of course divided.

In reality, CBDC infrastructure design choices come in three main categories:

- **Centralised**: this model typically involves a central authority, usually a central bank, managing the entire system and leveraging the existing banking infrastructure. This can streamline operations and simplify regulatory compliance but may pose challenges related to resilience and single points of failure.
- **Distributed**: this model often leverages DLT, which may improve system resilience and reduce the risk of a central point of failure. However, it may introduce complexities in governance and interoperability.
- **Hybrid**: this infrastructure choice combines elements of both centralised and decentralised models, aiming to balance control with resilience and flexibility.

The choice of infrastructure is pivotal in determining how effectively CBDCs can be implemented and managed. As we explore these infrastructure options, it's crucial for professionals, regulators, and policymakers to consider how these choices will interact with the architecture models previously discussed. Understanding the synergies and trade-offs between architecture and infrastructure is key to developing a cohesive and efficient CBDC ecosystem that meets the needs of all stakeholders.

Centralised infrastructure

This model typically involves leveraging core national banking infrastructure, such as the **Real-Time Gross Settlement System (RTGS)**. I won't cover RTGS here (please see my first book for this), but Figure 7.9 gives you an idea of what's involved.

Figure 7.9 highlights that in the centralised architecture, the CBDC ledger is in the central bank's domain and would operate in a very similar fashion to retail payment schemes inasmuch as transactions in a centralised CBDC system are typically settled through the RTGS system, which ensures the

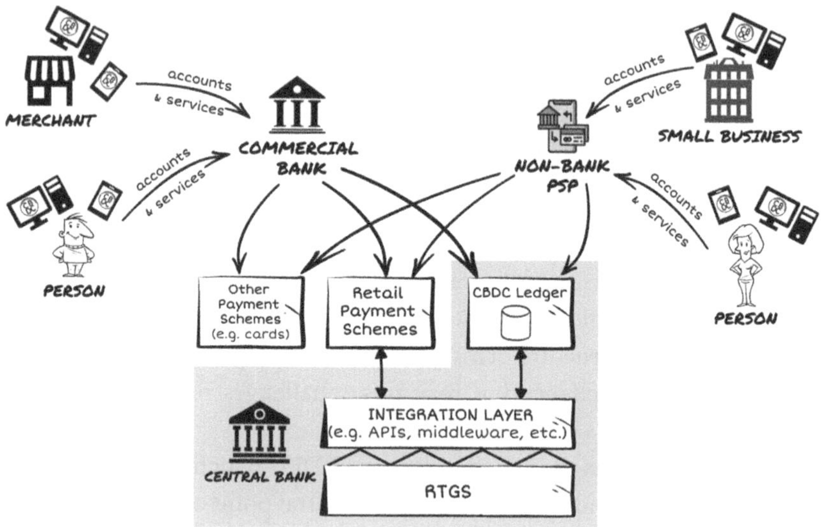

Figure 7.9 An example of centralised CBDC infrastructure. © 2024 Neira Jones.

security and consistency of interbank settlements. Accounts and services would typically be provided by intermediaries (e.g. commercial banks, non-bank PSPs) in a familiar fashion, as these would most probably modify their existing digital wallets to operate with the CBDC ledger in addition to the additional funding mechanisms they may offer (see Chapter 6, *Traditional digital wallets*).

BOX 7.1 JAMAICA'S JAM-DEX

The centralised CBDC model is used by the Bank of Jamaica (BoJ) for their JAM-DEX CBDC[24] which launched in 2022. The name, a contraction of "Jamaica Digital Exchange", was chosen to reflect both the country of origin and the digital, exchangeable nature of the currency (I guess eJMD would have been a bit boring...). It is an intermediated CBDC fully integrated with their JamClear® RTGS (Note from the author: BoJ calls their CBDC "hybrid", but as far as I can tell, it looks intermediated to me... Feel free to disagree. It is centralised nevertheless.).

BoJ partnered with technology firm ecurrency[25] who specialise in CBDC integration with existing wholesale and retail payments infrastructure, including ISO 20022 APIs and positioned their solution as "Unmatched by blockchain, distributed ledger and other technologies". BoJ's primary purpose for JAM-DEX is to reduce the replacement, storage, and handling costs of cash (several millions of US dollars per year).

BoJ has been actively promoting its CBDC and incentivising users with giveaways,[26] and in April 2022 the Government of Jamaica gave $2,500 worth of Jam-Dex to the first 100,000 users which totalled $250 million Jam-Dex.

With JAM-DEX, BoJ's plan was for all banks to offer CBDC wallets, but, at the time of writing, TFOB Limited, the operator of the Lynk mobile application, has been the sole digital wallet provider for JAM-DEX[27] from the start and is now questioning progress.[28] JN Bank Limited was onboarded in December 2022 as a digital wallet provider with JN Pay,[29] but deployment is still pending.[30] Several other financial institutions have expressed interest in developing wallets to support the CBDC, but the $500,000 development price tag may be putting them off.

In any instance, widespread adoption hasn't yet materialised, not helped by the fact that Jamaica's POS terminals, as used by merchants to accept payments, are not equipped to handle the CBDC QR codes. Consequently, In January 2024, the Jamaican government, two years after JAM-DEX's launch, pledged to invest in upgrading at least 20% of the total pool of payment terminals. BoJ's governor Richard Byles said: "I think it will be successful, eventually". Time will tell.

Professionals should remember the following:

- **Simplicity and proven technology**: centralised CBDC infrastructures often rely on existing, well-understood technologies that are easier to implement and manage compared to decentralised systems. This simplicity can reduce the complexity and risk associated with deploying a new currency system. However, the approach may limit innovation and flexibility, as it relies on established technologies that may not incorporate the latest advancements or support new use cases that decentralised systems might offer (in the appropriate context).

- **Scalability**: centralised systems can be designed to handle a large volume of transactions efficiently, making them suitable for nationwide implementation where high throughput and low latency are essential. However, these implementations may face bottlenecks if not properly managed, and scaling up can require significant investment in infrastructure to maintain performance as demand grows.
- **Cost effectiveness**: leveraging existing central bank infrastructure and technology can be more cost-effective than developing and maintaining a decentralised system. Additionally, a centralised CBDC infrastructure can lead to efficiencies in cash management by reducing the need for physical cash distribution and handling, thereby minimising expenses related to printing, transporting, and securing cash.
- **Data management and security**: a centralised infrastructure allows for centralised data management, which can simplify security protocols and data integrity measures, and central banks are generally proficient at managing systemically important infrastructures. This centralisation can enhance the ability to monitor and protect against fraud and cyber threats. However, centralised data systems might be more vulnerable to single points of failure or targeted attacks, potentially compromising the entire system if breached (evidently, resilience is a major concern for central banks).
- **Interoperability with existing systems**: a centralised approach allows the central bank to maintain direct control over system updates, maintenance, and upgrades, ensuring the infrastructure remains secure and up-to-date with technological advancements. In addition, centralised systems can be designed to interface with decentralised systems or other digital currencies through standardised protocols and APIs, enabling cross-platform transactions and enhancing the overall flexibility of the financial ecosystem. This interoperability can facilitate innovation and provide users with a seamless experience across different types of digital currencies. However, centralised control can lead to slower decision-making and implementation processes, as changes must go through centralised governance structures. This can hinder the ability to quickly adapt to new threats or opportunities. As an example, the BoJ might not have considered the impact on merchants and the fact that existing POS systems were not QR code-capable, which hindered deployment.

These considerations highlight the balance between the benefits of a centralised CBDC infrastructure and the potential trade-offs that central banks must weigh when making technological decisions. At the time of writing, JAM-DEX and China's eCNY[31] are the only examples of purely centralised CBDCs, and other deployments have opted for either distributed or hybrid infrastructure models, which will be covered in the next sections.

Distributed infrastructure

This model typically leverages DLT, particularly permissioned blockchains, to create a CBDC system that is more resilient and less reliant on a single point of control. Permissioned DLTs are preferred by central banks because they allow for controlled access, ensuring that only authorised participants can validate transactions, which enhances security and compliance. This setup may be suitable for both wholesale and retail CBDCs, and they both come with their own set of benefits and challenges. Wholesale CBDCs, used for interbank transactions, could benefit from the efficiency and security of a distributed ledger, whilst retail CBDCs, intended for public use, can leverage the transparency and accessibility features of DLT.

But first, let's get one thing clear:

Decentralisation and distribution are not the same thing. Decentralisation is about the distribution of power, control, or functions away from a central authority or location to multiple independent entities. Distribution, on the other hand, is about spreading or allocating resources, products, or information across different locations, entities, or individuals. Whilst CBDCs may be based on DLT, this doesn't mean that they are decentralised. At the time of writing, most DLT-based pilots leverage permissioned DLT (e.g. Hyperledger Fabric), which are, to all intents and purposes, centralised (see Chapter 1, *Blockchain types*). Many central banks are exploring or implementing CBDCs with DLT components to leverage the benefits of blockchain technology, such as transparency and security. However, these implementations often maintain central control to ensure regulatory compliance and monetary policy integration. By using permissioned DLT, central banks can control access and manage the network effectively, thus maintaining necessary control whilst still benefiting from the transparency and security features of DLT.

In any instance, the potential benefits of a CBDC-distributed infrastructure model are:

- **Programmability**: distributed systems, particularly those using DLT, allow for the implementation of smart contracts which can automate complex processes (see Chapter 2, *Smart contracts*), such as conditional payments and compliance checks, without the need for intermediaries. This capability is generally more advanced in distributed systems compared to centralised ones where implementing such automation is more challenging due to the reliance on central control and the lack of a decentralised execution environment.
- **Atomic settlement**: a distributed infrastructure can facilitate atomic settlement, where transactions are settled instantaneously and in a single operation. This reduces counterparty risk by ensuring that all parts of a transaction are completed simultaneously or not at all. Whilst centralised systems can achieve atomic settlement through mechanisms like **Payment versus Payment (PvP)** and **Delivery versus Payment (DvP)**, distributed systems inherently support atomic settlement through decentralisation, reducing the need for intermediaries, which potentially enhances efficiency and lowers costs. Additionally, distributed systems provide real-time processing and transparency, which are more challenging to achieve in centralised systems.
- **Transparency**: distributed CBDC infrastructures provide a transparent and immutable record of transactions, which can enhance trust among users and aid in regulatory compliance. This transparency can also help tackle crime and protect tax revenues by clamping down on money laundering and corruption. In centralised systems, transparency is often limited by the central authority's control over data visibility, making it harder to achieve the same level of openness and traceability as in distributed systems.
- **Enhanced availability and resilience**: in a distributed model, data is stored across multiple nodes, enhancing availability and resilience. This reduces the risk of data loss or service disruption due to a single point of failure, a risk more prevalent in centralised systems.
- **Cross-border integration**: the use of DLT can facilitate cross-border transactions by providing a shared, transparent platform for multiple

currencies and jurisdictions. This can potentially simplify and speed up international payments, which are often more cumbersome in centralised systems as they often require coordination among multiple intermediaries and jurisdictions, leading to increased complexity and slower processing times.

- **Innovation and composability**: distributed systems can potentially facilitate greater interoperability between different financial platforms and services, allowing for the seamless integration of CBDCs with a variety of digital financial services. This could enable the development of innovative solutions that can operate across multiple platforms and jurisdictions. However, distributed systems may face challenges in integrating smoothly with existing financial systems, requiring significant adaptation and collaboration with existing financial institutions to achieve interoperability. As such, centralised CBDCs may find it easier to integrate with existing infrastructure due to alignment with current technologies and regulatory frameworks, but they might not offer the same level of adaptability and innovation potential as distributed systems.
- **Enhanced privacy options**: distributed systems can offer more nuanced privacy features by allowing transactions to be verified without revealing all transaction details, using techniques like zero-knowledge proofs (see Chapter 1, *Privacy-focused blockchains*). This can provide privacy to users whilst still ensuring compliance with regulations. Centralised systems typically have less flexibility in privacy configurations, as they often require more comprehensive data collection and central oversight.

Let's examine how this model could be employed in both retail and wholesale CBDCs.

Figure 7.10 shows that from the perspective of an end-user (e.g. person, business), a distributed (i.e. DLT-based) CBDC is no different from centralised CBDC, as long as the access services (e.g. digital wallets, accounts) provided by the commercial banks and non-bank PSPs are fit for purpose. After all, this is only a technical choice, and whether the ledger is a database or a blockchain should be irrelevant (and invisible) to the end-user of a general-purpose CBDC.

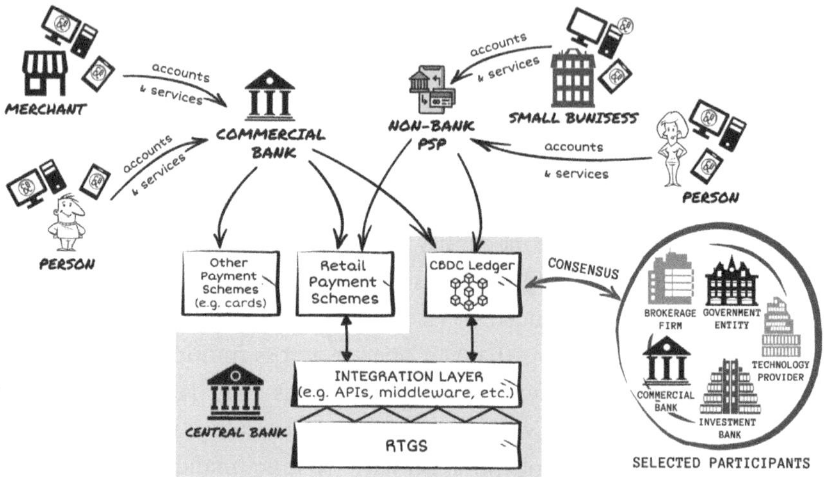

Figure 7.10 An example of distributed retail CBDC infrastructure. © 2024 Neira Jones.

A distributed infrastructure may not be the most suitable choice for a retail CBDC for several reasons:

- **Scalability and performance**: retail CBDCs must handle large transaction volumes with low latency to ensure a seamless user experience. Whilst distributed systems can offer resilience, they may struggle with scalability and performance issues, particularly in handling the high concurrency required for retail transactions.[32] Implementing scaling solutions (see Chapter 1, *Are blockchains scalable*), or optimising consensus mechanisms may help improve scalability and performance in distributed systems.
- **Interoperability with existing systems**: retail CBDCs must integrate smoothly with existing financial systems, services, and infrastructure. Distributed systems may face challenges in achieving this interoperability, as they often require significant adaptation. Developing and adopting standardised APIs and protocols, as well as collaborating with existing financial institutions, can facilitate smoother integration and interoperability.

- **Complexity and governance**: retail CBDCs require a high level of control and oversight to ensure regulatory compliance and consumer protection, which can be challenging to achieve in a fully distributed system.[33,34] To address these challenges, central banks may need to implement hybrid models that combine distributed technology with centralised oversight, ensuring compliance and consumer protection whilst leveraging the benefits of DLT.
- **Security and risk**: although distributed systems can reduce the risk of a single point of failure, they may introduce other security challenges, such as ensuring consensus and protecting against malicious actors. Retail CBDCs need robust security measures to protect consumers and maintain trust in the currency. Employing strong cryptographic techniques, regular security audits, and robust consensus algorithms can enhance security and mitigate risks in distributed systems.
- **Regulatory compliance**: central banks typically require a high level of control over retail CBDCs to ensure compliance with regulatory requirements and monetary policy objectives. A fully distributed infrastructure (i.e. permissionless blockchain) doesn't provide the necessary control and flexibility to meet these needs. Implementing a permissioned DLT framework may allow central banks to retain control over the network, ensuring compliance with regulatory standards whilst leveraging the benefits of DLT.

BOX 7.2 NIGERIA'S ENAIRA

The informal economy (aka shadow economy) in Nigeria, where 54% of transactions use cash (the remainder is 23% cash and 23% transfer), accounts for 58% of the country's GDP and 90% of employment.[35] The Central Bank of Nigeria (CBN) decided to redesign its monetary policy to promote financial inclusion, introduce cash efficiencies, as well as to improve cross-border transactions (as Nigeria's economy relies heavily on remittances). This included bank notes redesign and the introduction of a CBDC.

Nigeria launched Africa's first CBDC in October 2021 when 500 million eNaira were minted (about $320,000 at the time of writing), in partnership with Bitt[36] for the permissioned DLT infrastructure (based on Hyperledger Fabric) and the eNaira Speed Wallet.[37] In 2023, the CBN attempted to replace high-denomination bank notes with a new design aimed at curbing counterfeiting, but the CBN failed to print enough of the new notes. This led to a significant cash shortage as people withdrew their money or tried to exchange their old notes for the new design before the deadline of February 2023.[38] This part of the redesign policy failed and in November 2023, the Nigerian Supreme Court ruled that the old notes would remain legal tender and coexist with the new ones until further notice.[39]

In the intervening period, digital payment usage, including eNaira's, surged as people and businesses sought digital alternatives, but Nigeria's financial digital infrastructure wasn't capable of handling the increase, leading to failed or reversed transactions. This ultimately led to an estimated loss of 20 trillion Naira (~$40 billion) to the Nigerian economy.

As of March 2024, eNaira's adoption remained low, representing less than 1% of circulating currency,[40] and at the time of writing, Nigeria still ranked as the world's topmost cash-dominant economy.[41] In addition, interest in bitcoin and stablecoins increased as a hedge against inflation when the Naira's value plunged, particularly during the most extreme drops in June and July of 2023, making Nigeria one of the leading countries in cryptocurrency adoption.[42]

In fact, the popularity of cryptocurrencies in Nigeria far exceeds that of the eNaira as cryptocurrencies are perceived as more flexible and independent compared to the government-issued eNaira, which has struggled to offer unique advantages over traditional payment methods (for many Nigerians, it's much easier to open a crypto account than to open a bank account).

Whilst cryptocurrencies have gained widespread acceptance due to their perceived benefits in a volatile economic environment, the eNaira has struggled to achieve similar traction. The dominance of cash and the preference for cryptocurrencies present ongoing challenges to the eNaira's adoption. Efforts to improve infrastructure and merchant acceptance, increase public awareness, and offer incentives for using the eNaira are crucial for its success. However, despite government efforts, the current landscape suggests that the eNaira has a long way to go to match the adoption levels of other payment methods in Nigeria.[43]

The eNaira example, alongside the JAM_DEX example earlier (Box 7.1), underscores the fact that a retail CBDC implementation isn't just about technology, but also about how that technology is perceived and adopted by the public.

By contrast, wholesale CBDCs may help central banks derive efficiencies, and a distributed model may help with this.

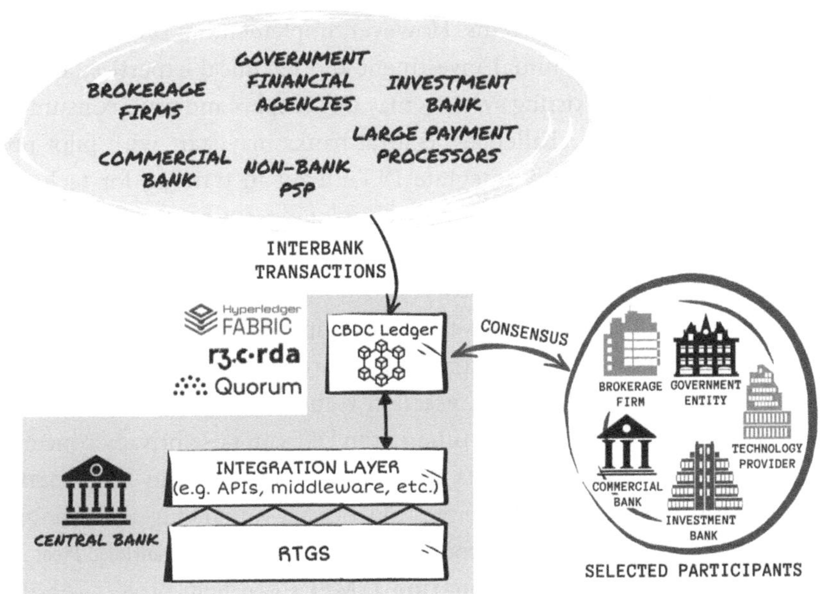

Figure 7.11 An example of distributed wholesale CBDC infrastructure. © 2024 Neira Jones.

In Figure 7.11, it is apparent that the end users (e.g. people, businesses) that were shown in Figure 7.10 are no longer part of the picture. This is because these users don't benefit directly from a wholesale CBDC (nor do they participate), whilst they might benefit indirectly from the potential efficiencies that this type of CBDC might bring to interbank settlements.

If we want to tie this all together with previous chapters, it becomes clear that for a central bank to retain the necessary control and oversight in interbank settlement, a permissioned blockchain is the most suitable model. Reading (or re-reading) Chapter 1, *Permissioned blockchain* and Chapter 2, *Permission blockchain platforms* will help consolidate understanding.

A distributed infrastructure may be a suitable choice for a wholesale CBDC for several reasons:

- **Efficiency in interbank settlement**: wholesale CBDCs are primarily used for interbank transactions, where DLT can enhance efficiency by providing real-time settlement and reducing the need for intermediaries. This can lead to faster transaction times and lower costs compared to traditional systems. However, implementing DLT systems can require significant initial investment and technical expertise, and the transition from existing systems may be complex and time-consuming. To mitigate these challenges, central banks may start with pilot programmes to gradually integrate DLT, invest in training for technical expertise, and collaborate with technology partners to streamline the transition process.
- **Transparency and auditability**: DLT offers a transparent and immutable record of transactions, which can improve auditability and reduce the risk of fraud. This transparency is particularly beneficial in wholesale markets where large transaction volumes and values are involved. However, the transparency inherent in DLT can raise privacy concerns, as sensitive transaction data may become accessible to more parties within the network. Implementing privacy-enhancing technologies, such as zero-knowledge proofs (see Chapter 1, *Zero-Knowledge Proof*) or **secure multi-party computation (SMPC)** can help protect sensitive data and transaction privacy whilst maintaining transparency.
- **Control**: whilst DLT provides a distributed infrastructure, wholesale CBDCs typically use permissioned DLT systems that allow central banks to maintain control over the network. This ensures that regulatory compliance and monetary policy objectives are met whilst leveraging the benefits of distribution. Balancing distribution with control can be challenging, as too much centralisation may negate the benefits of using DLT, whilst too much distribution can complicate governance and compliance. Establishing clear governance frameworks and using permissioned DLT can help maintain the necessary balance between control and distribution.
- **Scalability and performance**: wholesale transactions typically involve fewer participants than retail transactions, which can make scalability and performance more manageable on a DLT platform. The lower volume of transactions compared to retail CBDCs can be efficiently

handled by DLT systems. Despite lower transaction volumes in wholesale transactions, DLT systems may still face scalability challenges, particularly as the network grows or if real-time processing becomes a requirement. Employing scalable DLT solutions, such as layer 1 or layer 2 solutions (see Chapter 1, *Are blockchains scalable*), can enhance performance and handle increased transaction volumes.

- **Security, resilience, and risk management**: DLT can enhance security by distributing the ledger across multiple nodes, reducing the risk of a single point of failure. This distributed nature can also improve resilience against outages or cyberattacks, which is crucial for maintaining trust in wholesale financial markets. However, the distributed nature of DLT can introduce new security vulnerabilities, such as the risk of consensus attacks or the need for robust node management to prevent unauthorised access or manipulation. Implementing robust node validation processes, consensus mechanisms with high-security thresholds, and regular security audits can mitigate these risks.
- **Interoperability with existing systems**: DLT can be integrated with existing financial infrastructure through standardised protocols, facilitating interoperability. This is important for wholesale CBDCs, which need to work seamlessly with current payment and settlement systems. However, achieving interoperability can be complex and may require significant changes to existing systems, as well as the development of new standards and protocols. Engaging in international collaboration to develop and adopt standardised protocols may facilitate smoother integration and interoperability.
- **Regulatory compliance**: permissioned DLT systems allow central banks to enforce regulatory compliance by controlling access and participation in the network. This ensures that wholesale CBDCs meet necessary legal and regulatory standards whilst benefiting from the efficiencies of DLT. However, ensuring compliance across a distributed network can be challenging, particularly when dealing with cross-border transactions and differing regulatory environments. Establishing clear regulatory guidelines and fostering international regulatory cooperation can help address compliance challenges in a distributed network.

In summary, whilst distributed infrastructures offer certain advantages, such as resilience and innovation potential, the decentralisation inherent in permissionless blockchains doesn't align well with the requirements and objectives of a CBDC. This is why, typically, central banks exploring DLT-based CBDCs will opt for permissioned blockchain deployments if they choose the distributed CBDC model.

With CBDC distributed infrastructure, professionals should remember the following:

- **Resilience and security**: distributed CBDC infrastructures potentially benefit from increased resilience as they spread the ledger across multiple nodes, making these systems less vulnerable to single points of failure, potentially enabling them to better withstand cyberattacks. However, whilst distribution can enhance security, it also introduces new challenges, such as ensuring consensus and preventing malicious actors from gaining control. The trade-off involves balancing resilience with the complexity of managing a distributed network.
- **Governance complexity**: distributed systems require robust governance frameworks to manage the network and ensure all participants adhere to the rules. This can lead to challenges in decision-making and coordination, as consensus must be reached among a diverse group of stakeholders. This may also slow down the implementation of changes and updates (see Chapter 3).
- **Interoperability challenges**: whilst distributed infrastructures potentially offer enhanced flexibility, they may face difficulties in integrating with existing centralised financial systems. Achieving interoperability requires careful design and the use of standardised protocols, which can be complex and time-consuming to implement.
- **Innovation and flexibility**: the use of DLT and other distributed technologies can foster innovation by allowing for the development of new applications and services that leverage the unique capabilities of a distributed network. However, this flexibility can come at the cost of increased complexity and the need for specialised technical expertise. See Chapter 2, *Building blockchains and applications.*
- **Scalability concerns**: distributed systems can face scalability issues, particularly in handling large volumes of transactions quickly and efficiently. Whilst innovations in DLT aim to address these challenges, scaling a DLT-based CBDC to a national level may require significant technological advancements and investment.

These considerations highlight the balance between the potential benefits of a distributed CBDC infrastructure and the potential trade-offs that central banks must weigh when making technological decisions.

At the time of writing, in addition to Nigeria's eNaira, distributed CBDCs include The Bahamas Sand Dollar[44,45] (retail, deployed), Sweden's eKrona[46,47] (retail, pilot), and India's Digital Rupee[48] (retail and wholesale, pilot).

Hybrid infrastructure models offer another option to balance control, scalability, and security with the need for innovation and flexibility.

Hybrid infrastructure

A hybrid CBDC infrastructure may integrate both centralised and distributed components in order to balance control, scalability, security, and innovation. This is still an evolving area (see Figure 7.5), and most of the projects remain undecided on their infrastructure choices (e.g. Australia eAUD[49]).

In any instance, I'll attempt to list infrastructure components where centralisation vs. distribution may be a choice:

- **Ledger and transaction processing**: as shown earlier, the CBDC ledger can be centralised (e.g. eCNY, JAM-DEX) where a central database is managed by the central bank or a designated authority to handle transaction processing and maintain the authoritative ledger. This ensures efficient data handling and integration with existing financial systems. Conversely, a permissioned blockchain can be used for transaction validation and settlement (e.g. eNaira, Sand Dollar, Digital Rupee). Here, multiple authorised nodes, such as commercial banks, participate in the validation process, enhancing resilience and reducing the risk of a single point of failure.
- **CBDC Wallets**: we covered digital wallets in Chapter 6, *Digital wallets*. Accordingly, CBDC wallets can be deployed and managed in different ways. CBDC may come in three types, custodial wallets and non-custodial wallets (as covered in Chapter 6), and the new type of "bearer wallet" which relies on the possession of a physical form factor (e.g. smart card, smartphone). CBDC bearer wallets are a bit like reloadable prepaid cards for CBDCs and very similar to crypto hardware wallets (see Chapter 6, *Hardware wallets*). Tables 7.2 and 7.3 explain this:

Table 7.2 Comparing CBDC wallets. © 2024 Neira Jones

Feature	**Custodial CBDC Wallet**	**Non-custodial CBDC Wallet**	**CBDC Bearer Wallet**
Form factor	Digital accounts, apps, or online platforms provided by a central bank or financial services firms	Digital apps or hardware wallets managed by the user	Secure elements in devices like smartcards, smartphones, or specialised hardware
Issuer	Central banks or authorised financial institutions	Central banks or authorised financial institutions	Central banks or authorised financial institutions
Custody of keys	Issuer has control over private keys and funds management	Wallet holders have complete control over their funds and private keys	Keys are embedded within the secure hardware of the device, providing access to the stored funds. Ownership is determined by physical possession of the device
Funds storage	Funds are managed by the custodian and not stored on the user's device	Funds are not stored on the wallet; the wallet holds keys to access funds on a blockchain	Actual funds are stored on the device
Security	Custodian manages security	Wallet holders must manage their own security, including key storage	Security relies on the physical security of the device, such as a smartcard

Feature	Custodial CBDC Wallet	Non-custodial CBDC Wallet	CBDC Bearer Wallet
Connectivity	Typically requires an internet connection for transaction and management	Typically requires an internet connection for transaction and management	Does not require a permanent internet connection
Offline capability	Typically not designed to operate offline	Typically not designed to operate offline	Can operate offline, typically synchronises with ledger when wallet is back online
Privacy	Limited privacy. Transactions are visible to the custodian and potentially to regulatory authorities. May offer some privacy from third parties	Potentially higher privacy, depending on the blockchain design. Transactions may be pseudonymous, but wallet addresses could be linked to identities	Highest level of privacy. Transactions are typically anonymous and difficult to trace, similar to physical cash
User experience	Generally user-friendly with support from custodians, making it easier for less tech-savvy users to navigate	Requires more technical knowledge to manage security and funds, which can be challenging for some users	Can be user-friendly, but the need for physical possession and secure handling may complicate the experience for some users
Examples	eCNY, eNaira, JAM-DEX	No examples at the time of writing	eCNY has some offline features[50]

Table 7.3 Comparing hardware crypto wallets and CBDC bearer wallets. © 2024 Neira Jones

Feature	Crypto Hardware Wallet	CBDC Bearer Wallet
Purpose	Store and manage cryptocurrencies	Store and manage CBDCs issued by central banks
Offline capability	Designed for offline storage (cold storage), requires connection for transactions	Designed for offline payments, requires periodic synchronisation
Control over private keys	User has complete control	User has control, but centralised features are possible
Security features	Secure offline storage, immune to online threats	Embedded secure elements, high-security requirements
Design and accessibility	Standalone devices (e.g. USB sticks), smartcards, Bluetooth-enabled devices	Smartcards, USB-type devices, cards with displays and keypads, smartphones (Secure Element)
Currency support	Often supports multiple cryptocurrencies (some crypto-specific hardware wallets exist, such as Trezor Safe 5 for Bitcoin)	Specific to CBDCs
Typical costs	\$40–\$200	Varies, often provided by central banks

In the dynamic landscape of digital currencies, CBDC wallets are emerging as a pivotal tool for managing CBDCs. Whether central banks opt to deploy a custodial wallet with its convenient third-party management, a non-custodial wallet that puts users in the driver's seat, or a bearer wallet that combines the tactile assurance of physical possession with the flexibility of offline transactions, each type offers unique advantages. As central banks continue to research the field, these wallets may become an important component of how we interact with money.

- **Automated processes**: process automation and business logic can be handled by centralised systems in the usual way, but automation can also be achieved through smart contracts for DLT-based CBDCs.
- **Payment systems**: as seen earlier (see Figures 7.9–7.11), CBDCs must integrate with existing payment systems (e.g. RTGS), but decentralised systems may also be integrated for specific purposes (e.g. Ripple).
- **Identity services**: there are many ways to verify the identity of CBDC users, each with varying degrees of centralisation, and CBDCs may leverage existing infrastructure where present. Typically, identity services may include private digital ID systems (e.g. Alibaba and Tencent in China have developed private digital ID systems integrated with their payment platforms), collaborative public-private solutions (e.g. Norway BankID, Sweden BankID, Switzerland SwissID, Belgium itsme; Estonia's e-Residency program), market-driven systems (e.g. Germany Verimi, US ID.me,[51] UK Yoti,[52] Australia Digital ID by Australia Post[53]), government-issued digital ID programmes (e.g. India's Aadhaar,[54] Singapore's SingPass[55]), and decentralised digital ID systems (e.g. Sovrin,[56] Civic,[57] Worldcoin,[58] trinsic[59]).

BOX 7.3 DECENTRALISED IDENTITY

Because the concept of digital identity is closely linked to wallets, it's worth having a slight bifurcation from the flow of this section. I don't intend to provide a comprehensive account of decentralised identity here (as I cover this extensively in my next book, *Payments Unbound*), but it's worth introducing a few concepts. **Decentralised identity** is a digital identity management approach where identity data is not controlled by a single, centralised authority. Instead, it is distributed across multiple nodes or entities, often leveraging DLTs, to ensure security, privacy, and user control. This model allows individuals to have control over their identity data, enhancing privacy and security. Forms of decentralised identity include:

- **Self-Sovereign Identity (SSI)**: is a specific implementation of decentralised identity that specifically focuses on giving individuals full control over their identity data. SSI allows users to store their identity credentials in a digital wallet and share them selectively as needed. It is inherently decentralised because it focuses on user autonomy and minimises reliance on centralised authorities. SSI systems typically use decentralised identifiers (DIDs) and verifiable credentials (VCs) to ensure privacy and security. Some may argue that SSI is key to retail CBDC adoption[60] as it might be a way to address the duality of needs for user privacy (avoid government surveillance) and transparency for regulatory compliance (to curb financial crime).[61] For example, SSI is seen as a potential enabler for **open banking**.[62]

- **Blockchain-based identity systems**: some decentralised identity systems use blockchain technology to distribute identity data across a network. However, not all blockchain-based systems provide the level of user control and autonomy that SSI does. An example is Civic, which is used by many blockchain applications, including crypto exchanges.[63]
- **Decentralised identity platforms with centralised governance**: some platforms may use decentralised technologies for identity management but retain centralised control over governance and policy enforcement. For example, Singapore's TradeTrust is a digital utility that uses decentralised identity technologies with centralised governance to streamline trade documentation processes. This initiative aims to enhance transparency and efficiency in international trade, including payment settlements.[64]

Decentralised identity is not to be confused with federated identity systems which allow users to access multiple services using a single identity, managed by a trusted identity provider. Whilst they offer some decentralisation by reducing the number of credentials users need to manage, they still rely on a central authority for identity verification (e.g. Open ID Connect[65]).

Decentralised identity represents a shift towards more user-centric identity management, potentially offering enhanced privacy, security, and control. Whilst SSI is a specific form of decentralised identity that prioritises user autonomy, other decentralised identity approaches may incorporate different levels of centralisation and user control.

In a hybrid CBDC system, the central bank might use centralised systems for identity management and core transaction processing, ensuring fast and reliable operations. Simultaneously, a permissioned blockchain could be employed for transaction settlement and validation, involving multiple financial institutions as validating nodes. Automated processes, such as those facilitated by smart contracts, could streamline operations, and users might interact with the system through a combination of custodial, non-custodial, and bearer wallets.

This combination of centralised and distributed components allows the CBDC to benefit from the efficiency and control of centralised systems whilst leveraging the resilience, transparency, and innovation potential of distributed technologies. The hybrid model may provide a robust and flexible infrastructure capable of adapting to various use cases and requirements, balancing the need for control with the advantages of decentralisation. But as always, the proof of the pudding is in the eating…

Note from the author: I used Worldcoin, of Sam Altman[66]'s fame, as an example of a decentralised digital identity solution. Worldcoin has been the subject of much controversy and criticised by the industry and regulators for the privacy implications[67,68] of their iris-biometrics "orb", but in August 2024, it switched to secure multi-party computation[69] and deleted the old iris codes, attracting praise.[70,71]

Recap on CBDC infrastructure choices

Table 7.4 gives a quick recap on infrastructure choices for the different choices of CBDC infrastructure.

For the purpose of completeness, I included permissionless blockchains and stablecoin issuance by central banks as theoretical use cases, and these will be shaded in the table due to their current lack of suitability.

Access

When it comes to accessing CBDCs, think of it like choosing the best way to store and use your digital treasures. Just as you might choose between a secure vault, a personal safe, or a purse for your valuables, CBDC access models offer different methods to manage and use digital currencies. Each model has its own unique features and benefits, catering to different needs and preferences. There are three types of CBDC access models:

Table 7.4 Comparing CBDC infrastructures. © 2024 Neira Jones

Aspect	**Permissionless Blockchain Retail or Wholesale CBDC**	**Permissionless Blockchain, CBDC Issued as Stablecoin**	**Permissioned Blockchain Retail CBDC**	**Permissioned Blockchain Wholesale CBDC**	**Centralised CBDC Infrastructure**
Network participants	Anyone can join including central bank, commercial banks, non-bank PSPs, individuals, and businesses	Anyone can join including central bank, commercial banks, non-bank PSPs, individuals, and businesses	Central bank, commercial banks, non-bank PSPs, and selected financial institutions with permissioned access (e.g. specific fintech companies, licensed PSPs)	Central bank, commercial banks, and selected financial institutions with permissioned access (e.g. authorised wholesale banks, large financial institutions)	Central banks, regulated financial institutions, and selected third-party providers
Suitability for CBDC	Unsuitable for both retail and wholesale CBDCs	Potentially suitable for wholesale CBDC	Suitable for retail CBDC, balances security, control, and user experience	Highly suitable for wholesale CBDC, offers security and compliance with efficiency	Highly suitable for retail and wholesale CBDC due to control and compliance
Infrastructure examples	Bitcoin, Ethereum	No known examples, but discussions exist	Hyperledger Fabric, Corda, Quorum (permissioned blockchains)	Hyperledger Fabric, Corda, Quorum (permissioned blockchains)	Traditional databases and proprietary banking infrastructures

Aspect	Permissionless Blockchain Retail or Wholesale CBDC	Permissionless Blockchain, CBDC Issued as Stablecoin	Permissioned Blockchain Retail CBDC	Permissioned Blockchain Wholesale CBDC	Centralised CBDC Infrastructure
Monetary policy control	Limited control, difficult to manage distribution, inflation, and deflation due to decentralised nature	Limited control, whilst stablecoins can be pegged, decentralised issuance poses challenges for policy implementation	High control, central bank can effectively manage distribution, inflation, and deflation	High control, central bank can effectively manage distribution, inflation, and deflation	Complete control, central banks can directly manage distribution, inflation, and deflation
Services to end users	Custodial and non-custodial wallets, public access to blockchain explorers	Custodial and non-custodial wallets, integration with existing financial apps, and potentially tokenised assets	Custodial and non-custodial wallets, provided by banks and PSPs, integration with existing financial apps	Custodial and non-custodial wallets, provided by banks and financial institutions, integration with existing financial systems	Traditional digital wallets, provided by banks and financial institutions, integration with existing financial systems
Complexity and governance	High complexity with decentralised governance, consensus mechanisms needed	High complexity with decentralised governance, consensus mechanisms, etc.	Moderate complexity with centralised governance, easier to manage	Moderate complexity, centralised governance simplifies management	Lower complexity, governed within a centralised framework with clear guidelines

(Continued)

Table 7.4 (Continued)

Aspect	Permissionless Blockchain Retail or Wholesale CBDC	Permissionless Blockchain, CBDC Issued as Stablecoin	Permissioned Blockchain Retail CBDC	Permissioned Blockchain Wholesale CBDC	Centralised CBDC Infrastructure
Scalability and performance	Scalability issues, high transaction volume can lead to congestion for retail CBDC. May be more scalable for wholesale CBDC due to fewer participants but still faces performance challenges	Potential scalability issues, high transaction volume can lead to congestion	Better scalability, controlled environment allows for optimisation	High scalability, fewer participants and centralised control enhance performance	High scalability due to centralised management; optimised transaction speeds
Security and risk	High risk of attacks due to public nature, security relies on network size	High risk of attacks due to public nature, security relies on network size	Enhanced security through controlled access, easier to implement robust measures	High security due to limited, trusted participants and controlled access	Enhanced security through restricted access, robust measures can be implemented
Interoperability with existing systems	Challenging due to decentralised nature, requires significant adaptation	Challenging due to decentralised nature, requires significant adaptation	Easier integration with existing systems, standardised protocols can be used	Easier integration, aligns well with existing financial infrastructure	High interoperability as it is easier to adapt to existing financial systems

Aspect	Permissionless Blockchain Retail or Wholesale CBDC	Permissionless Blockchain, CBDC Issued as Stablecoin	Permissioned Blockchain Retail CBDC	Permissioned Blockchain Wholesale CBDC	Centralised CBDC Infrastructure
Regulatory compliance	Difficult to enforce due to anonymity and decentralisation	Difficult to enforce due to anonymity and decentralisation	Easier to ensure compliance, participants are known and regulated	High compliance, participants are regulated entities	Maximum compliance achieved as all participants are regulated entities (or selected third party providers)
User impact	High transparency, users have more control but face potential privacy issues	Users benefit from rapid transactions and stable value but face privacy concerns	Users benefit from security and privacy controls, less transparency	Minimal direct user impact, focuses on interbank transactions	Users face centralised control, may lead to less transparency but improves security
Examples	N/A	N/A	eNaira (Nigeria), Sand Dollar (Bahamas), DCash (Eastern Caribbean)	Project Jasper (Canada), Project Ubin (Singapore), Project Inthanon (Thailand)	e-CNY (China), JAM-DEX (Jamaica)

- **account-based**: this model involves accessing CBDC through a digital account managed by a central authority, requiring identity verification for transactions. It offers high security and traceability but requires robust infrastructure and may limit privacy.
- **token-based**: in this model, the CBDC is accessed via digital tokens, allowing transactions to occur anonymously without verifying the user's identity, similar to using cash. It provides greater privacy and inclusivity but poses challenges in preventing illicit activities.
- **hybrid**: this model combines features of both account-based and token-based systems, offering flexibility in how users manage and transact with CBDCs. It balances security and privacy but can be complex to implement and manage.

Let's explore these in more detail.

Account-based

The account-based model is similar to how traditional bank accounts work: individuals and businesses hold CBDC in accounts managed by a central authority, usually a central bank or an authorised financial institution (depending on the architecture model selected). Access to funds is authenticated through identity verification, ensuring that only the account holder can transact. This model offers a high level of security and allows for easy tracking of transactions, which can help prevent fraud and money laundering. However, it requires a robust infrastructure to manage accounts and verify identities. In addition, account-based CBDCs can't support offline transactions as they require verification of an associated account held at a third party.

Contrary to popular belief, an account-based CBDC access model can be either centralised or decentralised, but both are based on proof of identity (which may be provided by the private sector).

The two main implementations of this model include:

Centralised account-based access: this involves a trusted third party (e.g. financial services institution) managing accounts and performing identity proofing. This model aligns with traditional financial services practices for account management.

Distributed account-based access: this model may leverage DLT where a network of nodes participates in identity verification and is aligned with the concept of decentralised identity (see Box 7.3) and doesn't require the user to hold an account.

Figure 7.12 illustrates this.

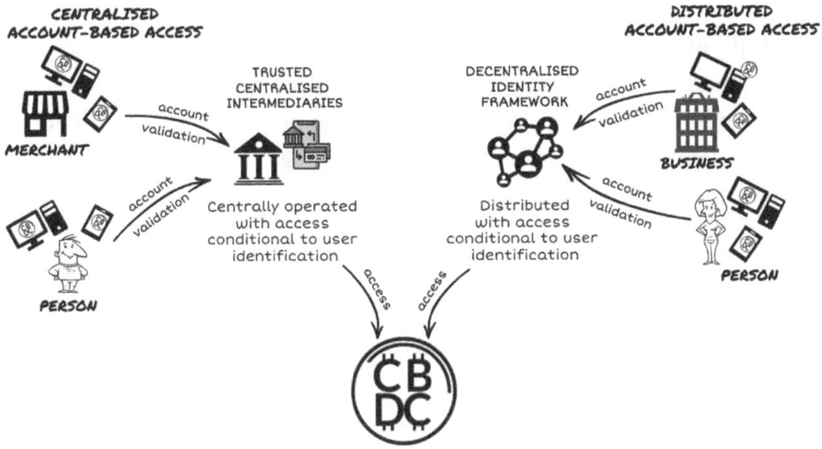

Figure 7.12 Account-based CBDC access. © 2024 Neira Jones.

Central banks may choose the account-based access model in support of their monetary policy for a variety of reasons:

- **Security and traceability**: this model offers enhanced security through robust identity verification and transaction monitoring, reducing fraud and illicit activities. However, this high level of traceability may raise privacy concerns for users who prefer more anonymous transactions.
- **Integration with existing systems**: this model can be easily integrated with current financial infrastructure, potentially simplifying implementation and lowering costs. On the flip side, implementing and maintaining a secure, large-scale account system requires significant technological resources.
- **Control and monetary policy**: account-based systems enable more direct control over the money supply and circulation, improving monetary policy implementation. Yet, this level of control might be seen as intrusive by some users.
- **Offline limitations**: unlike token-based models, account-based CBDCs can't support offline transactions as they require verification of an associated account held at a third party. This could be a significant drawback in areas with unreliable internet connectivity.

- **Inclusivity**: whilst this model can leverage existing financial systems, it may inadvertently exclude individuals without proper identification or those uncomfortable with digital account management.
- **Implementation options**: central banks may choose between centralised and distributed account-based access implementations, each with its own implications for identity management and system architecture. This flexibility allows for tailored solutions but may also increase complexity in decision-making and implementation.

Central banks may opt for the account-based access model to leverage existing financial infrastructure and enhance security through robust identity verification. This model offers strong traceability, which can help combat financial crimes, but it also raises privacy concerns and may exclude some users. Whilst it provides better control over monetary policy, it requires significant technological resources and can't support offline transactions. Central banks must carefully weigh these trade-offs, considering factors like financial inclusion, privacy protection, and integration with current systems. Ultimately, the choice between account-based, token-based, or hybrid models will depend on the specific needs and goals of each central bank and the communities they serve.

Token-based

The token-based model is akin to using cash. If you pay for a coffee with cash, the only thing the merchant needs to worry about is that the bank note I hand over is not fake. In particular, the merchant doesn't need to know anything about me. In the token-based model, the CBDC is represented as digital tokens that can be stored on a device, like a smartphone or a digital wallet (see Tables 7.2 and 7.3). Transactions are verified through the validity of the token itself rather than the identity of the user (just like a banknote). This model offers greater privacy and anonymity, as it doesn't require personal identification for each transaction. It's also more inclusive, as it doesn't necessitate having an account held by a third party. However, it may pose challenges in preventing illicit activities due to the anonymity it provides. **Token-based CBDCs can support both offline and online transactions**, enabling users to transact without an internet connection, which is particularly useful in areas with limited connectivity. This is important for retail CBDCs if these are to be used as cash alternatives.

Contrary to popular belief, a token-based CBDC access model can be either centralised or decentralised, but both are based on demonstrated knowledge (e.g. cryptographic keys) rather than proof of identity and as such, offer more privacy than account-based CBDCs.

Typical implementations of this model include:

Centralised token management: in this implementation, the central bank issues and manages digital tokens, maintaining a centralised ledger to track token issuance and transfers, ensuring oversight and control. This ensures that all transactions are recorded in a single, centralised system, allowing for comprehensive oversight and control.

Decentralised token infrastructure: alternatively, a decentralised system can be used, where tokens are managed on a DLT platform, allowing for peer-to-peer transactions without central authority intervention, typically using a decentralised identity framework (see Box 7.3).

Figure 7.13 illustrates this.

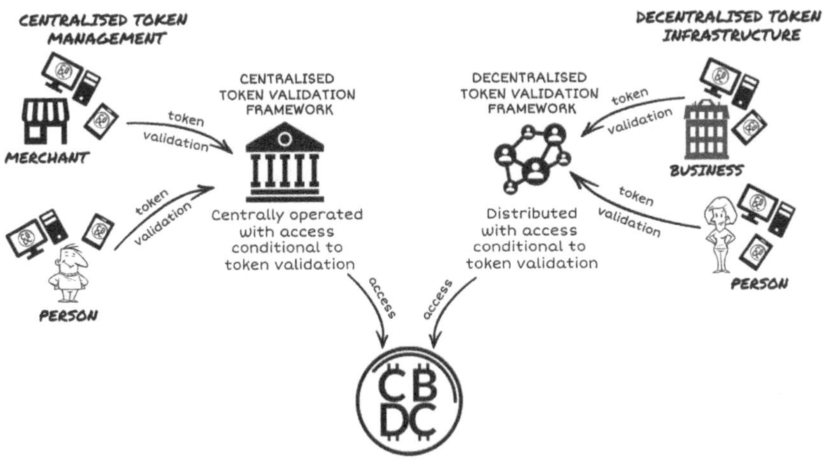

Figure 7.13 Token-based CBDC access. © 2024 Neira Jones.

Central banks may choose the token-based access model in support of their monetary policy for a variety of reasons:

- **Privacy and anonymity**: this model can offer varying degrees of privacy, making it suitable for low-value transactions where user identity verification is less critical.

- **Financial inclusion**: by not requiring users to have a financial account, token-based CBDCs can reach unbanked populations, facilitating broader financial inclusion and access to digital financial services.
- **Cash-like functionality**: token-based access mimics the ease and convenience of cash, allowing for quick, direct transactions without intermediaries, which is advantageous for everyday purchases and small transactions.
- **Flexibility in design**: central banks can choose between centralised or decentralised token management, tailoring the system to meet specific regulatory, security, and operational needs.
- **Support for innovative applications**: the programmable nature of digital tokens allows for integration with emerging technologies and services, such as micropayments and Internet of Things (IoT) applications, enhancing the scope of financial innovation.

Central banks may opt for the token-based access model to capitalise on these benefits, particularly in contexts where privacy, ease of access, and cash-like functionality are prioritised. The choice between centralised and decentralised management further allows central banks to align the system with their regulatory and operational objectives. This model is particularly suitable for retail CBDCs due to its ability to facilitate everyday transactions and reach unbanked populations. However, it may be less suitable for wholesale CBDCs, where transaction traceability and regulatory oversight are more critical. Central banks must consider the trade-offs between maintaining privacy and ensuring compliance with regulatory standards, as well as the potential complexity of managing a decentralised infrastructure.

Hybrid

The hybrid model combines elements of both account-based and token-based systems. It allows users to choose how they want to access and use CBDC, offering the flexibility of both account management and token transactions. This model can cater to a broader range of users, providing both the security and oversight of account-based systems and the privacy and inclusivity of token-based systems. The hybrid approach can be more complex to implement, as it requires maintaining both systems effectively. Typical implementations include:

- **Conditional access based on transaction type**: central banks might implement a system where low-value transactions use token-based access for speed and privacy, whilst high-value transactions may require account-based access for enhanced security and traceability.
- **Sector-specific access**: different sectors, such as retail and wholesale markets, might be assigned different access methods. For example, retail consumers might use token-based access for everyday transactions, whilst financial institutions might use account-based access for larger, regulated transactions.
- **Dynamic access switching**: the system could dynamically switch between account-based and token-based access depending on predefined criteria, such as transaction size, frequency, or user type, as determined by the central bank. Think of it as something similar to attempting a contactless transaction above the agreed limit and having to insert the card in the card reader for authentication.

Central banks may choose the hybrid model in support of their monetary policy for a variety of reasons:

- **Flexibility and efficiency**: by offering both access methods, central banks can efficiently cater to a wide range of transaction types and user needs, optimising the use of CBDCs across different scenarios.
- **Enhanced security and privacy balance**: the hybrid model allows central banks to balance the need for privacy in small, everyday transactions with the requirement for security and oversight in larger, more sensitive transactions.
- **Financial inclusion**: by supporting token-based access, central banks can reach unbanked populations, whilst account-based access ensures that those who prefer traditional banking security are also accommodated.
- **Regulatory compliance**: the ability to switch access methods based on transaction characteristics allows central banks to meet regulatory requirements and manage risks associated with different types of transactions.
- **Innovation and adaptability**: the hybrid model encourages innovation by allowing the private sector to develop solutions that leverage both access types, enhancing the overall functionality and appeal of the CBDC system.

Central banks may choose the hybrid access model to leverage its flexibility and efficiency, catering to a wide range of transaction types and user needs. By offering both account-based and token-based access, the hybrid model allows central banks to balance privacy and security, making it suitable for both retail and wholesale CBDCs. This approach supports financial inclusion by reaching unbanked populations through token-based access whilst accommodating those who prefer the security of account-based systems. Additionally, the hybrid model facilitates regulatory compliance by allowing dynamic switching between access methods based on transaction characteristics, thereby managing risks effectively. The model also fosters innovation and adaptability, enabling the private sector to develop solutions that enhance the overall functionality and appeal of the CBDC system. However, central banks must consider the complexity of implementing and maintaining both systems to ensure seamless operation and integration.

Recap on CBDC access models

Just as we have various ways to carry and spend money in the physical world, CBDC access models offer different approaches to managing digital currency. Think of the account-based model as a digital wallet tied to your identity, similar to your bank account or credit card. It's secure and traceable but requires you to verify who you are, just like when you use your debit card. The token-based model, on the other hand, is more like carrying digital cash in your pocket. It offers more privacy and doesn't require identification for every transaction, but like physical cash, it comes with its own set of risks and benefits.

CBDC access models have the potential to cater to diverse needs. The hybrid model, for instance, is like having a prepaid card that you can top up anonymously but still use for secure online purchases. As we move towards a more digital financial future, these CBDC access models may play a role in shaping how we interact with money. They'll need to strike a delicate balance between the convenience we've come to expect from modern payment systems, the security necessary to protect our assets, and the privacy we value in our financial transactions.

The choice of model will ultimately depend on how societies prioritise these different aspects of digital currency use, and the "money flower"[72] diagram from the Bank of International Settlements (BIS) illustrates this as shown in Figure 7.14.

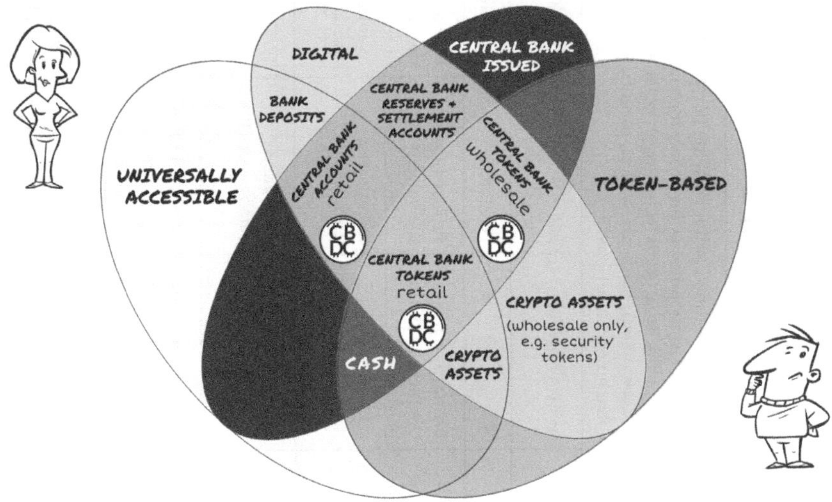

Figure 7.14 The money flower. © 2024 Neira Jones.

To wrap it all up, Table 7.5 compares traditional payments with CBDC access models.

Professionals should remember the following:

- **Balancing privacy and compliance**: account-based systems offer better traceability for anti-money laundering efforts, whilst token-based models provide more user anonymity. This balance is crucial for maintaining financial integrity whilst respecting individual privacy rights.
- **Infrastructure matters**: careful evaluation of the technology infrastructure required for each model is crucial. Account-based systems may necessitate more robust identity verification systems, whilst token-based models might require advanced cryptographic solutions. The chosen infrastructure will impact implementation costs, scalability, and long-term maintenance.
- **Financial inclusion**: token-based models could potentially serve unbanked populations more easily, as they don't require traditional bank accounts or extensive identity verification. This could be beneficial in regions with limited access to formal banking services. However, increasing financial inclusion may make it more challenging to implement anti-money laundering (AML) and KYC measures.

Table 7.5 Comparing traditional payments with CBDC access models. © 2024 Neira Jones

Access Model Feature	**Traditional Payments**				**CBDC**			
	Cash	**Bank Account**	**e-money**	**Mobile Money**	**Centralised Account-Based**	**Distributed Account-Based**	**Centralised Token-Based**	**Distributed Token-Based**
Form factor	Coins, banknotes	Online banking, mobile app, debit card, ATM, cheque	Mobile app, prepaid card, online account, QR code	Mobile phone-based services, often using USSD or SMS	Modified mobile banking apps, modified online banking portals, modified e-money wallets, modified ATMs, modified point-of-sale terminals, physical CBDC cards (which could include smart card technology), potentially modified wearable devices (e.g. smartwatches), hardware wallets, potentially modified IoT devices for machine-to-machine transactions			
User experience	Simple	Familiar	Familiar	Simple	Familiar	More complex	Familiar for digital natives	Complex
Offline capability	Yes	No	No	No	No	No	Possible	Possible
Verification Y	Authenticity of the banknotes and coins	Primarily verifies the identity of the user to authorise transactions	Primarily verifies the identity of the user to authorise transactions	Primarily verifies the identity of the user to authorise transactions	Primarily verifies the identity of the user to authorise transactions	Primarily verifies the identity of the user to authorise transactions	Primarily verifies the validity of the token to authorise transactions	Primarily verifies the validity of the token to authorise transactions
Infrastructure	None	Proprietary banking system	Proprietary payment platform	Proprietary telco platform	Centralised database	Typically DLT	Centralised database or DLT	Typically DLT
CBDC architecture suitability	N/A	N/A	N/A	N/A	Direct, intermediated, or hybrid CBDC			
Suitability for retail CBDC	N/A	N/A	N/A	N/A	Less common for retail, but still a potential option depending on specific goals	Potentially suitable, balancing distributed systems with familiar account structures	Highly suitable, balancing accessibility and control	Suitable, offering potential benefits in resilience and privacy

Access Model Feature	Traditional Payments				CBDC			
	Cash	**Bank Account**	**e-money**	**Mobile Money**	**Centralised Account-Based**	**Distributed Account-Based**	**Centralised Token-Based**	**Distributed Token-Based**
Suitability for wholesale CBDC	N/A	N/A	N/A	N/A	Highly suitable due to the need for direct control and oversight by the central bank	Potentially suitable, offering benefits in resilience and efficiency	Suitable, offering benefits of tokenisation whilst maintaining centralised control	Less common but potentially suitable for specific use cases
Anonymity	High	Low	Low to medium	Low to medium	Low	Low	Low to medium	Medium
User privacy	High	Low	Low to medium	Low to medium	Low	Low to medium	Medium	Medium to High
Transaction privacy	High	High	High	High	High	Medium to high	High	Medium to High
Financial inclusion	High	Medium	Medium to high	High	Medium to high	Medium to high	High	High
Examples	Any fiat currency	Any bank	PayPal, Revolut, Wise	M-Pesa, MTN Mobile Money, Orange Money	Nigeria eNaira, China eCNY, Jamaica JAM-DEX	No major implementation (see Note 1)	Bahamas Sand Dollar, Eastern Caribbean DCash, India Digital Rupee	No major implementations (see Note 1)

Note 1: it's important to note that for distributed CBDC implementations, a decentralised identity framework might be beneficial (see Box 7.3), and likely necessary in fully distributed implementations. Decentralised identity frameworks such as Sovrin, Civic, Worldcoin, or Trinsic are designed to work with distributed systems that align them well with the principles of DLT-based implementations, which are inherently distributed. However these solutions are still emerging and not yet suitable for highly regulated environments and identity and proof of uniqueness are key challenges in DLT adoption.[73] Some hybrid or partially distributed CBDC models might be able to function with more traditional identity systems, albeit potentially with reduced efficiency or security. Some CBDC designs are exploring ways to incorporate privacy and anonymity features even in more centralised models. This suggests that the specific identity solution chosen would depend on the overall design goals and regulatory requirements of the CBDC system.

- **Monetary policy implications**: account-based models may offer more direct control over money supply and circulation, potentially enhancing the effectiveness of monetary policy tools. This could provide central banks with more precise levers for economic management, but greater control for central banks could lead to concerns about privacy and government overreach in personal finances.
- **User adoption**: carefully designing the user experience is key as it will drive adoption rates. Token-based models might feel more familiar to cash users, potentially leading to faster adoption in some demographics. The ease of use and perceived benefits will greatly influence public acceptance of CBDCs. However, designing for familiarity and ease of use may limit the implementation of more advanced features or security measures.
- **Scalability**: account-based systems might face challenges with high transaction volumes, whilst token-based models could offer more efficient processing. The ability to handle increasing numbers of users and transactions is crucial for long-term success. Highly scalable systems may require more complex infrastructure or may sacrifice some level of transaction detail or control.
- **Interoperability**: interoperability with existing financial systems is an important consideration. The chosen access model will impact how easily the CBDC can integrate with current financial infrastructure and cross-border payment systems. Seamless integration could lead to wider acceptance and use, but prioritising interoperability may limit innovation or require compromises in the CBDC's unique features.
- **Resilience**: the resilience and offline capability of each model are crucial if the aim is to offer a cash alternative. Token-based systems may offer better offline capabilities, which could be crucial during network outages or in areas with limited connectivity. This ensures continuous access to financial services, even in challenging conditions. However, enhancing offline capabilities may increase security risks or complicate the reconciliation process when systems come back online.
- **Future-proofing**: the long-term maintenance and upgrade requirements should be considered at the outset, but designing for future flexibility may increase initial costs and complexity and could potentially delay launch or limit initial functionality. The chosen access model will influence the ongoing costs and complexity of managing and

evolving the CBDC system over time. A forward-thinking approach ensures the system remains relevant and efficient as technology and user needs evolve. All three launched CBDCs (JAM-DEX, eNaira, Sand Dollar) have not met central bank expectations and expected user adoption rates. The eCNY pilot hasn't met the original expectations of the PBOC either, but China is playing the long game and continues to evolve its CBDC.

As we've explored in this section, CBDC access models are like choosing the right key for your digital treasure chest. Just as we discussed how CBDC architecture forms the foundation and infrastructure provides the building blocks, access models determine how users interact with the digital currency. Whether it's the secure vault of account-based systems, the digital cash-like freedom of token-based models, or the versatile hybrid approach, each option offers unique benefits and challenges.

But our journey through the CBDC landscape doesn't end here. Much like how different keys might work with various locks, we need to consider how these digital currencies can work across different systems and borders. In our next section, we'll dive into CBDC interoperability models – think of it as creating a universal key that can open multiple treasure chests. We'll explore how CBDCs can communicate and transact with each other and existing financial systems, potentially unlocking a new era of seamless global transactions.

Interoperability

CBDCs, especially wholesale CBDCs, could enhance the efficiency of cross-border payments without creating a new global unit of account as envisioned in global stablecoin arrangements (unlike stablecoins, which are typically issued by private entities, CBDCs are backed by central banks, providing a higher level of trust and security). They may foster the seamless convertibility of one fiat currency into another and potentially tackle frictions in today's correspondent banking system, such as differences in the opening hours of payment systems, varying communication standards, and a lack of transparency around exchange rates or fees. For instance, traditional cross-border transactions often involve multiple intermediaries, leading to high costs and delays. By leveraging CBDCs, these transactions can become faster and more cost-effective, reducing reliance on intermediaries and improving financial inclusion.

This is where the concept of a **multi-CBDC (mCBDC)** arises, and there are three design models:

- **Enhanced compatibility**: separate CBDCs in each jurisdiction, each with their own regulations and governance frameworks, but with compatible regulatory technical standards and a multitude of privately offered correspondent and clearing services. Ensuring that all participating jurisdictions adhere to compatible technical standards can be complex, especially when dealing with varying levels of technological advancement and regulatory maturity. Additionally, coordinating privately offered services across borders requires robust oversight to ensure consistency and reliability.
- **Interlinking**: separate CBDCs in each jurisdiction, each with their own regulations and governance frameworks, with shared common interfaces or common clearing mechanisms. Establishing shared interfaces and clearing mechanisms requires significant collaboration and trust between jurisdictions. Moreover, maintaining seamless interoperability whilst respecting each country's regulatory autonomy demands careful policy coordination and ongoing dialogue.
- **Single system integration**: separate CBDCs in each jurisdiction, but all run on a single platform with a single infrastructure and ledger (e.g. mCBDC bridge), a single regulatory and governance framework, and a single set of participants across jurisdictions. The primary challenge is achieving consensus on a unified rulebook that respects the regulatory frameworks of all participating jurisdictions. Building and maintaining a single platform with a common infrastructure requires substantial investment and cooperation. Additionally, ensuring data security and privacy across a shared system is critical to maintaining trust among users.

The exploration of CBDC interoperability models highlights the potential to revolutionise cross-border payments by addressing existing inefficiencies within the correspondent banking system. The three models – enhanced compatibility, interlinking, and single system integration – offer distinct approaches to achieving seamless currency convertibility and operational harmony across jurisdictions. Each model presents unique benefits and challenges, which will be examined in the following sections. These sections will delve deeper into the specifics of each model, analysing their regulatory frameworks, technical standards, and the implications for global financial systems.

Enhanced compatibility

Imagine a world where each country has its own unique CBDC, like different instruments in a jazz band, but they all follow the same music sheet. With the enhanced compatibility model, each CBDC dances to its own regulatory tune, yet they all groove together with compatible technical standards, making cross-border transactions as smooth as a jazz ensemble.

> The four main characteristics of the enhanced compatibility model: multiple CBDCs on separate platforms, separate regulatory frameworks, compatible technical standards, and privately offered services compatible with the standards.

Figure 7.15 illustrates this.

Figure 7.15 mCBDC enhanced compatibility model. © 2024 Neira Jones.

Here are the main characteristics of this model:

- **Regulatory frameworks**: the Bank for International Settlements (BIS) has been working on harmonising regulatory frameworks to facilitate interoperability between CBDCs. This involves aligning AML and combating the financing of terrorism (CFT) regulations across jurisdictions.

- **Technical standards**: in the enhanced compatibility model, CBDC systems operate independently but adhere to common technical standards to facilitate interoperability. These standards include message formats, cryptographic techniques, and user interfaces, which help reduce the operational burden of participating in multiple systems.[74] For example, the ISO 20022 messaging standard is widely adopted to harmonise cross-border payments and improve communication between stakeholders.[75] This model emphasises the importance of aligning legal, regulatory, and supervisory standards to simplify processes such as KYC and transaction monitoring.[76]
- **Examples include**:
  - The **Universal Digital Payments Network (UDPN)**[77] is an example of a decentralised approach to interoperability, which aims to create a common messaging backbone for cross-border digital currency transactions.
  - **The Jasper-Ubin project**[78] between the Bank of Canada (CAD on Corda) and the Monetary Authority of Singapore (SGD on Quorum) used blockchain technology to test cross-border and cross-currency payments, enhancing clearing efficiency. This project is an example of enhanced compatibility, focusing on cross-border payment trials using blockchain technology.
  - **Project Aber**[79]: a collaboration between the central banks of Saudi Arabia and the United Arab Emirates, Project Aber tested the use of a single dual-issued digital currency as a unit of settlement between commercial banks in the two countries. This project focused on compatible technical standards whilst maintaining separate regulatory frameworks.
  - **Project Stella**[80]: a joint research project by the European Central Bank and the Bank of Japan, Project Stella explored the use of DLT to improve cross-border payment efficiency. It focused on ensuring compatibility between different CBDC systems whilst allowing for separate governance structures.

In the world of enhanced compatibility, CBDCs are like a global orchestra with each country playing its own instrument, yet all harmonising to create a symphony of seamless transactions.

Interlinking

Picture a network of bridges connecting islands of CBDCs, allowing them to exchange goods and ideas effortlessly. In this model, each CBDC island has its own customs and rules, but they all share common bridges (interfaces) that make cross-border payments as easy as a walk in the park.

> The four main characteristics of the interlinking model: multiple CBDCs on separate platforms, separate regulatory frameworks with policy coordination, compatible technical standards, and shared mechanisms (e.g. technical interfaces, clearing services).

Figure 7.16 illustrates this.

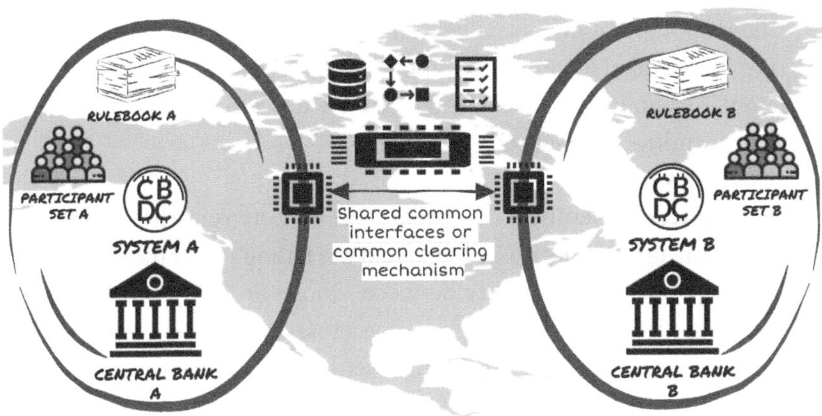

Figure 7.16 mCBDC interlinking model. © 2024 Neira Jones.

Here are the main characteristics of this model:

- **Regulatory frameworks**: the interlinking model encourages countries to adopt consistent and supportive regulations that facilitate cross-border transactions. This involves aligning certain regulatory aspects, such as AML and CFT requirements, to ensure seamless interoperability between systems. Each participating jurisdiction retains its regulatory autonomy, meaning that each country continues to regulate its CBDC according to its national laws and policies. Whilst countries maintain control over their monetary policy and financial stability there is a need for policy coordination to address cross-border regulatory challenges. This may involve establishing agreements on data sharing, privacy, and consumer protection to facilitate cross-border transactions without compromising national regulations whilst participating in the interlinking network. This collaborative governance model between central banks and regulatory authorities ensures that the system operates smoothly and efficiently. This includes setting guidelines for participation, managing access to the network, and addressing any regulatory issues that arise during cross-border transactions.

- **Technical standards**: The interlinking model requires CBDC systems to establish common technical interfaces and standards that enable information exchange and payments across different systems. This setup often involves using APIs and standardised messaging formats, such as ISO 20022, to facilitate communication between systems. Additionally, interlinking may involve a central clearing agent or a common clearing mechanism to simplify settlement between systems. An example is SWIFT's "hub and spoke" model, which acts as a clearing mechanism to streamline cross-border transactions.[81]
- **Examples include**:
  - **Project Ensemble**[82]: a collaboration between the Hong Kong Monetary Authority (HKMA) and the Banque de France designed to explore interoperability between wholesale CBDC infrastructures. The project focuses on real-time cross-border and cross-currency payments, aiming to optimise settlement efficiency and facilitate interoperability between financial market infrastructures in different jurisdictions.
  - **Project Jura**[83]: a collaboration between the Banque de France, the Swiss National Bank, and the BIS Innovation Hub, Project Jura tested the settlement of tokenised assets in wholesale CBDCs, demonstrating interoperability between different CBDC systems through shared technical interfaces.
  - **Project Mariana**[84]: led by the BIS Innovation Hub and the central banks of France, Singapore, and Switzerland, this project tested the cross-border trading and settlement of wholesale CBDCs using decentralised finance (DeFi) technologies. By using automated

market makers (see Chapter 6, Box 6.4) on a public blockchain, the project aimed to enhance interoperability between different CBDC systems.

- **Project Prosperus**[85]: an initiative focused on enhancing cross-border payments using CBDCs. The project involves a consortium including Banque de France, Banque Centrale de Tunisie, Bank Wormser Frères, BIAT, and BIAT France and aimed to demonstrate the potential of CBDCs for real-time remittance transfers between France and Tunisia. By leveraging DLT, Project Prosperus sought to improve the efficiency and security of cross-border transactions, facilitating seamless transfers between different financial systems and enhancing financial inclusion.
- **Project Nexus**: although not exclusively a CBDC project, Project Nexus by the BIS Innovation Hub aims to connect national payment systems to facilitate cross-border payments, aligning with the interlinking model's focus on shared interfaces and clearing mechanisms.

Interlinking is like a friendly neighbourhood of CBDCs, where everyone has their own house but shares the same roads and bridges. It's all about connecting the dots and simplifying cross-border payments.

Single system integration

Welcome to the CBDC superhighway, where all the lanes lead to a single, unified destination! In the single system integration model, every CBDC hops onto the same platform, sharing infrastructure, rules, and participants. It's like a global party where everyone speaks the same language and dances to the same beat.

> The four main characteristics of the single system integration model: multiple CBDCs on a single platform, separate regulatory frameworks with a unified rule book, shared technical standards, and shared mechanisms (e.g. technical interfaces, clearing services).

Figure 7.17 illustrates this.

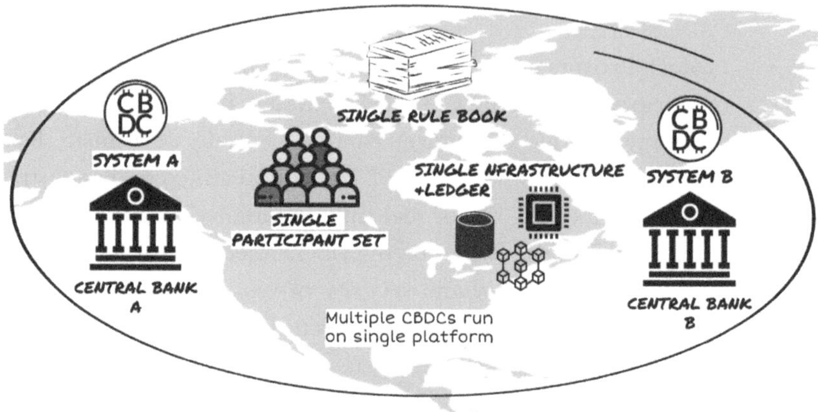

Figure 7.17 mCBDC single system integration model. © 2024 Neira Jones.

Here are the main characteristics of this model:

- **Regulatory frameworks**: whilst each country retains its regulatory framework, a unified rulebook seeks to align key legal and regulatory aspects to minimise friction. This might involve mutual recognition of regulatory standards or agreements on specific compliance measures (e.g. AML, CFT) necessary for participating in the platform and facilitating cross-border transactions. This unified rulebook serves as a collaborative agreement that outlines common standards and protocols, ensuring seamless interaction on the shared platform whilst allowing each jurisdiction to maintain its regulatory autonomy. The governance structure of the platform is designed to include representation from all participating jurisdictions, ensuring that decisions reflect the interests and regulatory requirements of each country, and helps maintain the integrity and legitimacy of the system. Building and maintaining a single platform with a common infrastructure requires substantial investment and cooperation. Additionally, ensuring data security and privacy across a shared system is critical to maintaining trust among users.
- **Technical standards**: in the single system integration model, multiple CBDCs operate on a single platform with standardised protocols and unified regulations. This model ensures consistency and reliability

in transactions across jurisdictions by using a single set of technical standards. Projects like the mCBDC Bridge and Project Dunbar exemplify this approach, where multiple countries collaborate to use a shared platform for their CBDCs, promoting uniformity and integration. This model allows for centralised clearing and settlement services, reducing complexity and enhancing efficiency by eliminating the need for multiple intermediaries, and also eliminates mismatches in communication standards and ensures seamless interoperability across the system.

- **Examples include**:
  - **mCBDC Bridge project**[86]: a prime example of single system integration involving the BIS Innovation Hub and the Bank of Thailand, the Central Bank of the United Arab Emirates, the Digital Currency Institute of the People's Bank of China, the Hong Kong Monetary Authority, and the Saudi Central Bank, aims to create a shared platform for cross-border CBDC transactions This project involves multiple CBDCs and is built on permissioned DLT, allowing for real-time, peer-to-peer cross-border payments and foreign exchange transactions. At the time of writing, the BIS decided to exit the mBridge project.[87]
  - **Project Dunbar**[88]: developed by the BIS Innovation Hub with the central banks of Australia, Malaysia, Singapore, and South Africa, this project created a shared platform for international settlements using multiple CBDCs.

In the single system integration universe, CBDCs come together on a grand stage, sharing the spotlight and making cross-border payments as synchronised as a well-rehearsed dance routine. Can this become a global celebration of unity and efficiency? All I can say is that all participating countries need to be really friendly to consider this model…

In any instance, the scarcity of examples in the single system integration interoperability model may suggest that it's damn hard!

One can't help but consider the BRICS nations (Brazil, Russia, India, China, and South Africa) and their exploration of ways to reduce their reliance on the US dollar due to geopolitical tensions and economic sanctions. This has led to discussions around the development of a shared digital currency or enhancing interoperability between their national currencies using CBDCs. The BRICS countries are motivated by a desire to increase their economic sovereignty and reduce the influence of US monetary policy on their economies. This is particularly relevant for countries like Russia, which face significant economic sanctions. **De-dollarisation** efforts aim to create alternative financial systems that bypass traditional US-centric infrastructures like SWIFT, thus reducing the impact of US sanctions. The use of CBDCs could present an opportunity for BRICS countries to facilitate cross-border transactions without relying on the US dollar as an intermediary currency. This can be achieved by developing interoperable CBDC systems that allow direct currency exchanges between member states. Whilst the mCBDC Bridge project itself isn't exclusively a BRICS initiative, it includes China, a key BRICS member, and could serve as a proof-of-concept for a multilateral CBDC system that BRICS countries hope to develop to counter US influence in global finance. Experts suggest that whilst creating a common BRICS currency might be challenging due to economic and political disparities among member countries, launching individual CBDCs and working towards interoperability is a more feasible approach.[89]

Special interoperability cases

THE DIGITAL EURO

Talking about friendliness, the digital euro presents a unique case in the context of CBDC interoperability, given that it is a single digital currency shared across multiple jurisdictions within the Eurozone. This situation provides an interesting use case for interoperability, as it involves harmonising across countries that already share the same currency and regulatory framework under the European Union. This doesn't fit neatly in any of the commonly accepted interoperability models.

> The four main characteristics of the digital euro model: one CBDC on a single platform, shared regulations, shared technical standards, and shared mechanisms (e.g. technical interfaces, clearing services).

The digital euro can be seen as a single-system integration model within the Eurozone, where a unified platform supports a single currency across multiple jurisdictions. This model benefits from the shared regulatory framework and existing payment infrastructure.

For transactions involving non-Eurozone countries, the digital euro might use interlinking models to ensure interoperability with other CBDCs. This would involve establishing shared interfaces and clearing mechanisms to facilitate cross-border payments.

The digital euro is expected to integrate with existing payment infrastructures such as TARGET2, the Eurosystem's RTGS. This integration will facilitate seamless transactions across the Eurozone by leveraging established payment rails. Whilst SWIFT is traditionally used for international payments, its infrastructure and standards could support the digital euro in facilitating cross-border transactions beyond the Eurozone, especially if interoperability with other CBDCs is pursued.

The implications and opportunities are two-fold:

- **Pan-European payments**: the digital euro aims to enhance pan-European payment solutions, promoting efficiency and innovation in retail payments. It serves as a public good that supports financial inclusion and accessibility across the Eurozone.
- **International role**: by providing a digital form of central bank money, the digital euro could strengthen the international role of the euro, supporting the EU's strategic autonomy in global finance.

In summary, the digital euro represents a significant step towards a unified digital payment system within the Eurozone, leveraging existing infrastructure and regulations to facilitate seamless interoperability. Its development highlights the potential for CBDCs to enhance cross-border payments and financial integration in a region with shared economic and regulatory frameworks.

As an aside, Project Helvetia,[90] conducted by the Swiss National Bank, the BIS Innovation Hub, and SIX Group, was primarily concerned with integrating a wholesale CBDC into Switzerland's existing financial market infrastructure. It explored the integration of tokenised assets and central bank money through a wholesale CBDC on a single platform, aligning with the single system integration model's use of a unified platform. But whilst Project Helvetia and the digital euro both explore CBDC integration, the digital euro represents a more unified approach across multiple jurisdictions, benefiting from shared currency and regulatory frameworks. Project Helvetia, meanwhile, focuses on national integration within Switzerland's financial system. I include it here for completeness.

THE REGULATED LIABILITY NETWORK (RLN)

Another special case, the Regulated Liability Network (RLN)[91] is a new concept in financial infrastructure that leverages DLT to facilitate the real-time, programmable settlement of financial transactions. It aims to integrate various forms of regulated money into a shared ledger. This integration aims to enhance the efficiency, security, and interoperability of financial transactions across different jurisdictions and institutions.

I agonised over the placement of the RLN in this chapter. Whilst the definition clearly specifies that it is aimed at "interoperability of financial transactions across different jurisdictions and institutions", all implementations at the time of writing are for a single currency. So I could have placed it earlier under *Hybrid infrastructure* when I talked about integration with existing payment systems (as is the purpose of the RLN pilots in the UK and Brazil). However, the US pilot of the RLN, whilst for a single currency (the dollar), is across many jurisdictions and focused not only on domestic interbank payments but also cross-border payments in USD. In the end, interoperability won, and it remains in this section. At least you understand my reasoning...

Key features of the RLN include:

- **Interoperability**: the RLN is designed to enable seamless transactions between different financial institutions and jurisdictions. Using a shared ledger, it allows for the integration of central bank money, commercial bank money, and CBDCs, creating a unified platform for financial settlements.
- **Real-time settlement**: the network aims to support instant settlement of transactions, operating 24/7, potentially reducing delays and improving liquidity management.
- **Programmability**: RLN transactions can be programmed to automate complex financial processes and compliance checks, aiming to offer a new level of convenience and efficiency.

- **Security and compliance**: the network incorporates advanced security measures and complies with existing financial regulations, ensuring safe and reliable transactions.

The RLN has seen some pilot deployments, including:

- **United States**: a proof of concept (PoC) was conducted to explore the RLN's feasibility for settling liabilities through a shared ledger.[92] This initiative involved major financial institutions such as BNY Mellon, Citi, HSBC, Mastercard, and others. The PoC focused on domestic interbank payments and cross-border payments in USD, demonstrating the potential of RLN to improve wholesale payment processing by enabling near-real-time settlement and enhancing interoperability across the financial ecosystem.
- **Brazil** is exploring the RLN architecture to support the settlement of tokenised assets and liabilities using tokenised deposits and the Real Digital, a wholesale CBDC.[93] This initiative includes advanced security features and aims to ensure interoperability with existing payment systems like PIX, Brazil's faster payment system. The Brazilian RLN proposal is part of a broader effort to modernise the country's financial infrastructure and integrate new technologies into its regulatory framework.
- **United Kingdom**[94]: the UK has undertaken a discovery phase to investigate the RLN's potential use cases and feasibility. This phase involved collaboration between UK Finance, EY, and various financial institutions. The focus was on identifying hypotheses for future experimentation, understanding business implications, and examining regulatory and legal considerations. The UK RLN aims to enhance domestic payments, cross-border payments, and securities settlement. The experimentation phase is expected to build on these findings and further explore the RLN's capabilities.

As another interoperability initiative in global financial systems, the RLN is seen as a potential global solution for financial settlement, addressing inefficiencies in traditional systems, and enabling a more inclusive and compliant financial ecosystem. It supports multiple currencies and asset types, which could significantly enhance cross-border payment efficiency and financial market integration. It could represent a step forward in leveraging blockchain technology to create a more efficient, secure, and interoperable global financial system.

Recap on CBDC interoperability models

In the rapidly evolving landscape of CBDCs, projects come and go (see Figure 7.5), but the interoperability of wholesale CBDCs could be a pivotal innovation with the potential to revolutionise cross-border payments. Understanding the various interoperability models is crucial for stakeholders aiming to harness the full potential of CBDCs. Each model has its distinct advantages and challenges.

Professionals should remember the following:

- **Technology impact**: Since CBDCs rely heavily on technology, it's essential to assess the current technological infrastructure and capabilities within a jurisdiction to determine the feasibility of various interoperability models, or if it is indeed realistic to even start a project at all. Factors such as existing payment systems, regulatory frameworks, network and telecoms infrastructure, and technological advancements all play a part. In addition, planning for scalability is also crucial for ensuring long-term viability, though it requires upfront investment and strategic planning.
- **Security and privacy**: this is a common feature of all settlement infrastructures, whichever form they take. Robust security measures, the development of advanced security protocols, and privacy protections should be prioritised whilst being mindful of the trade-off between security and user convenience and trust. This is especially critical when integrating CBDCs across multiple jurisdictions with varying regulatory standards.
- **Flexibility vs. standardisation**: each interoperability model has its own benefits and challenges. Enhanced compatibility allows jurisdictions to maintain their regulatory frameworks whilst adopting compatible technical standards, offering flexibility but potentially leading to inefficiencies due to the lack of a unified system. Interlinking improves interoperability through shared interfaces or clearing mechanisms,

fostering collaboration and trust, but requires significant policy coordination and investment, posing challenges in maintaining regulatory autonomy. Single system integration provides the most seamless interoperability with a unified platform, reducing transaction costs and times, yet demands high initial investment and consensus on a unified regulatory framework. Understanding these dynamics is key to navigating the complexities of CBDC implementation and maximising their potential benefits.

- **Innovation, regulations, and standards**: innovation should always be encouraged in the financial sector, but regulatory frameworks must be in place to manage risks. This balance can foster technological advancement whilst safeguarding financial stability and consumer protection. In addition, establishing or promoting common technical standards can enhance interoperability between different CBDCs, but this requires significant global collaboration, which in turn warrants recognising that trade-offs exist between achieving global coherence and respecting national regulatory autonomy.
- **Economic considerations**: the introduction of a CBDC can significantly impact monetary policy and financial stability, which are crucial for effective interoperability. A thorough economic analysis is necessary to understand these effects, as they influence the seamless integration of CBDCs across borders. By weighing the potential for economic growth against the risks of market disruption, stakeholders can ensure that CBDCs enhance financial systems without unintended consequences, thereby supporting stable and efficient cross-border transactions.
- **Cooperation is key**: this is about interoperability, which means engaging with a diverse range of stakeholders, including financial institutions and technology providers, in the CBDC development process to enhance the design and implementation of interoperable systems.
- **Observe and evolve**: continuously monitoring the development and impact of CBDCs, adapting strategies as new challenges and opportunities arise will help maintain a dynamic balance between innovation and regulation in the context of interoperability.

As we navigate the potentially promising yet complex landscape of CBDCs, understanding and implementing effective interoperability models is crucial for revolutionising cross-border payments. The enhanced compatibility, interlinking, and single-system integration models each offer distinct pathways to achieving seamless currency convertibility and operational harmony across jurisdictions. By carefully weighing the benefits and challenges of each model, stakeholders can make informed decisions that not only enhance efficiency but also uphold security and regulatory standards. As CBDCs continue to evolve, fostering international collaboration and innovation will be key to unlocking their full potential, ultimately paving the way for a more integrated and resilient global financial system.

Where could CBDCs help? (bridge over troubled water)

CBDCs have the potential to address several challenges in the current financial system whilst also presenting new opportunities for innovation. However, like any significant financial innovation, they come with their own set of challenges and criticisms.

One of the primary areas where CBDCs could make an impact is in **enhancing financial inclusion**. In many parts of the world, a significant portion of the population remains unbanked or underbanked. CBDCs could provide these individuals with easier access to digital financial services, potentially reducing reliance on cash and informal financial systems. The International Monetary Fund (IMF) has several publications.[95,96,97] This increased access could lead to greater economic participation and growth in underserved communities.

CBDCs also have the potential to **improve the efficiency and speed** of both domestic and cross-border payments. By leveraging digital technology, CBDCs could facilitate near-instantaneous transactions, reducing the time and cost associated with traditional payment methods. This could be particularly beneficial for remittances, which are often subject to high fees and long processing times.

Another area where CBDCs could prove valuable is in **combating financial crimes**. The digital nature of CBDCs allows for enhanced traceability of transactions, potentially making it easier for authorities to detect and prevent money laundering, tax evasion, and other illicit activities. But whilst the traceability of CBDCs could help combat financial crimes, it also raises questions about individual privacy and the potential for government overreach and surveillance.[98] Striking the right balance between privacy and regulatory oversight remains a key challenge in CBDC design.[99]

CBDCs could also provide central banks with new tools for implementing monetary policy. In times of economic crisis, for example, CBDCs could allow for the direct distribution of stimulus payments to citizens, potentially increasing the effectiveness of such measures.[100]

However, CBDCs are not without their critics and challenges. One of the primary concerns is the potential impact on the traditional banking system. If individuals can hold digital currency directly with the central bank, it could lead to a **reduction in bank deposits**, potentially affecting banks' ability to lend and their overall stability.[101]

There are also **technical challenges** to consider. Ensuring the security and resilience of CBDC systems against cyberattacks is crucial, as any breach could have severe consequences for the financial system and public trust.[102]

The **political landscape** surrounding CBDCs is equally complex. In the United States, for example, some political figures have taken strong stances against CBDCs. Former President Donald Trump has vowed to "never allow" the Federal Reserve to develop a CBDC if elected, citing concerns about government control over personal finances.[103] This political opposition highlights the contentious nature of CBDCs and the need for careful consideration of their implementation.

Advocates of CBDCs argue that these digital currencies could modernise the financial system, making it more efficient, inclusive, and resilient. They point to the potential for reduced transaction costs, improved monetary policy transmission, and enhanced financial stability.[104]

Critics, on the other hand, warn of the risks of centralised control over the monetary system and the potential for CBDCs to be used as tools for **surveillance and social control**. They argue that the benefits of CBDCs could be achieved through improvements to existing payment systems without the need for a new form of currency.[105]

In conclusion, CBDCs present both opportunities and challenges for the future of money and finance. Whilst they have the potential to address several shortcomings in the current financial system, their implementation requires careful consideration of technical, economic, and social factors. As the debate continues, it's clear that the development of CBDCs will play a role in shaping the future of global finance, if only through the benefits of research, discussions, and cooperation.

Central bank digital currencies (CBDCs) – conclusion (what next?)

In this whistle-stop tour of digital and CBDCs, we covered:

- The main characteristics of CBDCs
- The differences between retail and wholesale CBDCs
- Stablecoins versus CBDCs
- Design choices available to central banks in terms of architecture, infrastructure, access and interoperability
- Worldwide CBDC deployments, both launched and in pilot stage

I have tried to explain the jargon and debunk a few myths, and you'll find the key terms in the glossary for future reference. I have given you my opinion on some aspects of the mechanics and characteristics of the various CBDC aspects. In the absence of universally approved classification (although there are plenty of excellent reports and publications which I include as references), I offered categorisation frameworks, and I hope it goes some way towards clearing out misconceptions and misunderstandings. I hope these were helpful.

Throughout this book, I found it particularly helpful (if only to consolidate my own understanding 😉) to explain concepts and differences using comparative tables. I hope you have found these useful.

So here's one last table that puts CBDCs in the context of everything else I talked about in this book and my previous book (*Understanding Payments*).

If you read this book a few years from now, who knows how the CBDC landscape will have evolved? More research will be conducted, and improvements will be deployed (e.g. secure multi-party computation). New services will be developed on decentralised infrastructures, and these in turn will establish more links with other ecosystems, making the economic principles, mechanics, and governance even more confusing. Decentralised identity systems might even come of age. Ecosystem actors may benefit from some advancements, and not from others.

In any instance, it won't be boring, and I will watch how this develops with interest, as I'm sure you will.

As Table 7.6 was the last one in this book, I felt compelled to add one last figure, expanding on Chapter 6, Table 6.7…

Table 7.6 Virtual assets vs. traditional payments. © 2024 Neira Jones

Feature	Cash	Retail CBDC	Real-Time Payments	e-Money (Incl. Cards)	Stablecoin	Cryptocurrency
Safety as a settlement asset	Central bank liability	Central bank and intermediary liability (e.g. commercial bank, PSP)	Commercial bank or PSP liability	Issuer, or merchant or PSP liability	No (but more stable than cryptocurrency)	No
Finality of payment	Immediate on receipt	Immediate on verification	Immediate on authentication	Immediate on authorisation	After validation	After validation
Finality of underlying payment	No interbank settlement required	Central bank settlement	Deferred settlement or RTGS	Interbank, merchant settlement	DLT settlement	DLT settlement
Speed of settlement	Fast	Potentially fast	Depends on payment scheme	Depends on contract	Depends on DLT	Depends on DLT
Cost for users	None	Depends on central bank policy	Low, but depends on payment scheme	Low, but depends on product	Depends on DLT	Depends on DLT
Cost for merchants and businesses	Relatively low (cost of cash handling)	Low, but depends on design choices	Low, but depends on commercial bank or PSP	Medium to high, depends on service	Depends on DLT	Depends on DLT

(Continued)

Table 7.6 (Continued)

Feature	**Cash**	**Retail CBDC**	**Real-Time Payments**	**e-Money (Incl. Cards)**	**Stablecoin**	**Cryptocurrency**
Identification for access	No (some jurisdictions may require identification on high-value payments)	Design choice (account-based or token-based)	Yes	Yes	No	No
User anonymity	Yes	Design choice (account-based or token-based)	No	No	Can be achieved	Can be achieved
Offline payments	Yes	Design choice (account-based or token-based)	No	No	No	No
Cross-border use	Yes (physical transport)	Depends on design choices	Depends on payment scheme	Yes	Yes	Yes
New digital functions (e.g. programmability)	No	Yes	Yes	Yes	Yes	Yes
Transaction speed	Fast	Depends on design choices	Fast	Fast	Can be slow	Can be slow

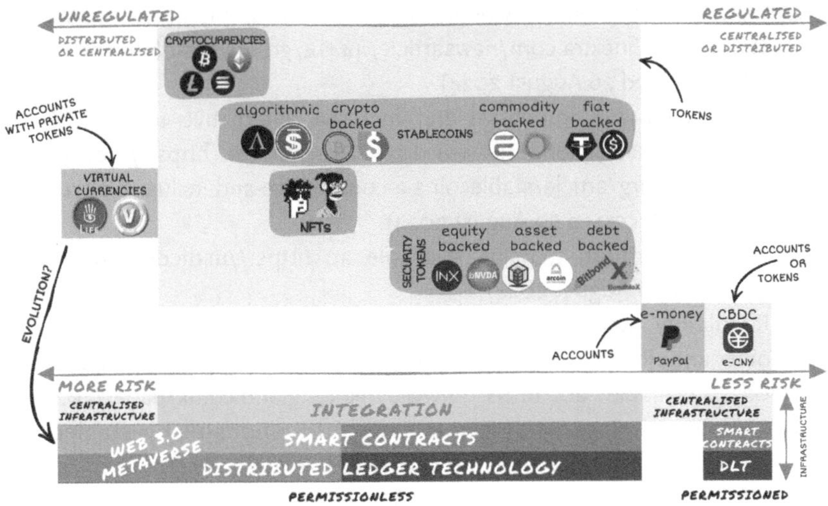

Figure 7.18 Recap on virtual assets, Part 2. © 2024 Neira Jones.

Figure 7.18 shows us that the payments world is not as clear cut as it appears on the surface, but you already knew that 😉. Not everything distributed will be risky or unregulated, and conversely, not everything centralised will be regulated or less risky. It all depends on context, and ultimately, it keeps policymakers in jobs. It will be interesting to see potential futures, such as traditional gaming and virtual currencies evolving into Web 3.0 and metaverse environments, but that's a story for another time.

And this concludes our tour of decentralised systems and how they apply to payments and inevitably intermingle with centralised financial systems. I hope you enjoyed this trip as much as I enjoyed being your guide!

Notes

1 "CBDC and the Operational Framework of Monetary Policy" BIS, 27 September 2023. Available at: https://www.bis.org/publ/work1126.htm (Accessed 6 August 2024).
2 Bjerg, O. (2017). *Designing New Money: The Policy Trilemma of Central Bank Digital Currency*. Copenhagen: Copenhagen Business School.
3 "Central Bank Digital Currencies: Putting a Big Idea into Practice" Bank for International Settlements, 31 March 2021. Available at: https://www.bis.org/speeches/sp210331.pdf (Accessed 19 August 2024).

4 "G+D Unveils Offline Payments Tech" *Finextra*, 4 July 2024. Available at: https://www.finextra.com/newsarticle/44414/gd-unveils-offline-payments-tech (Accessed 26 August 2024).
5 "Stablecoins: A Competitive and Inclusive Alternative to CBDCs" The payments Association, 19 April 2023. Available at: https://thepaymentsassociation.org/article/stablecoins-a-competitive-and-inclusive-alternative-to-cbdcs/ (Accessed 29 August 2024).
6 USDF consortium website. Available at: https://usdfconsortium.com/ (Accessed 26 August 2024).
7 "Regulatory Regime for Systemic Payment Systems Using Stablecoins and Related Service Providers" Bank of England, 6 November 2023. Available at: https://www.bankofengland.co.uk/paper/2023/dp/regulatory-regime-for-systemic-payment-systems-using-stablecoins-and-related-service-providers (Accessed 22 August 2024).
8 "Stablecoins' Role in Crypto and Beyond: Functions, Risks and Policy" European Central Bank website. Available at: https://www.ecb.europa.eu/press/financial-stability-publications/macroprudential-bulletin/html/ecb.mpbu202207_2~836f682ed7.en.html (Accessed 22 August 2024).
9 "Central Bank Digital Currencies: A Solution in Search of a Problem?" UK Parliament, 17 January 2022. Available at: https://publications.parliament.uk/pa/ld5802/ldselect/ldeconaf/131/13102.htm (Accessed 6 January 2024).
10 "Bank of England Begins Building Britcoin Team" *Finextra*, 11 April 2023. Available at: https://www.finextra.com/newsarticle/42117/bank-of-england-begins-building-britcoin-team (Accessed 6 August 2024).
11 "Response to the Bank of England and HM Treasury Consultation Paper – The Digital Pound: A New Form of Money for Households and Businesses?" Bank of England, 25 January 2024. Available at: https://www.bankofengland.co.uk/paper/2024/responses-to-the-digital-pound-consultation-paper (Accessed 6 August 2024).
12 "A Bank of Israel Digital Shekel" Bank of Israel, May 2021. Available at: https://www.boi.org.il/media/pscnnurd/2021-5-a-bank-of-israel-digital-shekel.pdf (Accessed 6 August 2024).
13 "Bank of Israel Remains Uncertain about Potential CBDC" Pymnts, 11 July 2024. Available at: https://www.pymnts.com/cbdc/2024/bank-israel-remains-uncertain-about-potential-cbdc/ (Accessed 6 August 2024).
14 "Donald Trump Vows to 'Never Allow' Central Bank Digital Currencies If Elected" *CoinDesk*, 18 January 2024. Available at: https://www.coindesk.com/policy/2024/01/18/donald-trump-promises-to-never-allow-central-bank-digital-currencies-cbdc-if-elected/ (Accessed 6 August 2024).

15 Collect Trump Cards website. Available at: https://collecttrumpcards.com/ (Accessed 25 September 2024).

16 "Trump proposes strategic national crypto stockpile: "Never sell your bitcoin" CNBC, 27 July 2024. Available at: https://www.cnbc.com/2024/07/27/trump-bitcoin-conference-harris.html (Accessed 25 September 2024).

17 "Central Bank Digital Currencies (CBDC)" Federal Reserve website, Board of Governors of the Federal Reserve System. Available at: https://www.federalreserve.gov/central-bank-digital-currency.htm (Accessed 6 August 2024).

18 "What's the state of China's digital yuan in 2023?" SCMP, 10 October 2023. Available at: https://www.scmp.com/economy/china-economy/article/3237317/whats-state-chinas-digital-yuan-2023 (Accessed 30 November 2024).

19 "China's Digital Yuan App Drops 'Pilot' Label, But No Announcement" *Ledger Insights*, 3 June 2024. Available at: https://www.ledgerinsights.com/chinas-digital-yuan-app-drops-pilot-label-but-no-announcement/ (Accessed 31 August 2024).

20 "Alipay Statistics 2023 – Market Share, Facts and Marketing Trends" EnterpriseAppsToday, 10 October 2023. Available at: https://www.enterpriseappstoday.com/stats/alipay-statistics.html (Accessed 6 August 2024).

21 "China's Digital Yuan Works Just Like Cash—With Added Surveillance" *Wired*, 8 November 2022. Available at: https://www.wired.com/story/chinas-digital-yuan-ecny-works-just-like-cash-surveillance/ (Accessed 6 August 2024).

22 European Central Bank website, Digital Euro. Available at: https://www.ecb.europa.eu/euro/digital_euro/html/index.en.html (Accessed 19 August 2024).

23 "Central Bank Digital Currency Tracker" Atlantic Council website. Available at: https://www.atlanticcouncil.org/cbdctracker/ (Accessed 6 August 2024).

24 "A Primer on BOJ's Central Bank Digital Currency" Bank of Jamaica, 31 March 2020. Available at: https://boj.org.jm/a-primer-on-bojs-central-bank-digital-currency/ (Accessed 21 August 2024).

25 ecurrency website. Available at: https://www.ecurrency.net/ (Accessed 21 August 2024).

26 "Jamaica's Central Bank Digital Currency (CBDC) – JAM-DEX" Bank of Jamaica, website. Available at: https://boj.org.jm/core-functions/currency/cbdc/ (Accessed 21 August 2024).

27 Lynk website. FAQs, CBDC. Available at: https://www.lynk.us/support?type=CBDC (Accessed 21 August 2024).

28 "Sole Jamaican CBDC Wallet Provider Questions JAM-DEX Progress" *Ledger Insights*, 14 August 2024. Available at: https://www.ledgerinsights.com/sole-jamaican-cbdc-wallet-provider-questions-jam-dex-progress/ (Accessed 21 August 2024).

29 "JN Bank Limited Onboarded as New Wallet Provider for JAM-DEX" Bank of Jamaica, 30 December 2022. Available at: https://boj.org.jm/jn-bank-limited-onboarded-as-new-wallet-provider-for-jam-dex/ (Accessed 21 August 2024).

30 "JN Bank Touts Digital Payments as it Finalises Digital Wallet" JN Bank, 27 February 2023. Available at: https://www.jnbank.com/jn-bank-touts-digital-payments-as-it-finalises-digital-wallet/ (Accessed 21 August 2024).

31 "China's Digital Currency: The Hopes and Fears of the e-CNY" China Research Center, 2023. Available at: https://www.chinacenter.net/2023/china-currents/22-1/chinas-digital-currency-the-hopes-and-fears-of-the-e-cny/ (Accessed 24 August 2024).

32 "How Finance Sector Treasurers Can Get Ready for CBDCs and Stablecoins" McKinsey & Company, 15 December 2022. Available at: https://www.mckinsey.com/capabilities/risk-and-resilience/our-insights/how-finance-sector-treasurers-can-get-ready-for-cbdcs-and-stablecoins (Accessed 22 August 2024).

33 "Summary of the Workshop on Technology for Retail Central Bank Digital Currency (CBDC)" BIS Innovation Hub, 25 May 2023. Available at: https://www.bis.org/innovation_hub/network/202305-cbdc-workshop.pdf (Accessed 22 August 2024).

34 "Decoding Retail CBDCs: Are Central Bank Digital Currencies Hype or Hope?" Edgar Dunn & Company, 1 August 2024. Available at: https://www.edgardunn.com/articles/decoding-retail-cbdcs-are-central-bank-digital-currencies-hype-or-hope (Accessed 22 August 2024).

35 "2024 Informal Economy Report" Moniepoint, 2024. Available at: https://informalreport.moniepoint.com/ (Accessed 24 August 2024).

36 Bitt website. Available at: https://www.bitt.com/ (Accessed 24 August 2024).

37 eNaira Speed Wallet website. Available at: https://enaira.gov.ng/speed-wallet-app/ (Accessed 24 August 2024).

38 "Nigeria Faces Shortages in Transition to New Paper Bills" Pymnts, 3 February 2023. Available at: https://www.pymnts.com/news/international/2023/nigeria-faces-shortages-in-transition-to-new-paper-bills/ (Accessed 24 August 2024).

39 "Tinubu to Review Buhari's Naira Redesign Policy Says Implementation Was Too Harsh" *The Guardian*, 29 May 2023. Available at: https://guardian.ng/news/tinubu-to-review-buharis-naira-redesign-policy-says-implementation-was-too-harsh/ (Accessed 24 August 2024).

40 "eNaira Adoption Remains Low, Representing Less Than 1% of Circulating Currency as of March 2024" *Fintech Magazine Africa*, July 2024. Available at: https://fintechmagazine.africa/2024/07/22/enaira-adoption-remains-low-representing-less-than-1-of-circulating-currency-as-of-march-2024/ (Accessed 24 August 2024).
41 "Report: Nigeria World's Topmost Cash Dominant Economy" *This Day*, July 2024. Available at: https://www.thisdaylive.com/index.php/2024/07/13/report-nigeria-worlds-topmost-cash-dominant-economy/ (Accessed 24 August 2024).
42 "Nigeria's Crypto Market Continues to Defy the Odds" *The Banker*, 13 October 2023. Available at: https://www.thebanker.com/Nigeria-s-crypto-market-continues-to-defy-the-odds-1697181653 (Accessed 24 August 2024).
43 "Why Did CBDC Fail in Nigeria? Valuable Lessons for Developing Countries" Modern Diplomacy, 22 October 2023. Available at: https://moderndiplomacy.eu/2023/10/22/why-did-cbdc-fail-in-nigeria-valuable-lessons-for-developing-countries/ (Accessed 24 August 2024).
44 "Project Sand Dollar: The Central Bank Identifies Preferred Technology Solutions Provider for Bahamas Digital Currency" Central Bank of The Bahamas, 1 March 2019. Available at: https://www.centralbankbahamas.com/news/press-releases/project-sand-dollar-the-central-bank-identifies-preferred-technology-solutions-provider-for-bahamas-digital-currency (Accessed 24 August 2024).
45 "Press Release: Public Update on The Bahamas Digital Currency—SandDollar" Central Bank of The Bahamas, 8 September 2023. Available at: https://www.centralbankbahamas.com/news/press-releases/press-release-public-update-on-the-bahamas-digital-currency-sanddollar-5 (Accessed 24 August 2024).
46 "The E-krona Pilot – Test of Technical Solution for the E-krona" Sveriges Riksbank website, 23 August 2023. Available at: https://www.riksbank.se/en-gb/payments--cash/e-krona/technical-solution-for-the-e-krona-pilot/ (Accessed 24 August 2024).
47 "E-krona Pilot Phase 4" Sveriges Riksbank website, 20 March 2024. Available at: https://www.riksbank.se/en-gb/payments--cash/e-krona/e-krona-reports/e-krona-pilot-phase-4/ (Accessed 24 August 2024).
48 "What Is Digital Rupee and How Does It Work" Bank of Baroda, 15 November 2023. Available at: https://www.bankofbaroda.in/banking-mantra/digital/articles/what-is-digital-rupee (Accessed 24 August 2024).
49 "Australian CBDC Pilot for Digital Finance Innovation" Reserve Bank of Australia, DFCRC, 2023. Available at: https://www.rba.gov.au/payments-and-infrastructure/central-bank-digital-currency/pdf/australian-cbdc-pilot-for-digital-finance-innovation-project-report.pdf (Accessed 31 August 2024).

50 "People's Bank of China Enables Offline Payments with Digital Yuan" Pymnts, 16 January 2023. Available at: https://www.pymnts.com/cbdc/2023/peoples-bank-of-china-enables-offline-payments-with-digital-yuan/ (Accessed 2 September 2024).

51 "ID.me Reaches a Major Milestone: 50 Million Users Have a Verified Identity Credential, Providing Rapid Access to Government Agencies, Healthcare Organizations, Banking and Consumer Brands via the ID.me Digital Wallet" *PR Newswire*, 30 January 2024. Available at: https://www.prnewswire.com/news-releases/idme-reaches-a-major-milestone-50-million-users-have-a-verified-identity-credential-providing-rapid-access-to-government-agencies-healthcare-organizations-banking-and-consumer-brands-via-the-idme-digital-wallet-302048074.html (Accessed 26 August 2024).

52 "Digital IDs from Lloyds and Yoti Accepted under PASS Scheme" *National Technology News*, 25 June 2024. Available at: https://nationaltechnology.co.uk/Digital_IDs_From_Lloyds_And_Yoti_Accepted_Under_PASS_Scheme.php (Accessed 26 August 2024).

53 Digital ID website. Available at: https://www.digitalid.com/ (Accessed 26 August 2024).

54 Aadhaar website, Unique Identification Authority of India. Available at: https://uidai.gov.in/en/ (Accessed 26 August 2026).

55 Singpass website. Available at: https://www.singpass.gov.sg/main (Accessed 26 August 2024).

56 Sovrin website. Available at: https://sovrin.org/ (Accessed 26 August 2024).

57 Civic website. Available at: https://www.civic.com/ (Accessed 26 August 2024).

58 Worldcoin website. Available at: https://worldcoin.org/ (Accessed 26 August 2024).

59 Trinsic website. Available at: https://trinsic.id/ (Accessed 26 August 2024).

60 "Self-Sovereign Decentralized Identity Is Key to Retail CBDC Adoption" *Forbes*, 7 August 2024. Available at: https://www.forbes.com/sites/alastairjohnson/2024/08/07/self-sovereign-decentralized-identity-is-key-to-retail-cbdc-adoption/ (Accessed 26 August 2024).

61 "Self-Sovereign Decentralized Identity Is Key to Retail CBDC Adoption" *Forbes*, 7 August 2024. Available at: https://www.forbes.com/sites/alastairjohnson/2024/08/07/self-sovereign-decentralized-identity-is-key-to-retail-cbdc-adoption/ (Accessed 26 August 2024).

62 "Decentralised Identity as an Enabler to Open Banking" techUK, 12 June 2024. Available at: https://www.techuk.org/resource/decentralised-identity-as-an-enabler-to-open-banking.html (Accessed 26 August 2024).
63 "Civic Announces Enhanced Identity Verification" *Civic*, 29 February 2024. Available at: https://www.civic.com/blog/civic-announces-enhanced-identity-verification/ (Accessed 26 August 2024).
64 "TradeTrust - Transform the Way You Trade" Singapore Government Developer Portal. Available at: https://www.developer.tech.gov.sg/products/categories/blockchain/tradetrust/overview.html (Accessed 26 August 2024).
65 Open ID website. Available at: https://openid.net/developers/how-connect-works/ (Accessed 26 August 2024).
66 Sam Altman's Wikipedia entry. Available at: https://en.wikipedia.org/wiki/Sam_Altman (Accessed 26 August 2024).
67 "The Web Needs a Way of Proving That You're a Real Person — Worldcoin Is Not the Solution" Forrester, 26 July 2023. Available at: https://www.forrester.com/blogs/the-web-needs-a-way-of-proving-that-youre-a-real-person-worldcoin-is-not-the-solution/ (Accessed 26 August 2024).
68 "Worldcoin Sets New Sign-Up Record in Argentina Despite Ongoing Investigation over Data Privacy" *Cryptonews*, 31 August 2023. Available at: https://cryptonews.com/news/worldcoin-sets-new-sign-up-record-in-argentina-despite-ongoing-investigation-over-data-privacy.htm (Accessed 26 August 2024).
69 "Worldcoin Foundation Unveils New SMPC System, Deletes Old Iris Codes" Worldcoin, 15 May 2024. Available at: https://worldcoin.org/blog/announcements/worldcoin-foundation-unveils-new-smpc-system-deletes-old-iris-codes (Accessed 26 August 2024).
70 "Worldcoin Beefs Up Security by Open-Sourcing Biometric Data System" *CoinTelegraph*, 15 May 2024. Available at: https://cointelegraph.com/news/worldcoin-beefs-up-security-open-sourcing-biometric-data (Accessed 26 August 2024).
71 "Biometric Honey. No More" David G. W. Birch, 16 August 2024. Available at: https://dgwbirch.substack.com/p/biometric-honey-no-more (Accessed 26 August 2024).
72 "Central Bank Digital Currencies" BIS, March 2018. Available at: https://www.bis.org/cpmi/publ/d174.pdf (Accessed 28 August 2024).
73 "Identity: A Key Bottleneck to Mass DLT Adoption" Kaspar Triebstok, 29 April 2023. Available at: https://redcurry.co/identity-a-key-bottleneck-to-mass-dlt-adoption/ (Accessed 29 August 2024).

74 "Cross-Border Interoperability of Central Bank Digital Currency" Deutsche Bundesbank, July 2022. Available at: https://www.bundesbank.de/resource/blob/895590/773444b7b7237c2cf436fefb586af46d/mL/2022-07-dzbg-data.pdf (Accessed 27 August 2024).

75 "Central Bank Digital Currencies for Cross-Border Payments" BIS, July 2021. Available at: https://www.bis.org/publ/bppdf/bispap115.pdf (Accessed 27 August 2024).

76 "Multi-CBDC Arrangements and the Future of Cross-Border Payments" BIS, March 2021. Available at: https://www.bis.org/publ/othp38.pdf (Accessed 27 August 2024).

77 UDPN website. Available at: https://www.udpn.io/home/io (Accessed 27 August 2024).

78 "Enabling Cross-Border High Value Transfer Using Distributed Ledger Technologies" Bank of Canada, Monetary Authority of Singapore, 2019. Available at: https://www.mas.gov.sg/-/media/Jasper-Ubin-Design-Paper.pdf (Accessed 27 August 2024).

79 "Project Aber – Final Report" Saudi Central Bank, Central Bank of the UAE. Available at: https://www.sama.gov.sa/en-US/News/Documents/Project_Aber_report-EN.pdf (Accessed 27 August 2024).

80 "Second Stella Report Published" European Central Bank website. Available at: https://www.ecb.europa.eu/press/intro/news/html/ecb.mipnews180327.en.html (Accessed 27 August 2024).

81 "CBDCs Will Need to Work across Borders. Here Are the Models Exploring How to Do It" Atlantic Council, 14 March 2024. Available at: https://www.atlanticcouncil.org/blogs/econographics/cbdcs-will-need-to-work-across-borders-here-are-the-models-exploring-how-to-do-it/ (Accessed 27 August 2024).

82 "Banque de France and HKMA Kick Off Cross-Border CBDC Project" *Finextra*, 8 July 2024. Available at: https://www.finextra.com/newsarticle/44424/banqe-de-france-and-hkma-kick-off-cross-border-cbdc-project (Accessed 27 August 2024).

83 "Project Jura – Cross-Border Settlement Using Wholesale CBDC" BIS website. Available at: https://www.bis.org/about/bisih/topics/cbdc/jura.htm (Accessed 27 August 2024).

84 "Project Mariana: BIS and Central Banks of France, Singapore and Switzerland Successfully Test Cross-Border Wholesale CBDCs" BIS, 28 September 2023. Available at: https://www.bis.org/about/bisih/topics/cbdc/mariana.htm (Accessed 27 August 2024).

85 "Central Banks of France, Tunisia in Wholesale Cross Border CBDC Trial" *Ledger Insights*, 19 July 2021. Available at: https://www.ledgerinsights.com/central-bank-of-france-tunisia-in-wholesale-cross-border-cbdc-trial/ (Accessed 27 August 2024).

86 BIS, 5 June 2024. Available at: https://www.bis.org/about/bisih/topics/cbdc/mcbdc_bridge.htm (Accessed 27 August 2024).

87 "Bank for International Settlements leaves Chinese CBDC project" The Global Treasurer, 1 November 2024. Available at: https://www.theglobaltreasurer.com/2024/11/01/bank-for-international-settlements-leaves-chinese-cbdc-project/ (Accessed 30 November 2024).

88 "Project Dunbar: International Settlements Using Multi-CBDCs" BIS website. Available at: https://www.bis.org/about/bisih/topics/cbdc/dunbar.htm (Accessed 27 August 2024).

89 "From De-Risking to De-Dollarisation: The BRICS Currency and the Future of the International Financial Order" The Tricontinental, 5 October 2023. Available at: https://thetricontinental.org/wenhua-zongheng-2024-1-derisking-dedollarisation-brics-currency/ (Accessed 27 August 2024).

90 "Swiss National Bank and SDX Extend Project Helvetia CBDC Project for Two More Years" Digital Pound Foundation, 21 June 2024. Available at: https://digitalpoundfoundation.com/swiss-national-bank-and-sdx-extend-project-helvetia-cbdc-project-for-two-more-years/ (Accessed 27 August 2024).

91 Regulated Liability Network website. Available at: https://regulatedliabilitynetwork.org/ (Accessed 27 August 2024).

92 "Facilitating Wholesale Digital Asset Settlement" Federal Reserve Bank of New York website. Available at: https://www.newyorkfed.org/aboutthefed/nyic/facilitating-wholesale-digital-asset-settlement (Accessed 27 August 2024).

93 "Proposal of a Regulated Liability Network (RLN) Architecture to Support Settlement of Tokenized Assets, Liabilities and Transactions Using Tokenized Deposits and Wholesale CBDC (Real Digital)" Microsoft Brazil, 2023. Available at: https://www.bcb.gov.br/conteudo/eventos/Documents/moedas_digitais/tokenizacao/WorkTOK-Mimeo-TECH_Multi_B_Proposal_RLN_architecture_to_support_Settlement_of_tokenized_assets_liabilities_transactions.pdf (Accessed 27 August 2024).

94 "Regulated Liability Network" UK Finance website. Available at: https://www.ukfinance.org.uk/regulated-liability-network (Accessed 27 August 2024).

95 "Central Bank Digital Currency and Financial Inclusion" International Monetary Fund, 17 March 2023. Available at: https://www.imf.org/en/Publications/WP/Issues/2023/03/18/Central-Bank-Digital-Currency-and-Financial-Inclusion-531104 (Accessed 29 August 2024).

96 "Central Bank Digital Currency's Role in Promoting Financial Inclusion" International Monetary Fund, 22 September 2023. Available at: https://www.imf.org/en/Publications/fintech-notes/Issues/2023/09/22/Central-Bank-Digital-Currency-s-Role-in-Promoting-Financial-Inclusion-538728 (Accessed 29 August 2024).

97 "Central Bank Digital Currencies Can Boost Middle East's Financial Inclusion, Payment Efficiency" IMF Blog, 18 June 2024. Available at: https://www.imf.org/en/Blogs/Articles/2024/06/18/central-bank-digital-currencies-can-boost-middle-easts-financial-inclusion-payment-efficiency (Accessed 29 August 2024).

98 "Opportunities and Challenges of New Technologies for AML/CFT" FATF, July 2021. Available at: https://www.fatf-gafi.org/content/dam/fatf-gafi/guidance/Opportunities-Challenges-of-New-Technologies-for-AML-CFT.pdf.coredownload.inline.pdf (Accessed 29 August 2024).

99 "Could CBDCs Destroy Privacy?" CFA Institute, 2024. Available at: https://www.cfainstitute.org/en/professional-insights-stories/could-cbdcs-destroy-privacy (Accessed 29 August 2024).

100 "Central Bank Digital Currency and the Future of Monetary Policy" National Bureau Of Economic Research, August 2017. Available at: https://www.nber.org/system/files/working_papers/w23711/w23711.pdf (Accessed 29 August 2024).

101 "Chapter 3: CBDC and the Monetary System" UK Parliament. Available at: https://publications.parliament.uk/pa/ld5802/ldselect/ldeconaf/131/13106.htm (Accessed 29 August 2024).

102 "Central Bank Digital Currency (CBDC) Information Security and Operational Risks to Central Banks" Bank of International Settlements, November 2023. Available at: https://www.bis.org/publ/othp81.pdf (Accessed 29 August 2024).

103 "Trump Pledges to Block Potential US Central Bank Digital Currency" Global Government Fintech, 22 January 2024. Available at: https://www.globalgovernmentfintech.com/trump-pledges-to-block-potential-us-central-bank-digital-currency/ (Accessed 29 January 2024).

104 "A Survey of Research on Retail Central Bank Digital Currency" International Monetary Fund, 26 June 2020. Available at: https://www.imf.org/en/Publications/WP/Issues/2020/06/26/A-Survey-of-Research-on-Retail-Central-Bank-Digital-Currency-49517 (Accessed 29 August 2024).

105 "Central Bank Digital Currencies and Freedom Are Incompatible" CATO Institute, 18 July 2022. Available at: https://www.cato.org/commentary/central-bank-digital-currencies-freedom-are-incompatible (Accessed 29 August 2024).

CONCLUSION (IS THIS THE END?)

Payment ecosystem convergence (meet me halfway)

The convergence of payment ecosystems is rapidly reshaping the financial landscape, with traditional payment systems and crypto platforms increasingly intertwining through strategic partnerships, mergers, and acquisitions. This trend is creating a more versatile payment environment, blending the stability and widespread acceptance of traditional finance with the innovation and potential efficiencies of blockchain infrastructures and crypto services beyond the already mainstream issuance of crypto debit and credit cards.

Banking

One notable example of this convergence is the partnership between Nubank, Latin America's largest digital bank, and Lightspark, a company specialising in Lightning Network solutions, announced in June 2024. This collaboration aims to explore integration possibilities and potential

DOI: 10.4324/9781003480761-9

product development, focusing on leveraging Lightspark's enterprise-grade entry point to the Lightning Network. This partnership could significantly expand the reach of the Lightning Network across Nubank's extensive customer base, potentially revolutionising how millions of users interact with Bitcoin and traditional financial services.

Traditional banks like JPMorgan Chase[1] and Goldman Sachs[2] offer crypto services, such as trading and custody, to their clients. They, however, are very much into centralised private distributed ledger systems. For example, JPMorgan Chase, despite its CEO's Jamie Dimon initial scepticism towards crypto assets, has developed its own digital coin called JPM Coin for instant payment settlements between institutional clients. In 2023, JPMorgan expanded its crypto offerings by launching a blockchain-based collateral settlement system.[3] Goldman Sachs initially launched a cryptocurrency trading desk in 2018 but scaled back its plans later that year due to regulatory uncertainty. In March 2021, Goldman Sachs announced the relaunch of its cryptocurrency trading desk, driven by increased demand from institutional clients.[4] Goldman Sachs also filed for SEC approval for a Bitcoin ETF in October 2023, but as of August 2024, it had not yet been launched.

HSBC, traditionally cautious about cryptocurrencies, entered the crypto space in 2023 by launching custody services for tokenised securities on its private blockchain.[5] In May 2024, HSBC took a significant step into the world of tokenised assets by launching its HSBC Orion platform, allowing institutional clients to issue digital bonds. This move by one of the world's largest banks underscores the growing acceptance of blockchain technology in traditional finance and highlights the potential for cryptocurrencies and tokenised assets to coexist with fiat currencies in a unified payment ecosystem.

In June 2024, Deutsche Bank partnered with Bitpanda to offer crypto trading services to its customers, signalling a cautious but significant shift towards digital assets by one of Europe's largest banks.

These developments reflect a broader acceptance of digital assets within the mainstream financial sector and demonstrate how established institutions are adapting to the changing landscape of finance. However, this integration comes with significant risks and challenges. Regulatory uncertainty remains a primary concern, as governments worldwide grapple with how to classify and regulate cryptocurrencies. Banks face the risk of reputational damage if crypto investments lead to substantial losses or if their platforms are used for illicit activities. Market volatility in the crypto space also poses a challenge, potentially affecting the stability of banks' balance sheets. Moreover, banks must invest heavily in cybersecurity to protect against the unique threats associated with digital assets. These factors contribute to a cautious approach by many institutions, balancing innovation with risk management to maintain consumer trust in both traditional and digital banking services.

As traditional banks dip their toes into the crypto pool, it's like watching your grandparents learn to use smartphones – a bit clumsy at first, but they're getting there!

PSPs

PayPal launched cryptocurrency buying and selling services in 2020 in partnership with Paxos and has since expanded its offerings. Following this, in 2021, PayPal introduced its "Checkout with Crypto" feature,[6] allowing users to pay for goods and services using cryptocurrencies at millions of online merchants. In 2023, PayPal developed its own stablecoin in-house, PayPal USD (PYUSD), also in partnership with Paxos, further integrating crypto into its payment ecosystem. PYUSD shows, at the time of writing, signs of becoming one of the largest stablecoins by market capitalisation. The integration of PYUSD by companies like Triple-A for cross-border payments demonstrates the growing acceptance of crypto-based solutions in traditional payment flows.[7] Additionally, PayPal expanded its services to allow crypto trading on Venmo,[8] users to transfer cryptocurrencies to external wallets.[9] This feature was developed in-house but leveraged the existing infrastructure established through its partnerships.

In April 2024, Stripe made moves in Web 3.0 with its integration with Avalanche for crypto on-ramping.[10] In Europe, the collaboration between Stripe and Bitstamp to expand crypto on-ramp services was announced in August 2024, making it easier for users to purchase cryptocurrencies using traditional payment methods, in compliance with EU regulations.[11] In addition, Stripe and Coinbase integrated their services,[12] allowing Coinbase users around the world to purchase cryptocurrencies using Stripe's payment infrastructure, further bridging the gap between traditional payments and the crypto world, highlighting Stripe's global approach to crypto integration.

Robinhood made several moves in the crypto space, including integrating with the Lightning Network in 2022[13] to enable faster Bitcoin transactions and significant strides through strategic acquisitions and expansions. Initially, it expanded its cryptocurrency offerings, allowing users to trade a variety of digital assets directly from its platform. In June 2024, in a major move to expand its global footprint, Robinhood acquired Bitstamp,[14] one of the oldest and most reputable crypto exchanges, for $200 million. This acquisition not only brought valuable experience and infrastructure to Robinhood but also over 50 active licenses across key markets in Europe, the US, and Asia, enhancing Robinhood's ability to serve both retail and institutional investors.

In April 2024, Paymentology, a global cloud-native issuer-processor, and Rain, a centralised crypto exchange, announced a partnership to accelerate the digital assets market in the MENA region.[15] The collaboration enables Rain to offer its users virtual and physical payment cards linked to their crypto wallets, allowing for seamless conversion and spending of digital assets in real-world transactions.

These developments demonstrate how established PSPs are adapting to include crypto services, making digital assets more accessible to mainstream users whilst also raising concerns about the increasing centralisation of crypto trading power. For small businesses, these integrations offer access to a global customer base and potentially lower transaction fees compared to traditional cross-border payments. Consumers benefit from increased payment options and the ability to seamlessly use cryptocurrencies for everyday purchases. However, the volatility of cryptocurrencies can pose challenges for pricing and accounting. As of early 2024, adoption rates varied widely by region and demographic, with younger, tech-savvy consumers leading the way. The ease of use provided by familiar PSPs has been a key factor in driving mainstream adoption of crypto payments.

With PSPs embracing crypto faster than a teenager adopts new slang, we might soon see "To Venmo" accompanied by "To crypto" in everyday language!

Card networks

Major card networks are also embracing crypto services. Visa has been particularly active in this space, partnering with various crypto companies to issue Visa-branded crypto debit cards. In 2021, Visa announced that it would allow the use of the USDC stablecoin to settle transactions on its payment network,[16] marking a significant step in the integration of digital currencies into the mainstream financial system. In the same year, Visa partnered with Consensys to build a bridge between Central Bank Digital Currencies (CBDCs) and traditional finance.[17] A year later, Visa expanded its crypto services by launching a crypto advisory practice to help financial institutions develop their cryptocurrency strategies. The card network also has a programme for crypto cards and, in May 2024, integrated with decentralised off-ramp service Gnosis Pay to launch a crypto debit card.[18]

Mastercard has also made strides in crypto integration. In February 2021, the company announced plans to support select cryptocurrencies directly on its network, allowing businesses to offer crypto products to their customers.[19] In 2024, Mastercard partnered with Ripple to pilot cross-border payments using XRP, aiming to reduce costs and increase speed for international transactions. Mastercard also has an extensive support programme for various crypto cards.[20]

The entry of Visa and Mastercard into the crypto space has sparked intense competition among card networks. Whilst Visa has taken a more aggressive approach with its USDC settlement capabilities and numerous crypto partnerships, Mastercard has focused on building a robust infrastructure for crypto support. Emerging players like Crypto.com and Binance are challenging the established networks by offering attractive rewards and seamless crypto-to-fiat conversions. This competition is driving innovation in areas such as instant settlement, programmable money, and integration with DeFi protocols. As a result, consumers are benefiting from a wider range of options and improved services in the rapidly evolving crypto card market.

As Visa and Mastercard race to crypto-fy their services, it's like watching two old dogs learn some very impressive new skills. Who said you can't teach them new tricks?

Compliance

As cryptocurrencies become more integrated into traditional payment systems, compliance challenges have emerged as regulators continue to focus on anti-money laundering (AML) and Know Your Customer (KYC) requirements for crypto transactions, in turn leading to innovative partnerships.

In 2021, Mastercard acquired CipherTrace,[21] a blockchain analytics company, allowing Mastercard to better monitor and manage the risks associated with cryptocurrency transactions to strengthen its compliance and risk management offerings in the crypto space. They subsequently launched a product called Crypto Secure that helps issuers assess the risk of crime associated with crypto merchants on its network.[22]

Sumsub, a KYC/AML service provider, partnered with Coinbase in 2023 to enhance compliance processes for the exchange, demonstrating the collaborative efforts within the industry to meet regulatory requirements. In May 2024, Sumsub also announced their collaboration with CODE,[23] a specialised compliance platform designed for DeFi and crypto businesses, to help DEXs and DeFi platforms comply with the FATF **Travel Rule**.

The compliance landscape for cryptocurrencies is rapidly evolving, with significant regulatory developments shaping the industry. The European Union's Markets in Crypto-Assets (MiCA) regulation, implemented in 2024, provides a comprehensive framework for crypto asset service providers, aiming to protect investors and maintain financial stability. In the United States, the Securities and Exchange Commission (SEC) has taken a more cautious approach, focusing on enforcement actions against projects it deems to be offering unregistered securities. The Financial Action Task Force (FATF) has also played a crucial role in setting global standards for anti-money laundering in the crypto space, particularly through its Travel Rule recommendations. These regulatory efforts are forcing businesses to invest heavily in compliance infrastructure, with potential fines and loss of operating licenses at stake for non-compliance.

In the wild west of crypto, compliance is the new sheriff in town. It's not the most exciting addition to the party, but someone's got to keep things from getting too rowdy!

What does this mean?

Industry experts have varying views on the convergence of payment ecosystems. Cuy Sheffield, head of crypto at Visa, has stated that

> crypto is not only a new asset class, but also a new payment network that can complement and enhance our existing offerings. We want to provide our users with more choice, convenience, and security when they interact with crypto, whether it's buying, selling, spending, or earning.[24]

The 2022 Binance partnership with Splyt[25] demonstrates the real-world impact of this convergence. The collaboration allows Binance users to pay for ride-hailing, food delivery, and other services directly with cryptocurrencies in over 150 countries. This integration showcases how businesses are adapting to the evolving landscape, providing seamless experiences that bridge traditional services with crypto payments.

For users, this convergence means greater flexibility and choice in how they manage and spend their money. The ability to seamlessly switch between fiat and cryptocurrencies, or to use blockchain-based payment solutions on traditional networks, is becoming a reality. This integration offers users the convenience of managing all their financial activities in one place, regardless of whether they're dealing with traditional currencies or digital assets.

However, this convergence also presents significant challenges and potential risks. The implementation of CBDCs, whilst promising, raises concerns about privacy and government control over individual finances. There's a delicate balance to be struck between the efficiency gains of digital currencies and the preservation of financial privacy that traditional cash offers.

Moreover, the integration of blockchain technology and smart contracts into mainstream finance could introduce new vulnerabilities. As financial systems become more interconnected and automated, they may also become more susceptible to large-scale cyberattacks or technical failures. Ensuring robust security measures and fail-safes will be crucial as these technologies are adopted more widely.

Regulatory bodies worldwide are grappling with how to approach this rapidly evolving landscape. The challenge lies in creating frameworks that foster innovation whilst also protecting consumers and maintaining financial stability. There's a risk that overly stringent regulations could stifle growth and innovation in the crypto space, whilst insufficient oversight could lead to market manipulation or financial crimes.

The concept of "programmable money" also raises ethical questions about the nature of currency and financial autonomy. Whilst it offers unprecedented flexibility and efficiency, it also introduces the possibility of external control over how and when money can be spent. This could have far-reaching implications for personal freedom and economic policy.

Furthermore, as traditional and crypto finance systems become more intertwined, there's a potential for increased market volatility. The crypto market's notorious price swings could have a more direct impact on traditional financial markets, potentially leading to broader economic instability.

Lastly, whilst these advancements promise a more interconnected global financial system, they also risk exacerbating existing economic inequalities. Those without access to the necessary technology or financial literacy could be left behind, widening the gap between the financially included and excluded.

As we move forward, it will be crucial to address these challenges proactively. This may involve developing new regulatory frameworks, investing in robust cybersecurity measures, and ensuring that the benefits of this financial revolution are accessible to all. The success of this convergence will depend on our ability to navigate these complex issues whilst harnessing the transformative potential of these new technologies.

The fusion of traditional finance and crypto is not just reshaping our financial landscape – it's creating a whole new financial universe. As we hurtle towards this brave new world of programmable money and blockchain-powered transactions, we're faced with a dizzying array of possibilities and pitfalls. Our wallets may be getting lighter, but our financial options are certainly getting heavier!

Will this convergence lead us to a utopia of financial inclusion and frictionless global commerce, or are we unwittingly constructing a digital panopticon of financial surveillance? Only time will tell. But one thing's certain: the future of money is being written right now, and it's up to us to ensure it's a bestseller, not a cautionary tale. So buckle up, folks – the financial rollercoaster is just getting started, and it promises to be one hell of a ride!

Notes

1 "JP Morgan Explains Why It Prefers Unified Ledger over Public Blockchain for Tokenization" 7 May 2024. Available at: https://www.ledgerinsights.com/jp-morgan-explains-why-it-prefers-unified-ledger-over-public-blockchain-for-tokenization/ (Accessed 17 August 2024).

2 "Goldman Sachs to Launch Three Tokenization Projects by End of Year, Says Digital Assets Chief" *Fortune*, 10 July 2024. Available at: https://fortune.com/crypto/2024/07/10/goldman-sachs-launch-tokenization-bitcoin-etfs-crypto-mcdermott/ (Accessed 17 August 2024).

3 "JPMorgan Announces First Client Trade on Tokenized Network" *Pymnts*, 11 October 2023. Available at: https://www.pymnts.com/blockchain/2023/jpmorgan-announces-first-client-trade-on-tokenized-network/ (Accessed 17 August 2024).

4 "Goldman Sachs Restarts Cryptocurrency Desk Amid Bitcoin Boom" *CNBC*, 1 March 2021. Available at: https://www.cnbc.com/2021/03/01/goldman-sachs-restarts-cryptocurrency-desk-amid-bitcoin-boom.html (Accessed 17 August 2024).

5 "HSBC to Launch Storage Services for Tokenized Securities as More Big Banks Warm to Blockchain" *CNBC*, 8 November 2023. Available at: https://www.cnbc.com/2023/11/08/hsbc-to-launch-custody-services-for-tokenized-securities.html (Accessed 17 August 2024).

6 "PayPal Launches "Checkout with Crypto"" Paypal, 30 March 2021. Available at: https://newsroom.paypal-corp.com/2021-03-30-PayPal-Launches-Checkout-with-Crypto (Accessed 17 August 2024).

7 "Triple-A Integrates PayPal USD for Cross-border Payments" *The Paypers*, 29 May 2024. Available at: https://thepaypers.com/cryptocurrencies/triple-a-integrates-paypal-usd-for-cross-border-payments--1268321 (Accessed 17 August).

8 "Introducing Crypto on Venmo" Paypal, 20 April 2021. Available at: https://newsroom.paypal-corp.com/2021-04-20-Introducing-Crypto-on-Venmo (Accessed 17 August 2024).

9 "PayPal Users Can Now Transfer, Send, and Receive Bitcoin, Ethereum, Bitcoin Cash, and Litecoin" Available at: https://newsroom.paypal-corp.com/2022-06-07-PayPal-Users-Can-Now-Transfer-Send-and-Receive-Bitcoin-Ethereum-Bitcoin-Cash-and-Litecoin (Accessed 17 August 2024).

10 "Avalanche Set to Gain Wider Reach with Its Stripe Integration" FXSTREET, 30 April 2024. Available at: https://www.fxstreet.com/cryptocurrencies/news/avalanche-set-to-gain-wider-reach-with-its-stripe-integration-202404300222 (Accessed 17 August 2024).

11 "Stripe and Bitstamp to Expand Crypto On-ramp in Europe" *The Paypers*, 8 August 2024. Available at: https://thepaypers.com/cryptocurrencies/stripe-and-bitstamp-to-expand-crypto-on-ramp-in-europe--1269553 (Accessed 17 August 2024).

12 "Stripe and Coinbase Integrate Crypto Services" *Pymnts*, 27 June 2024. Available at: https://www.pymnts.com/cryptocurrency/2024/stripe-and-coinbase-integrate-crypto-services/ (Accessed 17 August 2024).

13 "Robinhood Becomes Latest to Integrate Bitcoin's Lightning Network" *Yahoo! Finance*, 7 April 2022. Available at: https://finance.yahoo.com/news/robinhood-bitcoin-lightning-network-192503112.html (Accessed 17 August 2024).

14 "Robinhood bets big on crypto with $200 million deal for Bitstamp" Reuters, 6 June 2024. Available at: https://www.reuters.com/markets/deals/robinhood-bets-big-crypto-with-200-million-deal-bitstamp-2024-06-06/

15 "Paymentology and Rain Join Forces to Accelerate Digital Assets Market" *The Fintech Times*, 4 April 2024. Available at: https://thefintechtimes.com/paymentology-and-rain-join-forces-to-accelerate-digital-assets-market/ (Accessed 2 September 2024).

16 "Visa Becomes First Major Payments Network to Settle Transactions in USD Coin (USDC)" Visa, 29 March 2021. Available at: https://usa.visa.com/about-visa/newsroom/press-releases.releaseId.17821.html (Accessed 17 August 2024).
17 "Visa Partners with ConsenSys to Help Bridge CBDCs with Traditional Finance" *CoinDesk*, 13 January 2022. Available at: https://www.coindesk.com/business/2022/01/13/visa-partners-with-consensys-to-help-bridge-cbdcs-with-traditional-finance/ (Accessed 17 August 2024).
18 "Gnosis Pay and Visa to Launch Crypto-linked Debit Card in Europe" *The Paypers*, 29 May 2024. Available at: https://thepaypers.com/cryptocurrencies/gnosis-pay-and-visa-to-launch-crypto-linked-debit-card-in-europe--1268335 (Accessed 17 August 2024).
19 "Why Mastercard Is Bringing Crypto onto Its Network" Mastercard, 10 February 2021. Available at: https://www.mastercard.com/news/perspectives/2021/why-mastercard-is-bringing-crypto-onto-our-network/ (Accessed 17 August 2024).
20 "Enabling Consumers to Use Crypto Cards for Purchases" Mastercard website. Available at: https://www.mastercard.com/global/en/business/issuers/crypto/card-program.html (Accessed 17 August 2024).
21 "Mastercard Acquires CipherTrace to Enhance Crypto Capabilities" Mastercard, 9 September 2021. Available at: https://www.mastercard.com/news/press/2021/september/mastercard-acquires-ciphertrace-to-enhance-crypto-capabilities/ (Accessed 17 August 2024).
22 "Mastercard Pushes Deeper into Crypto with New Tool for Combating Fraud" *CNBC*, 4 October 2022. Available at: https://www.cnbc.com/2022/10/04/mastercard-deepens-crypto-push-with-tool-for-preventing-fraud.html (Accessed 17 August 2024).
23 "Sumsub and CODE Unite to Accelerate Crypto Travel Rule Compliance" Sumsub, 2 May 2024. Available at: https://sumsub.com/newsroom/sumsub-and-code-unite-to-accelerate-crypto-travel-rule-compliance/ (Accessed 17 August 2024).
24 "Cuy Sheffield: The Reason Visa Is 'Everywhere' in Crypto" *CoinDesk*, 4 December 2023. Available at: https://www.coindesk.com/consensus-magazine/2023/12/04/cuy-sheffield-the-reason-visa-is-everywhere-in-crypto/ (Accessed 2 September 2024).
25 "Cryptocurrency Platform Binance Partners with Splyt for Rides and Experiences" *PhocusWire*, 20 June 2022. Available at: https://www.phocuswire.com/binance-cryptocurrency-platform-enables-rides-experiences-through-splyt (Accessed 2 September 2024).

ACKNOWLEDGEMENTS

Eight months have passed since I started writing this book, and I hardly slept. At that time, I constantly had to revisit all chapters because an ecosystem actor did something interesting that I wanted to include, or because one simply went bust. I realised in August that this book was already getting too big, and I knew I had so much more to say. It struck me that this potentially marked the birth of the next book, and after some interesting discussions with my friend Tiffanny Anzai Hill, I decided on the next book, and we agreed on the new title: "Payments Unbound – Navigating Through the Perils and Potential of Decentralised Markets". I thank Rebecca Marsh at Routledge for being so understanding and supporting the idea. So here we are, the second book is completed. Did I answer all your questions? Some of them at least, I hope. But if you, like me, are curious about why some questions remain, I hope I have equipped you to go and find the answers. I've tried to remain unbiased and objective throughout. (Although sometimes, I couldn't help myself, and I thank David Parkinson at Musqet for the stimulating debate on Bitcoin! We'll talk again for the next book.) You may not always agree with me, and I'd love to hear from you. I'm sure there will be exciting discussions ahead. I also attempted to provide a comprehensive glossary for this brave new world, I hope you will find it useful.

I remain deeply passionate about the payments industry, and I hope I continue to instil some of that interest in you, Dear Reader. This is not a book for people completely new to payments, and the ducks will still paddle furiously, but I hope my contribution will help them find the world of decentralised payments less mystifying.

I am sure I will be compelled to update this edition in a couple of years from now when I will look at it fondly as some sort of historical document. Who knows what the fantastic brains out there will bring out?

I hope I have managed to do what I set out to do: write a book about the evolution of payments and decentralised infrastructures that isn't boring and that would appeal to those wanting to know more, warts and all.

This book wouldn't have been possible without the lovely people in my life. To all my industry friends, especially those who took the time to read the book, and endorse it: Flavia Alzetta, Tiffany Anzai Hill, Dave Birch, Stuart Campbell, Mike Chambers, Tony Craddock, John Davies, Janusz Diemko, Alison Donnelly, Paul Horlock, Ken Lipton, Rahul Matthan, Andy McDonald, Mark McMurtrie, Jeremy Nicholds, David Parkinson, Claire Pearson, Chris Skinner, Stanley Skoglund, Soteris Vasili, Jim Wadsworth, and Gary Yamamura. I am honoured to be in your crowd, and grateful for your help and support. Special thanks and gratitude are due to Roger Alexander, my friend and mentor for so many years. He is the reason why my books were ever written. Roger, I hope I continue to make you proud. Your friendship, support, and constant encouragement mean a lot to me. I would like to express my heartfelt gratitude to Tiffany Anzai Hill, my friend in Singapore, for her grace, tireless support, attention to detail, and help despite her very busy life. The "Tiffany Rules" are here to stay, and they made this book so much better! My gratitude goes to the Routledge team, especially to Rebecca Marsh for taking a chance on my first, second, and third books, and supporting my fourth book. Thanks also to Grace Collier and Emma Harder-Collins for being so efficient in making this book the best it can be. My gratitude and thanks to Natalia and Andy Ivanis not only for their friendship and support, but also for allowing me to launch my first book and this one at the fantastic, not-to-be-missed Merchant Payments Ecosystem conference in Berlin, the memories are eternal.

My thanks also go to my good friend Andrew Billings-Giles for creating "The Duck", it always makes me smile and is now a permanent fixture in my payments world. Ay up me duck! To all my friends and loved ones for their encouragement. To my sister, Aida Keehner, for never once looking bored with my daily (and long) payment ramblings and for actually reading everything I sent her. Sis, you're always the one in that Jesse Glynne song. I wish you lived closer. To my husband David for his constant love, you're my rock.

Finally, I thank you, Dear Reader, for accompanying me on this journey into the brave new world of decentralised payments, I hope it wasn't too bumpy a ride.

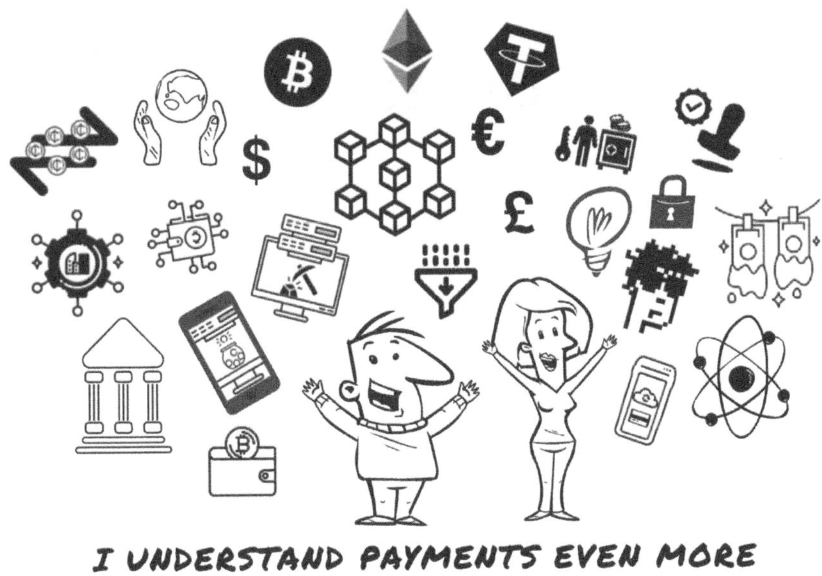

Drawing by the author. (It would look nice on a T-shirt, don't you think?)

All that remains is for me to say once more "Mind The Gap!" as you leave this train, and hopefully, you'll join me on the next platform for the next book, "Payments Unbound – Navigating Through the Perils and Potential of Decentralised Markets", but I'll have a little break before I do that. For those who can't wait, my next book should be available by the time you read this: "The A-to-Z of Payments – A Modern and Practical Glossary for the Curious and the Forgetful". It contains more than 1,600 entries, a first in the industry, so there'll be something for everyone...

Until next time,

Neira Jones

September 2024

GLOSSARY

2FA See two-factor authentication.

3DES Triple Data Encryption Standard. A *symmetric cryptography* algorithm.

3D Secure (3DS)[1] An *EMV* standard for the *authentication* of *e-commerce* transactions. Deployments include Mastercard's "SecureCode" and "Identity Check", Visa's "Visa Secure", and American Express' "SafeKey". 3D Secure stands for "3 Domain Secure" and refers to the three *ecosystem* domains involved in the process: the *acquirer* domain (acquirer and *merchant*), the *issuer* domain, and the interoperability domain (the *card scheme*).

A2A payment See *account-to-account payment*.

Aadhaar[2] A *digital identity* framework developed by the Unique Identification Authority of India (UIDAI)[3] on behalf of the Government of India. It consists of a 12-digit individual identification number and a set of rules governing the framework. The Aadhaar number serves as proof of identity and residence for any Indian resident, irrespective of age, and is valid for life. Through the Aadhaar deployment, the Indian government intends to promote *financial inclusion* for a largely rural and underbanked population by facilitating access to banking, mobile phone connections, and other government and non-government services. In March 2023, Aadhaar authentication transactions climbed to 2.31 billion, and UIDAI claims that its digital *KYC* (eKYC) deployment has significantly reduced customer acquisition costs for financial services institutions, telcos, and others.

account-based CBDC A *Central Bank Digital Currency* (CBDC) access model by which users access the CBDC through a *digital identity* scheme. Both *retail CBDCs* and *wholesale CBDCs* can use this access model. These CBDCs can run on either centralised (centralised CBDC account) or distributed (*DLT*-based CBDC account) infrastructure, and user identification may be provided by the private sector.

Account Information Service Provider (AISP) A *Third Party PSP* (TPP) that accesses information from a payment account (card account or bank account) on behalf of a *Payment System User* (PSU) on a read-only basis. In Europe, an AISP that has registered with their regulator is called a Registered AISP, or RAISP.

Account Servicing PSP (ASPSP) The payment *ecosystem* actor who manages the account belonging to the *Payment Service User* (PSU) account throughout its lifecycle, from creation to closure. This can be a *bank*, an *issuer*, or a *non-bank Payment Service Provider* (PSP).

account-to-account payment (A2A payment) A type of payment that allows funds to move from a *payer's bank account* to a *payee's* bank account. There are two types of A2A payments: *push payments* where the payer moves the money directly from their account to the payer's account (e.g. a bank transfer) and *pull payments* where the payee moves the money from the payer's account with the payer's prior agreement (e.g. a *direct debit*). A push payment is also referred to as "giro payment", "giro" and *credit transfer*.

Acquirer A *Payment Service Provider* (PSP) that enables a *merchant* to connect to a *card scheme*. Commonly referred to as an "acquiring bank", "merchant bank" (if they are also a bank), "Merchant Services Provider" (MSP), "merchant acquirer", "acquiring PSP", or "processor". Acquiring services are also referred to as "merchant services".

acquiring The process of acquiring card transactions from *merchants* to enable those merchants to take card payments for cards issued on a given *card scheme* (e.g. Visa, Mastercard). Acquiring connects merchants with card schemes. Also referred to as "merchant services".

AES Advanced Encryption Standard. A *symmetric cryptography* algorithm.

AI See artificial intelligence.

airdrop Also called "crypto airdrop". A marketing process used by *blockchain*-based projects and developers to raise interest in their initiatives by sending out free *tokens* to their community members. This concept is similar to receiving a free discount to encourage you to buy something or visit a new shop. Sometimes, a crypto airdrop is issued to users in exchange for completing a certain task, which may involve following an account on social media, sharing or retweeting one of their posts, sending or receiving a transaction (using a particular crypto platform or *crypto wallet*), or creating an account and agreeing to receive updates.

Airtel Money[4] A *mobile money* service popular in East, Central, and West Africa. Owned by Airtel Africa which is majority owned by Indian telecommunications company Bharti Airtel.

Algorand[5] A blockchain using the Proof of Stake consensus protocol.

Alipay[6] An *e-wallet*. One of the world's largest payment platforms, serving customers primarily in China and the broader Asia-Pacific region.

alternative payments A term coined by the card industry that is generally used to describe payments that are not traditional card payments.

AltFi See Alternative Finance.

Amazon Pay[7] An *e-wallet* provided by Amazon. A *staged digital wallet*.

American Express[8] A *card scheme* that operates according to the *three party model*.

AML See Anti-Money Laundering.

AML/CFT See Anti-Money Laundering.

AML/CTF See Anti-Money Laundering.

anonymity The state of being not identifiable within a set of subjects, allowing individuals to act or communicate without revealing their identity. In digital contexts, anonymity protects users' personal information and *privacy*, enabling them to engage in activities without fear of being tracked or recognised. This concept is crucial in various fields, including online communication, financial transactions, and *data protection*.

Android Pay A *mobile wallet* originally launched by Google and was subsequently replaced by *Google Pay* and *Google Wallet*.

Anti-Money Laundering (AML) The collection of laws, processes, and regulations that prevent illegally obtained money from entering the financial system. Increasingly, AML frameworks go beyond just *financial crime* to include Counter-Terrorism Financing (CTF) provisions as well as tax-related offences. Also referred to as AML/CFT or AML/CTF.

API See *Application Programming Interface.*

Apple Pay[9] A *mobile wallet* provided by Apple Inc. A *pass-through digital wallet.*

Application Programming Interface (API) A software interface allowing parties to communicate with each other through an agreed set of definitions and protocols. The document or standard that describes how to build or use such an interface is called an "API specification".

arbitrage The practice of buying an asset in one market where the price is low and simultaneously selling it in another market where the price is higher, thereby profiting from the price difference without taking on significant risk. In the context of *crypto assets*, arbitrage involves purchasing a crypto asset on one exchange where its price is lower and selling it on another exchange where its price is higher. This process takes advantage of price discrepancies across different cryptocurrency exchanges, allowing traders to earn a profit from the differences in market prices. See also *flash loan.*

arbitration A method of resolving disputes outside of traditional court systems, where an impartial third party (the arbitrator) reviews evidence, hears arguments, and makes a binding decision to settle the disagreement between two or more parties. This process is often faster, less formal, and more cost-effective than litigation. In the context of payment processes, arbitration refers to the resolution of disputes between parties involved in financial transactions, such as merchants, customers, or payment service providers. When conflicts arise over charges, refunds, or service quality, arbitration can be used to reach a fair settlement without resorting to legal action. Many payment platforms and financial institutions include arbitration clauses in their terms of service to manage disputes efficiently and maintain trust in their systems. For example, on the *card rails*, arbitration is a process that can be invoked by *card scheme* members to resolve a *chargeback*-related *dispute* between two members.

artificial intelligence (AI) A branch of computer science concerned with building smart machines capable of performing tasks that typically require human intelligence. See also *machine learning*, *deep learning*, and *large language model.*

asymmetric cryptography See *public key cryptography.*

asymmetric encryption See *public key cryptography.*

ATM See Automated Teller Machine.

atomic settlement A type of *settlement* which aims to mitigate *settlement risk* of traditional settlement systems, where the trade and settlement processes are separate and may occur on different days. To address the risk, the *Delivery-versus-Payment (DvP)* (for financial markets) and *Payment-versus-Payment (PvP)* (for FX markets) settlement arrangements were developed, whereby one leg of a transaction only settles if the other leg also settles on an "all-or-nothing" basis. A type of settlement that may also be facilitated by *blockchain* infrastructures on the basis of *smart contracts.* Transactions usually happen on a single ledger, although cross-ledger transactions may be possible. See also *atomic swap.*

atomic swap An emerging type of simultaneous *settlement* which aims to facilitate the exchange of crypto assets within a *blockchain* or more commonly across separate blockchains (and therefore separate ledgers) without the need for an intermediary such as a *crypto exchange.* Most atomic swap-enabled *crypto wallets* and blockchains use *smart contracts,* where the parties agree the price between themselves. Atomic swaps are useful if you only have one *cryptocurrency* but need to use another in a transaction. See also *atomic settlement.*

authentication The method used to verify the origin of a message or to verify the identity of a participant on a given *payment scheme.* This is the method by which a *cardholder* or bank account holder is authenticated. *Authentication* factors may take many forms, such as a password, an account number, a *PIN*, a signature, *biometrics*, etc. See also *two-factor authentication*, *multi-factor authentication*, *delegated authentication*, *decoupled authentication*, and *biometric authentication.*

authorisation A process by which an *Account Servicing PSP (ASPSP)* is asked to verify that a payer is genuine and allowed to make a payment transaction (e.g. sufficient funds) after the payer has given their consent (*payment instruction*) for the transaction. The process is different for *card rails* and bank rails, but generally involves an authorisation request made to the *ASPSP*, which will return their *authorisation decision.* See also *authentication.*

Automated Banking Machine (ABM) See *Automated Teller Machine.*

Automated Teller Machine (ATM) A self-service card terminal which allows cardholders to withdraw or deposit money, check their balances, transfer funds between accounts, pay bills, etc. Whilst all ATMs will allow cardholders to withdraw cash, not all ATMs will offer additional functionality. Sometimes referred to as an Automated Banking Machine (ABM), and historically, cash dispenser.

Avalanche[10] A blockchain using the *Proof of Stake consensus protocol.*

B2B See Business-to-Business.

B2C See Business-to-Consumer.

B2G See Business-to-Government.

BaaS See Banking-as-a-Service, Blockchain-as-a-Service.

bank A financial services institution that is authorised to accept deposits from customers, as well as lend money to customers and offer other financial services. In a payments context, a bank can be an *Account Servicing PSP (ASPSP)* on the bank rails, or an *issuer* on the *card rails*. Banks are defined as "credit institutions" in Europe and as "depository institutions" in the United States.

bank rails A term used to describe the bank payments *ecosystem*, its operating procedures and infrastructure.

bank rate See *Merchant Service Charge.*

bank run An event where the customers of a bank or other financial institution withdraw their deposits at the same time over fears about the bank's solvency, potentially leading the bank to fail. Silicon Valley Bank[11] and Credit Suisse[12] are recent examples.

bank transfer A *payment method* by which the funding mechanism is a bank account.

BankID A *digital identity* framework in Sweden[13] and Norway.[14] Whilst the name is the same in both countries, they are separate frameworks.

Banking-as-a-Service (BaaS) Technology provided by regulated institutions (e.g. banks) to *non-bank Payment Services Providers (PSPs)* to enable the latter to provide financial services to their customers. Also see *embedded finance.*

Bank Secrecy Act (BSA)[15] A US law requiring financial institutions to help government agencies in detecting and preventing *money laundering.*

batch processing In a payments context, the transmission or processing of a group of related *payment instructions.*

BATX An acronym for Baidu,[16] Alibaba,[17] Tencent,[18] and Xiaomi,[19] the four biggest tech firms in China. These platforms are increasingly involved in payments and financial services. See also *Big Tech, GAFA, FANG, MAMAA,* and *FAANG.*

Big Tech A collective term used to describe large technology companies and platforms. These platforms are increasingly involved in payments and financial services. See also *GAFA, BATX, FANG, MAMAA,* and *FAANG.*

BIN sponsorship The process by which BIN (Bank Identification Number) sponsors, which can be *acquirers* or *issuers*, enable other eligible organisations to issue cards by allowing them to use BIN ranges that they control (this is sometimes described as "BIN rental"). Working with a *principal* scheme member allows these eligible organisations to issue cards and adhere to the *card scheme* rules and regulatory requirements, giving them quick time to market. This is traditionally associated with the prepaid and *eMoney* markets. Also see *scheme membership*.

Binance[20] A centralised *crypto exchange*.

biometric authentication The use of *biometrics* for *authentication* purposes.

biometrics A term used to describe the biological measurements or physical characteristics of individuals. Common examples are fingerprint mapping, facial recognition, palm vein recognition, and retina scans. Behavioural biometrics is a subset of biometrics that analyses a user's digital physical and cognitive behaviour, such as phone movement, keyboard behaviour, touchscreen behaviour, mouse behaviour, phone pressure, gait, gesture, voice pattern, etc. In payments, biometrics may be used during the *authentication* of *Payment Service Users (PSU)*.

BIS[21] Bank for International Settlements. A bank whose mission is to support *central banks*' pursuit of monetary and financial stability through international cooperation, and to act as a bank for central banks.

Bitcoin (BTC)[22] A *cryptocurrency*, also a *coin*. Bitcoin also refers to the *layer 1 blockchain* infrastructure on which BTC operates (i.e. the Bitcoin blockchain). A *permissionless blockchain*. See also *Satoshi*.

Bitfinex[23] A centralised *crypto exchange*.

block 0 See *genesis block*.

blockchain A type of *Distributed Ledger Technology (DLT)* that uses *public key cryptography* to create and share transactions (the data blocks) across participants for validation. Time-stamped "blocks" of data are strung together (chain), and these blocks are intermittently validated (*consensus protocol*) by users of the network (i.e. *miners* or *validators*). These blocks of data are characterised as being *on-chain*. Blockchains can't access real-world data (*off-chain*) directly and need special services or data feeds for access to real-world information, such as *oracles*.

Blockchain-as-a-Service (BaaS) Cloud-based services offering a complete package for *blockchain* development, offering a pre-built blockchain infrastructure consisting of a managed network of *nodes*, the implementation of a specific *consensus protocol*, development tools (e.g. programming languages, *APIs*, and *SDKs*) and various security features (e.g. *encryption*, access management, and intrusion detection). Some BaaS providers may choose to support established *blockchain development frameworks.*

blockchain development framework A development environment specific to *permissionless blockchain* infrastructures. They offer (a) pre-built functionality in the form of pre-built modules and tools for common blockchain development tasks such as *consensus protocol* interaction, *smart contract* development, identity management, etc., (b) an abstraction layer to hide the complexities of the underlying blockchain protocol, allowing developers to focus on application logic, and (c) security features, as they will often prioritise security due to the nature of blockchain applications.

blockchain protocol The entire set of rules and specifications that govern the operation of a *blockchain.* It includes data structures, *cryptography algorithms, consensus protocols,* etc., how nodes communicate, and generally how the whole network operates.

blockchain settlement A *blockchain* mechanism by which transactions are settled (i.e. become final). This mechanism is decentralised and relies on a *consensus protocol* as a trust framework. Once a transaction has been confirmed and added to a block in a blockchain network, the transaction is considered "recorded". However, the transaction will generally be considered "final" (i.e. immutable) only after the *confirmation time* has passed. See also *block finality, immutability, and settlement.*

blockchain trilemma A concept coined by Ethereum's co-founder, Vitalik Buterin, describing the challenge faced by *blockchain* developers, **stating that optimal levels of decentralisation, security, and scalability are hard to achieve, as one of the three elements must be sacrificed in favour of the other two. Modern blockchains try to address this issue by using *scaling solutions.***

block finality See blockchain settlement.

block header In a *blockchain* context, a data construct is used to ensure the integrity of a block. As such, the block header will typically include a version number (referring to the validation rules used), the *hash* of the previous block, a *Merkle root* (for all transactions, including the *coinbase transaction*), a timestamp, the digital signature of the block creator, and additional fields specific to the protocol.

block interval The time it takes for a new block is added to a *blockchain.* For example, the Bitcoin blockchain has a block interval of about ten minutes, and the Ethereum blockchain claims 12 to 20 seconds (at the time of writing). See also *blockchain settlement* and *settlement cycle*.

block reward A term commonly used to describe the economic incentives that validating nodes receive for their participation in maintaining the *blockchain* network's security and integrity. In some blockchains, it is a combination of newly-minted coins and transaction fees, such as in the Bitcoin blockchain. In other blockchains, such as Ethereum, the block reward consists only of the newly minted coins, and transaction fees are a distinct component treated as additional incentives.

botnet A network of compromised computers or devices, known as "bots" or "zombies", that are controlled remotely by a malicious actor, often without the knowledge of the device owners. Botnets are typically created by infecting devices with malware, allowing the attacker to issue commands to the entire network. They are commonly used to conduct various cybercriminal activities, including *DDoS attacks*, spam distribution, data theft, and the propagation of additional malware. The scale and coordination of botnets can significantly amplify the impact of cyber threats.

BouncyCastle A *Java*-based *cryptography* library providing a similar *API* to *OpenSSL*, making it easier to port code between languages.

Bretton Woods agreement An agreements struck in July 1944 across 44 countries under which a new international monetary system was established, aiming to promote economic growth after World War II, stable exchange rates, and prevent competitive currency devaluations. At that point, the US dollar was pegged to gold at $35 per ounce, and other currencies were pegged to the US dollar, essentially creating an indirect gold standard system (dubbed the Bretton Woods system) and leading to the creation of the International Monetary Fund and the World Bank. Whilst agreed upon in 1944, the Bretton Woods system didn't become fully operational until 1958 and came under pressure in the 1960s due to increased circulation of the US dollar and economic growth in other countries. In 1971, President Richard Nixon announced the suspension of the US dollar convertibility into gold, effectively ending the Bretton Woods system, in a move commonly dubbed as the "Nixon Shock". Since then, the US dollar has been a *fiat currency*.

BRICS An intergovernmental organisation comprising Brazil, Russia, India, China, South Africa, Egypt, Ethiopia, Iran, Saudi Arabia, and the United Arab Emirates. In 2006, Brazil, Russia, India, and China created the "BRIC" group, and South Africa was added in 2010, making it "BRICS". Ethiopia, Iran, Saudi Arabia, and the United Arab Emirates joined in January 2024. These countries aim to act as a counterbalance to Western influence and aim to reduce their dependence on the US dollar, a process known as *de-dollarisation*.

BSA See Bank Secrecy Act.

burning In *blockchain*, burning refers to the permanent removal of *cryptocurrency* tokens or crypto assets from circulation by sending them to an unspendable address. This process effectively destroys the tokens, reducing the total supply. Burning is often used as a deflationary mechanism to increase scarcity, maintain price stability, or as part of governance processes in decentralised finance (DeFi) protocols. See also *minting*, *seigniorage*, and *tokenomics*.

Business-to-Business (B2B) A term used to describe a business model where one business makes a commercial transaction with another business.

Business-to-Consumer (B2C) A term used to describe the business model of selling products directly to customers without needed an intermediary (e.g. wholesalers, distributors, and intermediaries).

Business-to-Government (B2G) A term used to describe the trade between the business sector as a supplier and a government body as a customer.

bytecode In the context of *blockchains*, bytecode is a machine-readable instruction set designed for efficient execution by a *virtual machine* (*VM*). It acts as an intermediate representation derived from the original high-level smart contract code (e.g. Solidity for Ethereum). Unlike traditional compiled code specific to a particular hardware architecture, bytecode offers portability across different systems. The VM interprets the bytecode instructions and executes them within a secure sandbox environment, promoting security and isolation on the blockchain network. This standardised approach enables developers to write *smart contracts* in various languages and deploy them on compatible blockchain platforms.

Byzantine General's Problem A conceptual problem in distributed systems where components may fail and there is insufficient information on whether a component has failed, rendering decision-making difficult. The allegory stems from an example where a group of generals, each commanding a portion of an army, must coordinate an attack or retreat on a city. However, some generals may be traitors and might provide false or conflicting information to other generals, making coordination of the attack or retreat difficult. The challenge is for the loyal generals to reach a consensus despite the presence of traitors and potentially unreliable communication mechanisms in order to ensure that they either all attack or all retreat to avoid defeat. In the context of blockchains, the problem describes the challenge of achieving consensus among nodes in the presence of faulty or malicious actors. This is particularly relevant to *permissioned blockchains*, where participants are known and trusted entities and may abuse their influence through *Byzantine faults*. The consensus mechanism must therefore be resilient to malicious or compromised nodes who may send conflicting information, become unresponsive, or deliberately attempt to disrupt the network's operation. There are various mitigating features that a *blockchain protocol* may implement to resist Byzantine faults, such as thresholds on the number of nodes required to validate, node reputation systems, redundant communication channels, message replication, audits, network monitoring and intrusion detection, *cryptography*, etc.

Byzantine faults A type of malicious network attack. Byzantine faults include *sybil attacks*, *DDoS attacks*, *eclipse attacks*, packet tampering, time synchronisation attacks, *double-spending*, collusion, etc.

Byzantine Fault Tolerance (BFT) A *blockchain consensus protocol* popular in *permissioned blockchains*. Unlike *Proof of Work (PoW)* or *Proof of Stake (PoS)* blockchains who have a specific mechanism for achieving consensus (i.e. *mining* and *staking*), consensus protocols based on BFT rely on voting, quorum systems, and messaging within a (smaller) network of known entities and are designed to ensure that the blockchain can still achieve consensus and maintain its integrity and security even in the presence of *Byzantine faults*.

CApp Centralised Application. A broad term encompassing any application that interacts with a *blockchain* in some way and is controlled by a single entity. A CApp primarily operates on blockchain technology – leveraging one or more blockchains – but will have some elements built on traditional databases. A CApp may lack features like trustless transactions or native governance mechanisms, and the level of centralised control can vary depending on the implementation. An example could be a loyalty programme managed by a company that uses blockchain to store points but has centralised control over how they are issued and redeemed.

Cardano (ADA)[24] A layer 1 blockchain using the proof of stake consensus protocol. ADA is the native cryptocurrency for the Cardano blockchain.

card rails A term used to describe the card payments *ecosystem*, its *operating regulations*, and its infrastructure.

card scheme A *payment scheme* (or payment system) that provides an *ecosystem* for card payments.

cardholder A consumer or business that has a card account. A type of *payer* or *Payment Service User (PSU)*.

Cardholder Verification Method (CVM) The verification method used to confirm that a *payment instrument* used for a payment transaction is in the possession of the cardholder.

cash Banknotes and coins. Cash is a direct claim on a *central bank*.

Cash App[25] A *peer-to-peer payment app* provided by Block Inc.

CBDC See Central Bank Digital Currency.

CDD See Customer Due Diligence.

CeDeFi A contraction of *CeFi* and *DeFi*. A combination of centralised and decentralised finance in the crypto world. See also *TradFi*.

CeFi An abbreviation of "Centralised Finance". Used to describe centralised crypto businesses, such as centralised *crypto exchanges* or custodian *crypto wallets*. The CeFi platform serves as the custodian of the digital assets, and as such the service user relinquishes control of their *cryptocurrency* to the CeFi platform. The CeFi platform provides services and secures the assets for a fee. If the platform is compromised, the assets could be at risk. Ironically, one of the fundamental characteristics of *Distributed Ledger Technology (DLT)* is decentralisation, and CeFi introduces some degree of centralisation. Examples of CeFi platforms are *Binance* and *Coinbase*. Also see *custody*, *DeFi*, *CeDeFi*, and *TradFi*.

central bank An institution which has been given through a legal act the responsibility to conduct the monetary policy for a specific area.

Examples are the Bank of England, the Monetary Authority of Singapore, the Federal Reserve banks in the US, etc.

Central Bank Digital Currency (CBDC) A type of *virtual asset*. It is different from a *cryptocurrency* or *virtual currency*, as it is issued by a *central bank* and has *legal tender* status. CBDC implementations may use *Distributed Ledger Technology (DLT)*, but they don't have to, as they may use conventional centralised mechanisms, or a combination of both (hybrid infrastructure). Essentially the digital equivalent of notes and coins. See also *retail CBDC* and *wholesale CBDC*.

centralised exchange (CEX) See *crypto exchange*.

centralised ledger A database that is managed and controlled by a single trusted entity, or set thereof, such as a business, government body, or financial institution. In a centralised ledger system, such as traditional card or bank rails, all data is stored in one location, and access to that data is managed by trusted individuals or institutions. See also *distributed ledger*, *Distributed Ledger Technology*.

CEX Centralised Exchange. See *crypto exchange*.

chain analysis Also called *blockchain* analysis. A service that offers the ability to link *blockchain* addresses to real-world identities, which is particularly relevant in an *Anti-Money Laundering* context for *Virtual Asset Services Providers (VASPs)*. Not to be confused with *on-chain analysis*.

chainwork A cumulative measure of the total computational effort expended to create a *blockchain* up to a specific block. It represents the sum of the expected number of hash operations required to mine all blocks from the *genesis block* to the current one. Chainwork is used to determine the most valid chain in the case of *forks* and to assess the overall security of a *Proof-of-Work* blockchain network. It increases with each new block and is typically expressed as a large hexadecimal number.

chargeback A reversal of a payment made by a card *issuer* or payment processor at the request of a *cardholder*, typically initiated due to disputes over unauthorised transactions, fraud, or dissatisfaction with goods or services. Chargebacks are designed to protect consumers from fraudulent activity and ensure fair treatment in transactions, but they can also pose challenges for merchants, including financial losses and potential penalties from payment processors. A *cardholder* can invoke the chargeback process through their issuer to get the transaction amount back from the merchant for a disputed purchase, or it can be invoked directly by the card issuer when they suspect fraud. For merchants, chargebacks are most painful.

cheque A paper-based written *payment instruction* from a *payer* to a *payee* requiring the payer to pay a specified amount to the payee on presentment of the cheque. In markets with modern payment infrastructures, this payment instrument is slowly getting abandoned. Referred to as "check" in the US.

Chime[26] A *neo-bank*.

chip card A *credit card* or *debit card* that follows the *EMV Chip* standard. Also called an "EMV card" and historically a "smart card". Sometimes called *Integrated Circuit Card (ICC)*.

ciphertext Data that has been encrypted from its original state (plain text) using a *cryptography algorithm*. When using *public key cryptography* or *symmetric cryptography*, ciphertext can't be read until it has been decrypted (i.e. converted back to its original state or plain text) with a key. The decryption cipher is an algorithm that transforms the ciphertext back into plain text. Also spelt "ciphertext". See also *public key*, *private key*, *cryptography*, *hash*.

clearing The non-monetary exchange of transaction information. On the *card rails*, clearing is the process by which *merchant* transactions are reconciled with *cardholder* transactions. Merchant transactions are managed by the *acquirer*, and cardholder transactions are managed by the *issuer*, and the clearing process is orchestrated by the *card scheme*. On the bank rails, clearing is the process by which banking transactions are reconciled between banks. The banking transactions are managed by the sender's and receiver's banks, and the clearing process is orchestrated by the bank *payment scheme* for transaction reconciliation. Sometimes this term is used improperly to also include *settlement* (which is wrong since there is no actual funds movement at the clearing stage). In *blockchain* infrastructures, the concept of clearing differs across blockchain implementation and depends on the *consensus protocol*, and may include validation of transactions and blocks. See also *settlement*.

clearing account A deposit account held by a financial services institution at a *central bank*. Unlike *reserve accounts*, which institutions are required to maintain, clearing accounts are held by financial services institution if their required reserve balances are not large enough to cover the total value of their clearing activities and other transfers of funds through the central bank.

clearing cycle In theory, this describes how long it takes for the *clearing* of funds to complete. In practice, the term "clearing cycle" is often associated with cheques (as it takes a few days for cheques to clear). For digital payments (cards or bank accounts), the term "settlement cycle" is also used, meaning both *clearing* and *settlement*. The clearing cycle is more difficult to determine in *blockchain* infrastructures as it will be dependent on how the *mempool* is used, the *consensus protocol*, the *block interval*, etc.

closed loop Any system that is limited in its scope.

closed loop card A payment card that is limited in its scope. Examples are gift cards, fuel cards, and some store cards. These are not generally run on *card scheme* networks.

closed wallet See stored value digital wallet.

cloud mining See Mining-as-a-Service (MaaS).

COBOL Launched in 1959, COmmon Business-Oriented Language is a high-level programming language designed for business applications known for its English-like syntax, making it easier to read and maintain compared to more complex languages. COBOL remains widely used in enterprise systems for many tasks, including financial transactions processing (e.g. bank statements, managing accounts, and handling payments), inventory management (e.g. tracking stock levels, orders, and logistics), payroll processing (e.g. calculating salaries, deductions, and tax withholdings), data reporting (e.g. sales reports, expenses, and business metrics). COBOL's strength lies in its stability and ability to handle large datasets efficiently. Whilst newer languages are emerging, COBOL persists due to the vast amount of legacy code powering critical business operations.

codebase fork A copy of an existing software project's source code that is used to start a new, independent development effort. Unlike other types of forks, a codebase fork creates an entirely separate project with its own distinct history, often with different goals or features from the original. It typically does not share any ongoing development or transaction history with the original project after the point of forking. Commonly used term in *blockchain* ecosystems. See also *fork*.

coin In traditional payments a coin is physical *legal tender* and represents a claim on the issuing *central bank*. In decentralised systems, such as *blockchain* infrastructures, a coin is a *crypto asset* native to its blockchain such as Bitcoin (BTC) on the Bitcoin blockchain, or Ethereum (ETH) on the Ethereum blockchain. In practice, for blockchain infrastructures, the terms "coin" and "token" are often used interchangeably, although there is a technical difference.

Coinbase[27] A centralised *crypto exchange*.

coinbase transaction In a *blockchain* context, this is the first transaction in the block. It specifies the rewards that the block creator will get. It may include newly minted coins/tokens and transaction fees. The term is usually associated with *Proof of Work (PoW)* blockchains, as *Proof of Stake* blockchain tend to use the terms "staking reward transaction", "validator reward transaction", or "block reward transaction", although the term coinbase transaction may also be used. See also *genesis block*.

Coinomize[28] A *coin mixer*.

coin mixer Also known as "crypto currency tumbler" or "crypto mixer" or "crypto mixing service". A service that enables users to mix potentially traceable coins (for example, stolen coins) with other, clean coins in an effort to make it harder to trace them. Can be used for *money laundering* and increasingly attracting regulatory scrutiny. Also see *privacy coin* and *traceability*.

collusion A secret agreement or cooperation between two or more parties to deceive or defraud others, often for mutual benefit. In various contexts, such as business, politics, or cybersecurity, collusion can involve conspiring to manipulate outcomes, share sensitive information, or engage in anti-competitive practices. In decentralised systems, collusion among participants can undermine trust and fairness, leading to compromised integrity in processes like voting, *consensus protocols*, or resource allocation. Detecting and preventing collusion is crucial for maintaining transparency and accountability in any collaborative environment.

confirmation depth Usually expressed in minutes; this is the time taken for a specified number of blocks that must be added to the *blockchain* after the block containing the recorded transaction has been added. The value depends on the *blockchain* and its approach to security. This is a security measure rather than a technical one and is used to mitigate risk and fraud (e.g. the rough equivalent of managing *settlement risk* on traditional financial infrastructures). Sometimes called "confirmation number". See also *confirmation time*.

Confirmation of Payee (CoP) An *overlay service* implemented on top of a bank *payment scheme*. CoP enables payers to check the name and *sort code /* bank account number before they complete a bank payment. CoP is intended to help with reducing *authorised push payment fraud*.

confirmation time The time taken from the point at which a transaction is recorded (i.e. its containing block has been added to the blockchain) to the point when the required number of new blocks have been successfully added (i.e. the *confirmation depth*). This value is dependent on the average block creation time. This is a dynamic metric, and blockchain explorers usually track it. On some blockchains, confirmation times can be several hours or even days. See also *blockchain settlement*, *block finality*.

commodity A basic good or raw material that is interchangeable with other goods of the same type, typically used as inputs in the production of other goods or services. Commodities are often standardised and traded on exchanges, and they can be classified into two main categories: hard commodities (natural resources like oil, gold, and metals) and soft commodities (agricultural products like wheat, coffee, and livestock). The value of a commodity is primarily determined by supply and demand dynamics in the market.

Computer Misuse Act[29] A regulation in the UK which aims to protect the integrity and security of computer systems and data through criminalising systems or data access that is unauthorised by the owners of these systems or data.

consensus protocol The *blockchain* trust framework by which transactions are validated. *Nodes* "listen" to the network and gather valid transactions (i.e. legal, not *double-spending*, etc.) to fit in a block. These nodes may be called *miners* or *validators*, and they add valid transactions to their blocks. The consensus protocol (e.g. *Proof of Work (PoW)*, *Proof of Stake (PoS)*, etc.) determines which valid blocks get added to the chain, the ordering of validated blocks, and enables the blockchain network to be trustless. When the validated winning block is added to the chain, the transaction becomes irreversible. This is the equivalent of the *settlement* process on centralised payment systems. Also known as "consensus mechanism" and "consensus algorithm". See also *immutability*, *blockchain settlement*.

consortium blockchain A type of *permissioned blockchain* controlled by a group.

contact card A card that requires physical contact with a card reader or *payment terminal*. See also *Card Present*.

contactless card A card that doesn't require physical contact with a card reader or card terminal. See also *contactless payment* and *Card Present*.

contactless payment A method of payment where a cardholder pays for something by tapping or waiving their *contactless card* or contactless-enabled device (e.g. smart phone, card, key fob, other *wearables*, etc.) over a card terminal.

contagion risk A type of risk where the failure of one financial services institution (not necessarily a bank) may spill over to a large number of other financial services institutions and possibly the financial system as a whole. Also referred to as systemic risk. Recent examples are the collapse of Wirecard,[30] Terra/Luna[31] and FTX.[32]

CoP See Confirmation of Payee.

correspondent bank A *bank* authorised to provide services on behalf of another bank.

correspondent banking An arrangement under which one bank holds funds owned by another bank (the respondent bank) and provides payment and other services to that respondent bank. A "vostro account" is the term used by a correspondent to describe an account held on behalf of a foreign bank; the foreign bank would in turn regard this account as its "nostro account".

counterparty risk See *settlement risk*.

Counter-Terrorist Financing (CTF) The collection of laws, processes, and regulations that prevent the financing of terrorism. Also referred to as CFT (Combatting the Financing of Terrorism).

credit institution In the EU, this is the definition given to a *bank*.

credit risk The possibility of a financial loss happening due to a borrower's failure to repay a loan or to satisfy contractual obligations.

cross-border International. In payments terms, a cross-border payment or transaction is one where the *payer*'s account and the *payee*'s account are managed by entities in different jurisdictions.

cross-border settlement A *settlement* that takes place in a country other than where one or both counterparties to a transaction are located.

cross-chain staking In a *Proof of Stake* (PoS) context, this is where validators may participate in cross-chain *staking* protocols that enable them to stake their *coins/tokens* across multiple blockchains in order to maximise their stake and reduce their risk exposure to a single *blockchain*.

crowdfunding A method of raising capital through the collective efforts of a large number of individuals, typically via online platforms. It allows entrepreneurs, startups, and projects to solicit small contributions from a diverse pool of backers, often in exchange for rewards, equity, or other incentives. Crowdfunding democratises access to funding, enabling creators to finance their ideas whilst engaging with potential supporters and building a community around their projects.

crowdfunding platform A website, an application, or other software that is used to raise funds or *cryptocurrency* through donations.

crypto airdrop See *airdrop*.

crypto asset At a high level, a crypto asset is a type of *virtual asset* that lives on a *blockchain*, is secured by *cryptography*, and comes in five types: *cryptocurrency*, *Non-Fungible Token* (NFT), *utility token*, *stablecoin*, and *security token*. (Author's note: there is no formally accepted definition or classification of crypto assets.)

crypto ATM A crypto ATM (Automated Teller Machine) is a kiosk that allows users to buy and sometimes sell cryptocurrencies with cash or debit cards. These machines connect to digital wallets and use QR codes to process transactions, offering a familiar ATM-like experience for buying and selling cryptocurrencies.

crypto credit card A type of *credit card* that enables cardholders to earn *cryptocurrency* rewards on purchases instead of *cashback* or other rewards (e.g. points and travel rewards). The rewards earned are automatically used to purchase cryptocurrencies that are then deposited into the cardholder's connected cryptocurrency account (e.g. a *crypto wallet*). The type of cryptocurrency earned depends on the card *issuer* who will usually co-brand the card with a major *card scheme* (e.g. Visa, Mastercard, and American Express). They are called crypto credit cards because they earn cryptocurrency rewards, not because they use cryptocurrencies to make purchases. As cryptocurrencies are volatile, the cryptocurrency rewards earned could lose significant value from one day to the next (unlike standard credit card *cashback*) and may also be subject to tax in some jurisdictions. See also *crypto debit card* and *volatility*.

cryptocurrency A type of digital or virtual currency that uses *cryptography* for security. Cryptocurrencies are typically decentralised and operate on *blockchain* technology, ensuring transparency and security by recording all transactions on a public ledger maintained by a network of computers (*nodes*). A type of *crypto asset* intended to be used as a medium of exchange. This was the original purpose of *Bitcoin* (BTC), but over the years, BTC has morphed into a store of value used for speculative purposes. Some even refer to Bitcoin as "digital gold", which is a misnomer since gold is a stable asset and cryptocurrencies are highly volatile. To this day, no cryptocurrency can claim to be a true medium of exchange. Also spelt "crypto currency". See also *volatility*, *stablecoin*.

cryptocurrency tumbler See *coin mixer*.

crypto debit card A type of *prepaid card* that can be loaded with *cryptocurrency* to make payments online or face-to-face to entities that don't accept cryptocurrencies. This allows cryptocurrency holders to spend it without first having to convert it into *fiat currency* (i.e. without having to use another crypto *off-ramp* service). As with standard prepaid cards, cardholders will need to have cryptocurrency funds already available (this is referred to as *staking* and issuers may require cardholders to "stake" a particular *coin* or *token*) in their funding *crypto wallet* or investment account before they can use it to make payments. Crypto debit cards may also offer rewards on purchases (e.g. points and travel rewards) and issuers may co-brand the card with a major *card scheme* (e.g. Visa, Mastercard, and American Express). See also *crypto credit card*.

crypto exchange A service that allows customers to trade cryptocurrencies for other assets, such as *fiat money* or *cryptocurrency*. There are two types of crypto exchanges: centralised exchanges (CEX), where the exchange is in control of the user's private keys and therefore their crypto assets, and decentralised exchanges (DEX), where the user has full control of their keys and therefore their assets. A CEX, such as *Binance* or *Coinbase*, is also referred to as a "custodial exchange" because a third party has custody of the keys (not the user). A DEX, such as Uniswap and PancakeSwap, is also referred to as a "non-custodial exchange" as the user has custody of their keys. Users can connect their *crypto wallet* to a crypto exchange, and some crypto exchanges also provide crypto wallet services. Also called cryptocurrency exchange. There are also some specialised crypto exchanges called security exchanges which specifically deal with assets that are classified as securities (e.g. *security tokens* and tokenised real-world assets). Also see *CeFi*, *DeFi*, *crypto wallet*, *off-ramp*, and *on-ramp*.

cryptography The science of concealing messages between two parties with a secret code so that third parties are unable to read the message in its concealed form (the *ciphertext*). Although the term "cryptography" refers to the science and the term *encryption* describes the process by which the science is applied, nowadays, both terms are used interchangeably. Also see *cryptography algorithm*, *symmetric cryptography*, *public key cryptography*, *hash*, and *quantum cryptography*.

cryptography algorithm A mathematical function used to scramble plain text and make it unreadable (*ciphertext*). There are three types of cryptography algorithms: *public key cryptography*, *symmetric cryptography*, and hashing algorithms. Also referred to as "cryptographic algorithm". When referring to public key or symmetric cryptography, the algorithms are sometimes referred to as "encryption algorithm". Also see *public key*, *private key*, *cryptography*, *encryption*, *hash*, and *quantum cryptography*.

crypto mixer See *coin mixer*.

crypto mixing service See *coin mixer*.

crypto off-ramp See *off-ramp*.

crypto wallet A type of *digital wallet* used to store the user's *public keys* and *private keys* which act as a certificate of ownership for *crypto assets* that are stored on *Distributed Ledger Technology* (*DLT*), usually a *blockchain*. There are two types of crypto wallets: custodial wallets, where the third party is in control of the user's *private keys* and therefore their crypto assets, and non-custodial wallets, where the user has full control of their keys and therefore their assets. Also see *public key*, *private key*, *CeFi*, *DeFi*, and *crypto exchange*.

CTF See Counter-Terrorist Financing.

custodial exchange See *crypto exchange*.

custodial wallet See *crypto wallet*.

custody A term used to refer to the safekeeping and management of assets on behalf of others. In the traditional financial services world assets can be securities, financial instruments, etc. In the *blockchain* world, custody refers to the safeguarding of users' public and private keys. See also *crypto exchange* and *crypto wallet*.

Customer Due Diligence (CDD) The process by which businesses verify that their customers are who they say they are and is usually conducted at the *underwriting* stage, or when creating a new business relationship. CDD allows businesses to assess *money-laundering* and terrorism-financing risks to which customers may potentially expose them. A form of *due diligence*. See also *Enhanced Due Diligence (EDD)*.

Custom Virtual Machine (CVM) A software layer designed to execute code specifically for a particular platform or application. Unlike a standard *Virtual Machine (VM)*, a CVM isn't as common and requires dedicated development for its functionality.

CVM See Cardholder Verification Method or Custom Virtual Machine.

DAG See Directed Acyclic Graph.

DAO See Decentralised Autonomous Organisation.

dApp Decentralised Application. A software application built on *Distributed Ledger Technology (DLT)* (e.g. a *blockchain*) consisting of a *smart contract* at the backend and a front-end user interface. The user interface is just like any app and is usually built using traditional web technology. Since smart contracts are typically public on the blockchain, anyone can inspect the code and transactions associated with the dApp.

data breach A security violation where sensitive, protected, or confidential data is copied, transmitted, viewed, stolen, modified, or used by a fraudster or cybercriminal. Also described as unintentional information disclosure, data leak, information leakage, and data spill. See also *data protection* and *data privacy*.

data privacy A subset of *data protection*. The process by which access to personal data is controlled (e.g. through policies, technology). Personal data should be protected from those who should not have access to it and individuals should have the ability to control who can access their personal information. Nowadays, as the amount of data being created and stored is continuously increasing, data privacy has become a crucial part of any business strategy, especially in the payments world. Data privacy is recognised as a universal human right in the Universal Declaration of Human Rights (Article 12), the European Convention of Human Rights (Article 8), and the European Charter of Fundamental Rights (Article 7). See also *data protection*.

data protection The process of protecting sensitive information from damage, loss, unauthorised access, or corruption through processes, policies, and technology. Nowadays, as the amount of data being created and stored is continuously increasing, data protection has become a crucial part of any business strategy, especially in the payments world. Used interchangeably with "data security". See also *data privacy.*

decentralisation The distribution of power, control, or functions away from a central authority or location to multiple independent entities. Unlike mere *distribution*, which simply spreads resources or data across multiple points, decentralisation involves granting decision-making authority and autonomy to these dispersed entities. In technology and governance, decentralisation aims to reduce single points of failure, enhance resilience, and promote more democratic or collaborative systems. Whilst distribution focuses on the spread of resources, decentralisation emphasises the spread of control and authority.

Decentralised Autonomous Organisation (DAO) A group of people without a central leader or company dictating any of the decisions. Its structure and governance processes are built on a *blockchain* using *smart contracts* to enforce the rules. DAOs intend to give every member a voice, vote, and opportunity to propose initiatives, and DAO members often buy their way in by purchasing *governance tokens* specifically for the DAO.

decentralised exchange See *crypto exchange.*

decryption The process of converting encoded or encrypted data back into its original, readable format. This is achieved using a specific algorithm and a key, which are required to reverse the *encryption process.* Decryption is essential for accessing secure information that has been protected to ensure confidentiality and prevent unauthorised access.

de-dollarisation A term referring to the attempt at shrinking the US dollar influence on the economies of countries other than the US, specifically those belonging to the *BRICS* block. Even as some BRICS countries have called for the creation of a common currency across the block for trade and investment,[33] the dollar is still by far the most widely held reserve currency and remains essential for conducting international business.

DDoS attack A Distributed Denial of Service (DDoS) attack is a malicious attempt to disrupt the normal functioning of a targeted server, service, or network by overwhelming it with a flood of internet traffic from multiple sources. This coordinated attack uses numerous compromised computer systems as sources of attack traffic, often leveraging a botnet. The goal is to exhaust the target's resources, such as bandwidth, system memory, or processing capacity, rendering the service unavailable to legitimate users. DDoS attacks can cause significant downtime, financial losses, and reputational damage to organisations and networks.

deferred net settlement A settlement method where payment transactions are grouped and settled at specific times throughout the day, rather than immediately. This means the final exchange of funds between parties happens later, even though the sender's account might show a decrease initially. This allows for streamlined processing and reduced costs, but it can also introduce some temporary risk before the final settlement. See *settlement cycle, settlement risk.*

deferred settlement See *settlement cycle.*

DeFi A generic term for decentralised applications (*dApps*) providing financial services on a *blockchain* settlement layer. Examples of DeFi services include investments, insurance, asset management, payments, lending, and trading. DeFi services rely on *smart contracts* and are accessible through dApps, allowing users to buy, sell, store, and trade their funds without the need for a central authority and don't usually require a *KYC* process (although these may be implemented depending on features and regulatory requirements). DeFi emphasises user control and self-*custody*. See also *CeFi, CeDeFi,* and *TradFi.*

Delivery-versus-Payment (DvP) A common form of *settlement* used in the securities industry which guarantees the transfer of securities only happens after payment has been made, alleviating *settlement risk.* DvP specifies that the buyer's cash payment for securities must be made prior to or at the same time as the delivery of the security. See also *Payment-versus-Payment (PvP), atomic settlement,* and *atomic swap.*

delta-hedging A risk management strategy in options trading that aims to neutralise directional risk by continuously adjusting a portfolio to maintain a delta-neutral position. Delta measures the sensitivity of an option's price to changes in the underlying asset's price. In the context of *crypto assets,* delta-hedging is particularly valuable due to the high volatility of *cryptocurrencies,* allowing traders to manage risk and capitalise on price fluctuations without taking on significant directional exposure. See also *synthetic stablecoin.*

depository institution In the US, this is the definition given to a *bank.*

de-risking A process where banks or other financial services institutions either terminate some or all services, or restrict access to services from customers, sectors, or regions they determine to present unacceptable risk. This is a risk avoidance practice rather than a risk management one. Also spelt "derisking". See also a *de-banking*, *Politically Exposed Person (PEP)*, *sanction*.

DEX Decentralised Exchange. See *crypto exchange*.

difficulty target In *Proof of Work (PoW)* blockchains, a value representing the mining difficulty level set by the *blockchain protocol* that miners have to achieve when mining the block (i.e. find a *hash* that is below the difficulty target).

Diffie-Hellman key exchange A *public key cryptography* algorithm. Also known as "Diffie-Hellman key agreement protocol".

digital asset See *virtual asset*.

digital currency A broad term used to describe any currency, money, or money-like asset that exists purely in a digital form. There are several types of digital currencies and many ways of defining the subsets, sometimes conflicting. They can be regulated or unregulated, and some can be secured by *cryptography*. See also *cryptocurrency*, *CBCD*, *crypto asset*, *eMoney*, *virtual asset*, and *virtual currency*.

digital identity Information used digitally to represent real-world identities, including individuals, organisations, applications, and devices. Digital identity can be used for a range of purposes and may offer benefits, ranging from *authentication* and *authorisation* of users for access to information and resources to facilitating e-commerce and personalised digital experiences. Also see *eID*.

digital-only bank See *neo-bank*.

digital signature A cryptographic mechanism used to verify the authenticity, integrity, and non-repudiation of digital messages or documents. It is the electronic equivalent of a handwritten signature or seal, but with added security features. Using *public key cryptography*, a digital signature is created by encrypting a *hash* of the message with the sender's *private key*. Recipients can then use the sender's *public key* to decrypt the signature and verify that the message hasn't been altered and truly comes from the claimed sender. Digital signatures are widely used in various applications, including secure email, software distribution, and financial transactions, to ensure trust and security in digital communications.

digital wallet A broad term used to describe a digital payment facility that enables digital transactions. Digital wallets come in three types: *e-wallets*, *mobile wallets*, and *crypto wallets*.

direct CDBC A *CBDC* architecture model by which a CBDC is issued by a *central bank* who also maintains the ledger of all retail transactions, performs *retail settlement*, and offers accounts and services directly. *Onboarding*, *KYC*, and *authentication* may be performed by intermediaries. This model places significant operational and technical burden on the central bank and distracts from its main role of formulating monetary policy, acting as "bank to banks", being the "lender of last resort", and regulating the domestic banking system. There is no known deployment of this model, although Iceland explored this option. See also *intermediated CBDC (sCBDC)*, *multi-CBDC (mCBDC)*.

Directed Acyclic Graph (DAG) An implementation of *Distributed Ledger Technology (DLT)* designed as a mathematical construct offering a conceptual representation of the ordering of a series of activities which are represented by circles, some of which connected by lines representing the flow from one activity to another. Example of implementations are NANO,[34] Obyte,[35] and IOTA.[36] See also *blockchain*, *Hashgraph*, *Holochain*.

direct participant A term used to describe bank payment scheme participants that are directly connected to the bank payment scheme. See also *directly connected settling participant*, *directly connected non-settling participant*, *principal*, *indirect participant*.

direct payment instruction See *payment instruction*.

directly connected non-settling participant A bank *payment scheme* participant that can connect to the *payment scheme* but cannot settle funds directly with the payment scheme. These participants will settle funds through *directly connected settling participants*. These participants may offer payment scheme access services to *indirect participants*.

directly connected settling participant A bank *payment scheme* participant directly connected to the scheme and able to settle directly through the *settlement agent* for that scheme (a *central bank*) through their settlement account. These participants may offer payment scheme access and settlement services to *indirect participants* and *directly connected non-settling participants*. See also *RTGS account*.

distributed ledger A database that is shared, replicated, and synchronised across multiple locations or entities. Unlike traditional centralised databases, a distributed ledger allows all participants to have access to the same data in real-time, enhancing transparency and security. This technology underpins *cryptocurrencies* and various *blockchain* applications, enabling secure and tamper-proof record-keeping without the need for a central authority. See also *Distributed Ledger Technology*.

Distributed Ledger Technology (DLT) A type of distributed database enabling the storage, recording, and sharing of digital information between consenting parties where the data is spread across multiple sites, regions, or participants. Each of the data stores, the ledgers, has the same data records and is maintained and controlled through a distributed network of computer servers referred to as *nodes*. DLT is based on *peer-to-peer networking*, where peers communicate with each other without the need for a central authority or intermediary. The integrity and security of the ledger, as well as the validation of updates to the ledger, are governed by the *consensus protocol* of the system. *Blockchain* is a form of DLT, but there are others, such as Hashgraph, Directed Acyclic Graph (DAG), Holochain, and Tempo (Radix). See also *centralised ledger*.

distribution The process of spreading or allocating resources, products, or information across different locations, entities, or individuals. Unlike *decentralisation*, which focuses on dispersing control and decision-making authority, distribution primarily concerns the physical or logical arrangement of elements. Distribution can occur within centralised or decentralised systems and often involves the organised dissemination of goods, services, or data from a source to multiple recipients. In various contexts, distribution can refer to:

The delivery of products to consumers or businesses

The allocation of resources or wealth across a population

The geographic spread of natural phenomena or populations

The arrangement of data points in statistical analysis

Whilst decentralisation aims to redistribute power and control, distribution focuses on the efficient and effective spread of tangible or intangible assets without necessarily altering the underlying power structure.

DLT See Distributed Ledger Technology.

Doge The smallest subdivision of a *DOGE* where 100,000,000 Doge represent one DOGE. The unit of measurement for *Dogecoin* transaction costs. See also *gas price*.

Dogecoin (DOGE) A *layer 1 blockchain* using the *Proof of work consensus protocol*. A *permissionless blockchain*. Also refers to the native Dogecoin *cryptocurrency (coin)*, abbreviated as DOGE. See also *Doge*.

double-spending A term referring to the attempted spending of the same funds twice, which creates a discrepancy between the actual amount of funds available and how it is recorded on a ledger. Double-spending is extremely improbable in centralised payment systems because they have mature processes, established regulations, robust security, and trusted intermediaries who oversee all transactions, from *payment instruction* to *settlement*. Double-spending is an issue for blockchain infrastructures as they don't rely on trusted intermediaries and operate a distributed trust model where participating *nodes* ensure the integrity of the system. In order to prevent double-spending, blockchains use various mechanisms, including the *consensus protocol*, the validation of transactions by nodes before they are added to the blockchain ledger, and timestamping of transactions. See also *blockchain, node, replay attack.*

domestic settlement A *settlement* that takes place in the country where both counterparties to a transaction are located.

domestic transaction A transaction where the *payer's* and *payee's* payment accounts are managed by entities located in the same jurisdiction.

DSA Digital Signature Algorithm. A *public key cryptography* algorithm.

due diligence The process of conducting the relevant checks that a business or person should perform before entering into an agreement or contract with another party. See also *Customer Due Diligence, Enhanced Due Diligence.*

DvP See Delivery-versus-Payment.

dynamic gas fee A "base fee" set by some *blockchain protocols* which validating nodes must use to calculate the transaction fee (the base fee can be changed at any time through blockchain governance according to a number of factors, including network congestion). This is a governance method to manage blockchain operations. In this model, users don't set the *gas price.*

dynamic routing The process and technology used to simplify and optimise *payment acceptance* for businesses by routing payment transactions in real time to the most suitable *acquirer* or *PSP* (e.g. *payment gateway*), with the objective of enhancing *authorisation* success rates, reducing failed transactions, reducing downtime impact, distributing payment load, and lowering transaction processing costs. See also *payment orchestration.*

EBA See European Banking Authority.

ECB See European Central Bank.

ECDSA Elliptic Curve Digital Signature Algorithm. A *public key cryptography* algorithm.

eclipse attack A type of network-level threat in *peer-to-peer* systems where a malicious actor isolates a target node from the rest of the network by monopolising all of its connections. The attacker floods the target with connections to nodes under their control, effectively "eclipsing" the victim from legitimate network activity. This isolation allows the attacker to manipulate the target's view of the network, potentially enabling *double-spending*, disrupting *mining* operations, or compromising the node's ability to verify transactions accurately. Eclipse attacks exploit limitations in peer discovery and connection protocols, posing risks to *blockchain* networks' security and *decentralisation*.

e-commerce The sale or purchase of goods and services through electronic transactions conducted online over the internet or other digital networks. Also spelt "ecommerce".

ecosystem A business ecosystem is an arrangement by which participants will create value for a common set of customers and share the benefits of value creation. Every business ecosystem has participants, and at least one member acts as the orchestrator of the participants. The most famous ecosystem is Amazon. A notable difference between an ecosystem and a *value chain* is that an ecosystem is not necessarily built around a fixed chain of processes and is all about seizing opportunities and innovating. The payments industry is at various stages of transitioning between value chains and ecosystems.

EDD See Enhanced Due Diligence.

EDI See Electronic Data Interchange.

eID A generic term to describe electronic identification to ensure secure access to government services, other online services, or carry out payment transactions.

eIDAS[37] Electronic Identification and trust services. A European regulatory framework aiming to ensure that people and businesses can use their own national electronic identification schemes (eIDs) to access public services available online in other EU countries.

Electronic Data Interchange (EDI) A mature electronic data exchange format which has been around since the 1960s, used between organisations across industries, typically used to format and exchange business documents electronically (e.g. purchase orders, invoices, shipping notices, etc.). EDI represents a set of standards that are used in different industries, including manufacturing, healthcare, logistics, retail, and finance. The most well-known formats are ANSI X12 and EDIFACT. Whilst EDI is still used in financial services, there are other standards that are specifically focused on the financial services sector, such as ISO 8583 and ISO 20022. See also XML.

Electronic Funds Transfer (EFT) A catch-all term used to describe electronic transfer of funds between financial institutions.

electronic money See *eMoney*.

Electronic Money Institution (EMI) A regulated payment business allowed to manage *eMoney* on behalf of its users. In Europe, there are two types of eMoney institutions, the *Small eMoney Institution* (SEMI) and the *authorised eMoney Institution* (EMI). In some geographies, these may be referred to as a Money Service Business (MSB). Electronic money institutions may be called Payments Banks in India, or Fintech Banks in the US.

Electrum[38] A *crypto wallet*.

EMI See *Electronic Money Institution*.

eMoney A type of *virtual asset*. It is an electronic store of value that acts as a cash substitute and is issued by either a regulated entity called an *eMoney Institution* (EMI) or a bank. It may be used for making payments to entities other than the *issuer* (unlike a *virtual currency*). Types of eMoney include *prepaid cards*, electronic prepaid accounts, and virtual payment accounts for use online.

eMoney Institution See Electronic Money Institution.

EMV The set of standards for cards, managed by *EMVCo*.

EMV card A credit or debit card that follows the *EMV Chip* standard. Also called a "chip card" and historically a "smart card".

EMV Chip An *EMV* standard for *chip cards*. The EMV chip itself is an integrated circuit consisting of a microprocessor and a memory constructed according to ISO/IEC 7816 (contact) and ISO/IEC 14443 (contactless). The chip contains the data required for EMV transactions at the *Point-of-Sale* (POS).

EMVCo[39] A consortium controlled equally by Visa, Mastercard, American Express, UnionPay, and Discover. EMVCo is responsible for developing and maintaining EMV card standards. EMV takes its initials from Eurocard, Mastercard, and Visa, the original founders in 1999. In 2002,

Mastercard merged with Europay International SA, the owners of the Eurocard brand. Whilst the Europay name disappeared, the EMV name remains.

encryption The process by which data is encrypted and decrypted. See also *cryptography*, *Secure Element*.

Enhanced Due Diligence (EDD) The process by which businesses perform more stringent *Customer Due Diligence (CDD)* on customers at underwriting stage, or during the course of a business relationship. EDD is usually performed where the customer is not present when KYC is performed, when *Politically Exposed Persons (PEPs)* are involved, where the nature of the customer's business changes, where there is a high risk of *money laundering* or terrorism financing, or where the customer is in a high-risk country. See also *sanction*.

EPI See European Payments Initiative.

escrow A legal arrangement where a third party (the escrow agent/holder) holds assets, such as money or property, temporarily until specific conditions of a transaction are met, ensuring all parties fulfil their obligations before the assets are released.

ESG An acronym for Environmental, Social, and Governance. This term is often used interchangeably with "sustainability" and represents a set of standards measuring the impact a business has on the environment, society, and how transparent and accountable the business is. In recent years, investors increasingly consider ESG factors when making business investment decisions. Depending on the jurisdiction, businesses, especially large ones, may have regulatory obligations to report on some ESG factors (e.g. carbon footprint, diversity, and inclusion). See also *greenwashing*.

ETF See Exchange Traded Fund.

Ethereum (ETH)[40] A *layer 1 blockchain* using *the Proof of stake consensus protocol*. Prior to "The Merge" in September 2022, the Ethereum *blockchain* used the *Proof of work* (PoW) *consensus protocol*. Also refers to the native Ethereum *cryptocurrency (coin)*, abbreviated as ETH. See also *Gwei*.

Ethereum Virtual Machine See *EVM*.

eToro[41] A social trading and multi-asset investment company that is also a *crypto exchange*.

European Banking Authority (EBA)[42] An independent EU authority which works to ensure effective and consistent prudential regulation and supervision across the European banking sector.

European Central Bank (ECB)[43] Together with the national *central banks* of the EU Member States whose currency is the euro, the ECB defines and implements the monetary policy for the euro area.

European Payments Initiative (EPI)[44] In 31 February 2021 major European banks created a joint venture with *acquirers* Worldline and Nets (now owned by Nexi), aiming to build a pan-European network to rival Visa and Mastercard. In March 2022, the EPI seemingly disbanded, but in April 2023, at the time P27 collapsed, in a surprising move, the EPI acquired Dutch payment scheme iDeal and Belgian mobile payments App Payconiq, progress which was welcomed by the European Central Bank. Watch this space, as this may very well become the EU equivalent of the American *Zelle*.

Eurosystem The central banking system of the euro area. It comprises the ECB and the national central banks of those EU Member States whose currency is the euro.

EVM (Ethereum Virtual Machine) A *Virtual Machine (VM)* specific to the *Ethereum blockchain*. The EVM establishes a standard environment for *smart contract* execution, promoting interoperability and simplifying development. Additionally, the isolated execution within the EVM enhances security and fosters decentralisation by distributing smart contract execution across the network. Finally, the EVM offers a developer-friendly approach, allowing programmers to use existing tools and languages to create smart contracts, making blockchain development more accessible. In essence, the EVM acts as a virtual computer within the Ethereum blockchain, executing the code behind *dApps* in a secure, standardised, and developer-friendly manner.

e-wallet A web application that can be accessed from any connected device and is used to make payments, usually with several funding options (e.g. cards, bank accounts, etc.). PayPal is an example of an e-wallet. Also spelt "ewallet".

exchange token A type of *utility token* which is only used in a specific *crypto exchange*.

Exchange Traded Fund (ETF) A type of investment fund that is traded on stock exchanges, generally tracking a specific index, market, or group of markets. They are offered by funds managers, who charge a fee for their services, and investors usually use them for short-term returns and ETFs are taxed for capital gains. They are designed to provide investors with the flexibility to buy and sell a diversified portfolio of assets, such as stocks, bonds, commodities, or other financial instruments, in a single security. Increasingly, *cryptocurrency* ETFs have emerged where they track the performance of the underlying asset (e.g. *Bitcoin*), allowing investors to gain exposure to Bitcoin without actually owning the asset. Cryptocurrency ETFs are increasingly attracting regulatory scrutiny.

Exodus[45] A crypto wallet.

Face ID Apple's implementation of *biometrics* for facial recognition which can be used as a form of *authentication* for accessing accounts or making payments. See also *delegated authentication*.

FAANG An acronym for Facebook (now Meta), Apple, Amazon, Netflix, and Alphabet (Google's parent company). These platforms are increasingly involved in payments and financial services. See also *Big Tech*, *BATX*, *GAFA*, *MAMAA*, and *FANG*.

FANG An acronym for Facebook (now Meta), Amazon, Netflix, and Alphabet (Google's parent company). These platforms are increasingly involved in payments and financial services. See also *Big Tech*, *BATX*, *GAFA*, *MAMAA*, and *FAANG*.

Fast IDentity Online (FIDO)[46] A set of standards for *authentication* protocols ultimately aimed at eliminating passwords. The standards (e.g. WebAuthn) are managed by the FIDO Alliance, an open industry association with members from across the globe, including Amazon, Apple, Bank of America, American Express, Google, Intel, Idemia, Meta, PayPal, and many others.

Faster Payments System (FPS) A bank *payment scheme*. A UK domestic A *real-time payment system (RTP system)*, *retail payment system* (RPS). The FPS[47] launched in 2008 and is the UK *real-time payment* system for payments up to £1 million. It allows customers to make electronic payments almost instantaneously, 7 days/week, 24 h/day. FPS is managed by Pay.UK. Also an RPS in Hong Kong,[48] operated by HKICL. Also an RPS in Russia,[49] operated by CBR.

FATF See Financial Action Task Force.

FedNow[50] A US A *real-time payment system (RTP system)*, *retail payment system* (RPS) operated by the Federal Reserve Bank and governed by NACHA. A bank *payment scheme* that launched in July 2023.

Fedwire[51] A US *Large Value Payment System (LVPS)* governed by *NACHA* and operated by the Federal Reserve Bank. A bank *payment scheme*. See also *wire transfer*.

fiat currency Government-issued currency that is not backed by a physical commodity, such as gold or silver, but rather by the government that issued it. It derives its value from supply and demand and the stability of the issuing government. Fiat currency gives *central banks* greater control over the economy, as they can control how much money is printed. Fiat currency has therefore no intrinsic value, and it is often referred to as "paper money". Governments have to make it *legal tender* by setting it as the standard for debt repayment. Most modern currencies are fiat money. Also referred to as fiat money. See also *money*.

fiat on-ramp See *on-ramp*.

FIDO See Fast IDentity Online.

finality An irrevocable and unconditional transfer of funds from one party to another which occurs during *settlement*.

Financial Action Task Force (FATF)[52] An independent intergovernmental body that develops and promotes policies to protect the global financial system against *money laundering*, terrorist financing, and the financing of the proliferation of weapons of mass destruction. The FATF is also known as GAFI (Groupe d'Action Financière), and is headquartered in Paris. The FATF identifies countries with weak *anti-money laundering* controls and lists them in two public documents that are published three times a year: the *black list* and the *grey list*.

financial crime A term referring to all crimes committed by an individual or a group of individuals involving unlawfully obtaining *money* or other property that belongs to someone else to obtain a financial or professional gain. In regulatory terms, financial crime may include any offence involving (a) fraud or dishonesty; (b) misconduct in, or misuse of information relating to, a financial market; or (c) handling the proceeds of crime. See also *money laundering*.

financial inclusion Refers to the ability of individuals or businesses to have access to financial services.

fintech A very broad term used to describe any business that uses technology to improve, digitise, automate, or provide enablers to financial services aimed at businesses or consumers.

flash loan A type of uncollateralised lending in *DeFi* where a user borrows and repays funds within a single *blockchain* transaction. The loan is facilitated by *smart contracts*, requiring no collateral as the borrowed amount must be returned before the transaction completes, or the entire operation is reversed. Flash loans are often used for *arbitrage*, liquidations, or other complex DeFi strategies.

foreign exchange (FX, Forex) The conversion of a country's currency into another country's currency. Foreign exchange also refers to the global trading market whereby currencies are virtually exchanged around the clock, with the largest centres being based in London, New York, Tokyo, and Singapore.

foreign exchange rate The relative value between two currencies. In particular, it is the quantity of one currency required to buy or sell a unit of the other currency.

forex See foreign exchange.

fork A fork is a technical event when a *blockchain* diverges into two separate paths forward. Forks can be accidental, in which case they should be resolved by the blockchain protocol relatively quickly making the split temporary or intentional with the purpose of implementing new rules, reverse the effects of hacking, or resolve disagreements within the community. Forks are classified as either *soft forks* (backward-compatible changes) or *hard forks* (non-backward-compatible changes that may result in two distinct blockchains). How forks are resolved depends on the blockchain implementation and the intent. See also *codebase fork*.

form factor The medium with which a payment is made. It can be a plastic card, a mobile phone, a wearable item (e.g. smartwatch, ring, etc.), a virtual card, etc.

four-party model A two-sided economic model by which there is a separation between *acquirers* and *issuers*. This promotes competition, as commercial terms can be set on either side (*merchant* and *cardholder*) to the benefit of merchants and cardholders. This model is also referred to as "open loop". Examples of *card schemes* operating on this model are Visa and Mastercard. The four parties referred to are the cardholder, the merchant, the acquirer, and the issuer.

FPS See Faster Payments System.

fractional ownership A method of property ownership where multiple parties share rights to a valuable asset, each holding a percentage of the total. This model allows investors to own a portion of high-value assets they might not be able to afford entirely on their own. Fractional ownership can apply to various assets, including real estate, artwork, luxury goods, or even digital assets like *Non-Fungible Tokens (NFTs)*. It enables broader access to investment opportunities, diversification, and shared costs whilst potentially offering partial usage rights or returns proportional to the owned fraction. See also *tokenisation*.

fraud proof A cryptographic mechanism used in *blockchain* networks, particularly in *optimistic rollups*, to challenge and verify the validity of transactions or state transitions. It allows network participants to contest potentially fraudulent or incorrect data by providing evidence of its invalidity. If a fraud proof is successfully submitted within a specified challenge period, the disputed transactions are reverted, and the network returns to the last known valid state. This system operates on the assumption that all transactions are valid unless proven otherwise, enhancing scalability whilst maintaining security.

full node In *blockchain* networks, this is a type of node with special responsibilities and privileges. A full node stores the entire blockchain transaction history, participates in the transaction validation process and through the *consensus protocol*, ensures which valid blocks will be added to the blockchain, and relays them to other full nodes. Because of this, full nodes require a lot of storage space and computing power. Full nodes are essential for maintaining the integrity of the blockchain network. A blockchain's decentralisation and security increase proportionally with the number of full nodes it possesses. The *Bitcoin* blockchain has in excess of 16,000 full nodes (although this can't be accurately determined as this number is rather dynamic) and has never been hacked (although blockchain-related services, such as a *crypto-exchange*, can be compromised). See also *miner*, *validator*, *master node*, and *light node*.

fungibility A characteristic of assets which are substitutable on account of their being identical. A banknote is fungible, a fine art painting is not.

FX See foreign exchange.

G2C See Government-to-Consumer.

GAFA An acronym for Google, Apple, Facebook, and Amazon. These platforms are increasingly involved in payments and financial services. See also *Big Tech*, *BATX*, *FANG*, *MAMAA*, and *FAANG*.

GAFI See Financial Action Task Force.

GameFi A combination of gaming and *DeFi* that refers to *blockchain*-based games which allow players to earn cryptocurrencies or tradable digital assets through gameplay. These games typically incorporate *play-to-earn* (P2E) models, *non-fungible tokens* (NFTs), and other DeFi elements to create in-game economies where players can own, trade, and monetise virtual assets.

gas fee See *gas price*.

gas limit A term usually associated with Proof of Work (PoW) *blockchain* networks where it represents the cost that the sender of a transaction is willing to pay for the transaction to be processed by the network of *miners* or *validators*.

gas price In a *blockchain* context, this is the payment made by crypto traders to compensate *miners* or *validators* for the computing energy and effort required to process and validate transactions on a blockchain. This term is usually associated with *Proof of Work (PoW) blockchain* networks where it represents the cost of the computing power required by *miners* or *validators* to execute transactions. The gas price is set by the sender of the transaction and is denominated in the native *cryptocurrency* of the blockchain or subdivision thereof (e.g. *Satoshi* on the *Bitcoin* blockchain, *Gwei* on the *Ethereum* blockchain). For other blockchain infrastructures, this may also be referred to as "transaction fee", "gas fee", or "network fee" and may be calculated differently.

gas station service In a *blockchain* context, this is a facility that provides real-time information on current network conditions, number of unspent transactions, and recommended *gas price* for each transaction speed, enabling users to set competitive prices.

GDPR[53] The EU General Data Protection Regulation.

Gemini[54] A centralised *crypto exchange*.

genesis block Also known as "block 0", this is the very first block added to a *blockchain* after which every subsequent block is added. It is essentially the ancestor to which every other block can trace its lineage since every block contains a reference to the block preceding it. The genesis blocks mark the launch of a blockchain and defines the format of all subsequent blocks. It is created differently than all subsequent block and, in most blockchains, it will be hardcoded directly into the software, potentially including some initial coin/token supply (initial coinbase reward), and unlike regular blocks, the genesis block has no previous block to reference. In *PoW* blockchains, the genesis block may be pre-mined by the blockchain creator or a trusted group of individuals. In *PoS* blockchains, the genesis block might be "seeded" by validators, typically involving distributing the initial stake to the chosen validators. The genesis block data is usually publicly available for inspection. See also *coinbase transaction*.

Gini coefficient A statistical measure of income or wealth inequality within a population. It ranges from 0 to 1, where 0 represents perfect equality (everyone has the same income/wealth) and 1 represents perfect inequality (one person has all the income/wealth, others have none). The coefficient is based on the Lorenz curve, which plots the cumulative share of income against the cumulative share of the population. A Gini coefficient below 0.3 suggests relatively low inequality, 0.3–0.5 indicates moderate inequality, and above 0.5 signifies high inequality. The Gini coefficient can be adapted to assess the distribution of *cryptocurrency* or *token* ownership within a *blockchain* network. A lower Gini coefficient indicates a more equitable distribution of tokens, contributing to greater decentralisation. Conversely, a higher Gini coefficient suggests a more concentrated ownership, indicating less decentralisation. This metric helps evaluate the fairness and distribution of economic power within blockchain ecosystems.

Google Pay A *Digital Wallet* provided by Google. Now incorporated into *Google Wallet*.

Google Wallet[55] A multi-purpose *Digital Wallet* provided by Google. Enables users to store and use payment cards, tickets, passes, keys, and identities. A *staged digital wallet*.

governance token An upgraded version of a *utility token* which gives more rights to its holders (e.g. voting). See also *blockchain*, *Decentralised Autonomous Organisation*.

Government-to-Consumer (G2C) A term used to describe a business model where a government entity provides services directly to consumers (e.g. tax, registration, educational services, and employment help).

Gwei The smallest subdivision of one *Ethereum* (ETH) where 100,000,000 Gweis represent one ETH. The unit of measurement for ETH transaction costs. See also *gas price*.

hacking A type of *cybercrime* involving methods and techniques for breaching defences and exploiting vulnerabilities in computer systems, devices, or networks.

hard fork See *fork*.

hard peg See *peg*.

Hardware Security Module (HSM) A hardware device which secures and manages secrets, performs *encryption* and decryption functions used for digital signatures, strong *authentication*, and other functions of *cryptography*.

hash A mathematical function that converts an input of arbitrary length into an encrypted output of fixed length. This means that regardless of the original size of data used as input, the output is a unique hash that will always have the same size. Hashing is used to secure stored data (data at rest), thus ensuring the integrity and authenticity of the stored data. Hashed data can be checked against the original content to determine that the contents haven't been modified whilst in storage. Hashed data is different from encrypted data inasmuch as there is no decryption key (it is a one-way function). Popular hashing algorithms include MD-5 (one of the earliest, now considered unsafe), RIPEMD-160 (RACE Integrity Primitives Evaluation Message Digest, also an established one, still considered secure), and the SHA family (Secure Hash Algorithm, current version is SHA-3). Commonly used for password security and in *blockchain* infrastructures. See also *cryptography*.

Hashgraph An implementation of *Distributed Ledger Technology (DLT)* claiming to be more scalable than blockchains by virtue of having a validation mechanism (see consensus) based on virtual voting where participants continuously communicate with each other, sharing information about the transactions they receive. An example of implementation is Hedera.[56] See also *blockchain, Holochain, Directed Acyclic Graph (DAG)*.

hashing The process of converting input data of any size into a fixed-size string of characters, typically a sequence of numbers and letters, using a mathematical algorithm known as a *hash* function. This output, called a hash value or hash code, serves as a unique identifier for the original data. Hashing is commonly used in data integrity verification, password storage, and digital signatures, as it provides a one-way transformation that is computationally difficult to reverse.

hashing power In a *Proof of Work (PoW) blockchain* context, the computing resources are available for *mining*.

hashrate The measure of computational power used to solve complex mathematical problems in *Proof-of-Work* blockchain networks, typically expressed in hashes per second (H/s). It represents the speed at which a miner or mining network can perform cryptographic hash functions, with higher hashrates indicating greater mining capacity and network security. Hashrate is a key metric for assessing the overall strength and competitiveness of a *blockchain* network's *mining* ecosystem.

HCE See Host Card Emulation.

Herfindhal index Also known as the Herfindahl-Hirschman Index (HHI). A measure of market concentration used to determine the level of competition within an industry. It is calculated by summing the squares of the market shares of all firms within the market. The index ranges from 0 to 10,000, where a higher value indicates greater market concentration and less competition. An HHI below 1,500 suggests a competitive marketplace, 1,500–2,500 indicates moderate concentration, and above 2,500 signifies high concentration. In a *blockchain* context, the HHI can be adapted to assess the distribution of power or resources across network participants, such as validators, token holders, nodes, and governance contributors. A lower HHI indicates greater decentralisation, whilst a higher HHI suggests more concentration. This helps evaluate the decentralisation of consensus mechanisms, token distribution, node infrastructure, and governance within blockchain networks.

HHI See Herfindahl index.

HODL In crypto vernacular, an acronym for "Hold On for Dear Life" which means retaining crypto assets that you own for an extended period of time, even during a highly volatile market movement. Another version of the term's origin is a spelling mistake of the word "hold". See also *volatility*.

Holochain An implementation of *Distributed Ledger Technology* (*DLT*) claiming to be more scalable than blockchains because it doesn't require all participating nodes to store and validate all of the data, which creates a large amount of overhead and doesn't scale easily. The architecture is "agent-centric" rather than "data-centric", meaning that a Holochain application creates its own encrypted peer-to-peer network between users directly with a concept of mutual accountability. Holochain positions itself as a *Web*3.0 platform.

homomorphic encryption A cryptographic technique that allows computations to be performed directly on encrypted data without decrypting it first, allowing parties to compute functions on private data without revealing the actual data or to search for data without entirely decrypting it.

Host Card Emulation (HCE) The cloud-based technology that allows cardholders to make a payment at a PoS terminal using their mobile phone. The technology allows card details to be stored in a shared secure repository as opposed to being stored on the phone itself. A form of *Secure Element*.

HSM See Hardware Security Module.

Howey Test A legal framework established by the US Supreme Court in 1946 to determine whether a transaction qualifies as an "investment contract" and therefore is considered a security subject to disclosure and registration requirements. The test consists of four criteria: (1) an investment of money, (2) in a common enterprise, (3) with the expectation of profit, and (4) derived primarily from the efforts of others. The Howey Test has gained recognition and influence beyond the United States, though its application and interpretation may vary in different jurisdictions. European regulations tend to be more prescriptive and detailed, leaving less room for discretionary interpretation compared to the Howey Test. As the crypto industry has gained traction globally, regulators in various countries have turned to principles similar to the Howey Test to determine whether *cryptocurrencies* and *Initial Coin Offerings (ICOs)* should be classified as securities.

hybrid blockchain A *blockchain* offering features from both a *permissioned blockchain* and a *permissionless blockchain*. It is controlled by a central authority but also offers some permissionless elements. The controlling entity can make the blockchain accessible to everyone (through a public blockchain) whilst a permissioned blockchain controls ledger updates. See also *private blockchain* and *consortium blockchain*.

Hyperledger Fabric A *permissioned blockchain platform*. Created by the Linux Foundation, it is designed for building permissioned blockchains with a focus on scalability and security. Often used in enterprise settings.

IDE See Integrated Development Environment.

identity theft A type of *cybercrime* where fraudsters steal and use a victim's personal information to commit a variety of crimes, such as opening accounts in the victim's name, unauthorised use of existing accounts, illegally obtaining goods or services, etc. Also referred to as "ID theft".

immutability The state of not being able to change or be changed once created. A term used in the context of *blockchain* infrastructures where, once transactions are added to the blockchain, they become immutable. See also *blockchain settlement* and *finality*.

impermanent loss A financial concept that refers to the potential opportunity cost incurred when holding a volatile asset rather than holding a stable asset like cash. In the context of *decentralised crypto exchanges (DEXs)*, it refers to the loss in value experienced by *liquidity* providers when the price of the assets they contribute to a *liquidity pool* changes significantly compared to when they initially deposited them. This loss is realised when the liquidity provider withdraws their assets from the pool.

improvement proposal (IP) A *blockchain* improvement proposal is a formalised suggestion for changes or upgrades to a *blockchain protocol*, aimed at enhancing its functionality or addressing issues. Prominent improvement proposal processes include Bitcoin Improvement Proposals (BIPs), which outline changes to the Bitcoin protocol; Ethereum Improvement Proposals (EIPs), which suggest modifications to the Ethereum network; Cardano Improvement Proposals (CIPs) for the Cardano blockchain; Zcash Improvement Proposals (ZIPs) focused on Zcash enhancements; and the Tezos amendment process, which facilitates on-chain governance for protocol updates. These proposals typically undergo community discussion, peer review, and a consensus mechanism for adoption.

Independent Software Vendor (ISV) A business that develops and sells software products that may run on physical hardware devices, virtual machines or in the cloud. They supply technology enablers for specific markets, industries, etc. In a payments context, an ISV will sell software to integrate within a stakeholder's payment technology environment. Sometimes called "Integrated Software Vendor".

indirectly connected participant A bank *payment scheme* participant that is not directly connected to the payment scheme nor able to settle directly through the *settlement agent*. These participants will connect and settle funds through *directly connected settling participants*. This model is referred to as "agency banking" and gives financial services institutions the ability to offer payment services to their customers in locations where they don't have a physical presence or where they are unable to meet the regulatory requirements for direct access to a payment scheme. Also referred to as "indirect participant".

indirect participant See indirectly connected participant.

indirect payment instruction See *payment instruction.*

information asymmetry A situation in which one party in a transaction or relationship has more or better information than the other party. This imbalance in access to relevant information can lead to unfair advantages, market inefficiencies, or suboptimal decision-making. In economics and finance, information asymmetry can result in adverse selection, moral hazard, or market failure. It is a key concept in understanding market dynamics, contract theory, and the design of regulatory frameworks aimed at promoting fairness and efficiency in various contexts, including financial markets, insurance, and corporate governance.

Ingenico[57] A French technology company providing *merchant services* which expanded from manufacturing *Point of Sale (POS)* payment terminals to also include complete merchant payment SaaS and related services.

Initial Coin Offering (ICO) The *cryptocurrency* version of crowdfunding where anyone can invest, usually launched on the *blockchain* project's website. See also *tokenomics, Initial Exchange Offering, Security Token Offering, and airdrop.*

Initial DEX Offering (IDO) A fundraising method in which a cryptocurrency project launches its token directly through a *decentralised exchange (DEX)*. IDOs allow projects to raise capital and provide immediate liquidity by creating a trading pair with the newly minted token. This model offers a more decentralised, accessible, and often faster alternative to traditional *Initial Coin Offerings (ICOs)* or *Initial Exchange Offerings (IEOs)*, typically with lower barriers to entry for both projects and investors. See also *tokenomics, Security Token Offering*, and *airdrop*.

Initial Exchange Offering (IEO) A fundraising method in the *cryptocurrency* industry where a new project sells its tokens directly through an established cryptocurrency exchange. The exchange vets the project, manages the token sale process, and typically lists the tokens for trading immediately after the sale. IEOs aim to provide enhanced security and credibility compared to *Initial Coin Offerings (ICOs)* by leveraging the exchange's reputation and user base. See also *tokenomics, Security Token Offering*, and *airdrop*.

integer overflow A programming error where the result of calculations is too big or too small for the data type storing it. Imagine a counter that only goes up to 99, but you try to add 1. Instead of 100, it overflows and flips back to 0. In *smart contracts*, this error can lead to unexpected behaviour, like accidentally resetting a user's balance to zero instead of adding funds. Using bigger data types and checking for potential overflows can help prevent these issues.

Integrated Development Environment (IDE) A software application combining a variety of tools to help programmers develop software efficiently. IDEs may include features such as code editors, debuggers, compilers or build automation tools, version control, graphical user interface builders, testing tools, etc. They aim to improve productivity, reduce errors, increase code quality, and simplify collaboration. Popular IDEs include Visual Studio, Android Studio, and PyCharm.

interbank settlement Traditionally, a centralised function coordinated by the *payment scheme* concerned with the *settlement* of a large variety of payment types (e.g. *retail payments* and *wholesale payments*), sizes (e.g. high value and low value), and settlement times. On the *card rails*, interbank settlement is the process of moving funds between *issuers* and *acquirers* and is managed by the *card scheme* through their *settlement agents*. This is the first step of the settlement process for card payments (the second step being *merchant settlement*). On the bank rails, interbank settlement happens between banks through the *settlement agent* (a *central bank*) for a given bank *payment scheme*. More recently, interbank settlement can be performed using stablecoins, and traditional players may partner with *blockchain* service providers or *stablecoin issuers* for this. See also *retail settlement* and *wholesale settlement*.

interchange An *ecosystem* funding mechanism used on the *card rails*. It is a percentage of the card transaction value. In the *four-party model*, this amount flows from the *acquirer* to the *issuer* for card transactions. In some countries, such as the EU, interchange is regulated, but the interchange rules are specified by the *card schemes* (within applicable regulations). For ATM transactions, the interchange fee is paid to the ATM operator that processes the transaction on the ATM network by the issuer of the card. Also referred to as "interchange fee".

intermediated CBDC (sCBDC) A *CBDC* architecture model by which a *central bank* issues one CBDC, maintains the ledger, and performs wholesale *settlement* (direct liability). Private *issuers* (e.g. commercial banks and *non-bank PSPs*) issue a synthetic CBDC (sCBDC) and distribute it to consumers and businesses by offering accounts and services. Here, commercial banks and non-bank PSPs offering services hold CBDC accounts at the central bank and perform *retail settlement*. The central bank needs to honour claims of which it has no record since it has no visibility of retail balances. There is a variant of this model, where the central bank would periodically records retail balances. Although this offers protection for businesses and consumers, it creates similar problems for the central bank as in the *direct CBDC* architecture model, as the central bank would have to rely on the intermediaries to consistently report the retail balances. An sCBDC is used for retail purposes, and its operation is similar to how *eMoney* works. This model is also referred to as "indirect", "synthetic", or "two-tier". Also see *direct CBDC* and *multi-CBDC*.

Internet of Things (IoT) Describes the network of physical objects – things – that contain sensors, software, and other technologies enabling them to connect and exchange data with other devices and systems over the internet.

intrabank settlement See *on us*.

invisible payments This term refers to the idea that payments can be processed seamlessly without the customer having to interact with any payment instrument or device. Typically, in the background, the customer would need to set up an account and provide credentials in advance, but any subsequent payment interactions, through the use of technology such as *artificial intelligence* and *biometrics*, will seem invisible.

IoT See Internet of Things.

ISO 20022 A modern messaging standard for data interchange between financial institutions, and prior to its release in 2004, *large-value payment systems (LVPS)* used SWIFT messaging, and *retail payment systems* (RPSs) used ISO 8583. Unlike ISO 8583, ISO 20022 data is machine-readable (not sequential) and uses XML (Extensible Markup Language) and ASN.1 (Abstract Syntax Notation). It can significantly streamline payment messaging by providing richer data, more transparency, better interoperability (e.g. standardising non-Latin alphabets), and adapting to changing needs and business models. ISO 20022 involves the processing of much larger data volumes, and payment *ecosystem* actors need to update their infrastructures to manage the additional information, which means substantial investment. ISO 20022 is particularly fundamental to modern *real-time payment system* infrastructures. See also *Electronic Data Interchange*.

ISO 8583 The payment messaging standard used to communicate between card payment *ecosystem* actors. This legacy messaging standard is also used by other payment ecosystems (bank *payment schemes*). ISO 8583 is an old standard and uses a bitmap format where each data element is assigned a specific position and is processed sequentially (i.e. as it is being read). It has been used since 1987 and is now on its third version (2003). ISO 8583 is now considered a legacy standard, although *card schemes* use this protocol, and there is no evidence that they are planning to move away from it (for card transactions). See also *Electronic Data Interchange*.

issuer In traditional financial services, this is an *Account Servicing PSP (ASPSP)* on the *card rails*. They provide and manage the cardholder account. An issuer can be a *bank* or a *non-bank Payment Service Provider* (PSP). In decentralised (e.g. *blockchain*) systems, the term refers to the organisation issuing the *coins* or *tokens*.

issuing The process of creating and managing card products for cardholders. These products can be physical or virtual, and may take many forms, including consumer credit cards, commercial cards, and debit cards.

ISV See Independent Software Vendor.

itsme app[58] A privately led *digital identity* service in Belgium.

Java A popular software programming language that is platform independent.

key exchange The process of securely sharing cryptographic keys between parties to enable encrypted communications. See also *public key, private key, public key cryptography, symmetric cryptography, encryption*.

key pair A set of cryptographic keys, usually consisting of a *public key* and a *private key*, used for securing communications and authentication. See also *public key cryptography* and *encryption*.

Know Your Customer (KYC) A process to verify a customer's identity through an independent, reliable source. See also *Customer Due Diligence*.

Kraken[59] A centralised *crypto exchange*.

KYC See Know Your Customer.

Lamport The smallest subdivision of a *SOL* where 100,000,000 Lamports represent one SOL. The unit of measurement for *Solana* (SOL) transaction costs. See also *gas price*.

large-value payment system (LVPS) A bank *payment scheme* that is designed for high-value payments. Sometimes referred to as large-value transfer system (LVTS) or high value payment system (HVPS). See also *retail payment system*.

Layer 1 blockchain The term layer 1 *blockchain* is generally accepted as representing the base layer in a *permissionless blockchain* ecosystem that is for general purpose use. It serves as the base infrastructure for building various applications serving various use cases. Some definitions might encompass the use of *open source* technology for the underlying code and *consensus protocol*, whilst other might add the use of an established consensus protocol such as *Proof of Work* or *Proof of Stake*. The *Bitcoin*, *Ethereum*, and *Solana* blockchains are layer 1 blockchains. It is important to note that other interpretations exist: *Hyperledger Fabric* is often defined as a layer 1 blockchain although it is a framework used to develop *permissioned blockchains*, not a blockchain itself; Ripple is also sometimes defined as a layer 1 blockchain, although it is *permissioned blockchain*, with a proprietary consensus protocol, and is designed for a specific purpose (i.e. cross-border payments). In any instance, if we take the broad definition of a "base layer" blockchain, I think the industry agrees on the terms "mainchain", "mainnet", and "parent blockchain", regardless of whether they are classified as "layer 1" or not. See also *layer 2 blockchain*.

Layer 1 scaling solution See *scaling solution*.

Layer 2 scaling solution See *scaling solution*.

Ledger Wallet[60] A hardware *crypto wallet*.

legal tender A form of *money* that a government recognises as the standard for the repayment of debt and that a court of law is required to recognise as satisfactory payment of monetary debt. A *fiat currency* is made legal tender by the government that issues it. A *cryptocurrency* is not considered legal tender unless a government makes it so (e.g. El Salvador with Bitcoin).

light node In *blockchain* networks, this is a type of *node* with special responsibilities and privileges. A light node doesn't store the entire blockchain transaction history, like a *full node* does, but only block headers and specific transaction information. However, a light node participates in the transaction validation process and performs the same steps as other validating nodes. If the transaction passes all validation steps, a light node sends the transaction to a full node for validation and inclusion on the blockchain ledger. Typically, light nodes are less resource intensive than other nodes and can even be run on mobile devices, which is why they are considered more vulnerable to attacks than other nodes but also more affordable to run for users that don't have the resources to run full nodes. As such, light nodes rely on full nodes for most functionality. Also referred to as "lightweight node" or "simplified payment verification (SPV)" node, or "stateless clients". See also *miner*, *validator*, *full node*, and *master node*.

liquidation risk The potential for an asset or position to be forcibly sold or closed out due to an inability to meet financial obligations or maintain required collateral levels. In trading and lending, it refers to the risk of a position being automatically closed by a platform or lender when its value falls below a specified threshold, often resulting in significant losses for the holder. Liquidation risk is particularly relevant in leveraged trading, margin lending, and collateralised debt positions in both traditional finance and *decentralised finance (DeFi)* protocols.

liquidity A term describing the ease with which financial institutions can discharge their payment and settlement obligations. Financial institutions must ensure that they have sufficient funds at a reasonable cost to meet their obligations.

liquidity pool A liquidity pool is a collection of *cryptocurrency tokens* or assets locked in a *smart contract* on a *decentralised exchange (DEX)* to facilitate trading. It provides the necessary *liquidity* for users to trade directly with the pool rather than waiting for a matching counterparty. In traditional forex markets, large banks act as market makers, holding reserves of various currencies to facilitate exchanges. A liquidity pool in *DeFi* is similar to these bank reserves, but instead of being controlled by a central entity, it is managed by a smart contract and funded by multiple participants.

liquidity risk A type of risk that a financial institution may face if it will not discharge its payment and settlement obligations on the *due date*. This doesn't necessarily mean that the financial institution is insolvent, as it may be able to settle at some later point.

Linden Dollar A *virtual currency* used in the game Second Life.

Litecoin (LTC)[61] A *cryptocurrency*, also a *coin*. Litecoin also refers to the *layer 1 blockchain* infrastructure on which LTC operates (i.e. the Litecoin blockchain). A *permissionless blockchain*. See also *Litoshi*.

Litoshi The smallest subdivision of one *Litecoin (LTC)* where 100,000,000 Litoshis represent one LTC. The unit of measurement for LTC transaction costs (*Litecoin blockchain*). See also *gas price*.

Lovelace The smallest subdivision of one *ADA* where 100,000 Lovelace represent one ADA. The unit of measurement for ADA (the *Cardano cryptocurrency*) transaction costs. See also *gas price*.

loyalty programme See *merchant loyalty*.

LVPS See large-value payment system.

M1, M2, and M3 money See *money*.

MaaS See Mining-as-a-Service (MaaS).

mainchain See layer 1 blockchain.

mainnet See layer 1 blockchain.

malware A contraction of "malicious software". Any software designed to disrupt, damage, or gain unauthorised access to a computer system, leak private information, deprive access to information, or interfere with computer security and privacy. An example is *ransomware*.

man-in-the-middle (MITM) attack A type of cybersecurity threat where an attacker secretly intercepts and potentially alters the communication between two parties who believe they are directly communicating with each other. The attacker positions themselves between the victims, acting as a proxy to relay messages whilst having the ability to eavesdrop or modify the content. This attack can compromise the confidentiality and integrity of data transmission, potentially leading to information theft, unauthorised access, or the injection of malicious content. MITM attacks highlight the importance of secure, encrypted communications and proper *authentication* methods in digital interactions.

marketplace Traditionally, a marketplace is a trading environment, such as eBay, Amazon, or Etsy, which connects buyers with multiple sellers and maintains complete control over the payment transactions, their fulfilment, and the end-to-end customer experience. With a marketplace, a cardholder intends to buy a product or service, and the marketplace will offer these products or services from multiple sellers. Marketplaces also come in other forms on different infrastructures (e.g. *Web 3.0*, *blockchain*), such as NFT marketplaces.

Mastercard[62] A *card scheme* operating on the *four-party model*.

Maximum Extractable Value (MEV) In a blockchain context, this is the maximum additional profit a block producer (e.g. *miner* and *validator*) can extract from a block, beyond the standard block reward and transaction fees, by manipulating the order in which transactions are included within that block.

mCBDC See *multi-CBDC*.

MD-5 A legacy hashing algorithm now considered unsafe. See *cryptography*, *encryption*, and *hash*.

mempool A staging area used in *blockchain* infrastructures, where validating nodes verify transactions and build candidate blocks for addition to the blockchain. Think of it as temporary storage of pending transactions. After a node has verified the validity of a transaction, they pass it on to the other validating nodes, who also verify the transaction and add it to their mempool (depending on how they prioritise transaction processing). Transactions in the mempool are called "unspent" because they have not yet been added to the blockchain (i.e. they are pending). The mempool is slightly different in Proof of stake blockchains, and whilst the concept is similar (i.e. a staging area for unspent transaction), the transactions within are not validated. Sometimes referred to as the "transaction pool" As a parallel with centralised systems, the transaction in a mempool is partly "authorised" and partly "cleared", but not yet "settled". Each validating node maintains its own mempool and decides on their own computing configuration. See also *clearing*, *validation*, *settlement*.

merchant A term generally describing an entity that provides goods or services and is able to accept card payments. A merchant can be virtual (e.g. e-commerce) or physical (e.g. a brick-and-mortar shop). Increasingly, this term is also used to describe businesses that accept bank payments or other types of payments.

merchant settlement Traditionally, the second and final step of the *settlement* process on the *card rails*, by which the *acquirer* will credit the merchant account according to their commercial contract. Acquirers may decide to defer merchant settlement as a risk management tool for certain industries (e.g. airlines, hospitality). As other payment infrastructures gain in popularity (e.g. account-to-account *payment*, *blockchain*), this term may also describe how any business will be paid. Also see *settlement* and *settlement cycle*.

Merkle tree A mathematical construct used in *blockchain* infrastructures commonly used to ensure block integrity in various blockchain implementations. This data structure summarises the transactions within a block by hashing each transaction individually, and then the individual hashes are hashed again in pairs, repeating the process until a single hash is obtained representing all the transactions. This final hash is known as the "Merkle root", which is included in the *block header*. When other validating nodes receive the proposed block, they verify its integrity by recalculating the Merkle root using the received transactions and then check whether it matches the Merkle root included in the block header. This is an efficient way of validating block integrity without having to re-validate each transaction.

Merkle root See *Merkle tree*.

metaverse Defined as a virtual reality space in which users can interact with a computer-generated environment and other users. Also see *Web 3.0*.

MEV See Maximum Extractable Value.

MFA See multi-factor authentication.

miner A *node* in a *Proof of Work (PoW)* blockchain network who participates in the transaction validation process. A miner listens to the network and gathers valid transactions to fit in a block. Miners ensure the integrity and security of the blockchain network by completing tasks including verifying and processing transactions, ensuring consensus, and preventing *double-spending*. As miners do this all at the same time for all transactions, which blocks get added to the chain is determined by the *consensus protocol*. Miners are incentivised with *cryptocurrency* for their participation. See also *mining*, *validator*, *master node*, *full node*, and *light node*.

mining A process commonly associated with *Proof of Work (PoW)* consensus in *blockchain* networks through which new transactions are added to a blockchain. It involves solving complex mathematical problems or cryptographic puzzles to validate and confirm transactions. See also *miner*, *staking*, and *validator*.

Mining-as-a-Service (MaaS) In a *Proof of Work (PoW) blockchain context*, a *mining* model where service providers rent out their own hashing power (including hardware and software) to individuals or businesses interested in earning mining rewards. The fees charged to users and cryptocurrencies supported will depend on the service provider. For example, they may require an initial deposit representing the hashing power to be rented or offer pay-as-you-go options. The individual or business can then start mining in the usual way without having to incur the infrastructure outlay. Rewards are then paid out regularly, after service fees are deducted. Also known as "cloud mining".

mining farm In a *Proof of Work (PoW) blockchain context*, a type of mining model where a business creates a dedicated facility with specialised equipment (*mining rigs*) dedicated to mining cryptocurrencies in PoW networks. Unlike *mining pools* and *MaaS* providers, which are targeted at those with no or little access to resources, these primarily attract investors as they require a high initial investment and could potentially give high returns. Farms may also join mining pools to leverage collective power.

mining pool In a *Proof of Work (PoW) blockchain context*, a type of cooperative construct where individual miners combine their individual computing resources, known as their hashing power, into one pool that competes as one entity to solve the cryptographic puzzle. The more hashing power, the more chance the mining pool has to solve the puzzle faster and earn the block reward. Rewards are then distributed amongst the pool members according to their hashing power contribution.

mining rig A specialised computer specifically designed to help *Proof of Work (PoW) miners* solve the complex cryptographic puzzles required by the *consensus protocol*.

minimum fee requirement A threshold for transaction fees that may be set by a blockchain protocol to manage network operations.

minting The process of manufacturing or producing coins or other forms of currency. Traditionally, this refers to the creation of physical coins by stamping metal blanks with designs. In the context of *blockchain*, minting refers to the creation of new coins, tokens, or crypto assets. This can involve generating new coins as block rewards in *Proof-of-Work* blockchains, creating tokens in *Proof-of-Stake* networks, or producing *non-fungible tokens (NFTs)*. Blockchain minting is typically governed by the blockchain protocol, ensuring controlled issuance and distribution of digital assets. See also *seigniorage*, *tokenomics*, *burning*.

MitID[63] A *digital identity* framework in Denmark which replaced the NemID framework in June 2023.

MITM attack See man-in-the-middle attack.

Mobiilivarmenne[64] A *digital identity* framework in Finland which is a partnership between telcos.

obile money A way to store and manage money in an account linked to a mobile phone, similar to a bank account. Most mobile money services allow users to purchase items in shops or online, pay bills, school fees, and top up mobile airtime. Cash withdrawals can also be carried out at authorised agents. Most mobile money services are offered by local mobile telecom operators. A type of mobile payment that doesn't rely on a formal financial services infrastructure (e.g. bank accounts). Popular in developing countries. See also *e-money*.

mobile payment A broad term to describe payment facilities that have a mobile element. It encompasses mobile banking, *mobile wallets, mobile money*, and even mobile *payment acceptance*. Mobile payments can be classified in two categories: those that necessitate a formal payment instrument as the underlying payment mechanism (e.g. card or bank account), and those that don't (e.g. use of cash).

mobile wallet A payment facility tied to a mobile hardware device that usually uses cards as the funding option.

monetary system A framework established to manage a nation's *currency*, *money* supply, and interest rates, typically overseen by a *central bank*. It functions as a public good, serving the nation's interest by ensuring economic stability, facilitating trade, and promoting sustainable growth within the economy.

money Any medium of exchange that is accepted by people for the payment of goods and services and the repayment of debt. Historically, *barter systems* were used to exchange goods and services for other goods and services. But the lack of transferability and divisibility, as well as the variable desirability of goods and services when compared to other goods and services, led to the development of commodity money (e.g. dried pelts, grain, gold). Especially in the case of gold, everybody agrees on its perceived value, making it a good medium of exchange. This is why national currencies were backed by gold until recently (in the history of money). Fast forward to more modern times, most currencies are no longer backed by gold, but rather on supply and demand and the stability of the government that issues it. The US dollar hasn't been backed by gold since 1971, and the British Pound since 1931.

A currency that isn't baked by gold is called a fiat currency or *fiat money*. Economists classify money into three categories:

M1 money All physical representations, including notes and coins; bank accounts where money can be withdrawn immediately (i.e. on-demand); traveller's cheques; any other form of liquid deposits and assets.

M2 money All the M1 money, plus all time-related deposits, several types of retirement accounts, and non-institutional money market funds.

M3 money All the M1 and M2 money, with the addition of all large time deposits, institutional money market funds, short-term repurchase agreements, and other larger liquid assets. M3 represents a country's total money supply. In practice, the terms "money" and currency" are often used interchangeably, and from the definition above, you'll realise that currency (i.e. notes and coins) is only one representation of M1 money...

Moneygram[65] A Money Transfer Operator.

money laundering Concealing the origin of money obtained from illegal activities such as drug trafficking, corruption, embezzlement, or gambling (where illegal) by converting it into a legitimate source. There are three stages of money laundering – placement, layering, and integration – that allow illicit funds to enter the legitimate financial system, obfuscate their origins, and then to reintegrate them so as to appear as legal tender. A form of *financial crime*.

money remittance A payment service by which funds are sent by a *payer* to a *payee* where no payment account needs to be opened in the name of either the payer or payee.

Money Service Business (MSB) Outside of Europe, this term is used to describe an *Electronic Money Institution (EMI)* or *Payment Institution (PI)*.

Money Transfer Operator (MTO) A financial company (usually not a bank) engaged in *money remittance* including *cross-border* transfer of funds. MTOs use their internal systems and/or access to banking networks. The MTO will use their own banking relationships and each country's bank payment capabilities where they can.

Monzo[66] A UK *neo-bank*.

M-PESA[67] A *mobile money* service successful in Kenya and other African countries.

MPC See secure multi-party computation.

MSC See Merchant Service Charge.

MTO See Money Transfer Operator.

multi-CBDC (mCBDC) A *CBDC* interoperability model that aims to tackle *cross-border* payments inefficiencies and frictions in today's *correspondent banking* system, such as differences in *payment systems* opening hours, varying communication standards, and lack of transparency around exchange rates or fees. There are three implementation models for mCBDCs:

- **enhanced compatibility** The different jurisdictions agree on compatible regulatory technical standards, and there is a multitude of privately offered correspondent banking and *clearing* services. Each jurisdiction has its own CBDC regulation.
- **interlinking** The different jurisdictions agree to connect their separate CBDC infrastructures through shared technical interfaces or by use of common *clearing* mechanism (centralised or decentralised). Each jurisdiction has its own CBDC regulation.
- **single system integration** Multiple CBDCs can be run on a single platform for all participating jurisdictions. There is a single set of regulations for all participants and a single infrastructure and ledger. See also *intermediated CBDC (sCBDC)* and *direct CBDC.*

multi-factor authentication (MFA) The use of two or more *authentication* factors when authenticating payment account holders and users. See also *knowledge-based authentication.*

multi-party computation (MPC) See *secure multi-party computation.*

multi-rail A term used to describe payment services that enable operations across multiple payment channels, networks, or *payment schemes.*

MyGov.be[68] A government-issued *digital identity* scheme in Belgium.

N26[69] A *neo-bank.*

NemID[70] A *digital identity* framework in Denmark.

neo-bank A digital-only bank. A *fintech* firm that offers mobile apps, software, and financial services with only an online presence and no physical branches. Also referred to as a "digital bank".

Nexi (formerly Sia)[71] A financial services institution who operates bank payment schemes in Europe and is also an *acquirer.*

NFT See Non-Fungible Token.

node A term used in computing to refer to a physical device or *virtual machine* connected to a network capable of processing and/or transmitting data.

In *blockchain* infrastructures, a node is a computer that participates in the management and operation of the network by maintaining a copy of the distributed ledger and validating transactions. See also *blockchain, miner, validator, full node, master node,* and *deep learning.*

non-bank financial institution A financial institution that doesn't come under the definition of a "bank", which means other than a credit institution in Europe or a depository institution in the US. Sometimes referred to as "non-bank PSP".

non-bank PSP Non-bank Payment Service Provider. See *non-bank financial institution.*

nonce A contraction of "number used once". In a *blockchain* context, the nonce is a number that can only be used once, is included as a transaction input, and used as a security measure in the transaction validation process. It is commonly used in computer science and *cryptography*, particularly in the context of hashing and *cryptography protocols*. In some *blockchain* implementations, a nonce may be included in individual transactions by the user's crypto wallet (or other facility used to interact with the blockchain). The user's wallet keeps track of the nonce associated with their address (*public key*) and ensures that each transaction has a unique and sequentially increasing nonce. By having users include a nonce, blockchain networks ensure that transactions are processed in the correct order and prevent *replay attacks.* A nonce may also be used for a different purpose in *Proof of Work (PoW)* blockchains where it is a field in the block header. Here, validating nodes must find a value for the nonce that, when combined with the other block header data, produces a hash that meets certain criteria (specified by the blockchain *consensus protocol*). Miners adjust the nonce repeatedly (this is resource intensive) until a valid hash is found (i.e. below the *difficulty target*), signifying that they have successfully mined a block. See also *hash.*

non-custodial wallet See *crypto wallet.*

Non-Fungible Token (NFT) A type of *crypto asset* that has been tokenised on a *blockchain* and assigned a unique identification. Non-fungible means "unique", and therefore can't be replicated. An NFT is different from other crypto assets, or *fiat currencies*, which are interchangeable. NFTs are largely unregulated unless they come in scope of securities regulations.

off-chain Refers to processing that is not conducted on a *layer 1 blockchain*. Processing may include processing transactions, record keeping, computation, data storage, dispute resolution, security, and much more. See also *layer 2 scaling solution*, *on-chain*.

offline A state in which a device, system, or application is not connected to the internet or a network, preventing real-time communication or data exchange. In this context, offline can refer to the inability to access online services, resources, or updates and may also indicate that data is stored locally rather than in the cloud. Offline functionality is often designed to allow users to perform tasks without an internet connection, with changes synchronised once connectivity is restored.

off-ramp A service that allows users to convert *cryptocurrency* into *fiat money*. These services are typically provided by entities such as *crypto exchanges*, where they base the amount of the crypto-to-fiat transaction on current market rates. Essentially, off-ramp means leaving the decentralised, *blockchain*-based monetary system and entering into the traditional fiat monetary system. Also spelt "off ramp" and sometimes referred to as "crypto off ramp". See also *on-ramp*.

omnibus account An account held at a *central bank* that streamlines how financial institutions hold reserves at the central bank. Instead of each institution having its own separate account, they can all deposit funds into a single, consolidated account managed by the central bank. The central bank then keeps detailed records of how much each institution has deposited, ensuring everyone has access to their reserves whilst benefiting from a more efficient system.

onboarding The process consisting of all activities involved in introducing a new customer to a business's products and services. This process ensures regulatory, legal, and credit-related *due diligence* obligations. It includes KYC checks and procedures such as identity verification and document collection. Also referred to as "customer onboarding".

on-chain Refers to processing that is conducted on a *layer 1 blockchain*. Processing may include processing transactions, record keeping, computation, data storage, dispute resolution, security, and much more. See also *off-chain*.

on-chain analysis A service which provides *cryptocurrency* investors with charts and dashboards to better help them visualise *blockchain* data and track the movements of cryptocurrencies and individual wallets. See also *chain analysis*.

on-ramp A service that allows users to convert *fiat money* into *cryptocurrency*. These services are typically provided by providers such as *crypto exchanges* (the more commonly used), third-party service providers (which may also offer services such as *crypto debit cards*) where they base the amount of the fiat-crypto transaction on current market rates. Essentially, on-ramp means leaving the traditional fiat monetary system and enter into the decentralised, *blockchain*-based monetary system instead, just like entering a motorway or highway. Also spelt "on ramp" and sometimes referred to as "fiat on-ramp". See also *off-ramp*.

on us When a payment instruction is issued to one bank and credited to a different account within the same bank. On us payments don't require the use of a *payment scheme*, and settlement is performed using the bank's own infrastructure. Also referred to as "intrabank settlement".

One-Time Passcode (OTP) A one-time authorisation code or dynamic password that is valid for only one login session or transaction on a computer system or other digital device. Sometimes referred to as One-Time Password, One-Time PIN, or One-Time Authorisation Code (OTAC).

open API A communication interface that follows a public standard or set of standards that are publicly available for developers to use.

open banking A term referring to the use of *open APIs* that enable *Third Party PSPs (TPPs)* to build and provide account information or payment initiation services through data access to payment accounts managed by *Account Servicing PSPs (ASPSPs)*. Usually capitalised, but sometimes written as "open banking".

open banking payment A type of *A2A payment* that follows agreed standards of interoperability, such as *open APIs*.

open loop An economic model that promotes competition. An open-loop *payment instrument* enables the account holder to make payments without having to be part of the system itself, such as a public transport card that may only be used on a specific public transport network. See *four-party model*, *three-party model*, and *closed loop*.

open source A term related to software development to describe an approach whereby something (e.g. a project, a product, an initiative, software) can be shared and modified by anyone because it is publicly accessible, following the principle of open exchange. Nowadays, it primarily refers to open source software, which is computer code that anyone can inspect, modify, or otherwise enhance. This is different from proprietary software where only the original authors can inspect, modify, or enhance the code, and users of the software must agree that they will not do anything with it that is not expressively permitted by the authors/owners. Users of open source software must also agree to the terms of a licence agreement, but the terms are very different from those applying to proprietary software as they are usually related to how users may use, study, modify, or distribute the software. *Permissionless blockchains* use open source software. See also *blockchain*.

OpenSSL A mature and widely used *open source cryptography* library.

optimistic rollup (ORU) A *blockchain layer 2 scaling solution*. A type of *rollup*.

open wallet See pass-through digital wallet.

operating regulations This usually refers to the rules set by a *card scheme* for the operation and governance of their network. Sometimes referred to as "operating rules".

oracle A data feed that connects a *blockchain* to *off-chain* (real-world) information so that *smart contracts* can query real-world data. For example, a prediction market *dApp* may use oracles to settle payments based on events, such as asking users to bet *cryptocurrency* on who will become the next president of the United States. They'll use an oracle to confirm the outcome and payout to the winners.

ORU See optimistic rollup.

OTAC One-Time Authorisation Code. See *One-Time Passcode*.

OTP See One-Time Passcode.

overlay service A term generally used in the bank payment context, but also applies to the *card rails*. These are services implemented on top of an existing payment scheme. Some bank payment examples are *Confirmation of Payee*, *Request-to-Pay*, and *Variable Recurring Payment*. On the card rails, *3D Secure* can be considered and overlay service. In decentralised infrastructures such as *blockchain*, you could say that a *smart contract* is technically an overlay service on top of a blockchain *settlement* infrastructure.

P2P See peer-to-peer.

packet tampering A type of *cyberattack* where an unauthorised party intercepts, alters, or injects malicious data into network packets as they travel between a source and destination. This technique exploits vulnerabilities in network protocols or inadequate *encryption* to modify the content, routing information, or other attributes of data packets. Packet tampering can lead to various security breaches, including data theft, *man-in-the-middle attacks*, or service disruptions. It underscores the importance of secure communication protocols and encryption in maintaining data integrity and confidentiality across networks.

PancakeSwap[72] A decentralised *crypto exchange*.

parent blockchain See *layer 1 blockchain*.

pass-through digital wallet A *mobile wallet* where the card payment information is passed on directly to the *Account Servicing PSP (ASPSP)* (e.g. *issuer*) through the *payment scheme* (e.g. *card scheme*) to perform a payment transaction. Funds are never stored on this type of wallet. For example, if a Visa card is attached to a pass-through wallet, the payment transaction would be like any other Visa transaction. Technically, this type of wallet is not a *payment instrument* (i.e. the Visa card is), but only a technical service (i.e. a container, or the digital equivalent of a leather wallet). Apple Pay, Venmo, and Samsung Wallet are pass-through digital wallets. Also referred to as "open wallet".

payee The entity or person that gets paid. See also *Payment Service User*.

payer The entity or person who pays. See also *Payment Service User*.

payment A transfer of value from one party to another.

payment gateway The technology that enables merchants to accept online card payments on their websites. Provided by a *merchant's PSP* on the *card rails* (e.g. a payment gateway provider, an *acquirer*). Also see *payee's PSP*.

Payment Initiation Service Provider (PISP) A *Third Party PSP* (TPP) which initiates payments on behalf of a payer. Sometimes called a "payment originator".

payment institution (PI) In Europe, a regulated payment business that is able to receive payments, remit money, issue cards but can't store value. There are two types of payment institutions, the small payment institution (SPI) and the authorised payment institution (PI). In some geographies, may be referred to as a "money service business (MSB)".

payment instruction A directive provided by a payer detailing the specifics of a payment to be executed, including the amount, recipient's account details, and payment method. A direct payment instruction is given directly to the organisation holding the *payer's* financial account (e.g. a bank), whilst an indirect payment instruction is given to an intermediary (such as a payment service provider or fintech company) authorised to execute the payment on behalf of the account holder. Indirect instructions often involve additional steps or processes before the actual account-holding institution receives the instruction to move funds. Sometimes called "payment order".

payment instrument A physical or virtual facility allowing the payment account holder to transfer funds. Examples of payment instruments are cards, money orders, cheques, etc.

payment message A communication message that typically contains information related to a payment, such as the identities of the parties involved, account information, and the payment amount.

payment method A facility that a *payer* (e.g. cardholder or bank account holder) will use to make payments.

payment orchestration The process of integrating and managing several stakeholders in the payments value chain to simplify integration into merchant environments and payment processing. Payment orchestration platform providers typically offer these services through a single *API*, enabling businesses to connect to multiple payment gateways, *acquirers*, various PSPs, as well as providing other services such as risk management, *CRM*, *KYC*, etc. Increasingly, the term also applies to service providers offering payment services across multiple *blockchains*. See also *dynamic routing*.

payment order See *payment instruction*.

payment page The customer-facing part of a *virtual terminal* that is integrated into a merchant's environment (e.g. online shop). For telephone sales, a virtual terminal can be used by the merchant, and this is where they would enter the cardholder's details as supplied by the cardholder over the phone. See *payee's PSP*.

payment scheme Generally, this refers to the *ecosystem* actor which provides the centralised payments infrastructure and operating rules. For the *card rails*, examples of payment schemes are Visa, Mastercard, American Express, etc., and these are also referred to as *card schemes*, "card networks", or "card brands". For the bank rails, examples of payment schemes are UK FPS, US FedNow, etc. In Europe, however, a SEPA payment scheme only refers to the operating rules and technical specifications for the scheme (e.g. *SEPA credit transfer*). *SEPA* refers to the payment schemes mentioned above as *payment systems*.

Payment Services Provider (PSP) A very generic term referring to any entity providing a payment service in a payments *ecosystem*.

Payment Service User (PSU) The payment *ecosystem* actor which uses payment services. If the actor makes a payment, they are referred to as a "payer", and if they receive a payment, they are referred to as a "payee". On the *card rails*, the PSU can be the actor who pays with a card, referred to as a *cardholder*, or the PSU who gets paid with a card, referred to as a *merchant*. On the bank rails, the PSUs are bank account holders.

payment system See *payment scheme*.

payment terminal A payment facility to enable merchants to accept card payments. Payment terminals can be physical (hardware) or virtual (digital). See also *POS*, *EPOS*, *mPOS*, *SoftPOS*, *payment page*, *virtual terminal*, and *unattended payment terminal*.

Payment-versus-Payment (PvP) A common form of *settlement* used in foreign exchange transactions which guarantees the final transfer of one currency only happens after the final transfer of another currency also happens, alleviating *settlement risk*. See also *Delivery-versus-Payment (PvP)*, *atomic settlement*, and *atomic swap*.

PayNow[73] An *account-to-account* payment service in Singapore.

Paypal[74] An e-wallet, a staged digital wallet.

Paytm[75] A mobile wallet, a stored value digital wallet. India's leading payment app.

peer-to-peer (P2P) A generic term used to describe services, platforms, or facilities that seemingly enable interactions between peers. It is used interchangeably with Person-to-Person.

peer-to-peer money exchange A type of *fintech* company challenging traditional *Money Transfer Operators (MTOs)* and bank *wire transfers*. Instead of using *correspondent banking* and *cross-border* transactions, they "crowd-source" fund transfer matches in each of the countries involved in a fund transfer. And then, theoretically, they only need to perform *domestic* bank transactions at each end, making them cheaper.

peer-to-peer networking A principle by which peers communicate with each other without the need for a central authority or intermediary.

peer-to-peer (P2P) payment A misnomer. Used to describe digital payment apps such as Venmo or Zelle. To the users, it looks like they're making a payment directly to their friend (or supplier, etc.) without intermediaries (hence Peer-to-Peer). This is not the case. Regardless of the rails used (i.e. card or bank), these payments still need to go through the existing mechanisms (i.e. *Authorisation*, *Clearing*, and *Settlement*), and therefore through intermediaries. For true "Peer-to-Peer" payments, you must look at decentralised rails.

peg A fixed exchange rate between two currencies or assets. In the context of *stablecoins*, a peg refers to the intended fixed value of the stablecoin relative to its target asset, typically a *fiat currency* like the US dollar. Stablecoins can have a hard peg, which aims to maintain a strict 1:1 ratio, or a soft peg, which allows for minor fluctuations around the target value. The peg is crucial for ensuring the stablecoin's stability and utility as a medium of exchange and store of value in the *cryptocurrency* ecosystem.

permissioned blockchain A *blockchain* controlled by a central entity (or set of entities) where access is restricted to certain *nodes*, and rights also can be restricted. See also *consortium blockchain*, *private blockchain*, *hybrid blockchain*.

permissioned blockchain platform A development environment specifically designed to address the needs of permissioned blockchain development to control access, maintain privacy, and use consensus mechanisms suited for smaller groups of known participants, features which are often absent in frameworks built for open access and transparency.

permissionless blockchain A *blockchain* where any user can join (i.e. become a *node*). A public blockchain.

phishing A type of *social engineering* attack where fraudsters or cybercriminals deceive victims into revealing sensitive information, sending money, installing malicious software (e.g. *ransomware*), etc. Through phishing, malicious actors may pose as legitimate institutions, trusted individuals, etc. Usually conducted via email or other messaging services.

Pix[76] A real-time payment system (RTP system), retail payment system (RPS) in Brazil, operated by BCB.

PKI See Public Key Infrastructure.

plasma chain In a *blockchain* context, a layer 2 *scaling solution* introducing a hierarchy of blockchains, with a parent chain and child chains. The main blockchain acts as a secure foundation and sets the rules for the whole network, whereas the child chains handle transaction execution. A variant is the "nested blockchains" involving child chains which are closely coupled with the mainchain, usually implementing a modified version of the mainchain's protocol, or one that is specifically designed to work with the main blockchain. Because of their complexity, these have lost favour to other layer 2 scaling solutions. See also *rollup*, *side chain*, *state channel*.

play-to-earn (P2E) A gaming model in *blockchain*-based games where players can earn *cryptocurrency* tokens or other digital assets with real-world value by participating in gameplay activities. These rewards can be traded, sold, or used within the game ecosystem, allowing players to potentially generate income through their gaming engagement. See also *GameFi*.

Point-of-Sale (POS) A system used by businesses to manage sales transactions. In the past, a POS in a shop would consist of a cash register and a ledger to record purchases and sales. Today, we have dedicated electronic terminals and solutions to automate the processes – from customer purchases to inventory management. In the payments world, the term "POS" is used interchangeably with "POS terminal". Also called PIN Entry Device (PED) or PIN pad where PIN entry is available. Some merchants may have a separate device for cardholders to enter their PIN.

PoS See Proof of Stake.

POS See Point-of-Sale.

PoW See Proof of Work.

prepaid card Generally refers to open-loop prepaid cards which run on *card scheme* networks. They can be used in the same way as a debit card or credit cards. The key difference is that they need to be loaded up with funds in advance. A *stored value card*.

principal An entity that acts on its own behalf to conduct business activities. See also *principal member*. This term is also used in the context of *credit*, where it refers to the money that a borrower originally agreed to pay back. See also *interest*.

privacy The right and ability of individuals to control access to their personal information and to maintain a state of seclusion from public attention. Unlike *anonymity*, which focuses on concealing one's identity entirely, privacy allows individuals to selectively reveal information about themselves. Privacy encompasses the protection of personal data, communications, and activities from unauthorised access or intrusion, whilst still allowing for identified interactions when desired or necessary.

privacy coin A type of *cryptocurrency* used to perform private and anonymous *blockchain* transactions by obscuring their origin and destination.

Some of the techniques used in these anonymous cryptocurrencies include hiding a user's real *crypto wallet* balance and address and mixing multiple transactions with each other to elude *chain analysis*. Monero[77] and Zcash[78] are examples. Aimed at ensuring *data privacy* for investors, but often associated with *money laundering* activities and increasingly attracting regulatory scrutiny. Also see *coin mixer*.

private API A communication interface specific to one organisation. Its use can only be granted by that organisation.

private blockchain A type of *permissioned blockchain* controlled by one authority. An example is *Ripple*.

private key A code that may take several forms: a 256-character long binary code, a 64-digit hexadecimal code, a *QR code*, or a mnemonic phrase. A *cryptocurrency* transaction is encrypted using a *public key* but can only be decrypted by an associated private key. For a cryptocurrency transaction to be authenticated, the recipient must "sign it" with their private key, proving that they are the legitimate recipient of the funds. Through the *consensus protocol*, unauthenticated transactions will be rejected by the *blockchain* network. Conversely, authenticated transactions are irreversible. Public and private keys fit together and are known as "key pairs". Also see *cryptography*, *public key cryptography*, *encryption*, and *public key*.

PromptPay[79] An *account-to-account payment* service in Thailand.

Proof of Stake (PoS) A *blockchain consensus protocol* by which *validators* stake their own funds, a process referred to as *staking*. A *coin* or *token* is picked randomly from all staked funds. The owner of the "winning" coin gets to add their block to the *blockchain*. In order to discourage validators from misbehaving (e.g. being offline for too long, attacking the network), some blockchains implement a governance mechanism called *slashing* by which a predetermined percentage or a fixed quantity of the validator's stake is lost, the amount of which depends on the severity of the transgression. See also *Proof of Work (PoW)*.

Proof of Work (PoW) A *blockchain consensus protocol* by which *miners* compete to solve a cryptographic puzzle. Whomever solves the puzzle first gets to add their block to the chain. See also *Proof of Stake (PoS)*.

PSP See Payment Services Provider.

public blockchain A type of *permissionless blockchain*. The *Bitcoin* and *Ethereum* blockchains are examples.

public key A cryptographic code that allows a user to receive *cryptocurrency* transactions. Anyone can send transactions to a public key, which can be freely shared (a bit like an email address). The public key is generated from a *private key*, and there can be any number of public keys associated with a private key. A user needs a private key to "unlock" a received transaction and prove they are the owner of the cryptocurrency received in the transaction. Public and private keys fit together and are known as "key pairs". Also see *cryptography*, *public key cryptography*, *encryption*, *private key*.

public key cryptography An *encryption* method that uses two mathematically related, but not identical, keys – a *public key* and a *private key* – where each key performs a unique function. Public key cryptography is considered more secure and easier to manage than *symmetric cryptography*, but slower. Used by *blockchain* networks and anywhere digital signatures are desirable. Also known as "asymmetric cryptography", "public key encryption" and "asymmetric encryption". Well known public key cryptography algorithms include Rivest-Shamir-Adleman (RSA), Elliptic Curve Digital Signature Algorithm (ECDSA), Digital Signature Algorithm (DSA), and Diffie-Hellman key agreement protocol. See also *quantum cryptography*.

public key encryption See *public key cryptography*.

Public Key Infrastructure (PKI) A collective term representing the hardware, software, processes, policies, and procedures required to manage *public keys* for digital certificates and *encryption*, as commonly used for securing data transfers over the internet.

PvP See Payment-versus-Payment.

QR code Quick Response Code. QR codes are contactless, scannable matrix barcodes that direct consumers to websites, online checkouts, mobile apps, menus, and other digital channels. They can be used as an *authentication* method for payments. Particularly popular in Asia but gaining popularity in other parts of the world.

QR payment A payment, usually through a mobile device, made using a QR code.

quantum computing An emerging multi-disciplinary technology field incorporating aspects of computer science, hardware research, physics, application development, and mathematics harnessing the laws of quantum mechanics in an effort to solve problems too complex for classical computers (including existing super-computers). In conventional computers, data processing is done in a Central Processing Unit (CPU) whereas in quantum computers, data processing is done in a Quantum Processing Unit (QPU), which consists of a number of interconnected *qubits*, the quantum equivalent of a "bit" in traditional computing. Use cases include drugs and chemical research, as well as *cryptography*, which is critical for securing digital transactions and communications. Amazon, Microsoft, Google, and IBM are dominant players in this market.

quantum cryptography A form of *cryptography* that uses the naturally occurring properties of quantum mechanics to secure and transmit data. Unlike traditional cryptography, which relies on mathematics, the security model of quantum cryptography relies on physics. Quantum cryptography should also remain safe against those using *quantum computing* to compromise data. See also *cryptography* and *encryption*.

quantum money A theoretical form of currency that leverages the principles of quantum mechanics and *quantum cryptography*, making impossible to forge. The concept was first proposed in 1983.[80] See also *money*.

Qubit An abbreviation for "quantum bit". The basic unit of quantum data. Unlike classical bits, which can only have two states, 0 or 1, qubits can exist in multiple states at the same time, a condition described as "superposition", a key property of quantum computing. Another important property of qubits is "entanglement", which describes a state where two qubits become linked in such a way that the state of one is dependent on the state of the other. This property allows quantum computers to perform some calculations much faster than traditional computers.

Quorum[81] A *private blockchain* originally developed by JP Morgan and acquired in 2020 by ConsenSys. A *permissioned blockchain*.

quotation currency In a *foreign exchange* context, the second currency in a currency pair.

Radix See *Tempo*.

ransomware A type of *malware* whereby cyber criminals block access to the victim's (which may be a person or a business) personal data unless a ransom is paid. Whilst some simple ransomware may lock the system without damaging any files, more advanced versions may delete the files or cause other damage. A form of extortion. Perpetrators usually request the ransom to be paid in *cryptocurrency*, especially *privacy coins*.

RC4 Rivest Cipher. A *symmetric cryptography* algorithm.

real-time The processing of instructions on an individual basis as they are received rather than at some point in the future. Used interchangeably with "real time" or "realtime".

Real-Time Gross Settlement (RTGS) See *settlement cycle*.

Real-Time Gross Settlement account (RTGS account) An account held by a bank or authorised non-bank institution at a *central bank* or central monetary authority. Referred to as an RTGS account.

real-time payment system (RTP system) A bank *payment scheme* where settlement happens in real-time or near real-time. See also *retail payment system*, *large value payment system*, *settlement cycle*.

real-world asset (RWA) token Digital *tokens* that represent ownership of tangible or traditional assets, such as real estate, commodities, or financial instruments, on a *blockchain*. *Tokenisation* of these assets enhances liquidity, accessibility, and the ability to trade them in a decentralised manner. See also *security token exchange*.

recurring payment See *recurring transaction*.

recurring transaction A type of payment transaction where the payment account holder gives a payee (e.g. merchant) their payment account details (e.g. card account details), so they can take regular payments from them. Also referred to as "recurring payment". The payment will be made at a regular frequency, for example, once a year or once a month, without account holder intervention. In blockchain infrastructures, a recurring payment may be implemented through smart contracts.

reentrancy attack A security vulnerability in *smart contracts* that exploits the way transactions are processed on a *blockchain*. It specifically targets smart contracts that interact with external functions or calls (often to other smart contracts) during a single transaction. As blockchains process transactions in blocks, there's a delay between a transaction being submitted and it being finalised in a block, creating a window of opportunity for attackers. Before the transaction finishes, the attacker tricks the contract into repeating that action, essentially stealing those funds or manipulating the system a second time. Careful coding practices and security audits can help prevent these attacks. See also *replay attack*.

regulatory sandbox A safe environment provided by regulators to enable the testing of new, innovative technologies, services, or approaches which are not fully compliant with the existing legal and regulatory frameworks. This can take place using near-real-life data (synthetic) or real-life data.

remittance See *money remittance.*

eplay attack A form of network attack in which a valid data transmission is maliciously or fraudulently retransmitted or delayed. The attacker would intercept a valid transaction and retransmit it, often multiple times, in view of deceiving the recipient or gaining unauthorised access. In *blockchain* infrastructures, this is a type of attack where a valid transaction is fraudulently retransmitted, which may occur when an attacker intercepts and records a legitimate transaction between two parties and then later replays that transaction to one or more nodes on the blockchain network in view of manipulating the system. In traditional centralised financial systems, replay attacks are unlikely to succeed as these systems usually have security and robust security and fraud prevention measures, such as authentication, transaction verification, security standards, stringent regulations, and of course, centralised control. In decentralised systems, such as blockchain networks, replay attacks can be particularly problematic because of the distributed nature of the trust framework. See also *double-spending* and *reentrancy attack.*

Request-to-Pay (RtP) An *overlay service* on the bank rails; it is similar in intent to sending an invoice. RtP involves a payee (e.g. a supplier of goods or services) initiating a digital payment request from a payer, without having to send an invoice. It caters for modern behaviours. For example, the payer can receive the request through their mobile device, or their banking app, or via a *Third Party PSP (TPP)*. But RtP is not just about digital invoicing: it gives more flexibility to payers. For each payment request, a payer may choose to pay in full, in part (asking for more time), or decline to pay altogether. A payer can also communicate with the payee through this service. Because of this flexibility, and the hoped-for outcome that it would help people avoid falling into debt, it could save money at a national level. Not all bank payment schemes can support RtP, and of course banks and other *Payment Service Providers (PSPs)* need to deploy it for it to be available to bank account holders. A type of *pull payment.*

reserve account On the *card rails*, an account holding funds that an *acquirer* requires a merchant to maintain to support the provision of card services and for risk management purposes. The amount of funds for the reserve account depends on a number of factors, including transaction volumes, business type, and channel. Also refers to a non-interest-bearing account held at a *central bank* (or correspondent bank) by a financial services institution. A central bank requires banks to hold a certain amount of cash in reserve so that they never run short and have to refuse a customer's withdrawal, possibly triggering a *bank run*. A central bank may also use bank reserve levels as a tool in monetary policy.

respondent bank See *correspondent banking*.

retail CBDC (rCBDC) A type of *Central Bank Digital Currency* (CBDC) for general-purpose domestic use, including B2C, B2B, P2P, and G2C. Several architecture models can be used for retail CBDCs, such as *direct CBDC*, *intermediated CBDC*, and *Multi-CBDC* (mCBDC). There are also hybrid CBDC models that incorporate features of other models.

retail payments A term used to describe payments between consumers, businesses, and public authorities. They can be everyday consumer transactions but also include higher-value payments such as payroll and tax payments made by businesses. Often referred to as "consumer payments", they are characterised by high volumes of transactions. Examples are card transactions, *direct debit*, *standing orders*, cheque transactions, etc. Also see *Business-to-Consumer* (B2C), *Business-to-Business* (B2B), *Government-to-Consumer* (G2C), and *wholesale payments*.

retail payment system (RPS) A term used to describe bank payment schemes that typically handle high volumes of *retail payments*.

retail settlement A subset of *interbank settlement* referring to the *settlement* of *retail payments* and used on the *bank rails* to describe how funds will be moved to/from a bank account. This is the equivalent of *merchant settlement* on the *card rails* and happens after interbank settlement. However, whereas merchant settlement is contingent to contractual arrangements, retail settlement times apply to everyone in the same way according to the bank *payment scheme rules*. See also *wholesale settlement*.

RIPEMD-160 RACE Integrity Primitives Evaluation Message Digest is an established hashing algorithm. See also *cryptography*, *encryption*, and *hash*.

Ripple[82] A *Real-Time Gross Settlement* system, currency exchange and *remittance* network based on a *private blockchain* that is open to financial institutions worldwide and used to transfer funds across borders at a low cost. Created by Ripple Labs Inc. See also *settlement cycle*.

Robux[83] A *virtual currency* used in the game Roblox.

rollup In a *blockchain* context, a *layer 2 scaling solution* similar to *plasma chains* in principle, inasmuch as processing is offloaded from the *layer 1 blockchain* to the adjacent chain (rollup chain), but with some important differences. There are two types of rollups: optimistic rollups (ORU) and zero-knowledge rollups (zk-rollups). An ORU assumes that all transactions are valid by default (hence the optimism!), and therefore fraud proofs are a crucial element of their design (similarly to plasma chains), and the main chain verifies them and may potentially reverse and an entire set of transactions if the fraud is proven. A zk-rollup includes a *validity proof* for every transaction in the batch, which is implemented through *zero-knowledge proofs (ZKP)*. See also *side chain*, *state channel*, and *validium*.

RPS See retail payment system.

RSA Rivest-Shamir-Adleman. A *public key cryptography* algorithm. By far the most popular.

RTGS Real-Time Gross Settlement. A payment system that enables the immediate transfer of funds between banks or financial institutions on a gross basis, meaning that transactions are settled individually in real-time without netting debits against credits. This system is typically used for high-value transactions, ensuring that payments are completed instantly and securely, thereby reducing *settlement risk*. Increasingly, this method is also used for retail real-time payments. See also *settlement cycle*.

RTGS account See Real-Time Gross Settlement account.

RtP See Request-to-Pay.

RTP See *real-time payment system*.

RWA token See *Real-World Asset token*.

safeguarding A requirement on regulated firms to keep clients' funds completely separate from their operational funds. The bank account where customer funds are kept is referred to as a "safeguarding account" provided by a *custodian*. (Please note that the term "safeguarding" can be used more generically to mean "securing").

Samsung Pay[84] A *mobile wallet* provided by Samsung. A *pass-through digital wallet*.

Samsung Wallet[85] A multi-purpose *Digital Wallet* provided by Samsung. Enables users to store and use payment cards, bank accounts, passwords, tickets, keys, passes, keys, and identities.

sanction In an *Anti-Money Laundering (AML)* context, this is the imposition of trade or financial restrictions and penalties by one or more countries against another country, entity, or individual with the purpose of changing a behaviour in order to reduce *financial crime*. Economic sanctions can include actions such as tariffs, trade restrictions, and financial limitations. See also *Financial Action Task Force (FATF)*, Politically Exposed Person (PEP), *derisking*, and *debanking*.

SAR See Suspicious Activity Reporting.

Satoshi The smallest subdivision of a *Bitcoin* where 100,000,000 Satoshis represent one Bitcoin. The unit of measurement for Bitcoin transaction costs. See also *gas price*.

scaling solution In a *blockchain* context, these are improvements to a blockchain aimed at solving the *blockchain trilemma*. There are two types of blockchain scaling solutions: layer 1 and layer 2. Layer-1 scaling solutions augment the base layer of the *blockchain protocol* itself in order to improve scalability. They change the rules of the protocol directly to increase transaction capacity and speed, whilst accommodating more users and data (e.g. changing block data, changing *consensus protocol*, sharding). Layer 2 scaling solutions involve shifting a portion of a blockchain protocol's transactional burden to an adjacent system architecture, which then handles the brunt of the network's processing and only subsequently reports back to the main blockchain to finalise its results.

sCBDC See *intermediated CBDC*.

SDK See Software Development Kit.

SE See Secure Element.

Secure Element (SE) A *tamper-resistant* chip containing a microprocessor capable of storing sensitive data and running secure applications which can be embedded in any mobile device (such as a smartphone, IoT device, or crypto hardware wallet). The content of the SE is protected from malware attacks on the host (i.e. the mobile device operating system) and unauthorised access, as the SE acts as a secure vault. Typical applications that would use the SE are *authentication*, digital signature, mobile payments, IoT, secure and encrypted communications, etc. The SE can also be cloud-based, which is referred to as *Host Card Emulation (HCE)*. See also *encryption*, *cryptography*.

secure multi-party computation (SMPC) A *cryptography* protocol that allows multiple parties to collaboratively compute a function over their inputs whilst ensuring that these inputs remain private. This means that each party can contribute data to a computation without revealing their individual data to others involved. SMPC is designed to protect the privacy of each participant's data through advanced cryptographic techniques, ensuring that the final result is obtained without compromising individual input confidentiality. In the context of *Central Bank Digital Currencies (CBDCs)*, particularly *wholesale CBDCs*, SMPC plays a crucial role in maintaining the delicate balance between privacy and transparency. Wholesale CBDCs involve large-scale transactions between financial institutions, where safeguarding sensitive financial data is paramount. SMPC ensures that whilst the overall system remains transparent and auditable, individual transaction details remain confidential. This is particularly important in *distributed ledger technology (DLT)* systems, where data privacy must be preserved even as transaction records are shared across a network. By employing SMPC, central banks and financial institutions can perform necessary computations, such as transaction verification and balance calculations, without exposing sensitive underlying data, thus complying with privacy regulations and mitigating the risk of data breaches. SMPC may also be used by blockchain *oracles*.

security token A type of *crypto asset* that is an investment contract representing the legal ownership of a digital, physical, or intangible asset. Security token investors aim to generate a profit (e.g. dividend payments, interest, profit share, residual rights). Security tokens are regulated under applicable securities regulations and can only be traded on regulated platforms.

security token exchange A regulated *crypto exchange* that facilitates the buying, selling, and trading of *security tokens*, which are digital representations of ownership in an asset or company, typically backed by real-world assets. These exchanges ensure compliance with relevant securities laws and regulations, providing a secure environment for investors to trade tokenised securities. See also *tokenisation*.

Security Token Offering (STO) A regulated form of fundraising where digital tokens representing ownership in real-world assets (such as stocks, bonds, or real estate) are issued and sold to investors. STOs combine *blockchain* technology with traditional securities, offering increased liquidity and accessibility whilst complying with relevant securities laws and regulations. Unlike *Initial Coin Offerings* (ICOs) and *Initial Exchange Offerings* (IEOs), STOs provide investors with legal rights and protections associated with conventional securities. See also *tokenomics*.

seigniorage The profit a government or central bank makes from issuing currency, typically calculated as the difference between the face value of money and the cost to produce it. In traditional finance, this occurs when the production cost of coins or banknotes is less than their monetary value. In the context of *blockchain*, seigniorage refers to the revenue generated by a *blockchain protocol* through the creation and distribution of new tokens. This can include block rewards for miners or validators, as well as the profits from selling newly minted tokens. Blockchain seigniorage is often used to fund protocol development, incentivise network participants, or maintain the stability of algorithmic stablecoins. See also *minting*, *burning*, and *tokenomics*.

semantic web See *Web* 3.0.

SEMI See Electronic Money Institution.

semi-closed wallet See *staged digital wallet*.

SEPA See Single Euro Payment Area.

settlement The last step in the transfer of value between a *payer* and a *payee*. After settlement, the obligations of all the parties are fulfilled, and the transaction is considered complete. Settlement brings transaction *finality*. The settlement process will be different for centralised (e.g. *card rail* and *bank rail*) and decentralised infrastructures (e.g. *blockchain*).

settlement agent A bank which orchestrates the *finality* of the transfer of value between parties that hold accounts with them. On the *card rails*, settlement agents are usually commercial banks chosen by the *card schemes* according to their reputation, size, and geographic coverage (but may be a *central bank*). On the bank rails, the settlement agent is a central bank. This concept doesn't exist in *blockchain* infrastructures as the trust framework is distributed.

Settlement cycle Refers to the time it takes for payment transactions to be settled. On the bank rails, the settlement cycle is dependent on the bank payment scheme and can be performed in three ways.

In real-time: Real-Time Gross Settlement (RTGS) Where each payment is presented and settled immediately. This is used by most *large-value payment systems* (*LVPS*) and also by modern *retail payment systems* (RPS); or

In near real-time: deferred net settlement several times a day Where banks batch their transactions at several points during the day and submit the batch each time. This is used by a number or mature real-time RPS. To a payer, the settlement process is transparent, as the payments take place within seconds and look as though in "real-time"; or

In batch at the end of the day: deferred net settlement Where banks use transaction *batch processing* at the end of the day and submit them in one go, and this is used by (older) retail *ACH schemes*, and it usually takes a few days. On the *card rails*, the clearing and settlement processes are described in the *card scheme operating regulations*, and the settlement cycle is contingent to the contractual arrangements between parties. The settlement process on the card rails has two stages, *interbank settlement* (between *acquirers* and *issuers*), and *merchant settlement* (between the acquirer and the *merchant*). Merchant settlement can be deferred by the acquirer as a risk management tool for specific industries with longer purchase cycles (e.g. airline and hospitality). In blockchain infrastructures, the concept of settlement cycle is known as the *block interval*.

settlement risk A type of risk that may occur if one party of a financial transaction is not able to hold their end of the deal by failing to deliver the funds or the security required to complete a transaction after the other party (the counterparty) has already delivered the security or funds as per the transaction agreement. Settlement risk may also occur when there is a time lag in payment from one party, usually due to time zones. Also known as "counterparty risk". Also see *Delivery-versus Payment* and *Payment-versus-Payment*, *settlement and settlement cycle*.

SHA Secure Hash Algorithm (e.g. SHA-3) is an established family of hashing algorithms. See also *cryptography*, *encryption* and *hash*.

sharding A layer 1 *scaling solution* involving breaking the state of an entire *blockchain* network into distinct datasets called "shards" which are simultaneously processed in parallel by the network, allowing for sequential work on numerous transactions. Aimed to address the *blockchain trilemma*.

side chain In a *blockchain* context, a layer 2 *scaling solution* involving separate blockchains with their own consensus mechanism (e.g. PoS and PoA) that connect to a *layer 1 blockchain* through a gateway called a "bridge", which is usually implemented through a *smart contract*. See also *plasma chain*, *rollup*, *state channel*, and *validium*.

Single Euro Payment Area (SEPA)[86] An initiative that aims to enable payers anywhere in the EU (as well as in a number of other countries) to make fast, safe, and efficient cashless Euro credit transfers (introduced in 2008) and direct debits (introduced in 2009) to anywhere within the area, just like national payments.

slashing A penalty mechanism deployed in some *blockchain* infrastructures (mostly *Proof of Stake*) by which validators are punished for misbehaving (e.g. creating invalid blocks, voting twice) by slashing a portion of their *cryptocurrency* stake, meaning they permanently lose those funds. This discourages bad behaviour by making it financially risky for validators to cheat the system. Slashing helps maintain the integrity and security of the blockchain network. See also *staking*.

smart card A historical term for an *EMV* chip card, or any card containing a chip.

smart contract Code stored on a *blockchain* that automatically executes when its predefined conditions are met. Based on the "If, Then" principle, they are typically used to automate the execution of an agreement between participants in a trustless environment, without the need for intermediaries. One of the building blocks of *DeFi* and many other blockchain applications.

SMPC See secure multi-party computation.

social engineering A technique used by fraudsters and cyber criminals to psychologically manipulate victims into performing actions or divulging confidential information. Social engineering is more effective than compromising computer systems because it relies on human vulnerabilities rather than finding and exploiting technical vulnerabilities. See also *phishing*, *vishing*, *smishing*, and *ransomware*.

Society for Worldwide Interbank Financial Telecommunications (SWIFT)[87] A membership organisation that specifies a set of standard messages and formats that the financial services industry agrees on, thus minimising translation and counterparty verification costs, as well as improving security. SWIFT doesn't actually move funds; the bank *payment schemes* do that.

SoFi[88] A *neo-bank*.

soft fork See *fork*.

soft peg See *peg*.

SoftPOS A modern iteration of *Mobile Point-of-Sale (mPOS)* which doesn't rely on additional hardware and allows merchants to accept card payments directly on a standard consumer smart phone or tablet (i.e. Android or iOS).

Software Development Kit (SDK) A collection of software development tools provided in one installable package. An example is *SoftPOS* virtual card terminals which can be deployed on a merchant's own device (e.g. smart phone or tablet).

Solana (SOL)[89] A layer 1 blockchain. A permissionless blockchain. Also refers to the Solana cryptocurrency SOL. See also blockchain.

StaaS See Staking-as-a-Service.

stablecoin A type of *crypto asset* with the intended purpose to facilitate trades on *crypto exchanges*. Stablecoins were created to address the *volatility* risks associated with cryptocurrencies and can be either pegged to a collateral (e.g. *fiat currency*, commodity, another *cryptocurrency*) or rely on a "mint and burn" stabilising mechanism to control the supply. The former is referred to as a "collateralised stablecoin" and the latter as "non-collateralised" or "algorithmic". Stablecoins are becoming increasingly regulated. See also *coin* and *token*.

staged digital wallet A digital wallet that uses two stages (called back-to-back funding) to complete a payment transaction: the "funding" stage where the wallet collects funds from the payer's payment instrument (e.g. a card or a bank account), and the "payment" stage where the wallet provider pays out the funds to the payer. Wallet holders can transfer funds to other wallet holders on the same wallet network or make payments at merchants with which the wallet holder has an agreement. A staged wallet doesn't necessarily transmit information to the card *issuer*. Examples are PayPal, Square Cash, Bizum, Vipps, Amazon Pay, and Google Wallet. Historically called a "semi-closed wallet". (Note: Paypal also operates as a *stored value digital wallet* since PayPal account holders can have a balance on their account.) See also *pass-through digital wallet*.

stake delegation In a *Proof of Stake (PoS) blockchain* context, a *staking* model by which coin/token holders may delegate their stake (voting power and staking rights) to other validators or entities of their choice if they don't have the resources or expertise to run a validator node and still want to participate in the *consensus protocol* and earn staking rewards. Delegators retain control of their stake and can withdraw delegation at any time. Coin/token holders running validator nodes may also self-delegate to their own node to enhance their reputation and probability of being chosen.

Stakeholder In a payment *ecosystem*, these are the parties involved whose interests are affected by the operation of the *value chain*.

Staking In a *blockchain* context the process of reserving an amount of *cryptocurrency* for a particular purpose. In the *Proof of Stake* (PoS) blockchain *consensus protocol*, this is the governance process by which by which *validators* are governed on a particular blockchain (see also *cross-chain staking*). Another definition applies to *crypto debit cards* and *crypto credit cards*, where some issuers may require cardholders to stake a cryptocurrency amount to be able to use the card.

Staking-as-a-Service (StaaS) StaaS providers may offer infrastructure, node management, validator hosting, etc. to those unable to run their own *validator* node on *Proof of Stake* (PoS) networks who may leverage the infrastructure and expertise of these providers by delegating their stake to them to increase their chance of earning staking rewards. Participants have more flexibility and control over their stake when compared to *staking pools*. They typically charge a fee, which is deducted from the staking rewards which are distributed amongst participants according to their contribution. Increasingly attracting regulatory scrutiny.

Staking farm In a *Proof of Stake* (PoS) context, this is a large-scale *staking* operation and validators may delegate their stake to the farm's infrastructure in exchange for professional infrastructure management, security, risk management, optimisation services, and even portfolio management across multiple blockchains. Staking farms will charge a fee, which is deducted from the staking rewards which are distributed amongst participants according to their contribution.

Staking pool In a *Proof of Stake* (PoS) *blockchain* context, this is a concept similar to a *mining pool* in *Proof of Work* (PoW) blockchains, whereby validators can join or create staking pools where the pool operator aggregates the delegated stakes to operate a validator node on behalf of the pool members. An alternative model is where staking pools function as intermediaries, allowing users to delegate their stakes to validators chosen by the pool operator as the pool doesn't operate a validator node itself. Regardless, staking pools share rewards proportionally to their member's contribution and typically charge fees which are deducted from the staking rewards. These pools can be small (targeted at individual investors or validators) or large-scale operations (targeted at institutional investors), and depending on size, may offer professional infrastructure management, security, risk management, optimisation services, and even portfolio management across multiple blockchains. Participants in a staking pool have limited control over their staked assets, as they delegate their tokens to the pool.

State channel In a *blockchain* context, a layer 2 *scaling solution* involving separate transactional infrastructures (usually not blockchains) where participants can carry out multiple private transactions off-chain on a *peer-to-peer* basis, where only the first (open channel) and final (close channel) transactions are recorded on the underlying *layer 1 blockchain*. As such, they facilitate fast and cheap transactions without relying on the main chain for every transaction. See also *plasma chain*, *rollup*, *side chain*, and *validium*.

Stored value card A type of *prepaid card* where the funds can be increased as well as decreased.

Stored value digital wallet A type of *e-wallet* similar to a *prepaid card* inasmuch as they allocate a separate account to each wallet holder. Wallet holders can load funds into their wallet account using a funding mechanism (e.g. a card) and once the wallet account is funded, the wallet holder can perform transactions with sellers that are part of the wallet network, as well as transfer funds to other users within the network. Examples are Alipay, Amazon Pay, Paytm, and Venmo. Also referred to as a *closed wallet*. A variation of this model is the retailer-issued stored value wallet, such as provided by Starbucks[90] or Target.[91]

Straksclearing[92] A real-time payment system (RTP system), retail payment system (RPS) in Denmark.

Suspicious Activity Reporting (SAR) The process by which financial crimes are reported to the regulator.

SWIFT See Society for Worldwide Interbank Financial Telecommunications.

Sybil attack A type of security threat in *peer-to-peer* networks where a malicious actor creates multiple fake identities or *nodes* to gain disproportionate influence over the network. Named after the subject of a book about dissociative identity disorder, this attack aims to undermine the network's integrity by overwhelming it with seemingly independent participants that are actually controlled by a single entity. Sybil attacks can compromise the reliability of *consensus protocols*, reputation systems, and voting processes in decentralised systems, potentially leading to network manipulation or disruption.

symmetric cryptography An *encryption* method where both the sender and receiver use the same encryption key, which is used for both encrypting and decrypting the messages. Symmetric cryptography is considered less secure and more difficult to manage (i.e. key distribution and key management) than *public key cryptography* (aka asymmetric cryptography), but faster. Typically used for bulk encryption of large volumes of data, including in centralised payment applications (e.g. card transactions), or for securing data at rest. Also known as "symmetric encryption" or "secret key cryptography". Well known symmetric cryptography algorithms include Advanced Encryption Standard (AES), Triple Data Encryption Standard (3DES), and Rivest Cipher (RC4).

synthetic stablecoin A synthetic stablecoin is a type of *cryptocurrency* designed to maintain a stable value, typically soft-pegged to a fiat currency like the US dollar, without relying on traditional banking infrastructure. It achieves this stability through a *delta-hedging* strategy, which involves creating offsetting positions in derivatives to manage risk. This ensures that the value of the synthetic stablecoin remains stable despite market volatility by balancing gains and losses between the spot and derivative markets.

systemic risk See *contagion risk*.

tamper-evident The capacity of a device to show evidence of physical attack.

tamper-proof The proven capacity of a device to resist all attacks.

tamper-resistant The proven capacity of a device to resist physical attacks up to a certain point.

TARGET2[93] A real-time gross settlement system owned and operated by the Eurosystem. See *settlement cycle*.

TEE See Trusted Execution Environment.

Tempo (Radix) An implementation of *Distributed Ledger Technology (DLT)* that uses a data structure called Tempo, where nodes rely upon the passage of logical time to validate transactions. Radix positions itself as a *Web 3.0* platform. See also *blockchain*, *Hashgraph*, *Directed Acyclic Graph (DAG)*.

terrorist financing The provision of funds or financial support to terrorists. A form of *financial crime*. See also *money laundering*.

testnet A separate *blockchain* network used for testing and development purposes, allowing developers to deploy and experiment with *smart contracts* and applications without using real *cryptocurrency* or affecting the main blockchain (mainnet). Testnets simulate the mainnet environment, enabling developers to identify bugs, test features, and ensure functionality in a risk-free setting before launching on the main network.

Tether (USDT)[94] A *stablecoin*.

Third Party PSP (TPP) A payment *ecosystem* actor which provides *Payment Service Users (PSUs)* with access services to payment accounts.

time synchronisation attack A malicious attempt to manipulate or disrupt the clock synchronisation process in networked systems. The attacker aims to alter the perceived time of one or more *nodes*, potentially causing communication failures, security vulnerabilities, or system malfunctions. Common techniques include delaying or modifying timing messages, exploiting vulnerabilities in synchronisation protocols, or manipulating local system clocks. These attacks can impact critical operations in various domains, including financial transactions, industrial control systems, and distributed networks.

token In traditional centralised payments, a token is a representation of a payment account number that has no link with the original payment account number. It is a security measure that prevents fraudsters from gaining access to the real data. The relationship between the token and the account is maintained in token vaults which are provided by *Independent Software Vendors (ISVs)* referred to as *Token Service Providers (TSPs)*. In decentralised systems (e.g. *blockchain*), a token is a *crypto asset* that is foreign (i.e. not native) to the blockchain it lives on. Examples are Tether (USDT), Uniswap (UNI) or Chainlink (LINK).

token-based CBDC A *CBDC* access model by which users access the CBDC with a password-like digital signature using *public key cryptography* without requiring personal identification. Both *retail CBDCs* and *wholesale CBDCs* can use this access model.

tokenisation In traditional financial services, the process of replacing sensitive data with non-sensitive data. On the *card rails*, a process designed to enhance security by which a card *Primary Account Number*

(*PAN*) is replaced with a unique alternative value, or *token*, which can be used for payment transactions instead of the real PAN. This token can be used subsequently in *recurring transactions*. In decentralised systems, tokenisation is the process by which real-world assets, or ownership thereof, are represented digitally on a *blockchain*, which is why it is sometimes referred to as "asset tokenisation". Tokenisation service providers typically offer services such as asset evaluation and pricing, regulatory compliance, creation of tokens, investor/issuer funds management dashboards, Tokenised Asset Offerings (TAO), and listing on security exchanges (see *crypto exchange*).

tokenomics A contraction of "token" and "economics". A term used to describe the economic model used by a *blockchain* ecosystem. This includes token/coin supply (e.g. *mining*, *staking*, *burning*, inflation, deflationary measures, etc.), distribution (e.g. *airdrop*, *Initial Coin Offering*, etc.), utility (e.g. function, access, governance, incentives, etc.), and governance (e.g. voting, upgrades, etc.). To draw a parallel with centralised payment ecosystems, tokenomics encompasses rules and processes related to a particular *payment scheme*, the applicable regulations, and the monetary policy under which it operates.

Total Value Locked (TVL) The aggregate amount of *crypto assets* deposited in a *DeFi* protocol, typically expressed in USD. TVL serves as a key metric to measure the overall adoption and *liquidity* of DeFi platforms and the broader ecosystem.

Tornado Cash[95] A *coin mixer*.

TPP See Third Party PSP.

traceability The degree to which a payment transaction can be traced back to the *payer* or the *payee*.

TradFi An abbreviation of "Traditional Finance". A term used to describe the entire traditional financial, centralised, *ecosystems* such as *card rails*, *bank rails*, and traditional centralised *settlement* and financial market infrastructures. Also see *DeFi*, *CeFi*, *CeDeFi*, *and CApp*.

transaction fee There isn't a single definition of a transaction fee. See acquirer margin, address verification fee, assessment fee, ATM interchange fee, authorisation fee, card scheme fee, early termination fee, gas price, interchange, interest, IRS reporting fee, Merchant Service Charge, retrieval request fee, set-up fee, surcharge fee. This term is also used to describe the fees that users pay to transact on blockchain networks.

transaction pruning In a *blockchain* context, a *layer 1 scaling solution* involving the removal of transactions from a *blockchain* after a certain period of time determined by the protocol (meaning that most full nodes won't have to store an entire copy of the blockchain, thus increasing scalability). If a blockchain implements transaction pruning, most full nodes will be pruned nodes, whilst a number of archival nodes will still store an entire copy of the blockchain. Bitcoin introduces this option in release 0.11.0,[96] and Zcash may also have introduced this option.

travel rule A *Financial Action Task Force (FATF)* recommendation by which *Virtual Asset Service Providers (VASPs)* and other financial services institutions are required to share accurate *payer* and *payee* information. The FATF recommendations were updated in November 2023.[97]

Trezor[98] A crypto wallet.

Trusted Execution Environment (TEE) A secure zone within a computer specifically designed to safeguard the confidentiality and integrity of code and data. Isolated from the main system, it prevents unauthorised access or modification of the information processed within. Even during a system breach, cryptographic techniques and hardware security features keep the data hidden. Additionally, TEEs ensure data integrity, acting as guardians against tampering. This guarantees the authenticity and trustworthiness of computations performed within. In a *blockchain* context, TEEs are relevant for decentralised *oracles* handling sensitive data. TEEs provide a secure space for decentralised oracles to process confidential information before feeding it to *smart contracts*, even within a decentralised network.

tulip mania A period during the Dutch Golden Age in the early 17th century when the prices of some tulip bulbs reached extraordinarily high levels and then dramatically collapsed. It is often cited as one of the first recorded speculative bubbles.

TUPAS A *digital identity* framework in Finland which is a partnership between all Finnish banks. It expired in September 2019 to be replaced by the Finish Trust Network (FTN).

TVL See Total Value Locked.

two-factor authentication (2FA) A type of *multi-factor authentication* that uses two factors. The first factor is usually a password, and the second commonly includes a text with a code sent to a smartphone, or *biometrics*.

Unified Payment Interface (UPI)[99] Unified Payment Interface. A *real-time payment system (RTP system)*, *retail payment system* (RPS) in India, operated by NPCI. Also see *Aadhaar*.

Uniswap[100] A decentralised *crypto exchange*.

Unspent Transaction Output (UTXO) A *double-spending* prevention model in *blockchain* infrastructures where each output from an unspent (i.e. not settled) transaction becomes a UTXO associated with the address of the transaction initiation user. Users initiating transactions will reference one or more UTXOs as inputs to a new transaction to prove that they have funds available. The sum of the UTXOs must cover the amount being spent, and the excess is then sent back as change to the sender's address, creating new UTXOs. The UTXO model, commonly used in Proof of work blockchains (e.g. Bitcoin and Bitcoin-based blockchains) and some PoS blockchains (e.g. Cardano, Zilliqa, and Tezos), enables the blockchain to keep a consistent and unbroken chain of ownership through the tracking of UTXOs where every transaction can be traced back to its origin through the series of unspent outputs. The UTXO model is generally preferred by blockchain projects with a focus on privacy. This is in contrast to account-based models (e.g. *Ethereum*, *Solana*, and *Polygon*) which primarily consider the account balance rather than individual unspent outputs.

UPI See Unified Payment Interface.

USD Coin (USDC)[101] A *stablecoin*.

USDT See *Tether*.

utility In economics and finance, utility refers to the measure of satisfaction or benefit derived from consuming goods or services. It represents the value that an individual assigns to a product based on its ability to fulfil needs or desires. In the context of *cryptocurrency* and *blockchain*, utility often describes the practical uses of a *token* within a specific ecosystem, such as enabling transactions, accessing services, or participating in governance, distinguishing it from speculative or investment purposes.

utility token A type of *crypto asset* with the intended purpose of giving crypto-project developers the ability to raise interest in their project, encourage developers to create applications, and generally create value in a blockchain *ecosystem*. These tokens can be used to redeem a special service or receive special treatment and are often given out for free to promote the project. Utility tokens are unregulated. Also see *airdrop*.

UTXO See Unspent Transaction Output.

validating node In a *blockchain* context, a node who participates in the transaction validation process. See also *mining, miner, validator, staking, and mempool.*

validation A catch-all term referred to a processed of verifying validity. In a *blockchain* context, it may refer to transaction or block validation. See also *staking, mining, and mempool.*

validator A validating node in a *Proof of Stake (PoS) blockchain* network who listens and gathers valid transactions to fit in a block (e.g. no *double-spending*). Validators are chosen according to the consensus protocol through *staking* and participate in securing the blockchain in exchange for rewards. This term may be used interchangeably to refer to a *validating node* (i.e. not specifically referring to PoS blockchains). See also *miner, mining, and mempool.*

validity proof A cryptographic mechanism used in *blockchain* networks, particularly in *layer 2 scaling solutions*, to verify the correctness of *off-chain* computations without re-executing them *on-chain*. It allows a prover to demonstrate that a large batch of transactions or state transitions is valid, enabling the main blockchain to accept these changes as correct without processing each transaction individually. Validity proofs provide immediate finality and enhanced security compared to other scaling approaches, as they mathematically guarantee the accuracy of the proposed state update.

validium A *blockchain layer 2 scaling solution*. A validium processes transactions *off-chain* for faster processing and relies on the *layer 1 blockchain* for security but stores transaction data *off-chain* using Data Availability Committees (DACs) or Providers (DAPs). Validiums use cryptographic proofs to verify the validity of these off-chain transactions before submitting the proofs to layer 1 for finalisation. See also *plasma chain, side chain, state channel,* and *rollup.*

value chain A business model describing the steps involved in bringing a product or service to market, from design to distribution, and everything in between.

Variable Recurring Payment (VRP) A payment instruction issued by a bank account holder to their bank authorising a biller (e.g. a subscription service) to collect payments from their account at regular intervals (e.g. weekly, monthly, and yearly), within agreed limits, without the bank account holder's intervention after the first instruction. It is a bank payment scheme *overlay service* and is a type of *recurring transaction*, but it offers more flexibility and transparency than alternatives such as *direct debit* and card recurring transactions, as the bank account holder remains in control of the payment limits and the payment instruction's end date is agreed upfront. At any point up to *clearing* and *settlement*, the bank account holder can change any of the agreed parameters, enabling them to respond to changes in circumstances as they happen. See also *recurring payment*.

VASP See Virtual Asset Service Provider.

V-Bucks[102] A *virtual currency* used in the game Fortnite.

Venmo[103] A peer-to-peer payment app, a stored value digital wallet.

Virtual asset Refers to any digital representation of value that can be digitally traded, transferred, or used for payment or investment purposes. Also referred to as "digital asset".

Virtual Asset Service Provider (VASP) Defined by the *Financial Action Task Force (FATF)* as a business that conducts one or more of the following actions on behalf of its clients:

Exchange between *virtual assets* and *fiat currencies*;

Exchange between one or more forms of virtual assets;

Transfer of virtual assets;

Safekeeping and/or administration or virtual assets or instruments enabling control over virtual assets; or

Participating in and provision of financial services related to an *issuer's* offer and/or sale of a virtual asset.

This encompasses a range of crypto businesses, including *crypto exchanges*, crypto ATM operators, custodial wallets, and hedge funds.

virtual currency A type of *virtual asset* that is issued, managed, and controlled by private *issuers*, developers, or the founding organisation. A virtual currency is used in a specific community and relies on a system of trust defined by the private issuer. As such, it is a form of a *closed loop* medium of exchange. Gaming platforms use virtual currencies, such as *V-Bucks* and *Robux*.

Visa[104] A *card scheme* operating on the *four-party model*.

VisaNet The *Visa* network infrastructure.

volatility The rate at which the price of a financial asset increases or decreases over a period of time and refers to both the frequency at which the asset value changes and the degree to which it changes. Higher volatility often means higher risk. Cryptocurrencies such as Bitcoin are volatile.

VM See Virtual Machine.

VRP See Variable Recurring Payment (VRP).

wash trading A manipulative practice where a trader simultaneously buys and sells the same financial instrument to create artificial market activity. In traditional markets, it's illegal and used to mislead other traders by inflating volumes or manipulating prices. For *crypto assets*, wash trading is common due to less regulation, and it is often employed to artificially boost trading volumes, create false impressions of liquidity, or manipulate prices of digital assets and *tokens*.

wearables Wearable technology is any technology designed to be used when worn (as clothing or accessories), implanted in the body, tattooed on the skin, overlayed on fingernails, etc. Sometimes referred to as "wearable devices", but the use of "wearables" is the most common. Popular examples are smartwatches, which have a particular relevance in payments. See also *Internet of Things*.

Web 1.0 The first incarnation of the internet was characterised by websites that just pushed information to users. It was defined by Tim Berners-Lee in 1989 and provided basic connectivity and hyperlinks. Also referred to as the "static web" or "read-only web".

Web 2.0 The second (current) version of the internet. Instead of just static Web 1.0 websites that pushed information to users, Web 2.0 introduced new forms of interactivity and saw the rise of social media, blogs, and other forms of interactive platforms and technologies (e.g. *Java* and XML).

Web 3.0 The next version of the internet. The exact definition is still loose, but the general consensus is that it has a decentralised infrastructure built on *blockchain* technologies and applications, and *artificial intelligence*. Also referred to as the "semantic web" and "Web3". See also *metaverse*.

WebAuthn[105] An *authentication* standard published by the World Wide Web Consortium. See *FIDO*.

WeChat Pay[106] A *mobile wallet*.

Western Union[107] A Money Transfer Operator.

Whirlpool A popular hashing algorithm. See also *cryptography*, *encryption*, and *hash*.

white paper A *blockchain* white paper is a document explaining the primary purpose, technology, current state, and plans for a blockchain project. It should also give information about its participants, utility, and all the potential factors that might give its underlying *coin/token* economic value. It is meant as a high-level guide that enables investors to ascertain whether a project has future potential and to raise the interest of potential users. The oldest white paper is the Bitcoin white paper, entitled "Bitcoin: A Peer-to-Peer Electronic Cash System", and was written under the pseudonym of Satoshi Nakamoto in October 2008. More recently, the 2014 white paper "Zerocash: Decentralised Anonymous Payments from Bitcoin"[108] that described zk-proofs (see *Zero-Knowledge Proofs*), a cryptographic technique used by many *layer 2 scaling solutions*, received the IEEE "Test of Time" award for its "broad and lasting impact on both research and practice in computer security and privacy".

wholesale CBDC A type of *Central Bank Digital Currency* (CBDC) aimed at financial firms holding reserve deposits with a *central bank* and used for *interbank settlement* and other financial market transactions. Several architecture models can be used for wholesale CBDCs, such as *internediated CBDC (sCBDC)*, *multi-CBDC (mCBDC)*, and *direct CBDC*.

wholesale payments A term used to describe transactions between banks or other eligible financial institutions and as being typically large-value payments. Wholesale payments are small in number but are typically very high in value, and represent most of the value of payments. An example is money market transactions. See also *retail payments*.

wholesale settlement A subset of *interbank settlement* which primarily focuses on high-value transactions between financial services institutions (e.g. banks, investment firms), usually operating on a *Real-Time Gross Settlement* basis. See also *Large Value Payment System (LVPS)*.

Wire transfer A term used to describe a large-value payment system (LVPS) that generally operates on a Real-Time Gross Settlement (RTGS) basis. See also settlement cycle, real-time payment system (RTP system), retail payment system (RPS).

Wise[109] A financial services institution formerly known as TransferWise that started as a *Peer-to-Peer money exchange* and subsequently obtained further permissions in various geographies, such as the *Electronic Money Institution* (EMI) licence.

Worldline[110] An *acquirer.*

Worldpay[111] An *acquirer.*

WorldRemit[112] A peer-to-peer money exchange.

wrapped token A *cryptocurrency* token that represents a claim on another underlying asset or token, typically from a different blockchain. Wrapped tokens allow assets to be used on non-native blockchains, enabling cross-chain interoperability and liquidity. The original asset is held in custody whilst an equivalent wrapped version is minted on the target blockchain, maintaining a 1:1 peg with the underlying asset.

XML (Extensible Markup Language) A flexible text-based format for storing and sharing structured data. Unlike its rigid predecessors, such as the fixed-length record format used in ISO 8583, XML empowers users to define custom tags. This flexibility allows XML to represent a wide range of data types, from everyday configuration files to complex financial messaging standards like ISO 20022. Before XML, data exchange relied on inflexible formats. Imagine fixed-length text files where each data point occupies a specific number of characters, requiring meticulous manual editing for any modifications. Proprietary binary formats, specific to software and often undocumented, further hindered communication. Even early database systems often had their own data formats, creating hurdles when migrating information between databases. XML's structured yet versatile approach addresses these limitations, making it a cornerstone of modern data communication. Its ability to securely and efficiently structure and transport information across various platforms solidifies its prominent role.

XRP The *cryptocurrency* issued by Ripple on its private blockchain. Also a *utility token.*

yield farming A DeFi strategy where users provide liquidity to protocols by depositing or lending *crypto assets* in exchange for rewards, typically in the form of the protocol's native tokens or transaction fees. This practice aims to maximise returns on *cryptocurrency* holdings through various incentive mechanisms.

YooMoney[113] An *e-wallet* owned by Sberbank. Formerly known as Yandex. Money.

Yuan The basic unit of the renminbi, the official currency of China, but the word is also used to refer to the Chinese currency generally. Abbreviated CNY.

Zelle[114] A peer-to-peer payment app. A *pass-through digital wallet*. An *A2A* payment app.

Zero-Knowledge Proof (ZKP, zk-proof) A cryptographic tool allowing a user to prove they are in possession of specific information (e.g. sufficient funds for a transaction) without revealing the information itself to the validator, thus maintaining network integrity whilst protecting user privacy. A commonly used type of ZKP is zk-SNARK (Succinct Non-interactive Argument of Knowledge). Variances of ZKP include zk-SNARK ((Succinct Non-interactive Argument of Knowledge) and bulletproof.

zero-knowledge rollup (zk-rollup) A *blockchain layer 2 scaling solution*. See *rollup*.

Notes

1 EMVCo, 3D Secure website. https://www.emvco.com/emv-technologies/3-d-secure/ (Accessed 21 November 2023).
2 Unique Identification Authority of India website. https://uidai.gov.in/en/ (Accessed 21 November 2023).
3 Unique Identification Authority of India website. https://uidai.gov.in/en/ (Accessed 11 December 2023).
4 Airtel Money Nigeria website. https://www.airtel.com.ng/support/airtel_money (Accessed 21 November 2023).
5 Algorand website. https://algorandtechnologies.com/ (Accessed 1 December 2023).
6 Alipay website. https://global.alipay.com/platform/site/ihome (Accessed 21 November 2023).
7 Amazon Pay website. https://pay.amazon.com/ (Accessed 21 November 2023).
8 American Express website. https://www.americanexpress.com (Accessed 21 November 2023).
9 Apple Pay website. https://www.apple.com/uk/apple-pay/ (Accessed 21 November 2023).
10 Avalanche website. https://www.avax.network/ (Accessed 1 December 2023).
11 "'The First Twitter-Fuelled Bank Run': How Social Media Compounded SVB's Collapse" *The Guardian*, 16 March 2023. Available at: https://www.theguardian.com/business/2023/mar/16/the-first-twitter-fuelled-bank-run-how-social-media-compounded-svbs-collapse (Accessed 11 December 2023).

12 "£55bn Withdrawn from Credit Suisse before Rescue" *BBC News*, 24 April 2023. Available at: https://www.bbc.co.uk/news/business-65370751 (Accessed 11 December 2023).
13 BankID Sweden website. https://www.bankid.com/en/privat/skaffa-bankid (Accessed 21 November 2023).
14 BankID Norway website. https://bankid.no/ (Accessed 21 November 2023).
15 Office of the Comptroller of the Currency website (Bank Secrecy Acts). https://www.occ.treas.gov/topics/supervision-and-examination/bsa/index-bsa.html (Accessed 21 November 2023).
16 Baidu website. https://ir.baidu.com/ (Accessed 11 December 2023).
17 Alibaba website. https://www.alibaba.com/ (Accessed 11 December 2023).
18 Tencent website. https://www.tencent.com/en-us/ (Accessed 11 December 2023).
19 Xiaomi website. https://www.mi.com/ (Accessed 11 December 2023).
20 Binance website. https://www.binance.com (Accessed 21 November 2023).
21 Bank for International Settlements website. https://www.bis.org/ (Accessed 21 November 2023).
22 Bitcoin website. https://bitcoin.org/en/ (Accessed 21 November 2023).
23 Bitfinex website. https://www.bitfinex.com/ (Accessed 21 November 2023).
24 Cardano website. https://cardano.org/ (Accessed 1 December 2023).
25 Cash App website. https://cash.app/ (Accessed 21 November 2023).
26 Chime website. https://www.chime.com/ (Accessed 21 November 2023).
27 Coinbase website. https://www.coinbase.com/ (Accessed 21 November 2023).
28 Coinomize website. https://coinomize.biz/ (Accessed 16 December 2023).
29 Legislation.gov.uk (Computer Misuse Act 1990) website. https://www.legislation.gov.uk/ukpga/1990/18/contents (Accessed 21 November 2023).
30 "How the Biggest Fraud in German History Unravelled" *The New Yorker*, 27 February 2023. https://www.newyorker.com/magazine/2023/03/06/how-the-biggest-fraud-in-german-history-unravelled (Accessed 6 December 2023).
31 "Anatomy of a Run: The Terra Luna Crash" National Bureau of Economic Research, April 2023. https://www.nber.org/papers/w31160 (Accessed 6 December 2023).
32 "Why Did FTX Collapse? Here's What to Know" *The New York Times*, 10 November 2022. https://www.nytimes.com/2022/11/10/technology/ftx-binance-crypto-explained.html (Accessed 6 December 2023).

33 "What Is a BRICS Currency and Is the U.S. Dollar in Trouble?" *Reuters*, 24 August 2023. Available at: https://www.reuters.com/markets/currencies/what-is-brics-currency-could-one-be-adopted-2023-08-23/ (Accessed 9 January 2024).
34 NANO website. Available at: https://nano.org/en (Accessed 12 January 2024).
35 Obyte website. Available at: https://obyte.org/ (Accessed 12 January 2024).
36 IOTA website. Available at: https://www.iota.org/ (Accessed 12 January 2024).
37 European Commission website (eIDAS regulation). https://digital-strategy.ec.europa.eu/en/policies/eidas-regulation (Accessed 21 November 2023).
38 Electrum website. https://electrum.org/ (Accessed 21 November 2023).
39 EMVCo website. https://www.emvco.com/ (Accessed 21 November 2023).
40 Ethereum website. https://ethereum.org/en/ (Accessed 21 November 2023).
41 eToro website. https://www.etoro.com (Accessed 21 November 2023).
42 European Banking Authority website. https://www.eba.europa.eu/ (Accessed 21 November 2023).
43 European Central Bank website. https://www.ecb.europa.eu/home/html/index.en.html (Accessed 21 November 2023).
44 European Payments Initiative website. https://www.epicompany.eu/ (Accessed 21 November 2023).
45 Exodus website. https://www.exodus.com/ (Accessed 21 November 2023).
46 FIDO Alliance website. https://fidoalliance.org/ (Accessed 21 November 2023).
47 UK Faster Payment System website. https://www.wearepay.uk/what-we-do/payment-systems/faster-payment-system/ (Accessed 21 November 2023).
48 Hing Kong Interbank Clearing Limited website. https://fps.hkicl.com.hk/eng/fps/index.php (Accessed 21 November 2023).
49 Bank of Russia website. https://www.cbr.ru/eng/Psystem/payment_system/ (Accessed 21 November 2023).
50 Federal Reserve website (FedNow). https://www.frbservices.org/financial-services/fednow (Accessed 21 November 2023).
51 Federal Reserve website (Fedwire). https://www.frbservices.org/financial-services/wires (Accessed 21 November 2023).
52 Financial Action Task Force website. https://www.fatf-gafi.org/en/home.html (Accessed 21 November 2023).

53 EUR-Lex (General Data Protection Regulation). https://eur-lex.europa.eu/eli/reg/2016/679/oj (Accessed 21 November 2023).
54 Gemini website. https://www.gemini.com (Accessed 21 November 2023).
55 Google Wallet website. https://wallet.google/ (Accessed 21 November 2023).
56 Hedera website. Available at: https://hedera.com/ (Accessed 12 January 2024).
57 Ingenico website. https://ingenico.com/en (Accessed 21 November 2023).
58 Itsme website. https://www.itsme-id.com/en-BE (Accessed 21 November 2023).
59 Kraken website. https://www.kraken.com (Accessed 21 November 2023).
60 Ledger website. https://www.ledger.com/ (Accessed 21 November 2023).
61 Litecoin website. Available at: https://litecoin.org/ (Accessed 26 May 2024).
62 Mastercard website. https://www.mastercard.com (Accessed 21 November 2023).
63 MitID website. https://www.mitid.dk/ (Accessed 21 November 2023).
64 Mobiilivarmenne website. https://mobiilivarmenne.fi/ (Accessed 21 November 2023).
65 Moneygram website. https://www.moneygram.com/ (Accessed 21 November 2023).
66 Monzo website. https://monzo.com/ (Accessed 21 November 2023).
67 M-PESA website. https://www.vodafone.com/about-vodafone/what-we-do/consumer-products-and-services/m-pesa (Accessed 21 November 2023).
68 MyGov.be website https://mygov.be/ (Accessed 27 November 2024)
69 N26 website. https://n26.com/ (Accessed 21 November 2023).
70 NemID website. https://lifeindenmark.borger.dk/apps-and-digital-services/nemid (Accessed 21 November 2023).
71 Nexi website. https://www.nexigroup.com/ (Accessed 21 November 2023).
72 PancakeSwap website. https://pancakeswap.finance/ (Accessed 5 December 2023).
73 The Association of Banks of Singapore Website (PayNow). https://www.abs.org.sg/consumer-banking/pay-now (Accessed 21 November 2023).
74 PayPal website. https://www.paypal.com/ (Accessed 21 November 2023).
75 Paytm website. https://paytm.com/ (Accessed 21 November 2023).
76 Banco Central do Brasil website. https://www.bcb.gov.br/en/financial stability/pix_en (Accessed 21 November 2023).
77 Monero website. https://www.getmonero.org/ (Accessed 15 December 2023).

78 ZCash website. https://z.cash/ (Accessed 15 December 2023).
79 Bank of Thailand website (PromptPay). https://www.bot.or.th/en/financial-innovation/digital-finance/digital-payment/promptpay.html (Accessed 21 November 2023).
80 "Conjugate Coding" ACM Digital Library, Stephen Wiesner, 1 January 1983. Available at: Conjugate coding | ACM SIGACT News (Accessed 25 January 2024).
81 "What Is Consensys Quorum?" Consensys website, 8 June 2021. Available at: What is Consensys Quorum? | Consensys (Accessed 25 January 2024).
82 Ripple website. https://ripple.com/ (Accessed 21 November 2023).
83 Roblox website (Buy Robux). https://www.roblox.com/upgrades/robux (Accessed 21 November 2023).
84 Samsung website (Samsung Pay). https://www.samsung.com/uk/samsung-pay/ (Accessed 21 November 2023).
85 Samsung website (Samsung Wallet). https://www.samsung.com/uk/apps/samsung-wallet/ (Accessed 21 November 2023).
86 European Central Bank website (SEPA). https://www.ecb.europa.eu/paym/integration/retail/sepa/html/index.en.html (Accessed 21 November 2023).
87 SWIFT website. https://www.swift.com/ (Accessed 21 November 2023).
88 SoFi website. https://www.sofi.com/ (Accessed 21 November 2023).
89 Solana website. Available at: https://solana.com/ (Accessed 26 May 2024).
90 Starbucks app website. https://www.starbucks.com/rewards/mobile-apps/ (Accessed 1 December 2023).
91 Target app. https://www.target.com/c/target-app (Accessed December 2023).
92 Danmarks Nationalbank website. https://www.nationalbanken.dk/en/what-we-do/safe-and-efficient-payments/the-payments-infrastructure-in-denmark (Accessed 21 November 2023).
93 European Central Bank website (TARGET2). https://www.ecb.europa.eu/paym/target/target2/html/index.en.html (Accessed 21 November 2023).
94 Tether website. https://tether.to/en/ (Accessed 21 November 2023).
95 Tornado Cash website. https://tornadocash-eth.ipns.dweb.link/ (Accessed 1 December 2024).
96 "Bitcoin Core 0.11.00" Bitcoin Core website. Available at: https://bitcoincore.org/en/releases/0.11.0/ (Accessed 10 May 2024).
97 FATF recommendations. https://www.fatf-gafi.org/content/dam/fatf-gafi/recommendations/FATF%20Recommendations%202012.pdf.coredownload.inline.pdf (Accessed 21 November 2023).
98 Trezor website. https://trezor.io/ (Accessed 21 November 2023).

99 NPCI website (UPI). https://www.npci.org.in/what-we-do/upi/product-overview (Accessed 21 November 2023).
100 Uniswap website. https://app.uniswap.org/swap (Accessed 5 December 2023).
101 Circle website (USDC). https://www.circle.com/en/usdc (Accessed 21 November 2023).
102 Fortnite website (V-Bucks). https://www.fortnite.com/vbuckscard (Accessed 21 November 2023).
103 Venmo website. https://venmo.com/ (Accessed 21 November 2023).
104 Visa website. https://www.visa.com (Accessed 21 November 2023).
105 FIDO Alliance website (WebAuthn). https://fidoalliance.org/fido2-2/fido2-web-authentication-webauthn/ (Accessed 21 November 2023).
106 WeChat Pay website. https://pay.weixin.qq.com/index.php/public/wechatpay (Accessed 21 November 2023).
107 Western Union website. https://www.westernunion.com/ (Accessed 21 November 2023).
108 "White Paper That Birthed Crypto ZK-proofs Receives IEEE 'Test of Time' Award" *Cointelegraph*, 20 May 2024. Available at: https://cointelegraph.com/news/whitepaper-birthed-crypto-zk-proofs-receives-ieee-test-of-time-award (Accessed 24 May 2024).
109 Wise website. https://wise.com/ (Accessed 21 November 2023).
110 Worldline website. https://worldline.com/ (Accessed 21 November 2023).
111 FIS website (Worldpay). https://www.fisglobal.com/en-gb/merchant-solutions-worldpay (Accessed 21 November 2023).
112 WorldRemit website. https://www.worldremit.com/ (Accessed 21 November 2023).
113 YooMoney website. https://yoomoney.ru/ (Accessed 21 November 2023).
114 Zelle website. https://www.zellepay.com/ (Accessed 21 November 2023).

INDEX

Note: **Bold** page numbers refer to tables, *italic* page numbers refer to figures.

For Product Safety Concerns and Information please contact our EU representative GPSR@taylorandfrancis.com Taylor & Francis Verlag GmbH, Kaufingerstraße 24, 80331 München, Germany